CREATED *for* CONNECTION

—∿—

Your Calling as a Communicator in Today's World

CREATED *for* CONNECTION

Your Calling as a Communicator in Today's World

-FIRST EDITION-

DONALD H. ALBAN JR.

Associate Professor of Communication Studies
Liberty University

Cover design by Paul Segsworth.

Interior design by RJS Design Studio.

Previously printed and distributed by Snowfall Press.

www.kendallhunt.com
Send all inquiries to:
4050 Westmark Drive
Dubuque, IA 52004-1840

Copyright © 2011 by Donald H. Alban Jr.

ISBN 978-1-4652-0676-3

Printed in the United States of America
10 9 8 7 6 5 4 3 2 1

To my wife and soul mate, Evangeline, an authentic lover of God
whose compassionate heart regularly teaches me that redemption is something to be lived.

"A woman who fears the Lord will be greatly praised."
-Proverbs 30:31

and

To my parents, Donald and Joanne, whose lifetime of serving others
has taught me much more about redemptive communication than their words alone could relay.

"Let each generation tell its children of your mighty acts;
let them proclaim your power."
-Psalm 145:4

CONTENTS

PART 3: JOB FIELDS FOR REDEMPTIVE COMMUNICATORS

PART 1:
REDEMPTIVE
COMMUNICATION:

—⚙—

Basic Principles

A REDEMPTIVE PRAYER

God be in my head, and in my understanding;
God be in mine eyes, and in my looking;
God be in my mouth, and in my speaking;
God be in my heart, and in my thinking;
God be at mine end, and at my departing.

-the Sarum Primer (1538)

CHAPTER 1
COMMUNICATION

—⁊⁊⁊—

What Is It?

Overview: *We begin this study by considering what communication means. This chapter presents the word's literal meaning and then explains how this definition can be misunderstood unless further developed. After proposing a working definition of communication, we evaluate the process through which communication takes place. Blending concepts from a couple of classic communication theories, we review several major elements in this process and explore the way they work together to cause communication to occur. We then consider factors that can prevent communication from happening.*

A Closer Look: On a cool, overcast Good Friday morning not long ago, I sat in my office at Liberty University—a large, thriving Christian institution located in central Virginia—contemplating what steps I might take to determine whether my introductory communication theory students were truly learning the content I had directed them to study throughout the semester. With only minutes to go before the scheduled beginning of my next session with them, I quickly decided that at the very least, these students should be able to define one of the most basic terms to which their study had been devoted—communication. Moments later, I hastily grabbed my computer bag, bolted out the door, and strode down the stairs and across a courtyard to the classroom where our session was scheduled to begin.

After entering the classroom and positioning myself behind the lectern, I prepared my computer equipment for the session and then, as had been my custom, called the class to order with an opening word of prayer. After briefly addressing several course-related administrative matters, I asked the approximately 60 students to pull out a piece of paper. A few scattered groans sounded throughout the classroom as students prepared for what several of them apparently feared would be yet another pop quiz over the assigned reading for the day.

"Hey! Don't worry. This is not a quiz . . ." I assured them, hoping to put minds at ease. "But, I do have an important question for you to think about, one that I'd like you to answer in writing. You have spent nearly an entire semester studying communication theory. Now I would you to tell me in your own words—what does the term *communication* mean? A few students almost immediately set their pens to paper and hastily began to write. A few others stared blankly into empty space, as if locked in deep thought, before reviving and carefully etching the first words of their apparently pensive descriptions. Most students had completed their writing two minutes later, so I collected their work and placed it in my briefcase to review later that day.

Hours later, while sitting in my home office on a rainy afternoon, I perused the students' responses and noted, with some pleasure albeit not much surprise, that in a basic way at least, their descriptions of the concept were quite similar. Most had presented communication as a way in which people do exchange or can exchange information with each other. Although the respondents generally agreed with this basic idea, they were less unified in their appraisals of what, beyond this, the concept of communication involves. Some students painted communication in the broadest terms imaginable, presenting it as a phenomenon that, although applicable to humans, is not necessarily limited them. As one young scholar put it, "Communication is the exchange of information between people, animals, and things." A few of her peers similarly portrayed communication broadly, but characterized it more concisely as something uniquely human. "Communication is everything that exists between people" one wrote. "It is the process of people sharing information with each other," penned another. Several other students were even more specific. Communication, they claimed, is not merely the exchange of information among people, but the shared understanding that can result when the exchange occurs.

> ―∞―
> **Our word *communication* derives from the Latin term *communis,* which means common, general, universal, or public.**
> ―∞―

As I pondered these distinctions and others like them among the dozens of submitted definitions, I was impressed by the fact that although a professor's preliminary clarification of key terms does not totally eliminate differences in student understandings of the terms' meanings, taking this step is nonetheless an essential starting point in the study of any subject. I have observed during my years of teaching that presenting foundational definitions early in a course at least moves students closer to shared understandings of what they are studying and enables them to evaluate the study's content in a more meaningful, focused way.

Accordingly, I submit that it behooves us at the beginning of an introductory communication text like this one, to consider what communication is. Defining this core idea, as precisely and practically as possible, is the primary goal of this opening chapter. In the pages that follow, I further this goal, first, by considering *communication's* literal meaning in the light of the language that produced it, and then by reviewing the elements that work together as a process to make communication possible. After defining communication and showing how it comes into existence, we review a series of terms that scholars often use to distinguish different types of communication that enrich one's study of the topic. Knowing these types can help students develop a clearer sense of the communications area that most interests them as they prepare to be skillful communicators in their personal lives, church lives, academic lives, and careers.

THE ROOTS OF *COMMUNICATION*

One of the best places to go when trying to define an English word is to the word's roots, which often come to us from other languages like Latin, French, and German. Our word *communication* derives from the Latin term *communis,* which means common, general, universal, or public.[1] The presence of commonness, or of something shared, is a distinguishing feature of communication. Without the former, the latter does not exist. A communicative state exists when two or more people share or come to share a perception, an idea, a feeling, an attitude, or a value, among other applications. The same basic idea appears in several English words that resemble *communication* because they, too, derive from *communis.* A community or commune, for example, is a group of people who share something, whether physical space or common ideals, interests, or beliefs. A common or commissary is a place that people share or where they gather for a shared experience or type of experience. A communion service in church is an experience in which Christians assemble to focus as one on the significance of Christ's death. If you were to break down *communication* even further, you would note as well the root *unis* in this term, from which we derive such English words as unity, united, and uniform. The core concept once again is the idea of oneness. When a person believes, feels, values, or acts as one with another person *communis* exists.

Before considering an official definition of communication, we should note, in the light of *communis's* literal meaning, that your study of communication can be approached in at least two ways, both of which are utilized and encouraged as major thrusts of this book. The *expositional* approach identifies, analyzes, and attempts to explain the existence of attitudes, values, beliefs, feelings, or behaviors that unify people as a whole or that come to unify particular groups of people. Lots of things can bring and/or hold people together as units. Individuals might be unified, for example, by an apparently universal belief, such as belief in the law of gravity, or by an isolated but shared belief (e.g., that the earth is flat), conviction (e.g., that abortion is murder), appreciation (e.g., for classical music), or behavior (e.g., their subscription to the same magazine), among many other possibilities. The expositor is someone who identifies the things that unify groups and then explains how the unifiers came to have the mobilizing influence that they have. Among the other questions an expositor may attempt to answer while analyzing a group are the following: Are the points that unify this body something that is unique to this body or are they something that unifies people as a whole? Where did this unifier come from?

—∾—

The expositor is someone who identifies the things that unify groups and then explains how the unifiers came to have the mobilizing influence that they have.

—∾—

Questions like these can be answered in a variety of ways, and it shows in the sometimes radically different explanations that expositors offer in their quest to make sense of what they observe. As later chapters explain, an expositor's worldview—his or her most basic beliefs about the way things are—can especially impact the way he or she approaches such questions and the types of answers he or she offers in response to them.

---

[1] Lewis, Charlton T, and Hugh M. Kingery. *An Elementary Latin Dictionary, by Charlton T. Lewis. with an Appendix of Names of Persons and Places Met in the Latin Authors Commonly Studies in the First Two Years of the College Course, Comp. by Hugh Macmaster Kingery.* New York, American Book Company, 1915. 147-148. Print.

As a partly expositional project, this book focuses, starting in chapter 3, on one trait that appears to unify people as a whole, rather than just an isolated group of people—the longing for something supremely meaningful outside ourselves that nothing in this world is apparently capable of perfectly satisfying. We will consider in that segment how a Biblically Christian worldview accounts for this constant human yearning in a way that is not only sensible, but demonstrably preferable to alternative explanations. At the very least, this account provides a rich starting point for expositing human behavior, including human communicative behavior. As will be explained, this approach to making sense of human experience begins with the human realization, as Augustine expressed it in words directed to God, that "thou hast made us for thyself and restless is our heart until it comes to rest in thee." Whatever else the human drive to connect with others through communication may be, it is fundamentally a response to this most basic of all human desires.

—∞—

Communication, for the purpose of this project, is the transmission of meaningful information from one person or group of persons (the sender) to another person or group of persons (the recipient) in a way that generates shared attitudes, values, beliefs, feelings, or behaviors between the sender and recipient.

—∞—

The *rhetorical* approach to the study of communication, which this project also utilizes and encourages, is similar to the expositional approach but it has a different objective. Whereas exposition aims to identify and explain the existence of commonalities that already unify people, rhetorical analysis strives to identify and to explain the communicational steps people take in their various quests to establish points of oneness with others. To be more precise, the rhetorical approach concentrates especially on how communicators deliberately use information, particularly verbal information, in their quests to convince others to adopt their own attitudes, values, beliefs, feelings, or behaviors. People can be very creative in their uses of information for rhetorical purposes. First-year college students might notice this when coursework requires them to evaluate such diverse, rhetorically charged texts as speeches, essays, visual or musical works, movies, or plays. Sometimes the text's apparent purpose is to inform or to persuade. Other times its apparent purpose is to entertain. Whatever its apparent purpose may be, each text has as its overarching goal the creation of a connectedness of some sort between the text's creator and/or performer and its recipients. Showing that the text's creator and/or performer tries to do this and explaining why he or she does so is the expositor's task. Showing how he or she tries to do this and assessing whether he or she does so successfully is the rhetorical analyst's task.

How, then, shall we define communication? As you might anticipate, the answer to this question depends partly on whether we take the expositional or the rhetorical approach to making sense of human behavior. Because the expositor's primary focus is on making sense of existing connections among people, he or she will be less directly concerned than the rhetorical analyst with understanding how these links come about in every day experience. Even so, the expositor cannot completely avoid questions about *how* people achieve unity through their interactions with each other. In order to explain why people quest for connections with each other, the expositor will presuppose that this drive is caused by something. Whether the assumed cause is God, genetics, social influences, a combination of these, or something else, the expositor necessarily considers whether this cause continues to drive human quests for connection. Whatever his or her conclusion may be, the expositor must be prepared to justify this answer in a way that involves some consideration of rhetorical questions.

Similarly, a rhetorical analyst cannot explain how humans achieve connection without considering expositional questions. If the rhetorical analyst considers the variety of ways humans build connections with each other, he or she must also consider what causes humans to do this and what impact, if any, this cause continues to have on human connection-building practices. A sufficient definition of communication, then, addresses both expositional and rhetorical issues. It presents communication not only as a state of unity that exists among people in general and/or particular groups of people, but as something that has a cause. Not only does it identify this cause, it proceeds to consider what impact, if any, this cause continues to have on quests for personal connection. If the definition holds that the cause continues to drive these quests, it will explain how this impact works and how it manifests itself in the individual communicational situations that expositors and rhetorical analysts alike try to explain.

COMMUNICATION DEFINED

Communication, for the purpose of this project, is the transmission of meaningful information from one person or group of persons (the sender) to another person or group of persons (the recipient) in a way that generates shared attitudes, values, beliefs, feelings, or behaviors between the sender and recipient. This definition, which blends concepts from twentieth century theorists Claude Shannon and Warren Weaver[2] and Wilbur Schramm[3], implies several important points about communication that are explained in the paragraphs that follow:

—∾— Communication is personal.
—∾— Communication requires a message sender.
—∾— Communication requires a message recipient.
—∾— Communication requires the encoding, transmission, and decoding of a message.
—∾— Communication produces a state of unity.
—∾— Communication attempts can fail for a variety of reasons

Communication is personal. Indeed, what distinguishes communication from other information sending processes, like photosynthesis or magnetics, is the fact that its sending and receiving agents are persons. Unlike animals, plants, and moon rocks, people are fundamentally spiritual beings. This means they are intelligent and are capable of living without bodies. This view of personhood implies that although humans are the most obvious example of persons, the term may be applicable as well

---

[2] Shannon, Claude E, and Warren Weaver. *The Mathematical Theory of Communication.* Urbana: University of Illinois Press, 1949. Print.

[3] Schramm, Wilbur. "How Communication Works." *The Process and Effects of Communication.* Ed. Wilbur Schramm. Urbana: University of Illinois Press, 1954. 3-26. Print.

to other spiritual beings, whether they are angelic, demonic, or divine. As such, these beings, too, qualify as potential senders and/or receivers in the communication process. Chapter 3 explains the importance of this view of personhood in the Biblically Christian worldview, which recognizes God as the Creator who, through a series of communicative acts, set the world into motion and who continues to send intelligible information to persons via His creation and via His Word.

Communication requires a message sender. A communicative message may be sent by one or more persons. Sometimes a sender, acting alone, crafts and channels a message to the recipient, as typically happens when you say something to your roommate in an informal face-to-face conversation. The message may be intentional, such as when you purposefully say "What time is it?" to him or her. The message also may be unintentional, as when your subconscious frown informs your roommate that you are angry. On occasion, we work with others to craft and to send a communicative message, as happens when we work with peers to present a group project to the class or when a publishing team works together to create and circulate a print or digital publication with a message or set of messages for its intended readership. In any case, a message must have a sender in order to be a message. If it has no sender, it may be informational, but it is not a message in the personal sense that our definition of communication requires.

Communication requires a message recipient. If you think to yourself late one night, *I wish my roommate would turn off the light so I could get some sleep!,* but you keep the thought to yourself, you obviously have formed an idea, but this alone does not create communication. If you write the thought on a piece of paper, but you keep the paper to yourself and do not show it to your roommate, this veiled expression of the thought does not create communication. If you say aloud, *Apaga la luz!,* but your roommate does not understand Spanish, communication still has not been achieved. Communication occurs only if the expressed thought (the message) is received and understood and this, of course, can happen only if there is a recipient. The existence of a *potential* recipient does not create communication. The existence of an *actual* recipient—a person who, in fact, perceives and accurately decodes the message's meaning in a way that creates a unity of understanding—is what gives communication its existence.

Communication involves encoding, transmitting, and decoding. Implicit in the preceding descriptions is the fact that the sender's attitude, value, belief, or feeling must be encoded, transmitted, and decoded by the recipient. Encoding is the sender's act, whether intentional or unintentional, of expressing his or her attitude, value, belief, or feeling in a tangible form, one that a recipient can perceive and decode in a way that results in shared understanding. Humans generally encode their messages in forms that recipients can receive through one or more of the senses. A spoken message is meant to be heard. A written message is meant to be seen. A pat on the back is meant to be felt. A spray of perfume is meant to be smelled.

Whether humans can exchange meanings in extra-sensorial ways, such as via intuition, is questionable. Whether God communicates with humans via sensory channels and, if so, whether He uses only these means for communicating with humans are questions for theologians to debate. Some have argued, quite convincingly, that God does reveal information to people without channeling it through their senses. Natural law theorists, for example, support this idea by observing that people everywhere enter the world with some awarenesses already intact. Among these, some of them say, is the principle of non-contradiction—which holds that *A* cannot at the same time be *non-A* (e.g., that something cannot at the same time be both true and false). As will be explained in a later chapter, Biblically Christian theologians, too, believe that some divinely instilled human knowledge precedes sensory experience. They point for support to Biblical passages that indicate God has impressed certain awarenesses, such as an awareness that human life has a purpose, on the human heart without using sensory media to place them there (see, for example, Eccl. 3:11 and Rom. 2:14-15).

The amount of time that passes between a message's encoding, transmission, and decoding can vary. In our face-to-face interactions, the process is nearly instantaneous, with only a millisecond passing between the time when the sender says something and when the recipient hears and makes sense of it. On occasion, though, lots of time may pass before the process is complete. While doing research toward my Masters degree, during the mid-1990s, I visited an archive at the University of Oxford, in England, where I was permitted to review 200-year-old publications that appeared to be relevant to my research topic. Although the creators of these documents could not have known that I would read their work some day, they functioned nonetheless as senders of information that they encoded in print and that I, many years later, received and decoded in a way that effected understanding. On other occasions, we may receive a message one day but not consciously notice or make sense of it until a day or two later when its meaning occurs to us. Perhaps you heard your parents asking you to call them within the next day but you did not really grasp their words, even though your memory retained them, until a day later when the words came back to haunt you.

Just as time is not necessarily a barrier to communication, neither is the physical distance that separates a sender and recipient. I spent my earliest days in the jungles of western Brazil, where my parents worked among tribal people groups, some of whom had no formal written language. For members of these tribes, communication was a mostly oral practice that took place while participants were within range of each others' voices or faces. Except for simple systems of signs that are used in rituals or to mark their property claims, most of these people groups lacked other means for sending information to each other. To this day, many still have no written language, nor do they have the print, electronic, or digital media that enable people in Western cultures to communicate with each other from virtually anywhere on earth, even from outer space, in either real or delayed time. For the technologically dependent Westerner, the stark reality of daily life in an oral culture is unfathomable until experienced for an extended period of time.

—∞—

For the technologically dependent Westerner, the stark reality of daily life in an oral culture is unfathomable until experienced for an extended period of time.

—∞—

Communication produces a state of unity. As noted, communication is achieved when the recipient understands the attitude, value, belief, or feeling that the sender encoded and transmitted, whether intentionally or unintentionally. This unity of knowledge, or of understanding, may produce or help to produce additional unities between the sender and recipient, such as shared beliefs, feelings, attitudes, desires, intentions, or ways of acting. If you see a friend crying and infer from this and surrounding observations that she has lost a parent to cancer, this understanding (a unity of knowledge), might produce additional unities between you and her such as shared feelings of sadness and a shared desire for comfort.

The idea that people are capable of forming unities of this type is a tough idea for some critics to accept. Because nobody experiences life in exactly the same way as someone else, they object, no two people can ever come to view or to understand anything in exactly the same way. While this point may seem sensible at first, a closer look exposes several cracks in this way of thinking. First, this objection to the possibility of shared perspectives is self-discrediting. Let us suppose, for the sake of argument, that it is true that no two people can come to see something in exactly the same way. If this is so, as the critics argue, an important question emerges—how did these critics, despite supposedly being incapable of seeing the world as others see it, somehow manage to escape their standpoints in order to compare other human perspectives and to conclude that no two are alike? Indeed, how did they, despite their supposedly inescapable isolation, somehow become capable of knowing that shared perspectives are impossible to attain? While it is sensible to suppose that people do not always see things in exactly the same way, it is questionable to argue, as these critics do, that people are incapable of seeing at least some things in the same way.

> **While it is sensible to suppose that people do not always see things in exactly the same way, it is questionable to argue, as these critics do, that people are incapable of seeing at least some things in the same way.**

A second problem with the critics' objection is that it recklessly supposes that all human knowledge is experience-based. This is a blind assumption, for it dismisses without justification the possibility that humans enter the world with the shared knowledge of at least some things already intact and not contingent on what experience teaches us. We already have considered, among the possibilities for this type of shared knowledge, such widespread human awarenesses as the notion that something cannot, at the same time, be both true and not true and the notion that humans exist for a purpose.

A third problem with the critics' objection is their assumption that differences of perspective prevent people from sometimes seeing and responding to the same things. If my wife and I are driving down the highway, we have slightly different perspectives since we are riding in different seats. Although our vantage points may differ slightly, either of us can see the road's boundaries from where we are sitting and, if necessary, can steer the car in a way that avoids the boundaries and gets us to our destination. We may not see the road in exactly the same way, but our shared recognition and understanding of some things (boundaries, for example) can keep either of us moving down the road in the same direction, toward the same intended destination.

This is not to say that those who doubt the possibility of shared perspectives are entirely wrong. Our observations tell us that people often see things in very different ways, and this sometimes leads to misunderstandings and conflict. Indeed, if people saw all things identically, communication would be as constant a feature of human experience as breathing and circulation and not something to be created through encoding, transmitting, and decoding processes. In reality, lots of barriers can prevent communication from coming about. We consider some of these in the final segment of this definition section.

Communication attempts can fail for a variety of reasons. When we say communication is the result of a successful transmission of meaningful information from a sender to a recipient, we imply that attempts to communicate may not always be successful. These failures occur for several reasons that we pause to consider before moving into this definitional chapter's next segment. The term for factors that can disrupt meaningful transmissions of information between senders and potential recipients is noise, and it comes in several varieties.

Physical Barriers: Lots of things in the material world can prevent a sender's message from making its way to the receiver. A speaker's voice might not reach potential recipients because they are deaf, because they are out of the voice's range, or because another sound, like background noise, drowns out the speaker's voice. A visual impairment might prevent someone from reading a street sign, from seeing a friend's smile, or from reading words on a computer screen. Media malfunctions might block the transmission of messages via e-mail, text messaging, cell phone, webcast, or broadcast. Natural elements, like fire, water, moths, or decomposition, might consume or render unreadable an ancient manuscript, a tombstone inscription, an antiquarian book, an old greeting card, an audio recording, or an improperly stored film. The passing of outdated media technologies might prevent a recipient from receiving messages via outdated media like 8-track or reel-to-reel tapes. Given enough time and a little imagination, one could conjecture thousands of situations in which physical factors like these could prevent the successful transmission of meaningful information from a sender to a recipient.

> *Language,* **for the purpose of this study, denotes the system of verbal and non-verbal symbols that senders and recipients use to encode and to decode expressions of attitudes, values, beliefs, or feelings.**

Linguistic Barriers: Sometimes the obstacle that prevents a message's transmission from one person to another has nothing to do with material factors. Instead, the breakdown may occur because of differences that exist between the sender and the receiver's language systems. *Language,* for the purpose of this study, denotes the system of verbal and non-verbal symbols that senders and recipients use to encode and to decode expressions of attitudes, values, beliefs, or feelings. This tool for finding common ground with others can be both an asset and a liability. Positively, language enables people, through the use of the same or similar symbolic systems, to exchange meaningful messages in a way that results in mutual understanding. Negatively, language use can create misunderstanding because of differences that distinguish two or more people's language systems. The greater these differences, the greater the potential for misunderstanding between them.

In a world of nearly 7,000 documented verbal languages, imagining situations in which linguistic differences complicate attempts to communicate is not too difficult a task for most people.[4] Your personal experiences with miscommunication probably provide a rich reference point for the study of this topic. We know that speakers of radically different languages, like English and Mandarin Chinese, will face obvious challenges if each speaks to the other in a language he or she does not understand. To bridge their divide, they will need to learn the other's language, to use a translator, or to use an alternative language system, whether a formal verbal one like French or German or an informal non-verbal one that consists of little more than gestures and/or facial expressions.

Even within a single verbal language system, like English, verbal differences exist that can create misunderstandings. The differences between American English and British English illustrate this point. What an American calls a *cookie,* a Briton calls a *biscuit.* What an American calls *soccer,* a Briton calls *football.* What an American calls a *truck,* a Briton calls a *lorry.* What Americans call *pants,* a Briton calls *trousers.* What Americans call an *attorney* or *lawyer,* Britons call a *barrister.* Despite inconsistencies like these, Americans and Britons are usually able to converse with each other with little difficulty, but their verbal differences can create misunderstandings and function as barriers to communication.

As an important aside, labels like American English and British English are actually somewhat misleading because language differences do not stop at the national level. Some differences are regional. I still recall the confusion that I once experienced at a grocery store in southern West Virginia, while attending college there during the late 1980s. Shortly after I entered the store, a clerk who I had never met approached me and asked, "Would you like a poke?" *What a weird question!* I thought. *Why would you ask to jab a complete stranger with your finger?* After politely declining, I walked away perplexed. Days later the mystery dissolved when I learned from a friend that a *poke* is merely a local term for what I call a *shopping bag.*

One additional point must be made about linguistic barriers to communication. Language systems are not just verbal. People routinely use non-verbal signals like facial expressions, gestures, movement, proximity, touch, volume, tone, pitch, pauses, silence, artifacts like clothing styles, eyewear styles, and jewelry, and other non-verbal cues to encode and transmit messages to others. Just as differences in verbal language can result in misunderstandings, so can differences in non-verbal language. The American's thumbs-up and A-OK hand gestures may mean something positive in America, but they are seen as obscene gestures in other parts of the world. Repeatedly turning the head side-to-side means "no" in North America, but in parts of South Asia it means "yes." Making eye contact with and smiling at strangers in rural Indiana may be a friendly gesture, but in Navajo American culture may be seen as disrespectful and in New York City it may be seen as threatening. Being an effective communicator, then, requires the sender and recipient to be mindful of the fact that non-

---

[4] Gordon, Raymond G, and Barbara F. Grimes. *Ethnologue: Languages of the World.* Dallas, Tex: SIL International, 2005. Print.

verbal cues do not always signify what they have learned to think they mean.

Belief Barriers: Another type of obstacle that can prevent senders and recipients from establishing mutual understanding is their differences of belief about each other. What they assume about people in general, about people like each other, or about people with each other's individual histories can skew their interpretations of each other's communicative behaviors and messages and result in misunderstanding.

As the third chapter explains, a person's view about people in general profoundly impacts the way he or she makes sense of the world and responds to it. Are people basically good, evil, or neither? Are they selfish or selfless by nature? What motivates them to act toward other people as they do? A recipient with a generally positive view of and attitude toward people might see the sender's motives as they really are or else see them as something better intentioned than they really are. Conversely, the recipient with a generally negative view of and attitude toward people might see the sender's motives as they really are or else see them as something more sinister than they really are.

> —⁓—
> **Another type of obstacle that can prevent senders and recipients from establishing mutual understanding is their differences of belief about each other.**
> —⁓—

Sometimes a recipient misunderstands the sender's communicative message because of false preconceptions he or she has about people like the sender or about a person with the recipient's individual history. The human tendency to form careless beliefs about people based on their features or group identities is called *stereotyping.* People can be stereotyped and their message meanings and motives can be misunderstood, as a result, for many reasons—their age or physical features, their economic, educational, or marital statuses, or their ethnic, racial, national, regional, linguistic, or religious identities, among other possibilities. What makes a stereotype potentially damaging is that its assumption about someone is based on an uninformed hunch rather than on credible evidence. As such, a stereotype is distinguishable from an informed generalization. Unlike a stereotype, an informed generalization is an educated speculation about the sender's motives and message meanings, one that is based on credible evidence that these are, in fact, very likely what you suppose they are.

QUESTIONS FOR ANALYSIS

1. As this chapter explains, *communication* can be defined in lots of ways. Using credible published sources, locate and compare five distinct definitions of *communication.* Write them down. Be sure to quote them accurately and to properly document your sources.

2. Next, write a 100-200 word response in which you, first, explain how the 10 definitions resemble each other and, second, explain how they differ from each other and from this chapter's definition.

3. Evaluate this chapter's definition of communication. What are its strengths? What are its weaknesses? If you were asked to improve it in one way, by adding, subtracting, or modifying something, what would you change? Present your answer and explain the reasoning that justifies it in a 100-200 word response.

4. Recall an incident in which you or an acquaintance experienced a communication breakdown because of a verbal linguistic barrier. Chronicle this incident in a 150-250 word response.

5. Recall an incident in which you or an acquaintance experienced a communication breakdown because of a non-verbal linguistic barrier. Chronicle this incident in a 150-250 word response.

6. This chapter questions the statement that no people can see the same thing because the statement is self-discrediting. If the statement were true, the person making the statement would have no way of knowing that it is true since, by his or her own admission, he or she could never gain access to what other people see for the purpose of determining this. What do you think? Share your thoughts in a 150-250 word response.

7. Historian Louis Gottschalk once said: "Only part of what was observed in the past was remembered by those who observed it; only a part of what was remembered was recorded; only a part of what was recorded has survived; only a part of what has survived has come to the historians' attention; only a part of what has come to their attention is credible; only part of what is credible has been grasped; and only a part of what has been grasped can be expounded or narrated by the historian." [5]

With this quotation in mind, and in the light of what this chapter says about barriers to communication, provide examples of five physical, five linguistic, and five different belief obstacles that might prevent a historian from receiving and understanding the information in a historical text.

8. This chapter discusses stereotyping as a potential obstacle to communication. Provide five examples of stereotypes and explain, after each, how it can prevent communication from occurring.

---

[5] Gottschalk, Louis. *Understanding History: A Primer of Historical Method.* New York: Alfred E. Knopf, 1969. 45. Print.

CHAPTER 2
COMMUNICATION

—ʍ—

How Does It Happen?

Overview: *This chapter breaks communication into several categories that people should know in order to more fully appreciate the vital role communication plays in the human experience and in their lives. It begins with an overview of major verbal and non-verbal forms through which people channel meaningful information to others and concludes with a brief review of terms that distinguish communicational situations from each other.*

A Closer Look: Now that we more clearly understand what communication is, what makes it happen, and what can prevent it from happening, we turn our attention to a series of terms that scholars use to distinguish various types of communication from each other. Several of these terms appeared in the previous section. Knowing what they mean can increase not only your knowledge of communication's many forms, but also your appreciation for the vital role this phenomenon plays in the human experience and in your life.

The Forms of Communication

As noted in the section about communication's encoding process, people use many verbal and non-verbal forms to express themselves to others. Verbal expressions, by definition, involve the use of words. A *word,* as one source aptly puts it, is "a sound or a combination of sounds, or its representation in writing or printing, that symbolizes and communicates a meaning."[6] Nonverbal expressions, by contrast, involve the use of meaningful symbols other than words for expression. In the paragraphs that follow, we briefly survey these major classifications of communicative message forms.

---

[6] McArthur, Tom. *Living Words: Language, Lexicography, and the Knowledge Revolution.* Exeter: University of Exeter Press, 1998. 43. Print.

VERBAL MESSAGES: People use a variety of verbal forms to get information across to each other. Whether spoken, written, or printed, words or combinations of words are *literal* if they are used forthrightly to signify the person, place, thing, idea, action, or state of being that the words or combination of words evidently symbolize. If you announce to family members in an e-mail that your neighbor "bought the farm," "kicked the bucket," or "bit the big enchilada," and mean that your neighbor actually bought a farm, kicked a bucket, or bit a big enchilada, you are speaking literally. At other times the words are *figurative* because they are used to signify a secondary meaning that is not patently obvious when the words are taken at face value. If you say your neighbor "bought the farm," "kicked the bucket," or "bit the big enchilada," and mean through these non-literal expressions that the neighbor died, you are speaking figuratively.

Literal expressions are forthright. They say what they mean and have no hidden meanings. Figurative expressions come in many forms. The following list defines and provides examples of several especially common figurative forms:

Metaphor (A is B or substitutes B for A): A common figurative form, a metaphor identifies one thing in a way that symbolically stands for another thing.

"A mighty fortress is our God."—Martin Luther
"You are a mist that appears for a little time . . ." —James 4:14, ESV
"Time is a physician which heals every grief."—Diphilus

Simile (A is like or as B): A simile explicitly compares two otherwise dissimilar things, usually via the modifiers *like* or *as*.

"My love is like a red, red rose."—Robert Burns
"He was as idle as a horse doctor in Detroit"—Anonymous
"A face that looks like it had worn out four bodies."—Anonymous

Synecdoche: This figurative form alludes to something by either highlighting only one aspect of it or something broader that includes it.

Washington *as a reference to America's federal government*
Hollywood *as a reference to America's film industry*
Threads *as a reference to clothing*

Euphemism: A euphemism is the use of a mild term in place of a harsh term to relay the same basic idea in a more tasteful form.

Pro-choice *instead of pro-abortion*
Passed away *instead of died*
Restroom *instead of bathroom*

Dysphemism: The opposite of a euphemism, a dysphemism is the use of a harsh term instead of a mild term for an intended effect.

Ambulance chaser *instead of lawyer*
Rug rat *instead of small child*
Dinosaur *instead of old person*

Overstatement: Also called *hyperbole,* overstatement is the use of exaggerated terms for emphasis but not for literal meaning.

I am so hungry I could eat a horse.
He has a million things to do today.
We are so happy we could jump to the moon.

Understatement: The opposite of overstatement, understatement is the use of terms to diminish the seriousness or intensity of something.

"It was an interesting day."—George W. Bush recalling 9/11
It's no big deal. He only had a heart attack.
Hitler had a little problem with Jews. (He murdered 6 million.)

Idiom: An idiom is a combination of words that means something different than the words' literal meaning.

Business has hit the rocks *lately (reached a low point).*
Idioms drive me crazy *(frustrate me).*
You will do well if you play your cards right *(act correctly).*

Personification: To personify is to ascribe human qualities to something that is not human.

"The trees of the field shall clap their hands."—Isaiah 55:12, ESV
"The stars in the sky looked down where He lay."—Martin Luther
"The wind is a playful child."—Katherine Mansfield

Paradox: A paradox is a statement that appears to be self-refuting but that is, in fact, true or possibly true.

The more things change, the more they stay the same.
"I shut my eyes in order to see."—Paul Gauguin
"You are absolutely unique. Just like everyone else."—Margaret Mead

When evaluating a message's verbal content, a recipient will infer its meaning based on observations of not only the words (the text), but also the circumstances surrounding the encoding of the words (the context). Who is the speaker? Who is the audience? What is the topic? What is the setting? Which words were used? How were they stated? A recipient's answers to questions like these will impact how he or she interprets the words' meanings.

Because of their relevance, two additional important terms are noteworthy in at this point. A word or phrase's literal meaning is sometimes called its *denotative* meaning. This is the meaning of the word or phrase according a dictionary or other recognized authoritative sources. A word or phrase's *connotative* meaning, by contrast, is the secondary meaning a recipient takes it to have when used in a particular situation. Sometimes the connotative meaning matches the denotative meaning; other times it does not. When it does not match, it is often because the sender's non-verbal cues indicate that the word or phrase should not be taken literally.

NON-VERBAL MESSAGES: Whether literally and figuratively expressed, verbal messages play a vital role in the transmission of meanings from the sender to the receiver. Even so, verbal messages are less significant than non-verbal messages in human communication. A classic study by psychologists Albert Mehrabian and Susan Ferris, years ago, indicated that as much as 93 percent of communication is nonverbal. According to the study, 55 percent of communication involves facial expressions, 38 percent involves nonverbal vocal qualities, and only 7 percent involves verbal content.[7] Other researchers, during the decades since then, have estimated that about 80 percent of communication is non-verbal.

> **Nonverbal messages, by definition, involve the use of symbols other than words for meaningful expression.**

Nonverbal messages, by definition, involve the use of symbols other than words for meaningful expression. People try to send messages, including information about themselves, to each other in lots of non-verbal ways—smiling, waving, hugging, whispering, standing close to someone, keeping breath fresh with chewing gum, wearing clothes of a certain color and style. We even use our material possessions to make statements about ourselves that we hope others will notice. I recall being puzzled at a funeral service several years ago when a relative with a basic service-oriented job showed up for the procession in a luxury vehicle that workers in his field typically cannot afford. Several days later I learned that although he had presented the car as his own, he had actually borrowed it from a wealthy friend, apparently to create a more favorable impression of himself on family members. Before chuckling at people who do this, contemplate how often each of us does the same thing, in different ways, every day. We choose many of the things we wear or display in public not merely because they are practically useful, but because we think they will create ideas about us, in the minds of others, that we consider to be favorable.

[7] Mehrabian, Albert, and Susan R. Ferris. "Inference of Attitudes from Nonverbal Communication in Two Channels." *Journal Of Consulting Psychology.* 31.3 (1967): 248-252. Print.

Whereas verbal information comes to us principally through the senses of sight and sound, nonverbal information can come to us through virtually any of the five senses. To witness this, walk through a large grocery store sometime. The product manufacturers and the store present their products to you as they do for one basic purpose—to get you to buy them. As you walk the aisles, notice the persuasive messages that come to you through your eyes as you view store signs and product labels. Listen to the messages that channel to your ears through the music and voices on store's speaker system. Consider the appeals to taste that occur at the product sampling displays. Observe the appeals to smell on the scratch-n-sniff products on some of the shelves. Finally, notice the subtle appeals to touch on the packaging of products like toilet paper, which use words like "soft" to compel passersby to feel the product, to be impressed, and to buy it.

Just as words like *metaphor, simile,* and *personification* denote distinct types of verbal messages, a terminology exists that enables us to distinguish the different types of nonverbal messages and to consider how they work together, along with verbal messages, to impact interpretations of a message's meaning. Scholar Judee Burgoon has created perhaps the most recognized *typology,* or classification system, for this purpose. Definitions and descriptions of her categories of non-verbal communication follow:

—◊◊—
Experience teaches us that our bodily movements, or in some situations, that the absence of bodily movements, is by default a statement that, taken alone, may relay a message . . . .
—◊◊—

Vocalics: A person's use of volume, tone, pitch, accent, speaking pace, and silence can profoundly impact a recipient's interpretation of his or her message and motives. Throughout our lives, we learn which combinations of these qualities communicate specific meanings to certain audiences under certain circumstances. We also learn that the same vocalic features may mean one thing to one audience but something very different to another audience. One learns, for example, that the hushed tones that communicate love to a spouse might communicate insecurity or weirdness if directed to a stranger. We learn as well that although cheering loudly may relay enthusiasm at a football game, it may imply disrespect or immaturity if sounded during in a church service or a class session. We come to know, too, that what passes as a normal accent in New York City may come across as something strange or suspicious in Southern Mississippi, and vice versa. Learning what vocalic nuances like these represent in the minds of one's potential audiences is vital for a would-be communicator, for unless one gains this proficiency, he or she will be ill prepared to use vocalics in a way that establishes mutual understanding with an audience.

Kinesics: We generally place body language in three categories (gestures, facial expressions, and eye contact). Think for a moment about the many ways people use bodily movement to send information to each other: standing, sitting, kneeling, bowing, lying down, crying, jumping, skipping, dancing, shaking, moving the mouth, the tongue or the lips, winking, squinting, hugging, hitting, kicking, spitting, clapping, waving, pointing, motioning with the hand, head, or foot, etc. Experience teaches us that our bodily movements, or in some situations, that the absence of bodily movements, is by default a statement that, taken alone, may relay a message or that, when combined with verbal information, may relay a blended message. A simple wink of the eye can be meaningful by itself. It can also transform words that, when taken alone, are shocking, into a lighthearted statement that is offered in jest. A crossing of the arms can be meaningful by itself. It can also transform words that, taken alone, imply friendliness into a statement of apparent resentment.

Any given bodily movement can be read in diverse ways by multiple recipients. The key to effective kinetic communication is knowing which movements signify which meanings to which audiences, especially audiences with whom the sender aims to establish shared understanding. The prolonged eye contact through which a Midwesterner might signify friendliness might be received as invasive and rude among Navajo Indians in the Southwest. Miscommunications like these can result when senders neglect to speak in a kinetic code the recipient understands.

Proxemics: People send information to each other through their use of space. We become upset when someone cuts in line, tailgates us, or stands too close to us, or when a stranger parks his car on our yard without permission, because these behaviors violate rules concerning the use of space that we expect others to respect. In face-to-face interaction, our use of space implies something about the nature of our relationship with the other. Anthropologist Edward Hall made this point during the 1960s when he popularized the notion that people have invisible public, social, personal, and intimate zones that they expect other people to recognize and respect. In American culture, he suggested, the public space, which is 10 feet or more away, is where we generally expect strangers to stand during interaction. Social space, which is 4 to 10 feet away, is where we permit acquaintances who are not necessarily friends to stand. Personal space, which is 1.5 to 4 feet away, is where friends or comfortable acquaintances are permitted to position themselves in relation to us. Intimate space, which is zero to 1.5 feet away, is reserved for our closest relations.

The measurements for these zones are culturally relative. Some cultures, like those of southern Europe, the Arab world, and Latin America, have comparatively smaller personal/intimate space ranges than North Americans. Northern European and Asian cultures share the American cultural tendency to be more personal space conscious. Cultural differences of this type can be defined not just by geographic variables, but also by the race and sex of the group. Researchers Teresa J. Rosegrant and James C. McCroskey have shown that males establish greater interpersonal distance from each other than females do from each other and that blacks and whites establish greater interpersonal distance from each other than they do when speaking to someone of the same race.[8]

Interpersonal interactions are just one setting in which proxemics can impact communication. Proxemics extends to consider, as well, the broader concept of personal property and what happens in

---

[8] Rosegrant, Teresa J., and James C. McCroskey. "The Effects of Race and Sex on Proxemic Behavior in an Interview Setting." *Southern Speech Communication Journal.* 40. (1975): 408-419. Print.

communication when people violate each other's property-related expectations. A telemarketer might violate your sense of personal space by giving you an unwanted phone call. A friend might violate the same sense by posting an obnoxious message as an announcement on your social networking site. A dorm mate might play his or her music too loudly and violate supposed right to enjoy your room in silence. As with vocalics and kinesics, a would-be communicator must consider his or her audience's proxemic standards when developing a plan for interacting with them. One's failure to do so can adversely affect his or her attempt to establish shared understanding with that audience.

Haptics: Communication can be impacted as well by touch, or by the lack thereof, among people. Touch can include lots of things—hugging, kissing, tickling, pinching, scratching, slapping, punching, kicking, grasping, holding, squeezing, patting, or shaking, etc. How the touching is interpreted will depend on the situation in which it occurs and on the significance attached to it by the observer. Punching a stranger in a traffic jam may be more acceptable in one part of the world than it is in another part. In American culture, doing this is likely to been seen as a negative expression of anger or frustration, although punching an opponent in the boxing ring may be seen as a positive expression of competitiveness. Whether touch is acceptable in any culture is determined by the relationship of the people involved, the parts of the body that touch, how long they touch, the purpose of the touching, and other factors. A person's decision not to touch another is meaningful as well, although it may be viewed alternatively as perfectly appropriate or as expressive of coldness or indifference.

As with previous non-verbal forms, haptics is culturally relative. What might be regarding acceptable touching behavior in one region might be regarded as unacceptable elsewhere. Whereas opposite-sex handshakes are permissible in American culture, they are not acceptable in Arab culture. Although same-sex handholding is acceptable as an expression of friendship among males in Arab culture, this is generally unaccepted in American culture. Being aware of and respecting norms like these obviously increases a sender's likelihood for success in achieving his or her communication goals.

Chronemics: This non-verbal communication form concerns time as a communicative factor. The timing of our message transmissions to others can profoundly impact the recipient's reading of it. For example, students often assume a professor should respond to their e-mails or grade their work within what they assume is a reasonable timeframe. Whether the professor does so can impact the student's impression of the professor and, by extension, of anything else he or she has to say. Professors, too, may form their impressions of students partly in response to whether the student submits his or her work on time. The same principle applies in the workplace. Prospective employers and existing bosses alike expect us to respond to their communications in a timely fashion. For some, this means immediately while, for others, it means within 24 hours. Whether a person satisfies this expectation can profoundly impact the employer's impression of him or her and influence the way the employer responds to his or her future communications.

What qualifies as a timely response depends partly on the unspoken rules of the culture in which the communication occurs. *Monochronic cultures* view time in a highly structured manner, reducing life to a series of tasks that are generally accomplished, one at a time, in a designated sequence. Northern European and American culture are this way. Because of their structured nature, cultures like these tend to be more task-oriented and less tolerant of deviations from the schedule than others. Breaking from the schedule without having good reason for doing so is generally viewed as a negative in these settings. So is lateness.

Adjusting to a monochronic culture can be a challenge for international students who come to America from less schedule-oriented *polychronic cultures.* They quickly learn after beginning studies in American universities that a late assignment submission in a monochronic culture is considerably more likely not to be accepted or more likely to be penalized for lateness than would be the case in a polychronic setting. Although they might not realize it, students from polychronic cultures, by submitting their work after deadline, might be sending a message to their professor that they are undisciplined or incapable of satisfying university-level academic standards.

⁓

Americans are expected to increase their spending on cosmetic surgical procedures to $2.6 billion by the year 2014.

⁓

On the other hand, the monochronic American businessperson or missionary may struggle when adjusting to life in a polychronic cultural setting. He or she may be frustrated when a native colleague shows up two days late for a scheduled task, as might be the norm in that setting. Although this may be unacceptable in the United States, the American must be careful not to send the wrong message to the native by protesting the lateness. Whether they realize it or not, the American who protests local norms like this may actually create the impression among polychronic locals that he or she is impatient, unfriendly, or hostile. Understanding and accommodating his or her audience's chronemic standards will help him or her be effective in realizing his or her goals in that setting.

Chronemics factors more than just whether a person is on time according to the standards of a given culture. This category also concerns the impact of time variables on the meanings people associate with other communicational expressions. Whether two people acted appropriately in a given situation may depend, at least partly, on whether their conversation, their hug or kiss, their eye contact, etc. were too long or too short by the culture's standards for people with the relationship that they share. In mainstream American culture, you may perceive disinterest in the person whose eye contact is too brief and eccentricity in the person whose eye contact is too lengthy. As with the other nonverbal message forms, the rules that distinguish what it too long and what is too short are to some extent culturally relative, so a person should make sense of another person's chonemic behavior in the light of the cultural standards that have impacted the meanings that person has come to associate with this dimension of human behavior.

Physical Appearance: Although Aesop may have been correct when he observed that appearances are often deceiving, it is also true, in words taken from Scripture, that "man looks on the outward appearance" (1 Sam. 16:7, ESV). If people judge books by their cover and products on the shelf by their labels, they certainly judge people, at least initially, based on their physical features.

Research consistently demonstrates that a person's physical features can affect how people respond to him or her.

--∾- Attractive people earn 5 to 10 percent more than average looking people, according to a 1994 study.[9]

--∾- Men who are more than 6 feet tall are 50 percent more likely to be married or have a long-term relationship with a woman than men who are shorter than 5 feet 5 inches, according to a 2005 study.[10]

--∾- Highly obese women earn 24 percent less than thin women, according to a 2002 article.[11]

Not surprisingly, because physical attractiveness can significantly impact the way people respond to each other, people spend lots of money on products and procedures that are designed to make them more beautiful. Americans are expected to increase their spending on cosmetic surgical procedures to $2.6 billion by the year 2014.[12] These procedures include reshaping, implants, lifts and tucks, liposuction, injections, dermal resurfacing, laser treatments, injectable products, equipment, disposables, biological materials and polymers. Moreover, Americans' spending on cosmetic and toiletry products, which exceeded $47 billion in 2008, is projected to continue its yearly increase through the year 2019.[13]

Although there are obvious limitations to what we can do to change our looks, doing what we can to enhance our appearance in the eyes of a target audience can promote the realization of our communication objectives. While definitions of attractiveness are to some extent culturally relative, they are similar across cultures in a number of basic ways. For example, a recent study indicated that the distance between a woman's eyes and her nose is recognized across cultures as determinative of whether her face is considered appealing. According to this 2009 study, a female face is viewed as attractive if the distance between her mouth and eyes is about 36 percent of the face's length and if the distance between her eyes is approximately 46 percent of the face's width.[14] Research about what makes a male face physically attractive is less conclusive than this, although one prominent study, from 1990, indicates a female preference for male faces with large eyes, prominent cheek bones, a large chin, and a big smile.[15]

Nonetheless, definitions of physical attractiveness are culturally relative to some extent. For example, whereas obesity is generally regarded to a detractor from beauty in North America and Northern

[9] Hamermesh, Daniel S., and Jeff E. Biddle. "Beauty and the Labor Market." *American Economic Review.* 84.5 (1994): 1174-1194. Print.

[10] Herpin, Nicolas. "Love, Careers, and Heights in France." *Economics and Human Biology.* 01 Jan. 2005. Print.

[11] Kristen, Elizabeth. "Addressing the Problem of Weight Discrimination in Employment." *California Law Review.* 90.1 (2002): 57-109. Print.

[12] "Cosmetic Surgery Products: US Industry Study with Forecasts for 2014 & 2019." The Freedonia Group, December 2010. Web. 9 May 2011. <http://www.freedoniagroup.com/brochure/27xx/2712smwe.pdf>.

[13] "Perfumes, Cosmetics, and Other Toilet Preparations." Highbeam Business, n.d. Web. 9 May 2011. <http://business.highbeam.com/industry-reports/chemicals/perfumes-cosmetics-other-toilet-preparations>.

[14] University of Toronto. "New 'Golden Ratios' for Female Facial Beauty." *ScienceDaily,* 17 Dec. 2009. Web. 9 May 2011.

[15] Cunningham, Michael R., and Anita P. Barbee. "What Do Women Want? Facialmetric Assessment of Multiple Motives in the Perception of Male Facial Physical Attractiveness." *Journal of Personality and Social Psychology.* 59.1 (1990): 61-72. Print.

Europe, it is commonly considered to be an attractive quality, especially as a female feature, in parts of Africa, Asia, Latin America, and the Pacific Islands. Whether a physical feature is universal or culturally desirable, one thing about physical attractiveness is clearly established—it is a non-verbal factor that can impact the way a recipient responds to a sender.

Artifacts: People send lots of information about themselves to others through the material objects through which they express their identities. Regardless of whether intended, a sender transmits lots of information about himself or herself through his or her displays of clothing, headwear, eyewear, footwear, jewelry, makeup, badges, ribbons, buttons, tattoos, masks, makeup, hair coloring, and scents. People also sometimes use their material possessions to make statements to others. The funeral story that I shared earlier demonstrates how someone used another person's expensive car in an attempt to make himself look more accomplished than he feared people would believe him to be. People use messages on personalized license plates or use clothing that publicly links them with a popular brand and all that it apparently represents for the same general purpose.

Unlike physical appearance, which generally concerns a person's natural traits, artifacts as a category considers how people use material objects in a way that says something about their attitudes, values, beliefs, and feelings. Your choice of clothing alone can send lots of messages that impact the way people respond to you. Which colors do you wear? Which styles do you choose? Which name brands or symbols do you display? What do your colors, styles, and name brands or symbols say about you to your particular audience? Is this the kind of statement you want to make to them? If not, how should you modify your attire so it will send the right kind of message to them?

—⚬⚬—

The responsible communicator is someone who studies his or her audience to determine what he or she must do in order to encode the message meaningfully.

—⚬⚬—

Whether we like it or not, people form their initial impressions of us based largely on non-verbal factors like these. These first assessments can have lasting consequences, so it behooves us to be mindful of the way we present ourselves to others, not just in what we say but in how we say it. As this section demonstrates, your communications can be profoundly impacted by the way you use your voice, your movements, the space around you, your time, the way you appear, and the way you use material objects to make statements about yourself.

This chapter, so far, has identified several major verbal and non-verbal devices that people use when they interact with each other. These message filters, and others like them, enable people to exchange meaningful messages in a communicative way. Because of differences between senders and recipients' language systems, though, people sometimes assign different meanings to same message. Effective communication requires a sender to gain an understanding of variables like these that exist in the communication process. Armed with such an awareness, the responsible communicator is someone who studies his or her audience to determine what he or she must do in order to encode the message meaningfully.

THE MODES OF COMMUNICATION

Before moving into a study of communication's origin, purpose, value, and potential, we must famil-iarize ourselves with one additional way of looking at communication. Whereas the previous section reviewed verbal and non-verbal forms that messages sometimes assume, this segment briefly reviews several types of communicational situations and presents the terms commonly used to differentiate them. These situations are generally distinguished from each other by the number of people involved in the interaction, by the purpose of their interaction, by the whether their interaction is immediate, and by the role, if any, that media play in the interaction. You should note that although communica-tion scholars generally acknowledge these categories, they do not always agree about the precise meanings of the terms that distinguish them from each other.

Interpersonal Communication: This term applies to situations in which people socially interact, usually in a face-to-face environment, but possibly also in real-time virtual environments like through inter-active radio, phone, and computer programs. What makes the situation interpersonal is not so much the number of participants as it is the real-time interactive nature of their encounter. *Dyadic commu-nication,* a sub-concentration of this category, denotes interpersonal interaction that takes place be-tween two people.

Unless you live in complete isolation, you experience interpersonal communication almost every day. It happens when you're having an informal conversation with friends, family, classmates, neigh-bors, fellow church attendees, business associates, or with strangers. The conversation might be face-to-face or else be mediated by phone, computer, or another interactive medium.

Group Communication: This communicational situation occurs when three or more people come to-gether for a common purpose, whether formally, as in a work group, or informally, as in social situa-tions. Anytime three or more people come together for a common purpose and can interact and influence each other in the exercise of this purpose, a group communication situation exists. *Small group communication* refers more specifically to situations in which a group of 3-10 people advance the group's purpose in a largely but not necessarily exclusively informal manner.

You may have experienced group communication if you have been part of a work team, a sports team, a support group, a Sunday School class, or a committee. If the experience involved three or more people whose interactions advanced the realization of a common purpose, it qualifies as a group communication situation.

Public Communication: This term and *public speaking* are often used interchangeably, as if they mean the same thing. This is a mostly valid assumption, although some communication scholars include variations of mediated and mass communication in their definitions of this category. In public com-munication, a speaker formally addresses a group of typically 10 or more individuals in a face-to-face environment where interactivity is possible but generally not practiced. The face-to-face quality dis-tinguishes this mode from mediated communication. The potential for interactivity distinguishes it from mass communication.

Although you likely experience this communicational mode less frequently than you experience interpersonal or group communication, you may recall being in situations that clearly link to this category. Perhaps you listened to a pastor give a sermon, a teacher give a lecture, an administrator give school announcements, or a best man pay tribute to a groom.

Mediated Communication: This communicational mode concerns situations in which senders use technologies to channel messages to recipents, whether synchronously or asynchronously. *Synchronous transmissions* take place in real time. *Asynchronous transmissions* do not take place at the same time. The media through which the messages channel are diverse, but they can be broadly classified as written, printed, electronic, or digital. When you use a pen, a printing press, a keyboard, or a radio tower to channel meaningful information to someone, you are engaging in mediated communication.

Mass Communication: When people use a media technology to distribute information to a large group of physically detached people, they engage in mass communication. People use a variety of media types for this purpose. Possibilities include billboards, mass mailings, newspapers, magazines, website postings, e-mails, podcasts, and radio or TV broadcasts.

Other Recognized Modes: Scholars use additional terms to denote other types of communications and communicational situations. *Organizational communication* highlights situations in which people interact as members of large networks, like businesses. *Family communication,* as one might expect, considers the unique interactions that take place among people who are related by marriage, birth, or adoption. *Intercultural communication* considers situations in which individuals from significantly different people groups, each of these with a distinguishable identity, interact with each other. These are but a few of the many terms that people use to distinguish different modes of communication.

—✦—

When you use a pen, a printing press, a keyboard, or a radio tower to channel meaningful information to someone, you are engaging in mediated communication.

—✦—

Spiritual Communication: Unlike its mainstream alternatives, this textbook assumes that we have no reason for not supposing that personal beings other than humans are real and that they are justifiably factored in analyses like this one as potentially if not actually communicative. Moreover, one could reasonably argue that such beings do exist—leading philosophers and theologians have compellingly argued this point over the centuries—and that they are rightly factored, therefore, in studies such as this one. Accordingly, we conclude this definitional section with a review of several communicational types that standard communication texts do not consider.

The term *spiritual communication* denotes any situation in which fundamentally spiritual beings—that is, intelligent, moral beings who are capable of living without bodies—send meaningful messages to each other. Examples of this in the Biblically Christian tradition include message exchanges between God and humans, between God and angelic or demonic beings, between humans and angelic or demonic beings, and between angelic or demonic beings and each other. Technically, human-to-human message transmissions fall into this category, too, since humans are fundamentally spiritual beings.

Spiritual communication exists in several varieties. *Divine revelation* refers to situations in which God, whether directly or indirectly, imparts meaningful messages to humans. In Christian tradition, divine revelation assumes two basic forms. *General revelation* refers to the non-verbal messages that God has imprinted on human consciousness or that come into human consciousness in response to what God discloses through nature. *Special revelation* refers to the messages that God discloses supernaturally through His Holy Spirit or through Scripture via the agency of the Holy Spirit. It also includes His Biblically documented disclosures of information to humans via channels like miracles, dreams, soundings, appearances, etc.

Religious expression, by contrast, is the human attempt to connect with God, or with something apparently ultimately fulfilling like Him, especially but not exclusively through such overtly "religious" message forms as meditation, prayer, chanting, singing, reciting, dancing, fasting, almsgiving, body decoration, self-punishment, sacrifices, etc. A Biblical worldview sees a religious motivation not just in these expressive forms, but in virtually all human conduct since it holds that human behavior is driven, to a large extent, by a longing to reconnect with the God whose communion we were created to enjoy, yet from whom we have become estranged. In religious expression, understood in this broader sense, a person attempts to satisfy this longing by adopting and exhibiting attitudes, beliefs, and behaviors that he or she believes will plug this void. This quest for a God-like connection can appear in the person's pursuit of almost anything that seems capable of providing ultimate fulfillment—knowledge, wealth, power, fame, love, respect, sex, or amusement, to name but a few possibilities. Some people even turn to formal religion or to morality, rather than to God himself, to fill the void. In any of these cases, a person's ultimate passion shows itself in the way he or she does life. Whatever else your life may be, it is fundamentally a religious expression since it manifests your sense that something of ultimate worth exists and that it is worth pursuing.

> —⁂—
> **The redemptive communicator is one who submits to the realization that the God of Scripture is, in fact, the creator and sustainer of the universe and that everything in it, therefore, including communication, must be understood and engaged in the instructive light of what His *divine revelation* says about it.**
> —⁂—

Redemptive criticism is a term for the attempt to make sense of human communicative behavior and specific human communications in the light of divine revelation. You may recall the terms *exposition* and *rhetoric* from the first chapter. As was noted, the expositor tries to explain why people share certain attitudes, values, beliefs, feelings, or behaviors. He or she does this by explaining mysteries like the widespread human longing to connect with God or something God-like. The redemptive expositor aims to show how this yearning gives shape to human communications and tries to explain why the longing exists and why it works as it does, in the light of what divine revelation says about it. As a rhetorical analyst, however, the redemptive critic also considers how people find redemption and what role, if any, communication plays in the process. The critic considers, too, how the redeemed life functions as a message to others and how it impacts or can impact other people.

Redemptive communication resembles religious expression, but it differs from it in a major way.

Whereas *religion* is the human attempt to connect with God or with something God-like, *redemption* is the state of having actually connected with God in the God-centered way that enables one to start seeing things as He sees them and relating to them as He relates to them. The redemptive communicator is one who submits to the realization that the God of Scripture is, in fact, the creator and sustainer of the universe and that everything in it, therefore, including communication, must be understood and engaged in the instructive light of what His *divine revelation* says about it. This God-centered stance not only gives shape to his or her definition of communication, but also frames his or her understanding of what motivates people to communicate and impacts his or her own communication practices.

Now that we have a basic understanding of what communication is and how it works, we turn our attention to a series of interrelated questions that must be engaged if we are to appreciate the practical value of studying and practicing this topic. As you will see, people's differences of belief at the most basic level can help to steer them toward very different conclusions about matters like these. In contrast to disappointing alternatives, a Biblically Christian approach to communication provides a rich starting that avoids many of the pitfalls that beset so many of its alternatives.

QUESTIONS FOR ANALYSIS

1. Words are powerful communicational tools. Consider the following wisdom from James 3: 2-10:

"If we could control our tongues, we would be perfect and could also control ourselves in every other way. We can make a large horse go wherever we want by means of a small bit in its mouth. And a small rudder makes a huge ship turn wherever the pilot chooses to go, even though the winds are strong. In the same way, the tongue is a small thing that makes grand speeches. But a tiny spark can set a great forest on fire. And the tongue is a flame of fire. It is a whole world of wickedness, corrupting your entire body. It can set your whole life on fire, for it is set on fire by hell itself. People can tame all kinds of animals, birds, reptiles, and fish, but no one can tame the tongue. It is restless and evil, full of deadly poison. Sometimes it praises our Lord and Father, and sometimes it curses those who have been made in the image of God. And so blessing and cursing come pouring out of the same mouth. Surely, my brothers and sisters, this is not right!"

Drawing from your personal experience, write a 200-300 word essay in which you describe the power of words to be destructive and to be constructive.

2. Bring a product, as packaged for sale on a store shelf, to your next class session. Analyze it and be prepared to explain to your classmates how its creator blended verbal and non-verbal elements in a quest to make the product more appealing to prospective buyers and more likely to be sold. Among the variables you should consider are word choice, the number of words, the font, size,

color, placement, and relative size of the words, colors or symbols that appear elsewhere on the packaging, etc.

3. Share three examples of a strange regional word or expression that you or a friend has encountered during your lifetime. Be sure for each of these to identify your hometown or region and where you were when you encountered the strange expression. Who said it? What was his or her home region? What did you think when you first heard the expression? How did you learn the intended meaning of the strange expression? Which term do people from your home region use for the same thing?

4. In a paragraph or two, answer the following questions about your use of artifacts to send people information about yourself: a) Which colors to you like to wear? Which do you not like to wear?; b) Why do you like or not like them? Which ideas or feelings do or might they communicate to other people?

5. Write a 200-300 word response to the following statement by Cornelius LaPide, a 17th century Jesuit priest: "The face, therefore, is the image of the heart, and the eyes are the mirror of the soul and its affections. One finds this principally in tumultuous and vile men who conceal their badness for a long time, but when they are distracted and unaware, it suddenly appears in their face and eyes. Therefore, the face and the eyes indicate the joy or sadness of the soul, its love or hatred; so also, honesty or treachery and hypocrisy." You may agree, partly agree, or disagree with this observation. In either case, state your position, clearly and succinctly, and back it with supportive information, such as illustrations or examples from your personal experience or that of someone else.

CHAPTER 3
COMMUNICATION

—ɯɯ—

Why Does It Matter?

Overview: In this chapter, we consider why communication is significant. A person's answer to this question is influenced by his or her worldview, his or most basic beliefs about the world as it really is. This chapter reviews a couple of autonomous approaches to making sense of things and pauses to consider their limitations. We then review how Biblically Christian thinking answers the same basic questions and how these answers enhance its merits as an alternative to human-centered models.

A Closer Look: As we have established, communication is the transmission of meaningful information from one person or group of persons (the sender) to another person or group of persons (the recipient) in a way that generates shared attitudes, values, beliefs, feelings, or behaviors between the sender and recipient. People use verbal and non-verbal forms like the ones presented in the previous chapter, sometimes intentionally and other times unintentionally, to create these shared understandings.

Important as these foundational concepts are, they merely set the stage for a more meaningful study of communication. Among the additional questions one can consider are the following: Where did communication come from? What is its purpose, if indeed it has a purpose? What meaningful difference can it make in individual lives and in the world? What, if anything, makes a communicative act or a communicational message moral or good? What, if anything, makes it immoral or evil? Unless it serves practically significant questions like these, the study of communication has little value.

A person's answers to questions like these, about communication's significance, will be powerfully influenced by his or her *worldview*—an individual's most basic assumptions about the way things truly are. Your worldview is a composite of your beliefs about human origin (where we came from), human nature (what makes us human), human purpose (why we are here), and human destiny (where we are going). It also involves your beliefs about moral values (the rightness or wrongness of things) and aesthetic values (the desirability or undesirability of things). Your worldview is so basic to your way of viewing life that you instinctively just assume it unless something presses you to critically evaluate or to justify it.

WORLDVIEWS AND THE VALUE OF COMMUNICATION

What is your worldview? Your behavior does more to answer this question than the words you offer when you are asked to state your beliefs. A person who professes to be a follower of Jesus but who lives in a way that contradicts Christian principles may profess the Christian worldview, but this person's behavior suggests that his worldview is likelier hedonistic than it is Christian. Indeed, a worldview is the belief system that a person practices in daily life, not just the set of belief statements that he offers when asked to do so. If the beliefs a person professes contradict the beliefs he actually practices, one may reasonably infer from this that he is hypocritical, delusional, or else ignorant of his true belief system. A hypocrite is someone who is aware of and content to live with an inconsistency between the belief system he professes and the one he practices. A delusional person is someone who does not know that such an inconsistency exists because he chooses to disbelieve in its existence, even though he has reason for believing that it does. An ignorant person is someone who does not know that such an inconsistency exists because he has no reason to know that it does.

> *A worldview is the belief system that a person practices in daily life, not just the set of belief statements that he offers when asked to do so.*

People whose walk and talk are inconsistent are often unaware that this is so because they simplistically assume that they truly believe in what they say they believe, as many people do. Blind assumptions of this type can adversely affect them in a number of ways. Besides preventing them from seeing themselves and engaging the world as they really are, this misconception can persuade others who notice the inconsistency that those who hold them are untrustworthy. Biblically Christian thinking recognizes an even greater potential consequence of inauthentic statements of believe: "Just as you can identify a tree by its fruit, so you can identify people by their actions. Not everyone who calls out to me, 'Lord! Lord!' will enter the Kingdom of Heaven. Only those who actually do the will of my Father in heaven will enter" (Matt. 7:20-21).

How does a person's worldview develop? Several factors contribute to this. Perhaps the most obvious of these is his or her lifetime of *socialization*—the person's history of interactions with people whose input helps to shape the way he or she sees and acts toward the world. Parents, spiritual leaders, teachers, friends, and media personalities are the most obvious examples of these influential others. Through formal and informal interactions with other people, we derive our verbal and non-verbal languages, our behavioral patterns, our group and individual identities, and many of our values and beliefs. If your parents warned you to avoid the wrong crowd or to avoid watching certain types of TV programming when you were young, they likely did so because they recognized the powerful impact one's socialization experiences can have in fashioning what he or she becomes.

A second factor that may impact a person's worldview development is his or her *physical constitution*—the bodily dynamics, like neurological and biochemical processes, that help to shape the individual's personality and, by extension, his or her openness to certain types of ideas, feelings, and behaviors. Volumes of scholarly research affirm that a person's physical constitution can impact his or her levels of aggressiveness, agreeability, sociability, and impulsiveness, among other belief-expressive tendencies. The research also shows that when a person's constitution changes, his or her personality can change, too. Perhaps you have witnessed such a transformation in someone who has suffered a brain injury or whose brain arteries have hardened (a condition called atherosclerosis) as he or she has aged.

—\\\\—
Divine intervention, no less than socialization and physical constitution, can impact a person's worldview development.
—\\\\—

A third factor that may impact a person's worldview development is his or her *spiritual constitution.* While mainstream communication scholars disregard this as a factor in someone's worldview development, Biblically Christian thinking does not. The Bible teaches that people enter the world in a state of spiritual brokenness. Although we are inclined to seek something God-like, we are not inclined, on our own, to seek for God himself (see Rom. 3:9-26). Despite this tendency, God, in ways not necessarily understandable to humans, can open a person's eyes to otherwise indiscernible spiritual truths and use this revelation to transform a person's understanding of life's purpose and about the right approach to living (see John 6:37-40, 44, 63-65). Thus, divine intervention, no less than socialization and physical constitution, can impact a person's worldview development.

Worldviews can be distinguished from each other in lots of ways. At the most basic level, worldviews can be broken into two major categories. *Autonomous worldviews* are systems of belief that people develop primarily in response to what human standards have taught them to deem believable or acceptable. The autonomist's defining belief, in words from the ancient Greek philosopher Protagoras, is that "Man is the measure of all things." A *theocentric worldview*, by contrast, recognizes that God, the timeless, changeless source and sustainer of the universe and the source of all knowledge, discloses otherwise indiscernible foundational truths through Scripture and that these, therefore, rightly frame and give direction to human quests to make sense of anything, including communication.

In their quests to determine what is believable, acceptable, or true, autonomists validate beliefs through the use several types of human-centered proof standards. Rationalistic and empirical truth standards, for example, hold that a belief, feeling, or behavior is unacceptable if it is illogical or if it is at odds with what common human observations tell us is true. To the rationalistic/empirical mind, Biblical accounts of miracles—such as Jesus' feeding of the 5,000 with five loaves and two fishes, or His walking on water (Mark 6)—are difficult to accept since these accounts go against commonly observed, supposedly unchangeable laws of physics.

Pragmatic truth standards, by contrast, hold that a belief, feeling, or behavior is acceptable if it simply "works" for the person who holds it, regardless of whether it logically consists with anyone else's experiences and standards. The twentieth century libertarian Ayn Rand expressed this way of thinking when she claimed that "man must be the beneficiary of his own moral actions" and that the "actor must always be the beneficiary of his action and that man must act for his own rational self-interest"[16] Many pragmatists deny the idea that people come to know things in exactly the same way, so they reject the use of supposedly objective criteria, like rationalistic or empirical rules, for the purpose of determining whether a person's beliefs, feelings, or behaviors are acceptable. What matters to these pragmatists, at least in theory, is that individuals are free to discover or to create truth for themselves without being sidetracked by other people's standards. To the pragmatist, others' moral standards are little more than tools for manipulating other people, or what nineteenth century nihilist Friedrich Nietzsche's more cynically called "the best of all devices for leading mankind by the nose."[17]

Utilitarian truth standards, like pragmatic ones, hold that a belief, feeling, or behavior is acceptable if it "works," but differ radically from pragmatists in how they determine what works. For the utilitarian, a belief, feeling, or behavior that works is one that promotes the greatest good not for the individual, but for humanity as a whole. As Jeremy Bentham, an 18th century formulator of this model, put it, "Ethics at large [for the utilitarian] may be defined as the art of directing men's actions to the production of the greatest possible quantity of happiness, on the part of those whose interest is in view."[18] For a modern example of how utilitarian thinking works, one can review the writings of Peter Singer, a controversial ethics professor at Princeton University. Like a pragmatist, he rejects universal moral rules, such as the Biblical teaching that all human life is valuable. Instead, he uses utilitarian logic

---

[16] Rand, Ayn and Nathaniel Branden. *The Virtue of Selfishness: A New Concept of Egoism*. New York: Penguin Books, 1964. n.pag. Print.

[17] Nietzsche, Friedrich W, and H L. Mencken. *The Antichrist*. New York: A.A. Knopf, 1920. 127. Print.

[18] Bentham, Jeremy, *An Introduction to the Principles of Morals and Legislation*. 1907. Library of Economics and Liberty. 25 May 2011. <http://www.econlib.org/library/Bentham/bnthPML18.html>.

to argue, shockingly, that killing some birth defected babies is morally justified for utilitarian reasons. The following quote illustrates how his thinking operates: "When the death of a disabled infant will lead to the birth of another infant with better prospects of a happy life, the total amount of happiness will be greater if the disabled infant is killed. The loss of happy life for the first infant is outweighed by the gain of a happier life for the second. Therefore, if killing the hemophiliac infant has no adverse effect on others, it would, according to the total view, be right to kill him."[19] This is the utilitarian thinking in its rawest form.

Before presenting the theocentric approach's truth standard and contrasting it with the autonomous standards just presented, we must briefly review a couple of the autonomous approach's especially prominent worldview traditions—physical determinism and social constructionism. In doing so, we contrast what these sub-systems say about human origin, purpose, destiny, and values and consider the implications of these views for their adherents' answer to this chapter's guiding question, "Why does communication matter?"

AUTONOMOUS WORLDVIEWS AND COMMUNICATION

How many worldviews are there? Scholars differ in their answers to this question. Dennis McCallum, in his book *Christianity: The Faith that Makes Sense,* identifies five systems—physical determinism, pantheism, theism, spiritism and polytheism, and postmodernism. David Noebel, in his book, *Understanding the Times,* highlights six—Christianity, Islam, secular humanism, Marxism, cosmic humanism, and postmodernism. Anthony Steinbronn, in his book *Worldviews: A Christian Response to Religious Pluralism,* lists seven systems—Buddhism, Confucianism, Hinduism, Islam, tribalism, modernism, and a Biblical view. In the latest edition of his *The Universe Next Door,* which has sold more than 300,000 copies since its first edition, James Sire profiles nine worldview traditions—Christian theism, deism, physical determinism, nihilism, existentialism, Eastern pantheistic monism, New Age spirituality, postmodernism, and Islamic theism.

Obviously, some of these works are more meticulous than others in their approach to parsing the world's major basic belief systems. Despite differences like this, each of these treatments, and others like them, helpfully demonstrates how our fundamental assumptions about the world impact the way we distinguish things that matter from things that do not matter. Rather than pointlessly deeming one of these treatments to be better than the others—each affords an interesting, informative approach to the topic—I reduce their distinctions to two clearly distinguishable, autonomous ways of thinking and then contrast them with their theocentric alternative. My goal in an introductory text like this one is not to

---

[19] Singer, Peter. *Writings on an Ethical Life.* New York: Harper-Collins, 2001. 189. Print.

catalog every autonomous way of thinking or every worldview sub-system, but to briefly describe the overarching systems—physical determinism and social constructionism—that have most profoundly impacted Westerners' ways of thinking about life and about communication's significance.

Physical determinism: The late Carl Sagan's quip that "the Cosmos is all that is or ever was or ever will be" well expresses this system's guiding assumption.[20] Physical determinism sees the universe as a self-created, self-sustaining machine, consisting of material particles and processes and nothing more than this, that invariably follows the course that physics has programmed it to follow. Everything that happens, this view holds, happens because nature has programmed it to occur. History follows an inevitable course, and nothing can alter this.

Physical determinism denies the existence of a separate spiritual realm and of a Creator who can alter history's course as He wills. Spiritual beliefs, it maintains, are little more than biochemically preconditioned mechanisms that the human brain creates to enable people to cope with the harsh realities of a hostile world. This view denies the existence of spiritual beings, like God, and holds that although the universe has the features of an infinitely complex machine, it was not intelligently created. "It is all accident, all a matter of chance. No reason, no end, no purpose at all," as one prominent evolutionary biologist reportedly put it.[21]

—∞—
Physical determinism sees the universe as a self-created, self-sustaining machine, consisting of material particles and processes and nothing more than this, that invariably follows the course that physics has programmed it to follow.
—∞—

This view has become increasingly popular in Western culture since the beginning of the Enlightenment, in the 17th century, when European scholars began to investigate and to explain the world independently, inspired but not necessarily guided by Biblical precepts. Ironically, a number of this movement's early trailblazers were outstanding Christians who aimed, through direct investigations of the material world, simply to use their logical and observational powers to better understand the universe they realized God had created. Their task, in words commonly attributed to astronomer Johannes Kepler, was simply to "think God's thoughts after Him."

---

[20] Sagan, Carl. *Cosmos.* New York: Random House, 1980. 4. Print.

[21] *Gems from Martin Lloyd-Jones: An Anthology of Quotations from "The Doctor."* Colorado Springs: Paternoster, 2007. 76. Print.

Buoyed by their discoveries and successes, emboldened new scholars emerged during the centuries that followed who saw in the human powers of observation and reasoning the key to answering questions not just about the physical universe's elements and operations, but about virtually anything. The Biblical precepts that inspired many of their predecessors' investigations ceased to be revered as divinely disclosed and rightly authoritative and were themselves subjected to rationalistic and empirical truth standards for the purpose of judging their validity. The new thinkers recognized human experience as most people know it or can come to know it through observation as the standard for determining whether something is believable. Thus, they generated works like Thomas Jefferson's *The Life and Morals of Jesus of Nazareth, a* New Testament that retained Jesus' moral teachings but removed references to His miracles. This earthy way of looking at the world gradually emerged as the truth standard not just among intellectuals, but throughout mainstream culture. It remains popular today, especially in scientific circles, which continue to embrace rationalistic and empirical truth standards and to disregard the principles of divine revelation in their quests to explain such earthly wonders as human communication.

What motivates people to communicate as they do? Inspired by ideas that biologist Charles Darwin popularized during the mid-nineteenth century, physical determinists assume the drive to survive is fundamentally what moves individuals to interact with each other. As these theorists see it, human history is fundamentally the story of people working with or struggling against nature and each other in each individual's quest for self-preservation. Nature, they say, has somehow wired people to operate in this way. Physical determinists believe an individual instinctively communicates with other individuals to establish connections that boost his or her likelihood for survival. This, in a nutshell, is the naturalist's explanation of what makes human communication significant. It is seen as little more than a lifeline in a turbulent Darwinian ocean in which only the fittest survive. When they sink beneath the waters and drown, this view supposes, they simply cease to exist. There is no spiritual afterlife in the physical determinist's way of seeing things.

—∿—

Physical determinists hold that people are essentially machines—that because they are wired to behave as they do, they are unable to choose their actions freely or to determine what they will become.

—∿—

One more point about physical determinism is noteworthy in this description. Physical determinists hold that people are essentially machines—that because they are wired to behave as they do, they are unable to choose their actions freely or to determine what they will become. Instead, these theorists posit, people become only what genetic and environmental variables combine to dictate that they shall become. Determinists dismiss a person's belief that he or she is free to define his or her own destiny as a biochemically induced illusion. As the 18th century philosopher Benedict de Spinoza expressed this fatalistic belief, "In the mind there is no absolute or free will; but the mind is determined to wish this or that by a cause, which has also been determined by another cause, and this last by another cause, and so on to infinity."[22] More recently, Albert Einstein expressed the same core idea in the following words: "Everything is determined, the beginning as well as the end, by forces over which we have no control. It is determined for the insect as well as the star. Human beings, vegetables, or cosmic dust, we all dance to a mysterious tune, intoned in the distance by an invisible piper."[23]

A critical look at this way of thinking is in order at this point. If the universe and all that comprises it is an accident with no overarching purpose, as physical determinists assert, then people can have no more value, significance, or purpose than mice, fleas, or amoeba, because each is a product of the same accidental yet supposedly self-directed creative process. Physical determinism assigns humans no special status or significance in the universe. Thus, people's religious rituals and their charitable acts toward others are seen as biochemically programmed quests for self-preservation that have no eternal value. Human abuses, too—whether genocide, rape, or child molestation—are trivialized as little more than culturally relative, socially unaccepted acts in the ongoing struggle among living beings for survival. Physical determinism does not see the abuse of another person as being wrong in the principled, absolute sense that theocentrists do when they criticize the abuse as wrong.

—∾—
Physical determinism qualifies as autonomous because it begins with the blind rationalistic/ empirical assumption— and it is just an assumption—that people can credibly believe only in that which sense experience deems objectively believable.
—∾—

Physical determinism qualifies as autonomous because it begins with the blind rationalistic/empirical assumption—and it is just an assumption—that people can credibly believe only in that which sense experience deems objectively believable. If most people can see, hear, smell, taste, or feel something, it is sufficiently believable for the physical determinist. He or she then tries to make sense of this something by examining and explaining it as if it were a purely physical phenomenon.

This way of thinking is flawed for a couple of reasons. First, physical determinists can offer no physical evidence—the only type that counts, they say—to support their belief that

---

[22] Spinoza, Benedictus , and R H. M. Elwes. *The Chief Works of Benedict De Spinoza.* London: G. Bell, 1889. 119. Print.

[23] Carey, John. *Eyewitness to Science.* Cambridge: Harvard University Press, 1997. 274. Print.

everything in existence is entirely physical and that there is no separate spiritual dimension. This is a faith-based assumption, not a scientifically validated premise. Darwin himself, in a letter to a Harvard biologist, admitted that his attempt to explain life's origin in purely naturalistic terms relied heavily on guesswork: "I am quite conscious that my speculations run quite beyond the bounds of true science."[24] Second, physical determinists can offer no physical evidence to support their assumption that humans' sense perceptions give accurate pictures of things as they really are. Even if we assume that our sense perceptions are demonstrably accurate, determinists fail to show why we should also assume, as they do, that our senses can actually grasp and that our brains can accurately process the volume of data one would need in order to formulate accurate answers to the questions we autonomously explore. This, too, is a faith-based assumption.

Because it rests on speculations like these, physical determinism is not the obviously best way of looking at the world that its proponents believe it to be. Many people who recognize this have compared physical determinism to its worldview alternatives and have criticized it for being one of the worst belief systems, mainly because its portrayal of human existence is so bleak and its ethical implications for it are so dark. Indeed, this system's logic has been used throughout modern history to justify racism, sexism, and even mass murder. Peter Singer, for example, has used it to justify euthanasia:

> *Any discussion of the ethics of voluntary euthanasia must begin by considering whether it can ever be right to kill an innocent human being. The view that this can never be right gains its strongest support from religious doctrines that claim that only humans are made in the image of God, or that only humans have an immortal soul, or that God gave us dominion over the animals—meaning that we can kill them if we wish—but reserved to himself dominion over human beings.*
>
> *Reject these ideas, and it is difficult to think of any morally relevant properties that separate human beings with severe brain damage or other major intellectual disabilities from nonhuman animals at a similar mental level.*
>
> *For why should the fact that a being is a member of our species make it worse to kill that being than it is to kill a member of another species, if the two individuals have similar intellectual abilities or if the nonhuman has superior intellectual abilities?* [25]

This treatment of naturalism is necessarily brief in a text like this one. Suffice it to say,

---

[24] Gillespie, Neal C. *Charles Darwin and the Problem of Creation*. Chicago: University of Chicago Press, 1979. 2. Print.

[25] Singer, Peter. "Decisions about Death." *Free Inquiry* Aug/Sept 2005: n. pag. Web. 28 May 2011. <http://www.utilitarian.net/singer/by/200508--.htm>.

for these reasons as well as for others that have been expounded in greater detail by other critics, that physical determinism falls short as a model for making sense of human origin, nature, purpose, and destiny and as a framework for explaining human communication.

Social Constructionism. If physical determinism places too strong an emphasis on physical factors as shapers of what people do and what they can become, social constructionism places too heavy an emphasis on each person's unique experiences as determinative of what he or she can do or become. Like physical determinism, social constructionism is autonomous because it follows human standards, rather than divine precepts, in its attempt to answer questions about human origin, nature, purpose, and destiny. However, unlike physical determinists, who use a rationalistic and empirical truth standard when validating or invalidating answers to such questions, social constructionists typically use a pragmatic truth standard. This is so because constructionists reject the ideas, popular among physical determinists, that people can come to see the world in the same way, despite their different conditioning experiences.

> —⟋—
>
> **Social constructionists assume that because each person experiences the world in a unique way, no two persons can come to see the world in exactly the same way, no matter how hard they try to do so.**
>
> —⟋—

Social constructionists assume that because each person experiences the world in a unique way, no two persons can come to see the world in exactly the same way, no matter how hard they try to do so. They believe a person becomes what his or her socializing experiences precondition him or her to become. Whatever else it may be, a person's way of communicating is seen as an artifact of these unique experiences and is deemed appropriately interpreted as little more than this.

What motivates people to communicate as they do? Social constructionists provide a variety of answers to this question. Many of them share the Darwinian notion that human behavior is motivated primarily by the drive to survive. Some place a greater emphasis on the Nietzschean idea that human behavior is fundamentally motivated by the individual's appetite for power. Others subscribe to the Marxist idea that human behavior is primarily conditioned by the person's status in the ongoing struggle between society's haves and its have-nots. Some adopt the Freudian notion that human behavior is driven, above all, by sexual impulses. Still other constructionists are more agnostic about questions like these and assert that we cannot know whether human behavior has a primary motive or, if so, what the motive might be.

Social constructionists also disagree with each other about the question of whether people are free to choose their behaviors and their destinies. Two recent sub-traditions— existentialism and postmodernism—are noteworthy for their contrasting their views about this. Existentialists believe that although the material world may exist in a fixed form, with all its particles and processes, it is nonetheless removed from us, and we cannot have direct contact with it. All we can know about the world, they say, is what our perceptions tell us about it. Whether our perceptions of it are accurate or not, existentialists believe we come to see the world as we do by the people who influence us through socialization. They believe this neither has to be nor should be so, arguing that individuals are radically free to take control of their minds, to break away from stifling social influences, and to free themselves to see the world in authentic, uninhibited, self-directed ways. This movement's dislike for the other individuals' socializing influences on our ways of thinking is aptly expressed in the late leading twentieth century existentialist Jean-Paul Sartre's famous literary line: "Hell is other people!"

To the existentialist, then, communication tends to be negative. It is like a rope in tug-of-war, with the influencers who have shaped your mind pulling to keep you positioned where their lifetime of tugging has taken you. The existential response to this situation is not simply for you to pull in the opposite direction, but for you to release the rope they have assigned to you and to stop playing their game. Only by ridding yourself of external influences can you live life authentically and freely, they say. For atheistic versions of existentialism, this requires one to drop religious ideals, such as belief in God, which are dismissed as externally imposed barriers to thinking freely and to realizing, consequently, that everything is meaningless. Sartre explained his rationale for this way of thinking in the following statement:

> Nowhere is it written that the Good exists, that we must be honest, that we must not lie; because the fact is we are on a plane where there are only men. Dostoievsky said, "If God didn't exist, everything would be possible." That is the very starting point of existentialism. Indeed, everything is permissible if God does not exist, and as a result man is forlorn, because neither within him nor without does he find anything to cling to. He can't start making excuses for himself.[26]

To attain this existential type of freedom, Sartre proposed, one must bravely endure the pain that comes with realizing, as he claimed to believe, that everything, including one's communications with others, is pointless. *Nausea* is Sartre's term for the psychological pain one feels upon authentically realizing this belief. He also used the term to title a literary

---

[26] Cahoone, Lawrence E. *From Modernism to Postmodernism: An Anthology.* Malden, MA: Blackwell Pub, 2003. 171. Print.

work that he authored, a story in which the main character's realization that life is meaninglessness nauseates him in this existential way. Sartre's only remedy for this anxiety—if it can be called a solution—is self-actualization, which means doing what your raw impulses tell you to do without allowing your reasoning to get in the way.

Existentialism, like physical determinism, has been criticized for several reasons over the years. First, it is self-refuting. This system's thinkers—who argued that individuals should resist having their thoughts assigned to them by other people—attempted through their writings, ironically, to assign their own thoughts to other people. Thus, their walk simply did not match their talk, a glaring inconsistency that raises questions about the believability of the ideas they proposed. Existentialism has also been criticized for providing a bleak picture of human existence by giving people so little a reason for living and so little a motive for behaving ethically toward others. Sartre himself may have realized his system's flaws later in his life. In a 1974 interview, he offered a statement, in a published interview, that implies his worldview may have shifted by that point, late in his life: *"I do not feel that I am the product of chance, a speck of dust in the universe, but someone who was expected, prepared, prefigured. In short, a being whom only a creator could put here; and this idea of a creating hand refers to God."*[27]

Like existentialism, postmodernism, the second social constructionist sub-tradition that we consider, assumes that people act as they do and become what they become primarily, if not exclusively, as a reaction to their lifetime of conditioning experiences. Postmodernists, who are also called deconstructionists, are especially interested in the ways people use language to impact each other's ways of thinking, feeling, and acting. Many of these theorists share the existentialists' belief that the material world, if it is really there, exceeds our grasp. The only reality people can know, they say, is the one their minds construct in response to the world as language filters it to them.

How should one respond to his or her lifetime of conditioning experiences? Existentialists and postmodernists answer this question differently. Whereas existentialists urge people to rid themselves of their socially instilled ways of seeing the world and to follow their raw instincts instead, postmodernists focus elsewhere. Those with Marxist leanings explore how powerful people (the haves) use language and media as tools to suppress the weak (the have-nots) and call for solutions to this supposed problem. Those with feminist leanings investigate how men use language and media to dominate women and call for fixes to this. Many deconstructionists explore how other groups of haves (whether racially, ethnically, culturally,

---

[27] Critchley, Simon. *The Book of Dead Philosophers*. Carlton, Vic: Melbourne University Publishing, 2008. 252. Print.

religiously, or politically defined) use language and media to exploit corresponding groups of have-nots and call for remedies to this. The goals for the postmodernist in any of these cases is twofold: 1) exposition—showing how social influencers can impact what people become and how privileged groups use this to promote themselves at others' expense and; 2) emancipation—promoting remedies for these supposed misuses of power. Deterministic deconstructionists devote themselves only to exposition, believing calls for emancipation to be pointless since, they believe, people inevitably become what their social conditioning has predisposed them to become.

Beneath these concerns are assumptions that clearly identify postmodernism as an autonomous, social constructionist tradition. As already noted, deconstructionists believe there is no real world out there waiting to be discovered.

—*m*—

If anything is unknowable, we could never learn that it exists and is unknowable unless this were revealed to us by one who, unlike us, has access to it.

—*m*—

Reality, they propose, is something your mind constructs in response to the linguistically filtered perceptions that it gathers and synthesizes throughout your lifetime. You have no way of rising above these perceptions to access and know for certain that anything outside you truly exists. Whatever you believe to be true, real, meaningful, and right or wrong, they say, is just a mindset that you have formed in response to your conditioning experiences. Because these perceptions are unique—no one, they assert, can experience and see life as another person does—you must respect the "fact" that each individual creates his or her own truth. Accordingly, postmodernists contend, you must not try to impose your view of the world and your values on other people. Deconstructionists are especially prickly about violations of this principle in situations in which members of traditionally empowered groups consciously or subconsciously "impose" their views of the world on members of traditionally disempowered minority groups, whether they are ethnically, racially, religiously, or politically defined.

To the postmodernist, communication is a weapon that can be used to promote good or evil. The good, as he or she imagines it, is the advancement of his or her postmodern ideals and values, including the works of exposition and emancipation. The evil, not surprisingly, is the disregard of these ideas and values and the imposition of one person's values on another or of a majority viewpoint on minorities through language and media. Postmodernists would not state this point about themselves so directly—to state anything so objectively, after all, would be contrary to the relativistic ideals they profess—but it is clearly the implication of what they right.

This brings us to a discussion of postmodernism's merits as a framework for making sense of communication, or of anything else for that matter. If one assumes, as postmodernists contend, that there is no world outside our perceptions, we must ask how one could possibly know that this is so. As G. K. Chesterton, once observed, "We do not know enough about the unknown to know that it is unknowable."[28] If anything is unknowable, we could never learn that it exists and is unknowable unless this were revealed to us by one who, unlike us, has access to it. The same objection applies to postmodernism's contention that no two people see the world in exactly the same way. In order to say credibly that this is so, the postmodernist somehow must escape the supposedly inescapable prison of his own perceptions in order to compare its content with the content of other people's perceptions and to determine, consequently, that no two perspectives are alike. Postmodern theorists consistently fail to explain why we should assume that they somehow are exempt from the very limitations, such as this one, that they assign to everyone else.

Deconstructionists also fail to explain why anyone in a postmodern world should conduct himself or herself ethically toward others. If we assume that individuals create their own truth and their own morals in response to their unique perceptions, as postmodernists suggest, then we must ask whether it is fair to hold people accountable to a moral standard other than one's own. Such an idea has ominous implications, as C. S. Lewis observed in an essay that he penned while the Nazis threatened to overtake his British homeland during World War II:

> *Out of this apparently innocent idea comes the disease that will certainly end our species (and, in my view, damn our souls) if it is not crushed; the fatal superstition that men can create values, that a community can choose its "ideology" as men choose their clothes. Everyone is indignant when he hears the Germans define justice as that which is to the interest of the Third Reich. But it is not always remembered that this indignation is perfectly groundless if we ourselves regard morality as a subjective sentiment to be altered at will. Unless there is some objective standard of good, overarching Germans, Japanese, and ourselves alike whether any of us obey it or no, then of course the Germans are as competent to create their ideology as we are to create ours. If "good" and "better" are terms deriving their sole meaning from the ideology of each people, then of course ideologies themselves cannot be better or worse than one another. Unless the measuring rod is independent of the things measured, we can do no measuring.*[29]

---

[28] Chesterton, Gilbert Keith. *William Blake*. New York: Cosimo Books, 2005. 74. Print.

[29] Lewis, C. S. *Christian Reflections*. Grand Rapids: Wm. B. Eeerdmans,1994. 73. Print.

Postmodernists often argue that we must protect the beliefs and values of the have-nots from the supposedly corrupting, self-serving influence of the haves. However, if each person's moral values are personally constructed and if one person's values are not necessarily better than the next person's values, why must we protect the have-nots? Why should one not crush them instead if his or her personal values deem this appropriate? Deconstructionists provide no satisfactory answers to this question.

THE LIMITATIONS OF AUTONOMOUS REASONING

As this chapter demonstrates, autonomous approaches to explaining human origin, nature, purpose, and destiny and to providing meaningful reasons for appreciating communication are plagued by serious limitations. Some of these problems are intellectual. Others are ethical. From a Biblically Christian standpoint, these problems, although intellectual and ethical on their surface, are fundamentally spiritual.

> **Consequently, people live in a corrupted state, having divorced ourselves from the very one for whom we were created and in whom we find our completion.**

The Bible reveals that God alone—the timeless, changeless source and sustainer of the universe and our creator—knows everything that can be known: "O LORD, you have examined my heart and know everything about me. You know when I sit down or stand up. You know my thoughts even when I'm far away. You see me when I travel and when I rest at home. You know everything I do. You know what I am going to say even before I say it, LORD. You go before me and follow me. You place your hand of blessing on my head. Such knowledge is too wonderful for me, too great for me to understand!" (Psalm 139: 1-6). Humans simply cannot attain the perfect knowledge that only God has.

Still, God has made known or knowable to us essential facts about the universe He created and our place in it. Perhaps the most illuminating Biblical passage about this matter is the book of Romans, especially its first two chapters. This epistle tells us that people—"through everything God made . . .can clearly see his invisible qualities—his eternal power and divine nature. So they have no excuse for not knowing God" (Rom 1:20). Even though people "know the truth about God because he has made it obvious to them" (v. 19), people "suppress the truth by their wickedness" (v. 18).

This highlights the fact that people have an imperfect nature and do not seek after the God by whom and for whom we were created. This dilemma traces to our earliest history, when our ancestors first asserted their autonomy by questing to "be like God, knowing both good and evil" (Gen. 3:5). This decision to chase an egotistical lie had enduringly adverse effects, for "When Adam sinned, sin entered the world. Adam's sin brought death, so death spread to everyone, for everyone sinned. Yes, people sinned even before the law was given.

But it was not counted as sin because there was not yet any law to break" (Rom. 5: 12-13).

Consequently, people live in a corrupted state, having divorced ourselves from the very one for whom we were created and in whom we find our completion: "No one is righteous— not even one. No one is truly wise; no one is seeking God. All have turned away; all have become useless. No one does good, not a single one. Their talk is foul, like the stench from an open grave. Their tongues are filled with lies. Snake venom drips from their lips. Their mouths are full of cursing and bitterness. They rush to commit murder. Destruction and misery always follow them. They don't know where to find peace. They have no fear of God at all" (Rom. 3:10-18).

Although our Creator has given us intelligence that we can use, despite our brokenness, to make sense of some things about the universe and our place in it, this intelligence is considerably limited: "My thoughts are nothing like your thoughts," says the LORD. "And my ways are far beyond anything you could imagine. For just as the heavens are higher than the earth, so my ways are higher than your ways and my thoughts higher than your thoughts: (Isa. 57:8-9).

> **"If I find in myself a desire which no experience in this world can satisfy, the most probable explanation is that I was made for another world."**

Despite the stifling effects of our corruption, our sense that we are made for something perfect, unlike anything in this world, lingers in our souls. Indeed, although we do not long for God himself (cf. Rom. 3:11), a craving for this perfect something that eludes our grasp drives much of our behavior. We long to connect with it, not knowing what it is or where to find it. Instead of humbly acknowledging our limitations and turning for guidance to the all-knowing Creator whose restored presence alone can fill this void, we anesthetize the pain within us by chasing empty alternatives that temporarily create false feelings of satisfaction: "They traded the truth about God for a lie. So they worshiped and served the things God created instead of the Creator himself, who is worthy of eternal praise! Amen" (Rom. 1:25). Among the God-made things that we worship is our corrupted human intelligence, which we sometimes centralize in our quests for worldview-related answers that simply exceed our fallen grasp—answers to questions about human origin, nature, purpose destiny, and values. We justify the answers that these generate using rationalistic/empirical, pragmatic, and utilitarian truth standards, among others that our minds devise, as if our minds could independently generate trustworthy answers despite their brokenness. In the end, though, these intellectual saviors disappoint and fail to deliver what we our souls truly desire. The logical implication of this pattern is clear, as   C. S. Lewis explains: "If I find in myself a desire which no experience in this world can satisfy, the most probable explanation is that I was made for another world."[30]

The only real solution to this crisis begins when we sincerely acknowledge that on our own we are hopelessly autonomous, that our hearts and minds are helplessly impaired by this corruption, and that our only hope for escaping our brokenness and seeing anything as it truly is must be God-centered (theocentric) and initiated. Through His Son's redemptive death on the cross, God bridged the gap that separates us from Him and extended to us the offer of a cure for our brokenness, one that we receive when we humbly and repentantly centralize God's authority in our lives (cf. Psalm 51:16-18; John 1:12). When we surrender ourselves in this way, we commit to make sense of anything, including ourselves as communicators, and to conduct ourselves, communicatively or otherwise, in the instructive light of His revealed Word to us (cf. Psalm 119:105; 1 Thes. 2:13; 2 Tim. 3:16-17). The person who is thus redeemed does not become all-knowing like God. Nor does he or she necessarily become more knowledgeable about human experience. However, this transformation does give the person the corrective lens through which the human experience must be filtered if one hopes to avoid the logical shortsightedness and the ethical distortions that inevitably plague autonomous attempts to make sense of it.

> —∞—
> **I invite you to become a redemptive communicator— someone who sees the world as God, according to His revelation, intended it to be and who interacts with others in a way that, above all, promotes His redemptive purpose in their lives.**
> —∞—

The next chapter considers how this corrective lens impacts one's view of the world and of human communication. An authentically theocentric vantage point impacts not only the way one makes sense of communication, but also the way one practices it. As you contemplate this book's first three chapters and as you read through the fourth and fifth, I invite you to become a redemptive communicator—someone who sees the world as God, according to His revelation, intended it to be and who interacts with others in a way that, above all, promotes His redemptive purpose in their lives.

---

[30] Lewis, C. S. *Mere Christianity.* New York: Macmillan, 1986. 106. Print.

QUESTIONS FOR ANALYSIS

1. This chapter indicates that a person's worldview is not the beliefs he or she professes, but the beliefs his or her behavior suggests. State whether you agree or disagree with this statement in a 100-200 word response. Be sure to provide at least three different reasons, examples, illustrations, or other supportive material that clearly supports your stated position.

2. Read the following two poems. Then, using relevant terms from this chapter, write a 200-300 word response that identifies the worldview that each of these compositions appears most to express. Be sure to justify your answers with clear, logical explanations so it is obvious how you arrived at your conclusions.

FROM "PARACELSUS"

Truth is within ourselves; it takes no rise
From outward things, whate'er you may believe.
There is an inmost centre in us all,
Where truth abides in fullness; and around,
Wall upon wall, the gross flesh hems it in,
This perfect, clear perception—which is truth.
A baffling and perverting carnal mesh
Binds it, and makes all error: and, to know,
Rather consists in opening out a way
Whence the imprisoned splendour may escape,
Than in effecting entry for a light
Supposed to be without.

—Robert Browning (1812-1889)

OPEN MY EYES THAT I MAY SEE

Open my eyes, that I may see
Glimpses of truth Thou hast for me;
Place in my hands the wonderful key
That shall unclasp and set me free.

Silently now I wait for Thee,
Ready my God, Thy will to see,
Open my eyes, illumine me,
Spirit divine!

Open my ears, that I may hear
Voices of truth Thou sendest clear;
And while the wave notes fall on my ear,
Everything false will disappear.

Open my mouth, and let me bear,
Gladly the warm truth everywhere;
Open my heart and let me prepare
Love with Thy children thus to share.

— Clara H. Fiske Scott (1841-1897)

3. As mentioned in the chapter, Romans 1:25 states: "They traded the truth about God for a lie. So they worshiped and served the things God created instead of the Creator himself, who is worthy of eternal praise! Amen." The chapter highlights corrupted human intelligence as one of the God-made things that we worship instead of God himself. Make a list of at least five other God-like substitutes in human experience that people "worship" or serve rather than God himself. Explain why you placed each item on your list.

CHAPTER 4
COMMUNICATION

—⟪⟫—

A Biblically Redemptive Account

Overview: A redemptive communicator is someone who views communication through the lens of what God says about it through His special and common grace.

A Closer Look: Unlike autonomous worldviews, the Biblically Christian worldview is a set of beliefs about human origin, nature, purpose, destiny, and values that people hold primarily in response to what God has revealed to be true, regardless of whether this revelation satisfies rationalistic, empirical, pragmatic, or utilitarian truth standards. Truth, the Biblically informed theist understands, is not a biochemical illusion or a social construction, but that which actually is the case, regardless of how it is perceived. As such, it is something to be discovered and to which people are accountable, regardless of whether they choose to believe it exists. The law of gravity, for example, is as true for the lunatic who tries to fly off a cliff as it is for the common person who carefully descends a stairway. Laws of ethics, too, are as true for those who deny or ignore them as they are for those who recognize and respect them. Physical laws like gravity are laws not because we recognize them, but because they are divinely fixed projections of God's creativity.

—⟪⟫—

Truth, the Biblically informed theist understands, is not a biochemical illusion or a social construction, but that which actually is the case, regardless of how it is perceived.

—⟪⟫—

Ethical laws are laws not laws because we see or believe them, but because they are divinely fixed projections of God's perfect character. Regardless of whether we like it, all people are accountable to the physical and ethical laws that God has instituted. Those who deny or disregard them must endure the consequences of doing so.

This realistic outlook frames the way Christians answer the questions that distinguish worldview systems from each other. Who are we? Where did we come from, why are we here, and where are we going? What relevance, if any, do the answers to these questions have for the way we live or should be living our lives now? What is right and what is wrong, and what makes it right or wrong? What should we desire and not desire in life, and why?

The Biblically Christian answer to these questions, not surprisingly, derives primarily from what God—the all-knowing, purposeful, truthful, and immutable source and sustainer of the universe and of human life—discloses through Biblical revelation. Christian theists understand that God's Word, the Bible, is perfectly authoritative in anything that it addresses and that it rightly frames our quests to understand the universe and our place in it. Because its Author's knowledge and character are perfect and constant, His Word's truth claims are received as *fixed* (they do not change), *uniform* (they consist with each other), and *universal* in their sweep (they are true for all people at all times, even for people who deny or ignore them).

THE BIBLICALLY CHRISTIAN WORLDVIEW

Accordingly, as worldview scholar James Sire observes, Biblically Christian thinking recognizes the following revealed truths as foundational to our quests to make sense of anything, including human communication:

1. God is infinite and personal, triune, transcendent and immanent, omniscient, sovereign and good.

2. God created the cosmos *ex nihilo* to operate with a uniformity of cause and effect in an open system.

3. Human beings are created in the image of God and thus possess personality, self-transcendence, intelligence, morality, gregariousness, and creativity.

4. Human beings can know both the world around them and God himself because God has built into them the capacity to do so and because he takes an active role in communicating with them.

5. Human beings were created good, but through the Fall the image of God became defaced, though not so ruined as not to be capable of restoration; through the work of Christ, God redeemed humanity and began the process of restoring people to goodness, though some choose to reject that redemption.

6. For each person death is either the gate to life with God and his people or the gate to eternal separation from the only thing that will ultimately fulfill human aspirations.

7. Ethics is transcendent and is based on the character of God as good (holy and loving).

8. History is linear, a meaningful sequence of events leading to the fulfillment of God's purposes for humanity.[31]

The last of these premises raises a series of interrelated questions that we must address in order to understand why Biblically Christian thinking regards communication to be significant. Why did God place us here? What is His purpose for humanity as a whole? What is His purpose for your life and for mine? What must you or I do in order to realize this purpose?

In order to appreciate the answers to these questions, one must understand the human drama for what it fundamentally is—the true story about our Creator, despite our rejection of Him and the corruption that resulted from it, graciously giving us a second chance to have the purposeful lives for which He originally created us. Detailed accounts of this Biblical story emerge from many creeds and catechisms that Christians have crafted over the centuries in their attempts to express this story accurately yet concisely. Rather than reciting one of these creeds at this point (see Appendix 1 for several noteworthy examples of these), I proceed in the following pages to summarize the Biblical drama in my own words, albeit with plenty of Biblical proof texts, in a way that sets the stage for our subsequent focus on how communication plays a part in this story.

A BIBLICAL VIEW OF HUMAN PURPOSE

The physical universe and its components—living and non-living, visible and non-visible—were created (Gen. 1) by a personal God who has intellect (Gen. 18:19; Ex. 3:7; Acts 15:18), emotion (Gen. 6:6; Psalm 103:8-13; John 3:16), and willpower (Gen. 3:15; Psalm 115:3; 2 Peter 3:9) for the purposes of displaying his glory (Psalms 8:1; 19:1 and Isa. 40:5), and inspiring the reverence that is rightly His alone (Isa. 43:7; Rev. 4:11). He set the physical world into motion and enables it to continue operating as it does (Neh. 9:6; Col. 1:17; Heb. 1:3).

Humans have intelligence, emotions, and freedom to choose what is right because God created us after his own likeness (Gen. 1:26, 27; Gen. 9:6; James 3:9). Although He disclosed his moral will to the first persons intellectually (Gen. 2:16, 17) and intuitively (Gen.3:8-11; Rom. 1:20), God granted them the freedom to decide whether they would

---

[31] Sire, James. *The Universe Next Door: A Basic Worldview Catalog.* Downers Grove: Intervarsity Press, 2009. Print.

61

comply with this perfect will. The first humans, in history's original expression of human autonomy, corrupted themselves by choosing not to comply (Gen. 3:6). Their sinful act polluted the course of human history. It alienated humans from their Maker and sentenced them to both physical death (Gen. 3:19; Rom. 5:12; 1 Cor. 15:22) and a spiritual death that would forever separate them from the One whose presence they were created to enjoy (Rom. 5:21; Eph. 2:1-5). Their sin's lethal effects corrupted not just the first humans, but every person, since everyone inherited the first humans' sinful nature (Job 14:1-4; Rom. 2:12-14) and its consequences (John 3:18, 36; Rom. 6:23; 1 Cor. 15:22). Sin estranged people not only from God, but also from each other by generating such relational cancers as greed, hatred, envy, murder, quarreling, deception, malicious behavior, gossip, and backstabbing (Rom. 1:29-30). Sin also afflicted the earth's environment with death and corrosion (Gen. 3:17-19; Isa. 24:3-6; 19-20 and Rom. 8:19-22).

Despite humanity's self-inflicted state of spiritual brokenness, God extends certain undeserved graces to people. Although all people are thus corrupted (Rom. 3:23) and deserve death because of it (Rom. 6:23), God extends *special grace* by offering humans a remedy for their spiritual alienation from Him. He made this possible by taking human form as Jesus Christ (John 10:30; 14:10; Phil. 2:5-8), who was sinless (2 Cor. 5:21; Heb. 4:15; 1 Peter 2:22) and capable, therefore, of paying the penalty for human sinfulness that justice requires. Jesus paid this penalty through His death on the cross and thereby restored for humanity the hope of renewed spiritual life and of restored communion with God (Rom. 3:25, 26; 5:19). Though his redemptive work was sufficient for every human in history (John 3:16; Gal. 4:4, 5; 1 Tim. 4:10; 1 John 2:2), it ultimately benefits only those who by faith acknowledge his Lordship (Acts 16:31; Rom. 10:9) and submit to it repentantly (Acts 3:19;17:30, 31; Luke 13:2-5) before they die physically (Heb. 9:27; Luke 16:19-26).

> —∽—
> **Human communication is possible because of common grace.**
> —∽—

Whereas God's special grace benefits only those who turn to Him in this manner, His common grace benefits believers and unbelievers alike. The term *common grace* denotes God's undeserved act of giving humans immeasurable blessings that they, because of their corruption, have no right to expect from Him. The most obvious example of this is the fact that God permits people, despite their sinfulness, to live physically for a while rather than experiencing the immediate death that we deserve. He also allows them to notice, explore, understand, and enjoy many life experiences in ways they could not appreciate were it not for His merciful restraint.

Human communication is possible because of common grace. Despite our sinfulness, people remain capable of receiving and making sense of communicative messages that God discloses through nature, through conscience, and especially through His Word. We also can receive and make sense of messages from other people. Humans also remain capable of forming attitudes, values, feelings, and beliefs, encoding them in meaningful ways, and sending them to recipients who likewise remain capable of receiving the messages, deciphering them, and understanding their meanings.

Because of common grace, people can use communication to form personally meaningful connections with God and with each other and to do so in ways that manifest His true purpose for our lives.

—ɯ—

True surrender to God's absolute authority is all-encompassing.

—ɯ—

Anything true, honorable, right, pure, lovely, or admirable that humans experience is an expression of God's grace (Col. 4:8). Because He is gracious, our minds, although corrupted, are capable of conceptualizing God, self, sin, and the message of redemption that He offers us through Christ. Because God is gracious, our hearts, although darkened, can be stirred by His Spirit and freely choose to receive His Gospel. Because He is gracious, we can be spiritually redeemed and have restored communion with Him. Because God is gracious, spiritually redeemed people can relate to Him, to other people, and to the world as a whole in the God-centered manner His perfect standard requires, as He intended when He first made us. Indeed, the apostle Paul urges this in his epistle to the Colossians:

> Don't let anyone capture you with empty philosophies and high-sounding nonsense that come from human thinking and from the spiritual powers of this world, rather than from Christ. For in Christ lives all the fullness of God in a human body. So you also are complete through your union with Christ, who is the head over every ruler and authority. (Col. 2:8-10)

This, in a nutshell, is the Biblically Christian calling for human lives—to acknowledge that we are helplessly corrupted with autonomy and to find the only possible deliverance from this self-serving pit by repentantly surrendering to our Deliverer's rightful authority over every aspect of our being. True surrender to God's absolute authority is all-encompassing. It recognizes, as the Dutch statesman Abraham Kuyper once put it, that "There is no thumb-width of the entire domain of our human life of which the Christ, the Sovereign over everything, does not proclaim, 'It is mine!'"[32] When we surrender to this realization, God enables us to express His grace to others "in the full and vigorous prosecution of our life."

---

[32] Craig G. Bartholomew and Michael W. Goheen. *The Drama of Scripture: Finding Our Place in the Biblical Story.* Grand Rapids: Baker Academic, 2004. 220. Print.

The surrendered person understands that authentic God-centeredness permeates and gives color to "our feeling, our perception, our sensations, our thinking, our imagining, our willing, our acting, our speaking" and that it must "not stand as a foreign factor in our life, but must be the passion that breathes throughout our whole existence."[33]

How then does the surrendered person who loves God in this way view communication's significance? How and why should he or she value it? How should he or she interpret others' communicative messages and craft his or her own? At the most basic level, such a person considers, first, what God says about human purpose and ponders the implications of this for what we conclude about human behavior, including our communicative behavior. As the next chapter explains, the redeemed person realizes that God values communication because it opens channels through which we can connect with Him and with others in ways that can draw them closer to Him and that promote the things He values. We know otherwise indiscernible truths like these because God has disclosed them through Scripture. Still, we make sense of communication itself—the way it works, the way people use it, the way it affects people, etc.—based largely on what our direct observations of it tell us. We must remember that reasoning and observation, although incapable by themselves of telling us where we came from and why we are here, are nonetheless common graces through which we can gather and interpret reliable information about ourselves—information that becomes all the more meaningful when viewed in the light of what God reveals about human origin and purpose. God can use the information that we gather from His Word and from these raw observation processes to enrich our interpretation of communicational texts and to enhance our daily practice as creators of communicational texts.

—w—

The redeemed person realizes that God values communication because it opens channels through which we can connect with Him and with others in ways that can draw them closer to Him and that promote the things He values.

—w—

The fact that God enables us, through Scripture, observation, and reasoning, to make sense of communication does not mean we always will arrive at the same conclusions about it. Only God sees anything perfectly, according to His Word. By contrast, even when He has redeemed us, we continue our ongoing struggle against our corruption's lingering effects. Although God redeems us, we continue to act to battle our fleshly impulse to think and to act in autonomous ways that are contrary to God's perfect standards. Although we will never be like God, who alone knows things perfectly , we have the hope that someday we will see

---

[33] Kuyper, Abraham. *Lectures on Calvinism.* Grand Rapids: William B. Eerdmans, 1931, 5. Print.

things more clearly than we do while dwelling in this broken world. As the apostle Paul stated this, "Now we see things imperfectly as in a poor mirror, but then we will see everything with perfect clarity. All that I know now is partial and incomplete, but then I will know everything completely, just as God knows me now" (1 Cor. 13:12).

Nonetheless, the question must be addressed—what does it mean to make sense of communication in a Biblically redemptive way? This mystery is the thrust of the next chapter, which offers foundational insights into how redemptive thinkers make sense of human communication and how they construct communicative texts of their own.

QUESTIONS FOR ANALYSIS

1. Review this chapter's definition of God's common grace. Then list 5-7 specific examples of God-honoring common graces—not just the ones identified in the chapter—that God permits humans in general to experience despite the debilitating effects of our self-inflicted corruption. After listing these examples, be sure to explain why you believe each qualifies as a common grace in this chapter's sense of the term.

2. See the Apostle's Creed and the Nicene Creed in Appendix 1, toward the end of this book. Analyze their individual statements. Then compose a 200-350 word response in which you explain how the wording in these historic statements of Christian faith highlights God's interest in communicating (connecting or reconnecting) with humans.

3. Read Dr. Arne H. Fjeldstad's article "God the Communicator" in Appendix 2. Then compose a 200-350 word response in which you answer the following: (a) According to the article, in which senses can God be considered a communicator? (b) According to the article, why should people—Christians in particular—care about communication?

CHAPTER 5
COMMUNICATION

—w—

A Biblically Redemptive Approach

Overview: A redemptive communicator is someone who views communication through the lens of what God says about it and who, as an expression of authentic love for Him, interprets and crafts communicative texts in the light of what He values.

A Closer Look: What makes communication significant? As the third chapter indicated, a utilitarian would answer this by pointing to the communication's effects and deciding whether they advance something that is in society's best interest. A pragmatist would answer the question by considering whether the communication is something personally meaningful for the individual communicator, regardless of how it affects other people. Unlike these humanly devised approaches to answering the question, the Biblically Christian standard begins with God's timelessly, changelessly loving character. The apostle John could not have stated it more clearly: "God is love . . ." (1 John 4:26).

God's love for us is a dominant theme throughout Scripture. Because He loves us, He created us, even though He knew we would corrupt ourselves. Because He loves us, he assumed earthly form as Jesus Christ and paid a costly price to remedy our spiritual corruption and to make possible renewed communion with Him. As the apostle John affirms, "God showed how much he loved us by sending his one and only Son into the world so that we might have eternal life through him. This is real love—not that we loved God, but that he loved us and sent his Son as a sacrifice to take away our sins" (1 John 4:9-10). Other Biblical passages affirm the same principle (John 3:16; Rom. 5:8).

When we repentantly submit to His leadership and receive His liberation from our corruption, He enables us through His Holy Spirit, despite the lingering effects of our corruption, to reflect His love to others as we interact, or communicate, with them. Indeed, "God has given us his Spirit as proof that we live in him and he in us" for "God is love and all who live in love live in God, and God lives in them" (1 John 4:13, 16). If we love our spiritual brothers and sisters as we should, it is only because God's love has enabled us to do so (v. 19). Additionally, a person who professes to love God but who hates a spiritual brother or sister is a liar (v. 20). When we love each other as we should, God's love is perfectly expressed through us (v. 11). This love, Jesus said, makes a powerful communicative statement to those around us: "Your love for one another will prove to the world that you are my disciples" (John 13:35).

The person who loves God yearns to please Him and expresses this by living in a way that honors His timeless precepts (John 14:15). Foremost among these guiding principles, Jesus said, are two that encapsulate all the rest: "'You must love the LORD your God with all your heart, all your soul, and all your mind.' This is the first and greatest commandment. A second is equally important: 'Love your neighbor as yourself.' The entire law and all the demands of the prophets are based on these two commandments" (Matt. 22: 37-40). To love God, then, one must love other people, for as the apostle Paul explains, "If you love your neighbor, you will fulfill the requirements of God's law. For the commandments say, 'You must not commit adultery. You must not murder. You must not steal. You must not covet.' These—and other such commandments—are summed up in this one commandment: 'Love your neighbor as yourself' " (Rom. 13:8-9).

> ―∽―
> **Communication is significant to the Biblically Christian thinker, then, because it enables people, through divine revelation, to understand and to embrace their God-appointed purpose and to fulfill this purpose through expressions of authentic love for Him and for each other.**
> —∽—

Communication is significant to the Biblically Christian thinker, then, because it enables people, through divine revelation, to understand and to embrace their God-appointed purpose and to fulfill this purpose through expressions of authentic love for Him and for each other.

As important as this foundational concept is, it only raises another question that must be given extra emphasis in an instructional communication text like this one—how does authentically God-honoring love show itself in a person's communicational practices? Can someone express Godly love through the acts of receiving and decoding messages from others? Can he or she do so through the acts of encoding and sending messages to others? This book assumes that honoring God in these ways is possible. The question we must face, then, is a practical one—how can the study and practice of communication honor God? In the next two sections, we consider a couple of Biblically Christian responses to this question—redemptive criticism, which the receiving and decoding of messages, and redemptive communication, which involves the encoding and sending of messages.

REDEMPTIVE CRITICISM

You may recall, from chapter 1, that *redemptive criticism* is a term for the attempt to make sense of human communicative behavior and specific human communications in the light of divine revelation. This task involves an *expositional* and a *rhetorical* component. As previously noted, an expositor tries to explain why people share certain attitudes, values, beliefs, feelings, or behaviors. He or she does this by explaining mysteries like the widespread human longing to connect with God or something God-like. The redemptive expositor aims to show how this yearning gives shape to human communications and tries to explain why the longing exists and why it works as it does, in the light of what divine revelation says about it. As a rhetorical analyst, however, the redemptive critic also considers how people find redemption and what role, if any, communication plays in the process. The critic considers, too, how the redeemed life functions as a message to others and how it impacts or can impact other people.

> —⁂—
> **As a redemptive critic, the God-lover is one with a passion for truth and truth-telling who "speaks the truth in love" (Eph. 4:15) and who "rejoices whenever the truth wins out" (1 Cor. 13:8).**
> —⁂—

As a redemptive critic, the God-lover is one with a passion for truth and truth-telling who "speaks the truth in love" (Eph. 4:15) and who "rejoices whenever the truth wins out" (1 Cor. 13:8). As an expositor, this critic highlights "what is true, and honorable, and right, and pure, and lovely, and admirable" (Phil. 4:8) in his or her quests to describe things, including corrupted things, as they really are. When expositing human behaviors like communication, he or she goes beyond merely explaining how it works to emphasize its ultimate significance in the light of humanity's God-given purpose. With such an explanation as his or her goal, the critic recognizes and identifies God's common graces for what they are upon seeing them in a communicative text. Three such graces—humanity's widespread God-consciousness, purpose-consciousness, and ethical -consciousness—present especially rich discussion points in the redemptive expositor's analysis.

1) *God-consciousness.* Writing more than a century ago, John Henry Newman eloquently observed that "God has so implicated Himself with [the universe], and taken it into His very bosom, by His presence in it, His providence over it, His impressions upon it, and His influences through it, that we cannot truly or fully contemplate it without in some main aspects contemplating Him."[34] This statement highlights the fact that, whatever else it may

---

[34] Newman, John Henry and Frank Miller Turner. *The Idea of a University.* New Haven: Yale University Press, 1996. 45. Print.

be, nature is a text through which God proclaims His existence and His divine qualities to all thinking people. The Old Testament affirms this communicational principle throughout the psalms, among other passages:

> The heavens proclaim the glory of God.
>> The skies display his craftsmanship.
> Day after day they continue to speak;
>> night after night they make him known.
> They speak without a sound or word;
>> their voice is never heard.
> Yet their message has gone throughout the earth,
>> and their words to all the world. (Psalm 19:1-4)

My wife and I recently came to appreciate this passage's depth during an escape to Virginia's Shenandoah Valley for our tenth anniversary celebration. As we sat alone one evening, on our secluded Bed & Breakfast's shadowed porch, we watched in speechless wonder as the sunset slowly cast its darkening amber glaze on the surrounding distant mountains. Far above us, one by one, twinkling stars announced their presence, piercing brilliantly through the descending blackness. As the wind lazily whispered its way through a field of nearby tree tops, a scattered chorus of crickets enriched our sense of the moment's magic with a symphony that lasted long into the night. I am reminded, during moments like these, of words from another psalm:

—∞—

Whatever else it may be, nature is a text through which God proclaims His existence and His divine qualities to all thinking people.

—∞—

> When I look at the night sky and see the work of your fingers—
>> the moon and the stars you set in place—
> what are mere mortals that you should think about them,
>> human beings that you should care for them? (Psalm 8:3-4)

After raising these thoughts and others like them, the psalmist ends with a worshipful postscript that I have uttered many times while contemplating the wonders of God's world: "O LORD, our Lord, your majestic name fills the earth!" (Psalm 8:9).

The picture of nature as a common grace through which God expresses His existence and divine qualities to the world is not confined to the Old Testament. The apostle Paul affirms it throughout the New Testament, in statements he directs to both unbelievers (Acts 17:24) and believers (Rom. 1:18-32). God, through nature, has given all people reason to know of His existence, creativity, and power. Although this is so, His Word indicates that we are not inclined to seek after Him (Rom. 3:11). Still, as an expositor, the redemptive critic explains the human capacity to be awed by nature as a God-given clue to His existence and to the fact that the universe has a purpose.

2) *Purpose-consciousness.* People seem always to be questing for something more than they already have—a something that perfectly satisfies their craving to live meaningful, purposeful lives. They thirst for a God-like something in their lives that can quell the inner longing for ultimate meaning that God, as a common grace, has placed in our hearts (Rom. 1:23-25). Because we are autonomously inclined, we often follow this urge down self-serving paths to earthly solutions that inevitably fall short. Among the God-like substitutes we pursue in our quest to quench this sense of soul-thirst are knowledge, wealth, power, fame, love, respect, or gratification through food, alcohol, drugs, sex, and other physically or psychologically pleasurable indulgences.

The Biblically redemptive critic understands that God is perfect, or holy (Psalms 18:30; 145:17 and 1 Peter 1:16), that He created people in His perfect image (Gen. 1:27), and that people, although they have corrupted this divine image through deliberate disobedience (Rom. 3:23; 5:12), remain vaguely aware of the fact that they exist for a purpose, even if they do not know what the purpose is or that it is God-given. Whatever else may motivate it, human behavior is driven fundamentally by a thirst to satisfy this God-given longing for significance. As Augustine of Hippo famously expressed this point, "O Lord, you have made us for yourself, and our heart is restless until it finds its rest in you."[35] Blaise Pascal echoed the same point, centuries later, in these words:

> *What is it then that this desire and this inability proclaim to us, but that there was once in man a true happiness of which there now remains to him only the mark and empty trace, which he in vain tries to fill from all his surroundings, seeking from things absent the help he does not obtain in things present? But these are all inadequate, because the infinite abyss can only be filled by an infinite and immutable Object, that is to say, only by God Himself.[36]*

To say the human yearning for purpose is foundational to our behavior is not to suggest that this is the only motive for human behavior. Abraham Maslow, a prominent twentieth

---

[35] Augustine and Henry Chadwick. *Confessions.* Oxford: Oxford University Press, 1992. Print.

[36] Pascal, Blaise. *Thoughts.* New York: P. F. Collier and Son, 1910. 138-139. Print.

century psychologist, created a famous model—his Hierarchy of Needs—that, although limited by naturalistic assumptions, helpfully identifies other factors that motivate individuals to behave as they do. At the most basic level are physical needs, such as one's need for food, water, and air. If you cannot breathe, you likely will be motivated to behave in a way that gives you access to air. At the next level, people have safety needs, such as protection from physical forces, from disease, from other people, etc. When people buy insurance, lock their doors, or carry concealed weapons, their behavior is probably a response to their need for safety. Next, Maslow proposed, people have belongingness and love needs that motivate them to form and to maintain relationships. People also have esteem needs that may motivate them to buy expensive sports cars, to wear popular brands of clothes, or to take other steps that give them a sense of status or accomplishment. Finally, Maslow suggested, people have self-actualization needs—needs for personal growth and for realizing their potential—that may motivate them to do humanitarian work, to climb high mountains, and take other steps that give them a sense of personal fulfillment.[37]

The Polish anthropologist Bronislaw Malinowski proposed a similar model that identifies seven basic needs that motivate people, acting as groups more than as individuals, to conduct themselves as they do. The first of these, metabolism, denotes the human need for food, drink, and air. Reproduction references the human need for procreating. Bodily comforts is this model's term for the human need to protect people's bodies from distress or disrespect. People also have needs for safety, movement, growth, and health.[38] A person's behavior can be impacted by the drive to satisfy the needs of his or her family, community, culture, or other group in any of these areas.

The redemptive critic does not necessarily reject models like the ones Maslow and Malinowski proposed. To the contrary, these can actually be very useful tools for describing human behavior. If models like these are flawed, it is typically because they are short-sighted and omit from their analyses spiritual factors that influence human behavior. However, this does not discredit the fact that the models' other factors do actually influence human behavior. Because the redemptive critic's goal is to describe things as they truly are, including these factors in one's description of human communicative behavior may actually generate colorful details for his or her analyses.

Still, for an analysis of human behavior to be ultimately valuable, it must go beyond merely describing what direct observation tells us. It must also consider foundational questions about human origin and purpose and how this impacts the needs that seem to

---

[37] Maslow, Abraham H. *Motivation and Personality.* New York: Harper, 1954. Print.

[38] Malinowski, Bronislaw. *A Scientific Theory of Culture and Other Essays,* The University of North Carolina Press, Chapel Hill, 1944. Print.

drive our behavior. If indeed the drives to physically survive, to belong, to self-actualize, etc, impact our behavior, as Maslow and Malinowski propose, why is this so? Why do people care whether they survive, belong, or realize their potential? As the third chapter explained, autonomous worldviews provide disappointing answers to questions like these—blind guesses that often wield dark implications and that insufficiently address more basic questions. For example, if physical survival, belonging, and self-fulfillment drive human behavior, as autonomous theorists commonly suggest, why do people—including people who seem to have it all—commit suicide? Why do people who apparently have everything sometimes choose to sacrifice everything, including their lives, their families, and their personal wants, for higher causes?

—ᵐᵐ—

The Biblically redemptive critic understands that human behavior is driven by something deeper than what Maslow or Malinowski proposed.

—ᵐᵐ—

The Biblically redemptive critic understands that human behavior is driven by something deeper than what Maslow or Malinowski proposed. He or she knows, as Blaise Pascal put it, that "All men seek happiness. This is without exception. Whatever different means they employ, they all tend to this end. The cause of some going to war, and of others avoiding it, is the same desire in both, attended with different views. The will never takes the least step but to this object. This is the motive of every action of every man, even of those who hang themselves."[39]

The Biblically Christian critic understands that the happiness for which people long is one that cannot be satisfied by anything in their surroundings, but only by the Infinite Someone by whom and for whose company they were created. C. S. Lewis explained the reasoning for supposing this in the following words:

The Christian says, "Creatures are not born with desires unless satisfaction for those desires exists." A baby feels hunger: well, there is such a thing as food. A duckling wants to swim: well, there is such a thing as water. Men feel sexual desire: well, there is such a thing as sex. If I find in myself a desire which no experience in this world can satisfy, the most probable explanation is that I was made for another world. If none of my earthy pleasures satisfy it, that does not prove that the universe is a fraud. Probably earthly pleasures were never meant to satisfy it, but only to arouse

---

[39] Pascal, Blaise. *Thoughts.* New York: P. F. Collier and Son, 1910. 136. Print.

it, to suggest the real thing. If that is so, I must take care, on the one hand, never to despise, or be unthankful for, these earthly blessings, and on the other, never to mistake them for the something else of which they are only a kind of copy, or echo, or mirage. I must keep alive in myself the desire for my true country, which I shall not find till after death; I must never let it get snowed under or turned aside; I must make it the main object of life to press on to that other country and help others to do the same.[40]

The last sentence in Lewis's observation succinctly states the redemptive critic's guiding vision. As an expression of authentic love for God and for others, he or she interprets everything—including the content of our communications—in the light of His revealed design and purpose for humanity. Whatever else may drive people to communicate, the redemptive critic sees in this motivation a God-initiated, God-sustained channel through which people can lovingly connect with Him and with each other, and thus realize the purpose for which He created them and for which they thirst.

3) *Ethical-consciousness*. God's common grace to humans shows not just in our God and purpose consciousnesses, but also in our humanity's innate general awareness that some things are right and that some things are wrong for people in general and not just for ourselves. Even the person who claims to believe that nothing is right or wrong for everyone, by making this very statement, suggests that he or she does not really believe it, since the statement implies his or her belief that this view is the right one and that its alternatives are wrong. Such a person also betrays his or her stated view when he or she objects, on moral grounds, to thieves, reckless drivers, or anyone else who they feel has done them wrong.

God's Word discloses that humanity's ethical consciousness is divinely originated. As the apostle Paul observed, "Even Gentiles, who do not have God's written law, show that they know his law when they instinctively obey it, even without having heard it. They demonstrate that God's law is written in their hearts, for their own conscience and thoughts either accuse them or tell them they are doing right" (Rom. 2:14-15). Although their specific definitions of what is right or wrong may differ, people have a God-given awareness that a moral "oughtness" exists in the universe—that things should be a certain way—and that we must uphold or promote it. This moral sense shows itself, among other ways, in the stories we hear and tell throughout our lifetimes. Whether expressed via fairy tales, personal anecdotes,

---

[40] Lewis, C. S. *The Complete C. S. Lewis Signature Classics*. New York: HarperCollins, 2007. 114. Print.

song lyrics, stage productions, or movie scripts, our stories fixate on finding just solutions for problematic situations. The evil empire must be defeated. The underdog must win. The criminal must be caught and punished. When our stories lack what we recognize as just outcomes (outcomes that consist with our God-given sense of moral oughtness), we criticize them, sometimes passionately, for lacking the result that our Creator predisposes our hearts to crave.

This craving for justice, for the restoration of things as they were designed to be, makes a profound statement about our human nature. Why do we sense that something is wrong in the world or in a story? Why do we so strongly desire solutions for these crises? The redemptive critic recognizes this impulse as a statement about our divine design and purpose. J. R. R. Tolkien, the literary scholar and fantasy author, highlighted this idea throughout his work:

—⁂—

The stories that we live, that we create, and that we communicate to others, although skewed by our corruption, manifest our awarenesses that God has created things to be a certain way and that at least some things in creation fall short of this ideal.

—⁂—

> We have come from God, and inevitably the myths woven by us, though they contain error, will also reflect a splintered fragment of the true light, the eternal truth that is with God. Indeed only by myth-making, only by becoming "sub-creator" and inventing stories, can Man aspire to the state of perfection that he knew before the Fall. Our myths may be misguided, but they steer however shakily towards the true harbour, while materialistic "progress" leads only to a yawning abyss and the Iron Crown of the power of evil.[41]

Stated another way, Tolkien's idea is simply this—the stories that we live, that we create, and that we communicate to others, although skewed by our corruption, manifest our awarenesses that God has created things to be a certain way and that at least some things in creation fall short of this ideal. Although polluted by our corruption, their subtexts consistently exhibit their creators' God-given longing for something better than the brokenness that defines our lives and our stories' plots. The redemptive critic shows, through exposition, how our craving for perfect solutions to problems exists because God, as an expression of His common grace, has placed within our hearts a yearning for redemption, for

---

[41] Lewis, C.S. and Walter Hooper. *On Stories: And Other Essays on Literature*. New York: Houghton-Mifflin-Harcourt, 2002. xiv. Print.

a restoration of righteousness that He alone can deliver. Were it not for His common grace, our yearning for liberation would be something far less than the clue to our true purpose that God designed it to be.

One must note that, although humanity's moral consciousness bears its Creator's imprint, it is not a perfect expression of God's moral will. Humanity's corruption has smudged this thumbprint and rendered it only generally reliable as evidence of our divine design and purpose. Our corruption shows, among other ways, in our failure to live up to very standards that we know to be correct. Rather than relating to God and to each other in the selfless way He prescribes, humans are often self-centered and self-serving and inclined to suppress what moral sense He has given us.

The redemptive critic acknowledges this but puts it in a Biblical perspective. He or she recognizes our failure to live as we know we should as evidence that God has "abandoned [people] to their foolish thinking and let them do things that should never be done" (Rom. 1:28). The critic explains that our lives, consequently, have become "full of every kind of wickedness, sin, greed, hate, envy, murder, quarreling, deception, malicious behavior, and gossip." Apart from God's redemptive grace, we are "backstabbers, haters of God, insolent, proud, and boastful." We even "invent new ways of sinning, and . . . disobey [our] parents." Moreover, we "refuse to understand, break [our] promises, are heartless, and have no mercy. " Even though we realize "God's justice requires that those who do these things deserve to die . . . [we] do them anyway. Worse yet, [we] encourage others to do them, too" (Rom. 1: 28-32).

The redemptive critic explains these vices as evidence of the corruption from which we long to escape. He or she explains that because human conscience is flawed as a guide for determining right and wrong, God has given the corrective lens of Scripture partly to provide the reliable definition about moral matters that people otherwise lack. "How can a young person stay pure?" the psalmist asks. "By obeying your word . . . I have hidden your word in my heart that I might not sin against you" (Psalm 119: 9, 11). The apostle Paul makes the same point about the ethical function of God's Word: "All Scripture is inspired by God and is useful to teach us what is true and to make us realize what is wrong in our lives. It corrects us when we are wrong and teaches us to do what is right. God uses it to prepare and equip his people to do every good work." (2 Tim. 3:16-17).

REDEMPTIVE COMMUNICATION

How can one honor God in his or her practice of communication? The preceding section yields a partial answer to this question by showing how one can honor Him through the explanations he or she infers from the communicative behaviors he or she observes. The section that follows considers what it means to honor God when we behave as senders of messages toward others, whether we transmit the information verbally, non-verbally, or both. The primary focus here is on our communicative behavior toward people, rather than toward God. Suffice it to say, as we already have established, that one's expression of authentic love for God will flow through him or her to touch other people.

A person functions as a redemptive communicator when his or her verbal and/or non-verbal behavior manifests God's love to others in a way that promotes what God values in the world. Our words and actions indicate or communicate whether we love Him in this way. Jesus made this point as a rebuke to religious leaders who did the "right" things without being motivated to do so by an authentic love for God: "Whatever is in your heart determines what you say. A good person produces good things from the treasury of a good heart, and an evil person produces evil things from the treasury of an evil heart. And I tell you this, you must give an account on judgment day for every idle word you speak. The words you say will either acquit you or condemn you" (Matt. 12:34-37).

> **A person functions as a redemptive communicator when his or her verbal and/or non-verbal behavior manifests God's love to others in a way that promotes what God values in the world.**

God values communication that manifests an authentic love for Him. Such a love shows itself not only through a God-centeredness in our stated attitudes, values, and/or beliefs, but also through our actions—whether actions toward God, toward others, toward ourselves, or toward the world. The prophet Micah emphasized this all-encompassing understanding of authentic faith in his oft quoted synopsis of life's purpose: "This is what he requires of you: to do what is right, to love mercy, and to walk humbly with your God" (Micah 6:8). The apostle Paul underscored the same idea in his instructive words to the Colossians: "Let the message about Christ, in all its richness, fill your lives. Teach and counsel each other with all the wisdom he gives. Sing psalms and hymns and spiritual songs to God with thankful hearts. And whatever you do or say, do it as a representative of the Lord Jesus, giving thanks through him to God the Father" (Col. 3:16-17).

Although God may use a person's wrongly motivated communications to promote His redemptive purposes, one's use of words alone is worthless. Jesus, quoting the prophet Isaiah, questioned people who "say they are mine" and who "honor me with their lips," but whose "hearts are far from me. And their worship of me is nothing but man-made rules learned by rote" (Isa. 29:13; cf. Matt. 15:7-9 and Mark 7:5-7). Indeed, without the love of God as its motive, speaking the right words or performing the right actions has little value in God's eyes for, as the apostle Paul observed, for "if I gave everything I have to the poor and even sacrificed my body, I could boast about it; but if I didn't love others, I would have gained nothing" (1 Cor. 13:3).

The redemptive communicator, then, is someone who expresses an authentic love for God in visible ways. Yet, as vital an element as this motivation is, redemptive communication involves something more than this. To function redemptively, a communicator's expressions must also promote something God values in this world. Because God is timeless and changeless, the things He values are constant. They do not change. We learn much about these eternal values through what He discloses about Himself in His Word, the Bible. Among the many things that He values and that the redemptive communicator, as an expression of authentic love for God, promotes through his or her communications are the following, each of which appears with specific Biblical references that disclose it:

   1. God values His rightful authority over all things, including our bodies (Ezek. 18:4; 1 Cor. 3:16-19; 6:18-20; 2 Cor. 6:16-17), **our minds** (Isa. 55:7; Rom. 12:2; 2 Cor. 10:5), **and His creation** (Ex. 9:29; 19:5; Deut. 10:14; 1 Chron. 29:11-12; Job 41:11; Pss. 24:1; 50:10-12; 89:11; 95:4-5; 1 Cor. 10:26).

   2. God values truth as that which actually is the case (Num. 23:19; Pss. 31:5; 33:4; 89:14; 111:7; 119:160; Isa. 65:16; Micah 7:20; John 8:31-32; 14:6; 17:17; 2 Cor. 4:2; 2 Thes. 2:10-12; 2 Tim. 2:15; Titus 1:2; 3 John 4; Rev. 15:3). Truth sometimes can be legitimately applied in a variety of ways (Rom. 14; 1 Cor. 8; Gal. 5:13-14).

   3. God values His exclusive right to our worship (Ex. 20:3-5; 34:14; Deut. 4:24; 5:9; 6:14-15; Isa. 43:21; 44:22-23; 45:5-6; Jer. 13:11; Matt. 21:12-13; 1 Pet. 2:9; Rev. 4:8-11; 15:3-4).

   4. God values human life. (Gen. 1:26-27; 9:6; Ex. 20:13; 21:12, 22-25; Deut. 5:17; Prov. 6:16-17; 24:11-12; Amos 1:13; Acts 17:28-29; Rom. 1:29; James 2:11). This includes preborn human life (Isa. 44:24; 49:1-5; Jer. 1:5; Gal. 1:15-16), older human life (Lev. 19:32; Job 12:12; Prov. 16:31; Isa. 46:3-4), and impaired human life (Matt. 14:14; 15:30; 20:34; Luke 4:18; 7:22).

   5. God values animal life, albeit less than he values human life. (Gen. 1:28, 31; 9:8-13; Ex. 23:5 and 12; Deut. 5:14; 25:4, Job 12:10; Pss. 36:6; 37:5-6, 28; 104:10-14 and 24-25; Prov. 12:10; 27:23; Jer. 12:4; Matt. 6:26; 10:29-31; Luke 12:6; 1 Cor. 3:16-17).

6. God values the earth (Gen. 1:31; Deut. 10:14; Job 26:7-9, 11-14; Pss. 24:1; 89:11; 145:9; 1 Cor. 10:26; Col. 1:16-17). He values humans' care of the earth (Gen. 2:15; Ex. 23:10-11; Lev. 18:26-28; 25:2-5; Deut. 20:19).

7. God values justice (Deut. 10:17-18; 2 Chron. 19:7; Pss. 9:8; 10:17-18; 11:7; 36:6; 45:6-7; 67:4; 75:2; 89:14; 97:2; 98:9; Prov. 21:3; Isa. 61:8-11; Amos 5:14-15, and 24; Micah 6:8; Matt. 5:6; Acts 17:31; 2 Thes. 1:5-6).

8. God values mercy (Num. 14:18; Neh. 9:27; Job 20:19-20; Pss. 106:1; 107:1; 136:1-26; Isa. 54:7; Lam. 3:32; Amos 8:4-7; Micah 7:18; Matt. 5:7; 9:13; 12:7; 18:23-35; Eph. 2:4-7; 4:32; James 2:13; 1 Pet. 1:3)

9. God values humility (Pss. 18:27; 147:6; Prov. 3:34; 27:2; Isa. 5:21; 66:2; Micah 6:8; Matt. 18:3-4; Luke 1:52; 14:7-11; 18:9-14; 22:24-27; Mark 9:35; Rom. 12:3; 1 Cor. 3:19; 13:4; 2 Cor. 11:30; 12:6-10; Gal. 6:14; Eph. 4:2; Phil. 2:1-11; Col. 3:12; James 4:6; 1 Pet. 5:2-6). This humility shows, among other ways, when a person limits his or her freedom out of respect for another person's sensitivities (Rom. 14; 1 Cor. 8; Gal. 5:13-14).

10. God values peace (Ps. 34:14; 133; Isa. 2:1-5; 26:3; 55:12; Matt. 5:9; Rom. 12:18; 14:17-19; 2 Cor. 13:11; Gal. 5:22; Phil. 2:1-2; 2 Tim. 2:22; James 3:16-18), *although there are times when He authorizes war* (Deut. 20:1-4; Josh. 8:1-29; 2 Chron. 20:13-21; Ps. 144:1; Eccl. 3:8). He loathes interpersonal discord (Prov. 6:19; 18:6; 22:10; James 3:14-18).

11. God values honesty (Lev. 19:13, 35-37; Deut. 25:13-16; Prov. 11:1-5; Micah 6:10-13; 7:2-4; Luke 3:12-14; 1 Cor. 6:10; Eph. 4:28; 1 Thes. 4:6)

12. God values self-control (Prov. 16:32; 25:28; 1 Cor. 6:10; 9:24-27; Gal. 5:23; 1 Thes. 4:4-5; 1 Tim. 3:2, 11; Titus 1:8-9; 2:2, 12; 1 Pet. 1:13; 2 Pet. 1:6).

13. God values family (Psalms 127 and 128; Prov. 20:6-7; 31:10). He values reproduction (Gen. 1:22-28; 9:1-7; Deut. 7:12-14; Ps. 113:7-9; 127:3-5).

14. God values monogamous, heterosexual marriage (Gen. 2:22-24; Deut. 24:5; Prov. 5:18-19; 18:22; 19:14; Matt. 19:4-6; Mark 10:6-9; 1 Cor. 7:1-16; Eph. 5:22-23; Col. 3:18-19; Heb. 13:4). He loathes divorce (Matt. 5:32).

15. God values sexual purity. He loathes sexual activity that is premarital (Matt. 19:19; Rom. 1:29; 1 Cor. 7:1-5), adulterous (Ex. 20:14; Matt. 5:18; Heb. 13:4), homosexual (Lev. 18:22; 20:13; Rom. 1:23-28; 1 Tim. 1:10), or perverse (Lev. 18:23; Rom. 1:23-28; 1 Cor. 5:1-8; 6:9-10; Gal. 5:19-21; Eph. 5:3; 1 Thes. 4:3-5; Jude 7). This includes lust (Job 31:1-12; Matt. 5:28-29; 1 Cor. 7:9; Col 3:5; 2 Tim. 2:22; 2 Pet. 2:14-16).

16. God values the church as an equipper of believers for doing God's redemptive work in the world (Matt. 16:18; 1 Cor. 10:31-33; 12:12-26; Eph. 1:22-23; 2:19-22; 4:4-16; 5:25-32; Col. 1:17-20; 3:14-16; 1 Pet. 2:9-10).

17. God values government as an executor of His righteousness (1 Kings 10:9; 2 Chron. 9:8; Amos 5:15-24; Rom. 13:1-7; 1 Tim. 2:1-4; Titus 3:1; 1 Pet. 2:13-17). He values His authority over government (Col. 2:10, 15; Eph. 1:20-22).

18. God values our faith in Him (Gen. 15:6; Hab. 2:2; Matt. 17:20; 23:23; Mark 11:22; Luke 18:17; Rom. 1:17; 3:27-5:2; 10:6-10; Gal. 3:6-23; Heb. 11; James 2).

19. God values our love for others (John 13:34-35; 15:12-17; Rom. 12:10; 16:16; 1 Cor. 16:20; 2 Cor. 13:11-12; Gal. 5:13-15; Eph. 4:2, 16; Phil. 1:9; Heb. 10:24; 1 Thes. 3:12; 4:9; 5:13; 2 Thes. 1:3; Heb. 13:1; 1 Pet. 1:22; 4:8; 5:14; 1 John 2:7; 3:10-11, 18; 4:7-21; Rev. 2:4).

20. God values our compassion for others. This includes the poor and oppressed (Job 18:7; Isa. 58:7; Jer. 5:28; 22:16; Mal. 3:5; Matt. 4:23-25; 8:1-3; 9:1-8; 25:35; 1 Tim. 5:10; John 3:17), children (Matt. 18:1-14; 19:13-15; Luke 17:1-3; James 1:27; 2:6-9), , employees (Isa. 58:6); prisoners (2 Chron. 28:15; Matt. 25:39), widows and the fatherless (Job 31:16-22; Jer. 5:28; Mal. 3:5; 1 Tim. 5:1-12); strangers (Mal. 3:5; Matt. 25:31-46), the sick (Matt. 25:31-46).

21. God values our hospitality to others (Lev. 19:34; Job 31:32; Isa. 58:7; Matt. 25:35, 38; Luke 10:30-37; 14:12-14; Rom. 12:13; Heb. 13:2; James 2:15-17; Titus 1:7-8; 1 Pet. 4:9).

22. God values our impartiality (Acts 10:34; Rom. 2:11; Eph. 6:9). He loathes prejudice against the poor (Ex. 23:6; Job 18:8; James 2:2-9), against employees (Eph. 6:9; Col 4:1), against foreigners (Lev. 19:33; Deut. 10:17-19), against people of different races/ethnicities (Numbers 12; Rom. 3:9, 29-30; Gal. 2:11-16; 3:28), or against the opposite sex (Gen. 5:1-2; Gal. 3:26-29; Col. 3:18-19). This does not disregard the fact, in the case of opposite sex relations, that God assigns unique roles to males and females (Gen. 3:16-19; 1 Cor. 11:3-10; Eph. 5:21-30).

23. God values personal property rights (Ex. 20:15; Lev. 6:1-7; 19:11-13; Deut. 5:19; Judg. 11:15; Prov. 22:28; Eccl. 5:19; Amos 3:10; Zech. 5:3-4; Matt. 19:18; 25:14-30; 1 Cor. 6:10; Eph. 4:28).

24. God values our attempts to liberate the wrongly oppressed via speech (Ps. 82:3-4; Prov. 24:11-12; 31:8-9; Isa. 1:17; Jer. 22:3; Ezek. 33:8).

25. God values our attempts to communicate His gospel of forgiveness and redemption to those who do not know Him (Pss. 67:1-2; 96:2-3; Isa. 49:6; 52:7; Matt. 5:14-16; 28:18-20; Mark 13:9-10; 16:15; Acts 1:8; Rom. 10:14-15).

As an earlier chapter explained, r*edemptive communication* resembles religious expression, but it differs from it in a major way. Whereas *religion* is the human attempt to connect with God or with something God-like, *redemption* is the state of having actually connected with God in the God-centered way that enables one to start seeing things as He sees them and relating to them as He relates to them. The redemptive communicator is one who lovingly submits to the realization that the God of Scripture is, in fact, the creator and sustainer of the universe and that everything in it, therefore, including our communication practices, must be understood and engaged in the instructive light of what His *divine revelation* says about it.

Consider for a moment the prescriptive implications of God's values for your approach to interacting with other people. Which communicational situations should you seek, and which should you avoid? Which topics should you discuss? What should you say about these topics? How should you say this? In the light of what Scripture discloses about God's eternal values, how should you view and what should you say about the following controversial social issues of our day?

abortion, infanticide, mercy killing, or euthanasia
abuse (child, elder, self, spousal)
addictions/codependency/eating disorders
air, land, space, or water pollution
animal abuse or vivisection
bioethics (cloning, eugenics, stem cell research)
birth or population control
crime (street, juvenile, gang, or white collar)
criminal justice (capital punishment, prison crowding, recidivism)
discrimination (ageism, ethnocentrism, racism, sexism)
ecology (climate change, pollution, littering)
education (underachievement or illiteracy)
false beliefs
famine, drought, or diseases
immigration
intellectual property (copyright, patent, trademark, plagiarism)
labor issues (child labor or sweatshops)
legal issues (government regulation of anything)
marriage (divorce, cohabitation)
poverty (welfare, world hunger, or homelessness)
taxation
sex (pre-marital, extramarital, homosexual, pornographic)
slavery or human trafficking
substance abuse (drugs, alcohol)
war

Our supreme calling in the world is to honor God by seeing things in the light of His eternal plan and by lovingly promoting what He values in our communicative behavior toward others.

Remember, the spiritually redeemed individual understands, based on what God graciously discloses, that our supreme calling in the world is to honor God by seeing things in the light of His eternal plan and by lovingly promoting what He values in our communicative behavior toward others. This calling is not confined to one part of our lives. Rather, it applies to all of life. Whether as a family member, a friend, a church member, a student, a teacher, a citizen, an employer or employee, or in any other role, the redemptive communicator's goal is the same: "So whether you eat or drink, or whatever you do, do it all for the glory of God" (1 Cor. 10:31). Such a person understands that "the fear of the Lord is the beginning of knowledge" (Prov. 1:7), that "the wisdom of this world is foolishness to God" (1 Cor. 3:19), and that His wisdom is an essential foundation for ultimately significant communication. Indeed, as a Biblical writer put it, "from a wise mind comes wise speech; the words of the wise are persuasive." (Prov. 16:23)

FINDING YOUR REDEMPTIVE FIELD

So where do you go from here? How can you fulfill your life's purpose by glorifying God as a redemptive critic and communicator? The obvious answer is that you do not need to go anywhere to find opportunities for realizing this call in your life, for these surround us all the time. We receive and decode meaningful messages every day. We construct and encode meaningful messages anytime we interact with people.

Still, a textbook like this one—a text written primarily for college-aged students, most of whom are contemplating which direction to go in life—would be remiss not to consider how these principles relate to one's choice of an academic major and of an occupation.

Section two of this book is designed to enrich readers understanding of how dozens of believers, representing a variety of job fields, have used their vocations as platforms for advancing some of the things God values that we have highlighted in this chapter. These individuals represent job fields that students often consider when evaluating their degree and career options while in college. As the profiles in section two demonstrate, one's ability to function as a redemptive communicator is neither defined nor limited by one's vocation or location. It is one's consecration—one's depth of devotion to loving God in an active way—that makes a redemptive difference in the world.

Section three of the book provides readers with a current overview of the job fields that section two's profiles represent. These field descriptions, which are adapted from the Occupational Outlook Index, can help students intelligently find a field in which someone with their individual interests and abilities can make a redemptive difference. Each listing provides an overview of the job field, emphasizing the nature of its work, any qualifications or credentials required for one to practice it, the job field's current employment situation and its outlook for the future, and the earnings currently earned by practitioners in this field.

As you review sections two and three, recall the principles we have covered in this first section. You need not live the disappointing life that autonomous approaches to living promise to deliver. Instead, God calls you, through redemptive faith in Christ, to experience "life in all its fullness" (John 10:10) by submitting to His authority, receiving His forgiveness, embracing what He values, and practicing communication in a way that reflects this to others.

QUESTIONS FOR ANALYSIS

1. This chapter indicates that God values our attempts to liberate the wrongly oppressed via speech (Ps. 82:3-4; Prov. 24:11-12; 31:8-9; Isa. 1:17; Jer. 22:3; Ezek. 33:8). If you could speak out to liberate one particular group of wrongly oppressed people (oppressed for something God's Word does not present as sinful), as an expression of authentic love for God, which group would you choose? Then describe three specific steps you can take during the next month to put this vision into action.

2. This chapter also indicates that God values our attempts to communicate His gospel of forgiveness and redemption to those who do not know Him (Pss. 67:1-2; 96:2-3; Isa. 49:6; 52:7; Matt. 5:14-16; 28:18-20; Mark 13:9-10; 16:15; Acts 1:8; Rom. 10:14-15). Is it possible to do this without using words, as Francis of Assisi once suggested? Write a 100-150 word response in which you state and support your answer.

3. Choose one profile of a redemptive communicator in a Section 2 chapter that highlights a vocational field that interests you. Using principles from the present chapter, explain in 100-150 words how the story subject functioned as a redemptive communicator in his or her story.

4. Choose one additional profile and do the same thing the previous question asked you to do.

PART 2:
REDEMPTIVE COMMUNICATORS:

—⚍—

Profiles from Across the Job Fields

A REDEMPTIVE VISION

"The fellowship of being near unto God must become reality, in the full and vigorous prosecution of our life. It must permeate and give color to our feeling, our perception, our sensations, our thinking, our imagining, our willing, our acting, our speaking. It must not stand as a foreign factor in our life, but it must be the passion that breathes throughout our whole existence."

- Abraham Kuyper (1837-1920)

CHAPTER 6

Redemptive Communicators:

—∽—

RELIGION

Don Richardson

A famed missionary-author devises a strategy for evangelizing everyone.

The term *redemptive analogies* may be foreign to many, but not to Canadian-born Don Richardson. Best-selling author of four books including *Peace Child* and *Lords of the Earth,* and popular speaker at missions conferences across North America, he states the definition in simple terms: "Redemptive analogies are eye-openers that become heart-openers. They're cultural compasses that point mankind to Jesus."

Richardson, now in his seventies, discovered these redemptive analogies through personal experience. In 1962, he and his late wife Carol Joy embarked on a missionary career in Irian Jaya. They settled among the Sawi, a Stone-age tribe of cannibalistic headhunters. The couple's lifestyle fascinated the tribesmen, who regarded them as beings from another planet. Their modern technology—steel axes, machetes, nylon fish line, metal fish hooks, and medicine—amazed them.

Before long, however, a conflict arose. The two tribes living nearest to the Richardsons had been at war before the missionaries arrived. Now their competitive desire to live near the foreigners fueled their hatred for each other, and fighting escalated.

Don begged the tribesmen to end the killings and make peace. "You talk about making peace as though it's an easy thing to do," they said. "But the Sawi shed each other's blood, sever heads, save skulls as trophies, and eat each other's flesh. Once these things happen, making peace is not easy."

As Richardson tried to share the Gospel with the Sawi, he discovered that they regarded treachery as a virtue. In fact, they applauded Judas as the hero in the story of Jesus' death. With such high value placed on deceit, how then could they possibly trust each other for a peace settlement? He concluded that this culture was void of any mechanism for making peace and considered moving his family to a different location, hoping this would end the bloodshed. That's when Kaiyo intervened.

Kaiyo lived in Kamur, one of the two warring villages. "The two foreigners chose to live among us and help us," he reasoned. "They're learning our language. Perhaps when they learn it more completely, they will help us in ways beyond our comprehension. I cannot let the senseless violence of my people drive this man and woman away from us. I must make peace."

According to Sawi culture, there was only one means for warring tribes to do so: A man must give his son to be raised by a father in the enemy village. The Sawi believed no insincere person could do such a thing, therefore this sacrifice was a basis for mutual trust. As long as that child remained alive, the enemy village would be bound to the commitment of peace.

Kaiyo and his wife had one child. He picked up his infant Biakadon, hugged him, and then ran from Kamur towards the neighboring village holding the boy in his arms. Neighbors shouted encouragement, but his wife screamed in anguish when she realized what was happening. "Please—no! Change your mind! Bring my baby back to me!" she cried. In times past when a peace child was offered, he had always been the son of a man with several children. It never occurred to her that her husband, the father of one child, might make that sacrifice.

It was too late. Kaiyo had already scanned the men's faces in the enemy village and chosen Mahor. He placed the baby in Mahor's arms and said, "I give you my only son as a peace child. Do you promise to be an advocate for peace so long as this child remains alive in your house?"

Honored to be chosen as the adoptive father, Mahor said, "Kaiyo, you've made the greatest possible sacrifice by giving your only son. Yes, I will guard the peace between your village and mine so long as this child remains alive in my house." He turned and called to his villagers, "Come, lay your hands on this peace child, Kaiyo's only son." Men, women, and children responded saying, "I receive this child as a basis for peace." Then another father, deeply moved by Kaiyo's sacrifice, placed his infant son in Kaiyo's arms as a peace child for Kamur village.

Richardson watched the scene thinking, *Why is there something familiar about this?* And then the answer came: The Sawi's custom of giving a child to achieve reconciliation depicted God's sacrifice made to establish peace between Himself and man!

This was the breakthrough Richardson needed to effectively share the Gospel with the Sawi people. The day came when Hato, a one-eyed chief, said, "I'm ready to lay my hand on Jesus. How do I do that?" Don led Hato in prayer, inviting the Spirit of God's holy peace child to dwell within him and to keep him in the way of peace with God and man. Hato's four wives and their children committed their lives to Christ the same day. He later became Richardson's travel companion, telling about Jesus in villages throughout the region. Before long, every village had believers and all warfare ceased.

Inspired by the Biblical example of Paul, who used a redemptive analogy when presenting the Gospel to pagan Athenians (see Acts 17:22-34) and by his experience with the Sawi, Richardson began to study other cultures for other such connecting points for presenting the Gospel. He found that once a year, the Dyak tribe in Kalimantan brings two chickens—without spot or blemish—to the riverside near a village. They kill one bird and sprinkle its blood on the shore. They tether the live bird at the end of a dugout canoe and place a burning kerosene lantern at the opposite end. At sunset, as the chicken pecks at rice grains, every villager places something invisible, symbolic of their sin, in the canoe. Then two elders push the craft into the river's current.

The people watch and wait. If the canoe drifts back to shore or overturns in the water within sight of the village, they live in apprehension for another year. If it disappears around the river's bend, they raise their hands and exclaim, "We're safe! We're safe!" The ceremony must be repeated every year to remove their sins.

"This analogy reminds us of two goats in the Old Testament," explains Richardson. "One was sacrificed after the Jewish high priest laid his hands on its head, symbolically depositing his sins and the sins of the Israelites there. The second goat was led into the wilderness and released. The Jews had their scapegoat; the Dyaks have a scapeboat."

Richardson also discovered redemptive analogies in the Chinese writing system. For instance, the word for 'righteous' is written with two small pictures, one above and one below. The upper picture symbolizes a lamb. The lower represents first person singular pronoun. "When the Chinese write the word for 'righteous,' they're actually writing 'the lamb over me,'" explains Richardson. "The Chinese language contains 120 such words that have spiritually significant encoded messages."

More recently, Richardson has searched Islam for redemptive analogies to help believers effectively reach this culture with the Gospel. "Islam has historically been the most resistant force on earth," he says. "It's as though there's a firewall, to borrow computer terminology, separating the minds and hearts of Muslims from our Christian appeal."

After studying the Koran, he concludes, "Cultures worldwide contain redemptive analogies to point to Jesus—the sacrifice made to atone for our sin. But Islam is different because Mohammed said Jesus didn't die. If he was correct, there's no atonement. Redemptive analogies would have to point to something Mohammed denied, therefore, there are no such analogies in Islam."

So how can a believer introduce a Muslim to faith in Christ without a cultural compass to point him to the Savior? In his latest book, *Secrets of the Koran*, Richardson suggests asking strategic questions whose answers show how Mohammed discredited himself as a prophet. He says, "Ask why Mohammed told the story of the Exodus 27 times in the first 89 chapters of the Koran, and why he repeated the story of Noah and the flood 28 times in the first 57 chapters.

"By doing word searches, I learned that the Koran's length could be reduced by 45 per cent if each story repeated dozens of times was told only once. Since Muslims love to memorize the Koran, elimination would make it much easier for them. Most have never thought about this, and it surprises them. These eye-openers become heart-openers for Muslims as they search the Koran and the Hadith for the answers."

Richardson says millions of Muslims nowadays are telling of seeing Jesus in their dreams. This phenomenon provides a natural bridge for believers to speak with them about Christ. The subject can be approached by saying, "I've heard about people seeing a kind-faced man dressed in shining garments appear to them. I'd like to meet someone who's had that experience." The hearts of those seeing this dream are ready to hear the Gospel.

"Gentile culture is filled with things that relate to an aspect of God and His law," says Richardson. "Who arranges these? They don't happen by accident, nor do they come from the evil one. God, in His mercy, has given these things to people as a sign that echoes in their hearts saying 'Jesus is our Savior. He's for us.'"

⎯⎯

Tresha McKnight

Bringing hope to Romania's youngest AIDS patients

Four-year-old Costel looked like any other Romanian boy his age, but there was one difference—a silent killer, the HIV virus, lurked within his body. When his parents learned of their boy's illness, they dumped him into a garbage can and left him there to die.

Costel represents an estimated 30,000 other Romanian children and teens stricken with HIV/ AIDS today. Many were infected because their mothers received contaminated blood transfusions for anemia while pregnant. Scores were infected when medical personnel vaccinated them against childhood diseases using the same contaminated needle. Some were infected when they visited health clinics where HIV-infected patients were treated. There, as in the schools, professionals used one needle in treating multiple patients.

Shunned by society as modern-day lepers due to fear and ignorance about HIV and AIDS, these youngsters are banned from school and the workplace. Sometimes their parents force them to leave home because they're afraid the disease will spread to other family members or because they cannot afford costly medications. Many eventually die alone and are buried as paupers in unmarked graves—unless The Joshua Project intervenes.

Tresha McKnight is one of four career staff with The Joshua Project. "Society's attitude is, 'These kids are dying, so why bother with them?' But we regard them as kids who are living with, not dying from AIDS,'" she says. "It's our goal to care for them in practical ways and to do whatever's necessary to ensure they understand that Christ loves them and died for them."

The Joshua Project was founded in 1999 after two Christian women met at a tram stop in Romania. One of these women was McKnight, a 21-year-old home healthcare nurse from Texas. Three years prior, her aspirations to pursue a career in opera had ended when she suffered a grand mal seizure on stage during her largest concert. Several seizures followed within three months. Doctors suspected a brain tumor and said one more seizure would kill her.

McKnight sank into depression. In desperation, she cried to God, "Do something with my miserable life!" He answered by healing her body and directing her to pursue nurses' training rather than a career in opera.

As McKnight and the other woman—Claudia Udrea, a Romanian psychologist and social worker—conversed at the tram stop, they discovered a shared passion for helping the defenseless. Udrea was familiar with the plight of HIV-infected children in the local infectious disease hospital, so she invited McKnight to see it firsthand.

"That hospital required official nametags for entry, and a gatekeeper stood guard to keep everyone else out," McKnight recalls. "We waited until he wasn't looking, and then we slipped in unnoticed."

The children's desperate state gripped the women's hearts. The two visited the hospital regularly for more than three years. They brought homemade soup, French fries, ham, and fried eggs to supplement the youngsters' meager diet. They earned the nurses' trust and were allowed to take the kids home where they bathed, clothed, fed them, and took them to church on Sundays.

The ministry grew. Tresha married Andy McKnight, a building contractor from Northern Ireland, and Claudia married Tony Udrea, a former Romanian police officer. Both men shared their wives' passion to help the less fortunate. They eagerly pitched in when God supplied funds to purchase and remodel a dilapidated orphanage.

The building had dirt walls, a floor made of wooden slats covered in coal dust, no heat, and no hot water. Within weeks they'd transformed it into a warm and welcoming day center with bright walls and big windows. The main room houses up to 20 teens who gather for art therapy, ping-pong, snacks, Bible studies and worship, the chance to joke and wrestle with their friends, and to feel valued. There's also a counseling room and state-of-the-art dental office. The debt-free facility nestles on a residential street in a small city. To respect the patrons' privacy, it bears no sign to identify its presence.

Some of the center's visitors have been raised in group homes because their parents abandoned them. Most come from abusive family situations. One girl, 13-year-old Daniella, was set ablaze by her uncle when he discovered her illness. Nine-year-old Marinella was referred to the center for counseling after her neighbors burned down her family's home upon learning she had HIV. Four-year-old Costel, the little boy left to die in a garbage can, was found by a stranger and taken to a hospital where he lived for nearly seven years until McKnight claimed him as her foster son.

"These stories are sad, but they're just the small stuff compared to the abuses these kids experience day-to-day," says McKnight. "The saddest part is that they never did anything to warrant getting HIV/AIDS. We try to help them understand that it's not their fault, even though society tries to blame them."

The Joshua Project staff have ongoing contact with more than 400 children and teens at any given time. Besides offering the day center services, they distribute clothing to needy families, do home and hospital visitations, and provide grief counseling for families whose children have died. They host a worship service at the day center once each month, and they hold in-depth Bible studies twice weekly to study how God's Word applies to life.

The topic of suicide has generated the most response, says McKnight. She explains that many of the kids suffer from manic depression and will attempt suicide by refusing to eat or drink, or by stopping their medications. "When they refuse to eat or drink, they slip into a coma and never come back," she says. "If they stop their medications, the disease multiplies, the organs shut down, and they die within weeks.

"When we discuss suicide, they're amazed and humbled to learn that their lives are not their own. They were bought with a price. On one occasion, the kids stayed after the study and cried when they realized how much God loves them and how suicide hurts His heart."

Since The Joshua Project began, it has touched the lives of several thousand teenagers. Many of those have already died, but not without hope. "To our knowledge, only five have passed into eternity without Christ," says Tresha.

"These kids know what it's like to hunger for something more in life," adds Andy McKnight. "They only need someone to tell them about Jesus. That's what we do through words and actions."

Holding week-long evangelistic camps has proven to be an effective method for communicating the Gospel to the teens. Volunteers from North America serve as counselors, teaching three short Bible studies every day and leading discussion groups afterwards. Days are filled with crafts and physical activities. "We have great fun," says McKnight. "These kids soon learn that Christians are not blah and boring."

Because the majority of the youth with whom they have contact are now Christians, The Joshua Project launched week-long discipleship camps in 2008. A team of North American believers leads intensive Bible studies that address issues such as bitterness, anger, and forgiveness. The discipleship curriculum also includes teaching about Biblical servanthood and the responsibility to share Christ with others—even their families who may have abandoned them.

"One of the deepest questions asked was, 'How can I love someone who hates me?' That was really tough—I can't imagine the kind of hatred these kids have experienced. It takes a great deal of maturity to love someone who despises them," says McKnight. "The leaders learned that these kids hunger to be different. They want to love in spite of the hatred shown them. Only Christ can heal someone's heart that much."

These camps, which rely on the participation of volunteer short-term missionaries from North America, face an ongoing obstacle—lack of adequate accommodation. Most facilities will not permit a group of AIDS-infected youth on their premises. The Joshua Project has found only one suitable hotel that will allow them to stay, but it can host only 25 guests. And so, the project has a vision of someday building a facility that includes a big red barn in the countryside – a place where they can host two camps every month all year long.

"It's at these camps where our kids experience their biggest 'God moments,'" says McKnight. "Besides learning more about His Word, these kids are reassured of His love by knowing that North Americans have traveled several thousand miles to be with them, the modern-day lepers."

The two couples testify to the intensity of this ministry. Building relationships with youngsters destined for early death can wreak havoc on one's emotions. But they consider this a calling from God, a lifestyle that demands their availability especially when "their kids" are hospitalized and need advocates to ensure adequate treatment or to hold their hands as death approaches.

"These kids are an unreached people group," says McKnight. "Looking into their eyes and seeing the light of life when they pray to accept Jesus makes it all worthwhile. I wouldn't trade that for anything in the world."

Taylor Field
An Oklahoman reaches the destitute of inner city Manhattan.

Taylor Field sounds like the name of a high-end department store. But it actually is the name of a storefront minister. But given the fact that this inner-city man of the cloth takes his cues for ministry from the One who clothes the lilies of the field, Taylor's name is most appropriate. Like the Heavenly Father whose unconditional love of his creation translates into tailoring nature's garments and feeding the anxious-free sparrows, Taylor has a passion of people.

"Early on the Lord opened my eyes to the value in all people, but especially those in the city," the pastor of New York's East 7th Street Baptist Church says without hesitation. "I love the way Francis Schaeffer put it. He said people are precious to God, so cities must be his treasure."

While attending Wake Forest College, Taylor was following in his lawyer-father's footsteps. That included majoring in pre-law and spending a year as an exchange student in Europe. He chose Berlin. In addition to studying German, Taylor learned the emotional pain of loneliness in a depersonalized city firsthand. Not only did he discover what it feels like to overlooked by society, he began to realize his need of a personal Savior.

"I grew up in a Christian home in the Bible Belt of Oklahoma, but I never saw the importance of embracing my parents' faith, "Taylor recalls. "When I left for Berlin, I reluctantly packed a pocket size New Testament my mom had given me. When I got lonely, I'd pick it up. But since I didn't want my roommates to see, I read it in secret and hid it under my bed as if it were a pornographic magazine."

Taylor found more than familiar English words in that little Bible. He found a Father calling him to himself. Shortly after returning home for his senior year of college, he invited Jesus into his heart. Taylor soon knew he wanted to spend his life finding ways to show the Savior's love in practical ways.

While studying at a seminary in New Jersey, Taylor first visited the storefront outreach center in the Lower East Side of Manhattan that one day would call him as pastor. Although the brick exterior was covered with graffiti, Taylor saw more than spray painted slogans, pictures, and designs. He saw the hand of God.

"I was intrigued by these inner-city missionaries who were willing to do whatever it took to reach kids in their own subculture," Taylor admits. "Here was a group who initially tried to paint over gang graffiti on the front of the building. When the designs and slogans appeared the next day, these Spirit-led Christians chose to put down their paint brushes and pick up a spray can. They created their own graffiti with Christian oriented symbols and words."

With so many hours of hands-on ministry credits to fulfill, Taylor volunteered at Graffiti Outreach Center working with children and youth in literacy programs in a neighborhood comprised of abandoned buildings, drug traffic, and prostitution. As he walked the streets several worlds removed from his native Enid, Oklahoma, Taylor had no idea this run-down section of the Big Apple one day would become home.

Twelve years later while completing his doctorate at a seminary in California, Taylor contemplated what kind of ministry he should commit to. Although encouraged to take a traditional pastorate in suburbia, Taylor bristled at the idea. His heart still beat for broken people few ministries were reaching. A speaker in chapel challenged the students to have the courage to set out to do the thing that makes their hearts sing.

"That was such a freeing thought," Taylor recalls. "I knew what made my heart sing. It was expressing God's love in physical and tangible ways. I couldn't get the unique ministry at Graffiti out of my head. In a very real way the handwriting was on the wall. I knew that's where God wanted me."

Taylor arrived in Manhattan's "Alphabet City" in 1986 with his wife and two sons (a two-year-old and two-month-old). The 32-year-old was committed to serve the needs of those in his neighborhood before attempting to spell out the claims of Christ. For many, that meant teaching the alphabet and helping adults as well as children learn how to read. It also meant staking a claim in a neighborhood that literally was controlled by drug dealers.

"Initially I was concerned for my family's safety," Taylor confesses. "I remember watching my little boy pick up a hypodermic needle some addict had discarded. Another time I took my sons to the park. As they ran up to chase a squirrel, I realized it was a big rat."

Taylor learned he had to trust God for his own safety as well. His arrival as director of Graffiti Outreach Center was not appreciated by everyone on the Lower East Side. The drug lord was not pleased that those he'd controlled now had other options for income or protection. Someone tried to strangle him while someone else pulled a knife on him. A homeless woman even tried to attack him with a nail-pierced board.

Since Taylor and his family moved to New York City in 1986, the Graffiti Outreach Center became a full-fledged church. But East 7th Street Baptist Church is anything but your typical congregation. It worships in an abandoned Jewish Synogogue it purchased and recently refurbished. Between Sundays, it is involved in 26 hands-on ministries that include literacy training, after-school tutoring, soup kitchens, Bibles studies, drug rehab, and legal advocacy.

"Although we've been at Graffiti for 25 years, the last ten or so years have been the most difficult and the most fulfilling," Taylor muses. "Since our church is located only 5,000 feet from Ground Zero, September 11th opened up opportunities for ministry to our community exponentially. We have been deeply involved in the emotional and spiritual rebuilding of lives. The shadows of that terrible Tuesday continue to linger."

Stories of how Taylor and his team of 20-plus associates are being used by God to reach lost people as well as literally to redeem a community are told in *Mercy Streets*, a book published by Broadman and Holman. In addition to Taylor's candid reflections on how experiencing the trauma of September 11th impacted his young family, the book offers testimonies that validate the ministry to which Taylor has invested his life.

Asked if the ministry of Graffiti church is still causing his heart to sing, Taylor is quick to answer. "You better believe it! I'll be here as long as the Lord lets me."

CHAPTER 7

Redemptive Communicators:

—ɯ—

EDUCATION

Kenneth Elzinga

A distinguished economics professor uses Jesus as a model for teaching.

Kenneth G. Elzinga had a mother deeply committed to the Christian faith and a father whose hostility toward religion exhibited itself by moodiness on Sundays. Elzinga's mother's influence won out, and he attended church with her every Sunday while growing up.

As he continued the weekly practice of Sunday worship in graduate school, though, Elzinga discovered a different type of Christian: those who talked about a personal relationship with Jesus Christ as a defining element of their lives. Their example provoked Elzinga to ponder the difference between believing facts about God, which he did, and trusting in God, as his new church contacts did.

"If Jesus was who he said He was—and I had believed this for some time—His claim on my life needed to involve far more than regular church attendance," Elzinga says. Soon after, at a church missions conference, he surrendered his life to Christ. Ever since, Elzinga has sought to follow Jesus' example in all parts of his life.

Elzinga's main sphere of influence is as a University of Virginia professor of economics and researcher in Charlottesville. Right after he earned his doctorate at Michigan State University in 1967, Elzinga joined the faculty at the University of Virginia, where he has instructed 30,000 students.

Along the way, he has earned a reputation as a leading analyst of market structures and anti-trust policy. His many honors include winning a Phi Beta Kappa award for a text he co-authored on antitrust penalties, a Phi Eta Sigma teacher of the year award, a Commonwealth of Virginia outstanding faculty award and being honored with the first distinguished chair for teaching excellence in the history of the University of Virginia.

"I am firmly convinced that if I were not a follower of Jesus, I would not have received one of them," Elzinga says. "I recognize them all as God's grace to me, for taking someone who has no business, in terms of natural talents, receiving these honors."

Over the years, Elzinga has developed a philosophy that his authority as a teacher goes only as far as his willingness to serve his students. In addition, he believes that teaching is not confined to the classroom. It can take place in a professor's office, during lunch, or even in the teacher's residence.

A good teacher must know his material cold, Elzinga says. He doesn't allow lecturing about economics to become routine because he believes every year, students deserve to have him teaching at his best. He doesn't schedule any substantive activities before classes because he wants to use the time to prepare material. Elzinga doesn't rely on notes he scribbled 35 years ago. He looks at newspapers and scholarly journals to ensure that his lectures are relevant to today's society. Stories about OPEC come and go depending on the cartel's influence. He also keeps pace with technology. In addition to overhead transparencies and the chalkboard, he teaches with videos. He occasionally uses Bible stories to illustrate an economic principle.

"I'm reminded of the admonition, whatsoever you do, in word and deed, do it as unto the Lord,'" Elzinga says, referencing Colossians 3:17. "It would be an affront to the Lord if I did not try to teach economics excellently."

In smaller, upper-level courses, Elzinga teaches by the Socratic dialogue method in which students must be prepared to answer aloud questions about the day's assigned reading material. There is a give and take, a matching of wits.

By the semester's end, many shy students have been transformed into students who can confidently and clearly defend a line of reasoning.

"When this occurs, I experience the joy of teaching, and not simply the satisfaction of the task," says Elzinga, who prays in his office to the Lord before classes. "I sense a great dependence upon the Lord in teaching, especially the large classes," he says. "I do not have natural gifts to do this."

Beyond teaching excellence, Elzinga believes part of Jesus' example as a servant teacher means that he must likewise be available.

"A Christian professor can have a spiritual impact on a secular campus by exercising whatever gifts the Holy Spirit has given to that faculty member," Elzinga says. "For some, it is the gift of evangelism, for some prayer, for some hospitality."

Elzinga seems to have all three gifts. He stays after a lecture as long as there are students with questions. The commitment to students doesn't end in the classroom. On the days when Elzinga holds office hours, students visit non-stop from 2:30 to 6, longer if needed. He sees this as an exciting time to serve, dispensing not only lessons in economics but lessons in life. He gives biblical counsel to students, some of whom aren't even in his classes but are seeking spiritual direction.

"Their underlying problem is with broken relationships or broken lives," Elzinga says. "Their problem is not with economic analysis; it is with the fall of Adam." Not all problems are within his realm of understanding. At such times he asks students if they would mind if he prayed.

In part because his introductory economics course has a thousand students, the institution's largest class, Elzinga encourages students to phone him at home, much like a doctor on call. Elzinga and his wife, Terry, also open their home, located on the campus grounds, to a diverse lot of students, from rehearsals by a Jewish a capella group to a student who uses the kitchen to make baked Alaska for friends.

Sometimes they have students over for a late-night brownies and milk break. Foreign students may be treated to a Thanksgiving dinner. Elzinga says he learned hospitality from his first wife, Barbara, whom he married just out of graduate school. Barbara died after 12 years of marriage, of cancer, at age 33. She taught her husband about faith. "As the cancer advanced, her love for and trust in the Lord also grew," he recalls.

Terry, an architect, has continued the hospitality tradition. Elzinga says students at school crave a home in which they feel comfortable, either because they miss their own family or because they never had such a homey environment.

"We think opening our home is pretty important," Elzinga says. "It is a way of keeping our own selfishness in check. And it demonstrates to others that if they have a home someday they need not hold a tight rein on it but they can share it with others."

With all the kindness and generosity, Elzinga doesn't allow himself to become a doormat. For instance, he does not think it's his place to help a student who is transferring to another school pick courses or to guide a student through the completion of income tax forms.

Elzinga has never been accused of showing favoritism to Christian students. He has had to flunk a number of Christian students because of their lack of effort.

It is no secret on campus that Elzinga is a Christian. Annually he addresses groups ranging from Law Christian Fellowship to Chinese Christian Fellowship.

Elzinga suggests that Christian faculty members at public institutions have a Web site that identify themselves as a follower of Jesus, as he has done. "If you are a teacher, or have some other position of leadership, you shouldn't hide your light under a bushel by concealing from others the very focus of your life."

He also has advice for Christians working in any secular environment: "Be excellent in your work, so your colleagues cannot dismiss you as a shirker or someone who is no earthly good," he says. "Be loving, courteous, helpful, thoughtful, cheerful. Christians who do not work hard bug me. And they give an excuse to their colleagues to ignore the Gospel. Be particularly kind to colleagues who are suffering. Kindness can be the best apologetic in some circumstances."

Part of the reason Elzinga is at the University of Virginia is because he understands that secular institutions are powerful shapers of American culture because they train the majority of minds. "It would be a shame if Christians abandoned the very setting where so many young people are being educated," he says.

As a sideline, Elzinga has co-authored, with fellow economist William Breit, three mystery novels. The hero in *The Fatal Equilibrium*—now in its twentieth printing and used at more than 400 colleges and universities as a text—is an economist who solves the crime using economic theory.

Elzinga has had multiple offers to teach, do research or be an administrator elsewhere. And although many contemporaries have opted for early retirement, Elzinga has no such plans. His calling remains on the secular campus. "I have one of the greatest jobs in the world," Elzinga says. "I get to work with young people, I live in a beautiful part of the country, I have a lot of freedom to pick what I choose to research and write on, and I have a good church home."

Even after more than four decades Elzinga is having fun. "When one might expect boredom to set in, or at least the law of diminishing marginal utility to take its toll, teaching continues to be fresh, challenging, scary and rewarding."

⸻

Marvin Olasky

A former Marxist professor now promotes Biblical compassion.

Only now does Marvin Olasky understand God's grace, after his lengthy journey from Judaism to atheism to born-again Christianity. Along the way, Olasky, now in his sixties, has become a leading proponent in public life of espousing biblical solutions to societal problems.

His grandparents emigrated from Russia to Massachusetts. In Olasky's early years, the family kept religious customs and rituals as Orthodox Jews, including sending him to Hebrew school for seven years and his bar mitzvah at age 13. Yet as his parents became increasingly secularized during Olasky's childhood, he became increasingly skeptical about God. By 14 he considered himself an atheist.

The godless, materialistic books he read, including *History of the World* by H.G. Wells and *Future of an Illusion* by H.G. Wells contributed to his ideology.

"My own pride and arrogance fueled my heading toward atheism, too," Olasky says. He came to believe that only silly and pathetic people needed God. Olasky instead looked to human gods to right the ills of society.

A scholarship to Yale University cemented his confidence in atheism. Liberals and radicals dominated the late 1960s campus scene, and Olasky kept moving further left, both theologically and politically. After serving a brief stint the Bend Bulletin, a newspaper in Oregon, Olasky joined America's Communist party. He rode a Soviet freighter across the

Pacific Ocean and the Trans-Siberian Railroad across Russia in order to better relate to those living under Marxist-Leninist dogma.

He returned to the United States and fit right in at the *Boston Globe.* But becoming a professor became his real craving, and he headed to the University of Michigan at Ann Arbor to obtain his M.A. and Ph.D. degrees in an effort to be part of "the tenured left."

"That's where God surprised me," Olasky remembers. In November 1973, as he became disillusioned with communism and atheism, Olasky came to realize God does exist. A Russian New Testament he had read to brush up on his Russian had played a role in changing his mind. So did teaching a course in early American literature, which included Puritan sermons preaching to him from the grave.

"God changed my worldview, not through thunder or a whirlwind, but by means of a small whisper that became a repeated, resounding question in my brain: "What if Lenin is wrong? What if there is a God?'" Olasky says.

He went on to read the writings of C. S. Lewis and Francis Schaeffer, which laid the groundwork for his conversion. In 1976, just before moving to San Diego to teach, Olasky married his wife Susan. They selected a Baptist church from the Yellow Pages, heard sermons about being born-again, and received Christ as Savior.

In 1978, Olasky began a five-year job as an executive speech writer for the DuPont Company in Wilmington, Delaware. In 1983 he moved to the University of Texas at Austin, where he has been ever since. He only teaches two journalism courses per term, which leaves lots of time to write. His passion now is to promote biblical principles through his writing. He has authored 13 books and co-authored seven more.

As in the 1960s, today's college environment is rampant with liberal and radical faculty members, including many of the 2,000 who teach at the University of Texas-Austin.

"In the university environment, it's well-known that I'm a Christian," Olasky says. Nevertheless, he has, despite some opposition, become tenured and a full professor. While he would be receiving more recognition and making more money with politically correct writings, he prefers to write scholarly works from a distinctly biblical perspective. He lives out this commitment as a senior fellow with the Acton Institute for Religion and Liberty and as the editor of a Christian news magazine.

The publicity Olasky receives in the somewhat hostile academic environment only adds to his unique role. The student newspaper occasionally takes potshots at him for his conservative views. Sometimes graffiti are scrawled on the Christian posters he places on his office door.

Yet for the Christian students among the 50,000 on campus, Olasky is a rarity: a professor who doesn't attack them for their beliefs, someone who supports them and advises them.

For the many non-Christian students in his larger lectures, Olasky often shatters the stereotypical perceptions they have of Christianity.

Meanwhile, Olasky gained recognition in 1994 when the Republican congressional leadership adapted ideas from his book *The Tragedy of American Compassion* for inclusion in the welfare reform debate. He is known as a formulator of a compassionate social policy that attempts to bring a biblical perspective into American public life. This philosophy, unlike Social Darwinism, which teaches that society is better off if the poor are ignored, holds that all people have value and should be treated as such because all are created by God in His image.

"We are commanded not to look away from the psychologically and spiritually distressed," Olasky says. The book describes how Americans successfully fought poverty before the government took over with myriad programs. His 1996 book, *Renewing American Compassion,* reiterated the themes that the most efficient poverty programs are religion-based and that churches have a responsibility to care for the helpless, especially widows and orphans.

Thus, Olasky has played a role in the welfare rolls being trimmed in half since 1996 and in more adults finding jobs and working their way up the economic ladder.

"God is changing people's lives," he says. "Instead of growing up with a welfare mentality, kids are able to see their parents working, which makes an enormous impact."

As an offshoot of his biblical philosophy of compassion, Olasky also has been instrumental in defending unborn children's right to life, championing causes that will change hearts rather than merely legislate. The growth of the abstinence movement, the increasing use of ultrasound, and the promotion of adoption have contributed to the number of abortions dropping to 1.2 million annually from 1.6 million. One of Olasky's most recognized contributions to this trend is his 1992 book, *Abortion Rites: A Social History of Abortion in America.*

The youngest of the Olaskys' four children, Benjamin, is adopted, partly as an expression of Marvin and Susan's biblically-grounded convictions. "It is something I recommend to everyone," he says. "The sense of satisfaction from children is great whether they are born to you or whether they are adopted. In a sense they have been rescued." The Olaskys helped to start the Austin Crisis Pregnancy Center.

Now living in North Carolina, Olasky now advances Biblical compassion and ideals in his role as the editor-in-chief of *World* magazine.

Through it all, Olasky is enormously grateful that God saved him from ideologies that led nowhere.

"God knows what we need and gives us gifts even we don't know enough to ask for them," he says.

No longer at the University of Texas, Marvin Olasky now serves as the editor-in-chief of *World* magazine.

—m—

Vicki Caruana

An educator addresses her colleagues' spiritual needs.

"What do you want to be when you grow up?" From the time she was six years old, Vicki Caruana's answer to that question was always the same: "A teacher!"

And for good reason.

"Mrs. Robinson was my first grade teacher," Vicki recalls. "Her love for kids permeated the classroom. It was so obvious in how she taught, what she taught, in the way she treated people, in the atmosphere of the class. She made learning fun. I loved school because of her and I loved her. I decided I wanted to be just like her. I wanted to grow up to be the kind of person she was—to make other kids feel the way she made me feel, because it was so precious."

Few of us end up in the careers we aspire to in elementary school, but Vicki's determination never wavered. Growing up, she couldn't wait to inspire young hearts and minds. She longed to create that warm and loving environment in a classroom of her own. Caruana graduated from college with a master's degree in education and got her teaching certificate. She thought she was prepared. She felt she was ready.

But as it is for many beginning teachers, Vicki's first year in the classroom turned out to be a rude awakening. "You find out there's so much you *don't* know," Caruana says. "You feel ill-equipped, very inadequate. You don't know if you can really do this job that you signed up for, because so much of it has nothing to do with what you learned in books. Teaching is more of an art than a skill. So much of it is about dealing with people—not just students, but parents, colleagues, administrators. You're interacting, solving problems, being emotionally invested and then dealing with the repercussions of being emotionally invested. You get hurt, you get disillusioned, you get discouraged, and you don't know where to turn. It happens to almost every teacher that first year. It's a baptism by fire, and you have to decide how much you really love it. The desire to make an impact—is it strong enough to carry you?"

Caruana's first teaching assignment placed her in a troubled inner city school. Her students had severe learning disabilities. Not one of their parents showed up for Open House night. Vicki's classroom was vandalized repeatedly. She was so worried about the safety of her students that she had constant nightmares. It was a learning experience alright—though not the kind she had dreamed of. Yet somehow, knowing that she was making a difference in the life of one child kept her coming back day after day.

"There was one boy—I knew that every night when he went home, he wasn't sure if he'd be alive the next day, because of the circumstances in which he lived. But he loved being in my classroom because I was able to make it safe for him. He felt accepted there and loved there. He loved being in school and he loved to learn. I didn't know if he would ever make it past the third or fourth grade level—if he'd ever graduate. But he made the effort each and every day in his own limited way. This one little boy kept me going," Caruana reflects. "You just need one. One student who needs what you have to give. God always gave me at least one each year, and that's all it took."

As a young teacher, Vicki found her faith played a vital role in how she saw her career—her calling. Caruana had been raised in a Christian home. She says she always had an awareness of God, a sense of His presence in her life—though it wasn't until she was a teenager that she truly understood the Scriptures she had learned and what her faith was all about. Her relationship with Christ gave Vicki the focus, strength, and determination to take on the challenges she faced in the classroom.

"Being a Christian teacher enabled me to look at my students the way God would—especially the ones who seem the most unlovable and unteachable. I knew that God loved them and I asked Him to love them through me," Caruana says. "I came to understand that it was not a mistake, not a coincidence that these children were in my classroom—it was God-appointed. I was appointed to be their teacher and they were appointed to be my kids. It made such a difference to have that outlook. I also knew that the difficulties I had with parents or the demands of my administrators were opportunities to be a witness—to let them see Christ in me. It wasn't easy. It was such a great responsibility. But it was also a great privilege. I wouldn't have wanted it any other way."

Over the years, as she continued teaching in both public and private (Christian) schools, Caruana realized that her early experiences were not unique. New teachers everywhere face the same problems, challenges, and opportunities. They want to touch the hearts and lives of their students, but they are in desperate need of encouragement and inspiration themselves. Too many of them give up too soon.

In time, encouraging teachers became Vicki's new passion—her new calling. She began looking for ways to reach out to other teachers and minister to them. Today, Vicki travels around the country, speaking to teachers at conferences and conventions. She is the award-winning author of a number of best-selling devotional books for teachers, including *Apples and Chalkdust*, *One Heart at A Time*, *Recess for Teachers*, and *Prayers from a Teacher's Heart*. Caruana also serves adjunct professor at a teacher's college in Southwest Florida, teaching, training, and preparing aspiring teachers for the real-world challenges they will face.

As the mother of two teenage boys, Caruana has had the opportunity to reach out to her own sons' teachers as well. She encourages parents to get involved and become a part of their teacher's support team. "Ask how you can volunteer. Be willing to do whatever is needed—drivers on field trips, chaperones for parties, bulletin boards, decorating. Notes of encouragement are invaluable," she says. "I still have a big manila envelope with every one I ever received. They're reminders to me as a teacher, that I'm on the right track, that I'm doing what God's called me to do—even though I don't see the fruit of it very often.

"Find a teacher you used to have. I recently went online and discovered my fourth grade teacher in a nursing home, 82 years old. I contacted her and thanked her for what she did for me. She was overwhelmed—to her it meant everything. Write a note or an email or just say 'thank you' every once in a while. It means so much to know that you're appreciated."

A frequent guest on national radio and television programs, Caruana calls the Body of Christ to rally around the nation's teachers—to participate in organizations and events that support educators. She's thrilled to see many churches honor the teachers in their congregation with a "Back To School Sunday" prayer service—commissioning them and sending them out into the mission field that is their classroom.

Says Caruana, "The battle that's going on for the hearts and minds of this next generation is a spiritual battle, and teachers are on the front lines. Sometimes they're with our children more than we as parents are. They spend more waking hours with our kids than we do. They're called to encourage those children, and they can't do a very good job of it when they're discouraged and broken-hearted themselves. They really need us to pray for them, to support them, to encourage them, to build them up. They need prayer for direction and guidance, strength to stand firm and speak the truth in love. Even if you don't have children in school at this stage of your life, you're still called to pray. This next generation will be taking care of us soon. They'll be in charge, making all the decisions. We need to nurture our teachers so that they in turn can be nurturing our kids!"

The walls of Vicki Caruana's classroom have expanded far beyond the local elementary school. Her students now include teachers, parents, grandparents, families and communities around the world. It's obvious Caruana still loves to learn and make learning fun. She cares deeply for each and every life God has given her the opportunity to touch—she wants to make a difference in each one. That's the heart of a teacher.

CHAPTER 8
Redemptive Communicators:

—◊◊◊—

MEDIA

Lee Strobel

A journalistic doubter becomes a popular Christian apologist.

Lee Strobel felt betrayed and frightened when he discovered his wife, Leslie, the woman he had cherished since his youth had found a new love. In 1979, Leslie professed her devotion to that new love—Jesus Christ—and committed her life to Him.

"I was very upset she'd decided to take this path. I was afraid it would change our marriage. I felt like she'd switched bait on me," Lee Strobel recalls.

Strobel's fears were realized—the couple's marriage did change—but the transformation in his wife's life forced the then *Chicago Tribune* award-winning journalist to don his reporter's cap and pen and take note.

As he witnessed his wife becoming a more caring, compassionate and tender-hearted woman, Strobel began to investigate Jesus, undeniably the person most responsible for the subtle changes in her life.

"I knew she did not change as the result of some self-help course. There was something fundamentally changing in her very nature. Something very attractive and very beautiful. Leslie had always been beautiful, like a budding rose. But when I saw her in a relationship with Jesus Christ, she was more beautiful than ever, like a fully-blooming rose. I asked myself, 'What accounts for this?' "Strobel says.

His first step was to accompany Leslie to Willow Creek Community Church, where he listened as Pastor Bill Hybels taught the fundamentals of Christianity to a crowd of suspicious skeptics.

Strobel left that first service with one pressing thought—"I knew if what Hybels said were true, it had huge implications for my life," he recalls.

Armed with a Master of Studies in Law degree from Yale Law School, Strobel was skillfully trained in fact-finding. The challenge was set before him. He had to discover for himself—was there evidence to support a case for Christianity, or was God, as he suspected, only a myth?

For nearly two years following his wife's conversion, Strobel plowed through ancient literature, plodded through archaeology, plucked through the Bible, and purposefully interviewed some of the world's leading scholars, all in an effort to investigate the truth, if there was any, to Christianity.

He began by grilling Dr. Craig Blomberg, author of *The Historical Reliability of the Gospels,* widely considered one of the country's leading authorities on the biographies of Jesus. But Strobel wasn't content with just one man's discoveries.

Relentlessly, he interviewed many other scholarly notables, including Bruce Metzger, author and editor of 50 books regarding New Testament text, and historian Edwin Yamauchi, author of several books focusing on biblical archaeology. Strobel eventually interviewed more than a dozen scholars, finally culminating his quest with born-again philosopher J.P. Moreland.

His research would ultimately form the structure for his recently published book—*The Case for Christ* (Zondervan 1999). Compared by many to Josh McDowell's *Evidence That Demands a Verdict,* Strobel's book leads the reader on an intellectual trek that unearths the rudimentary evidence in support of Christianity.

It was a trek that led Strobel, himself, to the foot of the cross.

So what was the one discovery that clinched the case for Strobel?

"It was the evidence in support of the resurrection," he says.

The same resurrection that changed the lives of the disciples is still changing the lives of people some 2000 years later.

"Overall, that one fact had more impact on me than any other," he reports.

As a journalist, Strobel had read account after account of terrorists who were willing to lay down their lives for something they believed to be true. But the disciples didn't just have a hunch about the resurrection, Strobel noted, "they knew for a fact it had occurred."

"I couldn't find any examples in history of someone willing to die for a lie," he adds.

James, the half-brother of Jesus, was the one disciple who had a profound effect on Strobel.

"He was not in Jesus' camp. In fact, Jesus would have been an embarrassment to him. There was no incentive to James to report the resurrection as fact. But we know from secular history that James was put to death for his faith in Jesus. Why? Because after the resurrection, Jesus appeared to his half-brother. It changed James," Strobel says.

Changed him into a man willing to die for his faith, for something he not only believed to be was true, but knew to be fact because James had personally encountered the resurrected Christ.

When Strobel, who was logging his discoveries on a yellow legal pad, came across James's testimony, he recognized that to continue in his disbelief meant swimming upstream, against the torrent of evidence to the contrary.

"It was not a huge emotional moment. I was simply surprised and convinced by the truth of who God is. It was the single, most rational thing in my life," Strobel says of his own personal encounter with the resurrected Christ.

Years later, Strobel acknowledges God was orchestrating the entire discovery.

"My response to the evidence was not because I was clever, but because God used the evidence to open my eyes to the truth of who He is and showed me my need for a savior," he says.

Strobel's trek to the cross culminated in November of 1981. But it was only the first stop in the journey God had planned for him. Since 1987, Strobel has served as a teaching pastor at the church that challenged him with the Gospel, where he teaches some 17,000 suspicious skeptics, like he once was, who attend a weekly service for spiritual seekers.

"It's ironic that I teach at the same service where my investigation first began," he observes with a wry smile.

Christians, Strobel says, don't have to be intellectual scholars to be a witness. But, he cautioned, they should be prepared to give an answer when the occasion to discuss spiritual matters arises (2 Peter 3:15).

"Know why you believe," he says.

Then pray for opportunities to share that faith with others. Talk about God in everyday conversations.

"Have the courage to seize the opportunities," he says.

And, perhaps, most importantly, listen to the questions non-believers pose.

"Don't think you have to have all the answers, you don't," Strobel adds.

Perhaps there is no better evidence of the resurrected Christ than restored lives. Strobel can testify to this. It was his changed life that convinced his own daughter Alison, at age five, to embrace Christianity.

"For the first five years of her life, she knew me as a drunk and absent father, who was angry over life. It was not a good environment. It was so bad that if I entered the front door, Alison would gather her toys from the living room and head for the bedroom. I'm not proud of that, but it's the truth," he confesses.

But about six months after he became a Christian, Alison began to notice a change in her father's priorities and values.

"Even at her tender age, she could see I was becoming someone who was more loving, more positive, more caring. She thought, 'If God does this for people, why would I not want that for myself?' " Strobel says recalling his daughter's profession of faith.

It was the same question that confronted Strobel following Leslie's conversion. A question that all sincere seekers address eventually.

Today, the Strobel couple rejoice that both Alison and Kyle were raised in a household that demonstrates God's ability to restore lives.

"All the evidence doesn't matter if it isn't played out in the transformation of people's lives. Without a resurrection, it isn't worth the pursuit," Strobel concludes.

~~~

Cal Thomas

A leading syndicated columnist views journalism is his mission field.

Although he has been fired and downsized several times from a television and newspaper career that has spanned nearly five decades, Cal Thomas has become the world's most widely syndicated columnist, appearing in 517 newspapers. As a conservative Christian flourishing in a profession dominated by liberal commentators, Thomas wouldn't mind some company.

He believes too many Christians assume that the mass media are so collectively hostile to their beliefs and worldview that it's not worth engaging the media, even in a constructive way. Thomas, 58, knows better. "First you have to stop cursing the darkness," he says. "Nothing gets lighter when you curse the darkness. But if God is big enough to create the world, don't you think He's big enough to [place] a few people of His in various professions?"

According to Thomas, Christians need to rethink the definitions of "mission field" and "full-time Christian service." Believers ought to see themselves as already being in full-time Christian service, because the alternative—part-time Christianity—is clearly unbiblical. "The mission field is wherever God puts you," Thomas says. "It's not only a foreign country where you live among the natives in a grass shack. If that's where God is calling you, you should go. But it can also be in medicine, in law, in education, in the media."

Thomas long ago began to see his work as a missionary calling. "There was a time in my life when I saw the career as an end, supplying not only my physical needs but my emotional wants," Thomas says. "In the process of living and becoming a disciple of Jesus, I found that like so many other things with God, our ways are not His ways, and my perception has turned around. Now I see career as the means and the credibility that it gives me to share my faith among my colleagues . . . as the end. It is providing more contentment than I ever had when I was pursuing the elusive goals of what the world offers."

Thomas started working in radio as a news reader at age 16, before joining NBC's news division as a copyboy at 18 and working his way up from there. He didn't sense a need for church as he climbed the career ladder. By age 27 he had become one of the youngest people to have appeared regularly on the NBC radio and television networks.

As a child, Thomas had made a nominal profession of faith. "I did what my parents and grandparents expected of me when I was 12—I walked down an aisle, signed a card, went down dry and came up wet, and had my 'fire insurance policy' in my back pocket so I wouldn't fry when I died," Thomas recalls. Yet he rarely read the Bible while growing up, except for the time when his grandfather offered him a silver dollar if he would memorize the 23rd Psalm.

Despite his success working for NBC News in Washington, Thomas sensed a tremendous emptiness. "The more I got in terms of visibility and money, the less satisfied I was," Thomas says.

But his life changed, beginning with a prayer breakfast where he heard a federal judge testify about having a personal relationship with Jesus Christ. Then at a Bible study he heard pastor and later U.S. Senate Chaplain, Richard Halverson, teaching. "He got me out of religion and introduced me to Jesus," Thomas says of Halverson. Thomas committed his life to Christ at age 30, the night NBC News fired him. "God was working things out in me, including reliance on myself, so He could work himself into me and fit me for the column He was going to give me," Thomas says. "The firing forced me to make a commitment, which was a very gracious thing."

Thomas's faith deepened through the influence of philosopher-theologian Francis Schaeffer. "Francis Schaeffer renewed my mind and taught me how to think," Thomas says. "He pushed people to the logical conclusions of their presuppositions, which is one of the greatest debate tactics ever created."

Today, Thomas and his wife Ray sponsor dinners in their Alexandria, Virginia, home for journalism colleagues. The Thomases, who have four grown children, also hold an annual dinner the night before the National Prayer Breakfast where guests hear about the things of God.

Christianity should be evident in the lives of its followers, Thomas says: "Do we stay married? Are we an example to our children? Are we honest in our financial dealings? Do we humble ourselves? How many of us are clothing the naked, feeding the hungry, caring for widows and orphans, visiting those in prison?" (See Matt. 25)

Society is suffering, in part, Thomas believes, because too many Christians have segregated themselves from sinners, rather than interacting with them as Jesus did. "The people who really need the medicine—the unsaved, the unwashed—aren't getting it in sufficient numbers because not enough of our people hang out where they hang out. They don't go to our churches, so we have to go into the world to them."

Christian laypeople have a special responsibility to be salt and light in the workplace, says Thomas, who over the years has been a political commentator for CNBC and the Fox Network. In many cases, Christians can be more effective in mainstream careers, he says. He recalls meeting a Florida newspaper reporter frustrated with his working conditions. "He told me, 'I'm the only Christian on the staff, and I hardly ever get my views on the editorial page. I'm thinking of leaving and going into full-time Christian service,'" Thomas recalls. "I said, "Let me ask you a question: Do you know the name of your boss's wife? Your colleague who sits next to you, have you ever gotten her a cup of coffee in the morning? Could you go out to lunch with some of your buddies here and think that you had had an effective witness if the subject of God never came up? Sure, God will allow you to leave, but He [might not give you] this kind of responsibility again. Or you can get back in there and start loving your neighbor as yourself, being among your peers and seeing how God wants to work this out."

In 1980, Thomas became spokesman for Moral Majority. But by 1985, Thomas became concerned that many well-intentioned Christian conservatives had strayed from the church's spiritual calling after being seduced by political power. He believes spiritual regeneration is the key to the societal transformation that so many Christians desire. "We'll never have trickle-down morality," Thomas says. "In a free society, government reflects the soul of its people."

The *Los Angeles Times* took a chance on Thomas in 1984 by allowing him to start writing a column that challenged conventional wisdom by promoting a return to biblical morality. Thomas didn't rely solely on the sales staff to make the syndicate a success. "God doesn't reward slothfulness," he says. "I went out and met editors myself and hung out where they hang out. That's what Jesus did; He came down from heaven and became one of us."

For his outspoken articles, Thomas regularly receives hate mail accusing him of being a hypocrite, coward, liar, and bigot. The ungodly have occupied the territory surrendered by Christians, he believes. "They've intimidated anybody who thinks differently," he says, adding that Christians should be as passionate about truth as their antagonists are in their opposition to it.

In his writings, Thomas skillfully presents biblical truths without being sanctimonious. While his job is to express opinions and to make judgments, he must be careful not to be judgmental. This proves especially challenging when individual moral crises plague the political atmosphere.

Thomas is the author of many books, including *Occupied Territory, Liberals for Lunch, The Things That Matter Most, Uncommon Sense,* and *Blinded by Might* (co-authored by Pastor Ed Dobson). While writing *Blinded by Might,* Thomas says he became concerned that many Christians who strive to transform society do so without really knowing Scripture. Without a knowledge of Scripture, he contends, we tend to refashion the Gospel, supplanting the biblical emphasis of a world needful of spiritual redemption with agendas that, however admirable, will never be more important than the salvation of human souls.

"No human, fallen leader is going to save this country," Thomas says. "Only Jesus Christ saves individuals. Nations rise and fall. If America became a totalitarian state tomorrow, it would not change one thing that I am commanded or commissioned to do."

⸺

LaShawn Barber
A political commentator prevails in her struggle with alcoholism.

A fortuneteller once told me I had a curse hanging over my head and only she could lift it. "What kind of curse?" I asked, pressing for details. She wouldn't specify until I'd paid $50 up front and booked more sessions with her. I laughed, but cringed inside. While I didn't return to see the woman, I already knew what the curse was. I was 27, and I'd been drinking almost every day for nine years.

A few months before that 1994 visit to the fortuneteller, I'd had a blackout after one of my customary drinking binges. I don't recall how I got back to my building, but I remember looking up at a mountain of stairs leading to my third-story apartment. I gripped the rail and walked unsteadily up each step. When I got to the top, I lost my balance and fell backward to the bottom of the last flight of stairs. Stunned, I examined myself. Instead of the broken neck I should've had, I'd merely banged an elbow. With no idea how I got there, I awoke in my bed the next day with the sun intruding on my drunken slumber.

The fortuneteller was right. I had a curse hanging over my head—alcoholism.

I barely remember what life was like before I started drinking. I grew up in a marginally Christian home and believed the good I did outweighed the bad. As one of the "good" girls in high school, I didn't have sex, drink, or do drugs. But after my senior prom, a month before my eighteenth birthday, I had my first drink. I thought, *I deserve it. I've been good for 18 years!* After a few sips, my whole body reacted. The feeling was more gratifying than anything I'd ever known. The more I drank, the more pleasant the world looked. I spent the summer getting drunk—as well as the following four years.

Nearly every day of my college career was filled with drinking-related activities. Practically everyone drank, and I had all sorts of "friends." Days were filled with fun and frolic; nights with emptiness. Drinking caused my inhibitions to fall away, and I became promiscuous. Trying to recapture that first "buzz," I went through a series of relationships, jobs, and schools—even law school—in an alcoholic fog. I blamed my appalling behavior on drunken blackouts.

In early 1997, I was almost 30, unemployed, and living with my mother. Unknown to her, I drank myself to sleep every night and often feared I'd drink myself to death. I saw myself at age 50 still drinking—or dead—and realized I couldn't continue this lifestyle. I never was able to recapture that high from my initial drinking experience. For the first time in almost 12 years, I wanted to stop trying.

Although I wrestled with the decision, I decided to get sober by age 30. I couldn't imagine life without alcohol—my god, my savior, my friend. To no longer worship at its altar seemed unbearable, but *something* beyond me was pulling me away.

At the time, I thought it was sobriety. Suddenly, I didn't want to wake up with a hangover

CREATED FOR CONNECTION ～ DONALD H. ALBAN JR.

anymore. I was tired of waiting until everyone left the house before I threw empty beer cans into the outside garbage bin. On the night of March 18, 1997—two months shy of my thirtieth birthday—I had my last drink.

The next morning, I tossed my empty cans for the last time. The whole day I was tempted to give up. Alcohol occupied my every thought, and my thirst was strong and deep, like itching flesh under a cast. But I was determined to finish what I'd started.

At the end of the first week, I saw tangible evidence of my decision to stop drinking: A slight tremor in my right hand—an alcohol-withdrawal symptom that was my companion whenever I went more than a few hours between drinks—was gone. For the first time in years, I could hold a glass with one hand. I decided at that moment I didn't want mentors, meetings, or support; I wanted to do it on my own and get all the glory!

In September 1997—after six months of sobriety—I believed I'd obtained that glory. The months had been tough, but with a new outlook on life, I made plans for the future. Next to go was my sexual activity. I became abstinent—the perfect complement to my sobriety. I felt physically clean and believed I was becoming a good and moral person.

When I'd been sober almost a year, I moved to a different state, found a job, and got my own apartment. I felt confident and invincible. People called me the "Black Dr. Laura" because I sounded like her and listened to her faithfully. I told anyone who'd listen that they, too, could be moral if only they'd make the effort. A walking self-help book, I preached my new religion: "You have the power to change your own life!" Everything in my life was coming together because of my own efforts—or so I thought.

Toward the end of 1998, however, I came crashing down from my high. Although I was a sober, moral person, I was disheartened. I still was thirsty for alcohol, and remained frustrated, bitter, and ashamed about my past. My life didn't seem much better than it had been while I was drinking. I wondered why I didn't feel "good." Then, the hollow feeling that made me put down the bottle two years before returned.

My search for something to fill that empty space inside led me to my youngest sister, a Christian. I told her about my disillusionment, and she convinced me to buy a Bible. Reluctantly I did so. The book sat on my coffee table for months before I removed the plastic wrapper. God was a stranger, and I didn't think I needed Him. Whenever my sister told me she was praying for me, I laughed to cover my hostility.

Fueled by this skepticism and seduced by the existential philosophies I'd read in college, I questioned the point of life and my purpose in it. I rejected the notion I had to rely on something other than myself. I thought about all the lies I'd told and all the destructive things I'd done. *How will I carry it all?* I wondered. As I seriously considered getting on my knees and asking God for answers, I became distracted: In May of 1999, at the age of 32, I met a man.

I saw "Greg" almost every day at work, and he clearly was interested in me. He asked if he could call me, and we spoke on the telephone several times. Nothing remotely Christian came up in our conversations. I was flattered by his attention, but one question kept popping into my mind: *Is he a Christian?*

I didn't know what I believed about God, so I wondered why I was so curious about Greg's beliefs. But I asked him anyway. "I believe in Jesus, but I'm not living a perfect life," he said. Good. Neither was I! Before I could ask any more questions, he asked me out. While I was tempted to accept because I hadn't had a real date in years, I stalled in replying to Greg.

Once again I sought my sister's advice, and we spent hours discussing my potential relationship with Greg. Though I wasn't yet a Christian, I wanted to make wise choices. My sister helped me focus on what the Bible says about men, women, and relationships, and not what the world—or my body—says. She told me if I were to live as a Christian woman, the man in my life would need to be a Christian. Together we reasoned that if that were the case, the first thing Greg would have wanted to know was if I were a godly woman. I knew this was going to be the new standard by which I measured any potential partner.

While I was still drinking, I lived by my own morals. Now, I wanted to live by God's. I realized a "perfect" life isn't necessary; a surrendered life is. I never went out with Greg. I now believe God allowed him to come into my life to help me realize my need for a moral compass—and, more importantly, for a Savior.

Several months later, on December 23, 1999, I told God I knew sobriety and abstinence weren't enough to save me. I dedicated my life to *Him*. I asked Jesus Christ to forgive me of my sins, to release me from the burdens of bitterness and fear, and to fill my heart with trust. I surrendered my will to the Lord that night, finding comfort in Matthew 11:28: "Come unto me, all ye that labour and are heavy laden, and I will give you rest."

As I read the Bible, the Lord continues to open my spiritual eyes. Jesus didn't come to make bad people good; He came to make dead people alive! He says: "But whosoever drinketh of the water that I shall give him shall never thirst; but the water that I shall give him shall be in him a well of water springing up into everlasting life." (John 4:14).

Looking back, I see how God used my quest for goodness as a way to the Truth. Just as God used the Ten Commandments to show the Israelites their sins, he used my attempts to save myself to show me mine. I tried to apply moral principles to my life and failed. I'd been self-righteous and bold in telling others to live up to my standards instead of God's. Now I want to be bold for Christ.

Since my conversion, I've found fellowship with other believers in church and Bible study groups. While I'm not involved in a support group for alcoholics, one of my current goals is to speak to those battling addiction—Christians and non-Christians—and to share my story of hope. Our works are futile; in a thousand lifetimes, we never can be good enough to save ourselves. Only God's grace frees us from the bondage of sin and addiction. Even sobriety can become a form of bondage when it's worshiped as a god. Its "saving grace" is deceptive.

Today I struggle with a different issue: my singleness. I want to marry and have children, but remaining single might be God's will for my life. As with any problem or concern, I turn these desires over to God. According to the Bible, he has plans to prosper me and not to harm me (Jer. 29:11). He gives me hope and a future, and if that future requires my singleness, I'll glorify him as a single woman.

That long-ago fortuneteller was right in ways she couldn't imagine. I did have a curse hanging over my head. But the curse wasn't alcohol; it was my separation from God. That curse has been lifted. The Living Water that eluded me is now mine in abundance. I've been sober for a decade, and thanks to Christ, I no longer thirst.

~~~

Dick Wright
The political cartoonist with a pastoral heart

Pick up any newspaper in the United States and there's a one out of five chance that your eye will be caught by an editorial cartoon by Dick Wright. (His syndicated in about 300 of the nation's 1,500 newspapers.) Each cartoon's subject depends on the social and political issues of the date. In December 1998 you might have seen a drawing of the then-U.S. President sitting in a corner he'd painted himself into, surrounded by black paint cans labeled Lies. In March of 2001 one cartoon depicted the current U.S. President sitting with a donkey in a dilapidated Model-T on blocks. Printed on the jalopy's door: Social Security.

Whether someone agrees or disagrees with 56-year-old Dick Wright's point of view—and many liberal newspaper editors label it too conservative—most admit that he has a witty way of making a point with his pencil. He's been doing it for nearly 30 years.

Drawing Conclusions

When Dick talks about his career, he sometimes mentions his sixth-grade teacher's warnings that he was spending too much time doodling, rather than studying. Her prediction: If Dickie doesn't quit drawing in class, he'll never amount to anything.

That Pasadena, California elementary school teacher might be amazed to know that Dickie's doodling evolved into cartoons that are seen by millions of readers four times a week, material that made him a finalist for the Pulitzer Prize in 1983. (He's never been able to reach her to tell her.)

She might not be as amazed to know that her now much older former student who delivers zingers to politicians also boldly delivers the eternal truths of Scripture as the pastor of a Bible-believing congregation each Sunday. After all, it was at age 12 that Dick, raised in a devout Christian family (his father has taught Sunday School for 60 years), received Christ as his Savior. "Getting saved that young kept me out of an awful lot of trouble," Dick says. "My focus became the church and the things in the church. My salvation experience was very, very powerful, and it's changed the course of my life."

Dick's devotion to Christ and the authority of Scripture has long been strong. Although the Bible says little of direct relevance to the specific political issues that his cartoons usually address—Social Security reform, education funding, environmental policies, etc.—Dick turns to Scripture for principles that help guide him to the specific convictions about such issues that he expresses through his editorial cartoons.

His faith in Christ also led Dick, at age 18, to the church where he met the young woman who became the love of his life. When a new family came to church, Dick invited one of the boys to play fast pitch softball. On the field he asked Tim if he had any sisters. Tim replied, "Yes, but you wouldn't want to meet her." Dick chuckles as he says, "I did meet her and I married her." (Dick and Susan Wright have two grown daughters and four grandchildren.)

As a young man, Dick did freelance cartoons for various magazines at night but supported his family through his day job. He was a draftsman at NASA who helped design the fuel system for the Mariner project. That job caused him to decide to go back to college to become an engineer. But, while drawing cartoons for the university newspaper, he dreamed about making drawing cartoons a full-time career. He took his work to local newspapers where editors encouraged him. Eventually he got a job with the *San Diego Union* that launched his cartoonist career. He later became chief cartoonist for the Scripps Howard newspaper chain.

During his career, Dick has worked for several newspapers around the country and moved his family from the West Coast to the East. When it became clear that through syndication he didn't have to work on-site to be a paper's cartoonist, he chose as his home base Gainesville, Virginia, located in the Washington, DC area. It put him close to the many of the national events that he addresses via his cartoons.

Wright to the Point

Dick creates four cartoons each week in his basement home office. Each one usually takes four to five hours to get from idea stage to finished product. His ideas come from reading *The Washington Times* and *The Washington Post* early each morning and seeing breaking news on television. The drawing takes shape—and sometimes changes shape—on his 30 year-old draft board as he works with paper, pencils, erasers, and rulers. (Essentially the same tools he used in sixth grade.) After the image is clear he can use an overhead projector to alter its size. Then he scans it into his computer and sends it on its way to his syndicate editor at Tribune Media and the readers beyond.

On the theory of cartoon drawing, Dick explains the madness behind his method: "There are two schools of thought on editorial cartoons. One is to take current events and to see humor in that and make a light-hearted comment. The other is where I am. I believe an editorial cartoon should have a point to it. You use humor to get your point across. I'm attuned to what's going on and the consequences of the acts of politicians. Many times I'm very upset and do not like what's going on, and I have an opportunity to say that to the reader."

And the readers are able to talk back to him (he puts his e-mail address on each cartoon). Most have positive comments. The negative feedback comes more from newspaper staff members who don't like his politics or, sometimes, his religion.

Like the late Johnny Hart and other cartoonists who are Christians, Dick's faith influences his work in many ways. He isn't afraid to put an explicitly biblical message in his cartoons or take the flack that comes from it. Holidays give him an easy opening. For example, a cartoon he did in April 2001 showed two Roman soldiers looking back at a hill with three crosses on top and an empty tomb below. One says to the other: "Relax! In a hundred years, who'll care?"

Drawing Near

"I'm longing for the day I check out of this all together and just pastor," Dick Wright says with what sounds like a sigh. That may seem odd coming from a man so successful at what he does. Dick isn't burned out. He's not just tired of 30 years of deadline pressures. He's found a new passion—pastoring a local church.

Dick and some friends founded the Community Christian Fellowship in September 1999. They first began meeting in a home, then moved to a fire hall in New Baltimore, Virginia. The church has purchased five acres on the border of two counties (Faquier and Prince William), bought modular buildings from an army base for temporary space, and is building a sanctuary.

As you would expect from a pastor/cartoonist, things aren't somber in this church. "We're very casual in dress and relaxed," he says. "People are so taken by the fact we can have some fun in church."

The church especially tries to attract unchurched seekers, but Dick sees his congregation as a mixture of types of believers. After the first 18 months of meetings Dick was grateful that the church had 29 new converts and that many lives had been turned around.

While his political cartoons may be considered polarizing by some, Dick avoids anything divisive in his church. "We don't emphasize our differences. We stick with the main purpose of the church, which is to preach the Gospel, to disciple all people, and to love one another. If you do those things, you're not going to have a whole lot of trouble. . . That's where we're going and it's gone well."

Things have changed for the man who once wanted to do nothing but draw cartoons. "Drawing political cartoons is what I do for a living. I try to do the best job I can, but I'm not consumed by it," Dick says. "My focus has become more and more toward pastoring full-time and taking care of the needs of the church. That is a higher priority to me now than winning Pulitzer Prizes and journalistic awards and getting in more and more newspapers. That's not what drives me."

CHAPTER 9

Redemptive Communicators:

—W—

LAW & GOVERNMENT

Phillip Johnson

A distinguished law professor hammers evolutionary theory.

Shards of morning sunlight sliced through the windows overhead and sent shadows scampering under the pews. A thousand bodies shifted in their seats, a hundred voices whispered, one coughed. Then, into the light stepped a gentleman with white hair, rosy cheeks, and an easy smile. He didn't look like the leader of a revolution. He didn't even look like a lawyer. He looked a little like Santa Claus.

His fingers rested on the lectern. His smile widened. The crowd quieted. The man put a hand to the tie that hung crookedly from his neck. Then, he began to speak. And as he did, the noose of Darwinism that has choked our society for decades seemed to unravel. And that's when I knew that this was no Santa Claus. This was a man who is changing our world.

Phillip Johnson never dreamed that God would call him to spearhead the assault on Darwinism and the naturalistic philosophy that has enslaved our culture with skepticism toward biblical truth. As a young man, he believed he had life figured out. He graduated with prestige from Harvard and the University of Chicago. He had the rare honor of clerking for the Chief Justice of the United States Supreme Court, then Earl Warren, and later became a law professor at University of California at Berkeley. In the world's eyes, he had it all.

But when he received the Lord as his Savior, Johnson quickly found himself torn between two worlds—the world of academia and the world of the church. "In becoming a Christian, I was accepting as true some things which are assumed throughout the university world to be altogether false," he says. "So the question [of creation] required serious investigation. What was the truth I had accepted? Was it really truth? Or was it all imaginary? It seemed to be something that the really educated people discarded many years ago."

He found the distinction between secular academia and his new beliefs to be particularly acute at church where the pastors and members considered themselves to be a part of the university community. "They believed they were respected and accepted," says Johnson. But he knew the academic world well. He knew that Christians were neither respected nor accepted. "They assume that everything we stand for is false and even ridiculous," he reveals.

That discordance set Johnson on a path of investigation that eventually led to the publication in 1991 of *Darwin on Trial*, a book that rocked the academic world by exposing the flaws of evolutionary naturalism. Rather than primarily defending his own beliefs, Johnson chose, much like Paul at Athens (Acts 17), with this and his other books that have followed to go on the offensive against falsehood by forcing evolutionists to defend their own unquestioned assumptions. *Darwin on Trial,* which has been translated into Chinese, Spanish, French, Polish, Czech, and other languages, created such a ripple that it provoked sharp responses from such leading evolutionary thinkers as the now late Stephen Jay Gould of Harvard.

Why would an accomplished law professor devote the latter years of his life to addressing the creation question? "What else is there?" Johnson replies. How were we created? What is the truth about creation and evolution? To Johnson, these are among the most interesting and significant questions in the world.

Every culture, asserts Johnson, has a creation story and a priesthood who has the authority to tell that story. In our culture, Darwinian evolution has become our creation story, with scientists and TV anchors as its priests. They say evolution is real, and creation is not. They say, "In the beginning were the particles . . ." and relegate God to a place next to Tinkerbell and the Toothfairy. But then along comes Johnson, a respected professor from a prestigious university—a man who is one of the academy's own— and catches them off guard by publicly scrutinizing the culture's established creation myth.

"It's very difficult to challenge it," says Johnson. "If you do, you're accused of bringing up 'religion,' that is to say 'imaginary things,' in the viewpoint of the secular world." So, Johnson needed to devise a strategy to, as he says, "batter down the door, to split the log of dogma" that stands in the way of truth. And that is just what he did.

"Johnson's genius was in framing the debate to be about evidence. Not God. Evidence," says James Scott Bell, author of *The Darwin Conspiracy*. Though not a scientist himself, Johnson has shaken the evolutionary establishment by exposing flaws in evolutionary theory itself. Like a true prosecuting attorney, he has put the theory of evolution "on the stand" and has challenged its accuracy based on the facts themselves. He has turned the tables (or in this case, the fossils) on the evolutionary "priests" to show that their position requires more "faith" than that of "Intelligent Design." Much like Paul in Athens, Johnson uses what evolutionists understand—science—to challenge Darwinism. Science, he has found, is not the enemy of Creation, but in fact supports the idea of a Creator.

So, unlike many others before him, Johnson successfully defanged the opposition, approaching the question of origins in a manner that forces them to engage him as someone who is more than a "Bible-thumping religious fanatic."

"If you're going to challenge something as powerfully entrenched as the theory of evolution, you can't just have a strong feeling of 'well, I'm right.' You can't just have arguments that appeal to your own side. You must have an argument which has the capability of breaking through the opposition," says Johnson.

Through Johnson's leadership, this Wedge strategy (getting the wedge of truth into the scientific debate on origins), is making inroads into the once impenetrable realm of evolutionary thinking.

Johnson describes his Wedge strategy as an ax—he is the initial sharp edge, but behind him have now come a number of distinguished scientists and scholars, such as Michael Behe, Bill Dembski, Nancy Pearcey, and Jonathan Wells, who form the thicker part of the ax which is necessary to split the log.

The time is ripe, believes Johnson, to overturn the governing paradigm of the entire thinking world, to shatter the dominant belief that nature alone explains how we (and the universe) came into being.

Just as Johnson felt he was gaining ground, his life and career took a new turn in 2001. On Friday, July 13th, the world blurred, and the thing that Johnson had most relied on in his career and ministry—his brain—failed him. He had a stroke, a serious stroke. "It was the most devastating and frightening thing I could imagine," he shares, "more so than death even." He didn't know if he'd ever walk again, let alone debate evolutionists, or write books, or speak to crowds about his passion for God, the Creator.

Then, into his darkness and fear stepped a Christian friend named Kate. She stood by his bed in the Oakland Kaiser hospital and sang an old hymn: "On Christ the solid rock I stand, all other ground is sinking sand . . ." At that moment, a question whispered through Johnson's mind: "Am I actually standing on the solid rock?" he asked himself. And the answer he found was yes, he was, or at least he knew he had one foot on the solid rock. "But perhaps I was trying to make things a little better by getting an additional foothold on the shifting sand," he relates. "The sand was my brain, the brain that had taken me from a small town in Illinois to Harvard at the age of 17, had made me at the top of the legal profession and a professor at Berkeley—the brain that I thought would get me through any other trouble." This was not a moment of conversion, Johnson is quick to clarify, but of a deepening, solidifying commitment to Christ, and Christ alone.

And so today, with both feet planted firmly on the solid rock of Christ, Johnson stands before a church filled with people, with his tie slightly askew and his shoes tied by his wife, because he still hasn't relearned how to tie them. In the power of God alone, with the sun shining in his hair, he shares the truth about creation and evolution. God has granted him the grace to continue his mission, to keep on fighting, keep on declaring the reality of an Intelligent Designer.

"We may look back at him in a hundred years and say, 'He's the guy that unraveled

Darwinism in our culture," says James Scott Bell. And I have to agree. But it won't be because of Phillip Johnson's intellect, it will be because he dared, in the power God had given him, to ask the hard questions, the right questions. It will be because he stood up among the secular priests of Darwinism and boldly declared, "The emperor Evolution has no clothes!"

⟶

Mat Staver

A leading constitutional lawyer takes the culture war into the courtroom.

Mathew D. Staver is a driven man. He has a bachelor's degree in theology, a master's degree in religion, and a doctorate in law. He heads the Christian defense organization Liberty Counsel, shuttling between offices in Florida, Virginia, and Washington, D.C. He is a professor and dean of the law school at Liberty University. He produces a half-hour weekly TV program, *Law & Justice;* a 15-minute daily radio program, *Faith & Freedom;* and a 90-second daily radio program, *Freedom's Call.* Oh, and he's written 11 books.

"The Lord gives me a lot of energy," Staver says. "I work around a lot of talented people."

The dynamic and humble Staver models his work ethic after his mother, who as a single mom worked three jobs during his early childhood in rural Florida.

The only memories he has of his father are of a violent alcoholic who physically abused his mother. By the time he reached age 3, Staver's parents had divorced. His dad moved to Illinois with two of his siblings while Mat, the youngest, remained in Florida with his mom and four brothers and sisters. His mother operated a paper route before dawn, worked as a waitress in the day, and as a nurse's aide during the evening.

Staver grew up determined not to follow in the footsteps of his father, who died in middle age of cirrhosis of the liver. Mat became a record-setting placekicker on his Charlotte County high school football team and hoped to make the sport his profession. But a leg injury his senior year dashed his hopes.

After graduation, Staver attended an evangelistic revival service in Punta Gorda, Florida, an evening that would change the course of his life. Although he had attended church regularly throughout his youth, Staver didn't have a personal relationship with Jesus. At the meeting he committed his life to Christ as Savior. He determined to enter the ministry, and graduated cum laude from Southern University with a theology degree.

He later graduated summa cum laude, first in his class, from Andrews University Seminary with a master's degree in religion. One day in Lexington, Kentucky, where he served as a pastor, Staver attended a meeting with other local clergy. It became another gathering ormat:

that would change the course of his life. There, the ministers watched a video on abortion. For the first time, Staver saw an unborn child in the womb as well as the graphic aftermath of an abortion.

Immediately, Staver obtained as much information about abortion as he could from a local right-to-life organization. He visited the University of Kentucky law library and for the first time read a legal case—*Roe v. Wade*. At age 25, Staver became active in the pro-life movement.

As he prepared sermons each week at the seminary, Staver kept thinking about what he had learned at the law library across the street. Although he didn't understand why God might be diverting him from full-time ministry, Staver—who reads Hebrew, Greek, and Aramaic—sensed that God wanted him to become involved in the legal and public policy arenas of the sanctity of life movement.

Soon, Staver enrolled in the University of Kentucky Law School. After graduation—and marriage to his wife Anita—he moved to Orlando, Florida, and went to work for a private practice law firm, still engaged in right-to-life activities in his free time. Two years later, in 1989, Staver formed his own commercial law firm so that he could become more involved in pro-life issues on the side. Income from Staver & Associates financed Liberty Counsel, which initially focused on pro-life and religious liberties cases. Staver, who started out with only a secretary to help him in the Liberty Counsel office, became a pioneer in providing free Christian defense in the religious liberties movement, following John W. Whitehead who started the Rutherford Institute in Charlottesville, Virginia, in 1982.

Even working part-time for Liberty Counsel, Staver managed to litigate significant cases. In 1994, he argued *Madsen v. Women's Health Clinic*, an important "buffer zone" case for the free-speech rights of pro-lifers, before the U.S. Supreme Court. A judge in Melbourne, Florida, had ordered volunteer sidewalk counselor Judy Madsen and other pro-lifers to keep at least 36 feet away from an abortion facility. In addition, the judge approved a 300-foot zone around the building that would outlaw pro-life speech unless listeners showed an interest.

"In public areas, the Constitution does not require peaceful protesters to first obtain permission from those of the opposing viewpoint to speak," Staver argued. The high court ruled the attempts to silence sidewalk counselors unconstitutional.

Sanctity of life—all life—is important to Staver, whose father committed incest with one of his sisters. The rape resulted in the birth of a baby.

Anita, who had obtained a counseling degree, decided to obtain a law degree after the *Madsen* case so that she could work beside her husband. She has more than 30 published legal opinions.

Within a decade, Staver & Associates, the secular firm that bankrolled Liberty Counsel, had grown to 40 employees and included a branch in Tallahassee. The business law firm

127

attracted statewide clients in the insurance, hotel, restaurant, and hospital industries. But Staver found that the company's success acted as an impediment to Liberty Counsel. Staver had to spend too much of his time tending to commercial law matters, time he believed should have been devoted to Christian cases.

He sought counsel from Liberty Counsel board member Alfred Williams, a London pastor. Williams gave Staver three pieces of advice:

⟶ If he had peace in his heart about God wanting him to devote all his time to defending religious liberties and the sanctity of life, he should pursue it, even if he didn't know where he would obtain funding.

⟶ Satan is a master at delaying and distracting Christians from accomplishing visions God has imparted.

⟶ When God presents a plan of action, He may not speak again until the vision has been fulfilled.

Staver, indeed, had felt directed by God to start Liberty Counsel in 1989. But by 1999, he believed he had failed to completely trust God, instead hoping for a miraculous monetary gift to make the organization fully functional.

"In retrospect, I realized I hadn't been living in full dependence and faith on the Lord," Staver says.

So Mat and Anita took a leap of faith. They figured they would still have each other even if they lost all their possessions in closing Staver & Associates and its lucrative source of income.

God blessed the decision. A recently renovated office building the firm had purchased in Tallahassee had been on the market for 14 months without a single offer. It sold in six weeks. Staver & Associates sold its corporate airplane, two Mercedes Benzes, and several $20,000 copy machines. Outstanding receivables owed to the company were paid at a higher percentage rate than in the history of the firm. Within nine months, the company had paid off all its obligations.

Today, Liberty Counsel is fully funded by donations from individuals, churches, and organizations to provide pro bono legal services.

Staver has continued to argue cases that reach the U.S. Supreme Court. In 2000, he became involved in the history-making decision of *Bush vs. Gore* that cleared the way for George W. Bush to be elected president. Staver represented absentee voters who candidate Al Gore's campaign attempted to disenfranchise. In 2005, Staver defended a Ten Commandments display in county courthouses in *McCreary County v. ACLU of Kentucky*, but the Supreme Court ruled against him—on the same day the justices determined that a

Ten Commandments monument at the Texas State Capitol was constitutional.

In 2004, Staver took another faith step by helping found the Liberty University School of Law in Lynchburg, Virginia. For several years, Staver had written a column in *National Liberty Journal*, a monthly newspaper published by Liberty University founder Jerry Falwell. He also appeared on Falwell's weekly *Listen America* cable television talk show. Staver urged Falwell to start a law school in order to teach religious liberties to a new generation. Falwell didn't need much prodding; he had been thinking about it himself. The school began operation in 2004, headquartered in an 888,000-square-foot complex of buildings on 110 acres adjacent to Liberty University. Hobby Lobby founder David Green paid $10.3 million to a cellular telephone company moving operations overseas for the property.

In 2006, Staver relented to Falwell's persistent request that he become dean of the law school. Staver agreed, provided he could open a Liberty Counsel office on campus. The law school at Liberty University, where Staver also is a professor, serves as a training laboratory for future lawyers who hold a Christian worldview.

Liberty Counsel now also has offices in Texas and Washington, D.C. There are hundreds of affiliate attorneys around the country, in all 50 states. Ninety-five percent of Liberty Counsel's legal work is resolved without going to court. In its 20-year existence, Liberty Counsel has won 86 percent of the cases it has litigated, including 92 percent since 2004. Typical suits are filed to ensure that a Good News Club has a right to meet in a public school or to defend a second grader who had been prohibited from giving Bibles to his friends at school.

In addition to religious liberties and anti-abortion litigation, a third emphasis of Liberty Counsel for the past decade has been defense of the traditional family, marriage between one man and one woman. In 2008, Staver became the lead lawyer trying to overturn same-sex marriage in California. He needed bodyguards when arguing in court in San Francisco.

"My mission in life is to be a friend of God and to do His will in a Christ-like way, but to be uncompromising on principles of truth," Staver says. "So I'm not a friend of the world. A lot of people disagree with me."

Staver has attracted his most strident opposition from abortion-rights and homosexual-rights groups. He has endured vicious untrue attacks against his character from those who disrespect his biblical viewpoints.

Meanwhile, Staver is encouraged by the number of students at Liberty University who will be trained in law.

"The biggest legacy we can leave behind is the life of someone who is inspired to follow the will of God," Staver says. "The law school is training men and women in all areas of law—business, education public policy, public service, ministry. These people will become lawyers, judges, educators, policymakers, and world leaders."

Today, Liberty Counsel has a staff of 28, plus up to 20 student interns at any given time, most of them from Liberty University. During summer, the number of interns swells to 50.

"The synergy with Liberty University has solidified the future of Liberty Counsel," says Staver, now in his upper fifties.

A partnership between Liberty Counsel and Liberty University created the Liberty Center for Law and Policy in Washington, D.C., to train legislators. A similar collaboration expanded the Liberty Center for International Human Rights in 2009 after the entity had helped Christians in countries such as Romania, Malaysia, and China.

Of course the main concentration will continue to be on freedoms in the United States.

"Some people don't realize the serious threat against our liberties today, particularly from the homosexual agenda," Staver says. "Our job is to educate, motivate, and equip Christians to be able to engage the culture and advance the Kingdom."

~~

Gary Haugen

An accomplished attorney wars against the international slave trade.

When Gary Haugen was growing up in Sacremento, California he didn't have a care in the world. His father, a physician, provided a comfortable income for the family of eight. At school each morning as he stood to recite the Pledge of Allegiance, he had no idea the implications the phrase "and justice for all" would have on his life in years to come.

"In elementary school I was oblivious to the anti-war movement, the ongoing conflicts in Vietnam, and the racial tensions of that marked our nation in the early seventies," Gary admits. "What I read in my textbook about President Lincoln's passion to free the slaves was the only thing I knew about the denial of human rights."

It was not until Gary moved to Boston to begin his studies at Harvard in the fall of 1981 that his eyes were opened to the plight of people struggling to experience the comforts of life he'd always taken for granted.

"I saw homeless families living in alleyways as I went to class," Gary recalls. "It had a profound impact on me. As a member of our local campus Christian fellowship, I worked in a homeless shelter in Cambridge and helped to winterize the homes of the poor in Boston. It was an eye-opening experience for me."

But Gary's eyes weren't the only part of him that was impacted. His heart was too. By the time he graduated from Harvard in 1985 he felt called to live out his faith and education by investing in a cause bigger than himself. He traveled to South Africa and worked to promote human rights there. The months he spent working with the National Initiative for Reconciliation caused him to see the mandate for Christians to stand against injustice where it is found.

In the late eighties, after getting a law degree from the University of Chicago, Gary worked for the Lawyers Committee for Human Rights. In that role he investigated police and military misconduct in the in which civilians were murdered. The miscarriage of justice haunted the young lawyer whose core values were marked by Scripture he'd learned early on.

"My mom prayed with me to receive Christ as a young boy," Gary acknowledges with a smile. "I'm grateful to her for making sure my siblings and I were in church to hear of God's love. But I'm also grateful for the experiences God has allowed me that have helped me understand His passion for justice in the lives of helpless victims."

Another one of those experiences occurred after Gary went to work for the United States Department of Justice in Washington, D.C. In the aftermath of the Rwandan genocide in which 800,000 men, women and children were slaughtered in eight weeks time, Gary was sent to that blood-soaked African nation to investigate. His survey of mass-graves and eye-witness accounts caused him to return to the United States determined to do something.

"While some people asked where God was during such a human tragedy, I came home with another question burning in my gut," Gary admits. "I wanted to know where God's people were, [those who] could have stopped the needless slaughter of innocent lives. From the studies I conducted, it was obvious the genocide could have been prevented if certain people had done certain things."

Convinced Rwanda wasn't the only country where inhumane treatment of ordinary citizens was taking place, Gary left the Department of Justice to strike out on his own. In 1997 he founded International Justice Mission in suburban Washington with a simple vision. He wanted to work with local authorities to dig up evidence and bring prosecutions against those guilty of abuse and slavery in accordance with local laws.

Gary's vision was not only based on what he'd observed in South Africa, the Philippines and Rwanda. He was convinced by his reading of the Bible that God's heart beat on behalf of those denied fair treatment by those usurping control over them. A survey he'd conducted of 65 missionary organizations (representing more than 40,000 overseas workers) indicated they were aware of abuses of power but lacked the tools to oppose them. Gary was motivated to provide the tools because of his knowledge of God's Word.

"When you read the Scriptures with an eye for passages related to justice, you see it everywhere," Gary contends. "In Micah 6:8 God tells us that the bottom line agenda for his people is to do justice and love mercy and walk humbly with Him. Through Isaiah God bears his soul. 'Learn to do well; seek judgment, relieve the oppressed, judge the fatherless, plead for the widow' (Isa. 1:17). It's clear that God hates injustice and wants His people to confront it."

As he began IJM Gary found himself incensed about the trafficking in sex slaves that he observed taking place in Cambodia. IJM's undercover operatives shot video of children being offered for sale in brothels. When authorities were shown how young children were being forced into lurid behavior, brothels were raided and profiteers were arrested.

"We want to speak up for the abused and expose corrupt officials who turn a blind eye and hold out a greedy hand," the founder of IJM explains. "We exist to help missionaries and aid workers who discover criminal abuse but lack the resources or expertise to expose the perpetrators."

While sexual exploitation of women and children are one focus of IJM's agenda, the non-profit organization also opposes forced labor, illegal land seizures, illegal detention, and police brutality. Its overall purpose is to protect people from violence by securing rescue and restitution for victims and ensuring that public justice systems work for the disadvantaged.

The organization's mission has drawn attention. A steady stream of Christian lawyers and human rights activists have joined IJM's cause, convinced that their service matters more overseas than in a country rich with litigators. Today IJM (which 95 percent privately funded) has 16 offices in 12 countries and currently employs more than 260 individuals.

Gary's passion for his calling has resulted in many volunteer lawyers and investigators who leave their jobs for a few weeks to offer their skill in a country where abuses exist. Chicago-based lawyer Bob Mangan is one of those. When a U.S. Congressman asked Bob to attend a gathering in his home to hear Gary share his vision, Bob had no idea what would result.

"As I heard Gary speak about the plight of young girls being exploited in Peru, I knew I had to get involved," Bob recalls. "When Gary reported that Peru exceeds the rest of South America in its ambivalence towards the sexual abuse of women, I questioned how my involvement would make any difference. But upon going and serving in Jesus' name I came to believe that any justice served is service to a Holy God and is not without effect."

Gary's success in inspiring volunteers like Bob is an ongoing joy to him. But the husband and father of four refuses to let a ministry he feels passionate about undermine his effectiveness at home.

"I am very intentional about my work and travel schedule," Gary says without hesitation. "I won't travel more than six nights a month domestically and will not agree to more than three overseas trips a year. Not only do I need to avoid the potential for burnout, I want to be able to coach my kids' teams."

In light of his passion for justice, Gary has been called a modern-day Wilberforce. William Wilberforce, a nineteenth century British parliamentarian, is credited with bringing an end to his nation's slave trade. Although he does not deny the similarity of their concern, Gary is quick to note that the campaign against modern slavery is far from over.

"According to a recent *National Geographic* article, there are more slaves in the world today than there were in 400 years of trans-Atlantic slave trade," he observes. "My fear is that [we] celebrate what Wilberforce did in 1807 but overlook the far greater situation that exists 200 years later. Too many lives are at stake for Christians not to take action."

CHAPTER 10
Redemptive Communicators:

—◊◊—

BUSINESS & FINANCE

Dave Ramsey

A leading financial counselor shares wisdom from Scripture.

Growing up in the Nashville suburb of Antioch, Tennessee, Dave Ramsey had honest, hardworking parents who made a living as real estate agents. They were more likely to be attending an open house than a house of worship on Sundays.

Ramsey followed in his family's footsteps after graduating from the in 1982 with a degree in finance and real estate. Soon he and his wife Sharon, whom he met in college, started buying and selling property with aplomb. By age 26, Ramsey had amassed a $4 million real estate portfolio.

But the Ramseys borrowed too much money. And when another financial institution bought the bank that loaned them all the credit, the couple began to default on short-term loans. Within three years of making $200,000 annually, they filed for bankruptcy protection.

The financial turmoil naturally resulted in an emotional rift between the spouses, who by this time had two young children. They stayed together, in part, because they didn't have enough money to leave each other.

But more important, the couple had a spiritual walk that kept their marriage intact. At age 24, Ramsey attended a motivational sales training seminar in which the impressive and credible speaker ended his presentation with a challenge to the audience: anyone who really wants to be a success can't leave God out of his life.

Ramsey went home from the seminar and told his wife they needed to start attending church, which they did.

"I met God on the way up the real estate ladder, but I really got to know Him on the way down," says Ramsey, now in his fifties. "Pain and fear and hopelessness always lead you in a special way into the throne room."

Amid his despair, Ramsey devoured the Bible, became keenly aware of God's authority over his life, and asked Jesus to be his Savior. The Ramseys began teaching teenagers at church. Then the pastor asked Ramsey to teach a Sunday School class about money to those in college. By this time, Ramsey already had read all that Christian financial expert pioneers Larry Burkett and Ron Blue had written. He compiled his own book, the first version of *Financial Peace,* about God's way of handling money based on what he had learned from the mistakes he had made. The class's attendance swelled from 35 to 350.

Ramsey continued to sell real estate and—out of the trunk of his car—copies of *Financial Peace.* "It takes selling a lot of $12 books to eat," he says.

In 1992, Ramsey made a life-changing decision. He agreed to fill in as the host of a one-hour daily show at a radio station in financial straits. That evolved into the national "The Dave Ramsey Show," which continues today with the frank and humorous host serving as a personal money management expert.

Ramsey is a fast-talking, in-your-face kind of guy whose tough-love guidance over the airwaves from Nashville is connecting with a lot of Americans. Every few minutes on his three-hour weekday afternoon radio program, callers who recently paid off massive amounts of credit card obligations scream, "I'm debt free!"

Unlike most money experts who are Christian, Ramsey gained entrée into secular radio, resonating in a medium that reaches far beyond the evangelical world. He is syndicated on more than 300 radio stations, fewer than 15 of them Christian. He also is on subscription-based satellite radio. He has three million listeners each week. Dave has also been a Fox Business Network TV anchor since 2007.

"I sell a lot of books in Christian settings and speak in a lot of churches, but my calling is in the mainstream marketplace," Ramsey says.

Yet Ramsey, at intentionally strategic times, is overtly Christian and boldly proclaims his faith on the program. For instance, if a caller says he is a Christian and that his car has just been repossessed, Ramsey will quote a Scripture, such as Proverbs 22:7: "The rich rule over the poor, and the borrower is servant to the lender."

Sometimes Ramsey's Biblical paraphrases are more blunt: "If you sow stupid, you reap desperate and broke."

Ramsey doesn't have much patience for Christians looking for God to bail them out of the reckless financial decisions they've made in a society where pre-approved credit card applications arrive in the mail virtually every day. Ramsey says too many consumers have fallen prey to the sophisticated marketing schemes of financial institutions.

"We've come to believe debt is a way of life, that the way to prosper is through the use of a credit card, that you can't be a student without a student loan," Ramsey says. "I've cried over this stuff, too. I've done stupid with zeroes on the end. But our Heavenly Father loves us enough to show us the right way to do it, even if the path to get there is a little bit painful."

Ramsey believes he has made inroads into the mainstream market because of the credibility that he gained through the firsthand experience of failing to get a grip on his own finances.

"I went broke a few years ago," Ramsey says. "If somebody's hurting, I can relate. I'm a wounded healer."

In the couple of minutes or so of interaction that Ramsey has with each caller he says he must rely on the Holy Spirit's guidance to decipher whether a tender or brusque response is necessary. Whichever method fits the occasion, he wants the listener to emerge with a plan of action.

"I don't want to jump down the throat of a hopeless person," Ramsey says. "But I don't want to love on somebody too tenderly who is slothful. There are plenty of people who are poor because they are taken advantage of and oppressed, but one of the reasons the Bible says the poor will always be with us is because the lazy won't get up and work."

Still, the Ramseys have formed a program called Share It, which they finance heavily from their own income. Share It enables disadvantaged people—prisoners, unwed mothers, recovering drug addicts, those in low-income housing, victims of domestic violence—to attend classes for free to learn God's way of handing money.

More than 350,000 people have completed Ramsey's Financial Peace University, a 13-week course that he says enables the average family to pay off $5,300 in debt and save $2,700 in the first 91 days. In addition, 400,000 people have attended live events Ramsey has hosted to promote the rapid eradication of debt, based on his book *The Total Money Makeover*. At the end of his talks he always talks about the importance of the Lord.

"There's not one time in the Bible where God uses debt to bless His people," Ramsey says. "If you're a Christian and you use Scripture as your standard, every time debt is mentioned it's a curse and you're a slave."

Ramsey's no-nonsense approach to money has landed three of his books on *The New York Times* best-seller list. While thousands of Americans have heeded Ramsey's message, many others aren't listening.

"The statistics of pain are getting worse every year," Ramsey says. "We have more people getting behind on credit cards, more people filing bankruptcy, more people in foreclosure right now than we've ever had in this nation."

But numerous families are making better decisions and changing because of Ramsey's advice. And that means more people are saving—and giving money to their churches.

—⁓—

Anne Beiler

An entrepreneur retains eternal perspective amid remarkable success.

Anne F. Beiler's life went into a tailspin after the death of her 19-month-old daughter, Angela, who was run over by a farm tractor in 1975. Beiler, in her mid-twenties at the time, found herself depressed and, more than once, on the brink of suicide.

Despite being a faithful churchgoer, Beiler didn't feel as though she could share her pain with friends or family members. She and her husband, Jonas, whom she had wed at 19, drifted apart. The couple didn't talk about the tragedy and its ramifications. Instead, they remained silent partners who simply lived together. Anne determined to stay with her husband for the sake of their two other daughters. But she contemplated filing for divorce once LaWonna and LaVale grew up.

Seven years into the ordeal, Jonas convinced his wife to go with him for marriage counseling at their church.

"I really didn't want to go, even though my life was falling apart," she says. "But I had a breakthrough and in the process of counseling I saw how God loved me."

As God restored Anne, she and Jonas reconciled with each other. The Lord also revealed to the Beilers that many Christians around them suffered with a great deal of unspoken pain because of various crises in their lives.

After studying at EMERGE Ministries, founded by Dr. Richard Dobbins in Akron, Ohio, the Beilers began providing lay counseling as a way to help such broken people.

In order to make ends meet during those years, Anne relied upon the youthful baking experience she gained growing up on an Amish-Mennonite farm with seven siblings. Because Beiler had asthma as a child, she never ventured outdoors much. Thus, she inherited the role of cook and baker for the family. By age 12, she made as many as 70 pies and cakes from scratch each week for sale at a nearby farmer's market. She didn't skimp on the ingredients, and always carefully made sure the wares looked and tasted great.

"God often uses our history to fulfill His plan," Beiler says. "God was preparing me for the future."

As a financial means to supplement the counseling work she did with her husband, Beiler bought a concession stand at a farmer's market in Downington, Pennsylvania. She sold everything from pizza to ice cream, but it was the hand-rolled soft pretzels that customers gobbled up the fastest. Because of such demand, Beiler dropped the rest of the products and concentrated full time on the pretzels.

From that modest start she became one of the nation's leading entrepreneurs. Although the family's counseling center in Gap, Pennsylvania, has grown tremendously and today employs 17 people—handling more than 2,300 appointments annually—it's the baking business that has generated a much higher profile.

Auntie Anne's Hand-Rolled Soft Pretzels now rakes in $247 million in sales a year. In a quarter century, the company has grown from one outlet in a Pennsylvania farmer's market to more than 850 shops worldwide. Auntie Anne's, which likewise has headquarters in Gap, Pennsylvania, has found a niche among snack-seeking mall shoppers. The company has stores in 44 states.

In 1995, the business also began the process of allowing franchisees to open overseas. There are stores in 13 foreign countries, all because wealthy business people have sought Auntie Anne's out. The company doesn't advertise franchise opportunities, yet applications filter in on a daily basis. Today, the U.S. pretzel company is found in such unlikely spots as Indonesia, Thailand, Venezuela, and Saudi Arabia.

"The pretzel is a bread with a universal language," Beiler says. "The reaction is the same around the world."

The menu has expanded to offer more than pretzels. Customers want to dip their snacks into sauces, so a wide range is available, including cream cheese, marinara, caramel, and sweet mustard. And munching those pretzels can work up quite a thirst, so drinks include old-fashioned lemonade, gourmet coffee, and frozen beverages ranging from wild cherry to mocha.

But it's the pretzels—which are mixed, twisted, and baked in full view of customers—that keeps the franchise so popular. There are a dozen varieties, including cinnamon sugar, glazin' raisin, garlic, onion, and sour cream and onion. Yet the unadorned, lightly salted original remains the best seller.

Despite the great financial rewards, Beiler, now in her sixties, had no trouble keeping her faith in God at the forefront of her business dealings. She started Auntie Anne's without a high school education, business knowledge, or financial capital.

"My history is one of depending on God," she says. "I know who my Source is. The business is much bigger than I am."

Beiler says she based the company on the Book of Proverbs. The acronym LIGHT forms its statement of purpose: Lead by example; Invest in employees; Give freely; Honor God; and Treat all business contacts with integrity. She believes that God wants Christian men and women to open their own businesses and to find a higher purpose, as she and Jonas did. Jonas went on to found the non-profit Family Resource and Counseling Center, established in 1992.

"Without the love of my husband and God I wouldn't be here today," Anne says.

In 1999, Auntie Anne's began a foundation that provides funds to groups caring for children and families in need. The Angela Foundation, named after their deceased daughter, contributes money to charities and missionary organizations.

Ignoring early warnings from bankers that they were giving away too much of their profits, the Beilers have consistently donated more than a tenth of their corporate income to ministry causes.

In 2005, founders Anne and Jonas Beiler sold the company to Sam Beiler, a second cousin who had been Auntie Anne's president and chief operating officer since 2001. Anne and Jonas currently are focused on the development of the Gap Family Center to help needy children and families. Anne Beiler's image and likeness continue to be an integral part of the company.

~~~

David Green

A successful entrepreneur promotes eternal values through his creative centers.

The son of a financially strapped pastor, David Green began working in a five-and-dime store at age 15. He learned the ins and outs of merchandising and as a young adult worked his way up to become a supervisor of several stores.

But in 1970 Green and his wife, Barbara, dreamed of owning their own business and they borrowed $600 from a bank to buy a frame chopper and sticks of moldings. In the family's garage they started a miniature picture frame manufacturing company. Sons Mart and Steve assembled the frames while David and Barbara glued them together.

After a year and a half, they opened their first Hobby Lobby store, which had only 300 square feet of floor space. Although they soon moved into a building with 6,000 square feet, by the fifth year Barbara still couldn't draw a salary and David kept a full-time department store job to make ends meet.

"When you don't have money it takes forever," Green says. In that fifth year, 1974, the company did only $150,000 in sales.

The turning point came in 1975 when Green quit his other job and opened a second, larger store. Revenues in the sixth year totaled $750,000.

By branching out to other markets, Hobby Lobby found its niche. Although local ma and pa operations sold similar products, no specialized chain offered arts and crafts supplies, fashion fabrics, baskets, silk flowers, needlework, wearable art, picture framing, greeting cards, party supplies, furniture, and seasonal merchandise under one roof.

The company continued to expand and the Greens cultivated a growing clientele among wealthy homeowners looking to furnish their decors. But the 1985 oil bust almost put Hobby Lobby out of business. All of a sudden the upscale product line stopped moving off the shelves. The company lost $1 million. Banks threatened to foreclose.

The Green family spent much focused time in prayer seeking God's direction.

"It was one of the worst times, but also one of the best times in my life," Green says. "We found we had to depend more on God than in our abilities. Talents are of no value without His blessings on our business. God brought us through that time miraculously."

Within a year, Hobby Lobby again was turning a profit. Green has continued to find entrepreneurial success while growing in his faith through regular Bible reading, prayer and church attendance.

"God has a purpose in all our lives, but that purpose isn't just to gain assets that don't have a purpose for eternity," Green says. "Life is not just to gain riches for ourselves."

Through the years Green has bucked the trend of business owners in secular society who increasingly put profits ahead of God's priorities. In 1999, Hobby Lobby began an 18-month process of closing all its stores on Sundays.

Green figured the company couldn't be true to its statement of purpose if employees missed church and a day with their families because they had to work.

That statement of purpose is unabashedly Christian and includes a section that says the corporation is committed to "serving our employees and their families by establishing a work environment and company policies which build character, strengthen individuals, and nurture families."

At the time, Hobby Lobby did $100 million a year in Sunday revenues.

"I have no regrets," Green says.

The company's statement of purpose concludes: "We believe that it is God's grace and provision that Hobby lobby has endured. He has been faithful in the past, we trust Him for our future."

The company now stocks 60,000 items and is the largest privately held hobby and craft company in the United States. Hobby Lobby has nearly 500 stores in 27 Midwestern and Southern states. Green intends to keep growing.

"The larger the business, the larger our mission efforts," he says. "We can't get God's blessing unless we use our assets the way God wants us to use them. All that counts is what is eternal, not what's temporal."

Selling decorations for the home is the avenue for the Greens' real goal: spreading the Gospel. Hobby Lobby has purchased millions of dollars worth of real estate and buildings for Christian ministries, schools, and churches.

Its largest undertaking is underwriting an effort to print 180 million copies of *The Book of Hope* so that they may be distributed in more than 100 countries. The publication is a chronological rendering of the four gospels for young people and includes the prayer of salvation at the end. Hobby Lobby also has backed an Every Home for Christ campaign to place the Gospel in more than 40 million homes in Asia.

Part of Green's evangelistic outreach is through Hobby Lobby itself. On Christmas in 1993, Green read the Oklahoma City newspaper and in dismay realized how commercialized the holiday had become.

"I couldn't find any advertisement mentioning the real reason for Christmas," Green recalls. "All the ads said 'Season's Greetings' or 'Happy Holidays.'"

The next year, Hobby Lobby, at a cost of hundreds of thousands of dollars annually, began taking out full-page newspaper ads in every city where it has a store. On Christmas, the ads simply tell about the birth of Jesus and on Easter they explain the resurrection of Christ in succinct, poignant terms. Hundreds of readers have responded to a ministry phone number in the ads and received Christ as Savior.

At this writing, Green remains president of the business. Son Steve is executive vice president of Hobby Lobby. Son Mart is chief executive officer of Mardel Christian, Office, and Educational Supply, a 19-store chain. Daughter Darsee is involved in advertising and product development for Hobby Lobby and its eight affiliate companies.

"We're not planning to branch out to any more companies, but who knows?" Green says.

The corporation has its headquarters in a 2.7 million square-foot manufacturing, distribution, and office complex in Oklahoma City. Hobby Lobby did more than $2 billion in sales in 2009.

"My response is so what—if we didn't do something of eternal value," Green says.

~

Dan Cathy
Chick-fil-A continues its Biblical approach to business.

In a sense, Dan T. Cathy has been in the restaurant business his whole life—and then some.

Cathy likes to joke that he has been working at Chick-fil-A since being in the womb of his mother, Jeannette. The chicken chain started by his father, S. Truett Cathy, always has been a family business where everyone helps out. Four years ago Dan became president and chief operating officer of the company his father founded six decades ago.

Dan started his chicken career at age 9 by singing songs for customers at the original diner site, the Dwarf Grill. As a youth he performed a number of menial tasks at that Atlanta diner: picking up trash in the parking lot, washing dirty dishes, extracting chewing gum stuck underneath dining room tables, filling up ketchup and mustard bottles.

When Chick-fil-A began branching out in 1967 it concentrated on retail shopping malls. Over the years, restaurants have been added at locations such as college campuses, hospitals and airports. Now, the majority are built as freestanding stores. Dan says today's consumers often are incredibly busy, preferring to pick up food from their cars at a drive-through window rather than going inside a time-consuming mall.

Now in its sixtieth year, staying relevant to an ever-changing marketplace is a challenge for the Atlanta-based Chick-fil-A, which pioneered the boneless breast of chicken sandwich in the quick-service restaurant industry. Chick-fil-A has added fresh fruit and more salad entrees to its menu for a customer base demanding healthier and more nutritional meals. Chicken, of course, remains the staple item, with its preparation being in a multitude of creative ways.

What hasn't and won't change are the Biblical principles on which the company is based. That includes keeping stores closed on Sundays, a rare decision for a chain in the restaurant trade today. But Chick-fil-A insists that operators and their employees take Sundays off to be with their families, rest, and worship God, if they so choose. Even though that decision has meant a potential loss of 20 percent in business, the chain nevertheless has had 38 straight years of growth, with sales approaching $2 billion annually.

"Our corporate purpose for being is to glorify God by being a faithful steward of all that He has entrusted to us," Cathy says. "Because of being closed on Sunday we think our food tastes better on Monday."

Being a privately held corporation not beholden to shareholders is a chief reason Chick-fil-A can remain closed on Sundays.

"We're not answerable to a bunch of Wall Street analysts looking for higher earnings," Cathy says. "That pressure often causes businesses to make short-term decisions that aren't in the best long-term interests of the company."

Cathy credits the stability of the corporation's leadership and operators for keeping Chick-fil-A on course with its corporate purpose. The firm has more than a 96 percent annual stability rate with its franchise operators, and the corporate staff has an even higher retention rate.

In its management style, Cathy says the company focuses more on living out spiritual beliefs rather than propagating them.

"We aren't hesitant to share our Christian faith and biblical views, and we're thankful that in the Constitution our forefathers made provision for religious expression, even in the workplace," Cathy says. "However, the most potent way of sharing our faith with others is in the relationships we have in terms of compassion, kindness, and understanding in helping people accomplish their dreams, hopes, and ambitions."

Chick-fil-A offers several types of enrichment opportunities for its workers, including awarding a $1,000 scholarship to college-bound restaurant employees who have shown leadership, longevity with the chain, and demonstrate school and community involvement. More than $20 million has been awarded since the program started in 1973, resulting in Chick-fil-A scholarship recipients attending more than 1,200 institutions.

In 1984, S. Truett and Jeannette Cathy formed the WinShape Foundation, which provides a variety of services to support youth and marriages. That includes operating a two-week summer camp experience for 1,700 boys and girls every year; providing a loving, stable environment for more than 150 children in 14 foster homes; and sponsoring retreats for couples whose marriages need transformation.

While some other companies founded on Scriptural tenets have stopped being so outspoken in order to not offend an increasingly pluralistic society, Chick-fil-A continues to abide by the Golden Rule.

"Because Jesus Christ died for us all, that gives me the freedom and confidence to share this message of redemption in meaningful ways," Cathy says. "In the complete picture of what's going on, sharing our faith is not only not offensive, it can be incredibly winsome and endearing to others."

For children, Cathy also wants the meal experience to be more than just about food. Rather than a tie-in to the latest Hollywood movie, premiums with kid meals have a more positive, lasting impact with literacy or more values. Recently, a book from the Emmy Award-winning PBS program *Between the Lions* or an audiocassette from the Focus on the Family Adventures in Odyssey series has accompanied kids' meals. In addition to focusing on education and character development, the giveaways are designed to foster conversation between parents and child.

Work doesn't consume all of Cathy's time. Church has been a priority ever since he received Jesus Christ as Lord and Savior at age 12.

He has been playing trumpet for 43 years and he continues to practice nearly every day. He plays occasionally at weddings and sporting events, but every Sunday morning he is on the platform with the rest of the band at New Hope Baptist Church in Fayetteville, Georgia, a suburb of Atlanta.

"I take the responsibility of leading people in worship every seven days very seriously," says Cathy. "There's a difference between playing the notes and playing the music. People worship when the music is played." Jeannette Cathy, who also played the trumpet, instilled a love of the instrument for him as a young boy.

Another passion of Cathy's life is instructing 12th grade boys in Sunday School every week. He has been a Sunday School teacher for more than 30 years, also a discipline of his father's for nearly half a century. Cathy believes that church and Sunday School, unlike local civic organizations, help people develop an eternal outlook on the particulars of everyday life.

"It's a joy to serve the local church," Cathy says. "A local church ministry that impacts the lives of children, young people, and families in a positive way is the greatest community organization that we have."

Chick-fil-A now has more than 40,000 restaurant employees in 1,250 stores in 38 states and Washington, D.C. Cathy says putting a franchise in every state isn't a goal; the firm simply wants to be in markets where it makes business sense.

With his customary zeal, S. Truett Cathy, nearly 90 at the time of this writing, continues to work as chairman and chief executive officer at the conglomerate every day. Dan doesn't spend as much time around corporate headquarters because there aren't any chickens or cash registers there. While not home with Rhonda, his wife, he enjoys being with store employees and customers. He'll attend virtually all 65 openings of new Chick-fil-A restaurants this year.

CHAPTER 11
Redemptive Communicators:
—⚉—
MUSICAL ARTS

Harry Causey
Vision becomes reality for the National Christian Choir's founder.

C. Harry Causey began singing while still in the playpen. By age 4 he had learned to play the piano by ear. During elementary school he sang in a children's choir at the Presbyterian church in Rockingham, North Carolina, that his parents attended every week. The young boy loved to talk to his pastor about the Lord and the Bible.

In seventh grade, Causey sensed a calling to the ministry. At an evangelistic crusade conducted by Leighton Ford, Billy Graham's brother-in-law, Causey left his place in the choir and went forward to make a public profession of faith in Jesus Christ as Savior.

"I sought God's guidance as to whether to become a musician or a minister as an adult," Causey remembers. "At that point I never considered the possibility of doing both. I thought I could do only one or the other."

During high school, he became the assistant choir director for the adult choir at church, where he also played piano and organ. Yet during the late 1950s and early 1960s, Causey says he learned more about sacred music from his Christian teachers at high school than from church.

"In those days one could be open about faith in school," Causey says. "My teachers were good evangelists in their own way."

Although he possessed a great deal of musical talent, Causey sought to learn more. That's why he obtained bachelor of music degree from Davidson College, a master's degree in music composition from Florida State University, and a doctor in choral conducting from the University of Cincinnati.

During his college and post-graduate years, every summer Causey attended choral music workshops conducted by Lara Hoggard, who served as assistant conductor to popular bandleader Fred Waring.

Waring, leading the group called the Pennsylvanians, made choral music popular at the time. Through record albums, radio, television, and concert tours, Waring popularized both secular and sacred music.

Hoggard, a Christian known for his choral conducting, took an interest in Causey, who admired him tremendously. Causey considered the possibility of going into show business— in the hopes of becoming another Fred Waring—or writing music for TV dramas in Hollywood.

But after graduating with his final degree, Causey took a position as a full-time minister of music at a Cincinnati church. Soon after joining the staff at the church in 1969, Causey and his wife, Elizabeth, both reaffirmed their commitment to prioritizing God's call on their lives. Causey determined at that point to remain in music ministry.

Extra summer jobs helped convince him that he had made the right choice. He had been hired to prepare a choir for a Cincinnati Symphony Orchestra concert as well as another choir for a Presbyterian evangelical conference.

"As a newly recommitted Christian, I began to realize how fulfilled the people were who sang for the Lord and how unfulfilled the people were in the secular concerts," Causey says. "In the secular concert the personnel were bickering, complaining, and unhappy. But at the Christian concert they were singing for the Lord, still joyous in the parking lot afterwards."

In the early 1970s, Causey began to dream about forming a national Christian choir, which no one had done in evangelical circles, as a way to exalt Jesus Christ. Despite repeated attempts, he couldn't arrange any financial backing to get such an effort off the ground in Cincinnati.

In 1980, the same year he received his ministerial ordination from the Evangelical Church Alliance, Causey was recruited by Fourth Presbyterian Church minister Richard C. Halverson to become minister of music at that suburban Washington, D.C., church.

But a year into Causey's new position, Halverson received an appointment as chaplain of the U.S. Senate. Causey then became a freelance minister of music, starting a workshop and newsletter ministry called Music Revelation to help other music ministers.

"God used the move to Washington, D.C., for me to found the National Christian Choir," Causey says. "The nation's capital is the place for this ministry."

In 1983, Christian businessman Ron Doucette contacted Causey about heading up an innovative musical project. Doucette explained that he wanted to honor God by underwriting the expenses of renting Constitution Hall in downtown Washington, D.C., if Causey would enlist a choir and orchestra to present an evening of praise and worship. Causey in turn described his vision for the National Christian Choir and agreed to conduct the concert if the event served as the birth of the ministry. Doucette consented.

Causey convinced Christian radio stations in the area to run free public service announcements for choir auditions. He called his choir director friends around the city and auditions were held at five locations. By the time of the concert, 250 qualified singers had signed up.

"We were extremely diverse when we walked into the room, but within minutes we all realized that God had given us a gift of unity," Causey recalls. "Everyone there was a believer in Christ and we all had the same desire to honor Him."

The January 1984 concert proved to be a great success, and the NCC quickly formed a board of directors. The choir has been going strong ever since.

Although Causey is one of five full-time paid staff members, all choir members donate their time. They have weekly Monday night rehearsals at a Baptist church in Rockville, Maryland, during the school year, as well as four practices in the summer. Singers come from a wide geographic area, from Philadelphia in the north to Fredericksburg, Virginia, in the south. Some members drive three hours one way to attend rehearsal.

"They're called by God to this ministry," Causey says. "Every person involved takes commitment seriously."

The NCC performs about a dozen concerts a year around Once a year, the choir goes on tour for a long weekend somewhere in the United States. Every five years, the NCC goes on an extended trip, to places such as Alaska, Israel, or Eastern Europe. Choir members pay for their own airfare, hotel rooms, ground transportation, and most meals.

Those in the NCC for the most part aren't professional singers but "above average" church choir members, Causey says. They must show a certain amount of proficiency in an audition for reading music, controlling their voice, and blending their voice with others.

Members also must sign a statement of faith. "Even with our different worship styles, churches, backgrounds, traditions, and ages, we all have in common the belief that Jesus Christ is Lord and Savior," Causey says. "We celebrate a great deal of unity in the midst of diversity."

Only five members remain from the first concert 25 years ago, yet the majority have been part of the choir for more than 15 years. Causey says the nearly 200-member choir—which contains singers from 100 regional congregations—has an annual turnover rate of only half a dozen singers.

The choir has made two dozen audio recordings. Causey goes over thousands of new choral releases every year and whittles the list down to a few dozen favorites. In brainstorming sessions with his two accompanists and the rest of his music team, Causey determines what exactly to put on every year's particular compact disc. Each CD has a theme, whether it's hymns, patriotic music, Christmas carols, praise choruses, or inspirational numbers. Causey and his accompanists often arrange the selected pieces for the choir, and they have written a few compositions for the CD recordings themselves. Once the songs are finalized, Causey travels to Indianapolis to record the music in a studio (primarily with musicians from the Indianapolis Symphony Orchestra). Back in Washington, D.C., Causey records the choir voices. Then he returns to Indianapolis to mix the voices and instruments for the CD. The entire process—from looking for tunes to pressing a CD—typically takes three years.

The three most popular NCC CDs, with sales approaching 50,000, all deal with providing comfort, peace, and healing: *You are My Hiding Place, Wonderful Peace,* and *Balm in Gilead.* . "Those who are sick or who have experienced grief because of the death of a family member find the worshipful music quiets their souls," Causey says.

One of the outreaches of the NCC is a weekly radio program called *Psalm 95,* which began in 2002. Causey came up with the idea of an hour of choir singing interspersed with him offering Scripture readings and inspirational thoughts as host. The worship-laden Psalm 95 (which starts out "Come, let us sing for joy to the Lord; let us shout aloud to the Rock of our salvation") is the name of the program and helped convince WRBS, a Christian radio station in Baltimore, to carry it. Various choir members put together enough money to put the show on the air for its first 11 weeks. Gradually other radio stations—all of them non-profits that didn't require payment for commercials—have added the show. Now more than 375 non-profit stations in all 50 U.S. states and all 13 Canadian provinces carry *Psalm 95.* The program is rebroadcast in 177 foreign countries and on the Armed Forces Network.

Since 1990, the NCC has been sending music (first cassettes and now CDs) to soldiers overseas. Funds are donated by concertgoers to send the music to troops through the Music for Overseas Military program. More than 50,000 recordings have been sent to military personnel.

Causey says he receives letters frequently from two primary types of audiences who appreciate *Psalm 95.*

"There are elderly people who are unable to get to church or who feel disenfranchised because contemporary music dominates their church," he says. "We also hear from prisoners who tell us over and over that the show gives them hope, peace, and a sense of freedom behind bars."

Psalm 95 still is on WRBS, the only one that charges for airtime. Causey is hoping the NCC can raise funds to expand *Psalm 95* to other commercial stations.

Many choir members have told Causey they are drawn closer to the Lord through the NCC than by their own church.

"We don't want to be a church substitute," Causey says. "But because worship is our priority we have a lot of worship at rehearsals. Our presentations are more worship service than concert. The purpose of the NCC continues to be to glorify God and draw people into a deeper relationship with Him."

While some NCC music has a contemporary flavor, most of it is in the traditional inspirational style. Most listeners are 65 and older.

"This age group needs someone to preserve the music for them that they love," Causey says. "And I see the pendulum swinging back. There is a renewed interest in choral singing in churches that have abandoned choirs; in liturgical worship among those not liturgically minded; and a discovery of hymns among younger people who never heard hymns before."

Causey knows the day will come when he must pass off his baton.

"But I still have the stamina, health, drive, and desire to stay," he says. "Lord willing, I plan to keep going until I'm at least 75."

By necessity, Causey wears many hats at the NCC. He is music director, executive director, public relations marketing director, and resource development director. Elizabeth, his wife, does volunteer work for the choir, ranging from writing thank you notes to donors to being the orchestra music librarian.

Causey says he may keep some jobs once he can no longer direct.

It's not that Causey is bereft of ideas. He wants to see the NCC acquire a facility for rehearsals. He also wants the NCC to give birth to a national children's choir, youth choir, and adult ensemble.

"I will have to lay it down eventually, but those of us here now hope to leave a legacy," Causey says. "I love my work. I feel called to it."

—m—

Fernando Ortega

An award-winning musician revives a passion for the sacred.

After being challenged by a classmate to pronounce his faith publicly, a young and impassioned Fernando Ortega once stood on top a table and declared for all the art class to hear that Jesus is Lord of his life.

"It wasn't a very orthodox profession of faith," Ortega says, with a chuckle. "But I consider that the moment when I recognized my need for a Redeemer."

Today, this gifted musician seeks to deliver that same message in a less self-serving fashion.

"When I first became a Christian, I told everybody," Ortega recalled. "I was so vocal; it led to some really obnoxious, cringeable moments."

No one is cringing now. This award winning singer/songwriter is sought-after, and his compositions are admired by many. His artistry has been honored with two Dove Awards—one for Inspirational Album of the Year (2000's *Home*) and one for Bluegrass Recorded Song of the Year for "Children of a Living God" with Alison Krauss. Eight of his singles have reached number one on Christian music charts, and 12 have been nominated for Dove Awards. One of his latest recordings, *The Shadow of Your Wings,* which features the Turtle Island String Quartet, compels listeners to be mindful of God's presence.

Fernando has included at least two hymns on each of his recordings, but nearly half of this latest effort is devoted to hymns and sacred songs. Taking verses from centuries-old

Christian liturgy, he aimed to express these classic expressions of worship in music that is suitable for modern audiences. The experience proved to be a faith-building experience for him. Throughout the composition process, he often sensed the hand of God upon the project.

"There was a certain pronouncement, a bending of the knee. An acknowledgement that I can't even worship God unless he gives me breathe to do it," he recalls.

For those of us who grew up singing *Holy, Holy, Holy* or *Come, Thou Fount of Every Blessing* every Sunday, it is mind-boggling that many believers have never heard or do not recognize the lyrics of these sacred classics. When Fernando changed the chords and played his musically updated yet worshipful version of *Come, Thou Fount,* many in the congregation where he was leading worship assumed he had written the song. They had never heard the old hymns before.

These congregants were familiar with a more utilitarian style of music, Ortega says. A form of corporate worship involving simple choruses designed to illustrate the speaker's main point. Ortega found such music vacuous. Hymns cover more ground theologically, historically, and lyrically. Ortega defines his own musical style as heavy on the story line.

"My hope is that I'm able to take a song about my grandfather, or my wife, or my former landlady, Mildred, and say something about them in a universal way that means something to someone else. I hope I am writing and singing about things that resonate with others, and allows them to see how faith in God can be expressed not only in the most glorious, bet even the most mundane moments of our everyday lives."

A musician's life is not all glitz and glamour, and few artists meet with overnight success. Fernando was no child prodigy, but he was unusually talented from a very early age. As an undergraduate at the University of New Mexico, he earned the distinction of being one of the school's most outstanding musicians. "I thought I had a good shot at being a world class pianist if I worked hard enough," he recalls.

His vision abruptly fell short, however, when he auditioned for graduate school.

"As I was walking to the audition I heard one of the pieces I'd chosen to play—one of Chopin's ballades—being played far better than I could play it. I looked into the room and saw that it was being played masterfully by a young Korean girl, 12 to 14 years of age.

"I realized I could practice all I wanted and I would never be able to play like that. My musical gifts were elsewhere—writing music was my gift. That was a real defining moment for me. A moment that changed the course of my life. "

Eventually, Ortega went on staff with Campus Crusade for Christ, and led worship for the organization's founder, Dr. Bill Bright. That high-profile position earned him some name recognition and created opportunities for his musical ministry. He even managed to get a record deal with a company that, ironically, ended up going bankrupt.

After that record deal went belly up, Fernando abandoned his quest to make it big with a solo career. He was in his thirties and on staff at the South Coast Community Church in

Irvine, California. It was a great place to serve God and others, but it just wasn't the way Ortega envisioned his career unfolding.

"I experienced a death of a vision. At best, that vision was a pretty empty one," he says now. "Up until that point, my desire to make music was tinged with an ambition to be well-known. I hate to think I was that shallow, but playing concerts in front of large audiences was something I longed for. It was a vision that needed to die."

Fernando says he wasn't too upset at God over his failing quest for a musical career, but he was concerned about the fact that he still was single. Why hadn't God sent him the love of his life yet?

"I really wanted to be married. I was sick of living in apartments with roommates."

But before Fernando reached the state of frustration, God moved, as he so often does, in a mighty way. Ortega found the love of his life, literally, right before his nose.

"Margee came in with a friend and sat on the front row in a church where I was worship leader. It was a very social church, with constant chattering during worship, but Margee would be there with her eyes closed, really worshipping God. I found that beautiful."

Shortly afterward, they married, and Fernando's recording career took off.

Now that all that professional and personal striving is in his rearview mirror, Fernando devotes his energies to creating songs that minister God's grace. He has a particular compassion for those in mourning. When he first conceived his latest album, he had thought in terms of composing the content of a worship service.

"I wanted to do something liturgical for people who are mourning," Ortega said.

But the songs on *Shadow* go beyond grief. They are about shutting out the noise of the world and turning one's eyes upon Jesus. The songs grew out of Fernando's own heightened sense of frustration over life's clamor.

"This latest album is like a devotional. It takes concentration and requires you to be quiet and still," he says. "Our culture seems to be getting louder and louder. It's not only loud, it's in your face. Indicative, I think, of the influences of television and the Internet. Christian music has followed suit, getting more in your face. It is growing increasingly more difficult to be in a meditative state. I guess that's why I'm drawn to sacred music and hymns."

The other reasons might lie in the musical influences in Ortega's life. Gifted from an early age and raised in a nurturing Christian home, he began to take piano lessons at age 8 from Ralph Berkowitz, of Alburquerque, New Mexico. Berkowitz, an ardent classicist, introduced Ortega to the ballades of Chopin, and the concertos of Mozart and Brahms. Add to that, the Mexican and Italian folk songs that are a part of Fernando's Hispanic heritage, and the music education he received at the University of New Mexico, and the, and the result is an enormous talent with eclectic skill. All of which Ortega devotes to serving God.

Now that God has given him the desires of his heart, Ortega says he's learned a few more lessons about what it takes to succeed as an artist.

"It's way more work than I ever imagined, but incredibly fulfilling."

Still, he is keenly aware that all that he has, all that he is, is because of God's faithfulness, not his own.

"People have an elevated expectation of me as a person, as a Christian," he observes. "An expectation that, of course, is beyond my ability to rise to. I find that disappointing, but ultimately, it sends me to my knees and makes me recognize my need for God and my constant dependence on Him."

There's nothing complex about this for any of us—life at its fullest is just an old sweet tune about Jesus and His love.

~m~

Christopher Parkening
A world-class guitarist picks a heavenly tune.

Rapt silence grips the concert hall. All eyes are riveted on center stage as Christopher Parkening's hands trip masterfully up and down his guitar.

"Wow," whispers one captivated fan. "That's so awesome!" he quietly exclaims, while gleefully plucking his own "air guitar" right there in the plush velour seats of the symphony hall.

You wouldn't normally find such a scene at a classical music concert, listening to Joaquin Rodrigo's "Adagio" from *Concierto de Aranjuez*. But then, Christopher Parkening isn't the typical classical guitarist.

Arguably the world's best, Parkening hasn't just mastered the guitar technically; he *inspires* people with it. At intermission, admirers devour the man's CDs, videos, and method books, and then shift down the table like a herd of cattle to have them signed by the Grammy-nominated virtuoso. Unlike your garden-variety rock star, though, Parkening attracts a wide-ranging demographic. From a budding, slick-haired classical guitarist who wants to take a picture with his hero, to a bespectacled, balding grandfather seeking an autograph, it seems everybody can sense musical greatness in their midst.

Take a closer look, though, and you'll see a classical guitarist who isn't just an inspiring musician. There on the table, prominently arrayed in front of his autograph-signing area, are several CD-sized booklets. With every signature and handshake, Parkening offers one of these unassuming little items, and if you're not careful, you might miss the title that appears on them: "Life Story and Christian Testimony."

Talk to Parkening for five minutes and you quickly discern that his true passion is telling others about his relationship with Jesus Christ. Don't misunderstand: He loves his music.

He plays more than 50 concerts a year and has released more than 13 recordings. Yet in many ways his guitar is a means to an end.

"The Lord has opened up a million opportunities for me to share my faith in Christ," Parkening says.

In addition to distributing printed versions of his personal testimony, he delivers his testimony at churches across the country, presents the Gospel to students in his classes, and discusses it with his peers.

The man has a lot to be thankful for: he is a one-in-a-million talent, with droves of adoring fans, and a platform to influence them. Yet there was a time when he almost threw it all away — not for the Gospel, but for a trout stream in southwest Montana.

Mercurial rise to fame

A child of the post-World War II era, Parkening grew up in a God-fearing Southern California home. His mother and father took him to church regularly, and he learned many basic truths of the Christian faith.

"They told me I was a Christian, and I always believed that I was," he recalls.

Yet as with many who grow up in the church, knowing about Christ didn't affect his life much. He wasn't a rebellious kid. In fact, he was very disciplined, which could help explain his mercurial rise to fame by the age of 19. Yet it could also have fed some self-reliance that kept him from depending on God.

"I believed all the right facts, and I suppose that I even wanted a Savior to save me from hell," Parkening says, "but what I *did not* want was a Lord of my life that I should follow and trust and be obedient to."

No, as a kid his focus was his guitar. Parkening chose the instrument at age 11 and plunged in head-first. Encouraged by his father, he got up at 5:00 each morning and practiced for an hour-and-a-half before school, then put in another 90-minute session in the afternoon.

Within four years, he had landed a rare spot in a class being taught by Andres Segovia, generally regarded to be the greatest classical guitarist ever. At 15, Parkening was the youngest of only nine students in the select class.

Before he left his teens, the prodigy had been asked to start a guitar department at the University of Southern California, and had signed a six-album recording contract with Capitol Records. Soon he was touring the world, playing roughly 90 concerts a year and wowing audiences with his extraordinary talent.

But Parkening soon realized that the life of a touring solo musician wasn't for him.

"I hated it," he says. "One major city after the next; the monotony of the concerts; the pressure of them; the plane flights; the hotel rooms."

He still loved the music, but he was already burning out from the rigorous schedule of teaching, practicing, recording and touring that his newfound fame had brought.

"It was a means to an end for me," he says.

Early Retirement

The "end" that Parkening sought was retirement.

"My father had retired at the age of 47, so I thought that 30 would be a very good age to retire," he says. "I thought, *I'll still be in the prime of life.*"

Retirement would give him time to pursue his other passion: fly-fishing. As with his guitar playing, Parkening had become an expert fly-fisherman. It was an escape for him. He loved to wade into the cool water of a stream and enjoy the scenery as he fished for trout.

"I thought, *If I could buy a ranch someday with my own trout stream, and not have to work . . . I would be happy,*" Parkening remembers.

It was this dream that helped him endure what had become the drudgery of the concert life.

Come age 30, Parkening had reached his goal. Having made his fortune, he promptly set out to find his trout stream. And he found it, on a ranch in southwestern Montana. Parkening then called his record company, his concert promoter, and his university and told them he was walking away.

For a while, he lived—and loved—"the good life."

It took about a year, but the joy of retirement and fishing-til-you-drop finally began to wear off.

"I started thinking, *This is not what I thought it would be. I'm unfulfilled. I am unhappy,*" he says. "It was without purpose, and I sensed that."

"Lord, Lord"

Whether he realized it or not, his nagging lack of purpose set Parkening on a search for significance in his life. Yet he didn't take the easy road and fall back on his guitar. He stayed retired, for the time being.

During a visit to Southern California, a neighbor invited him to church. Having grown up in a church-going family, the decision to go was no big deal. In fact, he still regularly attended church in Montana. But this church — Grace Community Church in Sun Valley—was different from anything he had found.

"I was shocked that everybody had a Bible," Parkening recalls.

He got another jolt as he listened to the sermon that day. Speaking from Matthew 7, Pastor John MacArthur discussed Jesus' warning: "Not every one that saith unto me, Lord, Lord, shall enter into the kingdom of heaven; but he that doeth the will of my Father which is in heaven." The words hit Parkening squarely between the eyes. He realized immediately that simply going to church and knowing some facts about Jesus wasn't good enough.

That night, he recalls, Parkening received Christ as Savior.

Finding purpose

Parkening knew immediately upon receiving Christ that he had finally found the path to purpose in his life. He devoured MacArthur's sermon tapes, absorbing all the Bible teaching he could find.

Parkening grew so fond of MacArthur that one year he drove three Montana pastors down for a conference MacArthur was leading. When Parkening arrived, the pastor surprised the lapsed guitarist by asking him to perform and give his testimony.

The thought terrified Parkening. "First of all, I hadn't played in public for four years," he recalls. "Secondly, I'd never given my Christian testimony."

Yet he did it, and afterward MacArthur approached Parkening and encouraged him to pick up the guitar again — this time for a different purpose.

A different kind of fishing pole

Shortly after his talk with MacArthur, Parkening sensed God's call to more actively glorify Him with his life.

"There were only two things I knew how to do," he says. "One was fly-fishing for trout, and the other was playing the guitar. The latter seemed the better option to pursue."

So, in 1981, after four years away from playing professionally, Parkening called his recording and concert-management companies and told them he wanted back in.

There was no doubt Parkening was playing with newfound purpose and energy. With each concert, he sought not just to play with excellence, but to truly "honor the Creator" by playing his music "from the heart."

Yet as he grew in his faith, he realized God wanted more than just a soulful performance.

"I realized that as good a motive as that is, it is incomplete apart from making disciples for Christ," he says.

At first, he wondered how he could possibly share the Gospel as a concert guitarist. He could try preaching from the stage, but he wouldn't be invited back to many places if he did. Yet his heart was willing, and soon God began to open opportunities.

For example, he found that he had an audience whenever he taught a class. After the instruction was over, he frequently had the chance to tell his students what truly motivated him.

Parkening's stature as a musician also has given him an entree with his peers—such as leading film score composers John Williams and Elmer Bernstein—to present the Gospel.

Then there were the concerts, with their aspiring guitarists and adoring fans who were eager to soak up whatever wisdom the man has to offer.

"They will listen to anything you have to say," he says.

Now, he uses every occasion he gets to describe to others the life and purpose he has found in Christ. Which is undoubtedly why he lingers after each performance to sign autographs and pass out his printed testimony.

It's funny, when you think about it: The gift that a man once gave up so he could fish for trout is now a gift that God uses to fish for men.

∽

Diane Bish
The First Lady of the Pipe Organ

Fifteen-year-old organist Diane Bish weighed her options. Two churches desired her skills—one boasted a magnificent pipe organ and offered a tempting salary, the other housed a mediocre instrument and paid a lower wage.

God, show me Your will, prayed Bish. *Where do You want to best use the talent You've given me?* The teen recalled Matthew 6:33: "But seek ye first the kingdom of God, and his righteousness; and all these things shall be added unto you." Her passion for God tipped the scale. Bish chose the more menial job.

"It was a difficult decision, but I felt at home in that church," she recalls years later from her home in Bloomington, Indiana. "I felt I could worship wholeheartedly there. I think the Lord has blessed that decision throughout my life."

More than four decades after her humble beginnings, Bish is perhaps the world's most visible organist. Her recordings, compositions, and weekly television appearances on "The Joy of Music" have earned international acclaim. She performs approximately 35 classical concerts (regularly fighting nervous jitters) across North America annually. Critics applaud her performances as "stunning, virtuoso, fiery, and astonishing." In 1989, The National Federation of Music Clubs of America awarded Bish the National Citation—"the highest honor for distinguished service to the musical, artistic, and cultural life of the nation."

Piano lessons at age six began Bish's musical career. She practiced diligently and won numerous competitions, but before long, a different instrument fascinated her.

Every Sunday morning, her father's radio brought an organ's rich resonance into the family's home. And every week Bish admired the organ in her church sanctuary. She eyed the "king of instruments" and observed the musician's feet fly across its pedals. She watched her change its settings and listened to its majestic anthems. *Someday I'll play the organ, too,* she thought.

At age 14, her legs finally able to reach the pedals, Bish's dream came true. Her parents purchased an organ to facilitate her practice schedule. Before long she was playing concertos on her school's pipe organ and landed her first church organist position.

Bish continued her studies, winning national organ and composition competitions under Mildred Andrews's tutelage at the University of Oklahoma. She received Fulbright and French government grants for study in Amsterdam and Paris. Upon returning to the United States, Bish received a job offer from Dr. James Kennedy, pastor of Fort Lauderdale's Coral Ridge Presbyterian Church.

"I visited the church, saw its small organ, and declined. I took a teaching position at a university with a strong organ department instead," says Bish. "I worked there for a year, but throughout that entire time I sensed the Lord telling me I belonged at Coral Ridge."

Discovering that the church organist position was still available, Bish made the move. Her decision spawned a 20-year tenure filled with innovative methods for musically presenting the Gospel of Jesus Christ—a vision she'd embraced since receiving Christ as her Savior while attending a revival meeting at the age of five.

"Through grade school, junior high, and senior high, I wanted to spread God's Word," she says. "I witnessed whenever, wherever possible. I wanted to evangelize the world. I still do!"

Bish's extraordinary musical ability is her tool. When Coral Ridge built a bigger facility, she designed its 117-rank Ruffatti featuring 7,000 pipes, considered one of the world's greatest organs today. She then co-founded the largest church concert series in history. Averaging 14 concerts from November through April, the series draws people who don't normally attend church. Each concert attracts more than 1,000 folks. She clearly presents the Gospel message throughout the program.

Bish also founded the Church Music Explosion, an ongoing annual five-day workshop for national church and university musicians. Attendees study various aspects of music ministry: how to lead worship, how to hold a concert series in one's own church, how to use music as an evangelism tool, how to pursue musical excellence, and for church-goers who don't yet have a personal relationship with Jesus—how to become a Christian.

In 1982, Bish's expertise led to yet another evangelism opportunity through the launching of her television program, "The Joy of Music." The weekly show continues more than 20 years later, sponsored by donations totaling $400,000 annually. With satellite broadcasting, it reaches between 150 and 200 million viewers worldwide on both Christian and secular stations.

Bish's mandate? "To provide inspiration through great classical and sacred music and share the Gospel through the testimonies of classical artists who are Christian. I also want to feature famous cathedrals and organs, and tell the stories of faith behind them."

To accomplish that goal, she has produced 400 episodes of "The Joy of Music" in three categories. The first explores the Bible's teachings regarding music—the singing voice, the trumpet, the harp, the pipes, stringed instruments, and more. Outstanding artists sing or play corresponding instruments and tell their salvation testimony. The second category highlights renowned Christian composers' and artists' spiritual lives.

The third category takes viewers on musical journeys to stately palaces, museums, monasteries, and cathedrals around the world. Bish plays the organ, shows the artwork and Biblical paintings, and tells well-researched stories about the massive structures and the faith of those who built them.

"Other documentaries might teach about the world's historic cathedrals, but they don't mention the faith that built them, the faith that resonates from them, or the Creator God and Jesus Christ," says Bish. "'The Joy of Music' always acknowledges God as Creator and Inspirer of great art, of the Church, and the music that flows from it."

The television program regularly whisks its viewers to locations such as Hamburg, Germany, where St. Jacobi Church houses an organ played by musical masters including Bach. It transports them to the Market Church in Halle, Germany, where young Handel played for church services.

It carries them to Bish's favorite—St. Bavo Cathedral in Haarlem, Holland, located around the corner from Corrie ten Boom's father's clock shop. Chatting over breakfast one morning, Corrie told Bish that, as a young girl, she sat in that church and listened to the music being played.

"In my opinion, St. Bavo's 'Great Golden Organ' is the world's finest, rising 90 feet high and dating to 1737," says Bish. "It's an organist's mecca. Even Handel and Mozart made special trips to play this instrument."

Historical data fascinates Bish and the program's viewers, but the show offers more than interesting statistics. It reveals a spiritual heritage often wrought through physical suffering. In a typical episode, viewers might see Germany's Ulm cathedral, boasting the highest spire in Europe. Bish tells how the townspeople built it from their own sweat, tirelessly carrying stones and stacking them one atop the other.

"Some folks spent their entire lives building this place of worship in the city's center. They did all the work themselves; they didn't hire engineers or other people to do it. It was an extension of their faith, not just a place to visit once in a while. We dare not forget our fathers' faith that has brought us to where we are today," she says.

Many of her travelogues feature guest artists' testimonies and musical performances celebrating the Christian faith's great hymns. "Our spiritual heritage comes to us through the arts in many ways," says Bish. "We must not lose the great hymns. They're not folk— here today and gone tomorrow. They are statements of faith that flow from our Christian heritage.

"The hymns we've heard over the years often come from Scripture—we must not let them pass away. They're doctrine. They're strong."

Stating that she personally finds much encouragement not only in Scripture but also in hymns, Bish recites lyrics from "How Firm a Foundation," written in the 1700s:

> Fear not, I am with thee, O be not dismayed,
> For I am thy God, I will still give thee aid;
> I'll strengthen thee, help thee, and cause thee to stand,
> Upheld by My gracious, omnipotent hand.

On October 30, 2002, these lyrics gripped Bish afresh. That night, fire destroyed her home and consumed nearly every earthly possession—her grand piano and organ, car, clothing, her artist father's paintings, and photos. Devastated, Diane found comfort and hope in the lyrics she knows by heart.

It's her desire that others find the same hope and comfort through the One about whom the lyrics are written. But not everyone appreciates her evangelistic zeal.

"I've received numerous letters from public TV stations saying that 'The Joy of Music' is a great show, but they don't want Scripture readings. They don't want artists' salvation testimonies or God's name mentioned. I've had to choose between deleting the ministry part and remaining on secular stations or leaving it in and losing my place." True to her passion for God, Bish seeks His kingdom first and maintains the ministry focus.

"I believe we must honor God in the most excellent way possible," says Bish. "We must give Him our best efforts, glorifying Him with the talents He's given us." She's doing exactly that.

CHAPTER 12

Redemptive Communicators:

—⟋⟍—

PERFORMING ARTS

John David Ware

A filmmaker uses Scripture to help teach his craft.

John David Ware's vocational and spiritual trajectory changed forever in 1997 on the day his car got rear-ended by a vanload of missionaries. Ware had just moved to Los Angeles from Columbus, Ohio. It turned out the missionaries, returning from Mexico, were from the same church he attended in his native Columbus.

Ware and the missionaries began talking, and the missionaries soon discovered that while Ware accepted Jesus intellectually, he really had not made a commitment with his heart. He had tried to believe and to know, but he couldn't. But he was seeking.

"Accepting aspects like the Virgin Birth and the Resurrection had been difficult for me, because I was too logical," Ware recalls. "Actually believing the incredible story of Christ is a gift. He did prove himself to me."

Ware began attending Bel Air Presbyterian Church, where he co-founded SLATE: Salt and Light Aimed Toward Entertainment. He eventually founded the 168 Film Project, a competition that has furthered the careers of many emerging filmmakers. The faith-based speed program pits teams against each other to create a short film in just one week—that is, 168 hours. The films are shown at a festival, with top scripts vying for cash, prizes, and introductions to veteran Hollywood moviemakers.

Ware knew he was destined for Los Angeles when he graduated with a degree in mass communication and video production at Miami University in Ohio. As the son of two schoolteachers and the brother of two siblings who became psychiatrists, Ware fought the urge to go to Tinseltown. Instead he got a job in Ohio making instructional videos.

But the call to move to L.A. proved irresistible, even though he had no family and no friends there. Nevertheless, Ware quickly found production work on some major projects such as *Independence Day* and then did some screenwriting of his own. But as work on movies dried up, Ware discovered a knack for professional audio/video sales with manufacturer representatives in Los Angeles. In his first year, he sold more than $1 million worth of video and audio gear. More importantly, over seven years, he developed relationships with multiple manufacturers, such as Sony, Arri, and Eiki, that have become sponsors of the 168 Film Project.

Likewise, numerous actors, directors, and producers in the moviemaking business have come to recognize the professionalism and quality of the festival.

"We wanted to give people the chance to do something significant for their career based on God's Word," Ware says. "So we gave them seven days, which is plenty of time to shoot and edit an eleven-minute or less film. They also get ten days of preproduction after receiving their foundational Scripture. Giving them time to prepare means that they can walk away with a reel to be proud of, on both sides of the camera."

The first year, participants made 13 films and premiered to a standing-room-only crowd. Word of mouth spread that it could be a tremendous showcase for actors, producers, and directors wanting to break into the business. As of 2010, approximately 6,500 cast and crew have participated, including teams from nearly 30 countries, including China, Russia, Israel, Indonesia, and Cameroon. Around 300 Bushmen participated on missionary Greg Yost's team. By April 2011, more than 500 short films will have been made for the 168 Film Project. Contenders pay an entry fee of $168 to $298, depending on when they register.

"We don't allow writing before the verse is given," Ware says. "We want them to fall in love with Scripture over story, and to take the full opportunity to grow their faith and trust God to deliver a great story in a very short time."

The 168 hours—24 hours times seven days—refers to the actual shooting and editing time available to complete a short film that runs under 11 minutes. Here's how it works: Contestants are randomly assigned one of 70 Bible verses, connected to the year's theme (2010's was "Hearing God"), on which to build their film. While the verse itself doesn't necessarily have to be voiced or read in the picture, the subject matter clearly should reveal the message. Before filming, entrants have 10 days to do the writing and casting, as well as to pick the location and schedule for the one-week shooting. Some studios provide free locations for filming.

"Locally, we help them with a casting session, which speeds up the process," Ware says. "Callbacks are the same day and many productions are cast in just one day. We encourage those out of L.A. to mimic our process."

Many participants hire their own actors. And some wise actors even become producers, thereby creating tailor-made roles for themselves. Producers are responsible for raising their own budgets. Filming budgets range from next to nothing to up to $15,000.

Ware encourages prayer throughout the process, pairing teams with prayer partners with the help of local ministry via the Hollywood Prayer Network.

"We tell them they are going to need the prayer and most of them believe it before the contest," Ware says. "All of them believe it afterwards."

While many of those involved in the venture are Christians, it's not a requirement. Indeed, Ware notes that some agnostics have moved closer to the Christian faith upon completing a 168 Film Project. Entrants must follow rules that call for a respectful interpretation of Scripture without gratuitous sex, violence, or obscenity. Blasphemy and heresy aren't permitted. Yet the films aren't to be mere caricatures spouting Bible verses. Screenplays are expected to show authentic characters in redemptive, thought-provoking stories that honor God.

In 2008, *Coppelius* was produced in Germany by Travis, the only Christian on the team. His agnostic film school crew was excited — until they heard it was a Christian contest. Nevertheless, they went through the process diligently. Nowhere else would a group of agnostics find common ground with Christians studying 1 Peter 2:16 (Live as free men, but do not use your freedom as a cover-up for evil; live as servants for God). Travis's team shot in a bomb shelter, which had been inactive since World War II. After initial meetings, the curators mistakenly thought the filmmakers had written graffiti on the walls. The equation had been there for a long time, like a divine trail of breadcrumbs to these filmmakers: 12 x 14 + 168.

Later, after *Coppelius* won awards at the 168 Film Festival, Travis and the film's director Matthias told Ware that God had revealed himself through several other miracles as they made their film. "After 168, I consider myself a seeker because I can no longer deny the truth of the words of Jesus," Matthias told Ware. The last line in *Coppelius* is, "What is freedom's worth if not used for honoring God?"

Awards at the 168 Film Festival are given in 18 categories including director, actor, actress, screenplay, cinematography, editing, original score, makeup, newcomer, international film, and best gospel of Jesus presentation.

Some of the greatest prizes in the 168 Film Project are opportunities to interact with some industry players. Those judging in 2010 included producer Ralph Winter (*X-Men Origins: Wolverine* and *Fantastic Four*), writer-producer Luke Schlehaas (*Law and Order* and *Smallville*) and writer-producer Brian Bird (*Touched By an Angel* and *Not Easily Broken.*)

"Both Christian and non-Christian filmmakers love story," Ware says. "We're trying to teach them to be in love with Scripture, too, and to experience how a verse can guide their work and improve their art."

The films are shown in a jam-packed two-day festival, with awards announced on the final night. Once made, filmmakers own the rights to the movies. Some have taken them to other film festivals where they have won many awards.

"The films are a calling card to bigger things," Ware says. "We have launched and furthered many careers."

For instance, Robert Kirbyson, who produced two 168 Films, directed his first feature film in 2010, *Snowmen* (MPower Pictures).

Josh Weigel, who won eight awards at the 2008 festival, including best picture, won $100,000 with his film *The Butterfly Circus,* which has been downloaded more than five million times.

In October 2010, the 168 Film Project sponsored its second annual Write of Passage Screenwriting Competition. The mentored competition provides an amazing opportunity for writers to improve as they compete, with the goal of developing redemptive, inspirational stories that honor God. Writers don't have to create overtly Christian characters, but if they do, then authentic Christian characters are encouraged as opposed to one-dimensional caricatures. Writers are directed to create stories that at least hint of redemption, as the whole of the Bible points to Jesus as humanity's redemption. The contest is likewise Scripture-based: a theme, a verse a week.

What's next for Ware? He is working on expanding the 168 Film Project by adding a new film festival called Sermon Story, which targets church production staff. Films produced at any time are eligible, provided they have been made for a church and are no longer than 168 seconds. Winners will be crowned at a new exhibition in Las Vegas at the NAB Show Convention attended by 80,000 people.

"We know how hard church production staff work every week to entertain and illustrate sermons," Ware says. "We want to reward and recognize their excellence and dedication. The award is long overdue for this previously unheralded genre."

~

Ted Baehr
Transforming Tinseltown

Ted Baehr knows the entertainment industry. Having grown up the child of Robert "Ted" Allen and Evelyn Peirce—who were both successful stage, screen, and television actors— Ted understands it not only as an observer, but as one who functioned as part of the culture, performing as a child in commercials, movies, television and stage productions.

As others in the industry, Baehr adopted an skeptical view of religion as he grew older. By age 20, Baehr said, "I was pretty footloose and fancy free and slightly anti-Christian." Never did he imagine that one day he would be president of the Christian Film and Television Commission.

Religion was something than angered Baehr during his early years. He had been only 14 when his mother, a lukewarm Christian Scientist, who embraced the notion that doctors should be shunned in favor of faith-healing, died.

"That convinced me the whole religion thing was wrong," Baehr recalls. It was this attitude that Baehr packed up and took to Dartmouth College and New York University School of Law, where he earned his law degree.

But Baehr's life changed in 1975. Without an audience to applaud him, or TelePrompTer to lead him, Baehr received the living Christ after responding to a friend's challenge to read the Bible.

Baehr knew he believed the Gospel when he had read "about half-way through the Gospel of Matthew," he recalls. He knows it sounds simplistic, but for a man trained to find evidence, he needed to look no further than the Word of God itself to be persuaded by its message.

Baehr's relationship with Christ impacted his life in a profound way, but it did not take away his passion for the art of acting. Instead of tossing a blanket of condemnation on all things Hollywood, Baehr saw the entertainment industry as needful of God's grace.

"I had been involved in financing and producing films," he recalls. "I thought there had to be a way to be redemptive in the film industry."

Setting out to find that way, Baehr learned that prior to 1960 several Protestant churches had maintained their own film offices in Hollywood. A cadre of Christians wielded influence over the kinds of movies being produced.

"The church had been the predominate influence in Hollywood. After the church film offices were closed, the movies went south," Baehr says.

He set out to find a way to rebuild the temple. After consulting George Heimrich, who had been director of the Protestant Film Office, Baehr formed the Christian Film and Television Commission in 1986. Working along with Heimrich and other prominent members of the industry, Baehr continues to serve as a liaison between studio executives and the public-at-large.

"Our main mission is to redeem the values of media," Baehr said. The organization's purpose finds its basis in a challenge from Scripture, he says: "For though we walk in the flesh, we do not war after the flesh: (For the weapons of our warfare are not carnal, but mighty through God to the pulling down of strong holds;) Casting down imaginations, and every high thing that exalteth itself against the knowledge of God, and bringing into captivity every thought to the obedience of Christ" (2 Cor. 10:3-5).

As a father, Baehr personally understands the need for wholesome family entertainment. So each year, he selects the ten best family-friendly, and ten best morally-edifying films of the year and gives out awards to the producers, directors, writers and distribution companies of those films. Baehr also presents the coveted $25,000 Epiphany Prizes for the most inspiring movies and television programs.

"In the past 15 years we have seen the number of programs aimed at families rise from six percent to 40 percent. And 95 percent of those have a strong Christian context," Baehr reports. Money talks in Hollywood, so Baehr is careful to phrase his case for morally excellent productions in terms of box office receipts when he talks to industry officials.

Baehr understands that what he does requires a keen sensitivity to the scriptural challenge of being wise as serpents and harmless as doves (Matt. 10:16). He believes that simply bashing the TV tube and giving up on Hollywood altogether contradicts the example of Christ, who consistently engaged sinners of all stripes, helping them see the truth rather than giving up on them. Recalling a quote from C.S. Lewis, Baehr says, "The problem with evil for us as Christians is that we either become desensitized to it, or hypersensitive to it."

Recalling Paul and Peter's journeys in Acts, Baehr states, "They were driven to some pretty awful places, but God went with them. In order to redeem the people."

The message Hollywood needs to hear is a message of hope, Baehr concludes. "I don't think we are up against an unsolvable problem . . . [As Lewis observed] God's Word inspires us with the tools we need to overcome the world."

—∿—

Larry Poland
The Media Master

"Have you ever considered ministering to media people, those in the entertainment industry?" The question put to him in 1980 by a friend caught Dr. Larry Poland by surprise. A former pastor and once president of Miami Christian College, he headed the International Agape ministry of Campus Crusade for Christ, and believed he was in it for the long haul.

"No," he answered. "Why would I want to minister to Americans when so many people overseas are going to hell? Like other Americans, people in the media can hear the Gospel on radio and television, and they can't miss seeing John 3:16 painted somewhere on rocks and signs."

"But," the friend countered, "what about the influence of the media on values that are affecting people everywhere, including Christians? Larry, pray about it. It's a missionary field."

The challenge got to him. "I began to read everything I could get my hands on to understand how the entertainment industry works, who controls it, what the culture is," Larry says.

For six months, he and a team made phone calls to movers and shakers in the entertainment industry to determine how personal beliefs and faith (or the lack of it) affect their lives and decisions. "At the conclusion of the survey," he says, "I had a dramatic, new perspective of Hollywood. I had envisioned dark, smoke-filled rooms with people in black capes dancing around, saying, 'Bubble, bubble, how can we steal the soul of America?' But

I found no conspiracy. It would presuppose some kind of organization. And organizing Hollywood would be like herding cats."

He found that people in the entertainment business are "bright, fun people, but most of them are very lost." Hollywood and New York media people, he realized, were in a nearly century-long famine of God's Word and desperately needful of a witness to the good news of redemption and new life through Jesus Christ. "This," he says, "led to our ministry to media people, mainly those in the film and television industry."

Initially, Poland reached out to Hollywood under the Campus Crusade for Christ umbrella. Then in 1990 he began Mastermedia International, headquartered in Redlands, California, "to start a spiritual revolution in the media." According to its chairman and CEO, the stated mission of Mastermedia is "to build relationships with decision makers for the purpose of sharing Christ and discipling the people who respond, and to encourage and nurture Christians who work within the industry.

"The ultimate objective," he continues, "is to see the industry change, not by external pressure such as anger strategies, protests, boycott, sock-it-to 'em, but by the change of hearts of the people who run the industry." Poland, silver-haired and distinguished in appearance, directs a staff of about 20 people, including reps in Dallas, Chicago, and New York City.

He points out theirs is a classic missionary effort to an unreached people group, the most influential unreached people group in the world, he asserts. "The stuff these people produce," Larry contends, "contaminates every nation in the world. I've seen its effect in 77 countries. American media output has become the foremost moral and cultural pollutant on the planet."

To make contacts, Poland and his Mastermedia reps get appointments with key people—CEOs, presidents, vice presidents. Often many phone calls must be made. They ask for ten minutes—and usually get more time—to give free "marketing advice" about America's 70 million evangelical Christians. Entertainment executives show appreciation for the counsel and after eight minutes eagerly receive a demographic study. Then, with two minutes of appointment time left, the rep pops the question: "By the way, has there been a time in your life when you personally have prayed and established a personal relationship with Jesus Christ and invited Him to be the central person of your life?"

The question has led to many opportunities to present the Gospel, and some have professed faith in Christ. "I asked that question of the chairman of one of the most influential companies in television," recalls Larry Poland. "He replied, 'Well, I've never done that, but my wife and my mother both think I should.' Two appointments after that, a year and a half later, he prayed with me to receive Christ in his Manhattan office, and he is growing spiritually."

Poland finds women under 30 and men under 40 are "pretty much unreachable." They are buying a pack of lies that money, fame, and sex make for happiness, he says. "But after 30, women begin to realize that isn't true, and men do so after 40," he points out. "Then there are two other hard-to-reach groups—cynical, bitter feminists and in-your-face businessmen. The group easiest to reach is what I call the searchers, those spiritually open through trauma or because other life pursuits have left have left them unfulfilled."

In contacts, Mastermedia reps have discovered Christians at various levels in the media, and they seek to relate them to one another, so they can pray and network together. These people often refer Mastermedia reps to fellow workers. A senior executive, a believer, in one of the main Hollywood studios told Poland, "I feel so alone. I've never met one person at my level who is a Christian." Larry assured him there are believers in Hollywood who have not "bowed their knees to Baal." He introduced him to some of them.

"The guy came alive," Larry says with glee. "He called me and said, 'I found another one, another senior executive in our studio!' The two of them began a prayer group and Bible study in the board room of that studio. God is indeed at work in the entertainment industry! We have the names of some 2,500 Christians in the film and television business, and we've gotten many of these people together for encouragement and fellowship and strategy."

Some believers have become more bold. One Christian, Larry says, went to the chairman of his studio to discuss a film with sickening bathroom humor and the vulgar promotion that went with it. "It was exciting to realize that a few years ago this man would never have dared go to the chairman of his studio," Larry comments.

Mastermedia reps occasionally influence the content of films or TV programs, though reading and editing scripts is not their calling. A top program executive with a national TV network called. A relatively new Christian, he asked Larry for help. "My network is planning a special series on the subject of talking to God based on the experiences of a man who claims to be able to talk to the spirits of the dead."

"This kind of practice is strictly forbidden in Scripture," Poland responded. "Let me put together the biblical position and I'll fax it to you." Sometime afterward, the executive gave Larry a thumbs up: "Hey, we killed that project because of you!"

Why aren't we seeing a greater change in content? Over the next few years, Larry believes, the influence of believers within the industry will have a greater impact on TV programming and Hollywood films. "I compare this ministry to that reaching the sports world. They started in the nineteen-sixties and early seventies. We've been at it full time less than 20 years. Today, stick a mike in front of a football player and he praises Jesus. That will happen more and more in the entertainment industry.

"I see a spiritual awakening in the media," he says." Give us a few more years and there will be more good shows and more executives visible as Christians in the industry. We have them coming out of the woodwork and acknowledging that they are Christians, some high level people."

Most change is visible to us inside the industry, according to Poland. Only little bits of it show on the other side of the screen. But Poland acknowledges the "bad stuff" is getting worse. "We're not saying we can eliminate sin in the media output," he says, "for as long as there's a market for sin they'll produce products that will satisfy the demand for it. But in the future, there's going to be an increasing visibility of Christian people and redemptive content," he predicts.

"The Bible [says] to take the Gospel into the world," Poland says, pointing to the foundation of his ministry. "When the Gospel takes root, it will change people and their lifestyles. It's a change agent, the only one capable of changing the industry."

—m—

The Great Passion Play
America's most-attended outdoor drama event

Crickets are chirping in the rugged, rocky landscape as stars begin to twinkle in the sky. Suddenly, floodlights illuminate a panoramic 550-wide, three-story set. A shofar sounds to announce Jesus' triumphal Palm Sunday entry, whisking onlookers back nearly two millennia.

But this isn't Jerusalem; it's the Great Passion Play in the Ozark Mountains of Eureka Springs, Arkansas. About 130 nights each year, outdoor performances at the vast 4,100-seat amphitheater allow audiences to virtually experience the final week of Christ's life on earth, including a graphic flogging, realistic crucifixion, and the ascension, during which Jesus appears to miraculously soar into the trees, sky, and beyond.

The authentic-looking landscape is the equivalent in size of two football fields built into a hillside. As many as six scenes occur simultaneously, all with meticulously costumed actors. For instance, men mingle in the marketplace; women gather water at a well; Pharisees debate in the temple; Roman soldiers gallop on horses to maintain order; young boys chase sheep. In addition to roaring chariots and flying pigeons, the dusty, bustling city streets are filled with camels, horses, mules, and sheep.

Annually around 100,000 people make their way across winding, tree-lined two-lane roads to visit the rural theater tucked away in the northwest corner of . Since 1968, more than 7.5 million people have watched the Great Passion Play, which is the nation's most attended outdoor drama event.

Founders Gerald L.K. Smith and Elna M. Smith had been inspired by the passion play in Oberammergau, Germany. The Bavarian drama has been performed since 1634. The Smiths, using Jesus' words of John 12:32 ("And I, if I be lifted up from the earth, will draw all men unto ") as a guiding principle, figured if Americans could watch a similar play, it could transform their lives.

Although there isn't a formal altar call, officials at the Great Passion Play down through the years have heard various testimonies of how the Gospel presentation has impacted lives.

One such person is Forest "Bobo" Estes. Thirty-five years ago, Estes, then a firefighter in Baton Rouge, Louisiana, drove into Eureka Springs in a drunken stupor, finding little reason to go on living. The alcoholic Estes, separated from his wife, asked a clerk at a local motel what kind of attractions the town had to offer. The clerk told Estes about the Great Passion Play. Estes, thinking something with that title must surely involve pornographic entertainment, headed for the show. As soon as he returned to Louisiana, Estes called a local pastor, who led him in a prayer of salvation.

Estes reconciled with his wife and became involved in Bible studies at his church. He began to bring drug addicts and prostitutes in his nine-passenger station wagon, paying for their tickets to the Great Passion Play, not telling them of its spiritual implications. Eventually he brought hundreds of people to performances in a school bus. Before retiring, Estes organized several missions trips to build churches in Mexico. Estes and his wife celebrated their fiftieth anniversary in 2006—by attending a Great Passion Play presentation.

It takes 150 paid performers from a multitude of regional churches to make the show a reality. Ninety percent of the cast typically returns from the previous year. Eureka Springs has a population of only 2,300.

As long as there is no danger to the cast or audience, the show continues even if there are 30 mile per hour winds, torrential downpours, or temperatures that dip to near freezing. Prerecorded music plays throughout the performance and nearly all dialogue is directly from Scripture. The two-hour event occurs nearly every night May through October, with the exception of Sundays and Wednesdays, when most performers attend services at their own churches.

The two bearded men who alternately portray Jesus are both in their forties, yet they are hardly carbon copies.

Rick Mann is blond, blue-eyed and 6 feet, 2 inches. He is entering his 10th year depicting the Savior. At his church in nearby Berryville, Mann is worship leader and a Wednesday night Bible study teacher. Mann, who by day is a state housing maintenance mechanic, had theatrical training in high school and quickly adapted to the role of Jesus.

Although the dialogue portion of the performance is prerecorded, Mann initially still had to spend more than two months learning the lines to coordinate his movements. During dress rehearsal before his first performance the lights failed when he emerged from the tomb. During the actual show, the dazzling lights disoriented him and he walked smack into a stone wall.

Mann has learned to go with the flow. Once a pigeon landed on his head as he sat at the Last Supper table. He let the bird remain, reasoning that trying to shoo it away would detract from the character.

An inclement night sparked the most dramatic moment for him. One night as he hung on the cross and cried, "My God, My God, why have You forsaken Me?" thunder loudly clapped right behind him.

Mann is the more expressive of the two Jesus actors, so he holds nothing back when clearing the temple. "I want to show passion in a strong way," Mann says. "Any actor needs to communicate the role so that it's believable."

Joe Smith is the longer-tenured Jesus actor, the dark-haired one and at 6 feet, 7 inches, the taller one. A more soft-spoken, tender Christ figure, Smith has been in the play for more than two decades. It's apparent that this Jesus is a real-life schoolteacher during the week; during a scene teaching at the temple he comfortably interacts with children, placing a toddler on his lap. Smith had no acting experience when he began at the Great Passion Play after college, but he seems born for the role.

"At times I feel the strong presence of the Spirit of God," says Smith, who attends church in Washburn, Missouri. "I pray for that. I want to make a difference and do the best I can for Him."

Five evenings a week before the play, Smith conducts a 20-minute Parables of the Potter demonstration. As he molds a clay pot at his wheel, Smith relates several inspirational and evangelistic Scripture lessons. With his broad smile, piercing blue-gray eyes, calm demeanor, and expressive encouragement, Smith presents what amounts to an effective sermon.

The play provides a concise, direct explanation of the Gospel and it isn't designed just for evangelism, according to Marvin Peterson, the theater's director of operations. "It's not unusual to have discouraged pastors come and be touched by God," Peterson says. "It can be a turning point in a Christian's life."

There is more to the Great Passion Play grounds than the play itself. Visitors have the opportunity to visit a host of Bible-related sites.

The seven-story tall Christ of the Ozarks statue predates the play itself, having been completed in 1966. Emmet Sullivan, who worked on Mount Rushmore, sculpted the statue, which weighs more than two million pounds.

Gerald L.K. Smith and Elna M. Smith commissioned the statue as the first project on the site before they started the play and related attractions.

"In travels across the , the Smiths had seen great memorials to war heroes and politicians, but nowhere except in cemeteries had they seen a monument to Jesus Christ," says Peterson, who has been with the Great Passion Play since 1979. "They felt compelled by the Holy Spirit to erect a reminder of God's great love and mercy to all of humanity."

Attractions have been added at the Great Passion Play since its beginning. The New Holy Land tram tour features 30 exhibits recreating the history and culture of the ancient Middle East, including a life-sized reproduction of Moses' Tabernacle in the Wilderness. Along various stops, actors portray everyone from Simon Peter at the Sea of Galilee to Mary at the Bethlehem stable.

The Sacred Arts Center has exhibits dating back 1,200 years showing how artists have expressed their love of God. The Bible Museum contains more than 1,000 Bibles in 625 languages and dialects, several dating back nearly 500 years.

The Museum of Earth History has full-sized dinosaur skeleton displays and exhibits that reveal the scientific facts behind the Bible's historical Genesis account.

"We want to impact lives one at a time," Peterson says. "If we can continue to lift Jesus up as an extension of the church, people will be drawn to Him."

CHAPTER 13

Redemptive Communicators:

—⁓—

VISUAL ARTS

Michael Spielman

A graphic artist unmasks America's holocaust.

One of the federally protected liberties Americans have possessed since 1973 is the right to end the life of a baby before its birth, the result of the U.S. Supreme Court's *Roe v. Wade* decision. The debate since then often has devolved into political posturing about "choice." As a result, many people today don't understand what actually constitutes an abortion.

Michael G. Spielman's goal is to explain that grim reality.

Spielman's Web site, Abort73.com, has been able to accomplish what a lot of arguing elsewhere hasn't: enlightening and changing uninformed minds. With logical, conclusive evidence and graphic images, the site has led to numerous testimonials from readers who say they now comprehend why abortion is wrong.

Spielman devised the website in response to a transformation in his own thinking. He graduated from with a graphic design degree, then landed a job as a graphic designer at the *Nashville Business Journal*. While he made a good living, Spielman—who received Jesus as his Savior while in the seventh grade—felt he wanted to do something more ministry-oriented with his skills, something that would have more eternal significance.

A year into his new job, Spielman attended a seminar presented by Gregg Cunningham of the Center for Bioethical Reform (CBR). That event would be the catalyst he needed to find more meaning. Cunningham persuaded him that abortion isn't a political issue; it's a love-your-neighbor issue (See Matt. 22:38-40).

"I was struck by how clear-cut the case against abortion is from a purely secular standpoint," Spielman recalls. "The overwhelming medical and biological evidence establishes that human life begins at fertilization."

Like many Christians, Spielman had considered himself "pro-life" in his mind but he never really became engaged in the issue with his heart. In fact, he thought involvement in the movement would be a distraction from "real ministry."

In 1999 Spielman began more than five years of full-time work for CBR, fulfilling his longing to meaningfully combine vocation and ministry. Spielman spent a great deal of time on college campuses with CBR's Genocide Awareness Project, which features a huge photo mural exhibit comparing abortion with other crimes against humanity. Most of the posters are from first-trimester abortions, yet those are descriptive enough. The in-your-face encounters energized the low-key, soft-spoken Spielman.

"For the first time in my life I knew what it was to be utterly despised for my faith, and I knew the supernatural thrill of standing in the face of ridicule with nothing but love for the one spewing insults," Spielman says. "As I traveled the country debating the essence of life and death, I found that there are no insignificant conversations and no insignificant people."

Although many students indeed reacted with animosity, Spielman witnessed many others letting go of long-held unreasonable attitudes about abortion. Still, the process of visiting campus after campus proved to be a labor intensive, expensive, and slow-moving process.

"I wanted a way to simultaneously extend that education to students across the country, and to include high schoolers," Spielman says. "For the project to have a huge cultural impact, more than visits to individual campuses needed to be done."

So he decided to use technology as the means of reaching the masses. He began to devise a website to enable people to see the graphic reality of abortion from their own computers.

"It seemed like the more polished pro-life Web sites had a lot of details about their particular organization, but were thin when it came to actually educating about abortion," Spielman says. "I wanted a site that took better advantage of the educational opportunities provided by the World Wide Web, while giving pro-life students some practical tools."

Drawing upon his multimedia expertise, Spielman incorporated Loxafamosity Ministries in 2004 and Abort73.com soon followed. He continues to work for CBR part-time.

The Abort73.com site has various video, audio and text arguments against abortion. Reader blogs and message boards show abortion's destruction. Spielman outlines biological, psychological, financial, medical, theological and other reasons to avoid having an abortion. Along the way, those navigating Abort73.com learn about the Biblical foundation of life and are given opportunity to profess faith in Christ.

Spielman believes the facts about abortion need to be presented explicitly because that's what shook him from his complacency.

"When I went to that CBR seminar it was a graphic video that really hit me hard," Spielman remembers. "It was no longer abstract. The shocking pictures motivated me to get going. I want people to see what abortion does. Then the likelihood that they will go through with it decreases dramatically."

Spielman and his wife Carrie, whom he married in 2001, live in Rockford, Illinois, and attend Harvest Bible Chapel. They have two children, Seth and Melanie.

Having children has only reinforced Spielman's fortitude to contest the irrational views he encounters among abortion-rights advocates.

"Over and over I hear some variant of, 'Until a baby can survive on its own, it's not really a person,' " Spielman says. "As any parent knows, however, the smaller and more dependent a child is, the more care and protection we give to the baby."

As young children grow, the amount of direct oversight and provision they need decreases steadily, Spielman notes. But newborns need a great deal of care because they are so vulnerable and needy.

"As it relates to abortion, though, normal parental concern has been turned on its head," Spielman says. "The absolute dependence of unborn children has become the rationale, not for their protection, but for their destruction! The fact that so many mothers think of their child as a parasite is a scary indictment of our society."

Regularly Spielman receives e-mails from guilt-ridden girls confessing to their sin of destroying their offspring. The website has a section that allows women to tell how abortion traumatically affected them, in an effort to prevent others from following the same path.

Typical posted messages read, "Because of your website I chose not to kill my child" or "I showed your website to a lot of my friends and one of them was pregnant and it changed her mind completely."

Most visitors to the site are females of middle school, high school, and college age. In 2007, Spielman purposely began building in more social networking features on the Abort73.com site for students who are active in doing something about abortion. The site offers everything from digital videodiscs to T-shirts to give students basic tools to get the message out.

Spielman has discovered that the teen years are the best time to convince younger people that abortion is wrong.

"The older people get, the more they are entrenched in their belief system—and the likelier they are to have had a personal involvement in abortion," he says.

As might be expected, not everyone is thrilled with the revelations Spielman presents on the website. He has received angry and threatening e-mails from abortion defenders.

"Spiritual warfare accompanies this work since Satan has an interest in maintaining the abortion status quo," Spielman says. "I've done campus evangelism, but I've never faced such hatred and animosity in sharing the Gospel as I have when talking about abortion."

Spielman takes a great deal of time to address vitriolic remarks with humility and grace, but that often provokes only rage.

"Darkness hates the light," Spielman says "We're not only battling unwitting ignorance, but also chosen ignorance."

—m—

Matt Anderson

A card designer helps Christians encourage each other.

Ask Matt Anderson's children what their daddy does for a living and they'll answer, "He draws little angels with great big noses." But his job goes far beyond sketchbook doodles. The big-nosed angels are the trademark of Matt's greeting cards, "Heaven's Unofficial Greetings," and are found in Christian bookstores across North America. Since 1991 Matt's angels have delivered hugs from heaven—mini messages filled with hopeful reminders of biblical truths. Gentle reminders of God's love. Humorous tidbits of truth.

"People need encouragement—they can't get enough of it. I want people to be encouraged with the hope that comes from knowing the Lord," says Anderson.

"That goal is accomplished with a clever cover, a Scripture verse inside, and the back message pointing to the Source of hope."

Anderson's cartooning ability was obvious when he was a young boy. Growing up in Seattle, Washington, he spent hours drawing cartoon characters on a roll of butcher paper. Later, in college, he printed and sold several card designs. A crucial element was missing, however. "I could draw funny pictures but I had no message. My cards had no concept of life, truth, and encouragement."

While attending college in Tacoma, Washington, Anderson became sidetracked by mingling with the wrong crowd. "Although I wasn't raised in a Christian home, I'd always lived a clean life," he says. "I wanted to discover what I'd been missing." He found only emptiness.

"As soon as I started making bad choices, I knew I didn't want to live like that. I carried a terrible burden of guilt." He recalls praying, "God, I've really screwed up my life. I know You have the answer but I don't know what it is. Could You please tell me?" Matt bought a one-way ticket to Europe, embarking on a search for that answer.

His prayers continued while hitchhiking through Europe. While touring Spain's northern Basque country, he was suspected of being a foreign terrorist. With a machine gun to his back and soldiers rifling through his belongings, he prayed, "God, get me out of here!" The soldiers released him.

Later in Morocco, Matt suffered from a severe case of food poisoning.

Lying on his bed in a hostel, fearful of dying, he again cried to God for help. He recovered. "God, You must have something for me to do," he acknowledged. He returned home a few weeks later—still searching for spiritual reality, open to whatever it might be.

Upon his return, his parents gave him a Bible. "I read John 14:6 where Jesus says, 'I am the way, the truth and the life.' Deep inside my soul, something responded, 'Yes. This is the answer.'"

The search ended. Weeping, Anderson committed his life to Jesus Christ—"Whatever

You want, I'm Yours." He openly shared his newfound faith with his family. One after another, his parents and three siblings received Christ.

"As soon as I became a Christian I realized that, not only did I have peace and purpose, but I had a message to go with my gift for cartooning," says Anderson. "But I still didn't know how to put it all together." He received direction during a year-long tour with the Covenant Players, a Christian drama troupe. While on tour, he stayed in people's homes.

"For the first time I saw Christians not just in church but in their real surroundings. I witnessed the wide variety that exists in the body of Christ. Through listening to people talk about the struggles in their lives, the Lord showed me their common need for encouragement."

In 1986, one year after graduating from the University of Washington with a Bachelor's degree in Art, Matt sketched his first angel character. "I drew a little skier skiing off a cliff. His worried expression made me laugh out loud. Be anxious for nothing popped into my thoughts. It was as though the Lord said, 'Matt, this is what I want you to do.'"

"Heaven's Unofficial Greetings" had been conceived but it would be another five years before its birth. As Matt filled sketch books with ideas, he worked as a youth pastor intern for a year. One of his favorite cards was modeled after a plaque he made to encourage a boy in his youth group—the only kid in school who didn't receive a year-end award. On it, he sketched the boy's caricature and wrote the words 'Masterpiece in Progress.' After listing the boy's Christ-like qualities, he added, 'God is doing a good work in you.' The plaque made such a positive impact that he designed one for the boy's sister as well.

In 1988 he attended Multnomah Graduate School of Ministry in Portland, Oregon, for a year of graduate study in Bible and Theology. "If I was going to encourage people with God's word, I wanted to do it accurately," he says.

At Multnomah he met Kris Oman. They married on September 8, 1990. Matt did freelance artwork and custom illustrations while trying to design a card line but his earnings weren't enough to provide for a family. Kris' job as a dental receptionist provided their main source of income. He was still seeking the secret recipe for the cards when they discovered she was expecting their first child. Their faith faced a major challenge.

"Our prayers became very earnest," Matt admits. "I prayed, 'Lord, You know who You've made me to be and the gifts You've given me. I truly believe You have a purpose. I'm at Your service. I'm tired of trying to make this come together in my brain. You're going to have to do it and You're going to have to do it quickly."

Over the next two weeks, Matt sketched 40 card designs. "It was truly an answer to prayer. It came after releasing myself to what He wanted to do through me instead of what I wanted to do for Him." Anderson showed his cards to friends and family, making necessary changes until he saw the response he'd hoped for—people laughing, saying, "Oh, this is so true. I know someone who needs this!" The artwork and the message were finally working together. He photocopied his cards, hand-painted each design and sold them in nine local bookstores for several months. He visited each store frequently, keeping accurate sales records.

Kris quit her job at the end of November. Their first child was born in December. After seeing Anderson's sales records, a card company decided to launch "Heaven's Unofficial Greetings" nationwide in January. Matt was supporting his family within a month.

"I got letters from all across the country. People were hungry for humor and encouragement. I began learning that this business is simply about being a mouthpiece for the Lord to use for speaking encouragement to His people."

In January, 2000, as Matt put the finishing touches on several new card designs, he and his wife found their faith challenged and encouraged again. A doctor's diagnosis gave Kris a 50 percent chance of survival due to stage three tonsil cancer. One of Matt's new cards read, God's faithfulness means . . . every storm will pass. Another one read, When the challenge is God-sized . . . the solution will be, too. "I couldn't believe God's timing," Matt says. "He prepared us through the messages He'd given me for the cards."

As Kris underwent aggressive surgery, chemotherapy, and radiation, 'hugs from heaven' embraced them daily in a variety of ways. Encouragement came through God's Word, especially Psalm 20—"The LORD hear thee in the day of trouble; the name of the God of Jacob defend thee." Friends supported them by taking Kris to radiation treatments, homeschooling their three children, doing laundry, housecleaning, and meal preparation. Their help allowed Matt to care for Kris' physical needs and continue working as much as possible in Product Development at DaySpring Cards, the world's largest publisher of Christian greeting cards. Kris completed treatment five months after her diagnosis.

"The byline of my cards is 'Celebrating the Everyday Adventure of Faith,'" says Matt. "Kris' cancer was simply another part of the adventure of walking with Christ. Her illness wasn't about us. It was about Him revealing Himself to us. He was the same the day after her diagnosis as He was the day before. We prayed, 'Lord, just be who You are. No matter what the outcome is, we can deal with this if You are who You say You are.'"

Anderson quotes Romans 15:5,6: "Now the God of patience and consolation grant you to be likeminded one toward another according to Christ Jesus: That ye may with one mind and one mouth glorify God, even the Father of our Lord Jesus Christ."

"I love what's revealed in these verses—that God Himself gives encouragement! He often uses another person sharing His Word in love as the bodily form of His own expression of encouragement. The end result is that God is glorified. What an inspiration to me as I work to create products that people can use to encourage one another and ultimately bring glory to our awesome God!"

Randy Hofman

A sand sculpture presents the Gospel to Maryland beachgoers.

As a young child, Randy Hofman enjoyed playing in the sand. He and his eight siblings dug around the sandbox in the backyard of their suburban Washington, D.C., home. The family also took summer vacations to Ocean City, Maryland, where Hofman could build castles and roads on the white sandy beach. From the age of five, Hofman knew he wanted to be an artist.

Hofman grew up and faced a reality of adulthood: putting away childish dreams and making a living. He began to study advertising design and visual communications at the Pratt Institute in Brooklyn, New York, with plans of becoming a magazine art director. But after a couple of years of classes, Hofman determined such a career path would be too confining.

In 1974, Hofman returned to Ocean City, the site of his childhood summer vacations, to help sand artist Marc Altamar. For seven years, Hofman served as Altamar's apprentice. During that period, Hofman made a commitment to Jesus as his Savior. Since early childhood, Hofman had a head knowledge of the Lord. But at age 25, on the beach one night, he agreed to allow Jesus into his heart to guide his daily life.

"I had gone through a party phase in my life and I wanted to be done with that," Hofman says. "I didn't want to just trifle with the Lord anymore."

When Altamar moved to Florida in 1981, Hofman became the sole resident sand-sculpting artist on the Ocean City beachfront, turning it into a full-blown ministry.

The effort has grown more elaborate in the past quarter century. Initially, Hofman would take a few hours a day to build a sand painting. With overnight winds, it would be indistinguishable by the next day. Since 1990, a glue and water spray mixture has held sculptures intact for up to several weeks – and even months – if the elements or vandals don't damage them.

These days, Hofman puts in a lengthier workday at the beach. Using only a square shovel and plastic crab picking knife, he creates sculptures that can extend 40 feet wide and 10 feet tall. His most intricate and crowd-pleasing piece, depicting the Last Supper, sometimes takes 17 hours.

Once he begins work, Hofman keeps going until finished, stopping only for dinner and restroom breaks. He never abandons a project to rest and may continue working until dawn.

John and Hale Harrison, Christian brothers who operate the Plim Plaza Hotel in Ocean City, provide free water and electricity to Hofman so he can construct his artwork on a public beach about 25 feet off the boardwalk. The water is essential to make the sand pliable. The lights make the sculptures visible at night. The boardwalk stretches for 2.5 miles as part of the 10 miles of beach.

Hofman has a dozen basic Biblical themes for his work, including Noah and the ark,

Moses carrying the Ten Commandments, Samson crashing the temple pillars, David fighting Goliath, the Wise Men visiting the newborn Savior, and Jesus praying in the Garden. Hofman's favorite is an elaborate head of Jesus. A Biblical adage, such as "Wise men still seek Him" often is etched near the top of the carving, giving it the appearance of a newspaper headline.

"I want it to click so that even someone who is spiritually ignorant can understand," Hofman says.

In all, he has completed about 1,000 sculptures, each somewhat different than anything he's done in the past. The artwork and the Bible passage – plus the fact that tens of thousands of tourists are relaxed while on a family vacation—provide an atmosphere for evangelism. "Kids ask their parents what the sculpture is all about," Hofman says.

Sometimes Hofman will create thematic stories side by side, such as Jesus praying in the Garden, Christ dying on the Cross, and the appearance of the resurrected Lord.

Hofman, who also has been an ordained minister since 1985, engages inquisitive passersby in conversation about God. He sometimes preaches while he's sculpting. He also has distributed more than a million 32-page evangelistic tracts that are available next to his work at the beach.

Although Hofman has a jar beside the sand sculptures for tips, he survives financially by doing oil paintings, primarily individual portraits and landscapes. Hofman and his wife Marilynne, a registered nurse, live in nearby Berlin, Maryland.

There is room outside his spot near the hotel for four connecting scenes. Youth from a local church group, Son Spot Ministries, excavate the sand piles, digging with shovels to bring moist sand to the top to form a mound. Hofman creates his work at a 45-degree angle so that it's visible from the boardwalk to tourists who flock to Ocean City in the summer. Hofman crafts his designs on the beach, from the beginning of April to the end of October.

While Christians usually admire the sculpting mostly for its Biblical storytelling, non-Christians often are drawn by Hofman's craftsmanship. His attention to detail and classical portrayal of the human anatomy frequently impress those who are Biblically illiterate or skeptical.

If a storm or vandal spoils the work, Hofman sometimes takes a day or two to repair it. Few people intentionally destroy the work anymore because the glue makes it difficult to budge.

Still, Hofman occasionally encounters an antagonistic visitor questioning his beliefs—or sanity. "Some people just have a nasty disposition," Hofman says. "The sculptures I choose are about love of God and His generosity. If somebody is crabby about that, they're just crabby."

Although his age, the hot summer sun, and the backbreaking work sometimes take a toll on Hofman, he plans to continue in the artistry that has kept him occupied for more than three decades.

"I see this as the highest calling," says Hofman. "It seems to complete me."

CHAPTER 14

Redemptive Communicators:

—⚸—

MEDICINE

Jill Stanek

A nurse takes a courageous stand for life.

In the end, she actually wanted to get fired. It's true that she had spent the better part of a decade working toward this position, in this unit, in this hospital. And it's true that the job was a dream-come-true, the work both challenging and rewarding.

But Jill Stanek was tired of being whispered about, tiptoed around, and excluded from hallway chatter. Then came the written warnings, the suspension, and the anonymous hate mail.

After all, she was the one who, in 1999, blew the whistle on Chicago's renowned Christ Hospital. She exposed the fact that her employer was performing "live-birth abortions," in which pre-term labor is induced, a fully formed baby delivered intact, and—if still alive— left to die with no medical intervention.

Two years later—two years of constant scrutiny from her bosses and ostracism from her co-workers—Stanek was finally fired.

And, boy, was she relieved.

"I was just so happy and thankful to God," she said. "I was almost laughing."

Even though her job at Christ Hospital had come to an end, though, Stanek was really only beginning her battle for these tiny victims.

Almost immediately, people began to call, offering her writing and speaking engagements. She testified before Congress and dabbled in local politics. And twice she's visited the White House, at President Bush's invitation, to watch him sign pro-life legislation.

A Grisly Discovery

A self-described late bloomer, Stanek, already had school-aged children when she began working the night shift in labor and delivery section at Christ Hospital in Oak Lawn, Illinois. At first, she wasn't aware that the hospital performed labor-induced abortions; she'd already been there a year when a co-worker shared the devastating news.

Stanek learned the hospital had been performing the procedure for more than two decades by the time she came on staff. As sickened as she was by this information, she was even more disturbed by the thought that hundreds—maybe thousands—of hospital employees knew it was going on and had never said a word.

She attributed the silence to fear. Fear of losing a job, fear of what others might say, fear of a tarnished reputation. Stanek, too, was frightened into silence, not sure what to do.

So for three years she said nothing, until a "crisis of conscience" compelled her to take the risk she'd tried so hard to avoid.

Late one evening, Stanek opened the door that changed her life forever. It was the door to a hospital utility closet, where a co-worker—too busy to hold an aborted baby boy until he died—had left the child. By the time Stanek found the Down syndrome boy, abandoned and still breathing, it was too late to provide medical assistance. Huddled in a closet, surrounded by soiled laundry, she cradled him, rocked him—and 45 minutes later, felt his small body go limp in her arms.

Her dream job would never be the same.

"Having to walk by a room where people were aborting and I knew it was going on—not being able to do anything about it was such torture," she said.

Witnessing the devastating effects of late-term abortion was one thing. Knowing a secret the hospital attempted to hide was another. While Christ Hospital officials claimed this procedure was performed only on babies with fatal handicaps, Stanek knew the truth. There were others, perfectly formed, delivered before they had a chance to live.

Because the procedure is so controversial, it's difficult to know how many hospitals perform live-birth abortions, or even who's doing them. At Christ Hospital, Stanek said, they were referred to as "medically indicated" abortions: A pregnant woman was given a drug to dilate the cervix and induce labor. The pre-term babies were often delivered dead—but not always.

True to the procedure's name, some of these babies enter the world with their tiny arms flailing and fragile chests heaving, gasping for air, desperate for help. Yet the doctors and nurses only turn their backs.

Sometimes a nurse will hold them until they die. Sometimes a mother or father will rock their premature son or daughter until death. But many times, these little ones will take their final breaths alone, surrounded only by stark walls and sterile hospital equipment.

"You'll find this procedure going on in almost every major city, and people aren't saying anything about it," Stanek says. "They think that it's enough not to participate if you're pro-life. But it's not enough."

So began her one-woman crusade.

Going Public

Like her co-workers, Stanek could have simply looked the other way. But she decided that God had placed her in this position—and that alone was worth risking her job and professional reputation.

"I did want to leave," she said, "but my view was that there is no such thing as a coincidence. God had put me in that place for a reason. So every time I thought about leaving, I thought I was abandoning the position that Christ had put me in."

She handled matters privately at first, writing letters to and meeting with hospital administrators, urging them to change their policy on abortion. But the officials made it clear they had no intention of stopping.

That's when she went public.

Her pastor sent out a letter to about 70 churches and pro-life organizations, in and across the country. The news spread quickly, and before she knew it, Stanek was being interviewed by the *New York Times*, *Newsweek* and Fox News.

Through it all, she continued to work the night shift at Christ Hospital. Once-friendly co-workers now ignored her, doctors scheduled abortions when she wasn't around, and administrators monitored her every move, watching for any infraction that could merit termination.

For two years, Stanek was on probation for breaking an unspecified rule in her employment contract. And for two years, hospital staff couldn't come up with a compelling reason to fire her.

She knew she was being watched, but she was well past the point of intimidation. She testified twice before Congress about what she saw at . She campaigned for the federal Born Alive Infants Protection Act, which requires hospitals and doctors to treat all infants who are delivered alive—even those who were aborted—as persons deserving all necessary medical attention.

Stanek's lawyer, Liberty Counsel's Mat Staver, said she wasn't trying to cause controversy; she was just trying to be a good nurse and a good Christian.

"Jill made a decision," Staver says, "and that decision was to stand for principle and to stand for life and the unborn, and she put her entire career literally on the line."

"I Wasn't a Pro-Life Activist"

In August 2001, Stanek returned from vacation to discover that she had indeed been fired. Hospital officials claimed it had nothing to do with her pro-life views or all the negative publicity she brought to the hospital. Yet when they provided Stanek with written reasons for her termination, all pertained to her outspokenness.

Without her nursing career, Stanek devoted herself to full-time activism. Her speaking invitations increased, and she decided to get involved in local politics—running for the Illinois

General Assembly against her pro-abortion state representative only three months after leaving Christ Hospital.

Stanek lost the election, but the experience opened up even more opportunities to share her story. For the last three years, she has spoken extensively about her experiences, been quoted hundreds of times in the national media and currently writes a weekly column on important issues for *The Illinois Leader.*

On August 5, 2002, President Bush invited Stanek to the signing of the Born Alive Infants Protection Act, for which she testified. A year later, she was again in the room when Bush signed long-awaited legislation banning partial-birth abortion. And *World* magazine named her one of the 30 most prominent pro-life leaders of the past three decades.

But despite all that, Stanek doesn't see herself as a hero. Rather, she simply lives out the biblical duty to defend the cause of the helpless

"I've never tried to open my own door," she said. "God has opened doors I never would have thought possible. I wasn't a pro-life activist, I was just pro-life...My home is heaven... but as long as I'm here, I have a job to do."

—m—

James Blessman

A Christian doctor ministers to the physical needs of America's poor.

Tables and chairs are being set up in the waiting area. Ear-probe thermometers, blood pressure cuffs, and tongue depressors are prepared in the screening section. A toy box and children's videos are readied in an overflow room. It's 5:30 P.M. Thursday in the basement of a church in Des Moines, Iowa, and a beehive of active volunteers are transforming Sunday School rooms into a free clinic.

Although patients won't be seen for another half hour, they already are lining up for the first-come, first-served ministry. The church has designated a corner for medical exams and supplies storage. The weekly free clinic is the brainchild of Dr. James L. Blessman. As founder and executive director of the nonprofit Health Care Access Network, Blessman has started free weekly clinics in 17 Iowa locations.

HCAN reaches many Iowans who have jobs, but little or no health insurance. With the vision of using volunteers from local churches, Blessman in the past decade has recruited 200 doctors and 1,000 non-physician volunteers to donate their services. In addition to the free labor, the use of facilities is donated along with most of the equipment and medicines. The state covers malpractice insurance for the doctors providing the free care. The network of clinics provides free primary medical care, no strings attached, to those who likely don't have a regular doctor.

"We're just a tiny piece of the safety net," Blessman says. Many patients who wouldn't set foot in a church for a service don't mind doing so for free health care that is run as efficiently and professionally as commercial clinics. The patients who gather are a mixture, representing the neighborhood in northwest Des Moines: a white elderly woman, a Hispanic family of five, a black teenager. Typically, three nurses, one doctor, a medical student and half a dozen non-medical volunteers will be on hand from 6 to 8 P.M. All likely have put in a full day of work in their regular jobs.

An average of 15 patients are seen each Thursday night, receiving everything from bronchitis medication to measles immunizations. Sometimes a diagnosis and treatment can change a life. At one clinic, a doctor determined that a baby had phenylketonuria, a genetic disorder that results in mental retardation if not caught early and treated with a special diet.

Tonight's on-call physician is Dr. James P. Lovell, a cardiologist who has been volunteering monthly since the clinic opened eight years ago. For a specialist whose career involves the intricacies of the heart, treating a common cold is a bit of a departure.

"I'm just a cardiologist," says Lovell. Recalling Christ's challenge to treat people as if they were Christ Himself (Matt. 25: 31-45), he adds, "Sometimes I wonder if I should be seeing sick babies. But this is a place where God wants me to be. In a sense this is a missions outreach. This is the place where I can make a small contribution."

Blessman grew up attending a church and Sunday School where he never heard about salvation. But as an adult, his pastor asked him the question: If he were to die tonight would he go to heaven? Blessman pondered the question. Unsure of how to answer the question, he soon acknowledged his sinfulness and consequent need of salvation based on someone or something other than himself. He asked God to forgive him of his sins and received Christ, the only Savior, into his life (John 14:6). Although initially motivated to operate the clinics as a social service contribution to the community, Blessman eventually realized that he could serve Christ by serving others. As Jesus himself stated, "Inasmuch as ye have done it unto one of the least of these my brethren, ye have done it unto me" (Matt. 25:40).

Since then, counselors are available at clinics to offer prayer to patients before they leave. Nearly everyone agrees, and almost every week one or two patients decide to receive Jesus as Savior. Those who do receive a free Bible, discipleship materials, and local church information. Adding a spiritual component to the clinic has meant that the outreach can minister to the physical, emotional, and spiritual well-being of people.

The cost to HCAN for each patient is $21 per visit, one-tenth of the basic cost for a trip to a local hospital emergency room. The entire annual $313,000 HCAN budget comes from private funds and no government money is used. The clinics are dependent upon individuals, congregations, patient donations and private grants to keep going. Blessman is continually on the hunt for more corporate sponsors. The most ambitious free clinic is La Clínica de la

Esperanza (Clinic of Hope), opened by Blessman's group in 1994.

Now there are three local health care providers coordinating services at the facility, which is open every weekday and has three registered nurses on staff. The clinic is located in southeast Des Moines where many poor, undocumented Hispanics work in meat-packing plants. La Clínica is expected to treat 10,000 patients a year.

For years Blessman says he was a workaholic while he practiced family medicine and also operated a pain-relief center in Des Moines. "I spent the first 45 years of my life trusting in my own abilities, power and influence," Blessman says. "I thought I was very successful and living the best life that I possibly could. Looking back on the decision to turn my finances, work, time, family and relationships over to the Lord should have been easy, but I had a difficult time letting go of the control I thought I had."

Blessman left the lucrative medical profession in 2001 after overseas short-term missionary health care trips stirred his heart toward poor and spiritually lost people in Third World countries. At 58, he has reached the point in life where most doctors are winding down and looking forward to a comfortable retirement. Instead, he and his wife, Beth, last year became medical missionaries with HealthCare Ministries, based in Missouri. They take 10 annual two-week medical team and disaster response trips, bringing God's love and healing to people around the world.

"On most trips we get to openly share the Gospel," says Blessman, who has provided free medical care in countries such as El Salvador, Vietnam, and Zambia. "Now I know that this is what God wants me to do—reach out to poor people in countries where they might not receive much medical attention otherwise. We can provide medical care, which is temporary, but we can also share [about the Gospel of] Jesus, which is an eternal benefit."

⟶

Ron Hoekstra

A doctor ministers to the families of pre-maturely born babies.

While growing up in a conservative Christian home, Ron Hoekstra developed a respect for human life that is foundational to the worldview of many believers: All people are created in God's image and have worth, even people whose lives are limited by physical or mental handicaps, or babies who survive only for a few days. As Scripture teaches, "He giveth to all life, and breath, and all things . . . . For in him we live, and move, and have our being (Acts 17:25-28).

A neonatal specialist at Children's Hospital in Minneapolis since 1979, Hoekstra has had the opportunity to put his beliefs in action.

"Any life has tremendous value, no matter how imperfect, no matter how long," says the lifelong Minnesotan. "These [pre-maturely born] babies, from a human and medical perspective didn't work out. But they had a tremendous impact on numerous lives. There's no price tag on that."

Hoekstra finished his pediatric residency at the Mayo Clinic in Rochester, Minnesota, in an era when neonatology was not a recognized specialty. But drug and technological advances in the past three decades mean that a baby born at 28 weeks who previously had little chance of survival now is likely to live a full and productive life. These days, the medical consensus is that every effort should be made to save a child born at 24 weeks. Hoekstra, 59, goes further. He is willing to take a risk on a babies who, if they live, probably will end up with long-term disabilities.

"I feel powerless without faith in God," Hoekstra says. "There's not a day I walk into the neonatal intensive care that I don't ask God for wisdom to know what's right."

At the hospital, Hoekstra and his colleagues have tried to save the lives of 37 babies born at 22 weeks, a time in gestation at which a baby's anatomy has often not developed to a point of being compatible with survival outside the uterus. Before that a baby's anatomy has not had adequate time to develop properly. Ten 22-week preemies treated by Hoekstra have survived and four of those are severely handicapped. In 2000, Hoekstra cowrote with Daniel Taylor *Before Their Time: Lessons in Living from Those Born Too Soon* (InterVarsity Press). The book details the stories of six premature babies, some who lived and some who did not. A century ago such preemies died. They had no chance.

Many neonatologists won't even consider saving 22-week-old infants, who, if they survive, will typically end up staying in a hospital for three months at a cost of $400,000. They see no reason to hook up a child to expensive machines when the baby is likely to die anyway, or at least have physical handicaps. A *New England Journal of Medicine* study in 2000 found that half of the preemies born before the 26th week are disabled, with problems including seizures, mental retardation, and deafness.

Hoekstra himself has been roundly criticized by other neonatal doctors who view efforts to save extreme preemies as illogical and too expensive. Many physicians argue that medicine is a science dealing with practical logic, not nebulous miracles. Yet Hoekstra, who with his wife Claudia, a nurse, has three adult sons, sees events from a different perspective. Time and again Hoekstra has seen children survive who had been classified as hopeless. Standard answers in a scientific textbook ignore the reality of flesh and blood struggling for life.

"A lot of lives are saved that might otherwise have slipped into eternity with little notice," Hoekstra says.

While he concedes that those who survive have a much higher likelihood of debilitating problems such as brain damage, chronic lung disease, or vision problems, Hoekstra believes children who enter this world should be given a chance to make it.

Though he is a gifted pediatric specialist, Hoekstra understands that reliance on God is key to his work in the neonatal intensive care unit. In his care of a 20-ounce preemie, Hoekstra frankly tells parents that God has more to do with healing than anything he can do medically. Every time he scrubs up before examining a newborn, Hoekstra prays for the child and asks God for wisdom in how to proceed with treatment.

"Sometimes a baby will live or die depending on factors that have nothing at all to do with medicine," Hoekstra says. "Frequently it's not a question of skill, or of medical ethics, but simply a question of how one assesses the possibilities."

Many other doctors inquire starkly as to whether the parents want to save the child, assuming that the little body has no value if it is unwanted and has medical problems. Hoekstra believes that faith, prayer, and praising God have as much to do with survival as medical care. And the hope God offers often is the difference in getting the parents through as well.

For the passing of one crisis usually only brings temporary relief; likely there will be many other critical periods where life and death hang in the balance. The faith—and marriages—of parents is severely tested by such stress. Those who find strength in the Lord, learn to pray as never before and they pray more specifically, more confidently, and more boldly. There is little time for the trivial when one is pleading for the life of his or her baby. Just as the saying goes that there are no atheists in foxholes, there don't appear to be any in the neonatal intensive care unit either.

Hoekstra tries to maintain a balance between optimism and realism, a balance rooted in both his faith and medical experience. Even when everything is done for some babies they still die. Only God creates life and sustains it at such a young age. Hoekstra ultimately asks whether things are being done for the baby or simply to the baby. In nearly all cases, the Lord helps him realize whether it's time to discontinue treatment when a baby has made no effort to respond to medical treatment. There comes a point when the parents must decide to turn the baby over to God. "God is faithful in helping us make agonizing decisions," Hoekstra says.

"But if [people say] it must die because it is flawed, or because it will be difficult to care for or, God forbid, because it is too expensive, then something is wrong," Hoekstra says. "A baby's physical and cognitive life does not have to be perfect to have value and meaning." While such a baby can put the rest of the family under great stress, that child also can be a tremendous blessing and inspiration.

Hoekstra is grateful that God has equipped him to relate to people at the greatest crisis in their lives, for he notes that pain is not meant to be endured alone. God, who sent his Son to die an excruciating death, understands when people cry out in despair.

"I try to never forget that life is sacred," Hoekstra says. "It's a rare privilege to walk through the most critical period of the lives of these parents. To see how they respond to the situation is to learn what it means to have faith."

—m—

Jean Chamberlain-Froese

A Canadian doctor ministers to Uganda's mothers.

Grief sweeps over Dr. Jean Chamberlain Froese as she stands in the back hall of the university hospital in Kampala, Uganda. On a metal trolley before her lie five babies—three stillborn infants and two neonatal deaths. The wee bodies are wrapped in thin blankets. Name tags on each blanket identify the children's mothers.

The doctor reads the names and then thinks of another mother—one who died of pregnancy-related complications in the same hospital a few hours ago. Six needless deaths in one day, she thinks. If this happened in North America, authorities would launch an investigation and heads would roll. But here? Nothing happens.

Jean turns from the trolley with increased determination to save the lives of Uganda's mothers and children. A specialist in Obstetrics and Gynecology, she's committed to using her medical skills and her voice to make necessary changes, and she's succeeding. In 2005, Froese co-founded Save the Mothers, an international organization whose mission is to improve the quality of life for mothers in developing countries. If mothers enjoy good health, their children also benefit, she reasons. She bases her efforts on Proverbs 31:9: "Open thy mouth, judge righteously, and plead the cause of the poor and needy."

"As a follower of Christ, it's my responsibility to speak up for the rights of the destitute, for those who can't defend themselves," says Jean. "Ugandan mothers and children fall into this category." She quotes startling statistics to support her stance:

A woman in Africa has a 1 in 16 chance of dying from pregnancy-related complications—a stark contrast from the industrialized world where that figure is 1 in 4,000.

These medical difficulties claim the lives of approximately 17 Ugandan women each day, or 6,000 annually.

Most of these deaths are from severe bleeding. This could be remedied with a 33 cent medication, less than the price of a cup of coffee.

On the average, each woman who dies leaves four children behind. Those children are 3 to 10 times more likely to die within two years than those living with both parents.

Jean, an assistant professor at Canada's McMaster University, had practiced medicine in Zimbabwe, Zambia, Pakistan, and Russia before her first rural hospital posting in Uganda in 1998. Nothing had prepared her for the dire need she encountered: Water supply was sporadic. Forty patients shared one room. Flimsy mattresses covered the beds. Patients had to supply their own bedding, plastic gloves, and medications. Surgical equipment, including anesthesia, was either outdated or non-existent. Local doctors and nurses were overworked and often didn't want to be there, and their attitudes toward patients reflected their frustration. The combination of poor facilities and ill treatment frightened expectant mothers who, in turn, refused to visit the hospital for prenatal care or for their baby's safe delivery. This jeopardized the mothers' well-being, which in turn placed their babies and other children at risk.

Inadequate facilities and poor treatment contributed to the nation's high maternal mortality rate, but Jean soon discovered a deeper issue. "I realized that the root problem was how women are viewed within their community. If they're properly valued, then their communities will be willing to invest in medical services to ensure their health. Unfortunately, the opposite is usually true."

In this culture, Jean discovered, women are denied the freedom to make decisions about their own health. They must receive permission and money from their husbands before seeking medical care. If a woman needs a Caesarean section to deliver her child safely but her husband is not present to give permission, doctors refuse to operate. This usually results in the woman's death.

She also discovered cultural superstitions that endanger women and children. One myth says that women who need C-sections have been unfaithful to their husbands. That misunderstanding causes expectant mothers to stay far from hospitals. Another belief says that pregnancy is like a battle for each individual woman. She goes in and fights that battle. Some mothers win; some lose.

"You don't see the community rally around the woman if she has complications," says Jean. "No one says, 'Let's find transportation and take her to the hospital, and let's make sure the hospital provides decent care.' If the woman dies, it's because she lost her battle and she's considered a failure. Her family will spend one or two hundred dollars for her funeral, but no one donates a few dollars to save her life."

Because taking a rural woman to a hospital requires time, family members are often reluctant to help her. Jean says the common thought is, We can't afford to lose two weeks of work to save this mother's life. "She's not valued as highly important in the family, the one who raises the children and ensures their health. From an economic point of view, it makes sense to invest in a mother's health. It saves money in the long run, but people don't see it that way," she says. "People think short term: I'm going to lose two weeks now rather than If we don't commit two weeks now, we'll lose the mother of these children."

Jeans cites the story of a mother who hemorrhaged to death after childbirth. A film crew went to the funeral and interviewed the woman's 13-year-old daughter. "I don't know what to do," the girl said. "My mother was everything. She encouraged and comforted me. She taught me how to cook and do other everyday things. Now she's gone. I'll have to leave school to take over her responsibilities."

This scenario is commonplace. In many cases, the father sends his children to live with other families who are already struggling financially to feed and care for their own youngsters. The end result? Children's health is comprised, and medications are not affordable if diseases such as pneumonia or malaria strike them. "When the mother dies, the whole family suffers," says Jean, "and when the family breaks down, society follows. Satan loves to see this happen. But we can make a difference by praying intentionally and then doing something about the problem."

Following her own counsel, Jean and Dr. Florence Mirembi, former chair of the OB Gyn department at Uganda's Makerere University, established Save the Mothers. Their strategy is simple but effective: train leaders such as journalists, politicians, health workers, social workers, teachers, and pastors to educate others about the problem. In conjunction with the health program taught at the Ugandan Christian University, professionals earn a master's degree in Public Health Leadership. The course requires them to attend classes for three weeks, three times a year for two years. They must also complete a major project focused on safe motherhood in their own area of work.

"Basically, these leaders are being trained in preventative medicine," says Jean. "They're learning about the essentials needed to save a mother's life. But they're also learning to integrate their new knowledge with their daily lives. As a result of their influence, legislation has been passed to include maternal healthcare in the nation's budget and the public is learning about the problem through media coverage. Perhaps most importantly, these professionals are learning about the key to behavioral change – understanding that women are not just objects, they are valued people."

Alex, a student-leader enrolled in Save the Mothers, works for a non-governmental agency that serves people with HIV/AIDS. Upon completing one module, he returned to his village and met with women's groups to discuss their health issues. "A man meeting with women's groups is far from the norm in this culture, nevertheless the event was an overwhelming success," recalls Jean. "Alex later testified to being a changed person having taken the course. He said, 'I see women differently now.' That's exactly what I want to hear."

Her role as advocate for Ugandan mothers and children has given Jean a deeper understanding of God's love and concern for people within the context of a fallen world. "God values the poor and destitute, and He's moving people such as national professionals to get involved on their behalf. It's happening in , and we hope to establish Save the Mothers in as well. But we need more North Americans to come alongside and become advocates, too. Scripture says we're to pray to the Lord of the harvest to send forth laborers, so that's what we're doing. The North American Christian community can engage in this battle by learning more about the problem, praying for improvement, traveling to and other similar countries to see the struggle firsthand, financially supporting programs that care for the health of mothers and children, and telling others."

"Poor maternal care is a neglected tragedy," says Jean. "Rather than simply lamenting the issue, we, as believers, ought to cast a vision for a solution and then move forward on behalf of the poor and destitute."

~

Charles De Haan

A physician revives a traditional approach to health care.

Dr. Charles De Haan is a third-generation physician. His grandfather practiced medicine in in the early 1900s, but felt called to abandon his little black bag to study a big black leather-bound Bible. His grandfather's passion for the study of Scripture (coupled with his intrinsic concern for the spiritual well-being of people) resulted in the founding of Calvary Church in Grand Rapids and a media ministry known as The Radio Bible Class.

While one of Dr. M. R. De Haan's sons followed in his father's ministerial footsteps, another son took up the elder De Haan's medical mantle. It was into the latter son's family that Charles was born.

During the fifties and sixties, the life of a general practice physician in the western suburbs of Chicago was much like that of Marcus Welby, MD. Charles and his siblings would often accompany their doctor father as he called on his patients.

"Those occasions impacted me more than I realized at the time," Charles recalls. "Long before I had any interest in studying medicine or becoming a physician, I understood the significance of caring for someone in an environment in which they felt secure."

Still Charles did not grow up dreaming of stethoscopes and scalpels. It wasn't until his sophomore year at Taylor University he began to think increasingly about a future in medicine. He was surprised at his aptitude for math and science. For the first time in his life, Charles wondered if the Lord might indeed be calling him to practice medicine as a means of ministering the people's physical and spiritual needs.

After completing his undergraduate degree, the would-be doctor attended Chicago Medical School and then fulfilled his residency requirements at the University of Illinois family practice program in Rockford, Illinois. With a wife and three daughters to provide for, Charles settled in the Rockford area working in emergency medicine at a Swedish-American hospital. In addition to working in emergency medicine and becoming board certified, he worked in an occupational medicine program, also in Rockford.

After seven years of providing for the needs of walk-ins and critical-care patients at the ER, Charles began to wonder if there might be a better way of going about the task of doctoring. The discomfort and emotional trauma which required patients to seek urgent care was exacerbated by getting to the hospital. For elderly people in particular, having to wait in a crowded waiting room and then wade through the seemingly endless paperwork before being seen was incredibly stressful.

"In the emergency department where I worked, my colleagues and I saw many patients who would have been more appropriately cared for in their homes," Charles notes. "I couldn't help but think about the pattern my grandfather and my dad observed when meeting patients on their home turf. I wondered if a case couldn't be made for returning to the familiar practice that had been deemed obsolete."

Charles's inclinations led him to do some investigation. The studies he researched validated his hunches. They showed that 85 percent of patients in the ER didn't need to be there. They could just as easily have been treated in the comfort of their own home. Relying on his father's experiences and his own research, he evaluated the strengths and weaknesses of house calls in light of today's portable technology. In 1993, with the courage of a pioneer, Charles devised a new paradigm that he called his "back to the future" approach to home healthcare.

"In an increasingly impersonal culture, people can easily feel more like a number than an individual," Charles admits. "House calling is much more personal. My patients get to know me better and I get to know them better. What is more, their trust level goes up. They are impressed about doctors who will make the extra effort to care for them in this special way."

Based in Northern Illinois, this unique program is the first fulltime house call practice in the Midwest. It currently covers ten counties between Chicago and Rockford and primarily serves the elderly, disabled, and those who are housebound. A central office staffed by a fulltime nurse and administrative assistants attend to the initial calls for help and schedule visits. In addition they communicate with the families, dispatch home health care workers, and support the doctors in the field. On average 600 house calls are made each month.

"Essentially, our practice actually is just like any other primary care practice," Charles explains.

"The primary difference is that we see the patients in their home. But there are other differences. We also attempt to bring a spiritual component to our care."

As a responsible physician Charles insists that the physical health of his patients is his primary concern. But as a committed Christian and active member at Harvest Bible Church in Rockford, he launched the MD at Home program assuming that "in home" care would lend itself to serving the "whole" person. With that assumption, Matthew 25:36 was identified as a theme verse. Jesus' explanation that those who visit the sick and needy are actually ministering unto him seemed to capture both the physical and spiritual dimension of the program's non-traditional approach.

"Because we see people who are in such great physical need in their familiar surrounding, we have many opportunities to discuss more than just their health concerns," Charles observes. "Given the informal setting, it is only natural to discuss their spiritual and social concerns with them. We have had many opportunities to pray with our patients and have even prayed with some to receive the Lord."

In the decade since MD at Home began, Charles has become more adept at recognizing the Lord's presence while making house calls. As he's reviewed patients' charts, he's been able to trace the hand of God in unexpected ways. For example, while calling on one patient with Alzheimer's disease, he seized upon a brief lucid period of time and led her to profess faith in the Lord. "This specific example happened as my nurse practitioner was doing the house call in my absence," he recalls. "We found out later that the Christian Medical Society, of which I am a member, had us listed to pray for on the day when the patient professed faith in the Lord." On another occasion while stopping to check on a patient, he ended up participating in a home Bible Study.

In addition to the medical charts, Charles and his colleagues (there are five physicians that work with MD at Home) keep, they also make mental notes of the more unusual settings in which they've found themselves.

Given the severity of Midwestern winters, MD at Home doctors are often forced to navigate icy roads to reach a patient's home. On more than one occasion they have had to shovel a path from an unplowed driveway to the front door. But that isn't the only shoveling these doctors have been called to do in order to render service.

As might be expected, the homes of elderly house-bound patients are quite unlike a sterile hospital setting where everything is clean and organized. The homes and apartments of those who live alone are often cluttered and impassable. Before tending to the needs of the patient they've driven to see, these "physicians on wheels" have had to clear paths through hallways stacked two feet high with newspapers, magazines, boxes, and litter.

Once while going to see an elderly woman patient in 's inner city, Charles was approached by a rough looking gang. He nervously told the apparent leader he was a doctor and stated that he was seeing one of the elderly women in the neighborhood. Amazingly, the gang stepped aside and let him pass. As he cautiously made his way to the graffiti sprayed housing project, he worried about his car on the street. Although it was locked, there was expensive medical equipment that could easily be stolen from it, including an ultrasound and an EKG machine. Charles whispered a prayer as he entered the run-down building and cared for his patient with sensitivity. As he exited the building, Charles noticed the gang was waiting for him.

"My hands were sweaty when I saw them again," Charles recalls. "But I had nothing to worry about. They had hung around just to ask me some medical advice about one of their members who had AIDS. And they had been the means the Lord used to answer my prayer about my car. Without me knowing it, they had been guarding it."

Charles admits that he would not continue with his innovative approach to medical care were it not for his God-given desire to minister to patients' physical as well as spiritual needs. The complexity and inconvenience of the "house call" practice prevents most new doctors from even considering it. But he hopes those who view their medical calling as a ministry will at least look for ways to increase their personal contact with patients.

"Our calling as physicians gives us the privilege of responding to obvious needs of those who look to us," Charles contends. "But that is just the start. A doctor-patient relationship opens the door to share at a more personal level about less obvious needs our patients have. For me, making house calls in Jesus' name provides me with one open door after another."

CHAPTER 15
Redemptive Communicators:

—⚏—

MATH & SCIENCE

David Block

A Jewish astronomer's spiritual odyssey

The year was 1969. The event had been advertised on the radio again and again. I arose at four o'clock in the morning and watched a blazing comet with utter awe, as its tail stretched across the eastern skies. My love affair with astronomy had begun.

South African astronomer Jack Bennett, who discovered the comet and whose name the heavenly object bore, became my hero. The next day I telephoned him and asked him rather timidly, "May I meet with you?" To my surprise he said, "Yes, do come over." And it was really then that the little hidden flame which had been ignited began burning to understand the universe.

Shortly after this my father bought me a four-and-a-half inch reflector telescope. That was no little thing for a teenager. With that incredible instrument I could start to look at planets like Saturn and at some of the nebulae in which stars are born.

I wanted to pursue studies in astronomy and my father was my biggest supporter. Leon Block always encouraged me to question things, to look beyond the ordinary and to make up my own mind. After all, we were Jews and that was part of our tradition as well.

My Jewish Upbringing

Both of my parents' Orthodox Jewish families have their roots in Lithuania. And we certainly kept to all the traditions as well: My mother would light the Sabbath candles and we would have a traditional Sabbath meal together. I went to synagogue both on Friday night and Saturday. We kept Passover. I fasted on Yom Kippur. I was bar mitzvah. We were practicing Jews. And I did all the things expected of a good Jewish boy. Actually, I felt that I was doing the best that I knew how to live out my Jewish faith.

Now this didn't mean that I was unquestioning when it came to the things of God. On the contrary, I'd listen in synagogue as the rabbis expounded how God was a personal God and how God would speak to Moses, to Abraham, to Isaac, and to Jacob, and wonder how I fit into all of it. And by the time I entered university I became concerned over the fact that I had no assurance that God was indeed a personal God. I did know that he was a historical God and that he did deliver our people from the hands of Pharaoh. But that seemed far removed from me in this scientific age. Those were "stories," as it were.

Where was the personality and the vibrancy of a God who could speak to David Block? If God is truly God, I reasoned, then why had he suddenly changed his character? The seeds of doubt were sprouting.

University Years

In order to follow my interest in astronomy I entered the Witwatersrand University in Johannesburg (South Africa). I sought a Bachelor of Science degree in applied mathematics and computer science. As a professional astronomer, a background in mathematics and statistics would be essential.

While still a student, I was appointed to be a "demonstrator" on the staff—in other words, I would help students with their tutorial problems on a formal basis. And while a student I also became quite friendly with Lewis Hurst, then professor of genetics and of medicine. He had a great interest in astronomy, if only from an amateur point of view, and he asked if I would give him individual lessons.

Week by week, Lewis and I would sit around the table and I would discuss the complexities of the cosmos with him and also explain fundamental terms in astronomy such as "black holes" and "quasars." It was a full but private course I was giving him.

The friendship grew and I started sharing my feelings about the cosmos with him—that it is so beautiful, that God is so creative, that He's made this stunning world. I even shared my doubts with him:

"Are we, as Shakespeare said, just as a 'fleeting shadow to appear and then disappear'? What is our purpose for living? What's the *raison d'etre* for being here? Is there a Designer out there?"

Lewis listened thoughtfully and then spoke, "David, there is an answer to all your questions."

"You know, Lewis, what does concern me is that the universe is so large, it's so immense. Do we go anywhere when we die?"

"There's an answer to all the questions you're asking," Lewis repeated. "Would you be willing—I know you come from an Orthodox Jewish family—but would you be willing to meet with a dear friend of mine, the Reverend Mr. John Spyker?"

My parents had taught me to seek answers where they may be found and so I consented to meet with this Christian minister. Of course, in my heart, when I had put my telescope on Saturn, and saw it in all its majesty and splendor—its rings simply encircling that globe—I just knew that there was a Great Designer. In fact, I knew there must be a personal God.

The Reverend Mr. Spyker read to me from the New Testament book of Romans where Paul says that Y'shua (Jesus) is a stumbling block to Jewish people, but that those who would believe in Y'shua would never be ashamed.

Suddenly it all became very clear to me: Y'shua had fulfilled the messianic prophecies in the Hebrew Scriptures, such as where the Messiah would be born and how he was to die. While my people were still waiting for the Messiah, I suddenly knew that I knew that I knew that I knew that Jesus was the Messiah and is the Messiah. And I surrendered my heart and my soul to him that day. That was in October of 1976.

I gave Judaism a chance and I accepted Him who is fully, fully Jewish. Paul, before he believed in Jesus, was a student of the great rabbi, Gamaliel. He was a Hebrew of the Hebrews. He had studied. He had examined. Yet, when Paul met the Master face to face, the Master mastered him. The Master mastered me as well.

Faith and Science

It might seem strange to some that a scientist and a Jew could come to faith in Jesus. But faith is never a leap into the dark. It is always based on evidence. All people believe and all scientists believe. They don't all believe in a personal God, of course, but each one of us uses our own measure of faith. Each one of us has a personal world system, a personal belief system.

As a scientist, I always think logically and I reason things out. That was how my whole search for God began. I looked through my telescope at Saturn and said to myself, Isn't there a great God out there? And when I studied relativity, relativistic astrophysics, cosmology and all these beautiful areas of mathematics, they pointed me to the fact that this whole universe is masterfully made, finely-tuned and controlled by the Great Designer. The logical next step was to want to meet this Designer face-to-face.

Among astronomers today there is great theistic sentiment, where even if scientists don't say Jesus has made the universe, they are coming to the very distinct conclusion that the universe is not an accident. The "Big Bang" is not viewed as not a cosmological firecracker. As the physicist Freeman Dyson put it, the universe seemed to be acting in anticipation for the appearance of mankind.

So it is on the basis of logic that we can understand that we live in a universe made by a personal God. It's logic from start to finish.

When it comes to God, many scientists lean toward assumptions that are philosophically comfortable to them. For example, in the "Big Bang" universe there is an unverifiable assumption called the principle of homogeneity, which asserts that on a large scale there is "no preferred center"—each point is equivalent in every sense to every other point. This, then, is a drastic departure from the cozy framework early cosmologists had worked with in their geocentric universe models.

Let me explain: If we go back to the 1500s, before the impact of the work of Copernicus, the worldview of the universe was a geocentric one. The earth was the center and the sun went around the earth as did all the stars, and to many it was a very reassuring ideal to adopt. In 1543 Copernicus' *De Revolutionibus* was published and we perceived ourselves to be living in a heliocentric world, (although Ptolemy's earth-centered system was still taught at Harvard University in the first years after its founding in 1636). Mankind was dethroned from his central position in the universe.

Many astronomers have gone to extremes by saying we are simply a "zero" in this large cosmos. After all, there are 100,000 million stars in our Milky Way galaxy. That can make us feel very lonely and unimportant in the light of all the immensity. Yet a simple study shows the opposite is true.

The universe has not always existed. It had a definite beginning. God expanded our early universe at just the critical rate to avoid recollapse. Galaxies and stars then formed, but one must realize that half the stars in the night sky are members of binary or multiple star systems and are therefore unable to support life. (No stable planetary orbits could exist around such star systems.) Of the remaining half there are about 30 parameters which must be met in order for them to support life. With billions and billions of stars, it is improbable that all the conditions which must be met for the existence of life exist elsewhere. I would not be surprised if we were the only intelligent life species in the entire universe. In fact, leading evolutionists, such as Dobzhansky and others have agreed that there has not been enough time for mankind to have assembled spontaneously within the time span of our universe.

We have astronomical evidence that demands a verdict. And I have examined this evidence, not from an emotional point of view, but from a logical point of view. We have historical evidence that Jesus, the Jew, lived and died and rose again from the dead. When Albert Einstein was asked by a reporter whether he accepted the historical existence of Jesus, he responded, "Unquestionably! No one can read the Gospels without feeling the actual presence of Jesus. His personality pulsates in every word. No myth is filled with such life. I am enthralled by the luminous figure of the Nazarene."

To the person who is seriously seeking today I would say, read the gospels from an objective point of view, as Albert Einstein did. As Isaac Newton did. Don't let your emotions override or cloud your decision.

Seek after truth and don't let anyone make up your mind for you. It is far too important. It does matter what you believe.

—⚬—

Raymond Damadian

His invention revolutionized medicine and punctuated his faith in God.

Raymond Damadian realizes he could not have invented the magnetic resonance imaging (MRI) scanner, which has revolutionized the field of diagnostic medicine, without God's intervention. In a critical juncture in his business and personal life, Damadian chose to follow God's path rather than strike out on his own. The Lord has blessed him for his decision.

Damadian grew up in Queens, one of the five boroughs of New York City, and attended a church that taught virtue but did not emphasize the saving grace of Jesus Christ. It was clear from the beginning that Damadian was intelligent, and it showed in several of his pursuits, including music, sports, and academics. He studied violin at the Juilliard School of Music and received a bachelor of science degree in mathematics from the University of Wisconsin in 1956.

At the invitation of his friend—and future wife Donna Terry—Damadian attended the Billy Graham Crusade in Madison Square Garden in 1957. At the time he was a tennis pro. But the simple salvation message stirred his heart. "I went forward, and I was profoundly impressed by what Billy Graham had to say," Damadian recalls. At that point Damadian realized that simply being a good person was not a ticket to heaven. "As far as I was concerned, I was doing everything right. I was a good student, I did what I thought I ought to do in terms of being careful about the needs of others and I didn't have any special greedy ambitions. I thought I was a fine chap, which is maybe the most common failing of all for those who think they are living the Christian life, and that I could satisfy the Master's expectations of me with good works. But Scripture does not teach that."

Damadian and Terry married in 1960, just after he received his medical degree from Albert Einstein College of Medicine in New York. Forgetting about athletics and music, Damadian now focused on inventing a machine that could detect human cancer cells. Damadian rose in the academic world, doing work at Washington University, Harvard, and State University of New York. At such institutions Damadian came in contact with several strong-minded atheists, and he slowly drifted away from God. His training in medicine and physics led him to develop a new theory of the living cell, the Ion Exchanger Resin Theory. He then desperately pushed to make the MRI scanner a reality as a means of detecting disease. "We were climbing the summit of trying to make magnets scan the human body, which the great majority of the scientific world said was impossible," he says.

"And there were a lot of technological problems to be overcome. So I was working night and day, and at that point, that's all that mattered." Most of his fellow academicians in the secular scientific world had no belief in God. Instead, these university professors believed they fully understood the world, it was under their control and God didn't play a role, neither in creating the earth or seeing that it kept going. In short, He was not needed.

Asking God for guidance was not really a priority for Damadian at that point. "I was foolish," he says. "I had been taken in by the arguments of the secular scientific world, and the principle damage was the acceptance of evolution." Looking back, Damadian sees how such thinking could be the linchpin in destroying faith. "Once you destroy the foundation of Genesis, then all the rest of Scripture has to be qualified, and you don't have much left," he says. "Any time you don't like what something says, you write it off as allegorical or symbolical and you skirt the discomfort off confronting it."

By 1977, his life had drifted out of control because of his consuming desire to succeed in inventing the MRI scanner. "Because of the ill-begotten attitudes of the secular scientific world, I drifted away considerably," he remembers. "At one point telling my technician, to her horror, that there was no God." At the same time, with typically rebellious teenagers in his house, Damadian felt further alienated from God. "I wasn't the priest of the home that I should've been," he says.

Fortunately for Damadian, his family—his wife and his parents—still believed in God and believed God could redeem circumstances. They continued praying for him to return to the Lord, realizing that his accomplishments would only have lasting value if directed by God. Damadian went to his knees to seek the Lord's direction.

In July 1977, Damadian and his team achieved the first successful MRI scan of the human body. The following year he founded FONAR Corporation in Melville, New York, to manufacture the MRI scanner, which is now used in hundreds of medical institutions around the world. The MRI produces images of the interior of the body that are far more detailed than was possible with X-ray devices.

Since that time, Damadian has prayed and read Scripture every day. At his company, there is a prayer meeting every morning for employees who want to participate. "We try to do what the Lord would have us do in all that we do, which in business is not easy," he says.

Damadian is still facing cutthroat competition over patents. FONAR's rivals are huge multinational corporations General Electric, Siemens, Hitachi, and Toshiba. "These are companies we have to go toe-to-toe with or not eat," Damadian says. "We've looked to Malachi 3:11, which says 'For My people I will stop the devourer, and you will have the fruit of your vine.' That's the problem we've been facing as a small company. We need to be able to use our own seed corn, but the giants eat our seed corn as fast as we produce it."

FONAR now has 650 employees, including two of Damadian's sons. Timothy is an executive and Jevan is an electrical engineer. The youngest of three children, daughter Keira, is in nursing school and plans to use that training in missions. She has been on short-term mission trips to Burundi, Thailand and Mexico.

As he grows older, Damadian sees God's purpose in allowing him to invent the MRI. "I can be a voice within the scientific world and I am in a position to say that the biblical account of origins is the correct one," he says. "I am in a position to get people to take notice where they would normally not have any exposure at all. It's come to pass that God has made it possible for me to be a witness on an important subject."

Indeed, President Ronald Reagan bestowed the National Medal of Technology upon Damadian. And he has been inducted into the National Inventors Hall of Fame.

Unlike many of his colleagues, Damadian knows that God and science are compatible. "The greatest scientists of the nineteenth century and the early part of the twentieth century were all very godly men," he says. "Unless you have your eye on the Almighty, there's nothing directing you and encouraging you to take the daring steps to think big. Fear of the unknown is a strong current, especially when the fear of embarrassment is even greater. Only those who can trust in the Lord get beyond these fears to attempt big things. So many of the great accomplishments in science by people like Louis Pasteur, Isaac Newton and James Clerk Maxwell were made because these men were not turned inward to the shrunken confines of the human mind." Such thinkers, Damadian says, believed, as Johannes Kepler put it, that it was their duty to "think God's thoughts after Him" or as Newton said, "All of my discoveries came in response to prayer."

—⁊⁊—

LeRoy Dorminy

A veterinarian reaches people through animal science.

Dr. Leroy Dorminy may not always look like a man on a serious mission. He often wears plaid shirts, blue jeans, and walking shoes—suitable attire for a veterinarian like him who may be called upon to treat a dog with worms one minute and deliver a calf the next. But despite his modest appearance, Dorminy is a man who is serious about his vocation and about his faith in Christ.

Dorminy is the founder of Christian Veterinary Mission, (www.christianvetmission.org). The purpose of the non-profit organization is to challenge, empower, and facilitate veterinarians to serve others though their profession, living out their Christian faith on the job. The work is Christ-centered and veterinary focused.

CVM encourages members to be involved in ministry to the people of other countries. They do this through a variety of outreaches that involve evangelism, education, encouragement, modeling, and prayer. As the Lord himself, the mission seeks to address people's physical and spiritual needs.

So far, the organization has established outreach programs in more than 35 countries, including Haiti, Bolivia, Nepal, Bangladesh, Cambodia, Sudan and Kenya.

"One of the most amazing places I've gone into is Mongolia," Dorminy says. "It's astounding how CVM has been able to meet the needs in that area. Most of the people there are herders, of one form or another—sheep, goats, horses. They have lots of animals."

By teaching the natives of Mongolia how to better care for their livestock, CVM has been able to establish a broad-based ministry in the region. "Our professional skills have allowed us to minister to these people in a way that I never thought possible," Dorminy says.

They are currently 22 veterinarians serving through long-term missions for CVM, typically via three-year terms. And last year 125 veterinarians served on short-term overseas missions trips with CVM.

The vision for sending veterinarians into undeveloped countries as lay ministers came to Dorminy in 1975 during an international conference that his denomination held in Stockholm. More than 10,000 people from over 84 different countries were in attendance. Dorminy recalls the moment when the Lord first impressed him with the idea of a Christian veterinary mission.

"We were in a small Bible Study group and our discussion leader asked a woman from an emerging nation in Africa how Christians of the developed world could help her people. She replied, 'Come and teach us your skills that we may do things for ourselves.'"

Dorminy was struck by the profound simplicity of her suggestion.

"I was 53 when I attended that convention. I went looking for something. I wasn't completely satisfied with what I was doing. This lady's comment weighed on me. I was really bothered by it," Dorminy recalls.

The woman's challenge continued to gnaw at him even after he returned to his practice in rural Georgia. In response, he volunteered his services to a mission board for overseas service and soon found himself in Dominican Republic, where he performed short-term mission work alongside Charley Purtle, an agricultural missionary from Oklahoma. Purtle had requested help from someone with animal husbandry and veterinary skills. Dorminy was apparently God's answer to Purtle's plea. The experience proved to be life-changing for the former.

"That was the most satisfying two weeks I've ever spent, before or since," Dorminy claims. The opportunity to use his professional skills to minister to people in a practical hands-on fashion stirred something deep inside of Dorminy. The idea of getting more veterinarians into the fields as missionaries to needy people became an all-consuming goal. One that would not let him rest.

"I became less and less interested in my practice and more and more focused on CVM," Dorminy says. He wasn't intimidated by the idea of doing something that hadn't been done before.

"I'm a Type-A person. I don't go around many obstacles—I go through them," he says. So he hired another veterinarian to help run his Georgia office And he spent three or four hours a night on the phone, raising support and interest in his vision.

"Every night I would work these leads. In nine months time, I had 300 people with a real interest in CVM." Some of those original 300 folks continue to support the ministry today, Dorminy, now in his eighties, notes with pride.

"Not all Christians are interested in missions. That I was able to identify 300 people that were, in that short of a time period, is really amazing."

A native Georgian, Dorminy came to know Christ at an early age. "I could go to the exact spot where I was sitting when the preacher was preaching in 1935," Dorminy says, recalling the meeting where he professed faith in Christ.

It was a small country church in Enigma, Georgia, just outside Tifton. The preacher had delivered a fiery sermon.

"He cautioned us that we needed to prepare ourselves for eternity. I remember him asking if we knew how long eternal life is," Dorminy recalls.

Dorminy, then 12, straightened his back when the preacher explained that in the time it would take a bird to move the earth to the moon, flying back and forth carrying one grain of sand at a time, eternity would just be beginning.

"I didn't go down to the altar because I was frightened. I went down because God's Spirit had touched my heart and I wanted to prepare myself for an eternity with Him," Dorminy recalls.

A stint in the Navy during World War 2 helped nurture Dorminy's desire to work outdoors with the animals he'd loved since boyhood.

"I was so tired of living on a steel ship for two years, I wanted to get outdoors. I liked science. And I had always liked animals. I thought being a veterinarian would enable me to combine those two," he observes.

But he was nourishing another love as well—his relationship with God. He believes God has endowed each of us with a special gift that He intends for us to use for His name's sake.

"One verse I've always utilized is 1 Peter 4:10. Each of us is called upon to use our gifts in dispensing God's grace to others. I've often said every one of us has special skills. I think we are to use those special skills in God's Kingdom service, to help others with physical needs and to be a witness through that," Dorminy says.

And, he believes no one is better suited to helping underdeveloped nations and their people than veterinarians.

"Veterinarian medicine is a tough profession," Dorminy explains. "For a lot of reasons. You work with many species of animals—we can't focus on one. It's not very lucrative work, compared to human medicine. Vets have to be practical folks and they have to be problem-solvers. I've done caesarean sections in a stall covered in manure and saved both the cow and the calf. Conditions in veterinary practice are seldom ideal and that is the same for missionaries overseas if there is anything that describes missions, that's it—the need and ability to be practical and to utilize what you have. Veterinarians know how to do that."

CVM folks are doing life-saving work around the world, both for animals and for people. Before CVM arrived, Haiti was in dire need of skilled veterinarians, Dorminy says. "They only had about five vets in a country of five million people."

One of the ministry's goals has been to train locals as veterinary technicians. It gives the people a skill and helps the economy of the community as well by keeping their livestock healthy.

"These people can fulfill a need and perform useful skills," Dorminy observes, noting that CVM has trained more than a thousand such technicians in Haiti alone.

One day while feasting on a lunch of rice and beans with Keith Flannagan, one of CVM's missionaries, Dorminy asked the natives what they thought of the veterinarians' work in their country. A dark-skinned man put down his bowl and spoke up.

"Well, to be quite truthful with you, it's allowed me to make a living for my family. And more importantly, before I got into this program, I was lost. I didn't know what I was going to do. I'd lost all hope in life. This program has given me hope."

Dorminy has heard similar testimonials in every country in which CVM ministers. "In Nepal, veterinarian Karen Stoffer has been ministering to women. Nepal is one of the most notorious countries in the world for mistreatment of women. They are treated as mere chattel."

Dorminy said many times women are assigned away in marriage, often before they turn 14 years of age. "They are slaves to their own families," he says. "It's horrible to have to be married to a person you don't love and forced to have his children."

Stoffer befriended such a girl. When her husband ran off and left her with two children to care for, Stoffer stepped in to aid the distraught girl. "Karen was able to help this girl gain a skill and knowledge. She taught her how to read and write, which then enabled her to get a job to support her two boys," Dorminy says. "Karen was able to salvage this lady's life and the lives of her two boys by telling her about the hope Christ offers. I seldom read Karen's letters without shedding a tear. She writes the truth of what she encounters," Dorminy says.

It's truly gratifying to use one's professional skills to help people with physical, emotional and spiritual problems, he adds. "Our profession allows us to minister to people in many ways. It allows us to share hope with the world."

Hope is what Christ gave each of us when He suffered that painful death upon the Cross. Hope for a life that outlasts suffering, sorrow, or shame. A life that will last far longer than it takes for a bird to fly to the moon and back. A life that will last vastly longer than any of our sufferings. An eternal life.

That's the message that CVM strives to bring to the people of this world whose lives are touched daily by tremendous sorrows. "Everybody's needs to have hope," Dorminy says. "It really touches me that we've been a catalyst for change in people's lives. They have some hope because of what CVM has been able to accomplish."

Sometimes people ask Dorminy how it is he's able to motivate veterinarians to leave the USA and devote their lives to working in underdeveloped nations. He gives the same answer every time.

"They don't do it because of me. They do it because of their commitment to the Lord and their tenacity as veterinarians," he says. "Being a vet steels them and makes them persevere. They rise to the challenge that mission work presents."

They've also learned that the best way to minister the Love of Christ to another person is one-on-one. "If you are going to witness to somebody, you have to be involved with that person's life." Dorminy remarks. "You have to earn the right to witness to them. CVM does that by helping people with their animals. It allows us to minister in unbelievable ways."

—⁂—

George Barna

A statistician aims to make the church more self-aware.

During his childhood in Princeton, New Jersey, George Barna attended mass every Sunday, served as an altar boy, and went through catechism and confirmation classes. By the time he went to premarital counseling sessions, Barna wondered why his church believed certain tenets and performed certain rituals. The priest advised him to stop asking such probing questions, to just accept what the church teaches, and to believe that everything would work out fine.

He didn't realize it at the time, but Barna would go on to make it his life's work to examine the intricacies of Christian belief and behavior, often uncovering that what people claim with their mouths doesn't match how they act.

Barna, in graduate school as he prepared to wed in 1978, didn't think the priest's counsel to turn off his intellect sounded too reasonable. He and his new wife, Nancy, decided to go on their own quest to truly discover God.

They found a small Bible-believing church, where the pastor embarked on a pursuit they never had witnessed before: verse by verse detailed explanation of Scripture.

After a few weeks of the couple's attendance, the preacher came calling to the Barna home. He made a presentation of the Gospel message, ending with an invitation that they receive Jesus as Lord and Savior.

"I said I didn't think so," Barna recalls. "But I told the pastor if Jesus is as great as He claimed, I'd give Jesus a month to prove it." The preacher reluctantly agreed, provided that Barna attend Sunday morning church services, attend Wednesday evening Bible studies, read the Bible daily beginning with the Gospel of John, pray daily that God would reveal

Himself, and allow the pastor to visit him weekly.

Before the end of the month, Barna had committed his life to Jesus.

Yet within a few months, Barna learned he needed to adhere to a set of religious rules to be a "real Christian." The minister told Barna he must look like a believer, and that meant shaving off his beard and wearing his hair in a specific style. Barna protested, but his arguments fell on deaf ears.

While many new Christians might have walked away from the faith under such circumstances, Barna determined to find another church.

"I had grown in my relationship with Christ and realized that even if whacky stuff goes on in the way people live and the manmade rituals they practice, Jesus is still real," Barna says.

Meanwhile, after earning two master's degrees from Rutgers University, Barna began working as a pollster for political candidates. Later, as the lone Christian at a Los Angeles media research marketing firm, Barna received the assignment of helping several television ministries determine what worked and what didn't on the air.

That got Barna to thinking about full-time work in the field of studying Christian attitudes and actions. Although the Gallup Poll had long asked general religious questions, no one, until Barna came along, tracked in-depth responses about evangelical spiritual beliefs and behavior.

In 1984, he opened his own marketing research firm, The Barna Research Group, then based in Glendale, California. (The company since has expanded and been renamed The Barna Group and relocated to Ventura, California.) In the intervening years he has continued to hone his skills and methods in order to provide current, reliable, and accurate bite-sized information to ministries wanting to make strategic marketing decisions.

Early on, many hailed Barna as an innovative wunderkind, delivering much-needed tell-it-like-it-is research on church health, leadership, and trends. But by the time he wrote his third book, Barna's detractors had grown vociferous, suggesting that relying on researcb, marketing, and strategic plans to communicate the Gospel amounted to secular selling out.

"Marketing in and of itself has no moral content," Barna notes. "It's just a process in which connections are made with people and each other's needs are met through a transaction."

Despite the reservations of skeptics, many more people thought Barna's numbers, guided by Biblical principles, made sense in advancing the work of God's kingdom. They understood that marketing research figures, if used wisely, could be a tool, just as preaching is. Many recognized that research can help the church, in response to Jesus' words, function in a culture of wolves with the wisdom of serpents (see Matt. 10:16).

Barna's influence continued to grow. His work helped pastors become more realistic and objective about the actual state of affairs their congregations, rather than assuming everything would run smoothly perpetually.

Along the way, as he publishes research findings, conducts all-day seminars for church leaders, and writes books, Barna has become a widely quoted authority—both inside and outside the church—on Christianity. His three-dozen books include best sellers such as *The Frog in the Kettle, ,* and *Transforming Children into Spiritual Champions.*

He also has done much to challenge people to scrutinize the depth of their spirituality.

While a Christian remnant lives faithfully and behaves ethically, Barna has reams of data showing that a lot of Americans think they are going to heaven even though they have no relationship with the Lord.

"Jesus died on the cross not to make people feel happy or to fill church auditoriums, but so that we can be transformed and completely committed to serve Him and other people," Barna says. "If Christ truly lives in us and the Holy Spirit truly guides us, there should be evidence of progress toward a greater state of holiness. It's a continual journey."

At times Barna becomes disappointed with those who are unwilling to examine whether their practices are truly Biblical. Their criticisms can be disheartening, but Barna continues his work, guided by the belief that calls His people to evaluate themselves and that sometimes, as with the Old Testament prophets, He calls individuals to issue this call to the current culture.

"It's never really concerned me whether people accept what I put out there because I'm doing this for God," Barna says. "Truth and transformation always have been my main focus."

But he still finds a ready audience willing to listen to his warnings. His family often accompanies him when he travels for his busy speaking schedule. He and his wife, Nancy, have three adopted daughters: Samantha, Corban, and Christine.

Barna continues to keep challenging ministry and institutional leaders, even when they wish he would go away with his challenging forecast for the American church.

"I can't worry about my critics," Barna says. "Jesus expects me to use all the years and the resources He gave me to facilitate transformation."

CHAPTER 16
Redemptive Communicators:
—m—
ENGINEERING

R. G. LeTourneau
A successful engineer's earthly business had a heavenly motive.

During much of his life, Robert Gilmour (Bob) LeTourneau was indeed widely known as a "mover of men and mountains." For 25 years he drove or flew across and flew to several foreign countries, speaking in churches and auditoriums large and small, usually about six times a week.

He called himself "just a mechanic whom the Lord has blessed" and enthusiastically proclaimed to listeners that God needs business people as partners as well as preachers. Many began a partnership with God, especially after LeTourneau helped establish the Christian Business Men's Committee movement flourishing on a national and international basis. In his later years, he kept only 10 percent of his income and gave 90 percent to the Lord's work, and this undoubtedly moved many to tithe.

A blue-collar worker in his younger years, he had worked as an iron molder, a brick layer, a gold miner, a stump puller, an irrigation ditch digger, and an auto mechanic. But in his thirties he began to build earth-moving machines. His firm, R.G. LeTourneau, Inc., built huge earth movers that enabled him to "take part in and contribute to the development of those great, heavy construction machines that have helped produce our twentieth century," he claimed during the late 1950s.

His eight-wheeled digger could quickly produce work that previously had required thousands of hours in manual labor. Instead of men pushing 100-pound wheelbarrow loads to accomplish a task, the operator of the digger would push a button and the machine would pick up the loads of 1,500 wheelbarrows, rolling them off at 15 miles per hour (mph) instead of 2 mph.

When the Allies invaded the beaches of Normandy, France on June 6, 1944, Le Tourneau earth movers and other machinery accompanied the great invasion force. His equipment constituted about 50 percent of the equipment used in combat during World War 2.

"On D-Day, as on islands in the Pacific, the bulldozers wallowed ashore to push aside the tank traps and barbed wire, and then rush, with upraised blades fending off machine gun bullets, to storm pill boxes, burying the fire slits under tons of dirt and smothering the gun crews that refused to flee or surrender," Le Tourneau wrote. "They sliced through hedgerows of Normandy, cut new approaches to bombed-out bridges, plowed through the debris of bombed cities, and had a field day tearing up the dragon's teeth, gun emplacements, and pill boxes of the 'impregnable' Siegfried Line. One bulldozer, we were told, did the work a thousand men did with shovels in World War I," according to his autobiography.

Bob LeTourneau was born November 30, 1888 on a farm near Richford, Vermont, and was named after his father's best friend, Robert Gilmour. He grew to become a "restless, inquisitive, energetic, determined, and ambitious boy," according to his mother. His brothers had less-biased opinions of him, describing him as "destructive, willful, stubborn, and fanatically determined to amount to nothing."

He invented what might be called his first earth-moving machine when he was 12, a heifer-pulled snow plow to ease his job of plowing snow. It was a V-shaped board with curving sides to shove snow to the side and make a path. It might have worked had not the heifer kicked it and him before he could really find out, curing him forever of his reliance on animal power of any kind.

That summer Bob had an accident that revealed what a wild kid he was. He swam out to a rock some 100 yards from shore. To return to shore, he dived off the rock and hit a rock he hadn't seen, and was groggy until the 50-degree water brought him to. He made it to shore before rescuers could reach him, and ran home and collapsed. It took 16 stitches to sew up the gash in his head. His father's comment hurt him: "Only fools jump in where angels fear to tread."

In his early teens, young Bob clashed with his father, and sparks would fly. Dad prayed for Bob and worked on him harder than his brothers and sisters combined, serving to make Bob feel picked on. When he was 13, after his dad became furious with him for cutting up fence posts for firewood, and called him too dumb to recognize a fence post when he saw one, Bob ran away. He spent that cold fall night in a ravine and wondered how his father would feel when they found his frozen body.

Hunger pangs the next morning sent him a mile away to the home of a widow, Mrs. Spango, for whom he had done chores, and he became her hired man after she talked with his father. She was harder on him than Dad, making him wash until he felt his skin was wearing thin. He began milking cows before sunup and hauled in wood to carry the stove through the night. She pushed him out the door for school despite heavy snow, and he had to walk twice as far as he did while living at home. "There were no dumb Swedes in my family," Mrs. Spango declared, "and I won't have one now even if he does have a French name."

Thanksgiving came and Bob's sister Mattie coaxed him to join the family at the home of an aunt and uncle. While he was there, a heavy snow fell. Bob found himself following his father home as he broke a trail.

"In the morning I helped with chores, and discovered my father could make a fair batch of pancakes," LeTourneau wrote. "That led to my helping him cut wood . . . and on the job I made another discovery. As long as I was an eager and willing worker . . . Dad could be a mighty fine fellow. By noon I saw my running away from home and rebellious stand in all its pettiness, and I was one repentant boy."

He discovered his father's love and it changed his whole attitude.

Chores that he had hated and fought against resentfully, he did cheerfully because he wanted to serve his dad.

It's like that when you discover the Lord, and you don't grow up, LeTourneau told audiences. Your heavenly father is with you always and everywhere. If you aren't serving Him now, it's because you don't know Him, like I didn't really know my own father, he would assert. But when you do know Him, you'll love Him, and when you love Him, you'll serve Him, and find great happiness.

In his early years Bob attended services in a small Plymouth Brethren church but recalled that he "heard a lot about God but without learning a thing."

School was a drag until the fifth grade, when he discovered that arithmetic makes sense. And geography became exciting when he learned that pink, green, and yellow areas on the map were real places, perhaps with palm trees instead of the snow that he was so accustomed to in Vermont and Minnesota, where the family resettled in his boyhood. At the same time he took an interest in reading, enjoying all the fifth-grade books and most of those at sixth-grade level.

His teacher was delighted and his folks stunned, resulting in his skipping sixth grade and being promoted to the seventh. "What a mistake,"

LeTourneau wrote. "The seventh-graders had put in a long, earnest year on the subjects I had skimmed over so swiftly, and when it came to reciting, I wasn't in their league." At almost six feet tall, he was not only the biggest in the class, but "also the dumbest," he remembered, going on to say it resulted in his developing an inferiority complex. He quit trying and came to hate school.

After his family resettled again to Portland, Oregon, at age 14, he quit school following a heated session with his father. He soon was working as an apprentice molder at East Portland Iron Works, a place that "filled the bill for Dante's Inferno," he recalled facetiously. The boss set him to work with the comment, "It's a job for a strong back and a weak mind. There's a gondola full of sand. Shovel it into a wheelbarrow and bring it in here." He was advised "not to work hard but fast."

When he was 16, friend problems impacted Bob's life. First, the police came to him seeking information about a friend who was wanted for assault and battery. Then in rapid succession three other friends got into trouble with the law.

This sudden accumulation of troubles brought him face to face with himself. "I could tell myself all I was doing with my spare time was making a model steam engine, but I couldn't escape the fact that my closest associates were enrolled with the police," LeTourneau recalled in his autobiography. "'A man is know by the company he keeps,' said Dad."

The week before Christmas 1904, when Bob was 16, a citywide revival stirred Portland. He gave up working on his steam engine and decided to see if the revival could do anything for him. But after a week of concentrated singing and listening to sermons, he "didn't feel even a tremor of response." He told himself he might as well have stayed home and worked on his steam engine. When he confessed this to his mother, the look on her face made him realized he couldn't have hurt her more if he'd "stabbed her with a blunt knife."

"I gave myself a working over that night. No great flash of awareness. I just prayed to the Lord to save me," LeTourneau wrote. "All my bitterness was drained away. I was filled with such a vast relief that I could not contain it all. I ran to my mother. 'I'm saved,' I cried. "You don't have to worry about me anymore. I have felt the love of our Lord Jesus Christ."

After a long silence, followed by a deep sigh, his mother responded, "Robert, we knew it had to happen. Two years ago, when we discovered we couldn't guide you, we left it in God's hands." Then she added, "But He kept us waiting a long time."

Bob entered New Year's Day 1905 with high hopes. At church, he joined the choir but soon quit because his "foundry-trained voice" was deep enough but usually not on tune. At the young people's missionary society, led by his two sisters, he was so painfully inarticulate that he could only squeak when he was called on to pray.

So things were off to a disappointing start for the new year. Then in the fall the foundry where he was working burned down. Now he was without a job. He found himself planted at the family table "mooching free meals." He considered himself "big, dumb, unemployed, and unemployable."

It was in May 1921 when Bob LeTourneau, at the age of 32, hung out his sign "R.G. LeTourneau, Inc." at 122 Moss Avenue, Stockton, California and began what in time became a huge business—manufacturing huge earth-moving machines. The barn became his machine shop and the acre of land his open-air factory. But he joked, "I was in business for five years before I noticed it had started. It was that small." Over the years he put machinery on the market that contractors welcomed: the rooter, hopper wagons, bottom-dump carts, bulldozers, and semi-drag scrapers, to name a few.

However, before that sign went up, Bob had many bumps in the road, along with memorable adventures, that followed his conversion to Christ in late 1904.

A few weeks after that life-changing experience, Bob's father received a letter from a friend saying that a job awaited Bob in   if he wanted it. And so it was, after several job-related disappointments, left his family in Portland, Oregon, and began work in San Francisco as an apprentice at Moore and Scott Iron Works. Knowing that San Francisco could gobble up their 16-year-old son, Mom and Dad reminded him they would pray hard for him. He assured them that he knew he couldn't make it without calling on the Lord for help along the way. God was on his side, he asserted, but years later he realized he needed to be on God's side.

On Sundays he attended church and the Young People's Missionary Society. His sisters Sarah and Marie were studying to become missionaries to China, and Bob considered going to and opening a foundry to make farm equipment. But hearing his sisters try to pronounce Chinese words convinced him he could never learn the language, jesting that not even the Chinese could learn to speak their language.

He thought his life was over when, at 5:12 a.m. on April 18, 1906, an earthquake began to violently shake San Francisco. As buildings crumbled, Bob's bedroom dropped ten feet and his bed and the bureau swapped places.

Bob covered his head with a blanket and thought, "This is the end of the world. Thank God I am saved and going to heaven." Though fire swept much of and destroyed the foundry where he worked, he and his friends were unscathed.

Days later he landed a job with the Pacific Foundry in an unharmed part of the city. But he was let go when contracts expected to come out of reconstruction failed to materialize. Soon he went to work at an Oakland elevator company, but when the need for elevators faded, he was again out of a job. However, the four years of apprenticeship at the foundry made him a journeyman molder. After tromping the streets trying to find another job, Bob returned to Portland and worked for his brother, pulling stumps using a cable and a steam-powered engine.

By 1910 he had settled in Stockton, California, and soon had the reputation as the best mechanic in town. Two years later in an auto race at a county fair, to help sell Regals that he and a partner were selling, LeTourneau suffered a broken neck in an accident. Poor medical care caused him for a time to carry his head on his right shoulder "like a tote sack," resulting in his ear being rubbed raw. Though he got additional medical help, the injury caused him to go through life with a slightly tilted head.

LeTourneau's first successful invention brought in customers both young and old. He had bought a used welding torch and had become an expert welder through a six-month course. With his welding torch, he did tricks to turn automobiles into hotrods and by applying his torch to the muffler he provided drivers an ear-splitting noise when they pulled a wire.

One day at his garage LeTourneau thought God was calling him home. He was working in his grease pit, juicing up a car for an elderly man. The undercarriage was a mass of oil and grease. He asked Uncle Bob Gilmour, after whom he was named, to stand by with a pail of water in event of a fire as he used his torch on exhaust pipe. Sure enough, the oil-soaked floorboards of the car ignited. Uncle Bob grabbed a bucket that he thought was water and dumped the contents onto the fire. But it was gasoline. The whole pit burst into flames. "How I got out from under the car [without being burned] I have never figured out," LeTourneau wrote. "I knew I had been saved by the Lord Jesus, and my thanks were directed to Him."

The accident served as an illustration for LeTourneau when he answered people who asked what difference a man's religion makes as long as he is sincere. "I say it makes a big difference," he voiced. "The Bible says there is no other name under heaven whereby we can be saved but the name of Jesus. Uncle Bob was just as sincere as he could be, and he wouldn't have hurt me, his namesake, for the world, but his sincerity couldn't stop gas from exploding, nor save me from being in the midst of the explosion."

Finding a wife was an adventure LeTourneau would prefer to have been more traditional. Some years earlier he had boarded with the Oscar Peterson family when their daughter Evelyn was a child in high-buttoned shoes. Now she was wearing pumps and silk dresses, and was "something to behold." He fell in love with her, and her father said yes to his marrying her—if they waited five years. This did not set well with the young couple. Instead of waiting, they eloped in on an August evening in 1917. She was 16 at the time. Mr. Peterson filed charges of kidnapping against his now son-in-law. Finally he said, "All right, Bob, we're dropping charges, but so help me, don't do it again."

Oscar Peterson didn't speak to Bob for another seven years. Then one day in 1924 he came to Bob and said, "You're all right. I'm the one who's wrong in holding a grudge. Want to shake hands?" In a flash, Bob grabbed his hand. But then Oscar added, "It isn't Christian, and I was wrong for being sore for seven years. But I was right the first three months."

You might guess that the newlyweds lived happily ever after, but the early years were tough going. They began married life living in a room with a gas plate to heat food; a bathroom was down the hall.

Bob offered himself for military service but was turned down because of his neck injury. He went to work for a navy yard and became an electrical machinist. Evelyn rented an old farmhouse, where she raised her own vegetables. Bob came home often enough to split firewood for the kitchen range.

On October 30, 1918 their first child, Caleb, was born. But during a flu epidemic that swept the country, the child died the next February. It shook Bob to the extent that he reviewed his life and realized he had been "acting like a Christian but really serving myself" As a result, he refocused his life, determined to follow Matthew 6:33, "Seek ye first the kingdom of God and His righteousness, and all these things shall be added unto you." Over the ensuing years God gave Bob and Evelyn five more children, a daughter and four sons, each of whom went on to serve the Lord.

After joining a Christian and Missionary Alliance church at the invitation of a friend, LeTourneau became a strong supporter of missions and a local rescue mission, where he overcame his fear of speaking in public. He tithed his income, heeding the principle of Malachi 3:10: "Bring ye all the tithes into the storehouse. . . I will pour you out a blessing." Even when debts overwhelmed him, he still managed to keep his financial pledge to his church. Years later when he became wealthy, he and the family lived on 10 percent of his income, and he used 90 percent to further God's work. Evelyn worked as a nursemaid for a time to help Bob get started in his earth-moving business. Once he had so many contracts that he "felt like the little dog that chased freight trains and finally caught one." He built a scraper powered by electric motors that made earth-moving speedier, enabling him to honor his contracts.

In the mid-1930s he opened a manufacturing plant in Peoria, Illinois, and later put factories in Toccoa, Georgia; Vicksburg, Mississippi; and Longview, Texas. Today there are two plants, in Vicksburg and Longview.

To reach employees with the Gospel, he hired chaplains and held chapel services; attendance was voluntary. Plants closed Sundays.

In Toccoa he built a dormitory for Toccoa Falls Bible Institute and established a Christian conference center. In a foundation that he initiated gave birth to what is now with a current enrollment of some 3,400.

In Liberia and Peru he established missionary projects where his machines cleared land for people to grow food and where the Gospel was preached.

As the years passed, LeTourneau spoke to audiences across the nation. On May 12, 1937, he had a close call as he and his wife were en route to Bob Jones College in Cleveland, Tennessee. A speeding car crashed into the LeTourneau car, killing his veteran driver and another passenger. Both LeTourneau and his wife received severe injuries. He was in a cast "from head to foot" for months. While incapacitated he invented a stretcher that allowed him to be wheeled through his plant in Peoria.

Next he invented the Tournapull, a huge, ugly Diesel-powered machine but "a beauty when it went into action." After the bombing of Pearl Harbor, Tournapulls filled in bomb craters on runways, packing and spreading dirt so swiftly that the planes that had gone into the air to challenge the attackers were able to return to their own base.

In his 75th year, it became evident because of declining health that LeTourneau's traveling and speaking days were behind him. On March 17, 1969 he concluded his earthly ministry when he went to his heavenly home.

Thousands of times to thousands of listeners, R.G. LeTourneau had said, "If you're not serving the Lord, it proves you don't love Him; if you don't love Him, it proves you don't know Him. Because to know Him is to love Him, and to love Him is to serve Him."

The man who moved men and mountains had served the Savior well. He loved Him deeply.

—∿—

Allan McGuirl

An inventor's solar-powered radios reach the world's isolated peoples.

The 62-year-old woman sitting in her hut high in the mountains of central Mexico thought she heard an airplane flying low over her village. She went outside and noticed a small parachute with a little box attached dropping close by. Could it be an explosive device? Putting her fears aside, she investigated. Inside the box was a small red plastic radio with a pictorial set of instructions showing her how to operate it. The radio was turned on, broadcasting a Christian program in Spanish. It was preset to hear only KVOH, the Voice of Hope.

Soon she was for the first time in her life hearing the Gospel of Jesus Christ. God had come knocking at her door. For days she enjoyed the Christian music, Bible reading, and Gospel messages. In time she prayed to receive Christ as her Savior, following along on the radio as she invited Jesus Christ into her heart. Later, as a bonus, God healed her of a malady she had suffered for many years.

The woman became so excited that she found a Bible in Spanish and learned to read within nine days by following along with Bible readings. She began inviting relatives and friends to her hut for Bible study. Soon they had begun a house church.

The amazing facts of this story are that no missionary, pastor, or evangelist had ever been up in those rugged mountains to share about the Gospel. It all had happened through the little radio, a Galcom "Go-Ye" radio, dropped out of the sky by a missionary pilot.

Nearly 500,000 "Go-Ye" radios have been sent to some 120 countries by Galcom International, with offices in Hamilton, Ontario and Tampa, Florida. Approximately 2,000 radios are sent out monthly at a cost of about $36,500. The little radios are manufactured in Hamilton at a cost of just under $20.00 and operate on 700 milliamp industrial batteries that are kept charged by solar power.

"The solar panel on the radio puts out 100 milliamps of current and works off indoor lighting as well as outdoor lighting," explains Allan McGuirl, Galcom's international director. "The radios draw only 30 milliamps of energy and will operate in the sun without batteries. Battery power is used only if a listener has his/her radio on all night." "Go-Ye" radios will operate for as many as ten years.

"We are really dependent on supporters' prayers as we send out these little portable missionaries to reach the unreached in AM, FM, and short-wave frequencies," stresses McGuirl.

Galcom International came into being in February 1989 while McGuirl, Harold Kent, and

Ken Crowell were attending the National Religious Broadcasters annual convention. The Lord, they attest, had earlier brought them together through friends. All three had independently thought of using radios preset to Christian stations to use in evangelism—McGuirl, in Hamilton, Ontario; Crowell, in Israel; and Kent, in Tampa, Florida.

"We chose the name Galcom International partly based on Psalm 37:5, 'Commit thy way unto the Lord. . . .,'" McGuirl says. "Commit in Hebrew is *gal*. *Gal* is half of a wheel or a wave. *Gal* is rolling over to God daily. *Com* is for communications. International means worldwide. So Galcom International indicates our commitment to communicating the Gospel worldwide.

"We decided to call our little radios the 'Go-Ye' radios, based on the Great Commission, 'Go ye therefore, and teach all nations . . . (Matt. 28:19)'"

Allan McGuirl, an ordained minister, would seem to be an unlikely person to build a solar-powered radio, but he had built one a year or so before he met Kent and Crowell. He is dyslexic, and says that as a boy he struggled with reading and writing, but the Lord gave him a very creative mind.

"As a ten-year-old I rigged up a control so that I could open and close the door to my room from my bed," he reveals. "I had my desk wired up with alarms so no one could take my pens and pencils. I hooked up a radio so I could pick up programming from all over the world. I could look at circuitry and determine the way it should be put together. I look at my affliction as a strength and a weakness, making me totally dependent on the Lord."

As McGuirl traveled widely as Canadian Director of Gospel Recordings, an agency that uses hand-wind cassette players to evangelize in many languages, the idea of using preset radios became increasingly on his mind and heart. After he became acquainted with Crowell and Kent, he and his wife, Florrie, prayed much about it and he agreed to leave Gospel Recordings, to reach out with radio.

Ken Crowell, an American pastor and engineer, had gone with his wife, Margie, to Israel in 1978 as "tentmaker missionaries." They established Galtronics Electronics Ltd., in Tiberius, Israel on the Sea of Galilee, which today produces more than 40 million antennas a year for the worldwide cellular industry. Many employees have come to Christ and worship in three congregations begun by the Crowells.

It was in 1987 that Crowell worked on a fixed-tuned radio for evangelizing, but in his busy life he filed his plans away. Then in 1988 he ran across the folder and felt the Lord moving him to do something with the radio idea. A few days later a friend phoned him to come to Florida to meet Harold Kent, "a person who has a proposal that might interest you."

"It just happened that I was to fly to the USA that following week on business," recalls Crowell. "This is an example of the Lord's leading."

Harold Kent, head of a chain of feed mills who came to Christ at age 40, sat in an assembly at a Christian camp in 1966 with his wife, Jo Ann. "It was shortly after I received

Jesus as Lord of my life," he says. "As I listened to a message, I saw [in my mind] the world as a deep blue globe. I saw a dot of light appear, then another dot, until the whole earth was filled with dots of light. I [came to realize the symbolism] of this many years later," he recalls.

In 1988 he listened to a Christian radio broadcaster speak of desiring to broadcast radio programs on short wave so that the Gospel could be heard in unreached parts of the world. "The thought crossed my mind, 'How do you know if anyone is listening?'" Crowell recalls. "In many parts of the world people do not have electricity or access to a radio, and even those who have a short-wave receiver must by chance tune into a Gospel program. It was at that moment the Lord seemed to say, 'Make fix-tuned radios and distribute them around the world to people who have no other way of hearing the Gospel.'" He thought of the image he had envisioned years before and associated each dot of light with people reached with the Gospel by radio.

In organizing Galcom International, the three men decided that Crowell would finish engineering the radio and manufacture them, Kent would begin funding the project, and McGuirl would distribute the radios around the world. Production of the radios is now in Hamilton, as mentioned.

Many stories of the effectiveness of the radio ministry are chronicled in the paperback book *He Who Has Ears to Hear* by Gary Nelson, president of Galcom International USA. Included are stories from Central and South America, Africa, and the Middle Eastern Muslim lands.

In Haiti a missionary group heard the testimony of a man who had come to Christ through a Galcom radio; then he shared the radio with a friend, a witch doctor. The witch doctor also received the Lord.. As the father gave his testimony to the missionary group, other village people gathered and 17 professed faith in the Lord. Later, the visitors heard the testimony of the witch doctor, who said he was out of business as the village witch doctor. Twelve of his 13 children had received Christ.

A missionary pastor in Ecuador, Felix Lician, relates the following:

"A few weeks ago [a pastor] returned from a mission trip with young people from his church. They went to a village where they intended to do mission work; 98 percent of the villagers were professing Christians. Earlier someone had given them one Galcom fix-tuned radio and they had attached it to an external speaker so that the entire village could listen to the Gospel programming. They have been and continue to be discipled in Christ by that one missionary radio."

A similar story derives from a village in Panama. A villager asked a missionary he encountered to come to the village to serve communion to the Christians of the community. The Christian worker asked if any missionary, pastor, or evangelist had been to the village. The villager said no but that there were a large number of Christians in the village. They had come to Christ through a radio tuned to HCJB and now wanted someone to come and serve communion to them.

In Estonia some 600 hardened prisoners shared 120 radios that a pastor distributed. A couple of months later the warden called. "I've got good news: you've changed the atmosphere of this prison. The bad news is I've got 262 men who want to be baptized and I don't know what to do."

In Iraq Christian radio stations, called The Voice of Peace, have a potential listening audience of 1,250,000 Kurds. Thousands of Galcom fix-tuned radios have been distributed to the people in the country's northern region.

In Iraq a 16-year-old married Muslim woman received the Lord after listening to a radio broadcast, and her husband put her in prison with her infant son. That month she had lost her mom and only brother in a car accident. The local church stood by her in prayer. In court the judge asked her if she had become a Christian and she acknowledged she had come to Christ. The judge divorced her and allowed her to keep her child.

Zewar, a Christian taxi driver living in Zakho, in northwest Iraq, made a practice of giving Galcom radios to customers. In February 2002 a customer demanded that he renounce his faith, and when Zewar refused, the customer shot him 28 times, killing him. "It is our prayer that Zewar will be the last Christian martyr in Iraq," writes Gary Nelson, a highly decorated combat fighter pilot who served 29 years in the USAF before joining Galcom.

For more than ten years Galcom has established "suitcase radio stations," stations that technicians set up in remote areas to reach out as far as 80-100 miles. Some can download from satellites in English and Spanish programming. "The cost for these stations is about $10,000, including studio, transmitter, tower, and antenna," according to Allan McGuirl. "We have about 70 now, 90 percent of them being FM."

By the time you read this article Pygmies—the Bakas—will be hearing the Gospel via Galcom radios in such countries as The Republic of Congo, Gabon, and Cameroon. They live in small jungle villages, and when the area becomes depleted of food, they move on, making it difficult to evangelize them. Suitcase radio stations will reach out to them, likely operated by Campus Crusade for Christ.

In a sense, Galcom International is doing a work like the angel in Revelation 14:6: "And I saw another angel fly in the midst of heaven, having the everlasting gospel to preach unto them that dwell on the earth, and to every nation, and kindred, and tongue, and people." All with little "Go-Ye" radios.

Don Shoendorfer

A Ph.D. from MIT helps bring dignity to the world's crippled destitute.

Several years ago Don Schoendorfer was a 49-year-old husband and father who had achieved what many people associate with success. This mechanical engineer with a Ph. D. from MIT had a great marriage, three beautiful daughters, and lived in Orange County, California. In addition, Don had a number of patents with his name attached to them.

"I had tasted the flavors of worldly success, but really wasn't satisfied," Don admits. "I had an inner hunger for more. I wanted a life that was marked by significance more than success."

Don's search for significance began with an honest confession. His nominal Christianity did not equate to having a personal relationship with Christ.

"The Lord got my attention when one of my daughters admitted to having an eating disorder," Don admits. "My world spun out of control, and I realized I needed Him to bring order out of chaos. I credit that crisis with my openness to surrender my life and my family to Jesus."

Don and his wife, Laurie, began to attend church regularly. Seeing how God was working in their lives, they gradually surrendered to Him. It was about this time when Don's pastor gave a message on the rich fool from Luke 12. He realized he was like the man in Jesus' parable by waiting until he had everything before using his gifts for God. The Lord reminded Don of something he had seen 20 years previously while on vacation in Morocco. A paraplegic woman in blood-soaked and torn clothing clawed her fingers into the dirt in an attempt to gain traction. Her daring goal was to pull her lifeless legs across a road. The image of that woman kept surfacing in his thoughts.

"Sensing that my purpose in life was now to serve Jesus by helping others, I determined to do something for people like that poor woman in North Africa," Don acknowledges. "I was obsessed with finding a way to provide the gift of mobility that every person created in the image of God deserves."

Don's goal was to design a lightweight wheelchair that would be durable yet inexpensive. He started with a white plastic lawn chairs seen on most American's patios. Sawing off the chair legs, he then attached two 24-inch mountain bike tires. For several months Don tinkered with a prototype in his garage before and after work. After countless hours of redesign and tweaking, Don was pleased with the result.

In February 2001 Don was given an opportunity to travel with a ministry team from his church to India. Since he had assembled 100 wheelchairs in his garage, he got excited about taking all of them to distribute. Because of travel restrictions, though, he was only allowed to take four.

Initially Don was disappointed to only have a few chairs to give away. But as he got to

Chennai and saw the reaction of the crippled people who were given the chairs, he knew all his months of work was in keeping with God's purposes. Something inside him told him the other chairs would eventually find a home.

While Don was gone, the company for which he worked went bankrupt. Don was faced with a life-changing decision.

"I had a choice," Don admits. "If I looked for a new job, I would have to give it my full attention and have to give up on making wheelchairs. But after returning from India all I could think about was the reaction of the people who were granted dignity by sitting in a chair instead of crawling on the ground."

In spite of the financial challenges it would mean for his family, Don knew the Lord was calling him to dedicate himself fully to the wheelchair project. He emptied his savings account, leased a warehouse and established a non-profit ministry. Since the wheelchairs would be given away to those in need of one at no charge, he chose to call the new outreach Free Wheelchair Mission.

"I came to realize there are 100 million people in the world like that woman in Morocco," Don soberly admits. "That's mindboggling. Our goal as an organization is to distribute 20 million wheelchairs."

Another of Don's goals is to keep the cost of manufacturing and distributing each chair under $50. Thanks to using components that are produced in high volume, inexpensive labor in China, and distribution networks already in place, the price tag for each wheelchair is only $48.35.

In the summer of 2005 Don received a call from the White House indicating that President Bush wanted to meet him. After seeing the chair and hearing the how Don's mission began, the President praised his ingenuity and dedication.

In the summer of 2007 Don and a member of his board, Dr. Michael Bayer (the ministry's Medical Director), rode their bikes from coast to coast as a way of publicizing his organization. The 3,500 mile trek began in New York City with an appearance on "The Early Show" on CBS television and concluded with a celebration at Mariners Church near the Pacific Ocean. The six-week adventure achieved Don's dream. Donations to FWM for the year increased by 40 percent.

Now in his sixties, Don confesses amazement at how God has blessed his efforts. To date Free Wheelchair Mission has provided more than 335,000 wheelchairs to people with disabilities in more than 75 countries, all given free of charge to them.

In March of 2008 Don was one of three individuals chosen from across the nation to receive the Above and Beyond Citizens Award. The honor was presented by the Congressional Medal of Honor Committee at Arlington National Cemetery.

"I know that there are others more deserving an award like that than me," Don says humbly. "But I am honored to know that being obedient to what God asks you to do can be recognized on such a public platform. Because Free Wheelchair Mission is solely dependent on donations and grants, I am grateful for whatever means the Lord uses to get the word out."

CHAPTER 17

Redemptive Communicators:

—◊—

MILITARY

Daniel Hardin

A military officer's wound prepared him to help traumatized soldiers.

Just before the deployment of his Alaska-based airborne parachute infantry regiment to Iraq, Chaplain Capt. Daniel W. Hardin learned he needed surgery to repair torn knee cartilage. Hardin was disheartened when his unit, known as the Geronimos, left without him in October 2006.

After a couple of months of recuperation Hardin was well enough to go to Iraq. On Christmas Eve he stood in front of U.S. troops, preached, and served Communion. Twelve hours later two of the paratroopers from Hardin's forward operating base were dead. Their truck had struck an improvised explosive device (IED).

Dealing with death and its aftermath, Hardin quickly learned, was part of the assimilation process in Iraq with the 1st Battalion, 501st Parachute Infantry Regiment, 4th Brigade Combat Team (Airborne), 25th Infantry Division.

On Feb. 4, 2007, Hardin accompanied a convoy to an outpost to conduct a worship service and offer grief counseling for a platoon that had lost a paratrooper to sniper fire.

At approximately 8:30 p.m. on a road west of Baghdad outside Fallujah, the truck in which Hardin rode struck a pressure plate detonated IED. The blast knocked the driver unconscious, wounded the front-seat passenger commander in the leg, and tore a hole in the firewall of the crew compartment—where Hardin sat.

"It felt like the right side of my face was on fire," recalls Hardin.

Hardin exited the truck stunned, groping to find his way onto the nighttime roadway. Spc. Jemell Garris, an infantryman assigned to the battalion as the chaplain's assistant — with the primary duty of providing security for the unit ministry team — found Hardin.

The 6-foot-2-inch Garris carried Hardin to a medic and returned to extract other wounded soldiers from the burning vehicle. No one died or suffered permanent injuries in the explosion, despite extensive damage to the vehicle.

Hardin suffered facial burns, eyelid and chin cuts, and a punctured outer ear. After stitches and the removal of gravel embedded in his face, he returned to his duties within three days. Outward appearances indicate that Hardin mended quickly. But healing emotionally proved to be arduous.

Suddenly the textbook theology Hardin learned in the classroom didn't jibe so smoothly with real-life experience. The nagging hurt, the shattering of his notions about God, feeling alone and helpless, and wondering what others thought of him plagued him.

As the only chaplain for his base, Hardin sensed soldiers with no faith background were checking to see if he still believed in God. Some questioned what he had done to make God so mad. Others thought if God didn't bother to protect the chaplain from harm, how could the Almighty care about the rest of them?

For the first two months after the attack, Hardin wanted to escape the war as memories of the attack loomed. Regularly he broke out in cold sweats when he heard outgoing mortar fire. Sleep did not come easily and he imagined something or someone was going to smack him in the face.

Hardin began to doubt if he had the fortitude to last as a chaplain.

Compounding Hardin's turmoil was his struggle with homesickness and news his mother had breast cancer. His workload also required him repeatedly to conduct memorials for troops killed by IEDs or sniper fire. Other duties included counseling soldiers dealing with everything from crumbling marriages to thoughts of suicide. All of it left Hardin sullen.

Via e-mail, retired U.S. Army Col. Scott McChrystal, who spent seven years as senior chaplain at the U.S. Military Academy at West Point, persuaded Hardin to talk about the trauma with someone in person.

"People who are impacted by IEDs and live to tell about it will never forget," says McChrystal, who witnessed the horror of fellow soldiers dying from bamboo-shard booby traps as an infantry platoon leader in Vietnam. "The Lord helps in the healing process."

Hardin laid bare his innermost thoughts with other chaplains. They told him he didn't have to put on a game face.

"I was afraid if they knew the real me with all my wounds, fears, inadequacies, and sins I would be rejected," Hardin says.

McChrystal explained to Hardin that if he didn't take care of himself, if he didn't acknowledge his vulnerability, he would quickly burn out.

"How a chaplain recovers from psychological trauma is extremely important," McChrystal says. "When a chaplain gets wounded, other soldiers take notice."

McChrystal says it's no shock that clergy in a prolonged war might be temporarily racked with disillusionment. Emotional healing is a process, and there can be times of discouragement.

"David, the warrior king after God's own heart, shows God can handle us being real and transparent about our weaknesses," explains McChrystal.

While recovering from surgery, Hardin opened a free coffeehouse for soldiers in Iraq. *The Anchorage Daily News* sent newspapers for free distribution, plus provided a professional grade espresso machine and 100 pounds of specialty coffee. Congregations in the United States raised $6,000 to sustain the supply of beverages.

The Drop Zone Café opened in March 2007, dispensing coffee, cappuccino, lattes, and snow cones to about 55 soldiers daily.

The café featured two decked-out MacBook computers connected with wireless Internet that allow soldiers to e-mail family, watch movies, or listen to music.

Many paratroopers wandering into the coffeehouse sought spiritual counseling or prayer. Because of the sheer number of casualties and the nature of those deaths, U.S. troops in Iraq have a heightened sense of mortality. This creates within them an increased focus on spiritual matters, and soldiers typically view a chaplain as God's representative in camp.

Still, recovery proved to be a long process for the man of God dispensing biblical counsel.

Hardin returned to Alaska in November 2007. Within 40 days of 2008 beginning, Hardin's two grandmothers and an uncle died; he endured another knee surgery; and he was diagnosed with post traumatic stress disorder. Many soldiers have PTSD, which is related to surviving the threat of death or serious injury. Hardin's symptoms were typical: insomnia, being easily provoked to anger, lack of motivation, and a general mental fog.

A downcast Hardin attended a church workshop in March 2008, which further helped him heal psychologically from the trauma. Hardin, for the first time, began to speak in front of small groups of paratroopers suffering from the physical and psychological wounds of war. He frankly explained his struggles and victories.

At the urging of his superiors, Hardin documented his experiences by putting together a program to help soldiers understand and normalize trauma and how to position themselves for healing. The work was published in *The U.S. Army Chaplaincy Journal* in 2009.

In December 2008, Hardin was transferred to Fort Benning, Georgia, where he oversees small groups that specialize in bringing healing and comfort to those who struggle with the effects of trauma.

Ironically, Hardin believes the best part of deployment was that he and Ann, his wife, grew closer. They stayed connected with letters, e-mails, instant messaging, and the occasional phone call (which is expensive because soldiers must pay international rates). The couple prayed for each other in their almost daily contact. Still, the couple experienced separation anxiety as Ann, living on the Army post, tried to raise four children 12 time zones away from her husband. She taught their teenage son Matthew to drive and potty trained toddler Katherine. The couple has two other children, Elizabeth and Joshua.

Today, Hardin has a renewed zeal to pray and read the Bible. The psalms of lament and grief offer him special consolation. The lengthy recovery process reshaped Hardin's theology of pain and evil, which in turn has helped him aid others.

"God is near even when I don't sense him." Hardin says. "He is not so much interested in keeping us from harm as He is in helping us through it. All people, including spiritual leaders, will experience pain and suffering because they are human and live in a broken world."

Hardin believes his Iraq deployment and the aftermath taught him a great deal about life, marriage, and ministry.

"As long as my family can handle this vocation, I will serve as a chaplain in the Army," he says. "I was made for this."

~~

Clebe McClary

A wounded veteran helps wounded military personnel overcome despair.

First Lieutenant Clebe McClary clips off platitudes like he's ordering take-out from Sonny's Barbecue. He's picked his remarks from the menu of hardship, and he's got his favorites memorized: FIDO. "Forget about it and drive on," McClary explained.

That's the advice he gives to new recruits and old veterans on how to cope with the unpacked baggage they bring home from the battlefield. McClary knows what's inside those duffel bags—survivor's guilt, flashbacks, nightmares, lost limbs, fallen friends, the should'ves, could'ves and would'ves.

In September, 1967, McClary boarded a jet airliner out of Charleston, South Carolina. Two days later, the then 26-year-old Lieutenant arrived in DaNang, Vietnam. Attached to the First Marine Recon, McClary fought at DaNang, Quang Tri, and in the Tet Offensive. He was wounded twice in December, 1967, but not badly enough to leave the battle.

Yet, the day did come—March 3, 1968—when McClary's squad was overrun. Eight out of 13 squad members were wounded, and another three were killed. McClary recalled the moment when he was severely wounded.

"I was leading a patrol of 13 men into a valley where very few of our troops had been. We stopped for the night on the top of a hill. Three men dug a foxhole to my right. I got into a punji pit and another eight men were in large bomb crater about 50 meters behind me."

Sometime around midnight, McClary heard the whistle of incoming fire. He climbed out of the pit to see if the guys in the nearby foxhole had heard anything when a grenade exploded, striking him in the neck and shoulder. McClary grabbed his radio and began calling for artillery support, when he saw a suicide squad of about 10 North Vietnamese fighters, charging the hill, with grenades strapped to their waists and in their hands. Their sole mission—to destroy the patrol of U.S. Marines.

McClary aimed his 12-gauge and fired. An enemy soldier fell on McClary, knocking them both into the punji pit, where the Vietnamese's satchel charge exploded, blowing them back out of the hole.

"I reached back for my shotgun and that's when I realized my left arm had been blown off. Bone hanging there. Nothing else," McClary recalled.

His radio man and medic were nearby, dead. Another grenade explosion followed. The three fellows in the foxhole were hit. Private First Class Ralph Johnson was dead. Johnson had thrown himself on a grenade to save the lives of the other two Marines.

McClary began to crawl to the foxhole, but was stopped by yet another grenade. This one blew out his left eye and much of his teeth. He jumped up, running for the bomb crater where eight of his comrades were fighting but another explosion knocked McClary's feet out from under him. He wasn't sure if he would live to see another day.

McClary thought of his young bride, Deanne, and how badly he wanted to see her again. They were supposed to meet in Hawaii soon for some much-deserved rest and relaxation. *That isn't going to happen now,* McClary thought as he lay in a pool of blood.

A North Vietnamese soldier shoved the enemy flag into the ground about 15 feet from McClary's head. And one other walked up to him and shot him in the right arm at point-blank range.

"I thought it was all over," he said. But then, he heard the voice of a young private calling out, "Lieutenant! Lieutenant!"

An 18-year-old Marine had come to rescue him. McClary urged the boy to call for choppers. The chopper crew said they couldn't get in till daybreak, another hour away, at least.

"Tell them to forget it then," McClary said, disgusted. "We won't last that long. We are out of grenades."

The chopper showed up within minutes.

"They put my two dead men, the four wounded, and me on the first bird. The last seven men jumped on the next bird. As it lifted off, about 150 or more of the enemy swarmed over the top of the hill. A few more minutes there and not a one of us would have gotten off that hill alive."

As it is, three of the men who were rescued that day have since taken their own lives. Private Johnson, the only other South Carolinian on the patrol, was posthumously awarded the Medal of Honor, the nation's highest award for heroism.

"Ralph came from a family of 18 brothers and sisters. His mother was a cleaning lady. He didn't know his own daddy," McClary said, then pausing, added, "He was one of my closest friends."

Friendships forged in the fire of war retain their incandescent glow over the years, growing sharper even as memory dims.

If he had died that day, McClary says he would have "split the gates of hell wide open." Raised on a 10,000 acre plantation outside Georgetown, South Carolina, McClary had grown up in the church.

"Like a lot of Americans, I went to church. I had a lot of religion in my head but nothing in my heart. I didn't smoke, drink, or cuss. I was so good, I was good for nothing."

Still, McClary said that if he had returned home in a casket, everyone would have assumed he was saved.

"The church would've been packed out because of Mama and Daddy. And 90 percent of 'em would've said if anyone's in heaven, Clebe is. But I wouldn't have been. I didn't have a personal relationship with Jesus. I could not claim him as my Savior."

Flown from DaNang to Japan for medical treatment, McClary began a grueling recovery. He'd lost an arm and an eye, and doctors warned him that he'd never walk again.

There were times when McClary despaired.

"The doctors wouldn't let me look in the mirror because my injuries were so extensive. I was married to a beauty queen. I knew if I died she could do a lot better than me. I was in a lot of pain. I wanted to die."

But on one of those dark days, McClary received a visit from a pro-golfer, Billy Casper. McClary overheard the chaplain tell Casper not to bother because "He's not going to make it." But Casper walked over to McClary, and in all sincerity told him, "Marine, I love you. I'll be praying for you.'"

That one act of kindness gave McClary the will to live.

When he was well enough to travel, he was taken to Bethesda Naval Hospital for more surgery, more recovery, months worth. Deanna would drive up from South Carolina to sit by his side, and to map out new dreams. Sometimes he would leave with Deanna for day trips. Sometimes weekend trips.

It during one of those trips home to South Carolina, McClary discovered that New York Yankee Bobby Richardson would be making an appearance at the local football stadium.

"C'mon, get in the car! Let's go," McClary, a long-time sports buff, told his wife.

The two didn't know Billy Zeoli of Gospel Films would be preaching, too.

"He preached a sermon I'll never forget," McClary said. "He started off talking about Joshua and his troops, marching around the city of Jericho, shouting. Zeoli said if someone did that today we'd think they had a heat stroke."

"But Joshua was a fool. A fool for Christ. Zeoli said there are two kinds of fools in this world: either you're a fool for Christ or a fool for others. What kind of fool of you?"

McClary said there was no question in his heart whose fool he had been. "I had gone to Sunday School and church all my life because my father and mother made me. I had a lot of religion but I still needed a Savior."

At that stadium, with his wife praying beside him, McClary asked Jesus into his heart.

"I found the real joy, real life and real peace of a Living Savior. I didn't change much on the outside, but my heart was different. Jesus filled up the hole that was leaking inside me."

McClary reads five Psalms and one Proverb everyday, and has ever since he was saved. The Psalms teach us about our relationship with God and Proverbs teach us about our relationship with others, he explained. McClary believes that clean living and a disciplined lifestyle are necessary components for healing from any battle wounds.

Citing Roman 5:3-5, McClary said he is in pain everyday but that he's learned to put his suffering into perspective: "But we glory in tribulations also: knowing that tribulation worketh patience; and patience, experience; and experience, hope: and hope maketh not ashamed; because the love of God is shed abroad in our hearts by the Holy Ghost which is given unto us."

McClary knows, despite the platitudes he's so fond of quoting, that a soldier who has been in battle and watched his buddy exhale his last breath, will never ever forget it.

"I will take the memory of that to my grave. But I don't dwell on it," he said. "I learn from it because I have another war to fight."

This time he's fighting for his fellow soldiers. McClary devotes much of his time to working with veterans returning from Iraq and Afghanistan, sharing the lessons he's learned with a whole new generation of people broken by war. His message is simple, "They can find healing in Christ."

—⁂—

Jeff Struecker

An officer's spiritual passion for his fellow Army Rangers

"Get ready!" Sixty-four rigged soldiers on the C-130 recheck their equipment—straps, harnesses, and buckles.

One soldier's heart starts to pound. Thump thump, thump thump.

Two more commands are yelled over the roaring engines of the plane. Everyone stands.

"Hook up!" The soldier reaches, hooking his static line. *What if the chute doesn't open?* Thump thump, thump thump.

"Sound off for equipment check!" The relay starts. His shoulder is grabbed. "OK!" he yells. His hand lands on the shoulder in front of him. With the last OK, the ramp lowers. The screaming wind whips by at 130 mph. Thump thump. Thump thump.

"Stand by!" Twenty seconds left. Thump thump. First guy's in the doorway. Thump thump. Thump thump. Now they must trust the jumpmaster—the one who checked all the parachutes back on the ground.

The plane approaches the drop zone. *Thump thump. Thump thump. Thump thump.*

"Go!"

Silence. The hard part is over.

Capt. Jeff Struecker is a jumpmaster for the 82nd Airborne Division. If one soldier dies in this maneuver, he has failed.

His responsibilities as a chaplain carry the same weight. With the souls of 650-plus soldiers on the line, Jeff longs for each of them to have a personal relationship with Jesus Christ. And timing is everything.

Jeff's battalion maintains a two-hour recall status—they must stay within two hours of Fort Bragg, North Carolina.

"Within 18 hours we could be lifting off of Pope Air Force Base flying anywhere in the world," says Jeff. "But what my soldiers don't understand is they may never come back alive. I understand that all too well."

A decorated Army Ranger, Jeff served in Panama and Desert Storm and received a Bronze Star for Valor for his role in Mogadishu, Somalia, featured in the book and film *Black Hawk Down.* When he signs copies, Jeff describes the 1993 event as the most intense 24 hours of his life with Jesus Christ.

"It could happen in 50 other places in the world—like Kandahar, Saudi Arabia, or the Philippines," says Jeff, "and it could be tomorrow. Once my soldiers get on those airplanes I may never have a chance to share Christ with them again."

After experiencing the spiritual openness of the soldiers in Somalia, Jeff decided to become a chaplain. "I want to see soldiers in love with Christ. I want to see Him make the difference in their lives that He made in mine."

But Jeff is also known for being tough, hence his nickname: Evil Christian. In a real combat situation, he wants his soldiers to survive. One told Jeff's pastor, "Sir, he is the meanest Christian I know."

Jeff pushes soldiers to the brink of their limitations, never over.

Once, at an obstacle course, specialist Bucky Harris froze 30 feet above the ground. "I can't do it," Bucky said, staring at the rope just out of reach. "If I grab it I am gonna fall."

Immediately, Jeff climbed the obstacle course. *Oh no, here he comes,* Bucky thought.

Jeff surprised Bucky by coaxing him to sit down next to him.

"Just look out across the horizon. Let everyone go ahead," Jeff continued. Fifteen minutes later Bucky completed the course.

"There are times when I am in a tough situation," Bucky says with a Southern drawl, "and I think, *What would Jeff do?*"

Serving on active duty as a chaplain, the father of Aaron (9), Jacob (7), Joseph (6), Abigail (4) and Lydia (2), sleeps less than most. Up at exactly 4:35 A.M. to spend time in prayer and Bible study yet make it to the office by six, Jeff completes his required PT (physical training) on the base.

"He is one of the most mentally and physically tough soldiers I've ever met," says his commander, Lt. Col. Richard Clarke. Jeff runs longer than most soldiers, then crams in sit-ups, pushups and pull-ups. Just two days after starting to lead his battalion's PT he was asked to quit; the troops were too worn out.

In his afternoons, Jeff may visit a soldier in the hospital, plan a marriage seminar, or research Sunday's sermon. But when he visits his battalion on the field, he sheds his office-quality battle-dress uniform for another with frayed edges and faded camouflage green. With his unit out sweating and crawling in the dirt, Jeff explains that they will resent him if he shows up neatly pressed. One soldier told him he was the dirtiest chaplain he's ever seen. Jeff considered it a compliment.

With one glance at his badges, a serviceman or woman immediately knows Jeff's credentials; to most soldiers, those badges are the goal of their career.

Sitting in his office at a drab metal desk, he points to the chaplain's badge with a cross on his shoulder. "When I stand before God He's not going to be impressed by this or this or this," indicating his other badges. "Right here [the cross that represents Jesus Christ] is all that is going to matter."

"He is not looking for notoriety or acknowledgment of what he has done or where he is," says Gen. Joe Gray, national director of Campus Crusade for Christ's Military Ministry. "He wants to pass it on to someone else who will maybe go through the same experience."

Once unwelcome, the publicity of the *Black Hawk Down* book and subsequent film now provides Jeff opportunities to recount that experience and the message of Jesus Christ. With hundreds of requests during the past year, from churches and from Congress, Jeff takes advantage of this fleeting platform whenever possible. The urgency of Christ's message motivates him.

"I can share Christ with my soldiers 24/7 and not get through all 650 before half of them leave," says Jeff, "and another 300 show up." This is where Military Ministry's influence is vital.

"I don't have the budget or the personnel, and [other than] the Holy Spirit at work, it is an impossibility to adequately minister to this battalion," laments the brown-haired, blue-eyed Ranger. His role in the military assigns him all the responsibilities of a pastor. "But I praise God that the Holy Spirit is at work, and Military Ministry has products and resources just for chaplains."

One Military Ministry resource essential to him is the Rapid Deployment Kit. Inside a sandwich bag, a New Testament with Psalms and Proverbs, a devotional booklet, and a Gospel tract fit compactly enough for soldiers to put the RDK in their pocket. Since the Sept. 11, 2001 attacks on the United States, more than 250,000 RDKs have been given away by 375 military chaplains.

When his unit entered the desert for a two-week training, Jeff handed each person an RDK. He told them to read the Bible, read the Gospel tract, then think and pray about it.

"In the middle of their firing missions and shooting howitzers," Jeff beams, "I just pulled a couple of them aside and said, 'Let's have a field chapel service.'" Throughout those weeks at least 13 men received Christ.

Soldiers also seek Jeff for counseling—often for their marriages. Dana Greenly found himself frequently yelling at his family and generally unhappy since his father's death. He came to Jeff's office hoping baptism would make a difference.

As the two men sat face to face behind a closed door, Jeff pulled out a Gospel tract. "You know what?" Jeff asked. "You can go down in the water with sin in your life, and when you come back out, all you are is a sinner that just got wet."

Dana agreed: "You're right; you're absolutely right."

"What you need to do," Jeff continued, "is get your heart right first." He explained about receiving Christ by faith through prayer, but with an intense voice, Jeff warned Dana not to make the mistake of saying that prayer and not meaning it.

"I can make that commitment," Dana replied, "but I'm not going to be like you."

"I am not the standard by which you need to measure yourself," Jeff said. That day, Dana trusted Christ.

With every life that Jesus changes, Jeff gets fired up to keep going. But with the responsibilities of a large family and being husband to Dawn as his priority, the souls of his soldiers a close second, and constant speaking requests, Jeff struggles to find balance. "I have not had a day yet where I felt like I got it right," he says.

Throughout his career of leadership in the Army, and currently as a jumpmaster, his job is to prepare soldiers for combat—to prevent death. As a chaplain, he explains the purpose of life—to love Jesus Christ: "Every morning when I roll out of bed I think there's another soldier that I can see come to Christ."

Soon enough, Jeff knows each soldier will face the silence. They will all have to jump.

PART 3:
Job Fields *for* Redemptive Communicators

—⚏—

A REDEMPTIVE PASSION

"I have but one passion. It is He, it is He alone. The world is the field and the field is the world; and henceforth that country shall be my home where I can be most used in winning souls for Christ."

- Count Nicolaus Ludwig Zinzendorf (1700-1760)

The job descriptions that follow are adapted from the Bureau of Labor Statistics, U.S. Department of Labor, Occupational Outlook Handbook, 2010-11 Edition. *This resource is available on the Internet at http://www.bls.gov/oco.* Public domain.

EDUCATION

—⚭—

Teaching (Elementary and Secondary)

Nature of the Work

Teachers play an important role in fostering the intellectual and social development of children during their formative years. The education that students acquire is key to determining the future of those students. Whether in elementary or high schools or in private or public schools, teachers provide the tools and the environment for their students to develop into responsible adults.

Teachers act as facilitators or coaches, using classroom presentations or individual instruction to help students learn and apply concepts in subjects such as science, mathematics, and English. They plan, evaluate, and assign lessons; prepare, administer, and grade tests; listen to oral presentations; and maintain classroom discipline. Teachers observe and evaluate a student's performance and potential. They are increasingly asked to use new assessment methods. For example, teachers may examine a portfolio of a student's artwork or writing in order to judge the student's overall progress. They then can provide additional assistance in areas in which the student needs help. Teachers also grade papers, prepare report cards, and meet with parents and school staff to discuss a student's academic progress or personal problems.

Significant Points

❖ Public school teachers must be licensed, which typically requires a bachelor's degree and the completion of an approved teacher education program; private school teachers do not have to be licensed but may still need a bachelor's degree.

❖ Many States offer alternative licensing programs to attract people into teaching, especially for hard-to-fill positions.

❖ Teachers must have the ability to communicate, inspire trust and confidence, and motivate students, as well as understand students' educational and emotional needs.

❖ Job prospects are best for teachers in high-demand fields, such as mathematics, science, and bilingual education, and in less desirable urban or rural school districts.

Many teachers use a hands-on approach that utilizes props to help children understand abstract concepts, solve problems, and develop critical thinking skills. For example, they may teach the concepts of numbers or of addition and subtraction by playing board games. As the children get older, teachers use more sophisticated approaches, such as demonstrating science experiments or working with computers. They also encourage collaboration in solving problems by having students work in groups to discuss and solve the problems together. To be prepared for success later in life, students must be able to interact with others, adapt to new technology, and think through problems logically.

Kindergarten and elementary school teachers play a vital role in the development of children. What children learn and experience during their early years can shape their views of themselves and the world and can affect their later success or failure in school, work, and their personal lives. Kindergarten and elementary school teachers introduce children to mathematics, language, science, and social studies. They use games, music, artwork, films, books, computers, and other tools to teach basic skills.

Kindergarten teachers use play and hands-on teaching, but academics begin to take priority in kindergarten classrooms. Letter recognition, phonics, numbers, and awareness of nature and science, introduced at the preschool level, are taught primarily in kindergarten.

Most *elementary school teachers* instruct one class of children in several subjects. In some schools, two or more teachers work as a team and are jointly responsible for a group of students in at least one subject. In other schools, a teacher may teach one special subject—usually music, art, reading, science, arithmetic, or physical education—to a number of classes. A small but growing number of teachers instruct multilevel classrooms, with students at several different learning levels.

Middle school teachers and *secondary school teachers* help students delve more deeply into subjects introduced in elementary school and expose them to more information about the world. Middle and secondary school teachers specialize in a specific subject, such as English, Spanish, mathematics, history, or biology. They also may teach subjects that are career oriented. Additional responsibilities of middle and secondary school teachers may include career guidance and job placement, as well as following up with students after graduation.

In addition to conducting classroom activities, teachers oversee study halls and homerooms, supervise extracurricular activities, and accompany students on field trips. They may identify students who have physical or mental problems and refer the students to the proper authorities. Secondary school teachers occasionally assist students in choosing courses, colleges, and careers. Teachers also participate in education conferences and workshops.

Computers play an integral role in the education teachers provide. Resources such as educational software and the Internet expose students to a vast range of experiences and promote interactive learning. Through the Internet, students can communicate with other students anywhere in the world, allowing them to share experiences and viewpoints. Students also use the Internet for individual research projects and to gather information. Computers play a role in other classroom activities as well, from solving math problems to learning English as a second language. Teachers also may use computers to record grades and perform other administrative and clerical duties. They must continually update their skills so that they can instruct and use the latest technology in the classroom.

Teachers often work with students from varied ethnic, racial, and religious backgrounds. With growing minority populations in most parts of the country, it is important for teachers to work effectively with a diverse student population. Accordingly, some schools offer training to help teachers enhance their awareness and understanding of different cultures. Teachers may include multicultural programming in their lesson plans, to address the needs of all students, regardless of their cultural background.

In recent years, site-based management, which allows teachers and parents to participate actively in management decisions regarding school operations, has gained popularity. In many schools, teachers are increasingly becoming involved in making decisions regarding the budget, personnel, textbooks, curriculum design, and teaching methods.

Work environment. Seeing students develop new skills and gain an appreciation of knowledge and learning can be very rewarding. However, teaching may be frustrating when one is dealing with unmotivated or disrespectful students. Occasionally, teachers must cope with unruly behavior and violence in the schools. Teachers may experience stress in dealing with large classes, heavy workloads, or old schools that are run down and lack modern amenities. Accountability standards also may increase stress levels, with teachers expected to produce students who are able to exhibit a satisfactory performance on standardized tests in core subjects. Many teachers, particularly in public schools, also are frustrated by the lack of control they have over what they are required to teach.

Teachers in private schools generally enjoy smaller class sizes and more control over establishing the curriculum and setting standards for performance and discipline. Their students also tend to be more motivated, since private schools can be selective in their admissions processes.

Teachers are sometimes isolated from their colleagues because they work alone in a classroom of students. However, some schools allow teachers to work in teams and with mentors, to enhance their professional development.

Many teachers work more than 40 hours a week, including school duties performed outside the classroom. Part-time schedules are more common among kindergarten teachers. Although most school districts have gone to all-day kindergartens, some kindergarten teachers still teach two kindergarten classes a day. Most teachers work the traditional 10-month school year, with a 2-month vacation during the summer. During the vacation break, those on the

10-month schedule may teach in summer sessions, take other jobs, travel, or pursue personal interests. Many enroll in college courses or workshops to continue their education. Teachers in districts with a year-round schedule typically work 8 weeks, are on vacation for 1 week, and have a 5-week midwinter break.

Most states have tenure laws that prevent public school teachers from being fired without just cause and due process. Teachers may obtain tenure after they have satisfactorily completed a probationary period of teaching, normally 3 years. Tenure does not absolutely guarantee a job, but it does provide some security.

EDUCATION

—m—

Teaching (Post-Secondary)

Nature of the Work

Postsecondary teachers instruct students in a wide variety of academic and vocational subjects beyond the high school level. Most of these students are working toward a degree, but many others are studying for a certificate or certification to improve their knowledge or career skills. Postsecondary teachers include college and university faculty, postsecondary career and technical education teachers, and graduate teaching assistants. Teaching in any venue involves forming a lesson plan, presenting material to students, responding to students learning needs, and evaluating students' progress. In addition to teaching, postsecondary teachers, particularly those at 4-year colleges and universities, perform a significant amount of research in the subject they teach. They also must keep up with new developments in their field and may consult with government, business, nonprofit, and community organizations.

College and university faculty make up the majority of postsecondary teachers. Faculty usually are organized into departments or divisions based on academic subject or field. They typically teach several related courses in their subject—algebra, calculus, and statistics, for example. They may instruct undergraduate or graduate students or both. College and university faculty may give lectures to several

Significant Points

❖ Many postsecondary teachers find the environment intellectually stimulating and rewarding because they are surrounded by others who enjoy the subject.

❖ Educational qualifications range from expertise in a particular field to a Ph.D., depending on the subject taught and the type of educational institution.

❖ Competition is expected for tenure-track positions; better opportunities are expected for part-time or non-tenure-track positions.

❖ Ph.D. recipients should experience the best job prospects.

hundred students in large halls, lead small seminars, or supervise students in laboratories. They prepare lectures, exercises, and laboratory experiments; grade exams and papers; and advise and work with students individually. In universities, they also supervise graduate students' teaching and research. College faculty work with an increasingly varied student population made up of growing shares of part-time, older, and culturally and racially diverse students.

Faculty keep up with developments in their field by reading current literature, talking with colleagues, and participating in professional conferences. They also are encouraged to do their own research to expand knowledge in their field by performing experiments, collecting and analyzing data, or examining original documents, literature, and other source material. They publish their findings in scholarly journals, books, and electronic media.

Most postsecondary teachers use computer technology extensively, including the Internet, e-mail, and software programs. They may use computers in the classroom as teaching aids and may post course content, class notes, class schedules, and other information on the Internet. The use of e-mail, instant messages, and other computer utilities has improved communications greatly between students and teachers.

Some instructors use the Internet to teach courses to students at remote sites. These distance-learning courses are becoming an increasingly popular option for students who work while attending school. Faculty who teach these courses must be able to adapt existing courses to make them successful online or design a new course that takes advantage of the online format.

Most full-time faculty members serve on academic or administrative committees that deal with the policies of their institution, departmental matters, academic issues, curricula, budgets, purchases of equipment, and hiring. Some work with student and community organizations. Department chairpersons are faculty members who usually teach some courses but have heavier administrative responsibilities.

The proportion of time spent on research, teaching, administrative, and other duties varies by individual circumstance and type of institution. The teaching load often is heavier in 2-year colleges and somewhat lighter at 4-year institutions. At all types of institutions, full professors—those who have reached the highest level in their field—usually spend a larger portion of their time conducting research than do assistant professors, instructors, and lecturers.

An increasing number of postsecondary educators are working in alternative schools or in programs aimed at providing career-related education for working adults. Courses usually are offered online or on nights and weekends. Instructors at these programs generally work part time and are responsible only for teaching, with little to no administrative and research responsibilities.

Graduate teaching assistants, often referred to as *graduate TAs*, assist faculty, department chairs, or other professional staff at colleges and universities by teaching or performing teaching-related duties. In addition, assistants have their own school commitments as students working toward earning a graduate degree, such as a Ph.D. Some teaching assistants have full responsibility for teaching a course, usually one that is introductory. Such teaching can include preparing lectures and exams, as well as assigning final grades to students. Others help faculty members by doing a variety of tasks such as grading papers, monitoring exams, holding office hours or help sessions for students, conducting laboratory sessions, and administering quizzes to the class. Because each faculty member has his or her own needs, teaching assistants generally meet initially with the faculty member whom they are going to assist in order to determine exactly what is expected of them. For example, some faculty members prefer assistants to sit in on classes, whereas others assign them other tasks to do during class time. Graduate teaching assistants may work one-on-one with a faculty member, or, in large classes, they may be one of several assistants.

Work environment. Many postsecondary teachers find the environment intellectually stimulating and rewarding because they are surrounded by others who enjoy the subject. The ability to share their expertise with others also is appealing to many.

Most postsecondary teachers have flexible schedules. They must be present for classes, usually 12 to 16 hours per week, and for faculty and committee meetings. Most establish regular office hours for student consultations, usually 3 to 6 hours per week. Otherwise, teachers are free to decide when and where they will work and how much time to devote to course preparation, grading, study, research, graduate student supervision, and other activities.

Classes typically are scheduled to take place during weekdays, although some occur at night or on the weekend. For teachers at 2-year community colleges or institutions with large enrollments of older students who have full-time jobs or family responsibilities, night and weekend classes are common. Most colleges and universities require teachers to work 9 months of the year, which allows them time to teach additional courses, do research, travel, or pursue nonacademic interests during the summer and on school holidays.

About 29 percent of postsecondary teachers worked part time in 2008. Some part-timers, known as adjunct faculty, have primary jobs outside of academia—in government, private-industry, or nonprofit research organizations—and teach on the side. Others have multiple part-time teaching positions at different institutions. Most graduate teaching assistants work part time while pursuing their graduate studies. The number of hours that they work may vary with their assignments.

University faculty may experience a conflict between their responsibility to teach students and the pressure to do research and publish their findings. This may be a particular problem for young faculty seeking advancement in 4-year research universities. Also, recent cutbacks in support workers and the hiring of more part-time faculty have put a greater administrative burden on full-time faculty. In addition, requirements to teach online classes have added greatly to the workloads of postsecondary teachers. Many find that developing the courses to put online is very time consuming, especially when they have to familiarize themselves with the format and answer large amounts of e-mail.

Like college and university faculty, graduate TAs usually have flexibility in their work schedules, but they also must spend a considerable amount of time pursuing their own academic coursework and studies. Work may be stressful, particularly when assistants are given full responsibility for teaching a class. However, these types of positions allow graduate students the opportunity to gain valuable teaching experience, which is especially helpful for those who seek to become college faculty members after completing their degree.

Training, Other Qualifications, and Advancement

The education and training required of postsecondary teachers varies widely, depending on the subject taught and the educational institution employing them. Educational requirements for teachers generally are highest at research universities, where a Ph.D. is the most commonly held degree.

Education and training. Four-year colleges and universities usually require candidates for full-time, tenure-track positions to hold a doctoral degree. However, they may hire master's degree holders or doctoral candidates for certain disciplines, such as the arts, or for part-time and temporary jobs.

Doctoral programs take an average of 6 years of full-time study beyond the bachelor's degree, including time spent completing a master's degree and a dissertation. Some programs, such as those in the humanities, may take longer to complete; others, such as those in engineering, usually are shorter. Candidates specialize in a subfield of a discipline—for example, organic chemistry, counseling psychology, or European history—and also take courses covering the entire discipline. Programs typically include 20 or more increasingly specialized courses and seminars, plus comprehensive examinations in all major areas of the field. Candidates also must complete a dissertation—a paper on original research in the candidate's major field of study. The dissertation sets forth an original hypothesis or proposes a model and tests it. Students in the natural sciences and engineering often do theoretical or laboratory work; in the humanities, they study original documents and other published material. The dissertation is done under the guidance of one or more faculty advisors and usually takes 1 or 2 years of full-time work.

In 2-year colleges, master's degree holders fill most full-time teaching positions. However, in certain fields where there may be more applicants than available jobs, institutions can be more selective in their hiring practices. In these fields, master's degree holders may be passed over in favor of candidates holding Ph.D.s. Many 2-year institutions increasingly prefer job applicants to have some teaching experience or experience with distance learning. Preference also may be given to those holding dual master's degrees, especially at smaller institutions, because those with dual degrees can teach more subjects.

Other qualifications. Postsecondary teachers should communicate and relate well with students, enjoy working with them, and be able to motivate them. They should have inquiring and analytical minds and a strong desire to pursue and disseminate knowledge. In addition, they must be self-motivated and able to work in an environment in which they receive little direct supervision.

Obtaining a position as a graduate teaching assistant is a good way to gain college teaching experience. To qualify, candidates must be enrolled in a graduate school program. In addition, some colleges and universities require teaching assistants to attend classes or take some training prior to being given responsibility for a course.

Although graduate teaching assistants usually work at the institution and in the department where they are earning their degree, teaching or internship positions for graduate students at institutions that do not grant a graduate degree have become more common in recent years. For example, a program called Preparing Future Faculty, administered by the Association of American Colleges and Universities and the Council of Graduate Schools, has led to the creation of many programs that are now independent. These programs offer graduate students at research universities the opportunity to work as teaching assistants at other types of institutions, such as liberal arts or community colleges. Working with a mentor, graduate students teach classes and learn how to improve their teaching techniques. They may attend faculty and committee meetings, develop a curriculum, and learn how to balance the teaching, research, and administrative roles of faculty. These programs provide valuable learning opportunities for graduate students interested in teaching at the postsecondary level and also help to make these students aware of the differences among the various types of institutions at which they may someday work.

Some degree holders, particularly those with degrees in the natural sciences, do postdoctoral research before taking a faculty position. Some Ph.D.s are able to extend postdoctoral appointments or take new ones if they are unable to find a faculty job. Most of these appointments offer a nominal salary.

Advancement. For faculty a major goal in the traditional academic career is attaining tenure, which can take approximately 7 years, with faculty moving up the ranks in tenure-track positions as they meet specific criteria. The ranks are instructor, assistant professor, associate professor, and professor. Colleges and universities usually hire new tenure-track faculty as instructors or assistant professors under term contracts. At the end of the period, their record of teaching, research, and overall contribution to the institution is reviewed, and tenure may be granted if the review is favorable. Those denied tenure usually must leave the institution. Tenured professors cannot be fired without just cause and due process. Tenure protects the faculty member's academic freedom—the ability to advocate controversial or unpopular ideas through teaching and conducting research without fear of being fired. Tenure also gives both faculty and institutions the stability needed for effective research and teaching, and it provides financial security for faculty. Some institutions have adopted post-tenure review policies to encourage ongoing evaluation of tenured faculty.

The number of tenure-track positions is declining as institutions seek flexibility in dealing with financial matters and changing student interests. Institutions are relying more heavily on limited-term contracts and part-time, or adjunct, faculty, thus shrinking the total pool of tenured faculty. Limited-term contracts, typically for 2 to 5 years, may be terminated or extended when they expire and generally do not lead to the granting of tenure. In addition, some institutions have limited the percentage of the faculty that can be tenured.

For tenured postsecondary teachers, further advancement involves a move into an administrative or managerial position, such as departmental chairperson, dean, or president. At 4-year institutions, such advancement requires a doctoral degree. At 2-year colleges, a doctorate is helpful but not usually required for advancement, except for advancement to some top administrative positions, which generally required a doctorate.

Job Outlook

Job openings will stem from faster than the average employment growth and many expected retirements. Competition is expected for tenure-track positions; better opportunities are expected for part-time or non-tenure-track positions. Ph.D. recipients should experience the best job prospects.

Employment change. Postsecondary teachers are expected to grow by 15 percent between 2008 and 2018, which is faster than the average for all occupations. Projected growth in the occupation will be due primarily to increases in college and university enrollment over the next decade. This enrollment growth stems mainly from the expected increase in the population of 18- to 24-year-olds, who constitute the majority of students at postsecondary institutions, and from the increasing number of high school graduates who choose to attend these institutions. Adults returning to college to enhance their career prospects or to update their skills also will continue to create new opportunities for postsecondary teachers, particularly at community colleges and for-profit institutions that cater to working adults. However, many postsecondary educational institutions receive a significant portion of their funding from State and local governments, so expansion of public higher education will be limited by State and local budgets.

Job prospects. Competition is expected for tenure-track positions; better opportunities are expected for part-time or non-tenure-track positions. A significant number of openings in this occupation will be created by growth in enrollments and the need to replace the large numbers of postsecondary teachers who are likely to retire over the next decade. Many postsecondary teachers were hired in the late 1960s and the 1970s to teach members of the baby-boom generation, and they are expected to retire in growing numbers in the years ahead. Ph.D. recipients should experience the best job prospects.

Although competition will remain tight for tenure-track positions at 4-year colleges and universities, there will be available a considerable number of part-time and renewable term appointments at these institutions and at community colleges. Opportunities will be available for master's degree holders because there will be considerable growth at community colleges, career education programs, and other institutions that employ them.

Opportunities for graduate teaching assistants are expected to be good, reflecting expectations of higher undergraduate enrollments. Graduate teaching assistants play an integral role in the postsecondary education system, and they are expected to continue to do so in the future.

One of the main reasons students attend postsecondary institutions is to prepare themselves for careers, so the best job prospects for postsecondary teachers are likely to be in rapidly growing fields that offer many nonacademic career options, such as business, nursing and other health specialties, and biological sciences.

EDUCATION

—⁂—

Teaching (Special Education)

Nature of the Work

Special education teachers work with children and youths who have a variety of disabilities. A small number of special education teachers work with students with severe cognitive, emotional, or physical disabilities, primarily teaching them life skills and basic literacy. However, the majority of special education teachers work with children with mild to moderate disabilities, using or modifying the general education curriculum to meet the child's individual needs and providing required remedial instruction. Most special education teachers instruct students at the preschool, elementary, middle, and secondary school level, although some work with infants and toddlers.

The various types of disabilities that may qualify individuals for special education programs are as follows: specific learning disabilities, speech or language impairments, mental retardation, emotional disturbance, multiple disabilities, hearing impairments, orthopedic impairments, visual impairments, autism, combined deafness and blindness, traumatic brain injury, and other health impairments. Students are identified under one

Significant Points

❖ Special education teachers must be organized, patient, able to motivate students, understanding of their students' special needs, and accepting of differences in others.

❖ All States require teachers to be licensed; traditional licensing requires the completion of a special education teacher training program and at least a bachelor's degree, although some States require a master's degree.

❖ Many States offer alternative licensure programs to attract college graduates who do not have training in education.

❖ Excellent job prospects are expected due to rising enrollments of special education students and reported shortages of qualified teachers.

or more of these categories. Early identification of a child with special needs is an important part of a special education teacher's job, because early intervention is essential in educating children with disabilities.

Special education teachers use various techniques to promote learning. Depending on the student, teaching methods can include intensive individualized instruction, problem-solving assignments, and small-group work. When students need special accommodations to learn the general curriculum or to take a test, special education teachers ensure that appropriate accommodations are provided, such as having material read orally or lengthening the time allowed to take the test.

Special education teachers help to develop an Individualized Education Program (IEP) for each student receiving special education. The IEP sets personalized goals for the student and is tailored to that student's individual needs and abilities. When appropriate, the program includes a transition plan outlining specific steps to prepare students for middle school or high school or, in the case of older students, a job or postsecondary study. Teachers review the IEP with the student's parents, school administrators, and the student's general education teachers. Teachers work closely with parents to inform them of their children's progress and suggest techniques to promote learning outside of school.

Special education teachers design and teach appropriate curricula, assign work geared toward each student's needs and abilities, and grade papers and homework assignments. They are involved in the student's behavioral, social, and academic development, helping them develop emotionally and interact effectively in social situations. Preparing special education students for daily life after graduation also is an important aspect of the job. Teachers provide students with career counseling or help them learn life skills, such as balancing a checkbook.

As schools become more inclusive, special education teachers and general education teachers increasingly work together in general education classrooms. Special education teachers help general educators adapt curriculum materials and teaching techniques to meet the needs of students with disabilities. They coordinate the work of teachers, teacher assistants, and related personnel, such as therapists and social workers, to meet the individualized needs of the student within inclusive special education programs. A large part of a special education teacher's job involves communicating and coordinating with others involved in the child's well-being, including parents, social workers, school psychologists, occupational and physical therapists, school administrators, and other teachers.

Special education teachers work in a variety of settings. Some have their own classrooms and teach only special education students; others work as special education resource teachers and offer individualized help to students in general education classrooms; still others teach together with general education teachers in classes including both general and special education students. Some teachers work with special education students for several hours a day in a resource room, separate from their general education classroom. Considerably fewer special education teachers work in residential facilities or tutor students in homebound or hospital environments.

Some special education teachers work with infants and toddlers in the child's home with his or her parents. Many of these infants have challenges that slow or preclude normal development. Special education teachers help parents learn techniques and activities designed to stimulate the infant and encourage the growth and development of the child's skills. Toddlers usually receive their services at a preschool where special education teachers help them develop social, self-help, motor, language, and cognitive skills, often through the use of play.

Technology is becoming increasingly important in special education. Teachers use specialized equipment such as computers with synthesized speech, interactive educational software programs, and audiotapes to assist children.

Work environment. Special education teachers enjoy the challenge of working with students with disabilities and the opportunity to establish meaningful relationships with them. Although helping these students can be highly rewarding, the work also can be emotionally demanding and physically draining. Many special education teachers are under considerable stress due to heavy workloads and administrative tasks. They must produce a substantial amount of paperwork documenting each student's progress and work under the threat of litigation against the school or district by parents if correct procedures are not followed or if the parents feel that their child is not receiving an adequate education. Recently passed legislation, however, is intended to reduce the burden of paperwork and the threat of litigation. The physical and emotional demands of the job cause some special education teachers to leave the occupation.

Some schools offer year-round education for special education students, but most special education teachers work only the traditional 10-month school year.

Training, Other Qualifications, and Advancement

All States require special education teachers to be licensed, which typically requires at least a bachelor's degree and the completion of an approved training program in special education teaching. Some States require a master's degree. Most States have alternative methods for entry for bachelor's degree holders who do not have training in education.

Education and training. Many colleges and universities across the United States offer programs in special education at the undergraduate, master's, and doctoral degree levels. Special education teachers often undergo longer periods of training than do general education teachers. Most bachelor's degree programs last four years and include general and specialized courses in special education. However, an increasing number of institutions are requiring a fifth year or other graduate-level preparation. Some programs require specialization, while others offer generalized special education degrees. The last year of the program usually is spent student teaching in a classroom supervised by a certified special education teacher.

Licensure. All 50 States and the District of Columbia require special education teachers to be licensed. The State board of education or a licensure advisory committee usually grants licenses, and licensure varies by State. In some States, special education teachers receive a general education credential to teach kindergarten through grade 12. These teachers then train in a specialty, such as learning disabilities or behavioral disorders. Many States offer general special education licenses across a variety of disability categories, while others license several different specialties within special education.

For traditional licensing, all States require a bachelor's degree and the completion of an approved teacher preparation program with a prescribed number of subject and education credits and supervised practice teaching. However, some States also require a master's degree in special education, which involves at least 1 year of additional coursework, including a specialization, beyond the bachelor's degree. Most States require a prospective teacher to pass a professional assessment test as well. Some States have reciprocity agreements allowing special education teachers to transfer their licenses from one State to another, but many others still require that experienced teachers reapply and pass licensing requirements to work in the State.

Most States also offer alternative routes to licensing that are intended to attract people into teaching who do not fulfill traditional licensing standards. Most alternative licensure programs are open to anyone with a bachelor's degree, although some are designed for recent college graduates or professionals in other education occupations. Programs typically require the completion of a period of supervised preparation and instruction through a partnering college or university and passing an assessment test while teaching under supervision for a period of 1 to 2 years.

Other qualifications. Special education teachers must be organized, patient, able to motivate students, understanding of their students' special needs, and accepting of differences in others. Teachers must be creative and apply different types of teaching methods to reach students who are having difficulty learning. Communication and cooperation are essential skills because special education teachers spend a great deal of time interacting with others, including students, parents, and school faculty and administrators.

Advancement. Special education teachers can advance to become supervisors or administrators. They also may earn advanced degrees and become instructors in colleges that prepare others to teach special education. In some school systems, highly experienced teachers can become mentors to less experienced teachers.

Employment

Special education teachers held a total of about 473,000 jobs in 2008. Nearly all worked in public and private educational institutions. A few worked for individual and social assistance agencies or residential facilities, or in homebound or hospital environments.

Job Outlook

Employment is expected to increase faster than the average for all occupations. Job prospects should be excellent because many districts report problems finding adequate numbers of licensed special education teachers.

Employment change. The number of special education teachers is expected to increase by 17 percent from 2008 to 2018, which is faster than the average for all occupations. Although student enrollments in general are expected to grow more slowly than in the past, continued increases in the number of special education students needing services will generate a greater need for special education teachers.

The number of students requiring special education services has grown steadily in recent years because of improvements that have allowed learning disabilities to be diagnosed at earlier ages. In addition, legislation emphasizing training and employment for individuals with disabilities and educational reforms requiring higher standards for graduation have increased demand for special education services. Also, the percentage of foreign-born special education students is expected to grow as teachers become more adept in recognizing disabilities in that population. Finally, more parents are expected to seek special services for children who have difficulty meeting the new, higher standards required of students.

Job prospects. In addition to job openings resulting from growth, a large number of openings will result from the need to replace special education teachers who switch to teaching general education, change careers altogether, or retire. At the same time, many school districts report difficulty finding sufficient numbers of qualified teachers. As a result, special education teachers should have excellent job prospects.

The job outlook does vary by geographic area and specialty. Although most areas of the country report difficulty finding qualified applicants, positions in inner cities and rural areas usually are more plentiful than job openings in suburban or wealthy urban areas. Student populations also are expected to increase more rapidly in certain parts of the country, such as the South and West, resulting in increased demand for special education teachers in those regions. In addition, job opportunities may be better in certain specialties—for example, teachers who work with children with multiple disabilities or those who work with children with severe disabilities such as autism—because of large increases in the enrollment of special education students classified into those categories. Legislation encouraging early intervention and special education for infants, toddlers, and preschoolers has created a need for early childhood special education teachers. Bilingual special education teachers and those with multicultural experience also are needed, to work with an increasingly diverse student population.

Earnings

Median annual wages in May 2008 of special education teachers who worked primarily in preschools, kindergartens, and elementary schools were $50,020. The middle 50 percent earned between $40,480 and $63,500. The lowest 10 percent earned less than $33,770, and the highest 10 percent earned more than $78,980

Median annual wages of middle school special education teachers were $50,810. The middle 50 percent earned between $41,720 and $63,480. The lowest 10 percent earned less than $35,180, and the highest 10 percent earned more than $78,200.

Median annual wages of special education teachers who worked primarily in secondary schools were $51,340. The middle 50 percent earned between $41,810 and $65,680. The lowest 10 percent earned less than $35,150, and the highest 10 percent earned more than $82,000.

In 2008, about 64 percent of special education teachers belonged to unions or were covered by union contracts.

In most schools, teachers receive extra pay for coaching sports and working with students in extracurricular activities. Some teachers earn extra income during the summer, working in the school system or in other jobs.

EDUCATION

—〰—

Librarians

Nature of the Work

The traditional concept of a library is being redefined from a place to access paper records or books to one that also houses the most advanced electronic resources, including the Internet, digital libraries, and remote access to a wide range of information sources. Consequently, *librarians*, often called *information professionals*, combine traditional duties with tasks involving quickly changing technology. Librarians help people find information and use it effectively for personal and professional purposes. They must have knowledge of a wide variety of scholarly and public information sources and must follow trends related to publishing, computers, and the media to oversee the selection and organization of library materials. Librarians manage staff and develop and direct information programs and systems for the public and ensure that information is organized in a manner that meets users' needs.

Librarian positions focus on one of three aspects of library work: user services, technical services, and administrative services. Librarians in user services, such as reference and children's librarians, work with patrons to help them find the information they need. The job involves analyzing users' needs to determine what information is appropriate and searching for, acquiring, and providing the information. The job also includes an instructional role,

---

Significant Points

❖ Librarians use the latest information technology to perform research, classify materials, and help students and library patrons seek information.

❖ A master's degree in library science is required for most librarian positions, although school librarians also often need to meet State teaching license requirements.

❖ Growth is expected to be as fast as the average and job opportunities are expected to be favorable, as a large number of librarians are likely to retire in the coming decade.

such as showing users how to find and evaluate information. For example, librarians commonly help users navigate the Internet so they can search for and evaluate information efficiently. Librarians in technical services, such as acquisitions and cataloguing, acquire, prepare, and classify materials so patrons can find it easily. Some write abstracts and summaries. Often, these librarians do not deal directly with the public. Librarians in administrative services oversee the management and planning of libraries: they negotiate contracts for services, materials, and equipment; supervise library employees; perform public-relations and fundraising duties; prepare budgets; and direct activities to ensure that everything functions properly.

In small libraries or information centers, librarians usually handle all aspects of library operations. They read book reviews, publishers' announcements, and catalogues to keep up with current literature and other available resources, and they select and purchase materials from publishers, wholesalers, and distributors. Librarians prepare new materials, classifying them by subject matter and describing books and other library materials to make them easy to find. Librarians supervise assistants, who enter classification information and descriptions of materials into electronic catalogs. In large libraries, librarians often specialize in a single area, such as acquisitions, cataloguing, bibliography, reference, special collections, or administration. Therefore, good teamwork is important.

Librarians also recommend materials. Many analyze collections and compile lists of books, periodicals, articles, audiovisual materials, and electronic resources on particular subjects. They collect and organize books, pamphlets, manuscripts, and other materials in a specific field, such as rare books, genealogy, or music. In addition, they coordinate programs such as storytelling for children and literacy skills and book talks for adults. Some conduct classes, publicize services, write grants, and oversee other administrative matters.

Many libraries have access to remote databases and maintain their own computerized databases. The widespread use of electronic resources makes database-searching skills important for librarians. Librarians develop and index databases and help train users to develop searching skills. Some libraries are forming consortiums with other libraries to allow patrons to access a wider range of databases and to submit information requests to several libraries simultaneously. The Internet also has greatly expanded the amount of available reference information. Librarians must know how to use these resources and inform the public about the wealth of information they contain.

Librarians are classified according to the type of library in which they work: a public library; school library media center; college, university, or other academic library; or special library. Librarians in special libraries work in information centers or libraries maintained by government agencies or corporations, law firms, advertising agencies, museums, professional associations, unions, medical centers, hospitals, religious organizations, or research laboratories. They acquire and arrange an organization's information resources, which usually are limited to subjects of special interest to the organization. They can provide vital information services by preparing abstracts and indexes of current periodicals, organizing bibliographies, or analyzing background information and preparing reports on areas of particular interest. For example, a *special librarian* working for a corporation could provide the sales department with information on competitors or new developments affecting the field. A *medical librarian* may provide information about new medical treatments, clinical trials, and standard procedures to health professionals, patients, consumers, and corporations. *Government document librarians*, who work in a variety of depository libraries in each of the States, preserve and disseminate government publications, records, and other documents that make up a historical record of government actions.

Some librarians work with specific groups, such as children, young adults, adults, or the disadvantaged. In school library media centers, librarians—often called *school media specialists*—help teachers develop curricula and acquire materials for classroom instruction. They also conduct classes for students on how to use library resources for research projects.

Librarians with computer and information systems skills can work as *automated-systems librarians*, planning and operating computer systems, and as information architects, designing information storage and retrieval systems and developing procedures for collecting, organizing, interpreting, and classifying information. These librarians analyze and plan for future information needs. Automated information systems enable librarians to focus on administrative and budgeting responsibilities, grant writing, and specialized research requests, while delegating more routine services responsibilities to technicians.

More and more, librarians apply their information management and research skills to arenas outside of libraries—for example, database development, reference tool development, information systems, publishing, Internet coordination, marketing, Web content management and design, and training of database users. Entrepreneurial librarians sometimes start their own consulting practices, acting as freelance librarians or information brokers and providing services to other libraries, businesses, or government agencies.

Work environment. Librarians spend a significant portion of time at their desks or in front of computer terminals; extended work at video display terminals can cause eyestrain and headaches. Assisting users in obtaining information or books for their jobs, homework, or recreational reading can be challenging and satisfying, but working with users under deadlines can be demanding and stressful. Some librarians lift and carry books, and some climb ladders to reach high stacks, although most modern libraries have readily accessible stacks. Librarians in small settings without support staff sometimes shelve books themselves.

Twenty-five percent of librarians work part time. Public and college librarians often work weekends, evenings, and some holidays. School librarians usually have the same workday and vacation schedules as classroom teachers. Special librarians usually work normal business hours, but in fast-paced industries—such as advertising or legal services—they can work longer hours, when needed.

Training, Other Qualifications, and Advancement

A master's degree in library science (MLS) is necessary for librarian positions in most public, academic, and special libraries. School librarians may not need an MLS but must meet State teaching license requirements.

Education and training. Entry into a library science graduate program requires a bachelor's degree, but any undergraduate major is acceptable. Many colleges and universities offer library science programs, but employers often prefer graduates of the 49 schools in the United States accredited by the American Library Association. Most programs take 1 year to complete; some take 2. A typical graduate program includes courses in the foundations of library and information science, such as the history of books and printing, intellectual freedom and censorship, and the role of libraries and information in society. Other basic courses cover the selection and processing of materials, the organization of information, research methods and strategies, and user services. Prospective librarians also study online reference systems, Internet search methods, and automated circulation systems. Elective course options include resources for children or young adults; classification, cataloguing, indexing, and abstracting; and library administration. Computer-related course work is an increasingly important part of an MLS degree. Some programs offer interdisciplinary degrees combining technical courses in information science with traditional training in library science.

The MLS degree provides general preparation for library work, but some individuals specialize in a particular area, such as reference, technical services, or children's services. A Ph.D. in library and information science is advantageous for a college teaching position or a top administrative job in a college or university library or large public library system.

Licensure. States generally have certification requirements for librarians in public schools and local libraries, though there are wide variations among States. School librarians in 20 States need a master's degree, either an MLS or a master's in education with a specialization in library media. In addition, over half of all States require that school librarians hold teacher certifications, although not all require teaching experience. Some States may also require librarians to pass a comprehensive assessment. Most States also have developed certification standards for local public libraries, although in some States these guidelines are voluntary.

Other qualifications. In addition to an MLS degree, librarians in a special library, such as a law or corporate library, usually supplement their education with knowledge of the field in which they are specializing, sometimes earning a master's, doctoral, or professional degree in the subject. Areas of specialization include medicine, law, business, engineering, and the natural and social sciences. For example, a librarian working for a law firm may hold both library science and law degrees, while medical librarians should have a strong background in the sciences. In some jobs, knowledge of a foreign language is needed.

Librarians participate in continuing education and training to stay up to date with new information systems and technology.

Advancement. Experienced librarians can advance to administrative positions, such as department head, library director, or chief information officer.

Employment

Librarians held about 159,900 jobs in 2008. About 59 percent were employed by public and private educational institutions and 27 percent were employed by local government.

Job Outlook

Job growth is expected to be as fast as the average and job opportunities are expected to be favorable, as a large number of librarians are likely to retire in the coming decade.

Employment change. Employment of librarians is expected to grow by 8 percent between 2008 and 2018, which is as fast as the average for all occupations. Growth in the number of librarians will be limited by government budget constraints and the increasing use of electronic resources. Both will result in the hiring of fewer librarians and the replacement of librarians with less costly library technicians and assistants. As electronic resources become more common and patrons and support staff become more familiar with their use, fewer librarians are needed to maintain and assist users with these resources. In addition, many libraries are equipped for users to access library resources directly from their homes or offices through library Web sites. Some users bypass librarians altogether and conduct research on their own. However, librarians continue to be in demand to manage staff, help users develop database-searching techniques, address complicated reference requests, choose materials, and help users to define their needs.

Jobs for librarians outside traditional settings will grow the fastest over the decade. Nontraditional librarian jobs include working as information brokers and working for private corporations, nonprofit organizations, and consulting firms. Many companies are turning to librarians because of their research and organizational skills and their knowledge of computer databases and library automation systems. Librarians can review vast amounts of information and analyze, evaluate, and organize it according to a company's specific needs. Librarians also are hired by organizations to set up information on the Internet. Librarians working in these settings may be classified as systems analysts, database specialists and trainers, webmasters or Web developers, or local area network (LAN) coordinators.

Job prospects. Job prospects are expected to be favorable. On average, workers in this occupation tend to be older than workers in the rest of the economy. As a result, there may be more workers retiring from this occupation than other occupations. However, relatively large numbers of graduates from MLS programs may cause competition in some areas and for some jobs.

Earnings

Salaries of librarians vary according to the individual's qualifications and the type, size, and location of the library. Librarians with primarily administrative duties often have greater earnings. Median annual wages of librarians in May 2008 were $52,530. The middle 50 percent earned between $42,240 and $65,300. The lowest 10 percent earned less than $33,190, and the highest 10 percent earned more than $81,130.

EDUCATION

—ᴡ—

Education Administrators

Nature of the Work

Successful operation of an educational institution requires competent administrators. *Education administrators* provide instructional leadership and manage the day-to-day activities in schools, preschools, day care centers, and colleges and universities. They also direct the educational programs of businesses, correctional institutions, museums, and job training and community service organizations. (College presidents and school superintendents are covered in the *Handbook* statement on general managers and top executives.)

Education administrators set educational standards and goals and establish the policies and procedures required to achieve them.

Significant Points

❖ Many jobs require a master's or doctoral degree and experience in a related occupation, such as teaching or admissions counseling.

❖ Strong interpersonal and communication skills are essential because much of an administrator's job involves working and collaborating with others.

❖ Excellent opportunities are expected for most jobs.

They also supervise managers, support staff, teachers, counselors, librarians, coaches, and other employees. They develop academic programs, monitor students' educational progress, train and motivate teachers and other staff, manage career counseling and other student services, administer recordkeeping, prepare budgets, and perform many other duties. They also handle relations with parents, prospective and current students, employers, and the community. In a smaller organization such as a small day care center, one administrator may handle all these functions. In universities or large school systems, responsibilities are divided among many administrators, each with a specific function.

Educational administrators who manage elementary, middle, and secondary schools are called *principals*. They set the academic tone and work actively with teachers to develop and maintain high curriculum standards, formulate mission statements, and establish performance goals and objectives. Principals confer with staff to advise, explain, or answer procedural questions. They hire and evaluate teachers and other staff. They visit classrooms, observe teaching methods, review instructional objectives, and examine learning materials. Principals must use clear, objective guidelines for teacher appraisals, because principals' pay often is based on performance ratings.

Principals also meet with other administrators and students, parents, and representatives of community organizations. Decision making authority increasingly has shifted from school district central offices to individual schools. School principals have greater flexibility in setting school policies and goals, but when making administrative decisions, they must pay attention to the concerns of parents, teachers, and other members of the community.

Principals also are responsible for preparing budgets and reports on various subjects, such as finances, attendance and student performance. As school budgets become tighter, many principals have become more involved in public relations and fundraising to secure financial support for their schools from local businesses and the community.

Principals ensure that students meet national, State, and local academic standards. Many principals develop partnerships with local businesses and school-to-work transition programs for students. Principals must be sensitive to the needs of a rising number of non-English-speaking students and a culturally diverse student body. In some areas, growing enrollments are a cause for concern, because they lead to overcrowding at many schools. When addressing problems of inadequate resources, administrators serve as advocates for the building of new schools or the repair of existing ones. During the summer months, principals are responsible for planning for the upcoming year, overseeing summer school, participating in workshops for teachers and administrators, supervising building repairs and improvements, and working to make sure that the school has adequate staff for the upcoming school year.

Schools continue to be involved with students' emotional welfare as well as their academic achievement. As a result, principals face responsibilities outside of academics. For example, many schools have a large number of students from single-parent families, families in which both parents work outside the home or students who are teenage parents. To support these students and their families, some schools have established before- and after-school child care programs or family resource centers, which also may offer parenting classes and social service referrals. With the help of community organizations, some principals have established programs to combat increases in crime, drug and alcohol abuse, and sexually transmitted diseases among students.

Assistant principals aid the principal in the overall administration of the school. Some assistant principals hold the position for only a few years, during which time they prepare for advancement to principal; others are assistant principals throughout their careers. They are primarily responsible for scheduling student classes and ordering textbooks and supplies. They also coordinate transportation, custodial, cafeteria, and other support services. They usually handle student discipline and attendance problems, social and recreational programs, and matters of health and safety. In addition, they may counsel students on personal, educational, or vocational matters. With the advent of site-based management, assistant principals play a greater role in academic planning by helping to develop new curricula, evaluating teachers, and dealing with school-community relations—responsibilities previously assumed solely by the principal. The number of assistant principals that a school employs may vary with the number of students.

Administrators in school district central offices oversee public schools under their jurisdiction. This group of administrators includes those who direct subject-area programs such as English, music, vocational education, special education, and mathematics. They supervise instructional coordinators and curriculum specialists and work with them to evaluate curricula and teaching techniques and to develop programs and strategies to improve them. Some administrators may oversee career counseling programs. Others may administer testing that measures students' abilities and helps to place them in appropriate classes. Some may direct programs such as school psychology, athletics, curriculum and instruction, and professional development. With site-based management, administrators have transferred the primary responsibility for many of these programs to the principals, assistant principals, teachers, instructional coordinators, and other staff in the schools.

In preschools and child care centers, which are usually much smaller than other educational institutions, the *director* or *supervisor* of the school or center often serves as the sole administrator. The director's or supervisor's job is similar to that of other school administrators in that he or she oversees the school's daily activities and operation, hires and develops staff, and ensures that the school meets required regulations and educational standards.

In colleges and universities, *provosts*, also known as *chief academic officers*, assist presidents, make faculty appointments and tenure decisions, develop budgets, and establish academic policies and programs. With the assistance of *academic deans* and *deans of faculty*, provosts also direct and coordinate the activities of deans of individual colleges and chairpersons of academic departments. Fundraising is the chief responsibility of the *director of development* and also is becoming an essential part of the job for all administrators.

College or university department heads or *chairpersons* are in charge of departments that specialize in particular fields of study, such as English, biological science, or mathematics. In addition to teaching, they coordinate schedules of classes and teaching assignments; propose budgets; recruit, interview, and hire applicants for teaching positions; evaluate faculty members; encourage faculty development; serve on committees; and perform other administrative duties. In overseeing their departments, chairpersons must consider and balance the concerns of faculty, administrators, and students.

Higher education administrators also direct and coordinate the provision of student services. *Vice presidents of student affairs or student life, deans of students*, and *directors of student services* may direct and coordinate admissions, foreign student services, health and counseling services, career services, financial aid, and housing and residential life, as well as social, recreational, and related programs. In small colleges, they may counsel students. In larger colleges and universities, separate administrators may handle each of these services. *Registrars* are custodians of students' records. They register students, record grades, prepare student transcripts, evaluate academic records, assess and collect tuition and fees, plan and implement commencement exercises, oversee the preparation of college catalogs and schedules of classes, and analyze enrollment and demographic statistics. *Directors of admissions* manage the process of recruiting, evaluating, and admitting students, and work closely with *financial aid directors*, who oversee scholarship, fellowship, and loan programs. Registrars and admissions officers at most institutions need computer skills because they use electronic student information systems. For example, for those whose institutions present college catalogs, schedules, and other information on the Internet, knowledge of online resources, imaging, and other computer skills is important. *Athletic directors* plan and direct intramural and intercollegiate athletic activities, overseeing the publicity for athletic events, preparing budgets, and supervising coaches. Other increasingly important administrators direct public relations, distance learning, and technology.

Work environment. Education administrators hold leadership positions with significant responsibility. Most find working with students extremely rewarding, but as the responsibilities of administrators have increased in recent years, so has the stress. Coordinating and interacting with faculty, parents, students, community members, business leaders, and State and local policymakers can be fast paced and stimulating, but also stressful and demanding. Principals and assistant principals, whose duties include disciplining students, may find working with difficult students challenging. They also are increasingly being held accountable for their schools meeting State and Federal guidelines for student performance and teacher qualifications.

About 35 percent of education administrators worked more than 40 hours a week in 2008; they often supervise school activities at night and on weekends. Most administrators work year round, although some work only during the academic year.

Training, Other Qualifications, and Advancement

Most education administrators begin their careers as teachers and prepare for advancement into education administration by completing a master's or doctoral degree. Because of the diversity of duties and levels of responsibility, educational backgrounds and experience vary considerably among these workers.

Education and training. Principals, assistant principals, central office administrators, academic deans, and preschool directors usually have held teaching positions before moving into administration. Some teachers move directly into principal positions; others first become assistant principals or gain experience in other administrative jobs at either the school or district level in positions such as department head, curriculum specialist, or subject matter advisor.

In most public schools, principals, assistant principals, and school district administrators need a master's degree in education administration or educational leadership. Some principals and central office administrators have a doctorate or specialized degree in education administration. In private schools, some principals and assistant principals hold only a bachelor's degree, but the majority of principals have a master's or doctoral degree.

Educational requirements for administrators of preschools and child care centers vary with the setting of the program and the State of employment. Administrators who oversee preschool programs in public schools often are required to have at least a bachelor's degree. Child care directors who supervise private programs typically are not required to have a degree; however, most States require a preschool education credential, which often includes some postsecondary coursework.

College and university academic deans and chairpersons usually advance from professorships in their departments, for which they need a master's or doctoral degree; further education is not typically necessary. Admissions, student affairs, and financial aid directors and registrars sometimes start in related staff jobs with bachelor's degrees—any field usually is acceptable—and obtain advanced degrees in college student affairs, counseling, or higher education administration. A Ph.D. or Ed.D. usually is necessary for top student affairs positions. Computer literacy and a background in accounting or statistics may be assets in admissions, records, and financial work.

Advanced degrees in higher education administration, educational leadership, and college student affairs are offered in many colleges and universities. Education administration degree programs include courses in school leadership, school law, school finance and budgeting, curriculum development and evaluation, research design and data analysis, community relations, politics in education, and counseling. The National Council for Accreditation of Teacher Education (NCATE) and the Educational Leadership Constituent Council (ELCC) accredit programs designed for elementary and secondary school administrators. Although completion of an accredited program is not required, it may assist in fulfilling licensure requirements.

Licensure and certification. Most States require principals to be licensed as school administrators. License requirements vary by State, but nearly all States require either a master's degree or some other graduate-level training. Some States also require candidates for licensure to pass a test. On-the-job training, often with a mentor, is increasingly required or recommended for new school leaders. Some States require administrators to take continuing education courses to keep their license, thus ensuring that administrators have the most up-to-date skills. The number and types of courses required to maintain licensure vary by State. Principals in private schools are not subject to State licensure requirements.

Nearly all states require child care and preschool center directors to be licensed. Licensing usually requires a number of years of experience or hours of coursework or both. Sometimes, it requires a college degree. Often, directors also are required to earn a general preschool education credential, such as the Child Development Associate credential (CDA) sponsored by the Council for Professional Recognition, or some other credential designed specifically for directors. One credential designed specifically for directors is the National Administration Credential, offered by the National Child Care Association. The credential requires experience and training in child care center management.

There usually are no licensing requirements for administrators at postsecondary institutions.

Other qualifications. To be considered for education administrator positions, workers must first prove themselves in their current jobs. In evaluating candidates, supervisors look for leadership, determination, confidence, innovativeness, and motivation. The ability to make sound decisions and to organize and coordinate work efficiently is essential. Because much of an administrator's job involves interacting with others, a person in such a position must have strong interpersonal skills and be an effective communicator and motivator. Knowledge of leadership principles and practices, gained through work experience and formal education, is important. A familiarity with computer technology is a necessity for many of these workers as computers are used to perform their basic job duties and they may be responsible for coordinating technical resources for students, teachers, and classrooms.

Advancement. Education administrators advance through promotion to higher level administrative positions or by transferring to comparable positions at larger schools or systems. They also may become superintendents of school systems or presidents of educational institutions.

Employment

Education administrators held about 445,400 jobs in 2008. Of these, about 58,900 were held by preschool or child care administrators, about 230,600 by elementary or secondary school administrators, and 124,600 by postsecondary administrators. The great majority—more than 81 percent—worked in public or private educational institutions. Most of the remainder worked in child day care centers.

Job Outlook

Employment is projected to grow about as fast as the average for all occupations. Job opportunities should be excellent due to a large number of expected retirements and fewer applicants for some positions.

Employment change. Employment of education administrators is expected to grow by about 8 percent between 2008 and 2018, which is about as fast as the average for all occupations. Expected growth is primarily the result of growth in enrollments of school-aged children. Enrollment of students in elementary and secondary schools is expected to grow relatively slowly over the next decade, limiting the growth of principals and other administrators in these schools. However, the number of administrative positions will continue to increase as more administrative responsibilities are placed on individual schools, particularly with regard to monitoring student achievement. Preschool and child care center administrators are expected to experience substantial growth because of increasing enrollments in formal child care programs as fewer young children are cared for in private homes. In addition, as more States implement or expand public preschool programs, more preschool directors will be needed.

The number of students at the postsecondary level is projected to grow more rapidly than other student populations. Many of these schools cater to working adults who might not ordinarily participate in postsecondary education. Such schools allow students to earn a degree, receive job-specific training, or update their skills in a convenient manner, such as through part-time programs or distance learning. As the number of these schools continues to grow, more administrators will be needed to oversee them.

Job prospects. Job opportunities should be excellent due to a large number of expected retirements and fewer applicants for some positions. Principals and assistant principals should have excellent job prospects because a sharp increase in responsibilities in recent years has made the job more stressful and has discouraged some teachers from taking positions in administration. Principals are now being held more accountable for the performance of students and teachers, while at the same time they are required to adhere to a growing number of government regulations. In addition, overcrowded classrooms, safety issues, budgetary concerns, and teacher shortages in some areas are creating additional stress for administrators. Many teachers feel that the increase in pay for becoming an administrator is not high enough to compensate for the greater responsibilities.

Opportunities may vary by region of the country. Enrollments are expected to increase the fastest in the West and South, where the population is growing faster, and to decline or remain stable in the Northeast and the Midwest. School administrators also are in greater demand in rural and urban areas, where pay is generally lower than in the suburbs.

Fewer applicants are expected for nonacademic administrative jobs, such as director of admissions or director of student affairs. Furthermore, many people are discouraged from seeking administrator jobs by the requirement that they have a master's or doctoral degree in education administration—as well as by the opportunity to earn higher salaries in other occupations.

Earnings

In May 2008, preschool and child care program administrators had median annual wages of $39,940. The middle 50 percent earned between $31,290 and $54,680. The lowest 10 percent earned less than $25,910 and the highest 10 percent earned more than $77,150.

In May 2008, elementary and secondary school administrators had median annual wages of $83,880. The middle 50 percent earned between $68,360 and $102,830. The lowest 10 percent earned less than $55,580 and the highest 10 percent earned more than $124,250.

In May 2008, postsecondary school administrators had median annual wages of $80,670. The middle 50 percent earned between $58,940 and $113,860. The lowest 10 percent earned less than $45,050 and the highest 10 percent earned more than $160,500.

Salaries of education administrators depend on several factors, including the location and enrollment level of the school or school district.

MEDIA

—ɷ—

Announcers (TV & Radio)

Nature of the Work

Radio and television announcers perform a variety of tasks on and off the air. They announce station program information, such as program schedules and station breaks for commercials, or public-service information, and they introduce and close programs. Announcers read prepared scripts or make ad-lib commentary on the air as they present news, sports, the weather, the time, and commercials. If a written script is required, they may do the research and writing. Announcers also interview guests and moderate panels or discussions. Some provide commentary for the audience during sporting events, at parades, and on other occasions. Announcers often are well known to radio and television audiences and may make promotional appearances and do remote broadcasts for their stations.

Significant Points

❖ Competition for announcer jobs will continue to be keen.

❖ Jobs at small stations usually have low pay, but offer the best opportunities for inexperienced announcers.

❖ Applicants who have completed internships or have related work experience, and those with more advanced computer skills, may have an advantage in the job market.

❖ Employment is projected to decline slowly.

Announcers at smaller stations may have more off-air duties as well. They may operate the control board, monitor the transmitter, sell commercial time to advertisers, keep a log of the station's daily programming, and produce advertisements and other recorded material. At many radio stations, announcers do much of the work previously performed by editors and broadcast technicians, such as operating the control board, which is used to broadcast programming, commercials, and public-service announcements according to the station's schedule. radio and television announcers also are involved in station fundraising efforts.

Announcers frequently participate in community activities. Sports announcers, for example, may serve as masters of ceremony at sports club banquets or may greet customers at openings of sporting-goods stores.

Radio announcers who broadcast music often are called *disc jockeys (DJs)*. Some DJs specialize in one kind of music, announcing selections as they air them. Most DJs do not select much of the music they play (although they often did so in the past); instead, they follow schedules of commercials, talk, and music provided to them by management. While on the air, DJs comment on the music, weather, and traffic. They may take requests from listeners, interview guests, and manage listener contests. Many radio stations now require DJs to update their station Web site.

Some DJs announce and play music at clubs, dances, restaurants, and weddings. They often have their own equipment with which to play the music. Many are self-employed and rent their services out on a job-by-job basis.

Show hosts may specialize in a certain area of interest, such as politics, personal finance, sports, or health. They contribute to the preparation of the program's content, interview guests, and discuss issues with viewers, listeners, or the studio audience.

Public-address system announcers provide information to the audience at sporting, performing arts, and other events.

Work environment. Announcers usually work in well-lighted, air-conditioned, soundproof studios. Announcers often work within tight schedules, which can be physically and mentally stressful. For many announcers, the intangible rewards—creative work, many personal contacts, and the satisfaction of becoming widely known—far outweigh the disadvantages of irregular and often unpredictable hours, work pressures, and disrupted personal lives.

The broadcast day is long for radio and TV stations—many are on the air 24 hours a day—so announcers can expect to work unusual hours. Many present early-morning shows, when most people are getting ready for work or commuting, while others do late-night programs. The shifts, however, are not as varied as in the past, because new technology has allowed stations to eliminate most of the overnight hours. Many announcers work part time.

Training, Other Qualifications, and Advancement

Entry into this occupation is highly competitive, and postsecondary education or long-term on-the-job training is common. Trainees usually must have several years of experience in the industry before receiving an opportunity to work on the air. An applicant's delivery and—in television—appearance and style are important.

Education and training. Formal training in broadcasting from college or a technical school is valuable. These programs prepare students to work with the computer equipment and software to which they might otherwise not have access. In radio, many announcers will also need Web site editing skills. It is common for announcers to have a bachelor's degree in a subject such as communications, broadcasting, or journalism. High school and college courses in English, public speaking, drama, foreign languages, and computer science are valuable, and hobbies such as sports and music are additional assets.

There are many broadcast programs available and they have varying reputations. Individuals considering enrolling in a broadcasting school should contact personnel managers of radio and television stations, as well as broadcasting trade organizations, to determine the school's reputation for producing suitably trained candidates.

Announcers are often required to complete long-term on-the-job training. This can be accomplished at campus radio or TV facilities and at commercial stations while students serve as interns. Work experience at college or high school radio or TV stations is very valuable. Oftentimes, even for entry-level positions, employees need to have experience, which students can acquire at these stations. Paid or unpaid internships also provide students with hands-on training and the chance to establish contacts in the industry. Unpaid interns frequently receive college credit and are allowed to observe and assist station employees. This experience sometimes leads to paid internships which are valuable because interns may do work ordinarily performed by regular employees.

Once hired by a television station, an employee usually starts out as a production assistant, researcher, or reporter and is given a chance to move into announcing if he or she shows an aptitude for "on-air" work. A beginner's chance of landing an on-air job is remote. The best chances for an on-air job for inexperienced announcers may be as a substitute for a familiar announcer at a small radio station. In radio, newcomers usually start out taping interviews and operating equipment.

Other qualifications. Announcers must have a pleasant and well-controlled voice, good timing, excellent pronunciation, and correct grammar. College broadcasting programs offer courses, such as voice and diction, to help students improve their vocal qualities. Television announcers need a neat, pleasing appearance as well. Knowledge of theater, sports, music, business, politics, and other subjects likely to be covered in broadcasts improves one's chances for success. Announcers, especially those seeking radio careers, should have good information technology skills and be capable of using computers, editing equipment, and other broadcast-related devices because new advances in technology have made these abilities important. Announcers also need strong writing skills, because they normally write their own material. In addition, they should be able to ad lib all or part of a show and to work under tight deadlines. The most successful announcers attract a large audience by combining a pleasing personality and voice with an appealing style.

Advancement. Announcers usually begin at a station in a small community and, if they are qualified, may move to a better paying job in a large city. They also may advance by hosting a regular program as a disc jockey, sportscaster, or other specialist. Competition for employment by networks is particularly intense, and employees will need a college degree with at least several years of successful announcing experience if they wish to advance.

Employment

Announcers held about 67,400 jobs in 2008. About 51 percent were employed in radio and television broadcasting. Many other announcers were self-employed freelance announcers, who sold their services to networks and stations, advertising agencies, other independent producers, or to sponsors of local events.

Job Outlook

Competition for jobs as announcers will be keen because the broadcasting field attracts many more jobseekers than there are jobs. Furthermore, employment of announcers is projected to decline slowly. In some cases, announcers leave the field because they cannot advance to better paying jobs. Changes in station ownership, format, and ratings frequently cause periods of unemployment for many announcers.

Employment change. Employment of announcers is expected to decline by 4 percent from 2008 to 2018. Improving technology continues to increase the productivity of announcers, reducing the time required to edit material or perform other off-air technical and production work. The ability of radio announcers to broadcast a program live and record a show for another time has eliminated most late-night shifts and allowed multiple stations to use material from the same announcer. Increasing consolidation among broadcasting companies also may contribute to the increased use of syndicated programming and programs originating outside a station's viewing or listening area. The growth of alternative media sources, such as satellite radio, may contribute to the expected decline.

A possible positive area for radio announcers is hybrid digital (HD) radio, which broadcasters hope will increase in the coming years. HD radio offers more channels and could result in higher demand for on-air personalities. There will always be some demand for this occupation, because the public continues to desire local radio and television broadcasting and announcers play a necessary role in bringing it to them.

Job prospects. Some job openings will arise from the need to replace those who transfer to other kinds of work or leave the labor force. Nevertheless, competition for jobs as announcers will be keen because the broadcasting field attracts many more jobseekers than there are jobs. Small radio stations are more inclined to hire beginners, but the pay is low. Applicants who have completed internships and those with related work experience usually receive preference for available positions. Jobseekers with good computer and technical skills also will have an advantage. Large stations will seek announcers who have proven that they can attract and retain a sizable audience, because competition for ratings is so intense in major metropolitan areas. Announcers who are knowledgeable about business, consumer, and health news also may have an advantage over others. Although subject-matter specialization is more common at large stations and the networks, many small stations also encourage it. There will be some opportunities for self-employed DJs who provide music at clubs and special events, but most of these jobs will be part time.

Earnings

Salaries in broadcasting vary widely, but generally are relatively low, except for announcers who work for large stations in major markets or for networks. Earnings are higher in television than in radio and higher in commercial broadcasting than in public broadcasting.

Median hourly wages of radio and television announcers in May 2008 were $12.95. The middle 50 percent earned between $9.05 and $20.31. The lowest 10 percent earned less than $7.45, and the highest 10 percent earned more than $36.42. Median hourly wages of announcers in the radio and television broadcasting industry were $12.61.

Median hourly wages of public address and other system announcers in May 2008 were $13.18. The middle 50 percent earned between $8.82 and $21.04. The lowest 10 percent earned less than $7.51 and the highest 10 percent earned more than $33.58.

MEDIA

Authors, Writers, and Editors

Nature of the Work

Authors, writers and editors produce a wide variety of written materials in an increasing number of ways. They develop content using any number of multimedia formats that can be read, listened to, or viewed onscreen. Although many people write as part of their primary job, or on online chats or blogs, only writers and editors who are paid to primarily write or edit are included in this occupation.

Writers and authors develop original written materials for books, magazines, trade journals, online publications, company newsletters, and advertisements. Their works are classified broadly as either fiction or nonfiction and writers often are identified by the type of writing they do—for example,

> ### Significant Points
> ❖ Most jobs require a college degree, preferably in communications, journalism, or English.
>
> ❖ Keen competition is expected for writing and editing jobs as many people are attracted to this occupation.
>
> ❖ Online publications and services are growing in number and sophistication, spurring the demand for writers and editors with Web or multimedia experience.

novelists, playwrights, biographers, and *textbook writers*. Writers such as *songwriters, screenwriters*, or *scriptwriters*, produce content for radio and television broadcasts, motion pictures, and other types of performance. An increasing number of writers are producing scripted material directly for the Web and other communication devices.

Copy writers prepare advertising copy for use in publications or for broadcasting and they write other materials to promote the sale of a good or service. They often must work with the client to produce advertising themes or slogans and may be involved in the marketing of the product or service.

All writers conduct research on their topics, which they gather through personal observation, library and Internet research, and interviews. Some staff writers who work in the newspaper or magazine publishing industry are news analysts, reporters, and correspondents and like most writers are typically assigned articles to write by editors and publishers, and may propose their own story ideas. Writers, especially of nonfiction, are expected to establish their credibility with editors and readers through strong research and the use of appropriate sources and citations. Writers and authors then select the material they want to use, organize it, and use the written word to express story lines, ideas, or to convey information. With help from editors, they may revise or rewrite sections, searching for the best organization or the right phrasing.

Most writers and editors use desktop or electronic publishing software, scanners, and other electronic communications equipment in the production of their material. In addition, because many writers today prepare material directly for the Internet, such as online newspapers and text for video games, they should be knowledgeable about graphic design, page layout, and multimedia software. In addition, they should be familiar with interactive technologies of the Web so that they can blend text, graphics, and sound together. Some writers maintain blogs or issue text messages as a way of keeping in touch with readers or providing information to them quickly, but only those who are paid to write their blogs or send text messages may be considered writers.

An increasing number of writers today are *freelance writers*—that is, they are self-employed and make their living by selling their written content to book and magazine publishers, news organizations, advertising agencies, or movie, theater, or television producers or by working under contract with an organization. Some writers may be commissioned by a sponsor to write a script; others to write a book on the basis of a proposal in the form of a draft or an outline. Many freelance writers are hired to complete specific short-term or recurring assignments, such as contributing a column or a series of articles on a specific topic to a news agency or for an organization's newsletter.

Editors review, rewrite, and edit the work of writers. They also may do original writing. An editor's responsibilities vary with the employer and type and level of editorial position held. Editorial duties may include planning the content of books, journals, magazines, and other general-interest publications. Editors also review story ideas proposed by staff and freelance writers then decide what material will appeal to readers. They review and edit drafts of books and articles, offer comments to improve the work, and suggest possible titles. In addition, they may oversee the production of publications. In the book-publishing industry, an editor's primary responsibility is to review proposals for books and decide whether to buy the publication rights from the author.

Most editors begin work as writers. Those who are particularly adept at identifying stories, recognizing writing talent, and interacting with writers, may be interested in editing jobs.

Major newspapers and newsmagazines usually employ several types of editors. The *executive editor* oversees *assistant editors*, and generally has the final say about what stories are published and how they are covered. Assistant editors have responsibility for particular subjects, such as local news, international news, feature stories, or sports. The *managing editor* usually is responsible for the daily operation of the news department. *Assignment editors* determine which reporters will cover a given story.

In smaller organizations—such as small daily or weekly newspapers—a single editor may do everything or share responsibility with only a few other people. Executive and managing editors typically hire writers, reporters, and other employees. They also plan budgets and negotiate contracts with freelance writers, sometimes called "stringers" in the news industry. *Copy editors* review copy for errors in grammar, punctuation, and spelling and check the copy for readability, style, and agreement with editorial policy. They suggest revisions, such as changing words and rearranging sentences and paragraphs, to improve clarity or accuracy. They may also carry out research and confirm sources for writers and verify facts, dates, and statistics. In addition, they may arrange page layouts of articles, photographs, and advertising; compose headlines; and prepare copy for printing.

Editors often employ others, such as interns, fact checkers, or editorial assistants, for some entry-level positions. While gaining practical experience in a newsroom, they may carry out research and verify facts, dates, and statistics for other writers. In addition, they may arrange page layouts of articles, photographs, and advertising; compose headlines; and prepare copy for printing. *Publication assistants* who work for book publishing houses may read and evaluate manuscripts submitted by freelance writers, proofread printers' galleys, and answer inquiries about published material. Assistants on small newspapers or in smaller media markets may compile articles available from wire services or the Internet, answer phones, and proofread articles.

Work environment. Advances in electronic communications have changed the work environment for many writers. Laptop computers and wireless communications technologies allow growing numbers of writers and authors to work from home and on the road. The ability to send e-mail or text messages, transmit and download stories, perform research, or review materials using the Internet allows writers and editors greater flexibility in where and how they complete assignments. Still, some writers and authors work in offices and many travel to conduct on-site research on their topic.

Some writers keep regular office hours, either to maintain contact with sources and editors or to establish a writing routine, but most writers set their own hours. Many writers—especially freelance writers—are paid per assignment; therefore, they work any number of hours necessary to meet a deadline. As a result, writers must be willing to work evenings, nights, or weekends to produce a piece acceptable to an editor or client by the deadline.

While many freelance writers enjoy running their own businesses and the advantages of working flexible hours, most routinely face the pressures of juggling multiple projects with competing demands and the continual need to find new work. Deadline pressures and long, erratic work hours—often part of the daily routine in these jobs—may cause stress, fatigue, or burnout. In addition, the use of computers for extended periods may cause some individuals to experience back pain, eyestrain, or fatigue.

Editors' schedules generally are determined by the production schedule and the type of editorial position. Most salaried editors work in busy offices much of the time and have to deal with production deadline pressures and the stresses of ensuring that the information they publish is accurate. As a result, editors often work long hours, especially at those times leading up to a publication deadline, which can be daily or even more frequently when editing material for the Internet or for a live broadcast. Overseeing and coordinating multiple writing projects simultaneously is common in these jobs, which may lead to stress, fatigue, or other chronic problems. Freelance editors face the added pressures of finding work on an ongoing basis and continually adjusting to new work environments.

Training, Other Qualifications, and Advancement

A college degree generally is required for a position as an author, writer, or editor. Good facility with computers and communications equipment is necessary in order to stay in touch with sources, editors, and other writers while working on assignments, whether from home, an office, or while traveling.

Education and training. A bachelor's degree or higher is typically needed for a job as an author, writer, or editor. Because writing skills are essential in this occupation, many employers like to hire people with degrees in communications, journalism, or English, but those with other backgrounds and who can demonstrate good writing skills may also find jobs as writers. Writers who want to focus on writing about a particular topic may need formal training or experience related to that topic. For example, textbook writers and fashion editors may need expertise in their subject areas that they acquired either through formal academic training or work experience. The Internet and other media allow some people to gain writing experience through blog posts, text messages, or self-publishing software. Some of this writing may lead to paid assignments based upon the quality of the writing, unique perspective, or the size of the potential audience, without regard to the absence of a degree.

Training and experience for author, writer, and editor jobs can be obtained by working on high school and college newspapers, community newspapers, and radio and television stations and submissions to literary magazines. College theater and music programs offer playwrights and songwriters an opportunity for them to have their work performed. Many magazines, newspapers, and broadcast stations also have internships for students. Interns may write stories, conduct research and interviews, and learn about the publishing or broadcasting business.

Other qualifications. Authors, writers and editors must be able to express ideas clearly and logically and should enjoy writing. Creativity, curiosity, a broad range of knowledge, self-motivation, and perseverance are also valuable. Authors, writers, and editors must demonstrate good judgment and a strong sense of ethics in deciding what material to publish. In addition, the ability to concentrate and to work under pressure is essential. Editors also need tact and the ability to guide and encourage others in their work.

Familiarity with electronic publishing, graphics, Web design, and multimedia production increasingly is needed. Use of electronic and wireless communications equipment to send e-mail, transmit work, and review copy often is necessary. Online publications require knowledge of computer software and editing tools used to combine text with graphics, audio, video, and animation.

Advancement. Writers and authors generally advance by building a reputation, taking on more complex writing assignments, and getting published in more prestigious markets and publications. Examples of previously published work form the best route to advancement. Establishing a track record for meeting deadlines also makes it easier to get future assignments. Writing for smaller businesses, local newspapers, advertising agencies, or not-for-profit organizations either as a staff writer or on a freelance basis, allows beginning writers and authors to begin writing right away and take credit for their work. Opportunities for advancement within these organizations may be limited, because they either do not have enough regular work or do not need more advanced writing.

In larger businesses, jobs and promotions usually are more formally structured. Beginners often read submissions, do research, fact check articles, or copy edit drafts, and advance to writing and editing more substantive stories and articles.

Most editors begin work as writers. Those who are particularly adept at identifying stories, recognizing writing talent, and interacting with writers, may be interested in editing jobs. Except for copy editors, most editors hold management positions and must also enjoy making decisions related to running a business. For them, advancement generally means moving up the corporate ladder or to publications with larger circulation or greater prestige. Copy editors may move into original writing or substantive editing positions or become freelancers.

Employment

Authors, writers and editors held about 281,300 jobs in 2008. Writers and authors held about 151,700 jobs and editors held about 129,600 jobs. About 70 percent of writers and authors were self-employed, while 12 percent of editors were self-employed.

Among the 30 percent of salaried writers and authors, about half work in the professional, scientific, and technical services and in publishing (except Internet) industries. These industries include advertising, public relations and related services and newspaper, periodical, book, and directory publishers, respectively. Other salaried writers and authors work in broadcasting, professional and social organizations, and the motion picture and video industries.

While 51 percent of salaried editors worked in the publishing, except Internet industry (half of those for newspapers), a large number of editors were also employed in other industries. Business, professional and social organizations, information services, and educational institutions employed editors to work on their publications or Web content.

Jobs are somewhat concentrated in major media and entertainment markets—Boston, Chicago, Los Angeles, New York, and Washington, DC—but improved communications and Internet capabilities allow writers to work from almost anywhere. Many prefer to work outside these cities and travel regularly to meet with publishers and clients and to do research or conduct interviews in person. As a result, job location is less of a requirement for many writing or editing positions than it once was.

Job Outlook

Employment is expected to grow about as fast as average. Keen competition is expected for writing and editing jobs as many people are attracted to this occupation. At the same time, many employers are downsizing.

Employment change. Employment of authors, writers, and editors is expected to grow 8 percent, about as fast as the average for all occupations, from 2008 to 2018. Employment in salaried writing and editing positions is expected to increase slightly as jobs become more prevalent throughout the economy. Companies in a wide array of industries are using newer multimedia technologies and online media to reach a more technology friendly consumer and meet the growing demand for Web-based information. Online publications and services are growing in number and sophistication, spurring the demand for authors, writers, and editors, especially those with Web or multimedia experience. Businesses and organizations are adding text messaging services to expanded newsletters and Web sites as a way of attracting new customers. They may hire writers or editors on either a salaried or freelance basis to contribute additional content. Some publishing companies however, especially those that rely on advertising revenues and sales receipts to support large staffs of writers, will employ fewer writers and editors. But many experienced writers and editors will find work with nonprofit organizations and associations in their public relations offices, or in the public affairs departments of large companies or agencies. Others will find freelance work for newspaper, magazine, or journal publishers; some will write books.

Job prospects. Competition is expected for writing and editing jobs as many people are attracted to this occupation. Competition for jobs with established newspaper and magazines will be particularly keen as many organizations move their publication focus from a print to an online presence and as the publishing industry continues to contract. Writers and editors who have adapted to the new media and are comfortable writing for and working with a variety of electronic and digital tools will have an advantage in finding new work. The declining costs of self-publishing and the growing popularity of electronic books and book readers will allow many freelancers to get their work published. Some job openings will arise as experienced workers retire, transfer to other occupations, or leave the labor force.

MEDIA

—w—

Broadcast/Sound Engineering Technicians and Operators

Nature of the Work

Broadcast and sound engineering technicians and radio operators perform a wide variety of tasks. Their duties include setting up and maintaining the electrical equipment used in nearly all radio and television broadcasts, concerts, plays, sound recordings, and movies. There are many specialized occupations in this field.

Audio and video equipment technicians set up and operate audio and video equipment, including microphones, speakers, video screens, projectors, video monitors, and recording equipment. They also connect wires and cables and set up and operate sound and mixing boards and related electronic equipment for concerts, sports events, meetings and conventions, presentations, and news conferences. They may set up and operate associated spotlights and other custom lighting systems. They also are needed to install and maintain equipment in many large businesses and universities that are upgrading their facilities with audio and video equipment.

Broadcast technicians set up, operate, and maintain equipment that regulates the signal strength, the clarity, and the ranges of sounds and colors of radio or television broadcasts. These technicians also operate control panels to

Significant Points

❖ Job applicants will face keen competition for jobs in major metropolitan areas, where pay generally is higher; prospects are expected to be better in small cities and towns.

❖ Technical school, community college, or college training in broadcast technology, electronics, or computer networking provides the best preparation.

❖ About 29 percent of these workers are in broadcasting, mainly in radio and television stations, and 15 percent work in the motion picture, video, and sound recording industries.

❖ Evening, weekend, and holiday work is common.

select the source of the material. Technicians may switch from one camera or studio to another, from film to live programming, or from network to local programming.

Sound engineering technicians operate machines and equipment to record, synchronize, mix, or reproduce music, voices, or sound effects in recording studios, sporting arenas, theater productions, or movie and video productions.

Broadcast and sound engineering technicians and radio operators perform a variety of duties at small stations. At large stations and at the networks, technicians are more specialized, although job assignments may change from day to day. The terms "operator," "engineer," and "technician" often are used interchangeably to describe these workers. They may monitor and log outgoing signals and operate transmitters; set up, adjust, service, and repair electronic broadcasting equipment; and regulate fidelity, brightness, contrast, volume, and sound quality of television broadcasts.

Technicians also work in program production. *Recording engineers* operate and maintain video and sound recording equipment. They may operate equipment designed to produce special effects, such as the illusion of a bolt of lightning or a police siren. *Sound mixers* or *re-recording mixers* produce soundtracks for movies or television programs. After filming or recording is complete, these workers may use a process called "dubbing" to insert sounds. *Field technicians* set up and operate portable transmission equipment outside the studio. Because television news coverage requires so much electronic equipment and the technology is changing so rapidly, many stations assign technicians exclusively to news. *Chief engineers, transmission engineers*, and *broadcast field supervisors* oversee other technicians and maintain broadcasting equipment.

Radio operators mainly receive and transmit communications using a variety of tools. These workers also repair equipment, using such devices as electronic testing equipment, hand tools, and power tools. One of their major duties is to help ensure communication systems remain in good condition.

Work environment. Broadcast and sound engineering technicians and radio operators generally work indoors in pleasant surroundings. However, those who broadcast news and other programs from locations outside the studio may work outdoors in all types of weather or in other dangerous conditions. Technicians doing maintenance may climb poles or antenna towers, and those setting up equipment do heavy lifting.

Technicians at large stations and the networks usually work a 40-hour week under great pressure to meet broadcast deadlines, and may occasionally work overtime. Technicians at small stations routinely work more than 40 hours a week. Evening, weekend, and holiday work is usual because most stations are on the air 18 to 24 hours a day, 7 days a week. Some technicians need to be available on call whenever the station is broadcasting; technicians must handle any problems that occur during this time.

Technicians who work on motion pictures may be on a tight schedule and may work long hours to meet contractual deadlines.

Training, Other Qualifications, and Advancement

Broadcast and sound engineering technicians, as well as audio and video equipment technicians, should have some kind of formal training related to their field. Radio operators do not need an education beyond high school and can usually learn their jobs through several months of on-the-job training.

Education and training. Audio and video equipment technicians should complete a technical-training program related to the field, which may take several months to a year to complete. Many recent entrants to the field have also received an associate degree or bachelor's degree, although it is generally not required for entry-level positions. In addition to coursework, experience in high school or college audiovisual clubs can provide a student with good training for this occupation. Working as an assistant is a useful way to gain experience and knowledge for an entry-level employee.

For broadcast technicians an associate degree in broadcast technology, electronics, computer networking, or a related field is generally recommended. Because of the competitiveness of the broadcast industry, many jobs require a bachelor's degree. A four-year degree also gives employees much better prospects for advancement in the field.

Most entry-level employees find jobs in small markets or with small stations in big markets and can transfer to larger, better paying stations after gaining experience and learning the necessary skills. Small stations usually value more general skills since they have fewer employees doing less specialized work. Large stations almost never hire someone without previous experience, and they value more specialized skills. Working at a college radio or television station can be very advantageous for prospective employees.

Sound engineering technicians usually complete a vocational program, which can take about a year, although there are shorter programs. Prospective technicians should take high school courses in math, physics, and electronics. Technicians need to have excellent computer training to be successful in this field.

Radio operators are not usually required to complete any formal training. This is an entry-level position that generally requires on-the-job training.

In the motion picture industry, people are hired as apprentice editorial assistants and work their way up to jobs requiring higher level skills. Employers in the motion picture industry usually hire experienced freelance technicians on a picture-by-picture basis. Reputation and perseverance are important in getting jobs.

Continuing education to become familiar with emerging technologies is recommended for all broadcast and sound engineering technicians and radio operators.

Other qualifications. Broadcast and sound engineering technicians and radio operators need skills in information technology and electronics since most recording, editing, and broadcasting are done on computers. Prospective technicians must have manual dexterity and an aptitude for working with electrical, electronic, and mechanical systems and equipment.

Certification and advancement. Licensing is not required for broadcast technicians. However, certification by the Society of Broadcast Engineers is issued to experienced technicians who pass an examination, and the certification may help with advancement.

Experienced technicians can become supervisory technicians or chief engineers. A college degree in engineering is needed to become chief engineer at large television stations.

Employment

Broadcast and sound engineering technicians and radio operators held about 114,600 jobs in 2008.

About 29 percent of broadcast and sound engineering technicians and radio operators worked in broadcasting (except Internet broadcasting), and 15 percent worked in the motion picture, video, and sound recording industries. About 13 percent were self-employed. Television stations employ, on average, many more technicians than radio stations. Some technicians are employed in other industries, producing employee communications, sales, and training programs. Technician jobs in television and radio are located in virtually all U.S. cities; jobs in radio also are found in many small towns. The highest paying and most specialized jobs are concentrated in New York City, Los Angeles, Chicago, and Washington, DC—the headquarters of most network and news programs. Motion picture production jobs are concentrated in Los Angeles and New York City.

Job Outlook

Employment is expected to grow about as fast as the average through 2018. But people seeking entry-level jobs as technicians in broadcasting are expected to face keen competition in major metropolitan areas. Prospects are expected to be better in small cities and towns.

Employment change. Overall employment of broadcast and sound engineering technicians and radio operators is expected to grow by 8 percent over the 2008–18 decade, which is about as fast as the average of all occupations. Projected job growth varies among detailed occupations in this field. Employment of audio and video equipment technicians is expected to grow 13 percent, about as fast as average. Audio and video equipment is in heavy demand in many new buildings, especially new schools, and in existing schools as well. Many new technicians will be needed, not only to install, but to maintain and repair the equipment as well. A growing number of companies will plan permanent departments employing audio and video technicians. An increase in the use of digital signage will also lead to higher demand for audio and video equipment technicians. In the motion picture industry, employment for these workers will grow because they are needed to install digital movie screens.

Employment of broadcast technicians is expected to grow by 2 percent, signifying little or no change, and employment of sound engineering technicians is expected to grow by 6 percent, which is slower than average. Advancements in technology will enhance the capabilities of technicians to produce higher quality radio and television programming; however, this improved technology will also increase the productivity of technicians, which may hold down employment growth. Jobs in radio and television broadcasting will also be limited by further consolidation of stations and by labor-saving advances, such as computer-controlled programming. In the cable and pay portion of the broadcasting industry, employment is expected to grow as the range of products and services expands, including cable Internet access and video-on-demand. An area in which technicians will be in increasing demand over the next several years is mobile broadcasting.

Job prospects. People seeking entry-level jobs as broadcast technicians are expected to face keen competition because of the large number of people attracted by the glamour of working in television or radio. Competition will be stronger in large metropolitan areas where pay is generally higher and the number of job seekers usually exceeds the number of openings. Prospects for entry-level positions are expected to be better in small cities and towns, provided that the jobseeker has appropriate training.

Earnings

Television stations usually pay higher salaries than radio stations, commercial broadcasting usually pays more than non-commercial broadcasting, and stations in large markets pay more than those in small markets.

Median annual wages of audio and video equipment technicians in May 2008 were $38,050. The middle 50 percent earned between $28,130 and $51,780. The lowest 10 percent earned less than $21,500, and the highest 10 percent earned more than $66,030. Median annual wages in motion picture and video industries, which employed the largest number of audio and video equipment technicians, were $39,410.

Median annual wages of broadcast technicians in May 2008 were $32,900. The middle 50 percent earned between $22,900 and $49,340. The lowest 10 percent earned less than $17,510, and the highest 10 percent earned more than $66,550. Median annual wages in radio and television broadcasting, which employed the largest number of broadcast technicians, were $29,220.

Median annual wages of sound engineering technicians in May 2008 were $47,490. The middle 50 percent earned between $32,770 and $69,700. The lowest 10 percent earned less than $23,790, and the highest 10 percent earned more than $92,700.

Median annual wages of radio operators in May 2008 were $37,120. The middle 50 percent earned between $27,890 and $48,200. The lowest 10 percent earned less than

MEDIA

—ɱ—

Interpreters and Translators

Nature of the Work

Interpreters and translators facilitate the cross-cultural communication necessary in today's society by converting one language into another. However, these language specialists do more than simply translate words—they relay concepts and ideas between languages. They must thoroughly understand the subject matter in which they work in order to accurately convey information from one language into another. In addition, they must be sensitive to the cultures associated with their languages of expertise.

Although some people do both, interpreting and translation are different professions. Interpreters deal with spoken words, translators with written words. Each task requires a distinct set of skills and aptitudes, and most people are better suited for one or the other. While interpreters often interpret into and from both languages, translators generally translate only into their native language.

Interpreters convert one spoken language into another—or, in the case of sign-language interpreters, between spoken communication and sign language. Interpreting requires that one pay attention carefully, understand what is communicated in both languages, and express thoughts and ideas clearly. Strong research and analytical skills, mental dexterity, and an exceptional memory also are important.

There are two modes of interpreting: simultaneous, and consecutive. Simultaneous

> ### Significant Points
> ❖ About 26 percent of interpreters and translators are self-employed; many freelance and work in this occupation only sporadically.
>
> ❖ In addition to needing fluency in at least two languages, many interpreters and translators need a bachelor's degree.
>
> ❖ Employment is expected to grow much faster than average.
>
> ❖ Job prospects vary by specialty and language.

interpreting requires interpreters to listen and speak (or sign) at the same time someone is speaking or signing. Ideally, simultaneous interpreters should be so familiar with a subject that they are able to anticipate the end of the speaker's sentence. Because they need a high degree of concentration, simultaneous interpreters work in pairs, with each interpreting for 20-minute to 30-minute periods. This type of interpreting is required at international conferences and is sometimes used in the courts.

In contrast to the immediacy of simultaneous interpreting, consecutive interpreting begins only after the speaker has verbalized a group of words or sentences. Consecutive interpreters often take notes while listening to the speakers, so they must develop some type of note-taking or shorthand system. This form of interpreting is used most often for person-to-person communication, during which the interpreter is positioned near both parties.

Translators convert written materials from one language into another. They must have excellent writing and analytical ability, and because the translations that they produce must be accurate, they also need good editing skills.

Translating involves more than replacing a word with its equivalent in another language; sentences and ideas must be manipulated to flow with the same coherence as those in the source document so that the translation reads as though it originated in the target language. Translators also must bear in mind any cultural references that may need to be explained to the intended audience, such as colloquialisms, slang, and other expressions that do not translate literally. Some subjects may be more difficult than others to translate because words or passages may have multiple meanings that make several translations possible. Not surprisingly, translated work often goes through multiple revisions before final text is submitted.

Nearly all translation work is done on a computer, and most assignments are received and submitted electronically. This enables translators to work from almost anywhere, and a large percentage of them work from home. The Internet provides advanced research capabilities and valuable language resources, such as specialized dictionaries and glossaries. In some cases, use of computer-assisted translation—including memory tools that provide comparisons of previous translations with current work—helps save time and reduce repetition.

The services of interpreters and translators are needed in a number of subject areas. While these workers may not completely specialize in a particular field or industry, many do focus on one area of expertise. Some of the most common areas are described below; however, interpreters and translators may work in a variety of other areas also, including business, education, social services, and entertainment.

Judiciary interpreters and translators facilitate communication for people with limited English proficiency who find it challenging to communicate in a legal setting. Legal translators must be thoroughly familiar with the language and functions of the U.S. judicial system, as well as other countries' legal systems. Court interpreters work in a variety of legal settings, such as attorney-client meetings, preliminary hearings, arraignments, depositions, and trials. Success as a court interpreter requires an understanding of both legal terminology and colloquial language. In addition to interpreting what is said, court interpreters also may be required to read written documents aloud in a language other than that in which they were written, a task known as sight translation.

Medical interpreters and translator, sometimes referred to as healthcare interpreters and translators, provide language services to healthcare patients with limited English proficiency. Medical interpreters help patients to communicate with doctors, nurses, and other medical staff. Translators working in this specialty primarily convert patient materials and informational brochures issued by hospitals and medical facilities into the desired language. Interpreters in this field need a strong grasp of medical and colloquial terminology in both languages, along with cultural sensitivity to help the patient receive the information.

Sign-language interpreters facilitate communication between people who are deaf or hard of hearing and people who can hear. Sign-language interpreters must be fluent in English and in American Sign Language (ASL), which combines signing, finger spelling, and specific body language. Most sign-language interpreters either interpret, aiding communication between English and ASL, or transliterate, facilitating communication between English and contact signing—a form of signing that uses a more English language-based word order. Some interpreters specialize in oral interpreting for people who are deaf or hard of hearing and lip-read instead of sign. Other specialties include tactile signing, which is interpreting for people who are blind as well as deaf by making manual signs into their hands, using cued speech, and signing exact English.

Conference interpreters work at conferences that have non-English-speaking attendees. The work is often in the field of international business or diplomacy, although conference interpreters can interpret for any organization that works with speakers of foreign languages. Employers prefer high-level interpreters who have the ability to translate from at least two languages into one native language—for example, the ability to interpret from Spanish and French into English. For some positions, such as those with the United Nations, this qualification is mandatory.

Guide or escort interpreters accompany either U.S. visitors abroad or foreign visitors in the United States to ensure that they are able to communicate during their stay. These specialists interpret on a variety of subjects, both on an informal basis and on a professional level. Most of their interpreting is consecutive, and work is generally shared by two interpreters when the assignment requires more than an 8-hour day. Frequent travel, often for days or weeks at a time, is common, and it is an aspect of the job that some find particularly appealing.

Literary translators adapt written literature from one language into another. They may translate any number of documents, including journal articles, books, poetry, and short stories. Literary translation is related to creative writing; literary translators must create a new text in the target language that reproduces the content and style of the original. Whenever possible, literary translators work closely with authors to best capture their intended meanings and literary characteristics.

Localization translators completely adapt a product or service for use in a different language and culture. The goal of these specialists is to make it appear as though a product originated in the country where it will be sold and supported. At its earlier stages, this work dealt primarily with software localization, but the specialty has expanded to include the adaptation of Internet sites, marketing, publications, and products and services in manufacturing and other business sectors.

Work environment. Interpreters work in a wide variety of settings, such as schools, hospitals, courtrooms, and conference centers. Translators usually work alone, and they must frequently perform under pressure of deadlines and tight schedules. Technology allows translators to work from almost anywhere, and many choose to work from home.

Because many interpreters and translators freelance, their schedules often vary, with periods of limited work interspersed with periods requiring long, irregular hours. For those who freelance, a significant amount of time must be dedicated to looking for jobs. Interpreters who work over the telephone or through videoconferencing generally work in call centers in urban areas and keep to a standard 5-day, 40-hour workweek.

Training, Other Qualifications, and Advancement

Interpreters and translators must be fluent in at least two languages. Their educational backgrounds may vary widely, but many need a bachelor's degree. Many also complete job-specific training programs.

Education and training. The educational backgrounds of interpreters and translators vary. Knowing at least two languages is essential. Although it is not necessary to have been raised bilingual to succeed, many interpreters and translators grew up speaking two languages.

In high school, students can prepare for these careers by taking a broad range of courses that include English writing and comprehension, foreign languages, and basic computer proficiency. Other helpful pursuits include spending time abroad, engaging in direct contact with foreign cultures, and reading extensively on a variety of subjects in English and at least one other language.

Beyond high school, there are many educational options. Although a bachelor's degree is often required for jobs, majoring in a language is not always necessary. An educational background in a particular field of study can provide a natural area of subject-matter expertise. However, specialized training in how to do the work is generally required. Formal programs in interpreting and translation are available at colleges nationwide and through nonuniversity training programs, conferences, and courses. Many people who work as conference interpreters or in more technical areas—such as localization, engineering, or finance—have master's degrees, while those working in the community as court or medical interpreters or translators are more likely to complete job-specific training programs.

Other qualifications. Experience is an essential part of a successful career in either interpreting or translation. In fact, many agencies or companies use only the services of people who have worked in the field for 3 to 5 years or who have a degree in translation studies, or both.

A good way for translators to learn firsthand about the profession is to start out working in-house for a translation company; however, such jobs are not very numerous. People seeking to enter interpreter or translator jobs should begin by getting experience whatever way possible—even if it means doing informal or volunteer work.

Volunteer opportunities are available through community organizations, hospitals, and sporting events, such as marathons, that involve international competitors. The American Translators Association works with the Red Cross to provide volunteer interpreters in crisis situations. Any translation can be used as an example for potential clients, even translation done as practice.

Paid or unpaid internships and apprenticeships are other ways for interpreters and translators to get started. Escort interpreting may offer an opportunity for inexperienced candidates to work alongside a more seasoned interpreter. Interpreters might also find it easier to break into areas with particularly high demand for language services, such as court or medical interpreting.

Whatever path of entry they pursue, new interpreters and translators should establish mentoring relationships to build their skills, confidence, and professional network. Mentoring may be formal, such as through a professional association, or informal with a coworker or an acquaintance who has experience as an interpreter or translator. Both the American Translators Association and the Registry of Interpreters for the Deaf offer formal mentoring programs.

Translators working in localization need a solid grasp of the languages to be translated, a thorough understanding of technical concepts and vocabulary, and a high degree of knowledge about the intended target audience or users of the product. Because software often is involved, it is not uncommon for people who work in this area of translation to have a strong background in computer science or to have computer-related work experience.

Self-employed and freelance interpreters and translators need general business skills to successfully manage their finances and careers. They must set prices for their work, bill customers, keep financial records, and market their services to attract new business and build their client base.

Certification and advancement. There is currently no universal form of certification required of interpreters and translators in the United States. However there are a variety of different tests that workers can take to demonstrate proficiency, which may be helpful in gaining employment. For example, the American Translators Association provides certification in 24 language combinations involving English for its members.

Federal courts have certification for Spanish, Navajo, and Haitian Creole interpreters, and many State and municipal courts offer their own forms of certification. The National Association of Judiciary Interpreters and Translators also offers certification for court interpreting.

The U.S. Department of State has a three-test series for prospective interpreters—one test in simple consecutive interpreting (for escort work), another in simultaneous interpreting (for court or seminar work), and a third in conference-level interpreting (for international conferences)—as well as a test for prospective translators. These tests are not considered a credential, but successful completion indicates that a person has a significant level of skill in the field. Additionally, the International Association of Conference Interpreters offers certification for conference interpreters

The National Association of the Deaf and the Registry of Interpreters for the Deaf (RID) jointly offer certification for general sign interpreters. In addition, the registry offers specialty tests in legal interpreting, speech reading, and deaf-to-deaf interpreting—which includes interpreting among deaf speakers with different native languages and from ASL to tactile signing.

Once interpreters and translators have gained sufficient experience, they may then move up to more difficult or prestigious assignments, may seek certification, may be given editorial responsibility, or may eventually manage or start a translation agency.

Many self-employed interpreters and translators start businesses by submitting resumes and samples to many different translation and interpreting agencies and then wait to be contacted when an agency matches their skills with a job. Work is often acquired by word of mouth or through referrals from existing clients.

Employment

Interpreters and translators held about 50,900 jobs in 2008. However, the actual number of interpreters and translators is probably significantly higher because many work in the occupation only sporadically. Interpreters and translators are employed in a variety of industries, reflecting the diversity of employment options in the field. About 28 percent worked in public and private educational institutions, such as schools, colleges, and universities. About 13 percent worked in healthcare and social assistance, many of whom worked for hospitals. Another 9 percent worked in other areas of government, such as Federal, State, and local courts. Other employers of interpreters and translators include interpreting and translation agencies, publishing companies, telephone companies, and airlines.

About 26 percent of interpreters and translators are self-employed. Many who freelance in the occupation work only part time, relying on other sources of income to supplement earnings from interpreting or translation.

Job Outlook

Interpreters and translators can expect much faster than average employment growth. Job prospects vary by specialty and language.

Employment change. Employment of interpreters and translators is projected to increase 22 percent over the 2008–18 decade, which is much faster than the average for all occupations. Higher demand for interpreters and translators results directly from the broadening of international ties and the large increases in the number of non-English speaking people in the United States. Both of these trends are expected to continue throughout the projections period, contributing to relatively rapid growth in the number of jobs for interpreters and translators across all industries in the economy.

Demand will remain strong for translators of frequently translated languages, such as Portuguese, French, Italian, German, and Spanish. Demand should also be strong for translators of Arabic and other Middle Eastern languages and for the principal East Asian languages—Chinese, Japanese, and Korean. Demand for American Sign Language interpreters will grow rapidly, driven by the increasing use of video relay services, which allow individuals to conduct video calls using a sign language interpreter over an Internet connection.

Technology has made the work of interpreters and translators easier. However, technology is not likely to have a negative impact on employment of interpreters and translators because such innovations are incapable of producing work comparable with work produced by these professionals.

Job prospects. Urban areas, especially Washington, DC, New York, and cities in California, provide the largest numbers of employment possibilities, especially for interpreters; however, as the immigrant population spreads into more rural areas, jobs in smaller communities will become more widely available.

Job prospects for interpreters and translators vary by specialty and language. For example, interpreters and translators of Spanish should have good job opportunities because of expected increases in the Hispanic population in the United States. Demand is expected to be strong for interpreters and translators specializing in healthcare and law because it is critical that information be fully understood among all parties in these areas. Additionally, there should be demand for specialists in localization, driven by the globalization of business and the expansion of the Internet; however, demand may be dampened somewhat by outsourcing of localization work to other countries. Given the shortage of interpreters and translators meeting the desired skill level of employers, interpreters for the deaf will continue to have favorable employment prospects. On the other hand, competition can be expected for both conference interpreter and literary translator positions because of the small number of job opportunities in these specialties.

Earnings

Wage and salary interpreters and translators had median annual wages of $38,850 in May 2008. The middle 50 percent earned between $28,940 and $52,240. The lowest 10 percent earned less than $22,170, and the highest 10 percent earned more than $69,190. Individuals classified as language specialists in the Federal Government earned an average of $79,865 annually in March 2009.

Earnings depend on language, subject matter, skill, experience, education, certification, and type of employer, and salaries of interpreters and translators can vary widely. Interpreters and translators who know languages for which there is a greater demand, or which relatively few people can translate, often have higher earnings, as do those who perform services requiring a high level of skill, such as conference interpreters.

For those who are not salaried, earnings typically fluctuate, depending on the availability of work. Freelance interpreters usually earn an hourly rate, whereas translators who freelance typically earn a rate per word or per hour.

MEDIA

—∭—

News Analysts, Reporters, and Correspondents

Nature of the Work

News analysts, reporters, and correspondents gather information, prepare stories, and make broadcasts that inform the public about local, State, national, and international events; present points of view on current issues; and report on the actions of public officials, corporate executives, interest groups, and others who exercise power.

News analysts—also called *newscasters* or *news anchors*—examine, interpret, and broadcast news received from various sources. News anchors present news stories and introduce videotaped news or live transmissions from on-the-scene reporters. *News correspondents* report on news occurring in the large U.S. and foreign cities where they are stationed.

In covering a story, *reporters,* sometimes referred to as *journalists,* investigate leads and news tips, look at documents, observe events at the scene, and interview people. Reporters take notes and also may take photographs or shoot videos. At their office, they organize the material, determine the focus or emphasis, write their stories, and edit accompanying video material. Many reporters enter information or write stories on laptop computers and electronically submit the material to their offices from remote locations.

Significant Points

❖ Competition will be keen for jobs at large metropolitan and national newspapers, broadcast stations, and magazines; small publications and broadcast stations and online newspapers and magazines should provide the best opportunities.

❖ Most employers prefer individuals with a bachelor's degree in journalism or mass communications and experience gained at school newspapers or broadcasting stations or through internships with news organizations.

❖ Jobs often involve long, irregular hours and pressure to meet deadlines.

Increasingly, reporters are asked to maintain and produce material for a newspaper's Web site. In some cases, *newswriters* write a story from information collected and submitted by reporters. Radio and television reporters often compose stories and report "live" from the scene. At times, they later tape an introduction to or commentary on their story in the studio. Some journalists also interpret the news or offer opinions to readers, viewers, or listeners. In this role, they are called *commentators* or *columnists*.

Newscasters at large stations and networks usually specialize in a particular type of news, such as sports or weather. *Weathercasters*, also called weather reporters, report current and forecasted weather conditions. They gather information from national satellite weather services, wire services, and local and regional weather bureaus. Some weathercasters are trained meteorologists and can develop their own weather forecasts. *Sportscasters* select, write, and deliver sports news, which may include interviews with sports personalities and coverage of games and other sporting events.

General-assignment reporters write about newsworthy occurrences—such as accidents, political rallies, visits of celebrities, or business closings—as assigned. Large newspapers and radio and television stations assign reporters to gather news about specific topics—for example, crime or education. Some reporters specialize in fields such as health, politics, foreign affairs, sports, theater, consumer affairs, social events, science, business, or religion. Investigative reporters cover stories that may take many days or weeks of information gathering.

Some publications use teams of reporters instead of assigning each reporter one specific topic. As a member of a team, a reporter can cover a greater variety of stories. News teams may include reporters, editors, graphic artists, and photographers working together to complete a story.

Reporters on small publications cover all aspects of the news. They take photographs, write headlines, lay out pages, edit wire-service stories, and write editorials. Some also solicit advertisements, sell subscriptions, and perform general office work.

Work environment. The work of news analysts, reporters, and correspondents is usually hectic. They are under great pressure to meet deadlines. Broadcasts sometimes are aired with little or no time for preparation. Some news analysts, reporters, and correspondents work in comfortable, private offices; others work in large rooms filled with the sound of keyboards and computer printers, as well as the voices of other reporters. Curious onlookers, police, or other emergency workers can distract those reporting from the scene for radio and television. Covering wars, political uprisings, fires, floods, and similar events can be dangerous; however, the rate of injuries for reporters and correspondents is relatively low.

Work hours vary. Reporters on morning papers often work from late afternoon until midnight. Radio and television reporters usually are assigned to a day or evening shift. Magazine reporters usually work during the day.

Reporters sometimes have to change their work hours to meet a deadline or to follow late-breaking developments. Their work may require long hours, irregular schedules, and some travel. Because many stations and networks are on the air 24 hours a day, newscasters can expect to work unusual hours.

Training, Other Qualifications, and Advancement

Most employers prefer individuals with a bachelor's degree in journalism or mass communications, but some hire graduates with other majors. They look for experience at school newspapers or broadcasting stations, and internships with news organizations. Large-city newspapers and stations also may prefer candidates with a degree in a subject-matter specialty such as economics, political science, or business. Some large newspapers and broadcasters may hire only experienced reporters.

Education and training. More than 1,500 institutions offer programs in communications, journalism, and related programs. In 2008, more than 100 of these were accredited by the Accrediting Council on Education in Journalism and Mass Communications. Most of the courses in a typical curriculum are in liberal arts; the remaining courses are in journalism. The most important skills for journalism students to learn are writing and communication. Students planning a career in broadcasting take courses in radio and television news and production. Those planning newspaper or magazine careers usually specialize in more specific forms of writing. To create stories for online media, they need to learn to use computer software to combine online story text with audio and video elements and graphics.

Some schools also offer a master's or Ph.D. degree in journalism. Some graduate programs are intended primarily as preparation for news careers, while others prepare journalism teachers, researchers and theorists, and advertising and public-relations workers.

High school courses in English, journalism, and social studies provide a good foundation for college programs. Useful college liberal arts courses include English, with an emphasis on writing; sociology; political science; economics; history; and psychology. Courses in computer science, business, and speech are useful as well. Fluency in a foreign language is necessary in some jobs.

Employers report that practical experience is the most important part of education and training. Upon graduation, many students already have gained much practical experience through part-time or summer jobs or through internships with news organizations. Most newspapers, magazines, and broadcast news organizations offer reporting and editing internships. Work on high school and college newspapers, at broadcasting stations, or on community papers also provides practical training. In addition, journalism scholarships, fellowships, and assistantships awarded to college journalism students by universities, newspapers, foundations, and professional organizations are helpful. Experience as a freelancer or stringer—a part-time reporter who is paid only for stories printed—is advantageous.

Other qualifications. Reporters typically need more than good word-processing skills. Computer graphics and desktop-publishing skills are essential as well. Students should be completely proficient in all forms of multimedia. Computer-assisted reporting involves the use of computers to analyze data in search of a story. This technique and the interpretation of the results require computer skills and familiarity with databases. Knowledge of news photography also is valuable for entry-level positions, which sometimes combine the responsibilities of a reporter with those of a camera operator or photographer.

Reporters should be dedicated to providing accurate and impartial news. Accuracy is important both to serve the public and because untrue or libelous statements can lead to lawsuits. A nose for news, persistence, initiative, poise, resourcefulness, a good memory, and physical stamina are important, as is the emotional stability to deal with pressing deadlines, irregular hours, and dangerous assignments. Broadcast reporters and news analysts must be comfortable on camera. All reporters must be at ease in unfamiliar places and with a variety of people. Positions involving on-air work require a pleasant voice and appearance.

Advancement. Most reporters start at small publications or broadcast stations as general assignment reporters or copy editors. They are usually assigned to cover court proceedings and civic and club meetings, summarize speeches, and write obituaries. With experience, they report more difficult assignments or specialize in a particular field. Large publications and stations generally require new reporters to have several years of experience.

Some news analysts and reporters can advance by moving to larger newspapers or stations. A few experienced reporters become columnists, correspondents, writers, announcers, or public-relations specialists. Others become editors in print journalism or program managers in broadcast journalism, supervising reporters. Some eventually become broadcasting or publishing industry managers.

Employment

News analysts, reporters, and correspondents held about 69,300 jobs in 2008. About 53 percent worked for newspaper, periodical, book, and directory publishers. Another 21 percent worked in radio and television broadcasting. About 19 percent of news analysts, reporters, and correspondents were self-employed (freelancers or stringers).

Job Outlook

Employment is expected to decline moderately through 2018. Competition will continue to be keen for jobs on large metropolitan and national newspapers, broadcast stations and networks, and magazines. Small broadcast stations and publications and online newspapers and magazines should provide the best opportunities. Talented writers who can handle highly specialized scientific or technical subjects will have an advantage.

Employment change. Employment of news analysts, reporters, and correspondents is expected to decline 6 percent between 2008 and 2018. Many factors will contribute to the decline in this occupation. Consolidation and convergence should continue in the publishing and broadcasting industries. As a result, companies will be better able to allocate their news analysts, reporters, and correspondents to cover news stories. Since broadcasting and newspapers—the two industries employing most of these workers—are dependent on advertising revenue, employment growth will suffer during an economic downturn. Improving technology may eventually lead to more employment growth in this occupation by opening up new areas of work, such as online or mobile news divisions. The continued demand for news will create some job opportunities. Job openings also will result from the need to replace workers who leave their occupations permanently; some news analysts, reporters, and correspondents find the work too stressful and hectic or do not like the lifestyle, and transfer to other occupations.

Job prospects. Competition will continue to be keen for jobs at large metropolitan and national newspapers, broadcast stations and networks, and magazines. Job opportunities will be best for applicants in the expanding world of new media, such as online newspapers or magazines. Small local papers and news stations also will provide greater job prospects for potential reporters and news analysts. For beginning newspaper reporters, freelancing will supply more opportunities for employment as well. Students with a background in journalism as well as another subject, such as politics, economics, or biology, will have an advantage over those without additional background knowledge in moving beyond an entry-level position.

Journalism graduates have the background for work in closely related fields such as advertising and public relations or communications, and many take jobs in these fields. Other graduates accept sales, managerial, or other non-media positions.

Earnings

Salaries for news analysts, reporters, and correspondents vary widely. Median annual wages of reporters and correspondents were $34,850 in May 2008. The middle 50 percent earned between $25,760 and $52,160. The lowest 10 percent earned less than $20,180, and the highest 10 percent earned more than $77,480. Median annual wages of reporters and correspondents were $33,430 in newspaper, periodical, book, and directory publishing, and $37,710 in radio and television broadcasting.

Median annual wages of broadcast news analysts were $51,260 in May 2008. The middle 50 percent earned between $32,000 and $88,630. The lowest 10 percent earned less than $23,470, and the highest 10 percent earned more than $156,200. Median annual wages of broadcast news analysts were $51,890 in radio and television broadcasting.

MEDIA

—ɯ—

Public Relations Specialists

Nature of the Work

An organization's reputation, profitability, and its continued existence can depend on the degree to which its targeted public supports its goals and policies. Public relations specialists—also referred to as *communications specialists* and *media specialists*, among other titles—serve as advocates for clients seeking to build and maintain positive relationships with the public. Their clients include businesses, nonprofit associations, universities, hospitals, and other organizations, and build and maintain positive relationships with the public. As managers recognize the link between good public relations and the success of their organizations, they increasingly rely on public relations specialists for advice on the strategy and policy of their communications.

Public relations specialists handle organizational functions, such as media, community, consumer, industry, and governmental relations; political campaigns; interest-group representation; conflict mediation; and employee and investor relations. Public relations specialists must understand the attitudes and concerns of community, consumer, employee, and public interest groups to establish and maintain cooperative relationships between them and representatives from print and broadcast journalism.

Public relations specialists draft press releases and contact people in the media who

> ### Significant Points
>
> ❖ Although employment is projected to grow much faster than average, keen competition is expected for entry-level jobs.
>
> ❖ Opportunities should be best for college graduates who combine a degree in public relations, journalism, or another communications-related field with a public relations internship or other related work experience.
>
> ❖ Strong communication skills are essential.

might print or broadcast their material. Many radio or television special reports, newspaper stories, and magazine articles start at the desks of public relations specialists. Sometimes, the subject of a press release is an organization and its policies toward employees or its role in the community. For example, a press release might describe a public issue, such as health, energy, or the environment, and what an organization does to advance that issue.

Public relations specialists also arrange and conduct programs to maintain contact between organization representatives and the public. For example, public relations specialists set up speaking engagements and prepare speeches for officials. These media specialists represent employers at community projects; make film, slide, and other visual presentations for meetings and school assemblies; and plan conventions.

In government, public relations specialists may be called *press secretaries*. They keep the public informed about the activities of agencies and officials. For example, *public affairs specialists* in the U.S. Department of State alert the public of travel advisories and of U.S. positions on foreign issues. A press secretary for a member of Congress informs constituents of the representative's accomplishments.

In large organizations, the key public relations executive, who often is a vice president, may develop overall plans and policies with other executives. In addition, public relations departments employ public relations specialists to write, research, prepare materials, maintain contacts, and respond to inquiries.

People who handle publicity for an individual or who direct public relations for a small organization may deal with all aspects of the job. These public relations specialists contact people, plan and research, and prepare materials for distribution. They also may handle advertising or sales promotion work to support marketing efforts.

Work environment. Public relations specialists work in busy offices. The pressures of deadlines and tight work schedules can be stressful.

Some public relations specialists work a standard 35- to 40-hour week, but overtime is common, and work schedules can be irregular and are frequently interrupted. Occasionally, they must be at the job or on call around the clock, especially if there is an emergency or crisis. Schedules often have to be rearranged so workers can meet deadlines, deliver speeches, attend meetings and community activities, and travel.

Training, Other Qualifications, and Advancement

A bachelor's degree in a communications-related field combined with public relations experience is excellent preparation for a person interested in public relations work.

Education and training. Many entry-level public relations specialists have a college degree in public relations, journalism, marketing, or communications. Some firms seek college graduates who have worked in electronic or print journalism. Other employers seek applicants with demonstrated communication skills and training or experience in a field related to the firm's business—information technology, healthcare, science, engineering, sales, or finance, for example.

Many colleges and universities offer bachelor's and postsecondary programs leading to a degree in public relations, usually in a journalism or communications department. In addition, many other colleges offer courses in this field. Courses in advertising, business administration, finance, political science, psychology, sociology, and creative writing also are helpful. Specialties may be offered in public relations for business, government, and nonprofit organizations.

Internships in public relations provide students with valuable experience and training and are the best route to finding entry-level employment. Membership in local chapters of the Public Relations Student Society of America (affiliated with the Public Relations Society of America) or in student chapters of the International Association of Business Communicators provides an opportunity for students to exchange views with public relations specialists and to make professional contacts that may help them to find a full-time job after graduation.

Some organizations, particularly those with large public relations staffs, have formal training programs for new employees. In smaller organizations, new employees work under the guidance of experienced staff members. Entry-level workers often maintain files of material about company activities, skim newspapers and magazines for appropriate articles to clip, and assemble information for speeches and pamphlets. New workers also may answer calls from the press and the public, prepare invitation lists and details for press conferences, or escort visitors and clients. After gaining experience, they write news releases, speeches, and articles for publication or plan and carry out public relations programs. Public relations specialists in smaller firms usually get well-rounded experience, whereas those in larger firms become more specialized.

Other qualifications. In addition to the ability to communicate thoughts clearly and simply, public relations specialists must show creativity, initiative, and good judgment. Decision-making, problem-solving, and research skills also are important. People who choose public relations as a career should have an outgoing personality, self-confidence, an understanding of human psychology, and an enthusiasm for motivating people. They should be assertive but able to participate as part of a team and be open to new ideas.

Certification and advancement. The Universal Accreditation Board accredits public relations specialists who are members of the Public Relations Society of America and who participate in the Examination for Accreditation in Public Relations process. This process includes both a readiness review and an examination, which are designed for candidates who have at least 5 years of full-time work or teaching experience in public relations and who have earned a bachelor's degree in a communications-related field. The readiness review includes a written submission by each candidate, a portfolio review, and dialogue between the candidate and a three-member panel. Candidates who successfully advance through readiness review and pass the computer-based examination earn the Accredited in Public Relations (APR) designation.

The International Association of Business Communicators (IABC) also has an accreditation program for professionals in the communications field, including public relations specialists. Those who meet all the requirements of the program earn the Accredited Business Communicator (ABC) designation. Candidates must have at least 5 years of experience and a bachelor's degree in a communications field and must pass written and oral examinations. They also must submit a portfolio of work samples that demonstrate involvement in a range of communications projects and a thorough understanding of communications planning.

Employers may consider professional recognition through accreditation as a sign of competence in this field, and such designations could be especially helpful in a competitive job market.

Public relations specialists who show that they can handle more demanding assignments are more likely to be promoted to supervisory jobs than those who are unable to do so. In public relations firms, an entry-level worker might be hired as a junior account executive and be promoted over the course of a career to account executive, senior account executive, account manager, and, eventually, vice president. Specialists in corporate public relations follow a similar career path, although the job titles may differ.

Some experienced public relations specialists start their own consulting firms.

Employment

Public relations specialists held about 275,200 jobs in 2008. They are concentrated in service-providing industries, such as advertising and related services; healthcare and social assistance; educational services; and government. Others work for communications firms, financial institutions, and government agencies.

Public relations specialists are concentrated in large cities, where press services and other communications facilities are readily available and where many businesses and trade associations have their headquarters. Many public relations consulting firms, for example, are in New York, Los Angeles, San Francisco, Chicago, and Washington, D.C. There is a trend, however, toward public relations jobs to be dispersed throughout the Nation, closer to clients.

Job Outlook

Employment is projected to grow much faster than average; however, keen competition is expected for entry-level jobs.

Employment change. Employment of public relations specialists is expected to grow 24 percent from 2008 to 2018, much faster than the average for all occupations. The need for good public relations in an increasingly competitive and global business environment should spur demand for these workers, especially those with specialized knowledge or international experience. Employees who possess additional language capabilities also are in great demand.

The recent emergence of social media in the public relations is expected to increase job growth as well. Many public relations firms are expanding their use of these tools, and specialists with skills in them will be needed.

Employment in public relations firms is expected to grow as firms hire contractors to provide public relations services, rather than support more full-time staff when additional work is needed.

Among detailed industries, the largest job growth will continue to be in advertising and related services.

Job prospects. Keen competition likely will continue for entry-level public relations jobs, as the number of qualified applicants is expected to exceed the number of job openings. Many people are attracted to this profession because of the high-profile nature of the work. Opportunities should be best for college graduates who combine a degree in journalism, public relations, or another communications-related field with a public relations internship or other related work experience. Applicants who do not have the appropriate educational background or work experience will face the toughest obstacles.

Additional job opportunities should result from the need to replace public relations specialists who retire or leave the occupation for other reasons.

Earnings

Median annual wages for salaried public relations specialists were $51,280 in May 2008. The middle 50 percent earned between $38,400 and $71,670; the lowest 10 percent earned less than $30,140, and the top 10 percent earned more than $97,910.

MEDIA

—ɯ—

Technical Writers

Nature of the Work

Technical writers, also called *technical communicators*, put technical information into easily understandable language. They work primarily in information-technology-related industries, coordinating the development and dissemination of technical content for a variety of users; however, a growing number of technical communicators are using technical content to resolve business communications problems in a diversifying number of industries. Included in their products are operating instructions, how-to manuals, assembly instructions, and other documentation needed for online help and by technical support staff, consumers, and other users within the company or industry. Technical writers also develop documentation for computer programs and set up communications systems with consumers to assess customer satisfaction and quality control matters. In addition, they commonly work in engineering, scientific, healthcare, and other areas in which highly specialized material needs to be explained to a diverse audience, often of laypersons.

Technical writers often work with engineers, scientists, computer specialists, and software developers to manage the flow of information among project workgroups during development and testing. They also may work with product liability specialists and customer service or call center managers to improve the quality of product support and end-user assistance. Technical writers also oversee the preparation of illustrations, photographs, diagrams, and

Significant Points

❖ Most jobs in this occupation require a college degree—preferably in communications, journalism, or English—but a degree in a technical subject may be useful.

❖ Job prospects for most technical writing jobs are expected to be good, particularly for those with Web or multimedia experience.

❖ Excellent communications skills, curiosity, and attention to detail are highly desired traits.

charts. Technical writers increasingly are using a variety of multimedia formats to convey information in such a way that complex concepts can be understood easily by users of the information.

Applying their knowledge of the user of the product, technical writers may serve as part of a team conducting usability studies to help improve the design of a product that is in the prototype stage. Technical writers may conduct research on their topics through personal observation, library and Internet research, and discussions with technical specialists. They also are expected to demonstrate their understanding of the subject matter and establish their credibility with their colleagues.

Technical writers use computers and other electronic communications equipment extensively in performing their work. They also work regularly with desktop and other electronic publishing software and prepare material directly for the Internet. Technical writers may work with graphic design, page layout, and multimedia software; increasingly, they are preparing documents by using the interactive technologies of the Web to blend text, graphics, multidimensional images, and sound.

Some technical writers work on a freelance or contract basis. They either are self-employed or work for a technical consulting firm and may be hired to complete specific short-term or recurring assignments, such as writing about a new product or coordinating the work and communications of different units to keep a project on track. Whether a project is to be coordinated among an organization's departments or among autonomous companies, technical writers ensure that the different entities share information and mediate differences in favor of the end user in order to bring a product to market sooner.

Work environment. Advances in computer and communications technologies make it possible for technical writers to work from almost anywhere. Laptop computers and wireless communications permit technical writers to work from home, an office, or on the road. The ability to use the Internet to e-mail, transmit, and download information and assignments, conduct research, or review materials allows them greater flexibility in where and how they complete assignments.

Many technical writers work with people located around the world and with specialists in highly technical fields, such as science and engineering. As a result, they must be able to assimilate complex information quickly and be comfortable working with people from diverse professional and cultural backgrounds. Although most technical writers are employed directly by the companies that use their services, many freelance writers are paid on a project basis and routinely face the pressures of juggling multiple projects and the continual need to find new work. Technical writers may be expected to work evenings, nights, or weekends to coordinate with those in other time zones, meet deadlines, or produce information that complies with project requirements and is acceptable to the client.

Training, Other Qualifications, and Advancement

A college degree is required for a position as a technical writer. In addition, knowledge in a technical subject, as well as experience in Web design and computer graphics, is important.

Education and training. Employers look for candidates with a bachelor's degree, often preferring those with a major in communications, journalism, or English. Some technical writing jobs may require both experience and either a degree or knowledge in a specialized field—for example, engineering, medicine, or one of the sciences; others have broader requirements, such as a background in liberal arts. Knowledge of a second language is helpful for some positions. Experience in Web design and computer graphics also is helpful, because of the growing use of online technical documentation.

Other qualifications. Technical writers must have excellent writing and communication skills and be able to express ideas clearly and logically in a variety of media. Increasingly, technical writers need familiarity with electronic publishing, graphics, and sound and video production. Also needed is knowledge of computer software for combining online text with graphics, audio, video, and animation, as well as the ability to manage large, complex, and interconnected files.

Technical writers must be detail oriented, curious, persistent in solving problems, self-motivated, and able to understand complex material and explain it clearly. Technical writers also must demonstrate good working relationships and sensitivity toward others, especially those from different backgrounds. In addition, the ability to work under pressure and in a variety of work settings is essential.

Advancement. Some technical writers begin their careers not as writers, but as specialists in a technical field or as research assistants or trainees in a technical information department. By transferring or developing technical communication skills, they eventually assume primary responsibilities for technical writing. In small firms, beginning technical writers may work on projects right away; in larger companies with more standard procedures, beginners may observe experienced technical writers and interact with specialists before being assigned projects. Prospects for advancement generally include working on more complex projects, leading or training junior staff, and getting enough work to make it as a freelancer.

Many firms and freelancers provide technical writing services on a contract basis, often to small or not-for-profit organizations that do not have enough regular work to employ technical writers full time. Building a reputation and establishing a record for meeting deadlines also makes it easier to get future assignments. An experienced, credible, and reliable freelance technical writer or editor often is able to establish long-term dealings with the same companies.

Employment

Technical writers held about 48,900 jobs in 2008. There are technical writers in almost every industry, but they are concentrated in industries related to computer systems and software, publishing (except Internet), science, and engineering. The industry that employed the most technical writers in 2008 was the computer systems design industry, which had 18 percent of these workers. The second-largest employer was the computer and electronic manufacturing industry, with 8 percent of workers. Software publishers; architectural, engineering, and related services; management, scientific, and technical consulting services; and scientific research and development services industries also employed a sizeable number of technical writers. Two percent of technical writers were self-employed in 2008.

Jobs usually are concentrated in areas with high information technology or scientific and technical research industry employment, such as San Francisco and San Jose, CA; Boston, MA; and Washington, DC. However, technology permits technical writers to work in one location while communicating with clients and colleagues in another. As a result, geographic concentration is less of a requirement than it once was.

Job Outlook

Employment of technical writers is expected to grow faster than the average for all occupations as the need to explain a growing number of electronic and scientific products increases. Job prospects are expected to be good for those with solid writing and communications skills and a technical background.

Employment change. Employment of technical writers is expected to grow 18 percent, or faster than the average for all occupations, from 2008 to 2018. Demand over this decade is expected to increase because of the continuing expansion of scientific and technical information and the growing presence of customer service and Web-based product support networks. Legal, scientific, and technological developments and discoveries will generate demand for people who can interpret technical information for a general audience. Rapid growth and change in the high-technology and electronics industries will result in a greater need for people who can write users' guides, instruction manuals, and training materials in a variety of formats and communicate information clearly to others. This occupation requires workers who are both skilled writers and effective communicators and familiar with a specialized subject area.

Increasing acceptance of interactive media to provide nearly real-time information will create employment opportunities for technical writers because of the need to revise online information. Businesses and organizations are making more material available online often in formats that permit greater scrutiny and comparison of detailed information. The growing amount and complexity of information available on the Web will spur demand for technical writers. Professional, scientific, and technical services firms will continue to grow and should be a good source of new jobs even as the occupation finds acceptance in a broader range of industries, including data processing, hosting, and related services and educational services.

Job prospects. Job prospects, especially for applicants with solid communication and technical skills, are expected to be good. The growing reliance on technologically sophisticated products in the home and the workplace and the increasing complexity of medical or scientific information needed for daily living will create many new job opportunities for technical writers. However, competition will exist for technical writing positions with more desirable companies and for workers who are new to the occupation.

In addition to job openings created by employment growth, some openings will arise as experienced workers retire, transfer to other occupations, or leave the labor force. Also, many freelancers may not earn enough money by freelancing to remain in the occupation, thus generating additional job openings.

Earnings

Median annual wages for salaried technical writers were $61,620 in May 2008. The middle 50 percent earned between $47,100 and $78,910. The lowest 10 percent earned less than $36,500, and the highest 10 percent earned more than $97,460.

LAW & GOVERNMENT

—⁓—

Attorneys (Lawyers)

Nature of the Work

The legal system affects nearly every aspect of our society, from buying a home to crossing the street. *Lawyers* form the backbone of this system, linking it to society in numerous ways. They hold positions of great responsibility and are obligated to adhere to a strict code of ethics.

Lawyers, also called *attorneys*, act as both advocates and advisors in our society. As advocates, they represent one of the parties in criminal and civil trials by presenting evidence and arguing in court to support their client. As advisors, lawyers counsel their clients about their legal rights and obligations and suggest particular courses of action in business and personal matters. Whether acting as an advocate or an advisor, all attorneys research the intent of laws and judicial decisions and apply the law to the specific circumstances faced by their clients.

The more detailed aspects of a lawyer's job depend upon his or her field of specialization and position. Although all lawyers are licensed to represent parties in court, some appear in court more frequently than others. Trial lawyers spend the majority of their time outside the courtroom, conducting research, interviewing clients and witnesses, and handling other details in preparation for a trial.

Significant Points

❖ About 26 percent of lawyers are self-employed, either as partners in law firms or in solo practices.

❖ Formal requirements to become a lawyer usually include a 4-year college degree, 3 years of law school, and passing a written bar examination; however, some requirements may vary by State.

❖ Competition for admission to most law schools is intense.

❖ Competition for job openings should be keen because of the large number of students graduating from law school each year.

Lawyers may specialize in a number of areas, such as bankruptcy, probate, international, elder, or environmental law. Those specializing in, for example, environmental law may represent interest groups, waste disposal companies, or construction firms in their dealings with the U.S. Environmental Protection Agency and other Federal and State agencies. These lawyers help clients prepare and file for licenses and applications for approval before certain activities are permitted to occur. Some lawyers specialize in the growing field of intellectual property, helping to protect clients' claims to copyrights, artwork under contract, product designs, and computer programs. Other lawyers advise insurance companies about the legality of insurance transactions, guiding the company in writing insurance policies to conform to the law and to protect the companies from unwarranted claims. When claims are filed against insurance companies, these attorneys review the claims and represent the companies in court.

Most lawyers are in private practice, concentrating on criminal or civil law. In criminal law, lawyers represent individuals who have been charged with crimes and argue their cases in courts of law. Attorneys dealing with civil law assist clients with litigation, wills, trusts, contracts, mortgages, titles, and leases. Other lawyers handle only public-interest cases—civil or criminal—concentrating on particular causes and choosing cases that might have an impact on the way law is applied. Lawyers sometimes are employed full time by a single client. If the client is a corporation, the lawyer is known as "house counsel" and usually advises the company concerning legal issues related to its business activities. These issues might involve patents, government regulations, contracts with other companies, property interests, or collective-bargaining agreements with unions.

A significant number of attorneys are employed at the various levels of government. Some work for State attorneys general, prosecutors, and public defenders in criminal courts. At the Federal level, attorneys investigate cases for the U.S. Department of Justice and other agencies. Government lawyers also help develop programs, draft and interpret laws and legislation, establish enforcement procedures, and argue civil and criminal cases on behalf of the government.

Other lawyers work for legal aid societies—private, nonprofit organizations established to serve disadvantaged people. These lawyers generally handle civil, rather than criminal, cases.

Lawyers are increasingly using various forms of technology to perform more efficiently. Although all lawyers continue to use law libraries to prepare cases, most supplement conventional printed sources with computer sources, such as the Internet and legal databases. Software is used to search this legal literature automatically and to identify legal texts relevant to a specific case. In litigation involving many supporting documents, lawyers may use computers to organize and index materials. Lawyers must be geographically mobile and able to reach their clients in a timely matter, so they might use electronic filing, Web and videoconferencing, mobile electronic devices, and voice-recognition technology to share information more effectively.

Work environment. Lawyers do most of their work in offices, law libraries, and courtrooms. They sometimes meet in clients' homes or places of business and, when necessary, in hospitals or prisons. They may travel to attend meetings, gather evidence, and appear before courts, legislative bodies, and other authorities. They also may face particularly heavy pressure when a case is being tried. Preparation for court includes understanding the latest laws and judicial decisions.

Salaried lawyers usually have structured work schedules. Lawyers who are in private practice or those who work for large firms may work irregular hours, including weekends, while conducting research, conferring with clients, or preparing briefs during nonoffice hours. Lawyers often work long hours; of those who work full time, about 33 percent work 50 or more hours per week.

Training, Other Qualifications, and Advancement

Formal requirements to become a lawyer usually include a 4-year college degree, 3 years of law school, and passing a written bar examination; however, some requirements vary by State. Competition for admission to most law schools is intense. Federal courts and agencies set their own qualifications for those practicing before or in them.

Education and training. Becoming a lawyer usually takes 7 years of full-time study after high school—4 years of undergraduate study, followed by 3 years of law school. Law school applicants must have a bachelor's degree to qualify for admission. To meet the needs of students who can attend only part time, a number of law schools have night or part-time divisions.

Although there is no recommended "prelaw" undergraduate major, prospective lawyers should develop proficiency in writing and speaking, reading, researching, analyzing, and thinking logically—skills needed to succeed both in law school and in the law. Regardless of major, a multidisciplinary background is recommended. Courses in English, foreign languages, public speaking, government, philosophy, history, economics, mathematics, and computer science, among others, are useful. Students interested in a particular aspect of law may find related courses helpful. For example, prospective patent lawyers need a strong background in engineering or science, and future tax lawyers must have extensive knowledge of accounting.

Acceptance by most law schools depends on the applicant's ability to demonstrate an aptitude for the study of law, usually through undergraduate grades, the Law School Admission Test (LSAT), the quality of the applicant's undergraduate school, any prior work experience, and sometimes, a personal interview. However, law schools vary in the weight they place on each of these and other factors.

All law schools approved by the American Bar Association (ABA) require applicants to take the LSAT. As of June 2008, there were 200 ABA-accredited law schools; others were approved by State authorities only. Nearly all law schools require applicants to have certified transcripts sent to the Law School Data Assembly Service, which then submits the applicants' LSAT scores and their standardized records of college grades to the law schools of their choice. The Law School Admission Council administers both this service and the LSAT. Competition for admission to many law schools—especially the most prestigious ones—is usually intense, with the number of applicants greatly exceeding the number that can be admitted.

During the first year or year and a half of law school, students usually study core courses, such as constitutional law, contracts, property law, torts, civil procedure, and legal writing. In the remaining time, they may choose specialized courses in fields such as tax, labor, or corporate law. Law students often gain practical experience by participating in school-sponsored legal clinics; in the school's moot court competitions, in which students conduct appellate arguments; in practice trials under the supervision of experienced lawyers and judges; and through research and writing on legal issues for the school's law journals.

A number of law schools have clinical programs in which students gain legal experience through practice trials and projects under the supervision of lawyers and law school faculty. Law school clinical programs might include work in, for example, legal-aid offices or on legislative committees. Part-time or summer clerkships in law firms, government agencies, and corporate legal departments also provide valuable experience. Such training can lead directly to a job after graduation and can help students decide what kind of practice best suits them. Law school graduates receive the degree of *juris doctor* (J.D.), a first professional degree.

Advanced law degrees may be desirable for those planning to specialize, perform research, or teach. Some law students pursue joint degree programs, which usually require an additional semester or year of study. Joint degree programs are offered in a number of areas, including business administration or public administration.

After graduation, lawyers must keep informed about legal and nonlegal developments that affect their practices. In 2008, 46 States and jurisdictions required lawyers to participate in mandatory continuing legal education. Many law schools and State and local bar associations provide continuing education courses that help lawyers stay abreast of recent developments. Some States allow continuing education credits to be obtained through participation in seminars on the Internet.

Licensure. To practice law in the courts of any State or other jurisdiction, a person must be licensed, or admitted to its bar, under rules established by the jurisdiction's highest court. All States require that applicants for admission to the bar pass a written bar examination; most States also require applicants to pass a separate written ethics examination. Lawyers who have been admitted to the bar in one State occasionally may be admitted to the bar in another without taking another examination if they meet the latter jurisdiction's standards of good moral character and a specified period of legal experience. In most cases, however, lawyers must pass the bar examination in each State in which they plan to practice. Federal courts and agencies set their own qualifications for those practicing before or in them.

To qualify for the bar examination in most States, an applicant must earn a college degree and graduate from a law school accredited by the ABA or the proper State authorities. ABA accreditation signifies that the law school—particularly its library and faculty—meets certain standards. With certain exceptions, graduates of schools not approved by the ABA are restricted to taking the bar examination and practicing in the State or other jurisdiction in which the school is located; most of these schools are in California.

Although there is no nationwide bar examination, 48 States, the District of Columbia, Guam, the Northern Mariana Islands, Puerto Rico, and the Virgin Islands require the 6-hour Multistate Bar Examination (MBE) as part of their overall bar examination; the MBE is not required in Louisiana or Washington. The MBE covers a broad range of issues, and sometimes a locally prepared State bar examination is given in addition to it. The 3-hour Multistate Essay Examination (MEE) is used as part of the bar examination in several States. States vary in their use of MBE and MEE scores.

Many States also require the Multistate Performance Test to test the practical skills of beginning lawyers. Requirements vary by State, although the test usually is taken at the same time as the bar exam and is a one-time requirement.

In 2008, law school graduates in 52 jurisdictions were required to pass the Multistate Professional Responsibility Examination (MPRE), which tests their knowledge of the ABA codes on professional responsibility and judicial conduct. In some States, the MPRE may be taken during law school, usually after completing a course on legal ethics.

Other qualifications. The practice of law involves a great deal of responsibility. Individuals planning careers in law should like to work with people and be able to win the respect and confidence of their clients, associates, and the public. Perseverance, creativity, and reasoning ability also are essential to lawyers, who often analyze complex cases and handle new and unique legal problems.

Trial lawyers, who specialize in trial work, must be able to think quickly and speak with ease and authority. In addition, familiarity with courtroom rules and strategy is particularly important in trial work.

Advancement. Most beginning lawyers start in salaried positions. Newly hired attorneys usually start as associates and work with more experienced lawyers or judges. After several years, some lawyers are admitted to partnership in their firm, which means that they are partial owners of the firm, or go into practice for themselves. Some experienced lawyers are nominated or elected to judgeships. Others become full-time law school faculty or administrators; a growing number of these lawyers have advanced degrees in other fields as well.

Some attorneys use their legal training in administrative or managerial positions in various departments of large corporations. A transfer from a corporation's legal department to another department is often viewed as a way to gain administrative experience and rise in the ranks of management.

Employment

Lawyers held about 759,200 jobs in 2008. Approximately 26 percent of lawyers were self-employed, practicing either as partners in law firms or in solo practices. Most salaried lawyers held positions in government, in law firms or other corporations, or in nonprofit organizations. Most government-employed lawyers worked at the local level. In the Federal Government, lawyers worked for many different agencies, but were concentrated in the Departments of Justice, Treasury, and Defense. Many salaried lawyers working outside of government were employed as house counsel by public utilities, banks, insurance companies, real-estate agencies, manufacturing firms, and other business firms and nonprofit organizations. Some also had part-time independent practices, while others worked part time as lawyers and full time in another occupation.

A relatively small number of trained attorneys work in law schools and are not included in the employment estimate for lawyers. Most are faculty members who specialize in one or more subjects; however, some serve as administrators. Others work full time in nonacademic settings and teach part time.

Job Outlook

About as fast as the average employment growth is projected, but job competition is expected to be keen.

Employment change. Employment of lawyers is expected to grow 13 percent during the 2008-18 decade, about as fast as the average for all occupations. Growth in the population and in the level of business activity is expected to create more legal transactions, civil disputes, and criminal cases. Job growth among lawyers also will result from increasing demand for legal services in such areas as healthcare, intellectual property, bankruptcy, corporate and security litigation, antitrust law, and environmental law. In addition, the wider availability and affordability of legal clinics should result in increased use of legal services by middle-income people. However, growth in demand for lawyers will be constrained as businesses increasingly use large accounting firms and paralegals to perform some of the same functions that lawyers do. For example, accounting firms may provide employee-benefit counseling, process documents, or handle various other services previously performed by a law firm. Also, mediation and dispute resolution are increasingly being used as alternatives to litigation.

Job growth for lawyers will continue to be concentrated in salaried jobs as businesses and all levels of government employ a growing number of staff attorneys. Most salaried positions are in urban areas where government agencies, law firms, and big corporations are concentrated. The number of self-employed lawyers is expected to grow slowly, reflecting the difficulty of establishing a profitable new practice in the face of competition from larger, established law firms. Moreover, the growing complexity of the law, which encourages specialization, along with the cost of maintaining up-to-date legal research materials, favors larger firms.

Job prospects. Competition for job openings should continue to be keen because of the large number of students graduating from law school each year. Graduates with superior academic records from highly regarded law schools will have the best job opportunities. Perhaps as a result of competition for attorney positions, lawyers are increasingly finding work in less traditional areas for which legal training is an asset, but not normally a requirement—for example, administrative, managerial, and business positions in banks, insurance firms, real estate companies, government agencies, and other organizations. Employment opportunities are expected to continue to arise in these organizations at a growing rate.

As in the past, some graduates may have to accept positions outside of their field of interest or for which they feel overqualified. Some recent law school graduates who have been unable to find permanent positions are turning to the growing number of temporary staffing firms that place attorneys in short-term jobs. This service allows companies to hire lawyers on an "as-needed" basis and permits beginning lawyers to develop practical skills.

Because of the keen competition for jobs, a law graduate's geographic mobility and work experience are assuming greater importance. Willingness to relocate may be an advantage in getting a job, but to be licensed in another State, a lawyer may have to take an additional State bar examination. In addition, employers increasingly are seeking graduates who have advanced law degrees and experience in a specialty, such as tax, patent, or admiralty law.

Job opportunities often are adversely affected by cyclical swings in the economy. During recessions, demand declines for some discretionary legal services, such as planning estates, drafting wills, and handling real estate transactions. Also, corporations are less likely to litigate cases when declining sales and profits restrict their budgets. Some corporations and law firms will not hire new attorneys until business improves, and these establishments may even cut staff to contain costs. Several factors, however, mitigate the overall impact of recessions on lawyers; during recessions, for example, individuals and corporations face other legal problems, such as bankruptcies, foreclosures, and divorces—all requiring legal action.

For lawyers who wish to work independently, establishing a new practice will probably be easiest in small towns and expanding suburban areas. In such communities, competition from larger, established law firms is likely to be less than in big cities, and new lawyers may find it easier to establish a reputation among potential clients.

Earnings

In May 2008, the median annual wages of all wage-and-salaried lawyers were $110,590. The middle half of the occupation earned between $74,980 and $163,320.

Salaries of experienced attorneys vary widely according to the type, size, and location of their employer. Lawyers who own their own practices usually earn less than those who are partners in law firms. Lawyers starting their own practice may need to work part time in other occupations to supplement their income until their practice is well established.

LAW & GOVERNMENT

—⁓—

The Judiciary

Nature of the Work

Judges, magistrates, and other judicial workers apply the law and oversee the legal process in courts. They preside over cases concerning every aspect of society, from traffic offenses, to disputes over the management of professional sports, to issues concerning the rights of huge corporations. All judicial workers must ensure that trials and hearings are conducted fairly and that the court safeguards the legal rights of all parties involved.

The most visible responsibility of judges is presiding over trials or hearings and listening as attorneys represent their clients. Judges rule on the admissibility of evidence and the methods of conducting testimony, and they may be called on to settle disputes between opposing attorneys. Also, they ensure that rules and procedures are followed, and if unusual circumstances arise for which standard procedures have not been established, judges interpret the law to determine how the trial will proceed.

Judges often hold pretrial hearings for cases. They listen to allegations and determine whether the evidence presented merits a trial. In criminal cases, judges may decide that people charged with crimes should be held in jail pending trial, or they may set conditions for their release. In civil cases, judges and magistrates occasionally impose restrictions on

---

Significant Points

❖ A bachelor's degree and work experience are the minimum requirements for a judgeship or magistrate position, but most workers have law degrees and some are elected; training requirements for arbitrators, mediators, and conciliators vary.

❖ Overall employment is projected to grow more slowly than average, but this varies by occupational specialty.

❖ Competition is expected for judge or magistrate jobs because of the prestige associated with serving on the bench.

the parties until a trial is held.

In many trials, juries are selected to decide guilt or innocence in criminal cases, or liability and compensation in civil cases. Judges instruct juries on applicable laws, direct them to deduce the facts from the evidence presented, and hear their verdict. When the law does not require a jury trial or when the parties waive their right to a jury, judges decide cases. In such instances, the judge determines guilt in criminal cases and imposes sentences on the guilty; in civil cases, the judge awards relief—such as compensation for damages—to the winning parties to the lawsuit.

Judges also work outside the courtroom, in their chambers or private offices. There, judges read documents on pleadings and motions, research legal issues, write opinions, and oversee the court's operations. In some jurisdictions, judges also manage the court's administrative and clerical staff.

Judges' duties vary according to the extent of their jurisdictions and powers. General trial court judges of the Federal and State court systems have jurisdiction over any case in their system. They usually try civil cases that transcend the jurisdiction of lower courts and all cases involving felony offenses. Federal and State appellate court judges, although few in number, have the power to overrule decisions made by trial court judges or administrative law judges. Appellate court judges overrule decisions if they determine that legal errors were made in a case or if legal precedent does not support the judgment of the lower court. Appellate court judges rule on a small number of cases and rarely have direct contact with litigants—the people who bring the case or who are on trial. Instead, they usually base their decisions on the lower court's records and on lawyers' written and oral arguments.

Many State court judges hear only certain types of cases. A variety of titles are assigned to these judges; among the most common are *mu*nicipal court judge, county court judge, magistrate, and justice of the peace. Traffic violations, misdemeanors, small-claims cases, and pretrial hearings constitute the bulk of the work of these judges, but some States allow them to handle cases involving domestic relations, probate, contracts, and other selected areas of the law.

Administrative law judges, sometimes called *hearing officers* or *adjudicators*, are employed by government agencies to make determinations for administrative agencies. These judges make decisions on, for example, (1) a person's eligibility for various Social Security or workers' compensation benefits, (2) protection of the environment, (3) the enforcement of health and safety regulations, (4) employment discrimination, and (5) compliance with economic regulatory requirements.

Some people work as arbitrators, mediators, or conciliators instead of as judges or magistrates. They assist with alternative dispute resolution—a collection of processes used to settle disputes outside of court. All hearings are private and confidential, and the processes are less formal than a court trial. If no settlement is reached, no statements made during the proceedings are admissible as evidence in any subsequent litigation.

There are two main types of arbitration: compulsory and voluntary. During compulsory arbitration, opposing parties submit their dispute to one or more impartial persons, called arbitrators, for a final and nonbinding decision. Either party may reject the ruling and request a trial in court. Voluntary arbitration is a process in which opposing parties choose one or more arbitrators to hear their dispute and submit a final, binding decision.

Arbitrators usually are attorneys or businesspeople with expertise in a particular field. In arbitration, parties identify, in advance, the issues to be resolved, the scope of the relief to be awarded, and many of the procedural aspects of the process.

Mediators are neutral parties who help people to resolve their disputes outside of court. Parties to a dispute often use mediators when they wish to preserve their relationship. A mediator may offer suggestions, but resolution of the dispute rests with the parties themselves. Mediation proceedings also are confidential and private. If the parties are unable to reach a settlement, they are free to pursue other options. The parties usually decide in advance how they will share the cost of mediation. However, many mediators volunteer their services, or they may be court staff. Courts ask that mediators provide their services at the lowest possible rate and that the parties split the cost.

Conciliation, or facilitation, is similar to mediation. The conciliator's role is to guide the parties to a settlement. The parties must decide in advance whether they will be bound by the conciliator's recommendations.

Arbitrators, mediators, or conciliators also use other forms of dispute resolution, including executive minitrials, early neutral evaluations, and summary jury trials. An executive minitrial is a process that involves negotiation including senior executives who have no involvement with the issues that led to the disagreement. Senior executives from each side listen to a summary of key elements of the dispute presented by each of the parties. The presentations may be made to the executives on their own, or by agreement of the parties, a neutral third party may be present. In early neutral evaluation, a person experienced in the subject matter of a litigated dispute will hold a brief, nonbinding meeting to hear the parties outline the key elements of their cases. The evaluator will identify the main issues and explore the possibility of settlement. If a settlement can't be reached, the evaluator may assist the parties by indicating procedural recommendations. A summary jury trial is a form of alternative dispute resolution in which jurors are asked to render a nonbinding verdict after an expedited hearing. The verdict may be binding if the parties consent.

Work environment. Judges, magistrates, and other judicial workers do most of their work in offices, law libraries, and courtrooms. Work in these occupations presents few hazards, although sitting in the same position in the courtroom for long periods can be tiring. Most judges wear robes when they are in a courtroom. Judges typically work a standard 40-hour week, but many work more than 50 hours per week. Some judges with limited jurisdiction are employed part time and divide their time between their judicial responsibilities and other careers.

Arbitrators, mediators, and conciliators usually work in private offices or meeting rooms; no public record of the proceedings is kept. Arbitrators, mediators, and conciliators often travel to a site chosen for negotiations, but some work from home. Arbitrators, mediators, and conciliators usually work a standard 35- to 40-hour week. However, longer hours might be necessary when contract agreements are being prepared and negotiated.

Training, Other Qualifications, and Advancement

A bachelor's degree and work experience usually constitute the minimum requirements for judges and magistrates, but most workers have law degrees and some are elected. Training requirements for arbitrators, mediators, and conciliators vary.

Education and training. Most judges have been lawyers. In fact, Federal and State judges usually are required to be lawyers, which means that they have attended law school and passed an examination. About 40 States allow nonlawyers to hold limited-jurisdiction judgeships, but opportunities are better for those with law experience.

Federal administrative law judges must be lawyers and pass a competitive examination administered by the U.S. Office of Personnel Management. Some State administrative law judges and other hearing officials are not required to be lawyers.

All States have some type of orientation for newly elected or appointed judges. The Federal Judicial Center, American Bar Association, National Judicial College, and National Center for State Courts provide judicial education and training for judges and other judicial-branch personnel. General and continuing education courses usually last from a few days to 3 weeks. More than half of all States, as well as Puerto Rico, require judges to take continuing education courses while serving on the bench.

Training for arbitrators, mediators, and conciliators is available through independent mediation programs, national and local mediation membership organizations, and postsecondary schools. To practice in state-funded or court-funded mediation programs, mediators usually must meet specific training or experience standards, which vary by State and court. Most mediators complete a 40-hour basic course and a 20-hour advanced training course. Some people receive training by volunteering at a community mediation center or by co-mediating cases with an experienced mediator. Others go on to complete an advanced degree that consists of a 2-year master's program in dispute resolution or conflict management, a 4-year to 5-year doctoral program, or a certificate program in conflict resolution at a college or university. Many mediators have a law (JD) degree, but master's degrees in public policy, law, and related fields also provide good background for prospective arbitrators, mediators, and conciliators.

Licensure. There are no national credentials or licensure requirements for arbitrators, mediators, and conciliators. In fact, State regulatory requirements vary widely. Some States require arbitrators to be experienced lawyers. Some States license mediators while other States register or certify them. Currently, only five States—Florida, New Hampshire, North Carolina, South Carolina, and Virginia—have certification programs. In addition, at the Federal level, the U.S. Department of the Navy certifies mediators who have met the Department's requirements.

Increasingly, credentialing programs are being offered through professional organizations. For example, the American Arbitration Association requires mediators listed on its mediation panel to complete their training course, receive recommendations from the trainers, and complete an apprenticeship.

Other qualifications. Judges and magistrates must be appointed or elected a procedure that often takes political support. Federal administrative law judges are appointed by various Federal agencies, with virtually lifetime tenure. Federal magistrate judges are appointed by district judges—the life-tenured Federal judges of district courts—to serve in a U.S. district court for 8 years. A part-time Federal magistrate judge's term of office is 4 years. Some State judges are appointed, but the remainder are elected in partisan or nonpartisan State elections. Many State and local judges serve fixed renewable terms ranging from 4 to 6 years for some trial court judgeships to as long as 14 years or even life for other trial or appellate court judgeships. Judicial nominating commissions, composed of members of the bar and the public, are used to screen candidates for judgeships in many States and for some Federal judgeships.

Arbitrators, mediators, and conciliators must have knowledge of different mediation techniques and processes as well as knowledge of dispute resolution methods in order to be able to do their jobs successfully. They also must have good communication and listening skills and the ability to run successful meetings and negotiate a solution to a dispute. The ability to evaluate large amounts of information that are sometimes complex is essential. Good writing skills and technical problem-solving skills also is a must. Arbitrators, mediators, and conciliators who specialize in a particular area, such as construction or insurance, may need to have knowledge of that industry and must be able to relate well to people from different cultures and backgrounds.

Advancement. Some judicial workers move to higher courts or to courts with broader jurisdiction. Advancement for alternative-dispute workers includes taking on more complex cases, starting a business, practicing law, or becoming district court judges.

Employment

Judges, magistrates, and other judicial workers held 51,200 jobs in 2008. Judges, magistrate judges, and magistrates held 26,900 jobs, all in State and local governments. Administrative law judges, adjudicators, and hearing officers held 14,400 jobs, with 24 percent in the Federal Government. Arbitrators, mediators, and conciliators held another 9,900 jobs. Approximately 26 percent worked for State and local governments. The remainder worked for labor organizations, law offices, insurance carriers, and other private companies and organizations that specialize in providing dispute resolution services.

Job Outlook

Overall employment is projected to grow more slowly than average, but varies by specialty. Judges and magistrates are expected to encounter competition for jobs because of the prestige associated with serving on the bench.

Employment change. Overall employment of judges, magistrates, and other judicial workers is expected to grow 4 percent over the 2008–18 projection period, slower than the average for all occupations. Budgetary pressures at all levels of government are expected to hold down the hiring of judges despite rising caseloads, particularly in Federal courts. However, the continued need to cope with crime and settle disputes, as well as the public's willingness to go to court to settle disputes, should spur demand for judges.

Demographic shifts in the population also will spur demand for judges. For instance, the number of immigrants migrating to the United States will continue to rise, thereby increasing the demand for judges to handle the complex issues associated with immigrants. In addition, demand for judges will increase because, as the U.S. population ages, the courts are expected to reform guardianship policies and practices and develop new strategies to address elder abuse. Both the quantity and the complexity of judges' work have increased because of developments in information technology, medical science, electronic commerce, and globalization.

Employment of arbitrators, mediators, and conciliators is expected to grow faster than the average for all occupations through 2018. Many individuals and businesses try to avoid litigation, which can involve lengthy delays, high costs, unwanted publicity, and ill will. Arbitration and other alternatives to litigation usually are faster, less expensive, and more conclusive, spurring demand for the services of arbitrators, mediators, and conciliators. Demand also will continue to increase for arbitrators, mediators, and conciliators because all jurisdictions now have some type of alternative dispute resolution program. Some jurisdictions have programs requiring disputants to meet with a mediator in certain circumstances, such as when attempting to resolve child custody issues.

Job prospects. The prestige associated with serving on the bench will ensure continued competition for judge and magistrate positions. However, a growing number of candidates are choosing to forgo the bench and work in the private sector, where pay may be significantly higher. This trend may lessen the competition somewhat. Turnover is low among judges, and most job openings will arise as they retire. Additional openings will occur when new judgeships are authorized by law or when judges are elevated to higher judicial offices.

Jobs should be available for arbitrators, mediators, and conciliators, but opportunities may be limited because, as with judges, turnover is low. Once these workers have the appropriate qualifications and skills, they tend to remain in the occupation for many years. Those with certification and specialization in one or more areas of arbitration, mediation, or conciliation should have the best job opportunities.

Earnings

Judges, magistrate judges, and magistrates had median annual wages of $110,220 in May 2008. The middle 50 percent earned between $51,760 and $141,190. The top 10 percent earned more than $162,140, while the bottom 10 percent earned less than $32,290. Median annual wages in the industries employing the largest numbers of judges, magistrate judges, and magistrates in May 2008 were $126,080 in State government and $77,390 in local government. Administrative law judges, adjudicators, and hearing officers earned annual median wages of $76,940, and arbitrators, mediators, and conciliators earned an annual median of $50,660.

In the Federal court system, the Chief Justice of the U.S. Supreme Court earned $217,400 in January 2008, and the Associate Justices averaged $208,100. Federal court-of-appeals judges earned an average of $179,500 a year, while district court judges had average salaries of $169,300, as did judges in the Court of Federal Claims and the Court of International Trade. Federal judges with limited jurisdiction, such as magistrates and bankruptcy judges, had average salaries of $155,756.

According to a 2008 survey by the National Center for State Courts, salaries of chief justices of State highest courts averaged $150,850 and ranged from $107,404 to $228,856. Annual salaries of associate justices of the State highest courts averaged $145,194 and ranged from $106,185 to $218,237. Salaries of State intermediate appellate court judges averaged $141,263 and ranged from $105,050 to $204,599. Salaries of State judges of general jurisdiction trial courts averaged $130,533 and ranged from $99,234 to $178,789.

Most salaried judges are provided health, life, and dental insurance; pension plans; judicial immunity protection; expense accounts; vacation, holiday, and sick leave; and contributions to retirement plans made on their behalf. In many States, judicial compensation committees, which make recommendations on the amount of salary increases, determine judicial salaries. States without commissions have statutes that regulate judicial salaries, link judicial salaries to increases in pay for Federal judges, or adjust annual pay according to the change in the Consumer Price Index, calculated by the U.S. Bureau of Labor Statistics.

LAW & GOVERNMENT

—⚍—

Government (Federal)

Nature of the Industry

The Federal Government was established by the Constitution to provide services to the public. While these services vary considerably, all are designed to improve the lives of the United States population, as well as people around the world.

Goods and services. The Federal Government's essential duties include defending the United States from foreign aggression, representing U.S. interests abroad, crating and enforcing national laws and regulations, and administering domestic programs and agencies. Workers employed by the Federal Government are responsible for enacting and implementing the programs and performing the services that accomplish these goals, playing a vital role in many aspects of daily life.

Industry organization. More than 200 years ago, the founders of the United States gathered in Philadelphia to create a constitution for a new national government. The Constitution of the United States, ratified by the last of the 13 original States in 1791, created the three branches of the Federal Government and granted certain powers and responsibilities to each. The legislative, judicial, and executive branches were granted equal powers but very different responsibilities that act to keep their powers in balance.

The legislative branch is responsible for forming and amending the legal structure of the

---

Significant Points

❖ With about 2.0 million civilian employees, the Federal Government, excluding the Postal Service, is the Nation's largest employer.

❖ About 85 percent of Federal employees work outside the Washington, DC metropolitan area.

❖ A substantial number of job openings will arise as many Federal workers are expected to retire over the next decade; competition is high during times of economic uncertainty, however, when workers seek the stability of Federal employment.

Nation. Its largest component is Congress, the U.S. legislative body, which is made up of the Senate and the House of Representatives. This body includes senators, representatives, their staffs, and various support workers. The legislative branch employs only about 1 percent of Federal workers, nearly all of whom work in the Washington, DC area.

The judicial branch is responsible for interpreting the laws that are established by the legislative branch. The Supreme Court, the Nation's definitive judicial body, makes the highest rulings. Its decisions usually follow the appeal of a decision made by the one of the regional Courts of Appeal, which hear cases appealed from U.S. District Courts, the Court of Appeals for the Federal Circuit, or State Supreme Courts. U.S. District Courts are located in each State and are the first to hear most cases under Federal jurisdiction. The judicial branch employs about 2 percent of Federal workers, and unlike the legislative branch, its offices and employees are dispersed throughout the country.

Of the three branches, the executive branch has the widest range of responsibilities. Consequently, it employed about 97 percent of all Federal civilian employees (excluding Postal Service workers) in 2008. The executive branch is comprised of the Executive Office of the President, 15 executive Cabinet departments, and about 70 independent agencies, each of which has clearly defined duties. The Executive Office of the President is composed of several offices and councils that aid the President in policy decisions. These include the Office of Management and Budget, which oversees the administration of the Federal budget; the National Security Council, which advises the President on matters of national defense; and the Council of Economic Advisers, which makes economic policy recommendations.

Each of the 15 executive Cabinet departments administers programs that oversee an aspect of life in the United States. The highest departmental official of each Cabinet department, called the Secretary, is a member of the President's Cabinet. Each department, listed by employment size, is described below and in table 1.

Defense: Manages the military forces that protect our country and its interests, including the Departments of the Army, Navy, and Air Force and a number of smaller agencies. The civilian workforce employed by the Department of Defense performs various support activities, such as payroll and public relations.

Veterans Affairs: Administers programs to aid U.S. veterans and their families, runs the veterans' hospital system, and operates our national cemeteries.

Homeland Security: Works to prevent terrorist attacks within the United States, reduce vulnerability to terrorism, and minimize the damage from potential attacks and natural disasters. It also administers the country's immigration policies and oversees the Coast Guard.

Treasury: Regulates banks and other financial institutions, administers the public debt, prints currency, and collects Federal income taxes.

Justice: Works with State and local governments and other agencies to prevent and control crime and ensure public safety against threats, both domestic and foreign. It also enforces Federal laws, prosecutes cases in Federal courts, and runs Federal prisons.

Agriculture: Promotes U.S. agriculture domestically and internationally, manages forests, researches new ways to grow crops and conserve natural resources, ensures safe meat and poultry products, and leads the Federal anti-hunger programs, such as the Supplemental Nutrition Assistance Program (formerly known as the Food Stamp program) and the National School Lunch Program.

Health and Human Services: Performs health and social science research, assures the safety of drugs and foods other than meat and poultry, and administers Medicare, Medicaid, and numerous other social service programs.

Interior: Manages Federal lands, including the national parks, runs hydroelectric power systems, and promotes conservation of natural resources.

Transportation: Sets national transportation policy, plans and funds the construction of highways and mass transit systems, and regulates railroad, aviation, and maritime operations.

Commerce: Forecasts the weather, charts the oceans, regulates patents and trademarks, conducts the census, compiles economic statistics, and promotes U.S. economic growth by encouraging international trade.

Energy: Coordinates the national use and provision of energy, oversees the production and disposal of nuclear weapons, and plans for future energy needs.

Labor: Enforces laws guaranteeing fair pay, workplace safety, and equal job opportunity, administers unemployment insurance (UI) to State UI agencies, regulates pension funds; and collects and analyzes economic data.

State: Oversees the Nation's embassies and consulates, issues passports, monitors U.S. interests abroad, and represents the United States before international organizations.

Housing and Urban Development: Funds public housing projects, enforces equal housing laws, and insures and finances mortgages.

Education: Monitors and distributes financial aid to schools and students, collects and disseminates data on schools and other education matters, and prohibits discrimination in education.

Numerous independent agencies perform tasks that fall between the jurisdictions of the executive departments. Some smaller, but well- known, independent agencies include the Peace Corps, the Securities and Exchange Commission, and the Federal Communications Commission. Although the majority of these agencies are fairly small, employing fewer than 1,000 workers (many employ fewer than 100), some are quite large. The largest independent agencies are:

Social Security Administration: Operates old age, survivor, and disability insurance programs.

National Aeronautics and Space Administration: Oversees aviation research and conducts exploration and research beyond the Earth's atmosphere.

Environmental Protection Agency: Runs programs to control and reduce pollution of the Nation's water, air, and lands.

General Services Administration: Manages and protects Federal Government property and records.

Federal Deposit Insurance Corporation: Examines insuring deposits and promoting sound banking practices.

Office of Personnel Management: Oversees issues related to human resources, such as hiring practices, health insurance policies, and workforce performance evaluation.

Working Conditions

Hours. The vast majority of Federal employees work full time; some work on flexible schedules that allow workers more control over their work schedules. Some agencies also offer telecommuting programs, which allow selected workers to perform some job duties at home or from regional centers.

Work environment. Because of the wide range of Federal jobs, working conditions vary considerably. Most Federal employees work in office buildings, hospitals, or laboratories; but a large number also can be found at border crossings, airports, shipyards, military bases, construction sites, national parks, and other settings. Work environments vary from clean and comfortable to hazardous and stressful, such as those experienced by law enforcement officers and air traffic controllers.

Some Federal workers spend much of their time away from the offices in which they are based. For example, inspectors or compliance officers often visit businesses and worksites to ensure that laws and regulations are obeyed. Some Federal workers frequently travel long distances, spending days or weeks away from home. Auditors, for example, may spend weeks at a time in distant locations.

Employment

In 2008, the Federal Government, excluding the Postal Service, employed about 2.0 million civilian workers. The Federal Government is the Nation's single largest employer. Because data on employment in certain agencies cannot be released to the public for national security reasons, this total does not include employment for the Central Intelligence Agency, National Security Agency, Defense Intelligence Agency, and National Imagery and Mapping Agency.

The Federal Government makes an effort to have a workforce as diverse as the Nation's civilian labor force. The Federal Government serves as a model for all employers in abiding by equal employment opportunity legislation, which protects current and potential employees from discrimination based on race, color, religion, sex, national origin, disability, or age. The

Federal Government also makes a special effort to recruit and accommodate persons with disabilities.

Even though the headquarters of most Federal departments and agencies are based in the Washington, DC area, only 15 percent of Federal employees worked in the vicinity of the Nation's Capital in 2008. In addition to Federal employees working throughout the United States, about 35,000, which includes foreign nationals, are assigned overseas, mostly in embassies or defense installations.

Occupations in the Industry

Although the Federal Government employs workers in every major occupational group, workers are not employed in the same proportions in which they are employed throughout the economy as a whole. (See table 2.) The analytical and technical nature of many government agencies translates into a much higher proportion of professional, management, business, and financial occupations in the Federal Government, compared with all other industries combined.

Management, business, and financial occupations. Management, business, and financial workers made up about 34 percent of Federal employment in 2008. Managerial workers include a broad range of officials who, at the highest levels, lead Federal agencies or programs. Middle managers, on the other hand, usually oversee one activity or aspect of a program.

Business and financial occupations include *accountants and auditors*, who prepare and analyze financial reports, review and record revenues and expenditures, and investigate operations for fraud and inefficiency. *Management analysts* study government operations and systems and suggest improvements. *Compliance officers* make sure than contracts, licenses, and permits comply with Federal law, and *tax examiners, collectors, and revenue agents* determine and collect taxes.

Professional and related occupations. Professional and related occupations accounted for 33 percent of Federal employment (table 3). The largest groups of professional workers were in healthcare practitioner and technical occupations; life, physical, and social science occupations; and architecture and engineering occupations.

Health professionals, such as *licensed practical and licensed vocational nurses, registered nurses,* and *physicians and surgeons*, provide medical care at Federal hospitals, serving a wide range of individuals that include veterans of the nation's Armed Forces.

Life, physical, and social science occupations in the Federal government include *biological scientists, conservation scientists and foresters, environmental scientists and geoscientists,* and *forest and conservation technicians.* They perform tasks such as determining the effects of drugs on living organisms, preventing fires in national forests, and predicting earthquakes and hurricanes.

Architecture and engineering occupations include *aerospace, civil, electrical and electronics, and mechanical engineers.* Engineers were found in many departments of the executive branch, but the vast majority worked in the Department of Defense. Some worked in the National Aeronautics and Space Administration as well as other agencies. In general, they solve problems and provide advice on technical programs, such as building highway bridges or implementing agency-wide computer systems.

The Federal Government also employs a substantial number *lawyers, judges and related workers* who, interpret, administer and enforce many of the country's laws and regulations.

Computer specialists are also employed throughout the Federal Government. They write computer programs, analyze problems related to data processing, and protect computer systems from hackers, viruses, and other hazards.

Office and administrative support occupations. About 14 percent of Federal workers were in office and administrative support occupations. These employees aid management and other staff with administrative duties, such as scheduling appointments, drafting e-mail and other correspondence, maintaining financial documents, and executing purchase orders. Administrative support workers in the Federal Government include *information and record clerks, financial clerks,* and *secretaries and administrative assistants.*

Service occupations. Service workers hold a relatively small share of Federal employment, compared to their share of all industries combined. About 5 percent of service workers in the Federal Government were protective service workers, such as *correctional officers and jailers, detectives and criminal investigators,* and *police officers.* These workers protect the public from crime and oversee Federal prisons.

Installation, maintenance, and repair occupations. Federally employed workers in installation, maintenance, and repair occupations include *aircraft mechanics and service technicians* who fix and maintain all types of aircraft, and *electrical and electronic equipment mechanics, installers, and repairers,* who inspect, adjust, and repair electronic equipment such as industrial controls, transmitters, radar, radio, and navigation systems.

Other occupational groups. The Federal Government employed a relatively small number of workers in transportation, production, construction, sales and related, and farming, fishing, and forestry occupations. However, the Federal Government employs almost all or a significant share of some occupations, such as *air traffic controllers, agricultural inspectors,* and *bridge and lock tenders.*

Training and Advancement

The educational and training requirements for jobs in the Federal Government mirror those in the private sector for most major occupational groups. Many jobs in managerial or professional and related occupations, for example, require a 4-year college degree. Some, such as engineers, physicians and surgeons, and biological and physical scientists, require a bachelor's or higher degree in a specific field of study. In addition, many occupations, such as registered nurses or engineering technicians may require at least 2 years of training after high school. Many additional Federal jobs, such as those in office and administrative support, have more general requirements. Some have no formal educational requirement, while others require a high school diploma or some related experience.

In all but a few cases, applicants for Federal jobs must be U.S. citizens. Applicants who are veterans of military service also may be able to claim veteran's preference which gives them preferred status over other candidates with equal qualifications. For jobs requiring access to sensitive or classified materials, such as those relating to national security, applicants must undergo a background investigation. This investigation covers an individual's criminal, credit, and employment history, as well as other records. The scope of the investigation will vary depending on the nature of the position in the government and the sensitivity of the information involved.

Each Federal department or agency determines its own on-the-job training practices, and many offer workers opportunities to improve job skills or become qualified to advance to other jobs. These may include technical or skills training; tuition assistance or reimbursement; fellowship programs; and executive leadership and management training programs, seminars, and workshops. This training may be offered on the job, by another agency, or at local colleges and universities.

Advancement for most workers in the Federal Government is currently based on a system of occupational pay levels, or "grades." Workers typically enter the Federal civil service at the starting grade for an occupation and begin a series of promotions, called grade increases, until they reach the full-performance grade for that occupation. Pay grade increases through the full-performance level are usually given at regular intervals, as long as job performance is satisfactory. With each pay grade increase, an employee generally is given more responsibility and higher pay. The exact pay grades associated with a job's career ladder depend upon the occupation and specific job duties.

Once Federal workers reach the full-performance level of a position, they must compete for promotions, and advancement becomes more difficult. At this point, promotions occur as vacancies arise, and they are based solely on merit.

Outlook

Wage and salary employment in the Federal Government is projected to increase by 10 percent over the 2008-18 period. There will be a substantial number of job openings as many Federal workers are expected to retire over the next decade, although job prospects are expected to vary by occupation.

Employment change. Wage and salary employment in the Federal Government, except Post Office, is expected to increase by 10 percent over the coming decade, which is close to the 11 percent growth rate for all industries combined. Staffing levels in Federal Government can be subject to change in the long run because of changes in public policies as legislated by the Congress, which affect spending levels and hiring decisions for the various departments and agencies. In general, over the coming decade, domestic programs are likely to see an increase in employment.

While there will be growth in many occupations over the coming decade, demand will be especially strong for specialized workers in areas related to public health, information security, scientific research, law enforcement, and financial services. As a larger share of the U.S. population enters the older age brackets, demand for healthcare will increase. This will lead to a substantial number of new jobs in Federal hospitals and other healthcare facilities for registered nurses and physicians and surgeons. In addition, as cyber security becomes an increasingly important aspect of National defense, rapid growth will occur among information technology specialists, such as computer and information research scientists, who will be needed to devise defense methods, monitor computer networks, and execute security protocol. Furthermore, as global activity in scientific development increases, the Federal Government will add many physical science, life science, and engineering workers to remain competitive. Aside from these specific areas, numerous new jobs in other occupational areas will arise as the diverse Federal workforce continues to expand.

As financial and business transactions face increased scrutiny, a substantial number of compliance officers and claims adjusters, examiners, and investigators will be added to Federal payrolls. In addition, as the population grows and national security remains a priority, many new law enforcement officers, such as detectives and criminal investigators will be needed.

Job prospects. Job prospects in the Federal government are expected to vary by occupation. Over the next decade, a significant number of workers are expected to retire, which will create a large number of job openings. This may create favorable prospects in certain occupations, but jobseekers may face competition for positions in occupations with fewer retirements, or for popular jobs that attract many applicants.

Competition for Federal positions can increase during times of economic uncertainty, when workers seek the stability of Federal employment. In general, employment in the Federal government is considered to be relatively stable because it is less susceptible than private industries to fluctuations in the economy.

Earnings

Industry earnings. The majority of professional and administrative Federal workers are paid under the General Schedule (GS). The General Schedule, shown in table 4, has 15 grades of pay for civilian white-collar and service workers, and smaller within-grade step increases that occur based on length of service and quality of performance. New employees usually start at the first step of a grade, but if the position in question is difficult to fill, entrants may receive somewhat higher pay or special rates. Almost all physician and engineer positions, for example, fall into this category. In an effort to make Federal pay more responsive to local labor market conditions, Federal employees working in the continental United States receive locality pay. The specific amount of locality pay is determined by survey comparisons of private sector wage rates and Federal wage rates in the relevant geographic area. At its highest level, locality pay led to an increase of as much as 34 percent above the base salary in 2009.

For those in craft, repair, operator, and laborer jobs, the Federal Wage System (FWS) is used to determine worker pay. This schedule sets Federal wages so that they are comparable with prevailing regional wage rates for similar types of jobs. As a result, wage rates paid under the FWS can vary significantly from one locality to another.

Federal employees may also receive monetary bonuses and awards. Awards are generally bestowed for a special act or service, or for sustained high job performance. Some workers also may receive "premium" pay, which is granted when the employee must work overtime, on holidays, on weekends, at night, or under hazardous conditions.

Benefits and union membership. Benefits are an important part of Federal employee compensation. Federal employees generally receive health and life insurance options that are partially subsidized by the Government. In addition, workers hired after January 1, 1984, participate in the Federal Employees Retirement System (FERS), a three-tiered retirement plan including Social Security, a pension plan, and an optional Thrift Savings Plan—a savings program that is similar to many 401(k) plans. Worker participation in the Thrift Savings Plan is voluntary, but contributions are tax-deferred, and, up to a point, matched by the Federal Government. In addition to other benefits, some Federal agencies provide public transit subsidies in an effort to encourage employee use of public transportation.

Federal employees receive both vacation and sick leave. They earn 13 days of vacation leave a year for the first 3 years of service, 20 days a year for the next 12 years, and 26 days a year after their 15th year of service. Workers also receive 13 days of sick leave a year.

Law & Government

—☓—

Government (State or Local, Except Education & Health)

Nature of the Industry

Goods and services. State and local governments provide their constituents with vital services that may not be available otherwise, such as transportation, public safety, healthcare, education, utilities, and courts.

Industry organization. Excluding education and hospitals, State and local governments employ about 8.3 million workers, placing them among the largest employers in the economy. Seven out of 10 of these employees work for local governments, such as counties, cities, special districts, and towns. In addition, large numbers of State and local workers work in public education—a major part of the educational services industry

In addition to the 50 State governments, there were about 87,500 local governments in 2007, according to the U.S. Census Bureau. These included about 3,000 county governments; 19,500 municipal governments; 16,500 townships; 13,500 school districts; and 35,100 special districts. Illinois had the most local government units, with nearly 7,000; Hawaii had the fewest, with 19.

In many areas of the country, citizens are served by more than one local government unit. For example, most States have *counties,* which may contain various municipalities such as

---

Significant Points

❖ Local governments employ more than twice as many workers as State governments.

❖ Professional and service occupations accounted for more than half of all jobs; fire fighters and law enforcement workers, concentrated in local government, are among the largest occupations.

❖ Although job prospects vary by State and region, overall prospects are expected to be favorable.

❖ Employer-provided benefits are more common among State and local government employees than among workers in the private sector.

cities or towns, but which also often include unincorporated rural areas. *Townships,* which do not exist in some States, may or may not contain municipalities and often consist of suburban or rural areas. Supplementing these forms of local government, *special district* government bodies are independent, limited-purpose governmental units that usually perform a single function or activity. For example, fire districts and ambulatory services often are provided by a special district.

Working Conditions

Hours. Working conditions vary by occupation and, in some instances, by size and location of the State or local government. For example, chief executives in very small jurisdictions may work less than 20 hours a week; in larger jurisdictions, they often work more than 40 hours per week. Chief executives in large jurisdictions work full time year round, as do most county and city managers. Most State legislators work full time only when in session, usually for a few months a year, and work part time the rest of the year. Local elected officials in some small jurisdictions work part time.

Most professional, financial operations, and office and administrative support workers in State and local government work a standard 40-hour week in an office environment. However, workers in some of the most visible local government jobs have very different working conditions and schedules. Fire fighters' hours are longer and vary more widely than those of most workers. Many professional fire fighters are on duty for several days in a row, working over 50 hours a week, because some must be on duty at all times to respond to emergencies. They often eat and sleep at the fire station. Following this long shift, they are then off for several days in a row or for the entire next week. Some local fire districts also use the services of volunteer fire fighters, who tend to work shorter, regularly scheduled shifts, or remain on call for emergencies.

Most police and detectives work 40 hours a week, with paid overtime when they testify in court or work on an investigation. Because police protection must be provided around the clock, some officers must work weekends, holidays, and nights. Many officers are subject to call any time their services are needed and are expected to intervene whenever they observe a crime, even if they are off duty.

Bus drivers with regular routes and subway operators generally have consistent weekly work schedules. Those who do not have regular schedules may be on call and must be prepared to report for work on short notice. To accommodate commuters, many operators work split shifts, such as 6 a.m. to 10 a.m. and 3 p.m. to 7 p.m., with time off in between the two shifts.

A number of other State and local government jobs also require weekend or night work. For example, split, weekend, and night shifts are common for water and other public utility workers.

Work environment. Law enforcement work is potentially dangerous. The injury and fatality rates among law officers are higher than in many occupations, reflecting risks taken in apprehending suspected criminals and responding to various emergency situations such as traffic accidents. In addition to irregular hours, fire fighting can involve the risk of death or injury.

Most administrative positions are in climate controlled buildings. The nature of the work may lead to repetitive movement conditions, such as carpal tunnel syndrome.

Most driver/operator jobs in public transit systems are stressful and fatiguing because they involve dealing with passengers, tight schedules, and heavy traffic.

Employment

State and local governments, excluding education and hospitals, employed about 8.3 million people in 2008. About 70 percent of these workers were employed in local government.

Occupations in the Industry

Service occupations made up the largest share of employment in State and local governments, accounting for 32 percent of all jobs (chart 1). Of these, *police and sheriff's patrol officers, correctional officers and jailers,* and *fire fighters,* concentrated in local government, were the largest occupations (table 2). Professional and related occupations accounted for 21 percent of employment; office and administrative support occupations accounted for 19 percent; and management, business, and financial occupations constituted 12 percent.

State and local governments employ people in occupations found in nearly every industry in the economy, including chief executives, managers, engineers, computer specialists, secretaries, and health technicians. Certain occupations, however, are mainly or exclusively found in these governments, such as legislators; tax examiners, collectors, and revenue agents; urban and regional planners; judges, magistrates, and other judicial workers; police and sheriff's patrol officers; and correctional officers and jailers.

Chief executives, general and operations managers, and *legislators* establish government policy and develop laws, rules, and regulations. They are elected or appointed officials who either preside over units of government or make laws. Chief executives include governors, lieutenant governors, mayors, and city managers. General and operations managers include district managers and revenue directors. Legislators include State senators and representatives, county commissioners, and city council members.

Tax examiners, collectors, and revenue agents determine tax liability and collect past-due taxes from individuals or businesses. *Urban and regional planners* draft plans and recommend programs for the development and use of resources such as land and water. They also propose construction of physical facilities, such as schools and roads, under the authority of cities, counties, and metropolitan areas. Planners devise strategies outlining the best use of community land and identify the places in which residential, commercial, recreational, and other types of development should be located.

Judges arbitrate, advise, and administer justice in a court of law. They oversee legal processes in courts, apply the law to resolve civil disputes, and determine the sentence when guilt has been established in criminal cases. *Magistrates* resolve criminal cases not involving penitentiary sentences, as well as civil cases involving damages below a sum specified by State law.

Social workers counsel and assess the needs of clients, refer them to the appropriate sources of help, and monitor their progress. *Eligibility interviewers, government programs* interview and investigate applicants and recipients to determine eligibility to receive, or continue receiving, welfare and other types of social assistance. The duties of *social and human service assistants* vary with specific job titles. These workers include social service technicians, case management aides, social work assistants, residential counselors, alcoholism or drug abuse counseling aides, child abuse workers, community outreach workers, and gerontology aides. *Probation officers and correctional treatment specialists* assist in rehabilitation of law offenders in custody or on probation or parole.

Court, municipal, and license clerks perform a variety of State and local government administrative tasks. *Court clerks* prepare dockets of cases to be called, secure information for judges, and contact witnesses, lawyers, and attorneys to obtain information for the court. *Municipal clerks* draft agendas for town or city councils, record minutes of council meetings, answer official correspondence, keep fiscal records and accounts, and prepare reports on civic needs. *License clerks* keep records and help the public obtain motor vehicle ownership titles, operator permits, and a variety of other permits and licenses. State and local governments also employ many *secretaries and administrative assistants* and *general office clerks*.

Fire fighters control and extinguish fires, assist with emergency medical treatment, and help with the recovery from natural disasters such as earthquakes and tornadoes. *Fire inspectors* inspect public buildings for conditions that might present a fire hazard. *Emergency medical technicians and paramedics* assess injuries, administer emergency medical care, and extricate trapped individuals. They transport injured or sick persons to medical facilities.

Police and sheriff's patrol officers and *detectives and criminal investigators* have duties that range from controlling traffic to preventing and investigating crimes. They maintain order; enforce laws and ordinances; issue traffic summonses; investigate accidents; give evidence in court; serve legal documents for the court system; and apprehend, arrest, and process prisoners. State and local *correctional officers* guard inmates in jails, prisons, or juvenile detention institutions. *Bailiffs* keep order in courts.

Highway maintenance workers maintain highways, municipal and rural roads, airport runways, and rights-of-way. They patch broken or eroded pavement, repair guard rails and highway markers, plow snow, and mow or clear brush from along roads. *Bus drivers* pick up and deliver passengers at prearranged stops throughout their assigned routes. Operators may collect fares, answer questions about schedules and transfer points, and announce stops.

Training and Advancement

The educational level and experience needed by workers in State and local government varies by occupation. Voters elect most chief executives and legislators, so local support is very important. Taking part in volunteer work and helping to provide community services are good ways to establish vital community support. Those elected to chief executive and legislator positions come from a variety of backgrounds, but must conform to age, residency, and citizenship regulations regarding the positions that they seek. Advancement opportunities for most elected public officials are limited to other offices in the jurisdictions in which they live. For example, a local council member may run for mayor or for a position in State government, and State legislators may decide to run for State governor or for the U.S. Congress.

For city managers, a master's degree in public administration is widely recommended. Many cities prefer but do not require a master's degree. A bachelor's degree in business administration, public administration, finance, or a related field is usually required. City manager candidates may gain experience as management analysts or assistants in government departments, working with councils and mayors. They may also gain experience by moving to an executive position in a government agency or becoming a deputy or assistant city manager. They may initially be hired to manage a town or a small city and eventually become manager of larger cities.

For most professional jobs, a college degree is required. To obtain an entry-level urban or regional planning position, most State and local government agencies require 2 years of graduate study in urban and regional planning or the equivalent in work experience. To become a judge, particularly a State trial or appellate court judge, one usually is required to be a lawyer. Some State judges are appointed, while others are elected in partisan or nonpartisan elections. Most State and local judges serve fixed terms, usually ranging from 2 to 14 years. Appellate judges commonly serve longer terms than lower court judges.

Most applicants for firefighting jobs must have a high school education or its equivalent and pass a civil service examination. In addition, they need to pass a medical examination and tests of strength, physical stamina, coordination, and agility. Experience as a volunteer fire fighter or as a fire fighter in the Armed Forces is helpful, as is completion of community college courses in fire science. Recruits study fire fighting techniques, fire prevention, local building codes, emergency procedures, and the proper use of rescue equipment. Fire fighters may be promoted depending on written examination results and job performance.

Bus drivers must comply with Federal regulations that require drivers who operate vehicles designed to transport 16 or more passengers to obtain a commercial driver's license from the State in which they live. To qualify for a commercial driver's license, applicants must pass a written test on rules and regulations and demonstrate that they can operate a commercial vehicle safely. For subway and streetcar operator jobs, applicants with at least a high school education have the best chance. In some cities, prospective subway operators are required to work as bus drivers for a specified period. Successful applicants generally are in good health, possess good communication skills, and are able to make quick, sound judgments. Because bus drivers and subway operators deal with passengers, they need an even temperament and emotional stability. Driving in heavy, fast-moving, or stop-and-go traffic and dealing with passengers can be stressful.

Police departments in most areas require applicants to be U.S. citizens of good character, at least 20 years old, and able to meet rigorous physical and mental standards. Police departments increasingly encourage applicants to take college courses, and some require a college degree. Many community and junior colleges, as well as colleges and universities, offer programs in law enforcement or criminal justice. Officers usually attend a local or regional police academy that includes classroom instruction in constitutional law, civil rights, and State and local law. They also receive training in patrol, accident investigation, traffic control, using firearms, self-defense, first aid, and emergency management. Promotions for police officers are highly influenced by scores on a written civil service examination and subsequent performance evaluations by superiors.

Outlook

Although job prospects vary by State and region, overall prospects are expected to be favorable.

Employment change. Wage and salary employment in State and local government is projected to increase 8 percent during the 2008–18 period, slower than the 11 percent growth projected for all sectors of the economy combined.

Job growth will stem from the rising demand for services at the State and local levels, particularly demand for public safety and health services. Two factors are fueling the growth of these services: an increasing population and the assumption of responsibility by State and local governments for some services previously provided by the Federal Government. Despite the increased demand for the services of State and local governments, employment growth will continue to be dampened by budgetary constraints due to the rapidly increasing proportion of revenues devoted to the Medicaid program, and public resistance to tax increases. Outsourcing of government jobs to the private sector will also limit employment in State and local government. When economic times are good, many State and local governments increase spending on programs and employment.

Professional and service occupations accounted for over half of all jobs in State and local government. Most new jobs will stem from steady demand for community and social services, health services, and protective services, including law enforcement and fire fighting and prevention workers.

Employment of management, business, and financial occupations is projected to grow at about the same rate as overall employment in State and local government. Employment in office and administrative support occupations in State and local government is expected to remain close to current levels.

Job prospects. Although job prospects vary by State and region, overall prospects are expected to be favorable. In addition to job openings from employment growth, many opportunities will be created by workers who retire from the industry. Prospects with managerial experience will have better opportunities as a growing number of managers are expected to retire in the coming decade. Currently, some States and localities are being forced to reduce payrolls; however, as State and local budgets improve, new opportunities should arise.

Earnings

Industry earnings. Earnings and wages vary by occupation, size of the State or locality, and region of the country. As in most industries, professionals and managers earn more than other workers.

Benefits and union membership. Employer-provided benefits—including health and life insurance and retirement benefits—are more common among State and local government employees than among workers in the private sector. Although union membership data are not available, workers in State and local government have a relatively high rate of union membership.

LAW & GOVERNMENT

—ᴍ—

Law Enforcement

Nature of the Work

Police officers and *detectives* protect lives and property. *Law enforcement officer's* duties depend on the size and type of their organizations.

Police and detectives pursue and apprehend individuals who break the law and then issue citations or give warnings. A large proportion of their time is spent writing reports and maintaining records of incidents they encounter. Most police officers patrol their jurisdictions and investigate any suspicious activity they notice. They also respond to calls from individuals. Detectives, who often are called *agents* or *special agents*, perform investigative duties such as gathering facts and collecting evidence.

The daily activities of police and detectives vary with their occupational specialty—such as police officer, *game warden*, or detective—and whether they are working for a local, State, or Federal agency. Duties also differ substantially among various Federal agencies, which enforce different aspects of the law. Regardless of job duties or location, police officers and detectives at all levels must write reports and maintain meticulous records that will be needed if they testify in court.

State and Local Law Enforcement. Uniformed police officers have general law enforcement duties. They maintain regular patrols and respond to calls for service. Much of

> ### Significant Points
>
> ❖ Police work can be dangerous and stressful.
>
> ❖ Education requirements range from a high school diploma to a college degree or higher.
>
> ❖ Job opportunities in most local police departments will be favorable for qualified individuals, while competition is expected for jobs in State and Federal agencies.
>
> ❖ Bilingual applicants with college training in police science or with military police experience will have the best opportunities.

their time is spent responding to calls and doing paperwork. They may direct traffic at the scene of an accident, investigate a burglary, or give first aid to an accident victim. In large police departments, officers usually are assigned to a specific type of duty.

Many urban police agencies are involved in community policing—a practice in which an officer builds relationships with the citizens of local neighborhoods and mobilizes the public to help fight crime.

Police agencies are usually organized into geographic districts, with uniformed officers assigned to patrol a specific area. *Officers* in large agencies often patrol with a partner. They attempt to become familiar with their patrol area and remain alert for anything unusual. Suspicious circumstances and hazards to public safety are investigated or noted, and officers are dispatched to individual calls for assistance within their district. During their shift, they may identify, pursue, and arrest suspected criminals; resolve problems within the community; and enforce traffic laws.

Some agencies have special geographic jurisdictions and enforcement responsibilities. Public college and university police forces, public school district police, and agencies serving transportation systems and facilities are examples. Most law enforcement workers in special agencies are uniformed officers.

Some police officers specialize in a particular field, such as chemical and microscopic analysis, training and firearms instruction, or handwriting and fingerprint identification. Others work with special units, such as horseback, bicycle, motorcycle, or harbor patrol; canine corps; special weapons and tactics (SWAT); or emergency response teams. A few local and special law enforcement officers primarily perform jail-related duties or work in courts.

Sheriffs and *deputy sheriffs* enforce the law on the county level. Sheriffs usually are elected to their posts and perform duties similar to those of a local or county police chief. Sheriffs' departments tend to be relatively small, most having fewer than 50 sworn officers. Deputy sheriffs have law enforcement duties similar to those of officers in urban police departments. Police and sheriffs' deputies who provide security in city and county courts are sometimes called *bailiffs*.

State police officers, sometimes called *State troopers* or *highway patrol officers*, arrest criminals Statewide and patrol highways to enforce motor vehicle laws and regulations. State police officers often issue traffic citations to motorists. At the scene of accidents, they may direct traffic, give first aid, and call for emergency equipment. They also write reports used to determine the cause of the accident. State police officers frequently are called upon to render assistance to other law enforcement agencies, especially those in rural areas or small towns.

State highway patrols operate in every State except Hawaii. Most full-time sworn personnel are uniformed officers who regularly patrol and respond to calls for service. Others work as investigators, perform court-related duties, or carry out administrative or other assignments.

Detectives are plainclothes investigators who gather facts and collect evidence for criminal cases. Some are assigned to interagency task forces to combat specific types of crime. They conduct interviews, examine records, observe the activities of suspects, and participate in raids or arrests. Detectives usually specialize in investigating one type of violation, such as homicide or fraud. They are assigned cases on a rotating basis and work on them until an arrest and conviction is made or until the case is dropped.

Fish and game wardens enforce fishing, hunting, and boating laws. They patrol hunting and fishing areas, conduct search and rescue operations, investigate complaints and accidents, and aid in prosecuting court cases.

Federal Law Enforcement. *Federal Bureau of Investigation (FBI) agents* are the Government's principal investigators, responsible for investigating violations of more than 200 categories of Federal law and conducting sensitive national security investigations. Agents may conduct surveillance, monitor court-authorized wiretaps, examine business records, investigate white-collar crime, or participate in sensitive undercover assignments. The FBI investigates a wide range of criminal activity, including organized crime, public corruption, financial crime, bank robbery, kidnapping, terrorism, espionage, drug trafficking, and cybercrime.

There are many other Federal agencies that enforce particular types of laws. *U.S. Drug Enforcement Administration (DEA) agents* enforce laws and regulations relating to illegal drugs. *U.S. marshals and deputy marshals* provide security for the Federal courts and ensure the effective operation of the judicial system. *Bureau of Alcohol, Tobacco, Firearms, and Explosives agents* enforce and investigate violations of Federal firearms and explosives laws, as well as Federal alcohol and tobacco tax regulations. The U.S. Department of State *Bureau of Diplomatic Security special agents* are engaged in the battle against terrorism.

The *Department of Homeland Security* also employs numerous law enforcement officers within several different agencies, including Customs and Border Protection, Immigration and Customs Enforcement, and the U.S. Secret Service. *U.S. Border Patrol agents* protect more than 8,000 miles of international land and water boundaries. *Immigration inspectors* interview and examine people seeking entry into the United States and its territories. *Customs inspectors* enforce laws governing imports and exports by inspecting cargo, baggage, and articles worn or carried by people, vessels, vehicles, trains, and aircraft entering or leaving the United States. *Federal Air Marshals* provide air security by guarding against attacks targeting U.S. aircraft, passengers, and crews. *U.S. Secret Service special agents* and *U.S. Secret Service uniformed officers* protect the President, the Vice President, their immediate families, and other public officials. Secret Service special agents also investigate counterfeiting, forgery of Government checks or bonds, and fraudulent use of credit cards.

Other Federal agencies employ police and special agents with sworn arrest powers and the authority to carry firearms. These agencies include the Postal Service, the Bureau of Indian Affairs Office of Law Enforcement, the Forest Service, and the National Park Service.

Work environment. Police and detective work can be very dangerous and stressful. Police officers and detectives have one of the highest rates of on-the-job injury and illness. In addition to the obvious dangers of confrontations with criminals, police officers and detectives need to be constantly alert and ready to deal appropriately with a number of other threatening situations. Many law enforcement officers witness death and suffering resulting from accidents and criminal behavior. A career in law enforcement may take a toll on their private lives.

Uniformed officers, detectives, agents, and inspectors usually are scheduled to work 40-hour weeks, but paid overtime is common. Shift work is necessary because protection must be provided around the clock. Junior officers frequently work weekends, holidays, and nights. Police officers and detectives are required to work whenever they are needed and may work long hours during investigations. Officers in most jurisdictions, whether on or off duty, are expected to be armed and to exercise their authority when necessary.

The jobs of some Federal agents, such as U.S. Secret Service and DEA special agents, require extensive travel, often on very short notice. These agents may relocate a number of times over the course of their careers. Some special agents, such as those in the U.S. Border Patrol, may work outdoors in rugged terrain and in all kinds of weather.

Training, Other Qualifications, and Advancement

Education requirements range from a high school diploma to a college degree or higher. Most police and detectives learn much of what they need to know on the job, often in their agency's training academy. Civil service regulations govern the appointment of police and detectives in most States, large municipalities, and special police agencies, as well as in many smaller jurisdictions. Candidates must be U.S. citizens, usually at least 21 years old, and meet rigorous physical and personal qualifications.

Education and training. Applicants usually must have at least a high school education, and some departments require 1 or 2 years of college coursework or, in some cases, a college degree. Physical education classes and participation in sports are also helpful in developing the competitiveness, stamina, and agility needed for many law enforcement positions. Knowledge of a foreign language is an asset in many Federal agencies and urban departments.

State and local agencies encourage applicants to take courses or training related to law enforcement subjects after high school. Many entry-level applicants for police jobs have completed some formal postsecondary education, and a significant number are college graduates. Many junior colleges, colleges, and universities offer programs in law enforcement or administration of justice. Many agencies pay all or part of the tuition for officers to work toward degrees in criminal justice, police science, administration of justice, or public administration and pay higher salaries to those who earn one of those degrees.

Before their first assignments, officers usually go through a period of training. In State and large local police departments, recruits get training in their agency's police academy, often for 12 to 14 weeks. In small agencies, recruits often attend a regional or State academy. Training includes classroom instruction in constitutional law and civil rights, State laws and local ordinances, and accident investigation. Recruits also receive training and supervised experience in patrol, traffic control, use of firearms, self-defense, first aid, and emergency response. Police departments in some large cities hire high school graduates who are still in their teens as police cadets or trainees. They do clerical work and attend classes, usually for 1 to 2 years, until they reach the minimum age requirement and can be appointed to the regular force.

Fish and game wardens also must meet specific requirements. Most States require at least 2 years of college study. Once hired, fish and game wardens attend a training academy lasting from 3 to 12 months, sometimes followed by further training in the field.

Federal agencies require a bachelor's degree, related work experience, or a combination of the two. Federal law enforcement agents undergo extensive training, usually at the U.S. Marine Corps base in Quantico, Virginia, or the Federal Law Enforcement Training Center in Glynco, Georgia. The specific educational requirements, qualifications, and training information for a particular Federal agency can be found on its Web site. Many of these agencies are listed as sources of additional information at the end of this statement.

To be considered for appointment as an FBI agent, an applicant must be a college graduate and have at least 3 years of professional work experience or must have an advanced degree plus 2 years of professional work experience. An applicant who meets these criteria also must have one of the following: a college major in accounting, electrical engineering, information technology, or computer science; fluency in a foreign language; a degree from an accredited law school; or 3 years of related full-time work experience. All new FBI agents undergo 18 weeks of training at the FBI Academy on the U.S. Marine Corps base in Quantico, Virginia.

Other qualifications. Civil service regulations govern the appointment of police and detectives in most States, large municipalities, and special police agencies, as well as in many smaller jurisdictions. Candidates must be U.S. citizens, usually must be at least 21 years old, and must meet rigorous physical and personal qualifications. Physical examinations for entry into law enforcement often include tests of vision, hearing, strength, and agility. Eligibility for appointment usually depends on one's performance in competitive written examinations and previous education and experience.

Candidates should enjoy working with people and meeting the public. Because personal characteristics such as honesty, sound judgment, integrity, and a sense of responsibility are especially important in law enforcement, candidates are interviewed by senior officers and their character traits and backgrounds are investigated. A history of domestic violence may disqualify a candidate. In some agencies, candidates are interviewed by a psychiatrist or a psychologist or given a personality test. Most applicants are subjected to lie detector examinations or drug testing. Some agencies subject sworn personnel to random drug testing as a condition of continuing employment.

Although similar in nature, the requirements for Federal agents are generally more stringent and the background checks are more thorough. There are polygraph tests as well as interviews with references. Jobs that require security clearances have additional requirements.

Advancement. Police officers usually become eligible for promotion after a probationary period ranging from 6 months to 3 years. In large departments, promotion may enable an officer to become a detective or to specialize in one type of police work, such as working with juveniles. Promotions to corporal, sergeant, lieutenant, and captain usually are made according to a candidate's position on a promotion list, as determined by scores on a written examination and on-the-job performance.

Federal agents often are on the General Services (GS) pay scale. Most begin at the GS-5 or GS-7 level. As agents meet time-in-grade and knowledge and skills requirements, they move up the GS scale. Promotions at and above GS-13 are most often managerial positions. Many agencies hire internally for these supervisory positions. A few agents may be able to enter the Senior Executive Series ranks of upper management.

Continuing training helps police officers, detectives, and special agents improve their job performance. Through police department academies, regional centers for public safety employees established by the States, and Federal agency training centers, instructors provide annual training in self-defense tactics, firearms, use-of-force policies, sensitivity and communications skills, crowd-control techniques, relevant legal developments, and advances in law enforcement equipment.

Employment

Police and detectives held about 883,600 jobs in 2008. About 79 percent were employed by local governments. State police agencies employed about 11 percent. Various Federal agencies employ police and detectives.

According to the U.S. Bureau of Justice Statistics, police and detectives employed by local governments worked primarily in cities with more than 25,000 inhabitants. Some cities have very large police forces, while thousands of small communities employ fewer than 25 officers each.

Job Outlook

Job opportunities in most local police departments will be <u>favorable</u> for qualified individuals, whereas competition is expected for jobs in State and Federal agencies. As fast as average employment growth is expected.

Employment change. Employment of police and detectives is expected to grow 10 percent over the 2008–18 decade, about as fast as the average for all occupations. Population growth is the main source of demand for police services.

Job prospects. Overall opportunities in local police departments will be favorable for individuals who meet the psychological, personal, and physical qualifications. In addition to openings from employment growth, many openings will be created by the need to replace workers who retire and those who leave local agencies for Federal jobs and private-sector security jobs. Jobs in local police departments that offer relatively low salaries, or those in urban communities in which the crime rate is relatively high, may be the easiest to get. Some smaller departments may have fewer opportunities as budgets limit the ability to hire additional officers. Bilingual applicants with military experience or college training in police science will have the best opportunities in local and State departments.

There will be more competition for jobs in Federal and State law enforcement agencies than for jobs in local agencies. Bilingual applicants with a bachelor's degree and several years of law enforcement or military experience, especially investigative experience, will have the best opportunities in Federal agencies.

The level of government spending determines the level of employment for police and detectives. The number of job opportunities, therefore, can vary from year to year and from place to place. Layoffs are rare because retirements enable most staffing cuts to be handled through attrition. Trained law enforcement officers who lose their jobs because of budget cuts usually have little difficulty finding jobs with other agencies.

Earnings

Police and sheriff's patrol officers had median annual wages of $51,410 in May 2008. The middle 50 percent earned between $38,850 and $64,940. The lowest 10 percent earned less than $30,070, and the highest 10 percent earned more than $79,680. Median annual wages were $46,620 in Federal Government, $57,270 in State government, $51,020 in local government and $43,350 in educational services.

In May 2008, median annual wages of police and detective supervisors were $75,490. The middle 50 percent earned between $59,320 and $92,700. The lowest 10 percent earned less than $46,000, and the highest 10 percent earned more than $114,300. Median annual wages were $89,930 in Federal Government, $75,370 in State government, and $74,820 in local government.

In May 2008, median annual wages of detectives and criminal investigators were $60,910. The middle 50 percent earned between $45,930 and $81,490. The lowest 10 percent earned less than $36,500, and the highest 10 percent earned more than $97,870. Median annual wages were $73,170 in Federal Government, $53,910 in State government, and $55,930 in local government.

In May 2008, median annual wages of fish and game wardens were $48,930. The middle 50 percent earned between $37,500 and $61,290. The lowest 10 percent earned less than $30,400, and the highest 10 percent earned more than $81,710. Median annual wages were $48,960 in Federal Government, $50,440 in State government, and $35,810 in local government.

In May 2008, median annual wages of parking enforcement workers were $32,390. The middle 50 percent earned between $25,400 and $42,000. The lowest 10 percent earned less than $20,510, and the highest 10 percent earned more than $50,470. Median annual wages were $33,130 in local government and $27,640 in educational services.

In May 2008, median annual wages of transit and railroad police were $46,670. The middle 50 percent earned between $37,640 and $57,830. The lowest 10 percent earned less than $31,300, and the highest 10 percent earned more than $72,700. Median annual wages were $49,370 in State government, $43,720 in local government, and $56,300 in rail transportation.

Federal law provides special salary rates to Federal employees who serve in law enforcement. Additionally, Federal special agents and inspectors receive law enforcement availability pay (LEAP)—equal to 25 percent of the agent's grade and step—awarded because of the large amount of overtime that these agents are expected to work. Salaries were slightly higher in selected areas where the prevailing local pay level was higher. Because Federal agents may be eligible for a special law enforcement benefits package, applicants should ask their recruiter for more information.

Total earnings for local, State, and special police and detectives frequently exceed the stated salary because of payments for overtime, which can be significant.

In addition to the common benefits—paid vacation, sick leave, and medical and life insurance—most police and sheriffs' departments provide officers with special allowances for uniforms. Many police officers retire at half-pay after 20 years of service; others often are eligible to retire with 30 or fewer years of service.

BUSINESS & FINANCE

―ᴍ―

Advertising, Marketing, Promotions, Public Relations, and Sales Managers

Nature of the Work

Advertising, marketing, promotions, public relations, and sales managers coordinate their companies' market research, marketing strategy, sales, advertising, promotion, pricing, product development, and public relations activities. In small firms the owner or chief executive officer might assume all advertising, promotions, marketing, sales, and public relations responsibilities. In large firms, which may offer numerous products and services nationally or even worldwide, an executive vice president directs overall advertising, marketing, promotions, sales, and public relations policies.

Advertising managers. Advertising managers direct a firm's or group's advertising and promotional campaign. They can be found in advertising agencies that put together advertising campaigns for clients, in media firms that sell advertising space or time, and in companies that advertise heavily. They work with sales staff and others to generate ideas for the campaign, oversee a creative staff that develops the advertising, and work with the finance department to prepare a budget and cost estimates for the campaign. Often, these managers serve as liaisons between the firm requiring the advertising and an advertising or promotion agency that actually develops and places the ads. In larger firms with an extensive advertising

> ### Significant Points
>
> ❖ Keen competition is expected for these highly coveted jobs.
>
> ❖ College graduates with related experience, a high level of creativity, and strong communication and computer skills should have the best job opportunities.
>
> ❖ High earnings, substantial travel, and long hours, including evenings and weekends, are common.
>
> ❖ Because of the importance and high visibility of their jobs, these managers often are prime candidates for advancement to the highest ranks.

department, different advertising managers may oversee in-house accounts and creative and media services departments. The *account executive* manages account services departments in companies and assesses the need for advertising. In advertising agencies, account executives maintain the accounts of clients whereas the creative services department develops the subject matter and presentation of advertising. The *creative director* oversees the copy chief, art director, and associated staff. The *media director* oversees planning groups that select the communication medium—for example, radio, television, newspapers, magazines, the Internet, or outdoor signs—that will disseminate the advertising.

Marketing managers. Marketing managers work with advertising and promotion managers to promote the firm's or organization's products and services. With the help of lower level managers, including *product development managers* and *market research managers,* marketing managers estimate the demand for products and services offered by the firm and its competitors and identify potential markets for the firm's products. Marketing managers also develop pricing strategies to help firms maximize profits and market share while ensuring that the firms' customers are satisfied. In collaboration with sales, product development, and other managers, they monitor trends that indicate the need for new products and services and they oversee product development.

Promotions managers. Promotions managers direct promotions programs that combine advertising with purchasing incentives to increase sales. Often, the programs are executed through the use of direct mail, inserts in newspapers, Internet advertisements, in-store displays, product endorsements, or other special events. Purchasing incentives may include discounts, samples, gifts, rebates, coupons, sweepstakes, and contests.

Public relations managers. Public relations managers plan and direct public relations programs designed to create and maintain a favorable public image for the employer or client. For example, they might write press releases or sponsor corporate events to help maintain and improve the image and identity of the company or client. They also help to clarify the organization's point of view to their main constituency. They observe social, economic, and political trends that might ultimately affect the firm, and they make recommendations to enhance the firm's image on the basis of those trends. Public relations managers often specialize in a specific area, such as crisis management, or in a specific industry, such as healthcare.

In large organizations, public relations managers may supervise a staff of public relations specialists. They also work with advertising and marketing staffs to make sure that the advertising campaigns are compatible with the image the company or client is trying to portray. In addition, public relations managers may handle internal company communications, such as company newsletters, and may help financial managers produce company reports. They may assist company executives in drafting speeches, arranging interviews, and maintaining other forms of public contact; oversee company archives; and respond to requests for information. Some of these managers handle special events as well, such as the sponsorship of races, parties introducing new products, or other activities that the firm supports in order to gain public attention through the press without advertising directly.

Sales managers. Sales managers direct the distribution of the product or service to the customer. They assign sales territories, set sales goals, and establish training programs for the organization's sales representatives. Sales managers advise the sales representatives on ways to improve their sales performance. In large multiproduct firms, they oversee regional and local sales managers and their staffs. Sales managers maintain contact with dealers and distributors, and analyze sales statistics gathered by their staffs to determine sales potential and inventory requirements and to monitor customers' preferences. Such information is vital in the development of products and the maximization of profits.

Work environment. Advertising, marketing, promotions, public relations, and sales managers work in offices close to those of top managers. Working under pressure is unavoidable when schedules change and problems arise, but deadlines and goals still must be met.

Substantial travel may be required in order to meet with customers and consult with others in the industry. Sales managers travel to national, regional, and local offices and to the offices of various dealers and distributors. Advertising and promotions managers may travel to meet with clients or representatives of communications media. At times, public relations managers travel to meet with special-interest groups or government officials. Job transfers between headquarters and regional offices are common, particularly among sales managers.

Long hours, including evenings and weekends are common. In 2008, over 80 percent of advertising, marketing, promotions, public relations, and sales managers worked 40 hours or more a week.

Training, Other Qualifications, and Advancement

A wide range of educational backgrounds is suitable for entry into advertising, marketing, promotions, public relations, and sales manager jobs, but many employers prefer college graduates with experience in related occupations.

Education and training. For marketing, sales, and promotions management positions, employers often prefer a bachelor's or master's degree in business administration with an emphasis on marketing. Courses in business law, management, economics, accounting, finance, mathematics, and statistics are advantageous. In addition, the completion of an internship while the candidate is in school is highly recommended. In highly technical industries, such as computer and electronics manufacturing, a bachelor's degree in engineering or science, combined with a master's degree in business administration, is preferred.

For advertising management positions, some employers prefer a bachelor's degree in advertising or journalism. A relevant course of study might include classes in marketing, consumer behavior, market research, sales, communication methods and technology, visual arts, art history, and photography.

For public relations management positions, some employers prefer a bachelor's or master's degree in public relations or journalism. The applicant's curriculum should include courses in advertising, business administration, public affairs, public speaking, political science, and creative and technical writing.

Most advertising, marketing, promotions, public relations, and sales management positions are filled through promotions of experienced staff or related professional personnel. For example, many managers are former sales representatives; purchasing agents; buyers; or product, advertising, promotions, or public relations specialists. In small firms, in which the number of positions is limited, advancement to a management position usually comes slowly. In large firms, promotion may occur more quickly.

Other qualifications. Computer skills are necessary for recordkeeping and data management, and the ability to work in an Internet environment is becoming increasingly vital as more marketing, product promotion, and advertising is done through the Internet. Also, the ability to communicate in a foreign language may open up employment opportunities in many rapidly growing areas around the country, especially cities with large Spanish-speaking populations.

Persons interested in becoming advertising, marketing, promotions, public relations, and sales managers should be mature, creative, highly motivated, resistant to stress, flexible, and decisive. The ability to communicate persuasively, both orally and in writing, with other managers, staff, and the public is vital. These managers also need tact, good judgment, and exceptional ability to establish and maintain effective personal relationships with supervisory and professional staff members and client firms.

Certification and advancement. Some associations offer certification programs for these managers. Certification—an indication of competence and achievement—is particularly important in a competitive job market. Although relatively few advertising, marketing, promotions, public relations, and sales managers currently are certified, the number of managers who seek certification is expected to grow. Today, there are numerous management certification programs based on education and job performance. In addition, the Public Relations Society of America offers a certification program for public relations practitioners that is based on years of experience and performance on an examination.

Although experience, ability, and leadership are emphasized for promotion, advancement can be accelerated by participation in management training programs conducted by larger firms. Many firms also provide their employees with continuing education opportunities— either in-house or at local colleges and universities—and encourage employee participation in seminars and conferences, often held by professional societies. In collaboration with colleges and universities, numerous marketing and related associations sponsor national or local management training programs. Course subjects include brand and product management; international marketing; sales management evaluation; telemarketing and direct sales; interactive marketing; product promotion; marketing communication; market research; organizational communication; and data-processing systems, procedures, and management. Many firms pay all or part of the cost for employees who complete courses.

Because of the importance and high visibility of their jobs, advertising, marketing, promotions, public relations, and sales managers often are prime candidates for advancement to the highest ranks. Well-trained, experienced, and successful managers may be promoted to higher positions in their own or another firm; some become top executives. Managers with extensive experience and sufficient capital may open their own businesses.

Employment

Advertising, marketing, promotions, public relations, and sales managers held about 623,800 jobs in 2008.

These managers were found in virtually every industry. Sales managers held about 56 percent of the jobs; about 62 percent of sales managers were employed in wholesale trade, retail trade, manufacturing, and the finance and insurance industries. Marketing managers held approximately 28 percent of the jobs; the professional, scientific, and technical services, and the finance and insurance industries employed around 32 percent of marketing managers. About 27 percent of advertising and promotions managers worked in the professional, scientific, and technical services industries and wholesale trade. Around 48 percent of public relations managers were employed in service-providing industries, such as professional, scientific, and technical services; public and private educational services; finance and insurance; and healthcare and social assistance.

Job Outlook

Employment is projected to grow about as fast as average. As with most managerial jobs, keen competition is expected for these highly coveted positions.

Employment change. Overall employment of advertising, marketing, promotions, public relations, and sales managers is expected to increase by 13 percent through 2018. Job growth will be spurred by competition for a growing number of goods and services, both foreign and domestic, and the need to make one's product or service stand out in the crowd. In addition, as the influence of traditional advertising in newspapers, radio, and network television wanes, marketing professionals are being asked to develop new and different ways to advertise and promote products and services to better reach potential customers.

Sales and marketing managers and their departments constitute some of the most important personnel in an organization and are less subject to downsizing or outsourcing than are other types of managers, except in the case of companies that are consolidating. Employment of these managers, therefore, will vary primarily on the basis of the growth or contraction in the industries that employ them. For example, if, as is expected, the number of automobile dealers declines over the next decade, these major employers of sales managers will need fewer of them. Employment of marketing managers will grow about as fast as average at 12 percent between 2008 and 2018, and that of sales managers will grow faster than average at 15 percent over the same period.

Advertising and promotions managers are expected to experience little or no change in employment from 2008 to 2018. Despite large declines in the number of advertising managers in recent years, due mainly to the sharp reduction in the number of advertising agencies and newspaper and periodical publishers, which employ the greatest numbers of these managers, advertising and promotions managers are not expected to experience similar declines in the future. Because advertising is the primary source of revenue for most media, advertising departments are less affected in a downturn. An expected increase in the number of television and radio stations and a sharp increase in the amount of advertising in digital media, such as the Internet and wireless devices will generate a need for advertising managers to oversee new and innovative advertising programs. A number of these advertising managers will be self-employed.

Public relations managers are expected to see an increase in employment of 13 percent between 2008 and 2018, which is about as fast as average for all occupations, as organizations increasingly emphasize community outreach and customer relations as a way to enhance their reputation and visibility. Especially among the growing number of nonprofit organizations, such as education services, business and professional associations, and hospitals, where many of these workers are employed, public relations managers will be charged with promoting the mission of the organization and encouraging membership or use of the organization's services.

Job prospects. Most job openings for this occupation will be due to the need to replace workers who leave the occupation or retire. However, advertising, marketing, promotions, public relations, and sales manager jobs are highly coveted and are often sought by other managers or highly experienced professionals, resulting in keen competition. College graduates with related experience, a high level of creativity, and strong communication and computer skills should have the best job opportunities. In particular, employers will seek those who have the skills to conduct new types of advertising, marketing, promotions, public relations, and sales campaigns involving new media, particularly the Internet.

Earnings

Median annual wages in May 2008 were $80,220 for advertising and promotions managers, $108,580 for marketing managers, $97,260 for sales managers, and $89,430 for public relations managers.

Median annual wages of advertising and promotions managers in May 2008 in the advertising, public relations, and related services industry were $105,960.

Wages vary substantially, depending upon the employee's level of managerial responsibility, length of service, and education; the size and location of the firm; and the industry in which the firm operates. For example, manufacturing firms usually pay these managers higher salaries than nonmanufacturing firms. For sales managers, the size of their sales territory is another important determinant of salary. Many managers earn bonuses equal to 10 percent or more of their salaries.

According to a survey by the National Association of Colleges and Employers, starting salaries for marketing majors graduating in 2009 averaged $43,325.

BUSINESS & FINANCE

—⚏—

Accountants and Auditors

Nature of the Work

Accountants and auditors help to ensure that firms are run efficiently, public records kept accurately, and taxes paid properly and on time. They analyze and communicate financial information for various entities such as companies, individual clients, and Federal, State, and local governments. Beyond carrying out the fundamental tasks of the occupation—providing information to clients by preparing, analyzing, and verifying financial documents—many accountants also offer budget analysis, financial and investment planning, information technology consulting, and limited legal services.

Specific job duties vary widely among the four major fields of accounting and auditing: *public accounting, management accounting, government accounting,* and *internal auditing.*

Public accountants perform a broad range of accounting, auditing, tax, and consulting activities for their clients, which may be corporations, governments, nonprofit organizations, or individuals. For example, some public accountants concentrate on tax matters, such as advising companies about the tax advantages and disadvantages of certain business decisions and preparing individual income tax returns. Others offer advice in areas such as compensation or employee healthcare benefits, the design of accounting and data processing systems, and the selection of controls to safeguard assets. Still others audit clients' financial

> ### Significant Points
>
> ❖ Most jobs require at least a bachelor's degree in accounting or a related field.
>
> ❖ Job opportunities should be favorable; those who have earned professional recognition through certification or licensure, especially a CPA, should enjoy the best prospects.
>
> ❖ Much faster than average employment growth will result from an increase in the number of businesses, changing financial laws and regulations, and greater scrutiny of company finances.

statements and inform investors and authorities that the statements have been correctly prepared and reported. These accountants are also referred to as *external auditors*. Public accountants, many of whom are *Certified Public Accountants* (CPAs), generally have their own businesses or work for public accounting firms.

Some public accountants specialize in forensic accounting—investigating and interpreting white-collar crimes such as securities fraud and embezzlement, bankruptcies and contract disputes, and other complex and possibly criminal financial transactions, including money laundering by organized criminals. *Forensic accountants* combine their knowledge of accounting and finance with law and investigative techniques to determine whether an activity is illegal. Many forensic accountants work closely with law enforcement personnel and lawyers during investigations and often appear as expert witnesses during trials.

Management accountants—also called *cost, managerial, industrial, corporate, or private accountants*—record and analyze the financial information of the companies for which they work. Among their other responsibilities are budgeting, performance evaluation, cost management, and asset management. Usually, management accountants are part of executive teams involved in strategic planning or the development of new products. They analyze and interpret the financial information that corporate executives need to make sound business decisions. They also prepare financial reports for other groups, including stockholders, creditors, regulatory agencies, and tax authorities. Within accounting departments, management accountants may work in various areas, including financial analysis, planning and budgeting, and cost accounting.

Government accountants and auditors work in the public sector, maintaining and examining the records of government agencies and auditing private businesses and individuals whose activities are subject to government regulations or taxation. Accountants employed by Federal, State, and local governments ensure that revenues are received and expenditures are made in accordance with laws and regulations. Those employed by the Federal Government may work as Internal Revenue Service agents or in financial management, financial institution examination, or budget analysis and administration.

Internal auditors verify the effectiveness of their organization's internal controls and check for mismanagement, waste, or fraud. They examine and evaluate their firms' financial and information systems, management procedures, and internal controls to ensure that records are accurate and controls are adequate. They also review company operations, evaluating their efficiency, effectiveness, and compliance with corporate policies and government regulations. Because computer systems commonly automate transactions and make information readily available, internal auditors may also help management evaluate the effectiveness of their controls based on real-time data, rather than personal observation. They may recommend and review controls for their organization's computer systems, to ensure their reliability and integrity of the data. Internal auditors may also have specialty titles, such as *information technology auditors, environmental auditors, and compliance auditors.*

Technology is rapidly changing the nature of the work of most accountants and auditors. With the aid of special software packages, accountants summarize transactions in the standard formats of financial records and organize data in special formats employed in financial analysis. These accounting packages greatly reduce the tedious work associated with data management and recordkeeping. Computers enable accountants and auditors to be more mobile and to use their clients' computer systems to extract information from databases and the Internet. As a result, a growing number of accountants and auditors with extensive computer skills specialize in correcting problems with software or in developing software to meet unique data management and analytical needs. Accountants also are beginning to perform more technical duties, such as implementing, controlling, and auditing computer systems and networks and developing technology plans.

Work environment. Most accountants and auditors work in a typical office setting. Some may be able to do part of their work at home. Accountants and auditors employed by public accounting firms, government agencies, and organizations with multiple locations may travel frequently to perform audits at branches, clients' places of business, or government facilities.

Almost half of all accountants and auditors worked a standard 40-hour week in 2008, but many worked longer hours, particularly if they are self-employed and have numerous clients. Tax specialists often work long hours during the tax season.

Training, Other Qualifications, and Advancement

Most accountants and auditors need at least a bachelor's degree in accounting or a related field. Many accountants and auditors choose to obtain certification to help advance their careers, such as becoming a Certified Public Accountant (CPA).

Education and training. Most accountant and auditor positions require at least a bachelor's degree in accounting or a related field. Some employers prefer applicants with a master's degree in accounting, or with a master's degree in business administration with a concentration in accounting. Some universities and colleges are now offering programs to prepare students to work in growing specialty professions such as internal auditing. Many professional associations offer continuing professional education courses, conferences, and seminars.

Some graduates of junior colleges or business or correspondence schools, as well as bookkeepers and accounting clerks who meet the education and experience requirements set by their employers, can obtain junior accounting positions and advance to accountant positions by demonstrating their accounting skills on the job.

Most beginning accountants and auditors may work under supervision or closely with an experienced accountant or auditor before gaining more independence and responsibility.

Licensure and certification. Any accountant filing a report with the Securities and Exchange Commission (SEC) is required by law to be a Certified Public Accountant (CPA). This may include senior level accountants working for or on behalf of public companies that are registered with the SEC. CPAs are licensed by their State Board of Accountancy. Any accountant who passes a national exam and meets the other requirements of the State where they practice can become a CPA. The vast majority of States require CPA candidates to be college graduates, but a few States will substitute a number of years of public accounting experience for a college degree.

As of 2009, 46 States and the District of Columbia required CPA candidates to complete 150 semester hours of college coursework—an additional 30 hours beyond the usual 4-year bachelor's degree. California, Colorado, New Hampshire, and Vermont are the only States that do not require 150 semester hours for certification. Many schools offer a 5-year combined bachelor's and master's degree to meet the 150 semester hour requirement, but a master's degree is not required. Prospective accounting majors should carefully research accounting curricula and the requirements of any States in which they hope to become licensed.

All States use the four-part Uniform CPA Examination prepared by the American Institute of Certified Public Accountants (AICPA). The CPA examination is rigorous, and less than one-half of those who take it each year pass every part on the first try. Candidates are not required to pass all four parts at once, but most States require candidates to pass all four sections within 18 months of passing their first section. The CPA exam is now computerized and is offered 2 months out of every quarter at various testing centers throughout the United States. Most States also require applicants for a CPA license to have some accounting experience; however requirements vary by State or jurisdiction.

Nearly all States require CPAs and other public accountants to complete a certain number of hours of continuing professional education before their licenses can be renewed. The professional associations representing accountants sponsor numerous courses, seminars, group study programs, and other forms of continuing education.

Other qualifications. Previous experience in accounting or auditing can help an applicant get a job. Many colleges offer students the opportunity to gain experience through summer or part-time internship programs conducted by public accounting or business firms. In addition, as many business processes are now automated, practical knowledge of computers and their applications is a great asset for jobseekers in the accounting and auditing fields.

People planning a career in accounting and auditing should have an aptitude for mathematics and be able to analyze, compare, and interpret facts and figures quickly. They must be able to clearly communicate the results of their work to clients and managers both verbally and in writing. Accountants and auditors must be good at working with people, business systems, and computers. At a minimum, accountants and auditors should be familiar with basic accounting and computer software packages. Because financial decisions are made on the basis of their statements and services, accountants and auditors should have high standards of integrity.

Certification and advancement. Professional recognition through certification or other designation provides a distinct advantage in the job market. Certification can attest to professional competence in a specialized field of accounting and auditing. Accountants and auditors can seek credentials from a wide variety of professional societies.

The Institute of Management Accountants confers the Certified Management Accountant (CMA) designation upon applicants who complete a bachelor's degree or who attain a minimum score or higher on specified graduate school entrance exams. Applicants must have worked at least 2 years in management accounting, pass a four-part examination, agree to meet continuing education requirements, and comply with standards of professional conduct. The exam covers areas such as financial statement analysis, working-capital policy, capital structure, valuation issues, and risk management.

The Institute of Internal Auditors offers the Certified Internal Auditor (CIA) designation to graduates from accredited colleges and universities who have worked for 2 years as internal auditors and have passed a four-part examination. The IIA also offers the designations of Certified in Control Self-Assessment (CCSA), Certified Government Auditing Professional (CGAP), and Certified Financial Services Auditor (CFSA) to those who pass the exams and meet educational and experience requirements.

ISACA confers the Certified Information Systems Auditor (CISA) designation upon candidates who pass an examination and have 5 years of experience auditing information systems. Information systems experience, financial or operational auditing experience, or related college credit hours can be substituted for up to 2 years of information systems auditing, control or security experience.

For those accountants with their CPA, the AICPA offers the option to receive any or all of the Accredited in Business Valuation (ABV), Certified Information Technology Professional (CITP), or Personal Financial Specialist (PFS) designations. CPAs with these designations demonstrate a level of expertise in these areas in which accountants practice ever more frequently. The business valuation designation requires a written exam and the completion of a minimum of 10 business valuation projects that demonstrate a candidate's experience and competence. The technology designation requires the achievement of a set number of points awarded for business technology experience and education. Candidates for the personal financial specialist designation also must achieve a certain level of points based on experience and education, pass a written exam, and submit references.

Many senior corporation executives have a background in accounting, internal auditing, or finance. Beginning public accountants often advance to positions with more responsibility in 1 or 2 years and to senior positions within another few years. Those who excel may become supervisors, managers, or partners; open their own public accounting firm; or transfer to executive positions in management accounting or internal auditing in private firms.

Management accountants often start as cost accountants, junior internal auditors, or trainees for other accounting positions. As they rise through the organization, they may advance to accounting manager, chief cost accountant, budget director, or manager of internal auditing. Some become controllers, treasurers, financial vice presidents, chief financial officers, or corporation presidents.

Public accountants, management accountants, and internal auditors usually have much occupational mobility. Practitioners often shift into management accounting or internal auditing from public accounting, or between internal auditing and management accounting. It is less common for accountants and auditors to move from either management accounting or internal auditing into public accounting. Additionally, because they learn about and review the internal controls of various business units within a company, internal auditors often gain the experience needed to become upper-level managers.

Employment

Accountants and auditors held about 1.3 million jobs in 2008. They worked throughout private industry and government, but 24 percent of accountants and auditors worked for accounting, tax preparation, bookkeeping, and payroll services firms. Approximately 8 percent of accountants and auditors were self-employed.

Most accountants and auditors work in urban areas, where public accounting firms and central or regional offices of businesses are concentrated.

Some individuals with backgrounds in accounting and auditing are full-time college and university faculty; others teach part time while working as self-employed accountants or as accountants for private industry or in government.

Job Outlook

Accountants and auditors are expected to experience much faster than average employment growth from 2008-18. Job opportunities should be favorable; accountants and auditors who have a professional certification, especially CPAs, should have the best prospects.

Employment change. Employment of accountants and auditors is expected to grow by 22 percent between 2008 and 2018, which is much faster than the average for all occupations. This occupation will have a very large number of new jobs arise, about 279,400 over the projections decade. An increase in the number of businesses, changing financial laws and corporate governance regulations, and increased accountability for protecting an organization's stakeholders will drive job growth.

As the economy grows, the number of business establishments will increase, requiring more accountants and auditors to set up books, prepare taxes, and provide management advice. As these businesses grow, the volume and complexity of information reviewed by accountants and auditors regarding costs, expenditures, taxes, and internal controls will expand as well. The continued globalization of business also will lead to more demand for accounting expertise and services related to international trade and accounting rules and international mergers and acquisitions. Additionally, there is a growing movement towards International Financial Reporting Standards (IFRS), which uses a judgment-based system to determine the fair-market value of assets and liabilities, which should increase demand for accountants and auditors because of their specialized expertise.

An increased need for accountants and auditors also will arise from a greater emphasis on accountability, transparency, and controls in financial reporting. Increased scrutiny of company finances and accounting procedures will create opportunities for accountants and auditors, particularly CPAs, to audit financial records more thoroughly and completely. Management accountants and internal auditors increasingly will be needed to discover and eliminate fraud before audits, and ensure that important processes and procedures are documented accurately and thoroughly. Forensic accountants also will be needed to detect illegal financial activity by individuals, companies, and organized crime rings.

Job prospects. Job opportunities should be favorable. Accountants and auditors who have earned professional recognition through certification or other designation, especially a CPA, should have the best job prospects. Applicants with a master's degree in accounting or a master's degree in business administration with a concentration in accounting also may have an advantage.

Individuals who are proficient in accounting and auditing computer software and information systems or have expertise in specialized areas—such as international business, international financial reporting standards, or current legislation—may have an advantage in getting some accounting and auditing jobs. In addition, employers increasingly seek applicants with strong interpersonal and communication skills. Many accountants work on teams with others who have different backgrounds, so they must be able to communicate accounting and financial information clearly and concisely. Regardless of qualifications, however, competition will remain keen for the most prestigious jobs in major accounting and business firms.

In addition to openings from job growth, the need to replace accountants and auditors who retire or transfer to other occupations will produce numerous job openings in this large occupation.

Earnings

Median annual wages of wage and salary accountants and auditors were $59,430 in May 2008. The middle half of the occupation earned between $45,900 and $78,210. The bottom 10 percent earned less than $36,720, and the top 10 percent earned more than $102,380.

According to a salary survey conducted by the National Association of Colleges and Employers, bachelor's degree candidates in accounting received starting offers averaging $48,993 a year in July 2009; master's degree candidates in accounting were offered $49,786 initially.

Wage and salary accountants and auditors usually receive standard benefits, including health and medical insurance, life insurance, a 401(k) plan, and paid annual leave. High-level senior accountants may receive additional benefits, such as the use of a company car and an expense account.

BUSINESS & FINANCE

Budget Analysts

Nature of the Work

Budget analysts help organizations allocate their financial resources. They develop, analyze, and execute budgets, as well as estimate future financial needs for private businesses, nonprofit organizations, and government agencies. In private sector firms, a budget analyst's main responsibility is to examine the budget and seek new ways to improve efficiency and increase profits. In nonprofit and governmental organizations, which usually are not concerned with profits, analysts try to find the most efficient way to distribute funds and other resources among various departments and programs.

In addition to managing an organization's budget, analysts are often involved in program performance evaluation, policy analysis, and the drafting of budget-related legislation. At times, they also conduct training sessions for company or government personnel regarding new budget procedures.

At the beginning of each budget cycle, managers and department heads submit operational and financial proposals to budget analysts for review. These plans outline the organization's programs, estimate the financial needs of these programs, and propose funding initiatives to meet those needs. Analysts then examine these budget estimates and proposals for completeness, accuracy, and conformance with established procedures, regulations, and organizational objectives. Sometimes they employ cost-benefit analyses to review financial

Significant Points

❖ The need for sound financial analysis will spur job growth for budget analysts.

❖ A bachelor's degree generally is the minimum educational requirement, but some employers prefer or require a master's degree.

❖ Candidates with a master's degree are expected to have the best opportunities.

❖ About 41 percent of all budget analysts work in government.

requests, assess program tradeoffs, and explore alternative funding methods. They also examine past budgets and research economic and financial developments that affect the organization's income and expenditures.

After the initial review process, budget analysts consolidate individual departmental budgets into operating and capital budget summaries. These summaries contain statements that argue for or against funding requests. Budget summaries are then submitted to senior management, or as is often the case in government organizations, to appointed or elected officials. Budget analysts then help the chief operating officer, agency head, or other top managers analyze the proposed plan and devise possible alternatives if the projected results are unsatisfactory. The final decision to approve the budget usually is made by the organization head in a private firm, or by elected officials, such as State legislators, in government.

Throughout the year, analysts periodically monitor the budget by reviewing reports and accounting records to determine if allocated funds have been spent as specified. If deviations appear between the approved budget and actual spending, budget analysts may write a report explaining the variations and recommending revised procedures. To avoid or alleviate deficits, budget analysts may recommend program cuts or a reallocation of excess funds. They also inform program managers and others within the organization of the status and availability of funds in different accounts.

Data and statistical analysis software has greatly increased the amount of data and information that budget analysts can compile, review, and produce. Analysts use spreadsheet, database, and financial analysis software to improve their understanding of different budgeting options and to provide accurate, up-to-date information to agency leaders. In addition, many organizations are beginning to incorporate Enterprise Resource Planning (ERP) programs into their budget-making process. ERP programs can consolidate all of an organization's operating information into a single computer system, which helps analysts estimate the effects that a budget alteration will have on each part of an organization.

Work environment. Budget analysts usually work in a comfortable office setting. They spend the majority of their time working independently, compiling and analyzing data and preparing budget proposals. Some budget analysts travel to obtain budget details first-hand or to personally verify funding allocation.

The schedules of budget analysts vary throughout the budget cycle, and many are required to work additional hours during the initial development, mid-year reviews, and final reviews of budgets. The pressures of deadlines and tight work schedules can be stressful. In 2008, about 48 percent of budget analysts worked 40 hours per week, while about 11 percent worked more than 50 hours per week.

Training, Other Qualifications, and Advancement

A bachelor's degree usually is the minimum educational requirement for budget analyst jobs, but some organizations prefer or require a master's degree. Entry-level budget analysts usually begin with limited responsibilities but can be promoted to intermediate-level positions within 1 to 2 years, and to senior positions with additional experience.

Education and training. Employers generally require budget analysts to have at least a bachelor's degree, but some prefer or require a master's degree. Within the Federal Government, a bachelor's degree in any field is sufficient for an entry-level budget analyst position. State and local governments have varying requirements, but usually require a bachelor's degree in one of many areas, including accounting, finance, business, public administration, economics, statistics, political science, or sociology. Because developing a budget requires strong numerical and analytical skills, courses in statistics or accounting are helpful, regardless of the prospective budget analyst's major field of study. Some States may require a master's degree. Occasionally, budget-related or finance-related work experience can be substituted for formal education.

In most organizations, budget analysts usually learn the job by working through one complete budget cycle. During the cycle, which typically lasts 1 year, analysts become familiar with the various steps involved in the budgeting process. Many budget analysts also take professional development classes throughout their careers.

Other qualifications. Budget analysts must abide by strict ethical standards. Integrity, objectivity, and confidentiality are all essential when dealing with financial information, and budget analysts must avoid any personal conflicts of interest. Most budget analysts also need mathematical skills and should be able to use software packages, including spreadsheet, database, data-mining, and financial analysis programs. Strong oral and written communication skills also are essential, because budget analysts must prepare, present, and defend budget proposals to decision makers. In addition, budget analysts must be able to work under strict time constraints.

Certification and advancement. Entry-level budget analysts usually begin with limited responsibilities, working under close supervision. Capable analysts can be promoted to intermediate-level positions within 1 to 2 years, and to senior positions with additional experience. Because of the importance and high visibility of their jobs, senior budget analysts may be promoted to management positions in various parts of their organizations, or with other organizations with which they have worked.

Government budget analysts employed at the Federal, State, or local level may earn the Certified Government Financial Manager designation granted by Advancing Government Accountability, an organization that represents government accountability officers. To earn this designation, candidates must have a minimum of a bachelor's degree, 24 credit hours of study in financial management, and 2 years of professional-level experience in governmental financial management. They also must pass a series of three exams that cover topics on the governmental environment; governmental accounting, financial reporting, and budgeting; and governmental financial management and control. To maintain the designation, individuals must complete 80 hours of continuing professional education every 2 years.

Employment

Budget analysts held 67,200 jobs in 2008. Government is a major employer, accounting for 41 percent of budget analyst jobs. Budget analysts were also employed in manufacturing; management services; professional, scientific, and technical services; and schools.

Job Outlook

Budget analyst jobs are expected to increase faster than average. Candidates with a master's degree are expected to have the best opportunities.

Employment change. Employment of budget analysts is expected to increase by 15 percent between 2008 and 2018, faster than the average for all occupations. Employment growth will be driven by the continuing demand for sound financial analysis in both the public and the private sectors.

As businesses and other organizations become more complex and specialized, budget planning and financial control will demand greater attention. In recent years, computer applications used in budget analysis have become increasingly sophisticated, allowing more data to be analyzed and processed in a shorter amount of time. As a result, agency leaders have begun to demand more data, analyses, and other types of information relevant to the budgeting process. This has increased the workload of budget analysts, and created the need for more workers. As this process continues, demand for budget analysts will grow.

Job prospects. Job openings will result from employment growth and from the need to replace workers who retire or leave the occupation for other reasons. Candidates with a master's degree are expected to have the best opportunities. Familiarity with spreadsheet, database, data-mining, financial-analysis, and Enterprise Resource Planning software packages also should enhance a jobseeker's prospects.

Earnings

Wages of budget analysts vary by experience, education, and employer. Median annual wages of budget analysts in May 2008 were $65,320. The middle 50 percent earned between $52,290 and $82,150. The lowest 10 percent earned less than $42,470, and the highest 10 percent earned more than $100,360.

BUSINESS & FINANCE

—⚮—

Cost Estimators

Nature of the Work

Accurately forecasting the cost, size, and duration of future projects is vital to the survival of any business. *Cost estimators* develop the cost information that business owners and managers need to make a bid for a contract or to decide on the profitability of a proposed new project or product. They also determine which endeavors are making a profit.

Regardless of the industry in which they work, estimators collect and analyze data on all of the factors that can affect costs, such as materials, labor, location, duration of the project, and special machinery requirements, including computer hardware and software. Job duties vary widely depending on the type and size of the project.

The methods for estimating costs can also differ greatly by industry. On a large construction project, for example, the estimating process begins with the decision to submit a bid. After reviewing various preliminary drawings and specifications, the estimator visits the site of the proposed project. The estimator gathers information on access to the site; surface topography and drainage, and the availability of electricity, water, and other services. The estimator records this information, which may go in the final project estimate.

After the site visit, the estimator determines the quantity of materials and the labor required to complete the firm's part of the project. This process, called the quantity survey

Significant Points

❖ About 59 percent of cost estimators work in the construction industry, and another 15 percent are employed by manufacturers.

❖ Good job opportunities are expected; those with industry work experience and a bachelor's degree in a related field will have the best prospects.

❖ Voluntary certification can be beneficial to cost estimators; some employers may require professional certification for employment.

or "takeoff," involves completing standard estimating forms, filling in dimensions, numbers of units, and other information. A cost estimator working for a general contractor, for example, estimates the costs of all of the items that the contractor must provide. Although subcontractors estimate their costs as part of their own bidding process, the general contractor's cost estimator often analyzes bids made by subcontractors. Also during the takeoff process, the estimator must make decisions concerning equipment needs, the sequence of operations, the size of the crew required, and physical constraints at the site. Allowances for wasted materials, inclement weather, shipping delays, and other factors that may increase costs also must be incorporated in the estimate.

After completing the quantity surveys, the estimator prepares a cost summary for the entire project, which includes the costs of labor, equipment, materials, subcontractors, overhead, taxes, insurance, markup, and any additional costs that may affect the project. The chief estimator then prepares the bid proposal for submission to the owner. On large construction projects, there may be several estimators, each specializing in one area, such as electrical work or excavation, concrete, and forms.

Construction cost estimators also may be employed by the project's architect, engineering firm, or owner to help establish a budget, manage and control project costs, and to track actual costs relative to bid specifications as the project develops. During construction, estimators may be employed to manage the cost of change orders and negotiate and settle and extra costs or mitigate potential claims. Estimators may also be called upon as expert witness on cost in a construction dispute case.

In manufacturing, cost estimators usually are assigned to the engineering, cost, or pricing department. The estimator's goal is to accurately estimate the costs associated with developing and producing products. The job may begin when management requests an estimate of the costs associated with a major redesign of an existing product or the development of a new product or production process. For example, when estimating the cost of manufacturing a new product, the estimator works with engineers, first reviewing blueprints or conceptual drawings to determine the machining operations, tools, gauges, and materials that will be required. The estimator then prepares a parts list and determines whether it would be more efficient to produce or to purchase the parts. To do this, the estimator asks for price information from potential suppliers. The next step is to determine the cost of manufacturing each component of the product. Some high-technology products require a considerable amount of computer programming during the design phase. The cost of software development is one of the fastest growing and most difficult activities to estimate. As a result, some cost estimators now specialize in estimating only computer software development and related costs.

Thereafter, the cost estimator prepares time-phase charts and learning curves. Time-phase charts indicate the time required for tool design and fabrication, tool "debugging"—finding and correcting all problems—manufacturing of parts, assembly, and testing. Learning curves graphically represent the rate at which the performance of workers producing parts for the new product improves with practice. These curves are commonly called "cost reduction" curves, because many problems—such as engineering changes, rework, shortages of parts, and lack of operator skills—diminish as the number of units produced increases, resulting in lower unit costs.

Using all of this information, the estimator then calculates the standard labor hours necessary to produce a specified number of units. Standard labor hours are then converted to dollar values, to which are added factors for waste, overhead, and profit to yield the unit cost in dollars. The estimator compares the cost of purchasing parts with the firm's estimated cost of manufacturing them to determine which is less expensive.

Computers play a vital role in cost estimation because the process often involves complex mathematical calculations and requires advanced mathematical techniques. For example, to undertake a parametric analysis (a process used to estimate costs per unit based on square footage or other specific requirements of a project), cost estimators use a computer database containing information on the costs and conditions of many other similar projects. Although computers cannot be used for the entire estimating process, they can relieve estimators of much of the drudgery associated with routine, repetitive, and time-consuming calculations. New and improved cost estimating software has lead to more efficient computations, leaving estimators more time to visit and analyze projects.

Operations research, production control, cost, and price analysts who work for government agencies may do significant amounts of cost estimating in the course of their usual duties. In addition, the duties of construction managers may include estimating costs

Work environment. Estimators spend most of their time in offices, but visits to construction worksites and factory floors are often needed for their work. In some industries, there may be frequent travel between a firm's headquarters, its subsidiaries, and subcontractors.

Estimators usually work a 40-hour week, but overtime is common. Cost estimators often work under pressure and stress, especially when facing bid deadlines. Inaccurate estimating can cause a firm to lose a bid or to lose money on a job that was not accurately estimated.

Training, Other Qualifications, and Advancement

Job entry requirements for cost estimators will vary by industry. In the construction and manufacturing industries, employers increasingly prefer to hire cost estimators with a bachelor's degree in a related field, although it is also possible for experienced construction workers to become cost estimators. Voluntary certification can be beneficial to cost estimators; some employers, including the Federal Government, may require professional certification for employment.

Education and training. In the construction industry, employers increasingly prefer individuals with a degree in construction management, building science, or construction science, all of which usually include several courses in cost estimating. Most construction estimators also have considerable construction experience, gained through work in the industry, internships, or cooperative education programs; and for some estimators, years of experience can substitute for a degree in addition to taking classes in the field or getting an associate degree. Applicants with a thorough knowledge of construction materials, costs, and procedures in areas ranging from heavy construction to electrical work, plumbing systems, or masonry work have a competitive edge.

In manufacturing industries, employers prefer to hire individuals with a degree in engineering, physical science, operations research, mathematics, or statistics or in accounting, finance, business, economics, or a related subject. In most industries, experience in quantitative techniques is important.

Many colleges and universities include cost estimating as part of bachelor's and associate degree curriculums in civil engineering, industrial engineering, information systems development, and construction management or construction engineering technology. In addition, cost estimating is often part of master's degree programs in construction science or construction management. Organizations representing cost estimators, such as the American Society of Professional Estimators (ASPE), the Association for the Advancement of Cost Engineering (AACE International) and the Society of Cost Estimating and Analysis (SCEA), also sponsor educational and professional development programs. These programs help students, estimators-in-training, and experienced estimators learn about changes affecting the profession. Specialized courses and programs in cost-estimating techniques and procedures also are offered by many technical schools, community colleges, and universities.

Estimators also receive long-term training on the job because every company has its own way of handling estimates. Working with an experienced estimator, newcomers become familiar with each step in the process. Those with no experience reading construction specifications or blueprints first learn that aspect of the work. Subsequently, they may accompany an experienced estimator to the construction site or shop floor, where they observe the work being done, take measurements, or perform other routine tasks. As they become more knowledgeable, estimators learn how to tabulate quantities and dimensions from drawings and how to select the appropriate prices for materials.

Other qualifications. Cost estimators need to have an aptitude for mathematics, be able to analyze, compare, and interpret detailed but sometimes poorly defined information, and be able to make sound and accurate judgments based on this information. The ability to focus on details, while analyzing and managing larger obstacles, is vital. Assertiveness and self-assurance in presenting and supporting conclusions are also important, as are strong communications and interpersonal skills, because estimators may work as part of a team alongside managers, owners, engineers, and design professionals. Cost estimators also need to be proficient with computers and have skills in programming. Familiarity with cost estimation software, including commercial, and Building Information Modeling (BIM) software is beneficial. BIM software technology takes standard blueprints and creates three-dimensional models on the computer, allowing for better estimates of the building process. Proficiency in project management and the ability to incorporate work breakdown structure (WBS) techniques are increasingly important in cost estimating complex development projects.

Certification and advancement. Voluntary certification can be beneficial to cost estimators because it provides professional recognition of the estimator's competence and experience. In some instances, individual employers may even require professional certification for employment. The ASPE, AACE International, and SCEA administer certification programs. To become certified, estimators usually must have between 2 and 8 years of estimating experience and must pass a written examination. In addition, certification requirements may include the publication of at least one article or paper in the field.

For most estimators, advancement takes the form of higher pay and prestige. Some move into management positions, such as project manager for a construction firm, program manager for a government contractor, or manager of the industrial engineering department for a manufacturer. Others may go into business for themselves as consultants, providing estimating services for a fee to government or to construction or manufacturing firms.

Employment

Cost estimators held about 217,800 jobs in 2008. About 59 percent of estimators were in the construction industry and another 15 percent were employed in manufacturing. The remainder worked in a wide range of other industries.

Cost estimators work throughout the country, usually in or near major industrial, commercial, and government centers and in cities and suburban areas experiencing rapid change or development.

Job Outlook

Employment is projected to grow much faster than average. Overall, good job opportunities are expected; those with industry work experience and a bachelor's degree in a related field will have the best prospects.

Employment change. Employment of cost estimators is expected to grow by 25 percent between 2008 and 2018, much faster than average for all occupations. Growth in the construction industry will account for most new jobs in this occupation. In particular, construction and repair of highways, streets, bridges, subway systems, airports, water and sewage systems, and electric power plants and transmission lines will stimulate the need for more cost estimators. Similarly, an increasing population will result in more construction of residential homes, hospitals, schools, restaurants, and other structures that require cost estimators. As the population ages, the demand for nursing and extended-care facilities will also increase. The growing complexity of construction projects will also boost demand for cost estimators as more workers specialize in a particular area of construction.

Job prospects. Because there are no formal bachelor's degree programs in cost estimating, some employers have difficulty recruiting qualified cost estimators, resulting in good employment opportunities. Job prospects in construction should be best for those who have a degree in construction science, construction management, or building science or have years of practical experience in the various phases of construction or in a specialty craft area. Knowledge of Building Information Modeling software would also be helpful. For cost estimating jobs in manufacturing, those who have degrees in mathematics, statistics, engineering, accounting, business administration, or economics, and who are familiar with cost estimation software should have the best job prospects.

In addition to job openings arising from employment growth, many additional openings should result annually from the need to replace workers who transfer to other occupations due to the sometimes stressful nature of the work, or who retire or leave the occupation for other reasons.

Employment of cost estimators, like that of many other construction workers, is sensitive to the fluctuations of the economy. Workers in these trades may experience periods of unemployment when the overall level of construction falls. On the other hand, shortages of these workers may occur in some areas during peak periods of building activity.

Earnings

Salaries of cost estimators vary widely by experience, education, size of firm, and industry. Median annual wages of wage and salary cost estimators in May 2008 were $56,510. The middle 50 percent earned between $42,720 and $74,320. The lowest 10 percent earned less than $33,150, and the highest 10 percent earned more than $94,470.

BUSINESS & FINANCE

Financial Analysts

Nature of the Work

Financial analysts provide guidance to businesses and individuals making investment decisions. Financial analysts assess the performance of stocks, bonds, commodities, and other types of investments. Also called *securities analysts* and *investment analysts*, they work for banks, insurance companies, mutual and pension funds, securities firms, the business media, and other businesses, making investment decisions or recommendations. Financial analysts study company financial statements and analyze commodity prices, sales, costs, expenses, and tax rates to determine a company's value by projecting its future earnings. They often meet with company officials to gain a better insight into the firms' prospects and management.

Financial analysts can be divided into two categories: *buy side analysts* and *sell side analysts*. Analysts on the buy side work for companies that have a great deal of money to invest. These companies, called institutional investors, include mutual funds, hedge funds, insurance companies, independent money managers, and nonprofit organizations with large endowments. Buy side financial analysts devise investment strategies. Conversely, sell side analysts help securities dealers, such as banks and other firms, sell stocks, bonds, and other investments. The business media hire financial advisors that are supposed to be impartial, and occupy a role somewhere in the middle.

Financial analysts generally focus on trends impacting a specific industry, region, or type of product. For example, an analyst will focus on a subject area such as the utilities industry,

> ### Significant Points
> ❖ Financial analyst positions require a bachelor's or master's degree.
>
> ❖ Positions may also require professional licenses and certifications.
>
> ❖ Keen competition is anticipated for these highly paid positions.
>
> ❖ Financial analysts earn high wages.

an area such as Latin America, or the options market. Firms with larger research departments assign analysts even narrower subject areas. They must understand how new regulations, policies, and political and economic trends may impact the investments they are watching. *Risk analysts* evaluate the risk in portfolio decisions, project potential losses, and determine how to limit potential losses and volatility using diversification, currency futures, derivatives, short selling, and other investment decisions.

Some experienced analysts called *portfolio managers* supervise a team of analysts and select the mix of products, industries, and regions for their company's investment portfolio. Hedge fund and mutual fund managers are called *fund managers*. Fund and portfolio managers frequently make split-second buy or sell decisions in reaction to quickly changing market conditions. These managers are not only responsible for the overall portfolio, but are also expected to explain investment decisions and strategies in meetings with investors.

Ratings analysts evaluate the ability of companies or governments to pay their debts, including bonds. On the basis of their evaluation, a management team rates the risk of a company or government defaulting on its bonds. Other financial analysts perform budget, cost, and credit analysis as part of their responsibilities.

Financial analysts use spreadsheet and statistical software packages to analyze financial data, spot trends, create portfolios, and develop forecasts. Analysts also use the data they find to measure the financial risks associated with making a particular investment decision. On the basis of their results, they recommend whether to buy, hold, or sell particular investments.

Work environment. Financial analysts usually work in offices. They may work long hours, travel frequently to visit companies or potential investors, and face the pressure of deadlines. Much of their research must be done after office hours because their days are filled with telephone calls and meetings.

Training, Other Qualifications, and Advancement

Financial analysts must have a bachelor's degree. Many positions require a master's degree in finance or a Master of Business Administration (MBA). Positions may also require professional licenses and certifications. However, licenses and certifications are generally only earned after someone is hired.

Education and training. A bachelor's or graduate degree is required for financial analysts. Most companies require a bachelor's degree in a related field, such as finance, business, accounting, statistics, or economics. An understanding of statistics, economics, and business is essential, and knowledge of accounting policies and procedures, corporate budgeting, and financial analysis methods is recommended. An MBA or a master's degree in finance is often required. Advanced courses or knowledge of options pricing, bond valuation, and risk management are important.

Licensure. The Financial Industry Regulatory Authority (FINRA) is the main licensing organization for the securities industry. Depending on an individual's work, different licenses may be required, although buy side analysts are less likely to need licenses. The majority of these licenses require sponsorship by an employer, so companies do not expect individuals to have these licenses before starting a job. Experienced workers who change jobs will need to have their licenses renewed with the new company.

Other qualifications. Strong math, analytical, and problem-solving skills are essential qualifications for financial analysts. Good communication skills are necessary because these workers must present complex financial concepts and strategies. Self-confidence, maturity, and the ability to work independently are important. Financial analysts must be detail-oriented, motivated to seek out obscure information, and familiar with the workings of the economy, tax laws, and money markets. Although much of the software they use is proprietary, financial analysts must be comfortable working with spreadsheets and statistical packages.

With the increasing global diversification of investments, companies are assigning more financial analysts to cover foreign markets. These analysts normally specialize in one country, such as Brazil, or one region, such as Latin America. Companies prefer financial analysts to have the international experience necessary to understand the language, culture, business environment, and political conditions in the country or region that they cover.

Certification and advancement. Although not always required, certifications enhance professional standing and are recommended by employers. Certifications are becoming increasingly common. Financial analysts can earn the Chartered Financial Analyst (CFA) designation, sponsored by the CFA Institute. To qualify for this designation, applicants need a bachelor's degree, four years of related work experience, and must pass three exams. Applicants can take the exams while they are obtaining the required work experience. Passing the exams requires several hundred hours of self-study. These exams cover subjects such as accounting, economics, securities analysis, financial markets and instruments, corporate finance, asset valuation, and portfolio management. Additional certifications are helpful for financial analysts who specialize in specific areas, such as risk management.

Financial analysts advance by moving into positions where they are responsible for larger or more important products. They may supervise teams of financial analysts. They may become portfolio managers or fund managers, directing the investment portfolios of their companies or funds.

Employment

Financial analysts held 250,600 jobs in 2008. Many financial analysts work at large financial institutions based in New York City or other major financial centers. About 47 percent of financial analysts worked in the finance and insurance industries, including securities and commodity brokers, banks and credit institutions, and insurance carriers.

Others worked throughout private industry and government.

Job Outlook

Employment of financial analysts is expected to grow much faster than the average for all occupations. However, keen competition will continue for these well-paid jobs, especially for new entrants.

Employment change. As the level of investment increases, overall employment of financial analysts is expected to increase by 20 percent during the 2008–18 decade, which is much faster than the average for all occupations. Primary factors for this growth are increasing complexity and global diversification of investments and growth in the overall amount of assets under management. As the number and type of mutual and hedge funds and the amount of assets invested in these funds increase, companies will need more financial analysts to research and recommend investments. As the international investment increases, companies will need more analysts to cover the global range of investment options.

Job prospects. Despite employment growth, keen competition is expected for these high-paying jobs. Growth in financial services will create new positions, but there are still far more people who would like to enter the occupation. For those aspiring to financial analyst jobs, a strong academic background, including courses such as finance, accounting, and economics, is essential. Certifications and graduate degrees, such as a CFA certification or a master's degree in business or finance, significantly improve an applicant's prospects.

Earnings

Median annual wages, excluding bonuses, of wage and salary financial analysts were $73,150 in May 2008, which is more than double the national median wage. The middle 50 percent earned between $54,930 and $99,100. The lowest 10 percent earned less than $43,440, and the highest 10 percent earned more than $141,070. Annual performance bonuses are quite common and can be a significant part of their total earnings.

BUSINESS & FINANCE

—ɯ—

Human Resource Specialists

Nature of the Work

Every organization wants to attract, motivate, and retain the most qualified employees and match them to jobs for which they are best suited. Human resources, training, and labor relations managers and specialists provide this connection. In the past, these workers performed the administrative function of an organization, such as handling employee benefits questions or recruiting, interviewing, and hiring new staff in accordance with policies established by top management. Today's human resources workers manage these tasks, but, increasingly, they consult with top executives regarding strategic planning. They have moved from behind-the-scenes staff work to leading the company in suggesting and changing policies.

In an effort to enhance morale and productivity, limit job turnover, and help organizations increase performance and improve results, these workers also help their companies effectively use employee skills, provide training and development opportunities to improve those skills, and increase employees' satisfaction with their jobs and working conditions. Although some jobs in the human resources field require only limited contact with people outside the human resources office, dealing with people is an important part of the job.

There are many types of human resources, training, and labor relations managers and

---

Significant Points

❖ The educational backgrounds of these workers vary considerably, reflecting the diversity of duties and levels of responsibility.

❖ College graduates and those who have earned certification should have the best job and advancement opportunities.

❖ Human resources occupations require strong interpersonal skills.

❖ Much faster than average growth is expected during the projection period.

---

specialists. In a small organization, a human resources generalist may handle all aspects of human resources work, and thus require an extensive range of knowledge. The responsibilities of human resources generalists can vary widely, depending on their employer's needs.

In a large corporation, the director of human resources may supervise several departments, each headed by an experienced manager who most likely specializes in one human resources activity, such as employment and placement, compensation and benefits, training and development, or labor relations. The director may report to a top human resources executive.

Employment and placement. Employment and placement managers supervise the recruitment, hiring, and separation of employees. They also supervise employment, recruitment, and placement specialists, including employment interviewers. Employment, recruitment, and placement specialists recruit and place workers.

Recruitment specialists maintain contacts within the community and may travel considerably, often to job fairs and college campuses, to search for promising job applicants. Recruiters screen, interview, and occasionally test applicants. They also may check references and extend job offers. These workers must be thoroughly familiar with their organization, the work that is done, and the human resources policies of their company in order to discuss wages, working conditions and advancement opportunities with prospective employees. They also must stay informed about equal employment opportunity (EEO) and affirmative action guidelines and laws, such as the Americans with Disabilities Act.

Employment interviewers—whose many job titles include human resources consultants, human resources development specialists, *and* human resources coordinators—help to match employers with qualified jobseekers. Similarly, employer relations representatives, who usually work in government agencies or college career centers, maintain working relationships with prospective employers and promote the use of public employment programs and services.

Compensation, benefits, and job analysis. Compensation, benefits, and job analysis specialists administer compensation programs for employers and may specialize in specific areas such as pensions or position classifications. For example, job analysts, occasionally called position classifiers, collect and examine detailed information about job duties in order to prepare job descriptions. These descriptions explain the duties, training, and skills that each job requires. Whenever a large organization introduces a new job or reviews existing jobs, it calls upon the expert knowledge of job analysts.

Occupational analysts research occupational classification systems and study the effects of industry and occupational trends on worker relationships. They may serve as technical liaisons between companies or departments, government, and labor unions.

Establishing and maintaining a firm's pay structure is the principal job of compensation managers. Assisted by compensation analysts or specialists, compensation managers devise ways to ensure fair and equitable pay rates. They may participate in or purchase salary surveys to see how their firm's pay compares with others, and they ensure that the firm's pay scale complies with changing laws and regulations. In addition, compensation managers often oversee the compensation side of their company's performance management system. They may design reward systems such as pay-for-performance plans, which might include setting merit pay guidelines and bonus or incentive pay criteria. Compensation managers also might administer executive compensation programs or determine commission rates and other incentives for corporate sales staffs.

Employee benefits managers and specialists administer a company's employee benefits program, notably its health insurance and retirement plans. Expertise in designing, negotiating, and administering benefits programs continues to take on importance as employer-provided benefits account for a growing proportion of overall compensation costs, and as benefit plans increase in number and complexity. For example, retirement benefits might include defined benefit pension plans, defined contribution plans, such as 401(k) or thrift savings plans and profit-sharing or stock ownership plans. Health benefits might include medical, dental, and vision insurance and protection against catastrophic illness. Familiarity with health benefits is a top priority for employee benefits managers and specialists, because of the rising cost of providing healthcare benefits to employees and retirees. In addition to health insurance and retirement coverage, many firms offer employees life and accidental death and dismemberment insurance, disability insurance, and benefits designed to meet the needs of a changing workforce, such as parental leave, long-term nursing or home care insurance, wellness programs, and flexible benefits plans. Benefits managers must keep abreast of changing Federal and State regulations and legislation that may affect employee benefits. Working with employee assistance plan managers or work-life coordinators, many benefits managers work to integrate the growing number of programs that deal with mental and physical health, such as employee assistance, obesity, and smoking cessation, into their health benefits programs.

Employee assistance plan managers, also called employee welfare managers or work-life managers, are responsible for a wide array of programs to enhance employee safety and wellness and improve work-life balance. These may include occupational safety and health standards and practices, health promotion and physical fitness, medical examinations and minor health treatment, such as first aid, flexible work schedules, food service and recreation activities, carpooling and transportation programs such as transit subsidies, employee suggestion systems, child care and elder care, and counseling services. Child care and elder care are increasingly significant because of growth in the number of dual-income households and the older population. Counseling may help employees deal with emotional disorders, alcoholism, or marital, family, consumer, legal, and financial problems. Some employers offer career counseling and outplacement services. In some companies, certain programs, such as those dealing with physical security or information technology, may be coordinated in separate departments by other managers.

Training and development. Training and development managers and specialists create, procure, and conduct training and development programs for employees. Managers typically supervise specialists and make budget-impacting decisions in exchange for a reduced training portfolio. Increasingly, executives recognize that training offers a way of developing skills, enhancing productivity and quality of work, and building worker loyalty. Enhancing employee skills can increase individual and organizational performance and help to achieve business results. Increasingly, executives realize that developing the skills and knowledge of its workforce is a business imperative that can give them a competitive edge in recruiting and retaining high quality employees and can lead to business growth.

Other factors involved in determining whether training is needed include the complexity of the work environment, the rapid pace of organizational and technological change, and the growing number of jobs in fields that constantly generate new knowledge and, thus, require new skills. In addition, advances in learning theory have provided insights into how people learn and how training can be organized most effectively.

Training managers oversee development of training programs, contracts, and budgets. They may perform needs assessments of the types of training needed, determine the best means of delivering training, and create the content. They may provide employee training in a classroom, computer laboratory, or onsite production facility, or through a training film, Web video-on-demand, or self-paced or self-guided instructional guides. For live or in-person training, training managers ensure that teaching materials are prepared and the space appropriately set, training and instruction stimulate the class, and completion certificates are issued at the end of training. For computer-assisted or recorded training, trainers ensure that cameras, microphones, and other necessary technology platforms are functioning properly and that individual computers or other learning devices are configured for training purposes. They also have the responsibility for the entire learning process, and its environment, to ensure that the course meets its objectives and is measured and evaluated to understand how learning impacts performance.

Training specialists plan, organize, and direct a wide range of training activities. Trainers consult with training managers and employee supervisors to develop performance improvement measures, conduct orientation sessions, and arrange on-the-job training for new employees. They help employees maintain and improve their job skills and prepare for jobs requiring greater skill. They work with supervisors to improve their interpersonal skills and to deal effectively with employees. They may set up individualized training plans to strengthen employees' existing skills or teach new ones. Training specialists also may set up leadership or executive development programs for employees who aspire to move up in the organization. These programs are designed to develop or "groom" leaders to replace those leaving the organization and as part of a corporate succession plan. Trainers also lead programs to assist employees with job transitions as a result of mergers or consolidation, as well as retraining programs to develop new skills that may result from technological changes in the work place. In government-supported job-training programs, training specialists serve as case managers and provide basic job skills to prepare participants to function in the labor force. They assess the training needs of clients and guide them through the most appropriate training. After training, clients may either be referred to employer relations representatives or receive job placement assistance.

Planning and program development is an essential part of the training specialist's job. In order to identify and assess training needs, trainers may confer with managers and supervisors or conduct surveys. They also evaluate training effectiveness to ensure that employees actually learn and that the training they receive helps the organization meet its strategic goals and achieve results.

Depending on the size, goals, and nature of the organization, trainers may differ considerably in their responsibilities and in the methods they use. Training methods also vary by whether the training predominantly is knowledge-based or skill-based or sometimes a combination of the two. For example, much knowledge-based training is conducted in a classroom setting. Most skill training provides some combination of hands-on instruction, demonstration, and practice at doing something and usually is conducted on a shop floor, studio, or laboratory where trainees gain experience and confidence. Some on-the-job training methods could apply equally to knowledge or skill training and formal apprenticeship training programs combine classroom training and work experience. Increasingly, training programs involve interactive Internet-based training modules that can be downloaded for either individual or group instruction, for dissemination to a geographically dispersed class, or to be coordinated with other multimedia programs. These technologies allow participants to take advantage of distance learning alternatives and to attend conferences and seminars through satellite or Internet communications hookups, or use other computer-aided instructional technologies, such as those for the hearing-impaired or sight-impaired.

Employee relations. An organization's director of industrial relations forms labor policy, oversees industrial labor relations, negotiates collective bargaining agreements, and coordinates grievance procedures to handle complaints resulting from management disputes with employees. The director of industrial relations also advises and collaborates with the director of human resources, other managers, and members of their staffs, because all aspects of human resources policy—such as wages, benefits, pensions, and work practices—may be involved in drawing up a new or revised work rules that comply with a union contract.

Labor relations managers and their staffs implement industrial labor relations programs. Labor relations specialists prepare information for management to use during collective bargaining agreement negotiations, a process that requires the specialist to be familiar with economic and wage data and to have extensive knowledge of labor law and collective bargaining procedures. The labor relations staff interprets and administers the contract with respect to grievances, wages and salaries, employee welfare, healthcare, pensions, union and management practices, and other contractual stipulations. In the absence of a union, industrial relations personnel may work with employees individually or with employee association representatives.

Dispute resolution—attaining tacit or contractual agreements—has become increasingly significant as parties to a dispute attempt to avoid costly litigation, strikes, or other disruptions. Dispute resolution also has become more complex, involving employees, management, unions, other firms, and government agencies. Specialists involved in dispute resolution must be highly knowledgeable and experienced, and often report to the director of industrial relations. Mediators advise and counsel labor and management to prevent and, when necessary, resolve disputes over labor agreements or other labor relations issues. Arbitrators, occasionally called umpires or referees, decide disputes that bind both labor and management to specific terms and conditions of labor contracts. Labor relations specialists who work for unions perform many of the same functions on behalf of the union and its members.

EEO officers, representatives, or affirmative action coordinators handle equal employment opportunity matters. They investigate and resolve EEO grievances, examine corporate practices for possible violations, and compile and submit EEO statistical reports.

Other emerging specialties in human resources include international human resources managers, who handle human resources issues related to a company's overseas operations and human resources information system specialists, who develop and apply computer programs to process human resources information, match jobseekers with job openings, and handle other human resources matters; and total compensation or total rewards specialists, who determine an appropriate mix of compensation, benefits, and incentives.

Work environment. Human resources personnel usually work in clean, pleasant, and comfortable office settings. Arbitrators and mediators many of whom work independently may work out of home offices. Although most human resources, training, and labor relations managers and specialists work in the office, some travel extensively. For example, recruiters regularly attend professional meetings, participate in job fairs, and visit college campuses to interview prospective employees. Arbitrators and mediators often must travel to the site chosen for negotiations. Trainers and other specialists may travel to regional, satellite, or international offices of a company to meet with employees who work outside of the main corporate office.

Many human resources, training, and labor relations managers and specialists work a standard 40-hour week. However, longer hours might be necessary for some workers—for example, labor relations managers and specialists, arbitrators, and mediators—when contract agreements or dispute resolutions are being negotiated.

Training, Other Qualifications, and Advancement

The educational backgrounds of human resources, training, and labor relations managers and specialists vary considerably, reflecting the diversity of duties and levels of responsibility. In filling entry-level jobs, many employers seek college graduates who have majored in human resources, human resources administration, or industrial and labor relations. Other employers look for college graduates with a technical or business background or a well-rounded liberal arts education.

Education and training. Although a bachelor's degree is a typical path of entry into these occupations, many colleges and universities do not offer degree programs in personnel administration, human resources, or labor relations until the graduate degree level. However, many offer individual courses in these subjects at the undergraduate level in addition to concentrations in human resources administration or human resources management, training and development, organizational development, and compensation and benefits.

Because an interdisciplinary background is appropriate in this field, a combination of courses in the social sciences, business administration, and behavioral sciences is useful. Some jobs may require more technical or specialized backgrounds in engineering, science, finance, or law. Most prospective human resources specialists should take courses in principles of management, organizational structure, and industrial psychology; however, courses in accounting or finance are becoming increasingly important. Courses in labor law, collective bargaining, labor economics, and labor history also provide a valuable background for the prospective labor relations specialist. As in many other fields, knowledge of computers and information systems is useful.

An advanced degree is increasingly important for some jobs. Many labor relations jobs require graduate study in industrial or labor relations. A strong background in industrial relations and law is highly desirable for contract negotiators, mediators, and arbitrators; in fact, many people in these specialties have law degrees. A master's degree in human resources, labor relations, or in business administration with a concentration in human resources management is highly recommended for those seeking general and top management positions.

The duties given to entry-level workers will vary, depending on whether the new workers have a degree in human resource management, have completed an internship, or have some other type of human resources-related experience. Entry-level employees commonly learn by performing administrative duties—helping to enter data into computer systems, compiling employee handbooks, researching information for a supervisor, or answering phone calls and handling routine questions. Entry-level workers often enter on-the-job training programs in which they learn how to classify jobs, interview applicants, or administer employee benefits; they then are assigned to specific areas in the human resources department to gain experience. Later, they may advance to supervisory positions, overseeing a major element of the human resources program—compensation or training, for example.

Other qualifications. Experience is an asset for many specialties in the human resources area, and is essential for advancement to senior-level positions, including managers, arbitrators, and mediators. Many employers prefer entry-level workers who have gained some experience through an internship or work-study program while in school. Employees in human resources administration and human resources development need the ability to work well with individuals and a commitment to organizational goals. This field demands skills that people may have developed elsewhere—teaching, supervising, and volunteering, among others. Human resources work also offers clerical workers opportunities to advance to more responsible or professional positions. Some positions occasionally are filled by experienced individuals from other backgrounds, including business, government, education, social services administration, and the military.

The human resources field demands a range of personal qualities and skills. Human resources, training, and labor relations managers and specialists must speak and write effectively. Ever-changing technologies and the growing complexities inherent to the many services human resources personnel provide require that they be knowledgeable about computer systems, storage and retrieval software, and how to use a wide array of digital communications devices.

The growing diversity of the workforce requires that human resources managers and specialists work with or supervise people of various ages, cultural backgrounds, levels of education, and experience. Ability to speak a foreign language is an asset, especially if working in an industry with a large immigrant workforce or for a company with many overseas operations. Human resources employees must be able to cope with conflicting points of view, function under pressure, and demonstrate discretion, integrity, fair-mindedness, and a persuasive, genial personality. Because much of the information collected by these employees is confidential, they must also show the character and responsibility of dealing with sensitive employee information.

Certification and advancement. Most professional associations that specialize in human resources offer classes intended to enhance the skills of their members. Some organizations offer certification programs, which are signs of competence and credibility and can enhance advancement opportunities. For example, the International Foundation of Employee Benefit Plans confers a designation in three distinct areas of specialization—group benefit, retirement, and compensation—to persons who complete a series of college-level courses and pass exams. Candidates can earn a designation in each of the specialty tracks and, simultaneously, receive credit toward becoming a Certified Employee Benefits Specialist (CEBS). The American Society for Training and Development (ASTD) Certification Institute offers professional certification in the learning and performance field. Addressing nine areas of expertise, certification requires passing a knowledge-based exam and successful work experience. In addition, ASTD offers 16 short-term certificate and workshop programs covering a broad range of professional training and development topics. The Society for Human Resource Management offers two levels of certification, including the Professional in Human Resources (PHR) and the Senior Professional in Human Resources (SPHR). Additionally, the organization offers the Global Professional in Human Resources certification for those with international and cross-border responsibilities and the California Certification in Human Resources for those who plan to work in that State and become familiar with California's labor and human resources laws. All designations require experience and a passing score on a comprehensive exam. The WorldatWork Society of Certified Professionals offers four distinct designations in the areas of compensation, benefits, work-life, and global remuneration that comprise the total rewards management practice. Candidates obtain the designation of Certified Compensation Professional (CCP), Certified Benefits Professional (CBP), Global Remuneration Professional (GRP), and Work-Life Certified Professional (WLCP). Certification is achieved after passing a series of knowledge-based exams within each designation. Additionally, WorldatWork offers online and classroom education covering a broad range of total rewards topics.

Exceptional human resources workers may be promoted to director of human resources or industrial relations, which can eventually lead to a top managerial or executive position. Others may join a consulting or outsourcing firm or open their own business. A Ph.D. is an asset for teaching, writing, or consulting work.

Employment

Human resources, training, and labor relations managers and specialists held about 904,900 jobs in 2008.

Human resources, training, and labor relations managers and specialists were employed in virtually every industry. About 13 percent of human resources, training, and labor relations managers and specialists were employed in administrative and support services, 11 percent in professional, scientific, and technical services, 10 percent in healthcare and social assistance, and 9 percent in finance and insurance firms. About 12,900 managers and specialists were self-employed, working as consultants to public and private employers.

Job Outlook

Employment is expected to grow much faster than the average for all human resources, training, and labor relations managers and specialists occupations. College graduates and those who have earned certification should have the best job opportunities.

Employment change. Overall employment is projected to grow by 22 percent between 2008 and 2018, much faster than the average for all occupations. Legislation and court rulings revising standards in various areas—occupational safety and health, equal employment opportunity, wages, healthcare, retirement plans, and family leave, among others—will increase demand for human resources, training, and labor relations experts. Rising healthcare costs and a growing number of healthcare coverage options should continue to spur demand for specialists to develop creative compensation and benefits packages that companies can offer prospective employees.

Employment of labor relations staff, including arbitrators and mediators, should grow as companies attempt to resolve potentially costly labor-management disputes out of court. Additional job growth may stem from increasing demand for specialists in international human resources management and human resources information systems.

Job growth could be limited by the widespread use of computerized human resources information systems that make workers more productive. Like other workers, employment of human resources, training, and labor relations managers and specialists, particularly in larger companies, may be adversely affected by corporate downsizing, restructuring, and mergers; however, as companies once again expand operations, additional workers may be needed to manage company growth.

Demand may be particularly strong for certain specialists. For example, employers are expected to devote greater resources to job-specific training programs in response to the increasing complexity of many jobs and technological advances that can leave employees with obsolete skills. Additionally, as highly trained and skilled baby boomers retire, there should be strong demand for training and development specialists to impart needed skills to their replacements. In addition, increasing efforts throughout industry to recruit and retain quality employees should create many jobs for employment, recruitment, and placement specialists.

Among industries, firms involved in management, consulting, and employment services should offer many job opportunities, as businesses increasingly contract out human resources functions or hire human resources specialists on a temporary basis to deal with increasing costs and complexity of training and development programs. Demand for specialists also should increase in outsourcing firms that develop and administer complex employee benefits and compensation packages for other organizations.

Job prospects. College graduates and those who have earned certification should have the best job opportunities, particularly graduates with a bachelor's degree in human resources, human resources administration, or industrial and labor relations. Those with a technical or business background or a well-rounded liberal arts education also should find opportunities. Demand for human resources, training, and labor relations managers and specialists depends on general economic conditions and the business cycle as well as staffing needs of the companies in which they work. A rapidly expanding business is likely to hire additional human resources workers—either as permanent employees or consultants—while businesses that have consolidated operations or merged with another company may require fewer of these workers. Also, as human resources management becomes increasingly important to the success of an organization, some small and medium-size businesses that do not have separate human resources departments may assign various human resources responsibilities to some employees in addition to their usual responsibilities; others may contract with consulting firms to establish formal procedures and train current employees to administer programs on a long-term basis.

In addition to new human resources management and specialist jobs created over the 2008-2018 projection period, many job openings will arise from the need to replace workers who transfer to other occupations, retire, or leave the labor force for other reasons.

Earnings

Annual salary rates for human resources workers vary according to occupation, level of experience, training, location, and firm size.

Median annual wages of compensation and benefits managers were $86,500 in May 2008. The middle 50 percent earned between $64,930 and $113,480. The lowest 10 percent earned less than $49,350, and the highest 10 percent earned more than $147,050.

MUSICAL ARTS

—m—

Musicians, Singers, and Related Workers

Nature of the Work

Musicians, singers, and related workers play musical instruments, sing, compose or arrange music, or conduct groups in instrumental or vocal performances. They perform solo or as part of a group, mostly in front of live audiences in nightclubs, concert halls, and theaters. They also perform in recording or production studios for radio, TV, film, or video games. Regardless of the setting, they spend considerable time practicing alone and with their bands, orchestras, or other musical ensembles.

Musicians play one or more musical instruments. Many musicians learn to play several related instruments and can perform equally well in several musical styles. Instrumental musicians, for example, may play in a symphony orchestra, rock group, or jazz combo one night, appear in another ensemble the next, and work in a studio band the following day. Some play a variety of string, brass, woodwind, or percussion instruments or electronic synthesizers.

Singers use their knowledge of voice production, melody, and harmony to interpret music and text. They sing character parts or perform in their own individual styles. Singers often are classified according to their voice range—soprano, contralto, tenor, baritone, or bass—or by the type of music they sing, such as rock, pop, folk, opera, rap, or country.

Significant Points

❖ Part-time schedules—typically at night and on weekends—intermittent unemployment, and rejection when auditioning for work are common; many musicians and singers supplement their income with earnings from other sources.

❖ Aspiring musicians and singers begin studying an instrument or training their voice at an early age.

❖ Competition for jobs, especially full-time jobs, is keen; talented individuals who can play several instruments and perform a wide range of musical styles should enjoy the best job prospects.

Music directors and *conductors* conduct, direct, plan, and lead instrumental or vocal performances by musical groups such as orchestras, choirs, and glee clubs. These leaders audition and select musicians, choose the music most appropriate for their talents and abilities, and direct rehearsals and performances. *Choral directors* lead choirs and glee clubs, sometimes working with a band or an orchestra conductor. Directors audition and select singers and lead them at rehearsals and performances to achieve harmony, rhythm, tempo, shading, and other desired musical effects.

Composers create original music such as symphonies, operas, sonatas, radio and television jingles, film scores, and popular songs. They transcribe ideas into musical notation, using harmony, rhythm, melody, and tonal structure. Although most composers and songwriters practice their craft on instruments and transcribe the notes with pen and paper, some use computer software to compose and edit their music.

Arrangers transcribe and adapt musical compositions to a particular style for orchestras, bands, choral groups, or individuals. Components of music—including tempo, volume, and the mix of instruments needed—are arranged to express the composer's message. Although some arrangers write directly into a musical composition, others use computer software to make changes.

Work environment. Musicians typically perform at night and on weekends. They spend much additional time practicing or in rehearsal. Full-time musicians with long-term employment contracts, such as those with symphony orchestras or television and film production companies, enjoy steady work and less travel. Nightclub, solo, or recital musicians frequently travel to perform in a variety of local settings and may tour nationally or internationally. Because many musicians find only part-time or intermittent work and experience unemployment between engagements, they often supplement their income with other types of jobs. The stress of constantly looking for work leads many musicians to accept permanent full-time jobs in other occupations while working part time as musicians.

Most instrumental musicians work closely with a variety of other people, including colleagues, agents, employers, sponsors, and audiences. Although they usually work indoors, some perform outdoors for parades, concerts, and festivals. In some nightclubs and restaurants, smoke and odors may be present and lighting and ventilation may be poor.

Training, Other Qualifications, and Advancement

Long-term on-the-job training is the most common way people learn to become musicians or singers. Aspiring musicians begin studying an instrument at an early age. They may gain valuable experience playing in a school or community band or orchestra or with a group of friends. Singers usually start training when their voices mature. Participation in school musicals or choirs often provides good early training and experience. Composers and music directors usually require a bachelor's degree in a related field.

Education and training. Musicians need extensive and prolonged training and practice to acquire the skills and knowledge necessary to interpret music at a professional level. Like other artists, musicians and singers continually strive to improve their abilities. Formal training may be obtained through private study with an accomplished musician, in a college or university music program, or in a music conservatory. An audition generally is necessary to qualify for university or conservatory study. The National Association of Schools of Music is made up of 615 accredited college-level programs in music. Courses typically include music theory, music interpretation, composition, conducting, and performance, either with a particular instrument or a voice performance. Music directors, composers, conductors, and arrangers need considerable related work experience or advanced training in these subjects.

A master's or doctoral degree usually is required to teach advanced music courses in colleges and universities; a bachelor's degree may be sufficient to teach basic courses. A degree in music education qualifies graduates for a State certificate to teach music in public elementary or secondary schools. Musicians who do not meet public school music education requirements may teach in private schools and recreation associations or instruct individual students in private sessions.

Other qualifications. Musicians must be knowledgeable about a broad range of musical styles. Having a broader range of interest, knowledge, and training can help expand employment opportunities and musical abilities. Voice training and private instrumental lessons, especially when taken at a young age, also help develop technique and enhance one's performance.

Young persons considering careers in music should have musical talent, versatility, creativity, poise, and good stage presence. Self-discipline is vital because producing a quality performance on a consistent basis requires constant study and practice. Musicians who play in concerts or in nightclubs and those who tour must have physical stamina to endure frequent travel and an irregular performance schedule. Musicians and singers also must be prepared to face the anxiety of intermittent employment and of rejection when auditioning for work.

Advancement. Advancement for musicians usually means becoming better known, finding work more easily, and performing for higher earnings. Successful musicians often rely on agents or managers to find them performing engagements, negotiate contracts, and develop their careers.

Employment

Musicians, singers, and related workers held about 240,000 jobs in 2008, of which 186,400 were held by musicians and singers; 53,600 were music directors and composers. Around 43 percent worked part time; 50 percent were self-employed. Many found jobs in cities in which entertainment and recording activities are concentrated, such as New York,

Los Angeles, Las Vegas, Chicago, and Nashville.

Musicians, singers, and related workers are employed in a variety of settings. Of those who earn a wage or salary, 33 percent were employed by religious, grantmaking, civic, professional, and similar organizations and 12 percent by performing arts companies, such as professional orchestras, small chamber music groups, opera companies, musical theater companies, and ballet troupes. Musicians and singers also perform in nightclubs and restaurants and for weddings and other events. Well-known musicians and groups may perform in concerts, appear on radio and television broadcasts, and make recordings and music videos. The U.S. Armed Forces also offer careers in their bands and smaller musical groups.

Job Outlook

Employment is expected to grow as fast as average. Keen competition for jobs, especially full-time jobs, is expected to continue. Talented individuals who are skilled in multiple instruments and musical styles will have the best job prospects.

Employment change. Employment of musicians, singers, and related workers is expected to grow 8 percent during the 2008–18 decade, as fast as the average for all occupations. Most new wage-and-salary jobs for musicians will arise in religious organizations. Slower than average employment growth is expected for self-employed musicians, who generally perform in nightclubs, concert tours, and other venues. The Internet and other new forms of media may provide independent musicians and singers alternative methods for distributing music.

Job prospects. Growth in demand for musicians will generate a number of job opportunities, and many openings also will arise from the need to replace those who leave the field each year because they are unable to make a living solely as musicians or singers, as well as those who leave for other reasons.

Competition for jobs as musicians, singers, and related workers—especially full-time jobs—is expected to be keen. The vast number of people with the desire to perform will continue to greatly exceed the number of openings. New musicians or singers will have their best chance of landing a job with smaller, community-based performing arts groups or as freelance artists. Instrumentalists should have better opportunities than singers because of a larger pool of work. Talented individuals who are skilled in multiple instruments or musical styles will have the best job prospects. However, talent alone is no guarantee of success: many people start out to become musicians or singers but leave the profession because they find the work difficult, the discipline demanding, and the long periods of intermittent unemployment a hardship.

Earnings

Median hourly wages of wage-and-salary musicians and singers were $21.24 in May 2008. The middle 50 percent earned between $11.49 and $36.36. The lowest 10 percent earned less than $7.64, and the highest 10 percent earned more than $59.92. Median hourly wages were $23.68 in performing arts companies and $12.50 in religious organizations. Annual wage data for musicians and singers were not available because of the wide variation in the number of hours worked by musicians and singers and the short-term nature of many jobs. It is rare for musicians and singers to have guaranteed employment that exceeds 3 to 6 months.

Median annual wages of salaried music directors and composers were $41,270 in May 2008. The middle 50 percent earned between $26,480 and $63,200. The lowest 10 percent earned less than $16,750, and the highest 10 percent earned more than $107,280.

For self-employed musicians and singers, earnings typically reflect the number of jobs a freelance musician or singer played or the number of hours and weeks of contract work, in addition to a performer's professional reputation and setting. Performers who can fill large concert halls, arenas, or outdoor stadiums generally command higher pay than those who perform in local clubs. Soloists or headliners usually receive higher earnings than band members or opening acts. The most successful musicians earn performance or recording fees that far exceed the median earnings.

The American Federation of Musicians negotiates minimum contracts for major orchestras during the performing season. Each orchestra works out a separate contract with its local union, but individual musicians may negotiate higher salaries. In regional orchestras, minimum salaries often are less because fewer performances are scheduled. Regional orchestra musicians frequently are paid for their services without any guarantee of future employment. Community orchestras often have limited funding and offer salaries that are much lower for seasons of shorter duration.

Although musicians employed by some symphony orchestras work under master wage agreements, which guarantee a season's work up to 52 weeks, many other musicians face relatively long periods of unemployment between jobs. Even when employed, many musicians and singers work part time in unrelated occupations. Thus, their earnings for music usually are lower than earnings in many other occupations. Moreover, because they may not work steadily for one employer, some performers cannot qualify for unemployment compensation and few have typical benefits such as sick leave or paid vacations. For these reasons, many musicians give private lessons or take jobs unrelated to music to supplement their earnings as performers.

Many musicians belong to a local of the American Federation of Musicians. Professional singers who perform live often belong to a branch of the American Guild of Musical Artists; those who record for the broadcast industries may belong to the American Federation of Television and Radio Artists.

Performing Arts

—∿—

Actors, Producers, and Directors

Nature of the Work

Actors, producers, and directors express ideas and create images in theater, film, radio, television, and other performing arts media. They interpret a writer's script to entertain, inform, or instruct an audience. Although many actors, producers, and directors work in New York or Los Angeles, far more work in other places. They perform, direct, and produce in local or regional television studios, theaters, or film production companies, often creating advertising or training films or small-scale independent movies.

Actors perform in stage, radio, television, video, or motion picture productions. They also work in cabarets, nightclubs, and theme parks. Actors portray characters, and, for more complex roles, they research their character's traits and circumstances so that they can better understand a script.

Most actors struggle to find steady work and only a few achieve recognition as stars. Others work as "*extras*," with no lines to deliver. Some actors do voiceover and narration work for advertisements, animated features, books on tape, and other electronic media. They also teach in high school or university drama departments, acting conservatories, or public programs.

Producers are entrepreneurs who make the business and financial decisions involving a motion picture, television show, or stage production. They select scripts, approve the

---

Significant Points

❖ Actors endure long periods of unemployment, intense competition for roles, and frequent rejections in auditions.

❖ Formal training through a university or acting conservatory is typical; however, many actors, producers, and directors find work on the basis of their experience and talent alone.

❖ Because earnings may be erratic, many actors, producers, and directors supplement their incomes by holding jobs in other fields.

development of ideas, arrange financing, and determine the size and cost of the endeavor. Producers hire or approve directors, principal cast members, and key production staff members.

Large productions often have associate, assistant, or line producers who share responsibilities. The number of producers and their specific job duties vary with the size and budget of each production; however, all work is done under the overall direction of an executive producer. Together the producers coordinate the activities of writers, directors, managers, and agents to ensure that each project stays on schedule and within budget.

Directors are responsible for the overall creative decisions of a production. They interpret scripts, audition and select cast members, conduct rehearsals, and direct the work of cast and crew. They approve the design elements of a production, including the sets, costumes, choreography, and music. As with producers, large productions often have many levels of directors working on them. Assistant directors cue the performers and technicians, telling them when to make entrances or light, sound, or set changes. All directors must ultimately answer to the executive producer, who has the final say on all factors related to the production.

Work environment. Actors, producers, and directors work under constant pressure. Many face stress from the continual need to find their next job. To succeed, actors, producers, and directors need patience and commitment to their craft. Actors strive to deliver flawless performances, often while working under undesirable and unpleasant conditions. Producers and directors organize rehearsals and meet with writers, designers, financial backers, and production technicians. They experience stress not only from these activities, but also from the need to adhere to budgets, union work rules, and production schedules.

Work assignments typically are short term—ranging from 1 day to a few months—which means that workers frequently experience long periods of unemployment between jobs. The uncertain nature of the work results in unpredictable earnings and intense competition for jobs. Often, actors, producers, and directors must hold other jobs in order to sustain a living.

Work hours are often long and irregular—evening and weekend work is a regular part of life in the performing arts. Actors, producers, and directors who work in theater may travel with a touring show across the country, whereas those who work in film may work on location, sometimes under adverse weather conditions. Actors who perform in a television series often appear on camera with little preparation time, because scripts tend to be revised frequently or even written moments before taping. Those who appear live or before a studio audience must be able to handle impromptu situations and calmly ad lib, or substitute, lines when necessary.

Actors should be in good physical condition and have the necessary stamina and coordination to move about theater stages and large movie and television studio lots. They also need to maneuver about complex technical sets while staying in character and projecting their voices audibly. Actors must be fit to endure heat from stage or studio lights and the weight of heavy costumes. Producers and directors ensure the safety of actors by conducting extra rehearsals on the set so that the actors can learn the layout of set pieces and props, by allowing time for warm-ups and stretching exercises to guard against physical and vocal injuries, and by providing an adequate number of breaks to prevent heat exhaustion and dehydration.

Training, Other Qualifications, and Advancement

People who become actors, producers, and directors follow many paths to employment. The most important qualities employers look for are creative instincts, innate talent, and the intellectual capacity to perform. The best way to prepare for a career as an actor, especially in the theater, is through formal dramatic training, preferably obtained as part of a bachelor's degree program. Producers and especially directors need experience in the field, either as actors or in other related jobs.

Education and training. Formal dramatic training, either through an acting conservatory or a university program, generally is necessary for these jobs, but some people successfully enter the field without it. Most people studying for a bachelor's degree take courses in radio and television broadcasting, communications, film, theater, drama, or dramatic literature. Many stage actors continue their academic training and receive a Master of Fine Arts (MFA) degree. Advanced curricula may include courses in stage speech and movement, directing, playwriting, and design, as well as intensive acting workshops. The National Association of Schools of Theatre accredits over 150 programs in theater arts.

Most aspiring actors participate in high school and college plays, work at college radio or television stations, or perform with local community theater groups. Local and regional theater experience may also help many young actors hone their skills. In television and film, actors and directors typically start in smaller roles or independent movie production companies and then work their way up to larger productions. Actors, regardless of their level of experience, may pursue workshop training through acting conservatories or mentoring by a drama coach.

There are no specific training requirements for producers. They come from many different backgrounds. Actors, writers, film editors, and business managers commonly enter the field. Producers often start in a theatrical management office, working for a press agent, managing director, or business manager. Some start in a performing arts union or service organization. Others work behind the scenes with successful directors, serve on the boards of art companies, or promote their own projects. Although there are no formal training programs for producers, a number of colleges and universities offer degree programs in arts management and in managing nonprofit organizations.

Some directors have experience as actors or writers, while others gain experience in the field by assisting established directors. Many also have formal training in directing.

Other qualifications. Actors need talent and creativity that will enable them to portray different characters. Because competition for parts is fierce, versatility and a wide range of related performance skills, such as singing, dancing, skating, juggling, acrobatics, or miming are especially useful. Actors must have poise, stage presence, the ability to affect an audience, and the ability to follow direction. Modeling experience also may be helpful. Physical appearance, such as having certain features and being the specified size and weight, often is a deciding factor in who gets a particular role.

Some actors begin as movie extras. To become an extra, one usually must be listed by casting agencies that supply extras to the major movie studios in Hollywood. Applicants are accepted only when the number of people of a particular type on the list—for example, athletic young women, old men, or small children—falls below what is needed. In recent years, only a very small proportion of applicants have succeeded in being listed.

Like actors, directors and producers need talent and creativity. Directors need management ability because they are often in charge of a large number of people in a production. Producers need business acumen.

Advancement. As the reputations and box-office draw of actors, producers, and directors grow, some of them work on bigger budget productions, on network or syndicated broadcasts, in more prestigious theaters, or in larger markets. Actors may advance to lead roles and receive star billing. A few actors move into acting-related jobs, becoming drama coaches, directors, or producers. Some actors teach drama privately or in colleges and universities.

Employment

In May 2008, actors, producers, and directors held about 155,100 jobs, primarily in the motion picture and video, performing arts, and broadcast industries. This statistic does not capture large number of actors, producers, and directors who were available for work but were between jobs during the month in which data were collected. About 21 percent of actors, producers, and directors were self-employed.

Employment in motion pictures and in films for television is centered in New York and Los Angeles. However, small studios exist throughout the country. Many films are shot on location and may employ local professional and nonprofessional actors. In television, opportunities are concentrated in the network centers of New York and Los Angeles, but cable television services and local television stations around the country also employ many actors, producers, and directors.

Employment in the theater, and in other performing arts companies, is cyclical—higher in the fall and spring seasons—and concentrated in New York and other major cities with large commercial houses for musicals and touring productions. Also, many cities support established professional regional theaters that operate on a seasonal or year-round basis.

Actors, producers, and directors may find work in summer festivals, on cruise lines, and in theme parks. Many smaller, nonprofit professional companies, such as repertory companies, dinner theaters, and theaters affiliated with drama schools, acting conservatories, and universities, provide employment opportunities for local amateur talent and professional entertainers. Auditions typically are held in New York for many productions across the country and for shows that go on the road.

Job Outlook

Employment is expected to grow as fast as the average for all occupations. Competition for jobs will be keen. Although a growing number of people aspire to enter these professions, many will leave the field early because the work—when it is available—is hard, the hours are long, and the pay is often low.

Employment change. Employment in these occupations is expected to grow 11 percent during the 2008–18 decade, about as fast as the average for all occupations. Expanding cable and satellite television operations and increasing box-office receipts of major studio and independent films will increase the need for workers. Additionally, a rising demand for U.S. films in other countries should create more employment opportunities for actors, producers, and directors. Also fueling job growth is the continued development of interactive media, online movies, and mobile content produced for cell phones or other portable electronic devices. Attendance at live theater performances should continue to be steady, and drive employment of stage actors, producers and directors. However, station consolidation may restrict employment opportunities in the broadcasting industry for producers and directors.

Job prospects. Competition for acting jobs is intense, as the number of actors auditioning for roles greatly exceeds the number of parts that become available. Only performers with the most stamina and talent will find regular employment.

Venues for live entertainment, such as theaters, touring productions, and repertory theaters in many major metropolitan areas, as well as theme parks and resorts, are expected to offer many job opportunities. However, prospects in these venues are variable because they fluctuate with economic conditions.

Earnings

Many of the most successful actors, producers, and directors have extraordinarily high earnings, but many more of these professionals, faced with erratic earnings, supplement their income by holding jobs in other fields.

Median hourly wages of actors were $16.59 in May 2008. The middle 50 percent earned between $9.81 and $29.57. Median hourly wages were $14.48 in performing arts companies and $28.72 in the motion picture and video industry. Annual wage data for actors were not available because of the wide variation in the number of hours worked by actors and the short-term nature of many jobs, which may last for 1 day or 1 week; it is extremely rare for actors to have guaranteed employment that exceeds 3 to 6 months.

Median annual wages of producers and directors were $64,430 in 2008. The middle 50 percent earned between $41,890 and $105,070. Median annual wages were $85,940 in the motion picture and video industry and $55,380 in radio and television broadcasting.

Minimum salaries, hours of work, and other conditions of employment are often covered in collective bargaining agreements between the producers and the unions representing workers. While these unions generally determine minimum salaries, any actor or director may negotiate for a salary higher than the minimum.

A joint agreement between the Screen Actors Guild (SAG) and the American Federation of Television and Radio Artists (AFTRA) guarantees all unionized motion picture and television actors with speaking parts a minimum daily rate of $782 or $2,713 for a 5-day week as of June 2009. Actors also receive contributions to their health and pension plans and additional compensation for reruns and foreign telecasts of the productions in which they appear.

Some well-known actors earn well above the minimum; their salaries are many times the figures cited here, creating the false impression that all actors are highly paid. For example, of the nearly 100,000 SAG members, only about 50 might fall into this category. The average income that SAG members earn from acting is low because employment is sporadic and most actors must supplement their incomes by holding jobs in other occupations.

Actors Equity Association (AEA), which represents stage actors, has negotiated minimum weekly salary requirements for their members. Salaries vary depending on the theater or venue the actor is employed in. Many stage directors belong to the Society of Stage Directors and Choreographers (SSDC), and most film and television directors belong to the Directors Guild of America. Earnings of stage directors vary greatly. The SSDC usually negotiates salary contracts which include royalties (additional income based on the number of performances) with smaller theaters. Regional theaters may hire directors for longer periods, increasing compensation accordingly. The highest paid directors work on Broadway; in addition to their contract fee, they also receive payment in the form of royalties—a negotiated percentage of gross box-office receipts—that can exceed the contract fee for long-running box-office successes.

Stage producers seldom receive a set fee; instead, they get a percentage of a show's earnings or ticket sales.

PERFORMING ARTS

—ᙏᙎ—

Dancers and Choreographers

Nature of the Work

Complex movements and dances on stage and screen do not happen without a lot of hard work. *Dancers* spend years learning dances and honing skills, as do most *choreographers*. Together, they then translate those skills into movement that expresses ideas and stories.

Dancers perform in a variety of settings, including opera, musical theater, and other musical productions, and may present folk, ethnic, tap, jazz, or other popular kinds of dance. They also perform in television, movies, music videos, and commercials, in which they may sing and act. Dancers most often perform as part of a group, although a few top artists perform solo.

Choreographers create original dances and develop new interpretations of existing dances. They work in theaters, dance schools, dance and movie studios, and at fashion shows, and are involved in auditioning performers for dance parts. Because few dance routines are written down, choreographers instruct performers at rehearsals to achieve the desired effect, often by demonstrating the exact technique. Choreographers also work with performers other than dancers. For example, the complex martial arts scenes in movies are arranged by choreographers who specialize in the martial

Significant Points

❖ Many dancers stop performing by their late thirties, but some remain in the field as choreographers, dance teachers, or artistic directors.

❖ Most dancers begin formal training at an early age—between 5 and 15—and many have their first professional audition by age 17 or 18; becoming a choreographer usually requires years of experience.

❖ Dancers and choreographers face intense competition; only the most talented find regular work.

❖ Earnings from dancing are usually low because employment is irregular; dancers often supplement their income.

arts. Choreographers also may help coordinate costume design and lighting, as well as choose the music and sound effects that convey the intended message.

Work environment. Dance is strenuous. In fact, dancers have one of the highest rates of nonfatal on-the-job injury. Many dancers, as a result, stop performing by their late thirties because of the physical demands on the body. Nonetheless, some continue to work in the field as choreographers, artistic directors, and dance teachers and coaches, while a small number may move into administrative positions, such as company managers. A few celebrated dancers, however, continue performing most of their lives.

Many dance companies tour for part of the year to supplement a limited performance schedule at home. Dancers who perform in musical productions and other family entertainment spend much of their time on the road; others work in nightclubs or on cruise ships. Most dance performances are in the evening, whereas rehearsals and practice usually take place during the day. As a result, dancers often work very long and late hours. Generally, dancers and choreographers work in modern and temperature-controlled facilities; however, some studios may be older and less comfortable.

Training, Other Qualifications, and Advancement

Dancers generally need long-term on-the-job training to be successful. Most dancers begin formal training at an early age—between 5 and 15—and many have their first professional audition by age 17 or 18. Some earn a bachelor's degree or attend dance school, although neither is required. Becoming a choreographer usually requires years of experience.

Education and training. Training varies with the type of dance and is a continuous part of all dancers' careers. Many believe that dancers should start with a good foundation in classical technique before selecting a particular style. Ballet training for girls usually begins between the ages of 5 to 8 with a private teacher or through an independent ballet school, with more serious training beginning between the ages of 10 and 12. Boys often begin their ballet training between the ages of 10 and 15. Students who demonstrate potential in their early teens may seek out more intensive and advanced professional training. At about this time, students should begin to focus their training on a particular style and decide whether to pursue additional training through a dance company's school or a college dance program. Leading dance school companies often have summer training programs from which they select candidates for admission to their regular full-time training programs. Formal training for modern and culturally specific dances often begins later than training in ballet; however, many folk dance forms are taught to very young children. As a result, a good number of dancers have their first professional auditions by age 17 or 18.

Training is an important component of professional dancers' careers. Dancers normally spend 8 hours a day in class and rehearsal, keeping their bodies in shape and preparing for performances. Their daily training period usually includes time to warm up and cool down before and after classes and rehearsals.

Because of the strenuous and time-consuming training required, some dancers view formal education as secondary. However, a broad, general education including music, literature, history, and the visual arts is helpful in the interpretation of dramatic episodes, ideas, and feelings. Dancers sometimes conduct research to learn more about the part they are playing.

Many colleges and universities award bachelor's or master's degrees in dance, typically through departments of dance, theater, or fine arts. The National Association of Schools of Dance is made up of 74 accredited dance programs. Many programs concentrate on modern dance, but some also offer courses in jazz, culturally specific dance, ballet, or classical techniques. Courses in dance composition, history and criticism, and movement analysis are also available.

A college education is not essential for employment as a professional dancer; however, many dancers obtain degrees in unrelated fields to prepare themselves for careers after dance. The completion of a college program in dance and education is usually essential to qualify to teach dance in college, high school, or elementary school. Colleges and conservatories sometimes require graduate degrees but may accept performance experience. A college background is not necessary for teaching dance or choreography in local recreational programs. Studio schools prefer teachers to have experience as performers.

Choreographers should have a thorough understanding of the dance style that they arrange. This often is gained through years of performing and practicing. Some dance conservatories offer choreography courses.

Other qualifications. Because of the rigorous practice schedules of most dancers and choreographers, self-discipline, patience, perseverance, and a devotion to dance are essential for success in the field. Dancers and choreographers also must possess good problem-solving skills and an ability to work with people. Dancers, above all, must have good health and physical stamina, along with flexibility, agility, coordination, and grace, a sense of rhythm, a feeling for music, and a creative ability to express themselves through movement. Choreographers should possess many of the same attributes while also being able to plan and coordinate activities.

Because dancers and choreographers are typically members of an ensemble made up of other dancers, musicians, and directors or choreographers, they must be able to function as part of a team. They also should be highly motivated and prepared to face the anxiety of intermittent employment and rejections when looking for work.

Advancement. For dancers, advancement takes the form of a growing reputation, more frequent work, bigger and better roles, and higher pay. Some dancers may take on added responsibilities, such as by becoming a dance captain in musical theater or ballet master/ballet mistress in concert dance companies, by leading rehearsals, or by working with less experienced dancers in the absence of a choreographer.

Choreographers typically are experienced dancers with years of practice working in the theater. Through their performance as dancers, they develop reputations that often lead to opportunities to choreograph productions.

Employment

Professional dancers and choreographers held about 29,200 jobs in 2008. Many others were between engagements; as a result, the total number of people available for work as dancers over the course of the year was greater. Dancers and choreographers worked in a variety of industries, such as public and private educational services, which includes dance studios and schools, as well as colleges and universities; food services and drinking establishments; performing arts companies, which include dance, theater, and opera companies; and amusement and recreation venues, such as casinos and theme parks. About 14 percent of dancers and choreographers were self-employed.

Most major cities serve as home to major dance companies; however, many smaller communities across the Nation also support home-grown, full-time professional dance companies.

Job Outlook

Employment is expected to grow more slowly than the average. Dancers and choreographers face keen competition for jobs. Only the most talented find regular employment.

Employment change. Employment of dancers and choreographers is expected to grow 6 percent during the 2008-18 decade, more slowly than the average for all occupations. The public's interest in dance will sustain large and mid-size dance companies, but limited funding from public and private organizations is not expected to allow for additional dance companies. For many small organizations, the result will be fewer performances and more limited employment opportunities.

Job prospects. Because many people enjoy dance and would like to make their careers in dance, dancers and choreographers face intense competition for jobs. Only the most talented find regular employment.

Although job openings will arise each year because dancers and choreographers retire or leave the occupation for other reasons, the number of applicants will continue to vastly exceed the number of job openings.

National dance companies likely will continue to provide jobs in this field. Opera companies and dance groups affiliated with television and motion pictures also will offer some opportunities. Moreover, the growing popularity of dance for recreational and fitness purposes has resulted in increased opportunities to teach dance, especially for older dancers who may be transitioning to another field. Musicians will provide a small number of openings for both dancers and choreographers, and candidates are expected to face keen competition. Amusement parks and cruise ships should also provide some opportunities for dancers and choreographers.

Earnings

Median hourly wages of dancers were $12.22 in May 2008. The middle 50 percent earned between $8.03 and $18.82. The lowest 10 percent earned less than $7.28, and the highest 10 percent earned more than $27.26. Annual wage data for dancers were not available, because the wide variation in the number of hours worked by dancers and the short-term nature of many jobs—which may last for 1 day or 1 week—make it rare for dancers to have guaranteed employment that exceeds a few months.

Median annual wages of salaried choreographers were $38,520 in May 2008. The middle 50 percent earned between $25,320 and $55,360. The lowest 10 percent earned less than $17,880, and the highest 10 percent earned more than $67,160. Median annual wages were $37,570 in "other schools and instruction," the North American Industry Classification System category that includes dance studios and schools.

Dancers who were on tour usually received an additional allowance for room and board, as well as extra compensation for overtime. Earnings from dancing are usually low because employment is irregular. Dancers often supplement their income by working as guest artists with other dance companies, teaching dance, or taking jobs unrelated to the field.

Earnings of dancers at some of the largest companies and in commercial settings are governed by union contracts. Some dancers in major opera ballet, classical ballet, and modern dance corps belong to the American Guild of Musical Artists, Inc. of the AFL-CIO; those who appear on live or videotaped television programs belong to the American Federation of Television and Radio Artists; those who perform in films and on television belong to the Screen Actors Guild; and those in musical theater are members of the Actors' Equity Association. The unions and producers sign basic agreements specifying minimum salary rates, hours of work, benefits, and other conditions of employment. However, the contract each dancer signs with the producer of the show may be more favorable than the basic agreement.

Most salaried dancers and choreographers covered by union contracts receive some paid sick leave and various health and pension benefits, including extended sick pay and family-leave benefits provided by their unions. Employers contribute toward these benefits. Dancers and choreographers not covered by union contracts usually do not enjoy such benefits.

VISUAL ARTS

—ᵐ—

Graphic Designers

Nature of the Work

Graphic designers—or *graphic artists*—plan, analyze, and create visual solutions to communications problems. They find the most effective way to get messages across in print and electronic media using color, type, illustration, photography, animation, and various print and layout techniques. Graphic designers develop the overall layout and production design of magazines, newspapers, journals, corporate reports, and other publications. They also produce promotional displays, packaging, and marketing brochures for products and services, design distinctive logos for products and businesses, and develop signs and signage systems—called environmental graphics—for business and government. An increasing number of graphic designers also develop material for Internet Web pages, interactive media, and multimedia projects. Graphic designers also may produce the credits that appear before and after television programs and movies.

The first step in developing a new design is to determine the needs of the client, the message the design should portray, and its appeal to customers or users. Graphic designers consider cognitive, cultural, physical, and social factors in planning and executing designs for the target audience. Designers gather relevant information by meeting with clients, creative or art directors, and by performing their own research. Identifying the needs of consumers is becoming increasingly important for graphic designers as they continue to develop corporate communication strategies in addition to creating designs and layouts.

Significant Points

❖ Employment is expected to grow about as fast as the average, with many new jobs associated with interactive media.

❖ A bachelor's degree in graphic design is usually required.

❖ Jobseekers are expected to face keen competition; individuals with Web site design and animation experience will have the best opportunities.

Graphic designers prepare sketches or layouts—by hand or with the aid of a computer—to illustrate their vision for the design. They select colors, sound, artwork, photography, animation, style of type, and other visual elements for the design. Designers also select the size and arrangement of the different elements on the page or screen. They may create graphs and charts from data for use in publications, and they often consult with copywriters on any text that accompanies the design. Designers then present the completed design to their clients or art or creative director for approval. In printing and publishing firms, graphic designers also may assist the printers by selecting the type of paper and ink for the publication and reviewing the mock-up design for errors before final publication.

Graphic designers use specialized computer software packages to help them create layouts and design elements and to program animated graphics.

Graphic designers sometimes supervise assistants who follow instructions to complete parts of the design process. Designers who run their own businesses also may devote a considerable time to developing new business contacts, choosing equipment, and performing administrative tasks, such as reviewing catalogues and ordering samples. The need for up-to-date computer and communications equipment is an ongoing consideration for graphic designers.

Work environment. Working conditions and places of employment vary. Graphic designers employed by large advertising, publishing, or design firms generally work regular hours in well-lighted and comfortable settings. Designers in smaller design consulting firms and those who freelance generally work on a contract, or job, basis. They frequently adjust their workday to suit their clients' schedules and deadlines. Consultants and self-employed designers tend to work longer hours and in smaller, more congested, environments.

Designers may work in their own offices or studios or in clients' offices. Designers who are paid by the assignment are under pressure to please existing clients and to find new ones to maintain a steady income. All designers sometimes face frustration when their designs are rejected or when their work is not as creative as they wish. Graphic designers may work evenings or weekends to meet production schedules, especially in the printing and publishing industries where deadlines are shorter and more frequent.

Training, Other Qualifications, and Advancement

A bachelor's degree in graphic design is usually required. Creativity, communication, and problem-solving skills are important, as are a familiarity with computer graphics and design software.

Education and training. A bachelor's degree in graphic design is usually required for most entry-level and advanced graphic design positions. Bachelor's degree programs in fine arts or graphic design are offered at many colleges, universities, and private design schools. Most curriculums include studio art, principles of design, computerized design, commercial graphics production, printing techniques, and Web site design. In addition to design courses, a liberal arts education that includes courses in art history, writing, psychology, sociology, foreign languages and cultural studies, marketing, and business are useful in helping designers work effectively.

Associate degrees and certificates in graphic design also are available from 2-year and 3-year professional schools, and graduates of these programs normally qualify as assistants to graphic designers or for positions requiring technical skills only. Creative individuals who wish to pursue a career in graphic design—and who already possess a bachelor's degree in another field—can complete a 2-year or 3-year program in graphic design to learn the technical requirements.

The National Association of Schools of Art and Design accredits about 300 postsecondary institutions with programs in art and design. Most of these schools award a degree in graphic design. Many schools do not allow formal entry into a bachelor's degree program until a student has successfully finished a year of basic art and design courses, which can be completed in high school. Applicants may be required to submit sketches and other examples of their artistic ability.

Graphic designers must keep up with new and updated computer graphics and design software, either on their own or through formal software training programs.

Other qualifications. In addition to postsecondary training in graphic design, creativity, communication, and problem-solving skills are crucial. Graphic designers must be creative and able to communicate their ideas visually, verbally, and in writing. They also must have an eye for details. Designers show employers these traits by putting together a portfolio—a collection of examples of a person's best work. A good portfolio often is the deciding factor in getting a job.

Because consumer tastes can change fairly quickly, designers also need to be well read, open to new ideas and influences, and quick to react to changing trends. The abilities to work independently and under pressure are equally important traits. People in this field need self-discipline to start projects on their own, to budget their time, and to meet deadlines and production schedules. Good business sense and sales ability also are important, especially for those who freelance or run their own firms.

Advancement. Beginning graphic designers usually need 1 to 3 years of working experience before they can advance to higher positions. Experienced graphic designers in large firms may advance to chief designer, art or creative director, or other supervisory positions. Some designers leave the occupation to become teachers in design schools or in colleges and universities. Many faculty members continue to consult privately or operate small design studios to complement their classroom activities. Some experienced designers open their own firms or choose to specialize in one area of graphic design.

Employment

Graphic designers held about 286,100 jobs in 2008. Most graphic designers worked in specialized design services; advertising and related services; printing and related support activities; or newspaper, periodical, book, and directory publishers. A small number of designers produced computer graphics for computer systems design firms.

Some designers do freelance work—full time or part time—in addition to holding a salaried job in design or in another occupation.

Job Outlook

Employment is expected grow about as fast as average. Keen competition for jobs is expected; individuals with Web site design and animation experience will have the best opportunities.

Employment change. Employment of graphic designers is expected to grow 13 percent, as fast as the average for all occupations from 2008 to 2018, as demand for graphic design continues to increase from advertisers and computer design firms.

Moreover, graphic designers with Web site design and animation experience will especially be needed as demand increases for design projects for interactive media—Web sites, mobile phones, and other technology. Demand for graphic designers also will increase as advertising firms create print and Web marketing and promotional materials for a growing number of products and services. Growth in Internet advertising, in particular, is expected to increase the number of designers. However, growth may be tempered by reduced demand in the print publishing, where many graphic designers are employed.

Job prospects. Graphic designers are expected to face keen competition for available positions. Many talented individuals are attracted to careers as graphic designers. Individuals with Web site design and animation experience will have the best opportunities.

Graphic designers with a broad liberal arts education and experience in marketing and business management will be best suited for positions developing communication strategies.

Earnings

Median annual wages for graphic designers were $42,400 in May 2008. The middle 50 percent earned between $32,600 and $56,620. The lowest 10 percent earned less than $26,110, and the highest 10 percent earned more than $74,660.

According to the American Institute of Graphic Arts, median annual cash compensation for entry-level designers was $35,000 in 2008. Staff-level graphic designers earned a median of $45,000. Senior designers, who may supervise junior staff or have some decision-making authority that reflects their knowledge of graphic design, earned a median of $60,000. Solo designers who freelanced or worked under contract to another company reported median earnings of $57,000. Design directors, the creative heads of design firms or in-house corporate design departments, earned $95,000. Graphic designers with ownership or partnership interests in a firm or who were principals of the firm in some other capacity earned $95,000.

VISUAL ARTS

—ᴍ—

Artists and Related Workers

Nature of the Work

Artists create art to communicate ideas, thoughts, or feelings. They use a variety of methods—painting, sculpting, or illustration—and an assortment of materials, including oils, watercolors, acrylics, pastels, pencils, pen and ink, plaster, clay, and computers. Artists' works may be realistic, stylized, or abstract and may depict objects, people, nature, or events.

Artists generally fall into one of four categories. *Art directors* formulate design concepts and presentation approaches for visual communications. *Craft artists* create or reproduce handmade objects for sale or exhibition. *Fine artists, including painters, sculptors, and illustrators*, create original artwork, using a variety of media and techniques. *Multimedia artists and animators* create special effects, animation, or other visual images on film, on video, or with computers or other electronic media.

Art directors develop design concepts and review material that is to appear in periodicals, newspapers, and other printed or digital media. They control the overall visual direction of a project in fields such as advertising and publishing. They decide how best to present a concept visually, so that it is organized, eye catching, and appealing. Art directors decide which photographs or artwork to use and

---

Significant Points

❖ About 60 percent of artists and related workers are self-employed.

❖ Keen competition is expected for both salaried jobs and freelance work because the arts attract many talented people with creative ability.

❖ Artists usually develop their skills through a bachelor's degree program or other postsecondary training in art or design.

❖ Earnings for self-employed artists vary widely; some well-established artists earn more than salaried artists, while others find it difficult to rely solely on income earned from selling art.

oversee the design, layout, and production of material to be produced. They may direct workers engaged in artwork, design, layout, and copywriting.

Craft artists make a wide variety of objects, mostly by hand, that are sold in their own studios, in retail outlets, or at arts-and-crafts shows. Some craft artists display their works in galleries and museums. Craft artists work with many different materials, including ceramics, glass, textiles, wood, metal, and paper, to create unique pieces of art such as pottery, stained glass, quilts, tapestries, lace, candles, and clothing. Many craft artists also use fine-art techniques—for example, painting, sketching, and printing—to add finishing touches to their art.

Fine artists typically display their work in museums, commercial art galleries, corporate collections, and private homes. Some of their artwork may be commissioned (done on request from clients), but most is sold by the artist or through private art galleries or dealers. The gallery and the artist predetermine how much each will earn from the sale. Only the most successful fine artists are able to support themselves solely through the sale of their works. Most fine artists have at least one other job to support their art careers. Some work in museums or art galleries as fine-arts directors or as curators, planning and setting up art exhibits. A few artists work as art critics for newspapers or magazines or as consultants to foundations or institutional collectors. Other artists teach art classes or conduct workshops in schools or in their own studios. Some artists also hold full-time or part-time jobs unrelated to art and pursue fine art as a hobby or second career.

Usually, fine artists specialize in one or two art forms, such as painting, illustrating, sketching, sculpting, printmaking, and restoring. Painters, illustrators, cartoonists, and sketch artists work with two-dimensional art forms, using shading, perspective, and color to produce realistic scenes or abstractions.

Illustrators usually create pictures for books, magazines, and other publications and for commercial products such as textiles, wrapping paper, stationery, greeting cards, and calendars. Increasingly, illustrators are working in digital format—for example, creating scenery or objects for a video game. This has created new opportunities for illustrators to work with animators and in broadcast media.

Medical and scientific illustrators combine drawing skills with knowledge of biology or other sciences. Medical illustrators work digitally or traditionally to create images of human anatomy and surgical procedures as well as three-dimensional models and animations. Scientific illustrators draw animal and plant life, atomic and molecular structures, and geologic and planetary formations. These illustrations are used in medical and scientific publications and in audiovisual presentations for teaching purposes. Illustrators also work for lawyers, producing exhibits for court cases.

Cartoonists draw political, advertising, social, and sports cartoons. Some cartoonists work with others who create the idea or story and write captions. Some cartoonists write captions themselves. Most cartoonists have comic, critical, or dramatic talents in addition to drawing skills.

Sketch artists create likenesses of subjects with pencil, charcoal, or pastels. Sketches are used by law enforcement agencies to assist in identifying suspects, by the news media to depict courtroom scenes, and by individual patrons for their own enjoyment.

Sculptors design three-dimensional artworks, either by molding and joining materials such as clay, glass, wire, plastic, fabric, or metal, or by cutting and carving forms from a block of plaster, wood, or stone. Some sculptors combine various materials to create mixed-media installations. Some incorporate light, sound, and motion into their works.

Printmakers create printed images from designs cut or etched into wood, stone, or metal. After creating the design, the artist uses a printing press to roll the image onto paper or fabric. Some make prints by pressing the inked surface onto paper by hand or by graphically encoding and processing data, using a computer. The digitized images can then be printed onto paper.

Painting restorers preserve and restore damaged and faded paintings. They apply solvents and cleaning agents to clean the surfaces of the paintings, they reconstruct or retouch damaged areas, and they apply preservatives to protect the paintings. Restoration is highly detailed work and usually is reserved for experts in the field.

Multimedia artists and animators work primarily in motion picture and video industries, advertising, and computer systems design services. They draw by hand and use computers to create the series of pictures that form the animated images or special effects seen in movies, television programs, and computer games. Some draw storyboards for television commercials, movies, and animated features. Storyboards present television commercials in a series of scenes similar to a comic strip and allow an advertising agency to evaluate commercials proposed by advertising companies. Storyboards also serve as guides to placing actors and cameras on the television or motion picture set and to other production details. Many multimedia artists model objects in three dimensions by computer and work with programmers to make the images move.

Work environment. Many artists work in fine art or commercial art studios located in office buildings, warehouses, or lofts. Others work in private studios in their homes. Some fine artists share studio space, where they also may exhibit their work. Studio surroundings usually are well lighted and ventilated; however, fine artists may be exposed to fumes from glue, paint, ink, and other materials and to dust or other residue from filings, splattered paint, or spilled cleaners and other fluids. Artists who sit at drafting tables or who use computers for extended periods may experience back pain, eyestrain, or fatigue.

Artists employed by publishing companies, advertising agencies, and design firms generally work a standard workweek. During busy periods, they may work overtime to meet deadlines. Self-employed artists can set their own hours. They may spend much time and effort selling their artwork to potential customers or clients and building a reputation.

Training, Other Qualifications, and Advancement

Art directors usually have years of work experience and generally need at least a bachelor's degree. Because of the level of technical expertise demanded, multimedia artists and animators also need a bachelor's degree. Although formal schooling is not strictly required for craft and fine artists, it is very difficult to become skilled enough to make a living without some training.

Education and training. Many colleges and universities offer programs leading to a bachelor's or master's degree in fine arts. Courses usually include core subjects such as English, social science, and natural science, in addition to art history and studio art. Independent schools of art and design also offer postsecondary studio training in the craft, fine, and multimedia arts leading to certificates in the specialties or to an associate or bachelor's degree in fine arts. Typically, these programs focus more intensively on studio work than do the academic programs in a university setting. In 2009 the National Association of Schools of Art and Design accredited approximately 300 postsecondary institutions with programs in art and design; most of these schools award a degree in art.

Art directors usually begin as entry-level artists or designers in advertising, publishing, design, or motion picture production firms. An artist is promoted to art director after having demonstrated artistic and leadership abilities. Depending on the scope of their responsibilities, some art directors may pursue a degree in art administration or management, which teaches business skills such as project management and finance.

Many educational programs in art also provide training in computer techniques. Computers are used widely in the visual arts, and knowledge and training in computer graphics and other visual display software are critical elements of many jobs in these fields.

Medical illustrators must have both a demonstrated artistic ability and a detailed knowledge of living organisms, surgical and medical procedures, and human and animal anatomy. A bachelor's degree combining art and premedical courses usually is required. However, most medical illustrators also choose to pursue a master's degree in medical illustration. This degree is offered in four accredited schools in the United States.

Those who want to teach fine arts at public elementary or secondary schools usually must have a teaching certificate in addition to a bachelor's degree. An advanced degree in fine arts or arts administration is usually necessary for management or administrative positions in government or in foundations or for teaching in colleges and universities.

Other qualifications. Evidence of appropriate talent and skill, displayed in an artist's portfolio, is an important factor used by art directors, clients, and others in deciding whether to hire an individual or contract for his or her work. A portfolio is a collection of samples of the artist's best work. Assembling a successful portfolio requires skills usually developed through postsecondary training in art or visual communications. Internships also provide excellent opportunities for artists to develop and enhance their portfolios.

Advancement. Artists hired by firms often start with relatively routine work. While doing this work, however, they may observe other artists and practice their own skills.

Craft and fine artists advance professionally as their work circulates and as they establish a reputation for a particular style. Many of the most successful artists continually develop new ideas, and their work often evolves over time.

Many artists do freelance work while continuing to hold a full-time job until they are established. Others freelance part time while still in school to develop experience and to build a portfolio of published work.

Freelance artists try to develop a set of clients who regularly contract for work. Some freelance artists are widely recognized for their skill in specialties such as cartooning or children's book illustration. These artists may earn high incomes and can choose the type of work they do.

Employment

Artists held about 221,900 jobs in 2008. About 60 percent were self-employed.

Of the artists who were not self-employed, many worked for advertising and related services; newspaper, periodical, book, and software publishers; motion picture and video industries; specialized design services; and computer systems design and related services. Some self-employed artists offered their services to advertising agencies, design firms, publishing houses, and other businesses.

Job Outlook

Employment is projected to grow about as fast as the average. Competition for jobs is expected to be keen for both salaried and freelance jobs in all specialties because the number of people with creative ability and an interest in this career is expected to continue to exceed the number of available openings. Despite the competition, employers and individual clients are always on the lookout for talented and creative artists.

Employment change. Employment of artists and related workers is expected to grow 12 percent through 2018, about as fast as the average for all occupations. An increasing reliance on artists to create digital or multimedia artwork will drive growth.

Art directors will see an increase in jobs in advertising due to demand for the overall vision they bring to a project. However, declining opportunities in publishing will hold down job growth. With many magazines moving to an online-only format, art directors are used less in this field.

Demand for illustrators who work on a computer will increase as media companies use more detailed images and backgrounds in their designs. However, illustrators and cartoonists who work in publishing may see job opportunities decline as newspapers continue to cut staffs. Many are instead opting to post their work on political Web sites and online publications. The small number of medical illustrators will also be in greater demand as medical research continues to grow.

Demand for multimedia artists and animators will increase as consumers continue to demand more realistic video games, movie and television special effects, and 3D animated movies. Additional job openings will arise from an increasing need for computer graphics in the growing number of mobile technologies. The demand for animators is also increasing in alternative areas such as scientific research and design services. Some lower priority animation has been offshored, negatively affecting employment of animators.

Job prospects. Competition for jobs as artists and related workers will be keen because there are more qualified candidates than available jobs. Employers in all industries should be able to choose from among the most qualified candidates.

Despite the competition, studios, galleries, and individual clients are always on the lookout for artists who display outstanding talent, creativity, and style. Among craft and fine artists, talented individuals who have developed a mastery of artistic techniques and skills will have the best job prospects. Multimedia artists and animators should have better job opportunities than other artists but still will experience competition. Despite an expanding number of opportunities, art directors should experience keen competition for the available openings. Craft and fine artists work mostly on a freelance or commission basis and may find it difficult to earn a living solely by selling their artwork. Only the most successful craft and fine artists receive major commissions for their work. Competition among artists for the privilege of being shown in galleries is expected to remain intense, as will competition for grants from sponsors such as private foundations, State and local arts councils, and the National Endowment for the Arts. Because of their reliance on grants, and because the demand for artwork is dependent on consumers having disposable income, many of these artists will find that their income fluctuates with the overall economy.

Earnings

Median annual wages of salaried art directors were $76,980 in May 2008. The middle 50 percent earned between $54,490 and $108,090. The lowest 10 percent earned less than $40,730, and the highest 10 percent earned more than $154,840. Median annual wages were $80,170 in advertising, public relations and related services.

Median annual wages of salaried craft artists were $29,080. The middle 50 percent earned between $20,730 and $39,120. The lowest 10 percent earned less than $16,290, and the highest 10 percent earned more than $54,550.

Median annual wages of salaried fine artists, including painters, sculptors, and illustrators, were $42,650. The middle 50 percent earned between $29,230 and $60,650.

The lowest 10 percent earned less than $20,780, and the highest 10 percent earned more than $83,410.

Median annual wages of salaried multimedia artists and animators were $56,330. The middle 50 percent earned between $41,710 and $77,010. The lowest 10 percent earned less than $31,570, and the highest 10 percent earned more than $100,390. Median annual wages were $65,600 in motion picture and video industries, and $52,530 in advertising and related services.

Earnings for self-employed artists vary widely. Some charge only a nominal fee while they gain experience and build a reputation for their work. Others, such as well-established freelance fine artists and illustrators, can earn more than salaried artists. Many, however, find it difficult to rely solely on income earned from selling paintings or other works of art. Like other self-employed workers, freelance artists must provide their own benefits.

VISUAL ARTS

—m—

Fashion Designers

Nature of the Work

Fashion designers help create the billions of dresses, suits, shoes, and other clothing and accessories purchased every year by consumers. Designers study fashion trends, sketch designs of clothing and accessories, select colors and fabrics, and oversee the final production of their designs. *Clothing designers* create and help produce men's, women's, and children's apparel, including casual wear, suits, sportswear, formalwear, outerwear, maternity, and intimate apparel. *Footwear designers* help create and produce different styles of shoes and boots. *Accessory designers* help create and produce items such as handbags, belts, scarves, hats, hosiery, and eyewear, which add the finishing touches to an outfit. Some fashion designers specialize in clothing, footwear, or accessory design, but others create designs in all three fashion categories.

Significant Points

❖ The highest numbers of fashion designers were employed in New York and California.

❖ Employers usually seek designers with a 2-year or 4-year degree who are knowledgeable about textiles, fabrics, ornamentation, and fashion trends.

❖ Keen competition for jobs is expected as many applicants are attracted to the creativity and glamour associated with the occupation.

The design process from initial design concept to final production takes between 18 and 24 months. The first step in creating a design is researching current fashion and making predictions of future trends. Some designers conduct their own research, while others rely on trend reports published by fashion industry trade groups. Trend reports indicate what styles, colors, and fabrics will be popular for a particular season in the future. Textile manufacturers use these trend reports to begin designing fabrics and patterns while fashion designers begin to sketch preliminary designs. Designers then visit manufacturers or trade shows to procure samples of fabrics and decide which fabrics to use with which designs.

Once designs and fabrics are chosen, a prototype of the article using cheaper materials is created and then tried on a model to see what adjustments to the design need to be made. This also helps designers to narrow their choices of designs to offer for sale. After the final adjustments and selections have been made, samples of the article using the actual materials are sewn and then marketed to clothing retailers. Many designs are shown at fashion and trade shows a few times a year. Retailers at the shows place orders for certain items, which are then manufactured and distributed to stores.

Computer-aided design (CAD) is increasingly being used in the fashion design industry. Although most designers initially sketch designs by hand, a growing number also translate these hand sketches to the computer. CAD allows designers to view designs of clothing on virtual models and in various colors and shapes, thus saving time by requiring fewer adjustments of prototypes and samples later.

Depending on the size of their design firm and their experience, fashion designers may have varying levels of involvement in different aspects of design and production. In large design firms, fashion designers often are the lead designers who are responsible for creating the designs, choosing the colors and fabrics, and overseeing technical designers who turn the designs into a final product. They are responsible for creating the prototypes and patterns and work with the manufacturers and suppliers during the production stages. Large design houses also employ their own patternmakers, tailors, and sewers who create the master patterns for the design and sew the prototypes and samples. Designers working in small firms, or those new to the job, usually perform most of the technical, patternmaking, and sewing tasks, in addition to designing the clothing.

Fashion designers working for apparel wholesalers or manufacturers create designs for the mass market. These designs are manufactured in various sizes and colors. A small number of high-fashion (*haute couture*) designers are self-employed and create custom designs for individual clients, usually at very high prices. Other high-fashion designers sell their designs in their own retail stores or cater to specialty stores or high-fashion department stores. These designers create a mixture of original garments and those that follow established fashion trends.

Some fashion designers specialize in costume design for performing arts, motion picture, and television productions. The work of costume designers is similar to other fashion designers. Costume designers, however, perform extensive research on the styles worn during the period in which the performance takes place, or they work with directors to select and create appropriate attire. They make sketches of designs, select fabric and other materials, and oversee the production of the costumes. They also must stay within the costume budget for the particular production item.

Work environment. Fashion designers employed by manufacturing establishments, wholesalers, or design firms generally work regular hours in well-lighted and comfortable settings. Designers who freelance generally work on a contract, or by the job. They frequently adjust their workday to suit their clients' schedules and deadlines, meeting with the clients during evenings or weekends when necessary. Freelance designers tend to work longer hours and in smaller, more congested, environments, and are under pressure to please clients and to find new ones in order to maintain a steady income. Regardless of their work setting, all fashion designers occasionally work long hours to meet production deadlines or prepare for fashion shows.

The global nature of the fashion business requires constant communication with suppliers, manufacturers, and customers all over the United States and the world. Most fashion designers travel several times a year to trade and fashion shows to learn about the latest fashion trends. Designers also may travel frequently to meet with fabric and materials suppliers and with manufacturers who produce the final apparel products.

Training, Other Qualifications, and Advancement

In fashion design, employers usually seek individuals with a 2-year or 4-year degree who are knowledgeable about textiles, fabrics, ornamentation, and fashion trends.

Education and training. Fashion designers typically need an associate or a bachelor's degree in fashion design. Some fashion designers also combine a fashion design degree with a business, marketing, or fashion merchandising degree, especially those who want to run their own business or retail store. Basic coursework includes color, textiles, sewing and tailoring, pattern making, fashion history, computer-aided design (CAD), and design of different types of clothing such as menswear or footwear. Coursework in human anatomy, mathematics, and psychology also is useful.

The National Association of Schools of Art and Design accredits approximately 300 postsecondary institutions with programs in art and design. Most of these schools award degrees in fashion design. Many schools do not allow formal entry into a program until a student has successfully completed basic art and design courses. Applicants usually have to submit sketches and other examples of their artistic ability.

Aspiring fashion designers can learn these necessary skills through internships with design or manufacturing firms. Some designers also gain valuable experience working in retail stores, as personal stylists, or as custom tailors. Such experience can help designers gain sales and marketing skills while learning what styles and fabrics look good on different people.

Designers also can gain exposure to potential employers by entering their designs in student or amateur contests. Because of the global nature of the fashion industry, experience in one of the international fashion centers, such as Milan or Paris, can be useful.

Other qualifications. Designers must have a strong sense of the esthetic—an eye for color and detail, a sense of balance and proportion, and an appreciation for beauty. Fashion designers also need excellent communication and problem-solving skills. Despite the advancement of computer-aided design, sketching ability remains an important advantage in fashion design. A good portfolio—a collection of a person's best work—often is the deciding factor in getting a job.

In addition to creativity, fashion designers also need to have sewing and patternmaking skills, even if they do not perform these tasks themselves. Designers need to be able to understand these skills so they can give proper instruction in how the garment should be constructed. Fashion designers also need strong sales and presentation skills to persuade clients to purchase their designs. Good teamwork and communication skills also are necessary because increasingly the business requires constant contact with suppliers, manufacturers, and buyers around the world.

Advancement. Beginning fashion designers usually start out as pattern makers or sketching assistants for more experienced designers before advancing to higher level positions. Experienced designers may advance to chief designer, design department head, or another supervisory position. Some designers may start their own design company, or sell their designs in their own retail stores. A few of the most successful designers can work for high-fashion design houses that offer personalized design services to wealthy clients.

Employment

Fashion designers held about 22,700 jobs in 2008. About 31 percent of fashion designers worked for apparel, piece goods, and notions merchant wholesalers; and 13 percent worked for apparel manufacturers. Many others were self employed.

Employment of fashion designers tends to be concentrated in regional fashion centers. In 2008, the highest numbers of fashion designers were employed in New York and California.

Job Outlook

Little or no change in employment is projected. Competition for jobs is expected to be keen as many applicants are attracted to the creativity and glamour associated with the occupation.

Employment change. Employment of fashion designers is projected to grow by 1 percent between 2008 and 2018. Some new jobs will arise from an increasing population demanding more clothing, footwear, and accessories. Demand is increasing for stylish clothing that is affordable, especially among middle-income consumers which will increase the need for fashion designers among apparel wholesalers. However, job opportunities in cut and sew manufacturing will continue to decline as apparel is increasingly manufactured overseas. Employment of fashion designers in this industry will not decline as fast as other occupations because firms are more likely to keep design work in house.

Job prospects. Job competition is expected be keen as many applicants are attracted to the creativity and glamour associated with the occupation. The best job opportunities will be in design firms that design mass-market clothing sold in department stores and retail chain stores, such as apparel wholesale firms. Few employment opportunities are expected in design firms that cater to high-end department stores and specialty boutiques as demand for expensive, high-fashion design declines relative to other luxury goods and services.

Earnings

Median annual wages for salaried fashion designers were $61,160 in May 2008. The middle 50 percent earned between $42,150 and $87,120. The lowest 10 percent earned less than $32,150, and the highest 10 percent earned more than $124,780.

Earnings in fashion design can vary widely based on the employer and years of experience. Starting salaries in fashion design tend to be very low until designers are established in this occupation. Salaried fashion designers usually earn higher and more stable incomes than self-employed or freelance designers. However, a few of the most successful self-employed fashion designers may earn many times the salary of the highest paid salaried designers. Self-employed fashion designers must provide their own benefits and retirement.

MEDICINE

—ʍ—

Physicians & Surgeons

Nature of the Work

Physicians and surgeons diagnose illnesses and prescribe and administer treatment for people suffering from injury or disease. Physicians examine patients, obtain medical histories, and order, perform, and interpret diagnostic tests. They counsel patients on diet, hygiene, and preventive healthcare.

There are two types of physicians: *M.D.* (*Medical Doctor*) and *D.O.* (*Doctor of Osteopathic Medicine*). M.D.s also are known as *allopathic physicians*. While both M.D.s and D.O.s may use all accepted methods of treatment, including drugs and surgery, D.O.s place special emphasis on the body's musculoskeletal system, preventive medicine, and holistic patient care. D.O.s are most likely to be primary care specialists although they can be found in all specialties. About half of D.O.s practice general or family medicine, general internal medicine, or general pediatrics.

Significant Points

❖ Many physicians and surgeons work long, irregular hours.

❖ Acceptance to medical school is highly competitive.

❖ Formal education and training requirements—typically 4 years of undergraduate school, 4 years of medical school, and 3 to 8 years of internship and residency—are among the most demanding of any occupation, but earnings are among the highest.

❖ Job opportunities should be very good, particularly in rural and low-income areas.

Physicians work in one or more of several specialties, including, but not limited to, anesthesiology, family and general medicine, general internal medicine, general pediatrics, obstetrics and gynecology, psychiatry, and surgery.

Anesthesiologists focus on the care of surgical patients and pain relief. Like other physicians, they evaluate and treat patients and direct the efforts of their staffs. Through continual monitoring and assessment, these critical care specialists are responsible for maintenance of the patient's vital life functions—heart rate, body temperature, blood pressure, breathing—during surgery. They also work outside of the operating room, providing pain relief in the intensive care unit, during labor and delivery, and for those who suffer from chronic pain. Anesthesiologists confer with other physicians and surgeons about appropriate treatments and procedures before, during, and after operations.

Family and general physicians often provide the first point of contact for people seeking healthcare, by acting as the traditional family physician. They assess and treat a wide range of conditions, from sinus and respiratory infections to broken bones. Family and general physician typically have a base of regular, long-term patients. These doctors refer patients with more serious conditions to specialists or other healthcare facilities for more intensive care.

General internists diagnose and provide nonsurgical treatment for a wide range of problems that affect internal organ systems, such as the stomach, kidneys, liver, and digestive tract. Internists use a variety of diagnostic techniques to treat patients through medication or hospitalization. Like general practitioners, general internists commonly act as primary care specialists. They treat patients referred from other specialists and, in turn, they refer patients to other specialists when more complex care is required.

General pediatricians care for the health of infants, children, teenagers, and young adults. They specialize in the diagnosis and treatment of a variety of ailments specific to young people and track patients' growth to adulthood. Like most physicians, pediatricians work with different healthcare workers, such as nurses and other physicians, to assess and treat children with various ailments. Most of the work of pediatricians involves treating day-to-day illnesses—minor injuries, infectious diseases, and immunizations—that are common to children, much as a general practitioner treats adults. Some pediatricians specialize in pediatric surgery or serious medical conditions, such as autoimmune disorders or serious chronic ailments.

Obstetricians and gynecologists (OB/GYNs) specialize in women's health. They are responsible for women's general medical care, and they also provide care related to pregnancy and the reproductive system. Like general practitioners, OB/GYNs attempt to prevent, diagnose, and treat general health problems, but they focus on ailments specific to the female anatomy, such as cancers of the breast or cervix, urinary tract and pelvic disorders, and hormonal disorders. OB/GYNs also specialize in childbirth, which includes treating and counseling women throughout their pregnancy, from giving prenatal diagnoses to assisting with delivery and providing postpartum care.

Psychiatrists are the primary mental healthcaregivers. They assess and treat mental illnesses through a combination of psychotherapy, psychoanalysis, hospitalization, and medication. Psychotherapy involves regular discussions with patients about their problems;

the psychiatrist helps them find solutions through changes in their behavioral patterns, the exploration of their past experiences, or group and family therapy sessions. Psychoanalysis involves long-term psychotherapy and counseling for patients. In many cases, medications are administered to correct chemical imbalances that cause emotional problems.

Surgeons specialize in the treatment of injury, disease, and deformity through operations. Using a variety of instruments, and with patients under anesthesia, a surgeon corrects physical deformities, repairs bone and tissue after injuries, or performs preventive surgeries on patients with debilitating diseases or disorders. Although a large number perform general surgery, many surgeons choose to specialize in a specific area. One of the most prevalent specialties is orthopedic surgery: the treatment of the musculoskeletal system. Others include neurological surgery (treatment of the brain and nervous system), cardiovascular surgery, otolaryngology (treatment of the ear, nose, and throat), and plastic or reconstructive surgery. Like other physicians, surgeons also examine patients, perform and interpret diagnostic tests, and counsel patients on preventive healthcare.

Other physicians and surgeons work in a number of other medical and surgical specialists, including allergists, cardiologists, dermatologists, emergency physicians, gastroenterologists, ophthalmologists, pathologists, and radiologists.

Work environment. Many physicians—primarily general and family practitioners, general internists, pediatricians, OB/GYNs, and psychiatrists—work in small private offices or clinics, often assisted by a small staff of nurses and other administrative personnel. Increasingly, physicians are practicing in groups or healthcare organizations that provide backup coverage and allow for more time off. Physicians in a group practice or healthcare organization often work as part of a team that coordinates care for a number of patients; they are less independent than the solo practitioners of the past. Surgeons and anesthesiologists usually work in well-lighted, sterile environments while performing surgery and often stand for long periods. Most work in hospitals or in surgical outpatient centers.

Many physicians and surgeons work long, irregular hours. In 2008, 43 percent of all physicians and surgeons worked 50 or more hours a week. Nine percent of all physicians and surgeons worked part-time. Physicians and surgeons travel between office and hospital to care for their patients. While on call, a physician will deal with many patients' concerns over the phone and make emergency visits to hospitals or nursing homes.

Training, Other Qualifications, and Advancement

The common path to practicing as a physician requires 8 years of education beyond high school and 3 to 8 additional years of internship and residency. All States, the District of Columbia, and U.S. territories license physicians.

Education and training. Formal education and training requirements for physicians are among the most demanding of any occupation—4 years of undergraduate school, 4 years of medical school, and 3 to 8 years of internship and residency, depending on the specialty selected. A few medical schools offer combined undergraduate and medical school programs that last 6 or 7 years rather than the customary 8 years.

Premedical students must complete undergraduate work in physics, biology, mathematics, English, and inorganic and organic chemistry. Students also take courses in the humanities and the social sciences. Some students volunteer at local hospitals or clinics to gain practical experience in the health professions.

The minimum educational requirement for entry into medical school is 3 years of college; most applicants, however, have at least a bachelor's degree, and many have advanced degrees. In 2008, there were 129 medical schools accredited by the Liaison Committee on Medical Education (LCME). The LCME is the national accrediting body for M.D. medical education programs. The American Osteopathic Association accredits schools that award a D.O. degree; there were 25 schools accredited in 31 locations in 2008.

Acceptance to medical school is highly competitive. Most applicants must submit transcripts, scores from the Medical College Admission Test, and letters of recommendation. Schools also consider an applicant's character, personality, leadership qualities, and participation in extracurricular activities. Most schools require an interview with members of the admissions committee.

Students spend most of the first 2 years of medical school in laboratories and classrooms, taking courses such as anatomy, biochemistry, physiology, pharmacology, psychology, microbiology, pathology, medical ethics, and laws governing medicine. They also learn to take medical histories, examine patients, and diagnose illnesses. During their last 2 years, students work with patients under the supervision of experienced physicians in hospitals and clinics, learning acute, chronic, preventive, and rehabilitative care. Through rotations in internal medicine, family practice, obstetrics and gynecology, pediatrics, psychiatry, and surgery, they gain experience in the diagnosis and treatment of illness.

Following medical school, almost all M.D.s enter a residency—graduate medical education in a specialty that takes the form of paid on-the-job training, usually in a hospital. Most D.O.s serve a 12-month rotating internship after graduation and before entering a residency, which may last 2 to 6 years.

A physician's training is costly. According to the Association of American Medical Colleges, in 2007 85 percent of public medical school graduates and 86 percent of private medical school graduates were in debt for educational expenses.

Licensure and certification. To practice medicine as a physician, all States, the District of Columbia, and U.S. territories require licensing. All physicians and surgeons practicing in the United States must pass the United States Medical Licensing Examination (USMLE) or, for osteopathic physicians, the Comprehensive Osteopathic Medical Licensing Exam (COMLEX). To be eligible to take the USMLE or COMLEX, physicians must graduate from an accredited medical school. Although physicians licensed in one State usually can get a license to practice in another without further examination, some States limit reciprocity. Graduates of foreign medical schools generally can qualify for licensure after passing an examination and completing a U.S. residency. For specific information on licensing in a given State, contact that State's medical board.

M.D.s and D.O.s seeking board certification in a specialty may spend up to 7 years in residency training, depending on the specialty. A final examination immediately after residency or after 1 or 2 years of practice is also necessary for certification by a member board of the American Board of Medical Specialists (ABMS) or the American Osteopathic Association (AOA). The ABMS represents 24 boards related to medical specialties ranging from allergy and immunology to urology. The AOA has approved 18 specialty boards, ranging from anesthesiology to surgery. For certification in a subspecialty, physicians usually need another 1 to 2 years of residency.

Other qualifications. People who wish to become physicians must have a desire to serve patients, be self-motivated, and be able to survive the pressures and long hours of medical education and practice. Physicians also must have a good bedside manner, emotional stability, and the ability to make decisions in emergencies. Prospective physicians must be willing to study throughout their career to keep up with medical advances.

Advancement. Some physicians and surgeons advance by gaining expertise in specialties and subspecialties and by developing a reputation for excellence among their peers and patients. Physicians and surgeons may also start their own practice or join a group practice. Others teach residents and other new doctors, and some advance to supervisory and managerial roles in hospitals, clinics, and other settings.

Employment

Physicians and surgeons held about 661,400 jobs in 2008; approximately 12 percent were self-employed. About 53 percent of wage–and-salary physicians and surgeons worked in offices of physicians, and 19 percent were employed by hospitals. Others practiced in Federal, State, and local governments, educational services, and outpatient care centers.

According to 2007 data from the American Medical Association (AMA), 32 percent of physicians in patient care were in primary care, but not in a subspecialty of primary care.

A growing number of physicians are partners or wage-and-salary employees of group practices. Organized as clinics or as associations of physicians, medical groups can more easily afford expensive medical equipment, share support staff, and benefit from other business advantages.

According to the AMA, the New England and Middle Atlantic States have the highest ratios of physicians to population; the South Central and Mountain States have the lowest. Physicians tend to locate in urban areas, close to hospitals and education centers. AMA data showed that in 2007, about 75 percent of physicians in patient care were located in metropolitan areas while the remaining 25 percent were located in rural areas.

Job Outlook

Employment is expected to grow much faster than the average for all occupations. Job opportunities should be very good, particularly in rural and low-income areas.

Employment change. Employment of physicians and surgeons is projected to grow 22 percent from 2008 to 2018, much faster than the average for all occupations. Job growth will occur because of continued expansion of healthcare-related industries. The growing and aging population will drive overall growth in the demand for physician services, as consumers continue to demand high levels of care using the latest technologies, diagnostic tests, and therapies. Many medical schools are increasing their enrollments based on perceived new demand for physicians.

Despite growing demand for physicians and surgeons, some factors will temper growth. For example, new technologies allow physicians to be more productive. This means physicians can diagnose and treat more patients in the same amount of time. The rising cost of healthcare can dramatically affect demand for physicians' services. Physician assistants and nurse practitioners, who can perform many of the routine duties of physicians at a fraction of the cost, may be increasingly used. Furthermore, demand for physicians' services is highly sensitive to changes in healthcare reimbursement policies. If changes to health coverage result in higher out-of-pocket costs for consumers, they may demand fewer physician services.

Job prospects. Opportunities for individuals interested in becoming physicians and surgeons are expected to be very good. In addition to job openings from employment growth, openings will result from the need to replace the relatively high number of physicians and surgeons expected to retire over the 2008-18 decade.

Job prospects should be particularly good for physicians willing to practice in rural and low-income areas because these medically underserved areas typically have difficulty attracting these workers. Job prospects will also be especially good for physicians in specialties that afflict the rapidly growing elderly population. Examples of such specialties are cardiology and radiology because the risks for heart disease and cancer increase as people age.

Earnings

Earnings of physicians and surgeons are among the highest of any occupation. According to the Medical Group Management Association's Physician Compensation and Production Survey, median total compensation for physicians varied by their type of practice. In 2008, physicians practicing primary care had total median annual compensation of $186,044, and physicians practicing in medical specialties earned total median annual compensation of $339,738.

Self-employed physicians—those who own or are part owners of their medical practice—generally have higher median incomes than salaried physicians. Earnings vary according to number of years in practice, geographic region, hours worked, skill, personality, and professional reputation. Self-employed physicians and surgeons must provide for their own health insurance and retirement.

MEDICINE

—m—

Dentists

Nature of the Work

Dentists diagnose and treat problems with teeth and tissues in the mouth, along with giving advice and administering care to help prevent future problems. They provide instruction on diet, brushing, flossing, the use of fluorides, and other aspects of dental care. They remove tooth decay, fill cavities, examine x rays, place protective plastic sealants on children's teeth, straighten teeth, and repair fractured teeth. They also perform corrective surgery on gums and supporting bones to treat gum diseases. Dentists extract teeth and make models and measurements for dentures to replace missing teeth. They also administer anesthetics and write prescriptions for antibiotics and other medications.

Dentists use a variety of equipment, including x-ray machines, drills, mouth mirrors, probes, forceps, brushes, and scalpels. Lasers, digital scanners, and other computer technologies also may be used. Dentists wear masks, gloves, and safety glasses to protect themselves and their patients from infectious diseases.

Dentists in private practice oversee a variety of administrative tasks, including bookkeeping and the buying of equipment and supplies. They may employ and supervise dental hygienists, dental assistants, dental laboratory technicians, and receptionists.

Most dentists are general practitioners, handling a variety of dental needs. Other dentists

Significant Points

❖ About 3 out of 4 dentists are solo practitioners.

❖ Dentists must graduate from an accredited dental school and pass written and practical examinations; competition for admission to dental school is keen.

❖ Faster than average employment growth is projected.

❖ Job prospects should be good, reflecting the need to replace the large number of dentists expected to retire.

practice in any of nine specialty areas. *Orthodontists,* the largest group of specialists, straighten teeth by applying pressure to the teeth with braces or other appliances. The next largest group, *oral* and *maxillofacial surgeons*, operates on the mouth, jaws, teeth, gums, neck, and head. The remainder may specialize as *pediatric dentists* (focusing on dentistry for children and special-needs patients); *periodontists* (treating gums and bone supporting the teeth); *prosthodontists* (replacing missing teeth with permanent fixtures, such as crowns and bridges, or with removable fixtures such as dentures); *endodontists* (performing root-canal therapy); *oral pathologists* (diagnosing oral diseases); *oral* and *maxillofacial radiologists* (diagnosing diseases in the head and neck through the use of imaging technologies); or *dental public health specialists* (promoting good dental health and preventing dental diseases within the community).

Work environment. Most dentists are solo practitioners, meaning that they own their own businesses and work alone or with a small staff. Some dentists have partners, and a few work for other dentists as associate dentists.

Most dentists work 4 or 5 days a week. Some work evenings and weekends to meet their patients' needs. The number of hours worked varies greatly among dentists. Most full-time dentists work between 35 and 40 hours a week. However, others, especially those who are trying to establish a new practice, work more. Also, experienced dentists often work fewer hours. It is common for dentists to continue in part-time practice well beyond the usual retirement age.

Dentists usually work in the safety of an office environment. However, work-related injuries can occur, such as those resulting from the use of hand-held tools when performing dental work on patients.

Training, Other Qualifications, and Advancement

All 50 States and the District of Columbia require dentists to be licensed. To qualify for a license in most States, candidates must graduate from an accredited dental school and pass written and practical examinations.

Education and training. In 2008, there were 57 dental schools in the United States accredited by the American Dental Association's (ADA's) Commission on Dental Accreditation. Dental schools require a minimum of 2 years of college-level predental education prior to admittance. Most dental students have at least a bachelor's degree before entering dental school, although a few applicants are accepted to dental school after 2 or 3 years of college and complete their bachelor's degree while attending dental school. According to the ADA, 85 percent of dental students had a bachelor's degree prior to beginning their dental program in the 2006-07 academic year.

High school and college students who want to become dentists should take courses in biology, chemistry, physics, health, and mathematics. College undergraduates planning on applying to dental school are required to take many science courses. Because of this, some choose a major in a science, such as biology or chemistry, whereas others take the required science coursework while pursuing a major in another subject.

All dental schools require applicants to take the Dental Admissions Test (DAT). When selecting students, schools consider scores earned on the DAT, applicants' grade point averages, and information gathered through recommendations and interviews. Competition for admission to dental school is keen.

Dental school usually lasts 4 academic years. Studies begin with classroom instruction and laboratory work in science, including anatomy, microbiology, biochemistry, and physiology. Beginning courses in clinical sciences, including laboratory techniques, are also completed. During the last 2 years, students treat patients, usually in dental clinics, under the supervision of licensed dentists. Most dental schools award the degree of Doctor of Dental Surgery (DDS). Others award an equivalent degree, Doctor of Dental Medicine (DMD).

Licensure. Licensing is required to practice as a dentist. In most States, licensure requires passing written and practical examinations in addition to having a degree from an accredited dental school. Candidates may fulfill the written part of the State licensing requirements by passing the National Board Dental Examinations. Individual States or regional testing agencies administer the written or practical examinations.

Individuals can be licensed to practice any of the 9 recognized specialties in all 50 States and the District of Columbia. Requirements include 2 to 4 years of postgraduate education and, in some cases, the completion of a special State examination. A postgraduate residency term also may be required, usually lasting up to 2 years. Most State licenses permit dentists to engage in both general and specialized practice.

Other qualifications. Dentistry requires diagnostic ability and manual skills. Dentists should have good visual memory; excellent judgment regarding space, shape, and color; a high degree of manual dexterity; and scientific ability. Good business sense, self-discipline, and good communication skills are helpful for success in private practice.

Advancement. Dentists and aspiring dentists who want to teach or conduct research full time usually spend an additional 2 to 5 years in advanced dental training, in programs operated by dental schools or hospitals. Many private practitioners also teach part time, including supervising students in dental school clinics.

Some dental school graduates work for established dentists as associates for 1 to 2 years to gain experience and save money to equip an office of their own. Most dental school graduates, however, purchase an established practice or open a new one immediately after graduation.

Employment

Dentists held about 141,900 jobs in 2008.

Approximately 15 percent of all dentists were specialists. About 28 percent of dentists were self-employed and not incorporated. Very few salaried dentists worked in hospitals and offices of physicians. Almost all dentists work in private practice. According to the American Dental Association, about 3 out of 4 dentists in private practice are solo proprietors, and almost 15 percent belonged to a partnership.

Job Outlook

Employment is projected to grow faster than the average. Job prospects should be good, reflecting the need to replace the large number of dentists expected to retire.

Employment change. Employment of dentists is projected to grow by 16 percent through 2018, which is faster than the average for all occupations. The demand for dental services is expected to continue to increase. The overall U.S. population is growing, and the elderly segment of the population is growing even faster; these phenomena will increase the demand for dental care. Many members of the baby-boom generation will need complicated dental work. In addition, elderly people are more likely to retain their teeth than were their predecessors, so they will require much more care than in the past. The younger generation will continue to need preventive checkups despite an overall increase in the dental health of the public over the last few decades. Recently, some private insurance providers have increased their dental coverage. If this trend continues, people with new or expanded dental insurance will be more likely to visit a dentist than in the past. Also, although they are currently a small proportion of dental expenditures, cosmetic dental services, such as providing teeth-whitening treatments, will become increasingly popular. This trend is expected to continue as new technologies allow these procedures to take less time and be much less invasive.

However, employment of dentists is not expected to keep pace with the increased demand for dental services. Productivity increases from new technology, as well as the tendency to assign more tasks to dental hygienists and assistants, will allow dentists to perform more work than they have in the past. As their practices expand, dentists are likely to hire more hygienists and dental assistants to handle routine services.

Dentists will increasingly provide care and instruction aimed at preventing the loss of teeth, rather than simply providing treatments such as fillings. Improvements in dental technology also will allow dentists to offer more effective and less painful treatment to their patients.

Job prospects. As an increasing number of dentists from the baby-boom generation reach retirement age, many of them will retire or work fewer hours and stop taking on new patients. Furthermore, the number of applicants to, and graduates from, dental schools has increased in recent years. Job prospects should be good, because younger dentists will be able to take over the work of older dentists who retire or cut back on hours, as well as provide dental services to accommodate the growing demand.

Demand for dental services tends to follow the business cycle, primarily because these services usually are paid for either by the patient or by private insurance companies. As a result, during slow times in the economy, demand for dental services can decrease; consequently, dentists may have difficulty finding employment, or if already in an established practice, they may work fewer hours because of reduced demand.

Earnings

Median annual wages of salaried general dentists were $142,870 in May 2008. Earnings vary according to number of years in practice, location, hours worked, and specialty. Self-employed dentists in private practice tend to earn more than salaried dentists.

Dentists who are salaried often receive benefits paid by their employer, with health insurance and malpractice insurance being among the most common. However, like other business owners, self-employed dentists must provide their own health insurance, life insurance, retirement plans, and other benefits.

MEDICINE

—ᵐ—

Registered Nurses

Nature of the Work

Registered nurses (*RNs*), regardless of specialty or work setting, treat patients, educate patients and the public about various medical conditions, and provide advice and emotional support to patients' family members. RNs record patients' medical histories and symptoms, help perform diagnostic tests and analyze results, operate medical machinery, administer treatment and medications, and help with patient follow-up and rehabilitation.

RNs teach patients and their families how to manage their illnesses or injuries, explaining post-treatment home care needs; diet, nutrition, and exercise programs; and self-administration of medication and physical therapy. Some RNs may work to promote general health by educating the public on warning signs and symptoms of disease. RNs also might run general health screening or immunization clinics, blood drives, and public seminars on various conditions.

When caring for patients, RNs establish a care plan or contribute to an existing plan. Plans may include numerous activities, such

Significant Points

❖ Registered nurses (RNs) constitute the largest healthcare occupation, with 2.6 million jobs.

❖ About 60 percent of RN jobs are in hospitals.

❖ The three typical educational paths to registered nursing are a bachelor's degree, an associate degree, and a diploma from an approved nursing program; advanced practice nurses—clinical nurse specialists, nurse anesthetists, nurse-midwives, and nurse practitioners—need a master's degree.

❖ Overall job opportunities are expected to be excellent, but may vary by employment and geographic setting; some employers report difficulty in attracting and retaining an adequate number of RNs.

as administering medication, including careful checking of dosages and avoiding interactions; starting, maintaining, and discontinuing intravenous (IV) lines for fluid, medication, blood, and blood products; administering therapies and treatments; observing the patient and recording those observations; and consulting with physicians and other healthcare clinicians. Some RNs provide direction to licensed practical nurses and nursing aides regarding patient care. RNs with advanced educational preparation and training may perform diagnostic and therapeutic procedures and may have prescriptive authority.

Specific work responsibilities will vary from one RN to the next. An RN's duties and title are often determined by their work setting or patient population served. RNs can specialize in one or more areas of patient care. There generally are four ways to specialize. RNs may work a particular setting or type of treatment, such as *perioperative nurses*, who work in operating rooms and assist surgeons. RNs may specialize in specific health conditions, as do *diabetes management nurses*, who assist patients to manage diabetes. Other RNs specialize in working with one or more organs or body system types, such as *dermatology nurses*, who work with patients who have skin disorders. RNs may also specialize with a well-defined population, such as *geriatric nurses*, who work with the elderly. Some RNs may combine specialties. For example, *pediatric oncology nurses* deal with children and adolescents who have cancer. The opportunities for specialization in registered nursing are extensive and are often determined on the job.

There are many options for RNs who specialize in a work setting or type of treatment. *Ambulatory care nurses* provide preventive care and treat patients with a variety of illnesses and injuries in physicians' offices or in clinics. Some ambulatory care nurses are involved in telehealth, providing care and advice through electronic communications media such as videoconferencing, the Internet, or by telephone. *Critical care nurses* provide care to patients with serious, complex, and acute illnesses or injuries that require very close monitoring and extensive medication protocols and therapies. Critical care nurses often work in critical or intensive care hospital units. *Emergency*, or *trauma, nurses* work in hospital or stand-alone emergency departments, providing initial assessments and care for patients with life-threatening conditions. Some emergency nurses may become qualified to serve as *transport nurses*, who provide medical care to patients who are transported by helicopter or airplane to the nearest medical facility. *Holistic nurses* provide care such as acupuncture, massage and aroma therapy, and biofeedback, which are meant to treat patients' mental and spiritual health in addition to their physical health. *Home healthcare nurses* provide at-home nursing care for patients, often as follow-up care after discharge from a hospital or from a rehabilitation, long-term care, or skilled nursing facility. *Hospice and palliative care nurses* provide care, most often in home or hospice settings, focused on maintaining quality of life for terminally ill patients. *Infusion nurses* administer medications, fluids, and blood to patients through injections into patients' veins. *Long- term care nurses* provide healthcare services on a recurring basis to patients with chronic physical or mental disorders, often in long-term care or skilled nursing facilities. *Medical-surgical nurses* provide health promotion and basic medical care to patients with various medical and surgical diagnoses. *Occupational health nurses* seek to prevent job-related injuries and illnesses, provide monitoring and emergency care services, and help employers implement health and safety standards. *Perianesthesia nurses* provide preoperative and postoperative care to patients undergoing anesthesia during surgery or other procedure. *Perioperative nurses* assist surgeons by selecting and handling instruments, controlling bleeding, and suturing incisions. Some of these nurses also can specialize in plastic and reconstructive surgery. *Psychiatric-mental health nurses* treat patients with personality and mood disorders. *Radiology nurses* provide care to patients undergoing diagnostic radiation procedures such as ultrasounds, magnetic resonance imaging, and radiation therapy for oncology diagnoses. *Rehabilitation nurses* care for patients with temporary and permanent disabilities. *Transplant nurses* care for both transplant recipients and living donors and monitor signs of organ rejection.

RNs specializing in a particular disease, ailment, or healthcare condition are employed in virtually all work settings, including physicians' offices, outpatient treatment facilities, home healthcare agencies, and hospitals. *Addictions nurses* care for patients seeking help with alcohol, drug, tobacco, and other addictions. *Intellectual and developmental disabilities nurses* provide care for patients with physical, mental, or behavioral disabilities; care may include help with feeding, controlling bodily functions, sitting or standing independently, and speaking or other communication. *Diabetes management nurses* help diabetics to manage their disease by teaching them proper nutrition and showing them how to test blood sugar levels and administer insulin injections. *Genetics nurses* provide early detection screenings, counseling, and treatment of patients with genetic disorders, including cystic fibrosis and Huntington's disease. *HIV/AIDS nurses* care for patients diagnosed with HIV and AIDS. *Oncology nurses* care for patients with various types of cancer and may assist in the administration of radiation and chemotherapies and follow-up monitoring. *Wound, ostomy, and continence nurses* treat patients with wounds caused by traumatic injury, ulcers, or arterial disease; provide postoperative care for patients with openings that allow for alternative methods of bodily waste elimination; and treat patients with urinary and fecal incontinence.

RNs specializing in treatment of a particular organ or body system usually are employed in hospital specialty or critical care units, specialty clinics, and outpatient care facilities. *Cardiovascular nurses* treat patients with coronary heart disease and those who have had heart surgery, providing services such as postoperative rehabilitation. *Dermatology nurses* treat patients with disorders of the skin, such as skin cancer and psoriasis. *Gastroenterology nurses* treat patients with digestive and intestinal disorders, including ulcers, acid reflux disease, and abdominal bleeding. Some nurses in this field also assist in specialized procedures such as endoscopies, which look inside the gastrointestinal tract using a tube equipped with a light and a camera that can capture images of diseased tissue. *Gynecology nurses* provide care to women with disorders of the reproductive system, including endometriosis, cancer, and sexually transmitted diseases. *Nephrology nurses* care for patients with kidney disease caused by diabetes, hypertension, or substance abuse. *Neuroscience nurses* care for patients with dysfunctions of the nervous system, including brain and spinal cord injuries and seizures. *Ophthalmic nurses* provide care to patients with disorders of the eyes, including blindness and glaucoma, and to patients undergoing eye surgery. *Orthopedic nurses* care for patients with muscular and skeletal problems, including arthritis, bone fractures, and muscular dystrophy. *Otorhinolaryngology nurses* care for patients with ear, nose, and throat disorders, such as cleft palates, allergies, and sinus disorders. *Respiratory nurses* provide care to patients with respiratory disorders such as asthma, tuberculosis, and cystic fibrosis. *Urology nurses* care for patients with disorders of the kidneys, urinary tract, and male reproductive organs, including infections, kidney and bladder stones, and cancers.

RNs who specialize by population provide preventive and acute care in all healthcare settings to the segment of the population in which they specialize, including newborns (neonatology), children and adolescents (pediatrics), adults, and the elderly (gerontology or geriatrics). RNs also may provide basic healthcare to patients outside of healthcare settings in such venues as including correctional facilities, schools, summer camps, and the military. Some RNs travel around the United States and throughout the world providing care to patients in areas with shortages of healthcare workers.

Most RNs work as staff nurses as members of a team providing critical healthcare. However, some RNs choose to become advanced practice nurses, who work independently or in collaboration with physicians, and may focus on the provision of primary care services. *Clinical nurse specialists* provide direct patient care and expert consultations in one of many nursing specialties, such as psychiatric-mental health. *Nurse anesthetists* provide anesthesia and related care before and after surgical, therapeutic, diagnostic and obstetrical procedures. They also provide pain management and emergency services, such as airway management. *Nurse-midwives* provide primary care to women, including gynecological exams, family planning advice, prenatal care, assistance in labor and delivery, and neonatal care. *Nurse practitioners* serve as primary and specialty care providers, providing a blend of nursing and healthcare services to patients and families. The most common specialty areas for nurse practitioners are family practice, adult practice, women's health, pediatrics, acute care, and geriatrics. However, there are a variety of other specialties that nurse practitioners can choose, including neonatology and mental health. Advanced practice nurses can prescribe medications in all States and in the District of Columbia.

Some nurses have jobs that require little or no direct patient care, but still require an active RN license. *Forensics nurses* participate in the scientific investigation and treatment of abuse victims, violence, criminal activity, and traumatic accident. *Infection control nurses* identify, track, and control infectious outbreaks in healthcare facilities and develop programs for outbreak prevention and response to biological terrorism. *Nurse educators* plan, develop, implement, and evaluate educational programs and curricula for the professional development of student nurses and RNs. *Nurse informaticists* manage and communicate nursing data and information to improve decision making by consumers, patients, nurses, and other healthcare providers. RNs also may work as healthcare consultants, public policy advisors, pharmaceutical and medical supply researchers and salespersons, and medical writers and editors.

Work environment. Most RNs work in well-lit, comfortable healthcare facilities. Home health and public health nurses travel to patients' homes, schools, community centers, and other sites. RNs may spend considerable time walking, bending, stretching, and standing. Patients in hospitals and nursing care facilities require 24-hour care; consequently, nurses in these institutions may work nights, weekends, and holidays. RNs also may be on call—available to work on short notice. Nurses who work in offices, schools, and other settings that do not provide 24-hour care are more likely to work regular business hours. About 20 percent of RNs worked part time in 2008.

RNs may be in close contact with individuals who have infectious diseases and with toxic, harmful, or potentially hazardous compounds, solutions, and medications. RNs must observe rigid, standardized guidelines to guard against disease and other dangers, such as those posed by radiation, accidental needle sticks, chemicals used to sterilize instruments, and anesthetics. In addition, they are vulnerable to back injury when moving patients.

Training, Other Qualifications, and Advancement

The three typical educational paths to registered nursing are a bachelor's degree, an associate degree, and a diploma from an approved nursing program. Nurses most commonly enter the occupation by completing an associate degree or bachelor's degree program. Individuals then must complete a national licensing examination in order to obtain a nursing license. Advanced practice nurses—clinical nurse specialists, nurse anesthetists, nurse-midwives, and nurse practitioners—need a master's degree.

Education and training. There are three typical educational paths to registered nursing—a bachelor's of science degree in nursing (BSN), an associate degree in nursing (ADN), and a diploma. BSN programs, offered by colleges and universities, take about 4 years to complete. ADN programs, offered by community and junior colleges, take about 2 to 3 years to complete. Diploma programs, administered in hospitals, last about 3 years. Generally, licensed graduates of any of the three types of educational programs qualify for entry-level positions as a staff nurse. There are hundreds of registered nursing programs that result in an ADN or BSN; however, there are relatively few diploma programs.

Individuals considering a career in nursing should carefully weigh the advantages and disadvantages of enrolling in each type of education program. Advancement opportunities may be more limited for ADN and diploma holders compared to RNs who obtain a BSN or higher. Individuals who complete a bachelor's degree receive more training in areas such as communication, leadership, and critical thinking, all of which are becoming more important as nursing practice becomes more complex. Additionally, bachelor's degree programs offer more clinical experience in nonhospital settings. A bachelor's or higher degree is often necessary for administrative positions, research, consulting, and teaching

Many RNs with an ADN or diploma later enter bachelor's degree programs to prepare for a broader scope of nursing practice. Often, they can find an entry-level position and then take advantage of tuition reimbursement benefits to work toward a BSN by completing an RN-to-BSN program. Accelerated master's degree in nursing (MSN) programs also are available. They typically take 3-4 years to complete full time and result in the award of both the BSN and MSN.

There are education programs available for people interested in switching to a career in nursing as well. Individuals who already hold a bachelor's degree in another field may enroll in an accelerated BSN program. Accelerated BSN programs last 12 to 18 months and provide the fastest route to a BSN for individuals who already hold a degree. MSN programs also are available for individuals who hold a bachelor's or higher degree in another field; master's degree programs usually last 2 years.

All nursing education programs include classroom instruction and supervised clinical experience in hospitals and other healthcare facilities. Students take courses in anatomy, physiology, microbiology, chemistry, nutrition, psychology and other behavioral sciences, and nursing. Coursework also includes the liberal arts for ADN and BSN students.

Supervised clinical experience is provided in hospital departments such as pediatrics, psychiatry, maternity, and surgery. A number of programs include clinical experience in nursing care facilities, public health departments, home health agencies, and ambulatory clinics.

Licensure and certification. In all States, the District of Columbia, and U.S. territories, students must graduate from an approved nursing program and pass a national licensing examination, known as the National Council Licensure Examination, or NCLEX-RN, in order to obtain a nursing license. Other eligibility requirements for licensure vary by State. Contact your State's board of nursing for details.

Other qualifications. Nurses should be caring, sympathetic, responsible, and detail oriented. They must be able to direct or supervise others, correctly assess patients' conditions, and determine when consultation is required. They need emotional stability to cope with human suffering, emergencies, and other stresses.

RNs should enjoy learning because continuing education credits are required by some States and/or employers at regular intervals. Career-long learning is a distinct reality for RNs.

Some nurses may become credentialed in specialties such as ambulatory care, gerontology, informatics, pediatrics, and many others. Credentialing for RNs is available from the American Nursing Credentialing Center, the National League for Nursing, and many others. Although credentialing is usually voluntary, it demonstrates adherence to a higher standard and some employers may require it.

Advancement. Most RNs begin as staff nurses in hospitals and, with experience and good performance, often move to other settings or are promoted to positions with more responsibility. In management, nurses can advance from assistant unit manager or head nurse to more senior-level administrative roles of assistant director, director, vice president, or chief of nursing. Increasingly, management-level nursing positions require a graduate or an advanced degree in nursing or health services administration. Administrative positions require leadership, communication and negotiation skills, and good judgment.

Some RNs choose to become advanced practice nurses, who work independently or in collaboration with physicians, and may focus on providing primary care services. There are four types of advanced practice nurses: clinical nurse specialists, nurse anesthetists, nurse-midwives, and nurse practitioners. Clinical nurse specialists provide direct patient care and expert consultations in one of many nursing specialties, such as psychiatric-mental health. Nurse anesthetists provide anesthesia and related care before and after surgical, therapeutic, diagnostic, and obstetrical procedures. They also provide pain management and emergency services, such as airway management. Nurse-midwives provide primary care to women, including gynecological exams, family planning advice, prenatal care, assistance in labor and delivery, and neonatal care. Nurse practitioners serve as primary and specialty care providers, providing a blend of nursing and healthcare services to patients and families.

All four types of advanced practice nurses require at least a master's degree. In addition, all States specifically define requirements for registered nurses in advanced practice roles. Advanced practice nurses may prescribe medicine, but the authority to prescribe varies by State. Contact your State's board of nursing for specific regulations regarding advanced practice nurses.

Some nurses move into the business side of healthcare. Their nursing expertise and experience on a healthcare team equip them to manage ambulatory, acute, home-based, and chronic care businesses. Employers—including hospitals, insurance companies, pharmaceutical manufacturers, and managed care organizations, among others—need RNs for health planning and development, marketing, consulting, policy development, and quality assurance. Other nurses work as college and university faculty or conduct research.

Employment

As the largest healthcare occupation, registered nurses held about 2.6 million jobs in 2008. Hospitals employed the majority of RNs, with 60 percent of such jobs. About 8 percent of jobs were in offices of physicians, 5 percent in home healthcare services, 5 percent in nursing care facilities, and 3 percent in employment services. The remainder worked mostly in government agencies, social assistance agencies, and educational services.

Job Outlook

Overall job opportunities for registered nurses are expected to be excellent, but may vary by employment and geographic setting. Some employers report difficulty in attracting and retaining an adequate number of RNs. Employment of RNs is expected to grow much faster than the average and, because the occupation is very large, 581,500 new jobs will result, among the largest number of new jobs for any occupation. Additionally, hundreds of thousands of job openings will result from the need to replace experienced nurses who leave the occupation.

Employment change. Employment of registered nurses is expected to grow by 22 percent from 2008 to 2018, much faster than the average for all occupations. Growth will be driven by technological advances in patient care, which permit a greater number of health problems to be treated, and by an increasing emphasis on preventive care. In addition, the number of older people, who are much more likely than younger people to need nursing care, is projected to grow rapidly.

However, employment of RNs will not grow at the same rate in every industry.

Employment is expected to grow more slowly in hospitals—healthcare's largest industry—than in most other healthcare industries. While the intensity of nursing care is likely to increase, requiring more nurses per patient, the number of inpatients (those who remain in the hospital for more than 24 hours) is not likely to grow by much. Patients are being discharged earlier, and more procedures are being done on an outpatient basis, both inside and outside hospitals. Rapid growth is expected in hospital outpatient facilities, such as those providing same-day surgery, rehabilitation, and chemotherapy.

More and more sophisticated procedures, once performed only in hospitals, are being performed in physicians' offices and in outpatient care centers, such as freestanding ambulatory surgical and emergency centers. Accordingly, employment is expected to grow fast in these places as healthcare in general expands.

Employment in nursing care facilities is expected to grow because of increases in the number of older persons, many of whom require long-term care. Many elderly patients want to be treated at home or in residential care facilities, which will drive demand for RNs in those settings. The financial pressure on hospitals to discharge patients as soon as possible should produce more admissions to nursing and residential care facilities and referrals to home healthcare. Job growth also is expected in units that provide specialized long-term rehabilitation for stroke and head injury patients, as well as units that treat Alzheimer's victims.

Employment in home healthcare is expected to increase in response to the growing number of older persons with functional disabilities, consumer preference for care in the home, and technological advances that make it possible to bring increasingly complex treatments into the home. The type of care demanded will require nurses who are able to perform complex procedures.

Job prospects. Overall job opportunities are expected to be excellent for registered nurses. Employers in some parts of the country and in certain employment settings report difficulty in attracting and retaining an adequate number of RNs, primarily because of an aging RN workforce and a lack of younger workers to fill positions. Qualified applicants to nursing schools are being turned away because of a shortage of nursing faculty. The need for nursing faculty will only increase as many instructors near retirement. Despite the slower employment growth in hospitals, job opportunities should still be excellent because of the relatively high turnover of hospital nurses. To attract and retain qualified nurses, hospitals may offer signing bonuses, family-friendly work schedules, or subsidized training. Although faster employment growth is projected in physicians' offices and outpatient care centers, RNs may face greater competition for these positions because they generally offer regular working hours and more comfortable working environments. Generally, RNs with at least a bachelor's degree will have better job prospects than those without a bachelor's. In addition, all four advanced practice specialties—clinical nurse specialists, nurse practitioners, nurse-midwives, and nurse anesthetists—will be in high demand, particularly in medically underserved areas such as inner cities and rural areas. Relative to physicians, these RNs increasingly serve as lower-cost primary care providers.

Earnings

Median annual wages of registered nurses were $62,450 in May 2008. The middle 50 percent earned between $51,640 and $76,570. The lowest 10 percent earned less than $43,410, and the highest 10 percent earned more than $92,240.

Many employers offer flexible work schedules, child care, educational benefits, and bonuses. About 21 percent of registered nurses are union members or covered by union contract.

MEDICINE

Pharmacists

Nature of the Work

Pharmacists distribute prescription drugs to individuals. They also advise their patients, physicians, and other health practitioners on the selection, dosages, interactions, and side effects of medications, as well as monitor the health and progress of those patients to ensure that they are using their medications safely and effectively. Compounding—the actual mixing of ingredients to form medications—is a small part of a pharmacist's practice, because most medicines are produced by pharmaceutical companies in standard dosages and drug delivery forms. Most pharmacists work in a community setting, such as a retail drugstore, or in a healthcare facility, such as a hospital.

Pharmacists in community pharmacies dispense medications, counsel patients on the use of prescription and over-the-counter medications, and advise physicians about medication therapy. They also advise patients about general health topics, such as diet, exercise, and stress management, and provide information on products, such as durable medical equipment or home healthcare supplies. In addition, they often complete third-party insurance forms and other paperwork. Those who own or manage community pharmacies may sell non-health-related merchandise, hire and supervise personnel, and oversee the general operation of the pharmacy. Some community pharmacists provide specialized services to help patients with conditions such as diabetes,

> ### Significant Points
>
> ❖ Excellent job opportunities are expected.
>
> ❖ Earnings are relatively high, but some pharmacists are required to work nights, weekends, and holidays.
>
> ❖ Pharmacists are becoming more involved in counseling patients and planning drug therapy programs.
>
> ❖ Pharmacists must graduate from an accredited college of pharmacy and pass a series of examinations to be licensed.

asthma, smoking cessation, or high blood pressure. Some pharmacists are trained to administer vaccinations.

Pharmacists in healthcare facilities dispense medications and advise the medical staff on the selection and effects of drugs. They may make sterile solutions to be administered intravenously. They also plan, monitor, and evaluate drug programs or regimens. They may counsel hospitalized patients on the use of drugs before the patients are discharged.

Some pharmacists specialize in specific drug therapy areas, such as intravenous nutrition support, oncology (cancer), nuclear pharmacy (used for chemotherapy), geriatric pharmacy, and psychiatric pharmacy (the use of drugs to treat mental disorders).

Most pharmacists keep confidential computerized records of patients' drug therapies to prevent harmful drug interactions. Pharmacists are responsible for the accuracy of every prescription that is filled, but they often rely upon pharmacy technicians to assist them in the dispensing medications. Thus, the pharmacist may delegate prescription-filling and administrative tasks and supervise their completion. Pharmacists also frequently oversee pharmacy students serving as interns.

Some pharmacists are involved in research for pharmaceutical manufacturers, developing new drugs and testing their effects. Others work in marketing or sales, providing clients with expertise on the use, effectiveness, and possible side effects of drugs. Some pharmacists work for health insurance companies, developing pharmacy benefit packages and carrying out cost-benefit analyses on certain drugs. Other pharmacists work for the government, managed care organizations, public healthcare services, or the armed services. Finally, some pharmacists are employed full time or part time as college faculty, teaching classes and performing research in a wide range of areas.

Work environment. Pharmacists work in clean, well-lighted, and well-ventilated areas. Many pharmacists spend most of their workday on their feet. When working with sterile or dangerous pharmaceutical products, pharmacists wear gloves, masks, and other protective equipment.

Most pharmacists work about 40 hours a week, but about 12 percent worked more than 50 hours per week in 2008. In addition, about 19 percent of pharmacists worked part-time. Many community and hospital pharmacies are open for extended hours, so pharmacists may be required to work nights, weekends, and holidays. Consultant pharmacists may travel to healthcare facilities to monitor patients' drug therapies.

Training, Other Qualifications, and Advancement

A license is required in all States and the District of Columbia, as well as in Guam, Puerto Rico, and the U.S. Virgin Islands. In order to obtain a license, pharmacists generally must earn a Doctor of Pharmacy (Pharm.D.) degree from a college of pharmacy and pass several examinations.

Education and training. Pharmacists who are trained in the United States must earn a Pharm.D. degree from an accredited college or school of pharmacy. The Pharm.D. degree has replaced the Bachelor of Pharmacy degree, which is no longer being awarded. To be admitted to a Pharm.D. program, an applicant must have completed at least 2 years of specific professional study. This requirement generally includes courses in mathematics and natural sciences, such as chemistry, biology, and physics, as well as courses in the humanities and social sciences. In addition, most applicants have completed 3 or more years at a college or university before moving on to a Pharm.D. program, although this is not specifically required.

Pharm.D. programs generally take 4 years to complete. The courses offered are designed to teach students about all aspects of drug therapy. In addition, students learn how to communicate with patients and other healthcare providers about drug information and patient care. Students also learn professional ethics, concepts of public health, and business management. In addition to receiving classroom instruction, students in Pharm.D. programs spend time working with licensed pharmacists in a variety of practice settings.

Some Pharm.D. graduates obtain further training through 1-year or 2-year residency programs or fellowships. Pharmacy residencies are postgraduate training programs in pharmacy practice and usually require the completion of a research project. The programs are often mandatory for pharmacists who wish to work in a clinical setting. Pharmacy fellowships are highly individualized programs that are designed to prepare participants to work in a specialized area of pharmacy, such clinical practice or research laboratories. Some pharmacists who own their own pharmacy obtain a master's degree in business administration (MBA). Others may obtain a degree in public administration or public health.

Licensure. A license to practice pharmacy is required in all States and the District of Columbia, as well as in Guam, Puerto Rico, and the U.S. Virgin Islands. To obtain a license, a prospective pharmacist generally must obtain a Pharm.D. degree from a college of pharmacy that has been approved by the Accreditation Council for Pharmacy Education. After obtaining the Pharm.D. degree, the individual must pass a series of examinations. All States, U.S. territories, and the District of Columbia require the North American Pharmacist Licensure Exam (NAPLEX), which tests pharmacy skills and knowledge. Forty-four States and the District of Columbia also require the Multistate Pharmacy Jurisprudence Exam (MPJE), which tests pharmacy law. Both exams are administered by the National Association of Boards of Pharmacy (NABP). Each of the eight States and territories that do not require the MJPE has its own pharmacy law exam. Besides requiring the NAPLEX and law examination, some States and territories require additional exams that are unique to their jurisdictions. All jurisdictions also require a specified number of hours of experience in a practice setting before a license is awarded. In most jurisdictions, this requirement can be met while obtaining the Pharm.D. In many States, applicants must meet an age requirement before a license can be obtained, and some States require a criminal background check.

All States and U.S. territories except Puerto Rico permit licensure for graduates of foreign pharmacy schools. These individuals must apply for certification from the Foreign Pharmacy Graduate Examination Committee (FPGEC). Once certified, they must pass the Foreign Pharmacy Graduate Equivalency Examination (FPGEE), Test of English as a Foreign Language (TOEFL) exam, and Test of Spoken English (TSE) exam. Then they must pass all of the exams required by the licensing jurisdiction, such as the NAPLEX and MJPE, and meet the requirements for practical experience. In some States, applicants who graduated from programs accredited by the Canadian Council for Accreditation of Pharmacy Programs (CCAPP) between 1993 and 2004 are exempt from FPGEC certification and examination requirements.

Other qualifications. Prospective pharmacists should have scientific aptitude, good interpersonal skills, and a desire to help others. They also must be conscientious and pay close attention to detail, because the decisions they make affect human lives.

Advancement. In community pharmacies, pharmacists usually begin at the staff level. Pharmacists in chain drugstores may be promoted to pharmacy supervisor or store manager. Some pharmacists may be promoted to manager at the district or regional level and, later, to an executive position within the chain's headquarters. Hospital pharmacists may advance to supervisory or administrative positions. Some pharmacists become owners or part owners of independent pharmacies. Pharmacists in the pharmaceutical industry may advance in marketing, sales, research, quality control, production, or other areas.

Employment

Pharmacists held about 269,900 jobs in 2008. About 65 percent worked in retail settings. Most of these were salaried employees, but a small number were self-employed owners. About 22 percent of pharmacists worked in hospitals. A small proportion worked in mail-order and Internet pharmacies, pharmaceutical wholesalers, offices of physicians, and the Federal Government.

Job Outlook

Employment is expected to increase faster than the average. As a result of job growth, the need to replace workers who leave the occupation, and the limited capacity of training programs, job prospects should be excellent.

Employment change. Employment of pharmacists is expected to grow by 17 percent between 2008 and 2018, which is faster than the average for all occupations. The increasing numbers of middle-aged and elderly people—who use more prescription drugs than younger people—will continue to spur demand for pharmacists throughout the projection period. In addition, as scientific advances lead to new drug products, and as an increasing number of people obtain prescription drug coverage, the need for these workers will continue to expand.

Pharmacists also are becoming more involved in patient care. As prescription drugs become more complex, and as the number of people taking multiple medications increases, the potential for dangerous drug interactions will grow. Pharmacists will be needed to counsel patients on the proper use of medication, assist in drug selection and dosage, and monitor complex drug regimens. This need will lead to rapid growth for pharmacists in medical care establishments, such as doctors' offices, outpatient care centers, and nursing care facilities.

Demand also will increase in mail-order pharmacies, which often are more efficient than pharmacies in other practice settings. Employment also will continue to grow in hospitals, drugstores, grocery stores, and mass retailers, because pharmacies in these settings will continue to process the majority of all prescriptions and increasingly will offer patient care services, such as the administration of vaccines.

Job prospects. Job prospects are expected to be excellent over the 2008–18 period. Employers in many parts of the country report difficulty in attracting and retaining adequate numbers of pharmacists—primarily the result of the limited training capacity of Pharm.D. programs. In addition, as a larger percentage of pharmacists elects to work part time, more individuals will be needed to fill the same number of prescriptions. Job openings also will result from faster than average employment growth and from the need to replace workers who retire or leave the occupation for other reasons.

Earnings

Median annual wages of wage and salary pharmacists in May 2008 were $106,410. The middle 50 percent earned between $92,670 and $121,310 a year. The lowest 10 percent earned less than $77,390, and the highest 10 percent earned more than $131,440 a year.

MEDICINE

—ꟽ—

Occupational Therapists

Nature of the Work

Occupational therapists help patients improve their ability to perform tasks in living and working environments. They work with individuals who suffer from a mentally, physically, developmentally, or emotionally disabling condition. Occupational therapists use treatments to develop, recover, or maintain the daily living and work skills of their patients. The therapist helps clients not only to improve their basic motor functions and reasoning abilities, but also to compensate for permanent loss of function. The goal is to help clients have independent, productive, and satisfying lives.

Occupational therapists help clients to perform all types of activities, from using a computer to caring for daily needs such as dressing, cooking, and eating. Physical exercises may be used to increase strength and dexterity, while other activities may be chosen to improve visual acuity or the ability to discern patterns. For example, a client with short-term memory loss might be encouraged to make lists to aid recall, and a person with coordination problems might be assigned exercises to improve hand-eye coordination. Occupational therapists also use computer programs to help clients improve decision-making, abstract-reasoning, problem-solving, and perceptual skills, as well as memory, sequencing, and coordination—all of which are important for independent living.

Patients with permanent disabilities, such as spinal cord injuries, cerebral palsy, or

> ### Significant Points
> ❖ Employment is expected to grow much faster than average, and job opportunities should be good, especially for therapists treating the elderly.
>
> ❖ Occupational therapists are regulated in all 50 States; requirements vary by State.
>
> ❖ Occupational therapists are increasingly taking on supervisory roles, allowing assistants and aides to work more closely with clients under the guidance of a therapist.

muscular dystrophy, often need special instruction to master certain daily tasks. For these individuals, therapists demonstrate the use of adaptive equipment, including wheelchairs, orthoses, eating aids, and dressing aids. They also design or build special equipment needed at home or at work, including computer-aided adaptive equipment. They teach clients how to use the equipment to improve communication and control various situations in their environment.

Some occupational therapists treat individuals whose ability to function in a work environment has been impaired. These practitioners might arrange employment, evaluate the work space, plan work activities, and assess the client's progress. Therapists also may collaborate with the client and the employer to modify the work environment so that the client can succeed at work.

Assessing and recording a client's activities and progress is an important part of an occupational therapist's job. Accurate records are essential for evaluating clients, for billing, and for reporting to physicians and other healthcare providers.

Occupational therapists may work exclusively with individuals in a particular age group or with a particular disability. In schools, for example, they evaluate children's capabilities, recommend and provide therapy, modify classroom equipment, and help children participate in school activities. A therapist may work with children individually, lead small groups in the classroom, consult with a teacher, or serve on an administrative committee. Some therapists provide early intervention therapy to infants and toddlers who have, or are at risk of having, developmental delays. Therapies may include facilitating the use of the hands and promoting skills for listening, following directions, social play, dressing, or grooming.

Other occupational therapists work with elderly patients. These therapists help the elderly lead more productive, active, and independent lives through a variety of methods. Therapists with specialized training in driver rehabilitation assess an individual's ability to drive using both clinical and on-the-road tests. The evaluations allow the therapist to make recommendations for adaptive equipment, training to prolong driving independence, and alternative transportation options. Occupational therapists also work with clients to assess their homes for hazards and to identify environmental factors that contribute to falls.

Occupational therapists in mental health settings treat individuals who are mentally ill, developmentally challenged, or emotionally disturbed. To treat these problems, therapists choose activities that help people learn to engage in and cope with daily life. Activities might include time management skills, budgeting, shopping, homemaking, and the use of public transportation. Occupational therapists also work with individuals who are dealing with alcoholism, drug abuse, depression, eating disorders, or stress-related disorders.

Work environment. In large rehabilitation centers, therapists may work in spacious rooms equipped with machines, tools, and other devices generating noise. The work can be tiring because therapists are on their feet much of the time. Therapists also face hazards such as back strain from lifting and moving clients and equipment.

Occupational therapists working for one employer full-time usually work a 40-hour week. Around 31 percent of occupational therapists worked part-time. It is not uncommon for occupational therapists to work for more than one employer at multiple facilities, which may involve significant travel time. Those in schools may participate in meetings and other activities during and after the school day.

Training, Other Qualifications, and Advancement

Occupational therapists are regulated in all 50 States. Individuals pursuing a career as an occupational therapist usually need to earn a post-baccalaureate degree from an accredited college or university or education deemed equivalent.

Education and training. A master's degree or higher in occupational therapy is the typical minimum requirement for entry into the field. In addition, occupational therapists must attend an academic program accredited by the Accreditation Council for Occupational Therapy Education (ACOTE) in order to sit for the national certifying exam. In 2009, 150 master's degree programs or combined bachelor's and master's degree programs were accredited, and 4 doctoral degree programs were accredited. Most schools have full-time programs, although a growing number are offering weekend or part-time programs as well. Coursework in occupational therapy programs include the physical, biological, and behavioral sciences as well as the application of occupational therapy theory and skills. All accredited programs require at least 24 weeks of supervised fieldwork as part of the academic curriculum.

People considering this profession should take high school courses in biology, chemistry, physics, health, art, and the social sciences. College admissions offices also look favorably on paid or volunteer experience in the healthcare field. Relevant undergraduate majors include biology, psychology, sociology, anthropology, liberal arts, and anatomy.

Licensure. All States regulate the practice of occupational therapy. To obtain a license, applicants must graduate from an accredited educational program and pass a national certification examination. Those who pass the exam are awarded the title "Occupational Therapist Registered (OTR)." Specific eligibility requirements for licensure vary by State; contact your State's licensing board for details.

Some States have additional requirements for therapists who work in schools or early intervention programs. These requirements may include education-related classes, an education practice certificate, or early intervention certification.

Certification and other qualifications. Certification is voluntary. The National Board for Certifying Occupational Therapy certifies occupational therapists through a national certifying exam. Those who pass the test are awarded the title Occupational Therapist Registered (OTR). In some States, the national certifying exam meets requirements for regulation while other

States have their own licensing exam.

Occupational therapists are expected to continue their professional development by participating in continuing education courses and workshops. In fact, a number of States require continuing education as a condition of maintaining licensure.

Occupational therapists need patience and strong interpersonal skills to inspire trust and respect in their clients. Patience is necessary because many clients may not show immediate improvement. Ingenuity and imagination in adapting activities to individual needs are assets. Those working in home healthcare services also must be able to adapt to a variety of settings.

Advancement. Therapists are increasingly taking on supervisory roles in addition to their supervision of occupational therapy assistants and aides. Occupational therapists may advance their careers by taking on administrative duties at hospitals or rehabilitation centers.

Occupational therapists also can advance by specializing in a clinical area and gaining expertise in treating a certain type of patient or ailment. Therapists may specialize in gerontology, mental health, pediatrics, and physical rehabilitation. In addition, some occupational therapists choose to teach classes in accredited occupational therapy educational programs.

Employment

Occupational therapists held about 104,500 jobs in 2008. The largest number of occupational therapist jobs was in ambulatory healthcare services, which employed about 29 percent of occupational therapists. Other major employers were hospitals, offices of other health practitioners (including offices of occupational therapists), public and private educational services, and nursing care facilities. Some occupational therapists were employed by home healthcare services, outpatient care centers, offices of physicians, individual and family services, community care facilities for the elderly, and government agencies.

A small number of occupational therapists were self-employed in private practice. These practitioners treated clients referred by other health professionals. They also provided contract or consulting services to nursing care facilities, schools, adult day care programs, and home healthcare agencies.

Job Outlook

Employment is expected to grow much faster than average. Job opportunities should be good, especially for occupational therapists treating the elderly.

Employment change. Employment of occupational therapists is expected to increase by 26 percent between 2008 and 2018, much faster than the average for all occupations. The increasing elderly population will drive growth in the demand for occupational therapy services. The demand for occupational therapists should continue to rise as a result of the increasing number of individuals with disabilities or limited function who require therapy services. Older persons have an increased incidence of heart attack and stroke, which will spur demand for therapeutic services. Growth in the population 75 years and older—an age group that suffers from high incidences of disabling conditions—also will increase demand for therapeutic services. In addition, medical advances now enable more patients with critical problems to survive—patients who ultimately may need extensive therapy. However, growth may be dampened by the impact of Federal legislation imposing limits on reimbursement for therapy services.

Hospitals will continue to employ a large number of occupational therapists to provide therapy services to acutely ill inpatients. Hospitals also will need occupational therapists to staff their outpatient rehabilitation programs.

Employment growth in schools will result from the expansion of the school-age population and the federally funded extension of services for disabled students. Therapists will be needed to help children with disabilities prepare to enter special education programs.

Job prospects. Job opportunities should be good for licensed occupational therapists in all settings, particularly in acute hospital, rehabilitation, and orthopedic settings because the elderly receive most of their treatment in these settings. Occupational therapists with specialized knowledge in a treatment area also will have increased job prospects. Driver rehabilitation, training for the elderly, and ergonomic consulting are emerging practice areas for occupational therapy.

Earnings

Median annual wages of occupational therapists were $66,780 in May 2008. The middle 50 percent earned between $55,090 and $81,290. The lowest 10 percent earned less than $42,820, and the highest 10 percent earned more than $98,310.

MEDICINE

—ɯɯ—

Physical Therapists

Nature of the Work

Physical therapists, sometimes referred to as simply *PTs*, are healthcare professionals who diagnose and treat individuals of all ages, from newborns to the very oldest, who have medical problems or other health-related conditions, illnesses, or injuries that limits their abilities to move and perform functional activities as well as they would like in their daily lives. Physical therapists examine each individual and develop a plan using treatment techniques to promote the ability to move, reduce pain, restore function, and prevent disability. In addition, PTs work with individuals to prevent the loss of mobility before it occurs by developing fitness and wellness-oriented programs for healthier and more active lifestyles.

Significant Points
- ❖ Employment is expected to grow much faster than average.

- ❖ Job opportunities should be good.

- ❖ Today's entrants to this profession need a post-baccalaureate degree from an accredited physical therapist program.

- ❖ About 60 percent of physical therapists work in hospitals or in offices of other health practitioners.

Physical therapists provide care to people of all ages who have functional problems resulting from, for example, back and neck injuries, sprains/strains and fractures, arthritis, burns, amputations, stroke, multiple sclerosis, conditions such as cerebral palsy and spina bifida, and injuries related to work and sports. Physical therapy care and services are provided by physical therapists and physical therapist assistants who work under the direction and supervision of a physical therapist. Physical therapists evaluate and diagnose movement dysfunction and use interventions to treat patient/clients. Interventions may include therapeutic exercise, functional training, manual therapy techniques, assistive and adaptive devices and equipment, and physical agents and electrotherapeutic modalities.

Physical therapists often consult and practice with a variety of other professionals, such as physicians, dentists, nurses, educators, social workers, occupational therapists, speech-language pathologists, and audiologists.

Work environment. Physical therapists practice in hospitals, outpatient clinics, and private offices that have specially equipped facilities. These jobs can be physically demanding, because therapists may have to stoop, kneel, crouch, lift, and stand for long periods. In addition, physical therapists move heavy equipment and lift patients or help them turn, stand, or walk.

In 2008, most full-time physical therapists worked a 40-hour week; some worked evenings and weekends to fit their patients' schedules. About 27 percent of physical therapists worked part-time.

Training, Other Qualifications, and Advancement

Today's entrants to this profession need a post-baccalaureate degree from an accredited physical therapy program. All States regulate the practice of physical therapy, which usually requires passing scores on national and State examinations.

Education and training. The American Physical Therapy Association's accrediting body, called the Commission on Accreditation of Physical Therapy Education (CAPTE), accredits entry-level academic programs in physical therapy. In 2009, there were 212 physical therapist education programs. Of these accredited programs, 12 awarded master's degrees; and 200 awarded doctoral degrees. Currently, only graduate degree physical therapist programs are accredited. Master's degree programs typically are 2 to 2.5 years in length, while doctoral degree programs last 3 years.

Physical therapist education programs include foundational science courses, such as biology, anatomy, physiology, cellular histology, exercise physiology, neuroscience, biomechanics, pharmacology, pathology, and radiology/imaging, as well as behavioral science courses, such as evidence-based practice and clinical reasoning. Some of the clinically-based courses include medical screening, examination tests and measures, diagnostic process, therapeutic interventions, outcomes assessment, and practice management. In addition to classroom and laboratory instruction, students receive supervised clinical experience.

Among the undergraduate courses that are useful when one applies to a physical therapist education program are anatomy, biology, chemistry, physics, social science, mathematics, and statistics. Before granting admission, many programs require volunteer experience in the physical therapy department of a hospital or clinic.

Licensure. All States regulate the practice of physical therapy. Eligibility requirements vary by State. Typical requirements for physical therapists include graduation from an accredited physical therapy education program; passing the National Physical Therapy

Examination; and fulfilling State requirements such as jurisprudence exams. A number of States require continuing education as a condition of maintaining licensure.

Other qualifications. Physical therapists should have strong interpersonal and communication skills, so they can educate patients about their condition and physical therapy treatments and communicate with patients' families. Physical therapists also should be compassionate and possess a desire to help patients.

Advancement. Physical therapists are expected to continue their professional development by participating in continuing education courses and workshops. Some physical therapists become board certified in a clinical specialty. Opportunities for physical therapists exist in academia and research. Some become self-employed, providing contract services or opening a private practice.

Employment

Physical therapists held about 185,500 jobs in 2008. The number of physical therapist jobs is probably greater than the number of practicing physical therapists, because some physical therapists work part time, holding two or more jobs. For example, some may work in a private practice, but also work part time in another healthcare facility.

About 60 percent of physical therapists worked in hospitals or in offices of other health practitioners. Other jobs were in the home healthcare services industry, nursing care facilities, outpatient care centers, and offices of physicians. Some physical therapists were self-employed in private practices, seeing individual patients and contracting to provide services in hospitals, rehabilitation centers, nursing care facilities, home healthcare agencies, adult day care programs, and schools. Physical therapists also teach in academic institutions and conduct research.

Job Outlook

Employment is expected to grow much faster than average. Job opportunities should be good.

Employment change. Employment of physical therapists is expected to grow by 30 percent from 2008 to 2018, much faster than the average for all occupations. Changes to restrictions on reimbursement for physical therapy services by third-party payers will increase patient access to services and, thus, increase demand. The increasing elderly population will drive growth in the demand for physical therapy services. The elderly population is particularly vulnerable to chronic and debilitating conditions that require therapeutic services. Also, the baby-boom generation is entering the prime age for heart attacks and strokes, increasing the demand for cardiac and physical rehabilitation. Medical and technological developments will permit a greater percentage of trauma victims and newborns with birth defects to survive, creating additional demand for rehabilitative care. In addition, growth may result from advances in medical technology and the use of evidence-base practices, which could permit the treatment of an increasing number of disabling conditions that were untreatable in the past.

In addition, the federally mandated Individuals with Disabilities Education Act guarantees that students have access to services from physical therapists and other therapeutic and rehabilitative services. Demand for physical therapists will continue in schools.

Job prospects. Job opportunities will be good for licensed physical therapists in all settings. Job opportunities should be particularly good in acute hospital, skilled nursing, and orthopedic settings, where the elderly are most often treated. Job prospects should be especially favorable in rural areas as many physical therapists tend to cluster in highly populated urban and suburban areas.

Earnings

Median annual wages of physical therapists were $72,790 in May 2008. The middle 50 percent earned between $60,300 and $85,540. The lowest 10 percent earned less than $50,350, and the highest 10 percent earned more than $104,350.

MEDICINE

—ᴍ—

Dieticians and Nutritionists

Nature of the Work

Dietitians and *nutritionists* plan food and nutrition programs, supervise meal preparation, and oversee the serving of meals. They prevent and treat illnesses by promoting healthy eating habits and recommending dietary modifications. For example, dietitians might teach a patient with high blood pressure how to use less salt when preparing meals, or create a diet reduced in fat and sugar for an overweight patient.

Dietitians manage food service systems for institutions such as hospitals and schools, promote sound eating habits through education, and conduct research. Many dietitians specialize, becoming a clinical dietitian, community dietitian, management dietitian, or consultant.

Clinical dietitians provide nutritional services to patients in hospitals, nursing care facilities, and other institutions. They assess patients' nutritional needs, develop and implement nutrition programs, and evaluate and report the results. They also confer with doctors and other healthcare professionals to coordinate medical and nutritional needs. Some clinical dietitians specialize in managing the weight of overweight patients or in the care of renal (kidney), diabetic, or critically ill patients. In addition, clinical dietitians in nursing care facilities, small hospitals, or correctional facilities may manage the food service department.

Significant Points

❖ Most jobs are in hospitals, nursing care facilities, outpatient care centers, and offices of physicians or other health practitioners.

❖ Dietitians and nutritionists need at least a bachelor's degree; licensure, certification, or registration requirements vary by State.

❖ Applicants with specialized training, an advanced degree, or certifications beyond the particular State's minimum requirement should enjoy the best job opportunities.

Community dietitians counsel individuals and groups on nutritional practices designed to prevent disease and promote health. Working in places such as public health clinics, home health agencies, and health maintenance organizations, community dietitians evaluate individual needs, develop nutritional care plans, and instruct individuals and their families. Dietitians working in home health agencies provide instruction on grocery shopping and food preparation to the elderly, children, and individuals with special needs.

Increased public interest in nutrition has led to job opportunities in food manufacturing, advertising, and marketing. In these areas, dietitians analyze foods, prepare literature for distribution, or report on issues such as dietary fiber, vitamin supplements, or the nutritional content of recipes.

Management dietitians oversee large-scale meal planning and preparation in healthcare facilities, company cafeterias, prisons, and schools. They hire, train, and direct other dietitians and food service workers; budget for and purchase food, equipment, and supplies; enforce sanitary and safety regulations; and prepare records and reports.

Consultant dietitians work under contract with healthcare facilities or in their own private practice. They perform nutrition screenings for their clients and offer advice on diet-related concerns such as weight loss and cholesterol reduction. Some work for wellness programs, sports teams, supermarkets, and other nutrition-related businesses. They may consult with food service managers, providing expertise in sanitation, safety procedures, menu development, budgeting, and planning.

Work environment. Dietitians and nutritionists usually work in clean, well-lighted, and well-ventilated areas. However, some work in hot, congested kitchens. Many dietitians and nutritionists are on their feet for much of the workday.

Most full-time dietitians and nutritionists work a standard 40-hour week, although some work weekends. About 19 percent worked part time in 2008.

Training, Other Qualifications, and Advancement

Dietitians and nutritionists need at least a bachelor's degree. Licensure, certification, or registration requirements vary by State.

Education and training. Becoming a dietitian or nutritionist usually requires at least a bachelor's degree in dietetics, foods and nutrition, food service systems management, or a related area. Graduate degrees also are available. College students in these majors take courses in foods, nutrition, institution management, chemistry, biochemistry, biology, microbiology, and physiology. Other suggested courses include business, mathematics, statistics, computer science, psychology, sociology, and economics. High school students interested in becoming a dietitian or nutritionist should take courses in biology, chemistry, mathematics, health, and communications.

As of 2008, there were 279 bachelor's degree programs and 18 master's degree programs approved by the American Dietetic Association's Commission on Accreditation for Dietetics Education.

Licensure. Of the 46 States and jurisdictions with laws governing dietetics, 33 require licensure, 12 require statutory certification, and 1 requires registration. Specific requirements vary by State. As a result, interested candidates should determine the requirements of the State in which they want to work before sitting for any exam.

In States that require licensure, only people who are licensed can work as dietitians and nutritionists. States that require statutory certification limit the use of occupational titles to people who meet certain requirements; individuals without certification can still practice as a dietitian or nutritionist but without using certain titles. Registration is the least restrictive form of State regulation of dietitians and nutritionists. Unregistered people are permitted to practice as a dietitian or nutritionist.

Certification and other qualifications. Although not required, the Commission on Dietetic Registration of the American Dietetic Association awards the Registered Dietitian credential to those who pass an exam after completing academic coursework and a supervised internship. This certification is different from the statutory certification regulated by some States and discussed in the previous section. To maintain a Registered Dietitian status, workers must complete at least 75 credit hours in approved continuing education classes every 5 years.

A supervised internship, required for certification, can be completed in one of two ways. The first requires the completion of a program accredited by the Commission on Dietetic Registration. As of September 2009, there were 51 accredited programs that combined academic and supervised practice experience and generally lasted 4 to 5 years. The second option requires the completion of 900 hours of supervised practice experience in any of the 243 accredited internships. These internships may be full-time programs lasting 6 to 12 months or part-time programs lasting 2 years.

Advancement. Experienced dietitians may advance to management positions, such as assistant director, associate director, or director of a dietetic department, or may become self-employed. Some dietitians specialize in areas such as renal, diabetic, cardiovascular, or pediatric dietetics. Others leave the occupation to become sales representatives for equipment, pharmaceutical, or food manufacturers. A master's degree can help some workers to advance their careers, particularly in career paths related to research, advanced clinical positions, or public health.

Employment

Dietitians and nutritionists held about 60,300 jobs in 2008. More than half of all jobs were in hospitals, nursing care facilities, outpatient care centers, or offices of physicians and other health practitioners. State and local government agencies provided additional jobs—mostly in correctional facilities, health departments, and other public-health-related areas. Some dietitians and nutritionists were employed in special food services, an industry made up of firms providing food services on contract to facilities such as colleges and universities, airlines, correctional facilities, and company cafeterias.

Other jobs were in public and private educational services, community care facilities for the elderly (which includes assisted-living facilities), individual and family services, home healthcare services, and the Federal Government—mostly in the U.S. Department of Veterans Affairs. Some dietitians were self-employed, working as consultants to facilities such as hospitals and nursing care facilities or providing dietary counseling to individuals.

Job Outlook

Average employment growth is projected. Applicants with specialized training, an advanced degree, or certifications beyond the particular State's minimum requirement should enjoy the best job opportunities.

Employment change. Employment of dietitians and nutritionists is expected to increase 9 percent during the 2008-18 projection decade, about as fast as the average for all occupations. Job growth will result from an increasing emphasis on disease prevention through improved dietary habits. A growing and aging population will boost demand for nutritional counseling and treatment in hospitals, residential care facilities, schools, prisons, community health programs, and home healthcare agencies. Public interest in nutrition and increased emphasis on health education and prudent lifestyles also will spur demand, especially in food service management.

Also, with increased public awareness of obesity and diabetes, Medicare coverage has been expanded to include medical nutrition therapy for renal and diabetic patients, creating job growth for dietitians and nutritionists specializing in those diseases.

Employment growth, however, may be constrained if some employers substitute other workers, such as health educators, food service managers, and dietetic technicians, to do work related to nutrition. Also, demand for nutritional therapy services is related to the ability of patients to pay, either out-of-pocket or through health insurance, and although more insurance plans now cover nutritional therapy services, the extent of such coverage varies among plans. Growth may be curbed by limitations on insurance reimbursement for dietetic services.

Hospitals will continue to employ a large number of dietitians and nutritionists to provide medical nutritional therapy and plan meals. But hospitals also will continue to contract with outside agencies for food service and move medical nutritional therapy to outpatient care facilities, slowing job growth in hospitals relative to food service, outpatient facilities, and other employers.

Finally, the number of dietitian positions in nursing care facilities is expected to decline, as these establishments continue to contract with outside agencies for food services. However, employment is expected to grow rapidly in contract providers of food services, in outpatient care centers, and in offices of physicians and other health practitioners.

Job prospects. In addition to employment growth, job openings will result from the need to replace experienced workers who retire or leave the occupation for other reasons. Applicants with specialized training, an advanced degree, or certifications beyond the particular State's minimum requirement should enjoy the best job opportunities. Demand for dietitians should be particularly strong in outpatient care facilities, offices of physicians, and food service management. Applicants without a bachelor's degree will face keen competition for jobs.

Dietitians with specialized training, an advanced degree, or certifications beyond the particular State's minimum requirement will experience the best job opportunities. Those specializing in renal and diabetic nutrition or gerontological nutrition will benefit from the growing number of diabetics and the aging of the population.

Median annual wages of dietitians and nutritionists were $50,590 in May 2008. The middle 50 percent earned between $41,060 and $61,790. The lowest 10 percent earned less than $31,460, and the highest 10 percent earned more than $73,410.

MATH & SCIENCE

—m—

Mathematicians

Nature of the Work

Mathematics is one of the oldest and most fundamental sciences. *Mathematicians* use mathematical theory, computational techniques, algorithms, and the latest computer technology to solve economic, scientific, engineering, and business problems. The work of mathematicians falls into two broad classes: theoretical (pure) mathematics and applied mathematics. These classes, however, are not sharply defined and often overlap.

Theoretical mathematicians advance mathematical knowledge by developing new principles and recognizing previously unknown relationships between existing principles of mathematics. Although these workers seek to increase basic knowledge without necessarily considering its practical use, such pure and abstract knowledge has been instrumental in producing or furthering many scientific and engineering achievements. Many theoretical mathematicians are employed as university faculty, dividing their time between teaching and conducting research.

Applied mathematicians use theories and techniques, such as mathematical modeling and computational methods, to formulate and solve practical problems in business, government, engineering, and the physical, life, and social sciences. For example, they may analyze the most efficient way to schedule airline routes between cities, the effects and

Significant Points

❖ A Ph.D. in mathematics usually is the minimum educational requirement, except in the Federal Government.

❖ Much faster than average employment growth is expected for mathematicians.

❖ Keen competition for jobs is expected.

❖ Ph.D. holders with a strong background in mathematics and a related field, such as computer science or engineering, should have better employment opportunities in related occupations.

safety of new drugs, the aerodynamic characteristics of an experimental automobile, or the cost-effectiveness of alternative manufacturing processes.

Applied mathematicians working in industrial research and development may develop or enhance mathematical methods when solving a difficult problem. Some mathematicians, called cryptanalysts, analyze and decipher encryption systems—codes—designed to transmit military, political, financial, or law-enforcement-related information.

Applied mathematicians start with a practical problem, envision its separate elements, and then reduce the elements to mathematical variables. They often use computers to analyze relationships among the variables, and they solve complex problems by developing models with alternative solutions.

Individuals with titles other than mathematician also do work in applied mathematics. In fact, because mathematics is the foundation on which so many other academic disciplines are built, the number of workers using mathematical techniques is much greater than the number formally called mathematicians. For example, engineers, computer scientists, physicists, and economists are among those who use mathematics extensively. Some professionals, including statisticians, actuaries, and operations research analysts, are actually specialists in a particular branch of mathematics. Applied mathematicians frequently are required to collaborate with other workers in their organizations to find common solutions to problems.

Work environment. Mathematicians usually work in comfortable offices. They often are part of interdisciplinary teams that may include economists, engineers, computer scientists, physicists, technicians, and others. Deadlines, overtime work, special requests for information or analysis, and prolonged travel to attend seminars or conferences may be part of their jobs.

Training, Other Qualifications, and Advancement

A Ph.D. degree in mathematics usually is the minimum educational requirement for prospective mathematicians, except in the Federal Government.

Education and training. In private industry, candidates for mathematician jobs typically need a Ph.D., although there may be opportunities for those with a master's degree. Most of the positions designated for mathematicians are in research-and-development laboratories, as part of technical teams.

In the Federal Government, entry-level job candidates usually must have at least a bachelor's degree with a major in mathematics or 24 semester hours of mathematics courses. Outside the Federal Government, bachelor's degree holders in mathematics usually are not qualified for most jobs, and many seek advanced degrees in mathematics or a related discipline. However, bachelor's degree holders who meet State certification requirements may become primary or secondary school mathematics teachers.

Most colleges and universities offer a bachelor's degree in mathematics, and many universities offer master's and doctoral degrees in pure or applied mathematics. Courses usually required for these programs include calculus, differential equations, and linear and abstract algebra. Additional courses might include probability theory and statistics, mathematical analysis, numerical analysis, topology, discrete mathematics, and mathematical logic. In graduate programs, students also conduct research and take advanced courses, usually specializing in a subfield of mathematics.

Many colleges and universities advise or require students majoring in mathematics to take courses in a closely related field, such as computer science, engineering, life science, physical science, or economics. A double major in mathematics and another related discipline is particularly desirable to many employers. High school students who are prospective college mathematics majors should take as many mathematics courses as possible while in high school.

Other qualifications. For jobs in applied mathematics, training in the field in which mathematics will be used is very important. Mathematics is used extensively in physics, actuarial science, statistics, engineering, and operations research. Computer science, business and industrial management, economics, finance, chemistry, geology, life sciences, and behavioral sciences are likewise dependent on applied mathematics. Mathematicians also should have substantial knowledge of computer programming, because most complex mathematical computation and much mathematical modeling are done on a computer.

Mathematicians need to have good reasoning to identify, analyze, and apply basic principles to technical problems. Communication skills also are important, because mathematicians must be able to interact and discuss proposed solutions with people who may not have extensive knowledge of mathematics.

Advancement. The majority of those with a master's degree in mathematics who work in private industry do so not as mathematicians but in related fields, such as computer science, where they have titles such as computer programmer, systems analyst, or systems engineer. In these occupations, workers can advance to management positions.

Employment

Mathematicians held about 2,900 jobs in 2008. Many people with mathematical backgrounds also worked in other occupations. For example, there were about 54,800 jobs for postsecondary mathematical science teachers in 2008.

Many mathematicians work for the Federal Government, primarily in the U.S. Department of Defense which accounts for about 81 percent of the mathematicians employed by the Federal Government. Many of the other mathematicians employed by the Federal Government work for the National Institute of Standards and Technology (NIST) or the National Aeronautics and Space Administration (NASA).

In the private sector, major employers include scientific research and development services and management, scientific, and technical consulting services. Some mathematicians also work for insurance carriers.

Job Outlook

Employment of mathematicians is expected to grow much faster than average. However, keen competition for jobs is expected.

Employment change. Employment of mathematicians is expected to increase by 22 percent during the 2008–18 decade, which is much faster than average for all occupations. Advancements in technology usually lead to expanding applications of mathematics, and more workers with knowledge of mathematics will be required in the future. However, jobs in industry and government often require advanced knowledge of related scientific disciplines in addition to mathematics. The most common fields in which mathematicians study and find work are computer science and software development, physics, engineering, and operations research. Many mathematicians also are involved in financial analysis and in life sciences research.

Job prospects. Job competition will remain keen because employment in this occupation is relatively small and few new jobs are expected. Ph.D. holders with a strong background in mathematics and a related discipline, such as engineering or computer science, and who apply mathematical theory to real-world problems will have the best job prospects in related occupations. In addition, mathematicians with experience in computer programming will better their job prospects in many occupations.

Holders of a master's degree in mathematics will face very strong competition for jobs in theoretical research. Because the number of Ph.D. degrees awarded in mathematics continues to exceed the number of available university positions—especially tenure-track positions—many graduates will need to find employment in industry and government.

Employment in theoretical mathematical research is sensitive to general economic fluctuations and to changes in government spending. Job prospects will be greatly influenced by changes in public and private funding for research and development.

Mathematicians who work in academia usually have a mix of teaching and research responsibilities. These mathematicians may conduct research by themselves or in close collaboration with other mathematicians. Collaborators may work together at the same institution or from different locations, using technology such as e-mail to communicate. Mathematicians in academia also may be aided by graduate students.

Earnings

Median annual wages of mathematicians were $95,150 in May 2008. The middle 50 percent earned between $71,430 and $119,480. The lowest 10 percent had earnings of less than $53,570, while the highest 10 percent earned more than $140,500.

In March 2009, the average annual salary in the Federal Government was $107,051 for mathematicians; $107,015 for mathematical statisticians; and $101,645 for cryptanalysts.

Math & Science

—m—

Statisticians

Nature of the Work

Statistics is the scientific application of mathematical principles to the collection, analysis, and presentation of numerical data. *Statisticians* apply their mathematical and statistical knowledge to the design of surveys and experiments; the collection, processing, and analysis of data; and the interpretation of experiments and survey results. Opinion polls, statements about the accuracy of scales and other measuring devices, and information about average earnings in an occupation are all usually the work of statisticians.

Statisticians may apply their knowledge of statistical methods to a variety of subject areas, such as biology, economics, engineering, medicine, public health, psychology, marketing, education, and sports. Many economic, social, political, and military decisions cannot be made without statistical techniques, such as the design of experiments to gain Federal approval of a newly manufactured drug. Statistics might be needed to show whether the seemingly good results of a drug were likely because of the drug rather than just the effect of random variation in patient outcomes.

One technique that is especially useful to statisticians is sampling—obtaining information about a population of people or of a group of things by surveying a small portion of the total. For example, to determine the size of the audience for particular programs, television-rating services survey only a few thousand families, rather than all viewers. Statisticians decide

Significant Points

❖ About 30 percent of statisticians work for Federal, State, and local governments; private-industry employers include scientific research and development services, insurance carriers, and pharmaceutical and medicine manufacturing.

❖ A master's degree in statistics or mathematics is the minimum educational requirement for most jobs. Individuals with a degree in statistics are likely to have opportunities in a variety of fields.

where and how to gather the data, determine the type and size of the sample group, and develop the survey questionnaire or reporting form. They also prepare instructions for workers who will collect and tabulate the data. Finally, statisticians analyze, interpret, and summarize the data with the use of computer software.

In business and industry, statisticians play an important role in quality control and in product development and improvement. In an automobile company, for example, statisticians might design experiments in which engines are run until failure and breakdown in order to determine the failure time of engines exposed to extreme weather conditions. Working for a pharmaceutical company, statisticians might develop and evaluate the results of clinical trials to determine the safety and effectiveness of new medications. At a computer software firm, statisticians might help construct new statistical software packages to analyze data more accurately and efficiently. In addition to designing experiments for product development and testing, some statisticians are involved in deciding what products to manufacture, how much to charge for them, and to whom the products should be marketed. Statisticians also may manage assets and liabilities, determining the risks and returns of certain investments.

Nearly every government agency employs statisticians. Some government statisticians develop surveys that measure population growth, consumer prices, or unemployment. Other statisticians work for scientific, environmental, and agricultural agencies and may help figure out the average level of pesticides in drinking water, the number of endangered species living in a particular area, or the number of people afflicted with a certain disease. Statisticians also are employed in national defense agencies, determining the accuracy of new weapons and the likely effectiveness of defense strategies.

Because statistical specialists are employed in so many different kinds of work, specialists who use statistics often have different professional designations. For example, a person using statistical methods to analyze economic data may be called an *econometrician*, while statisticians in public health and medicine may hold titles such as *biostatistician* or *biometrician*.

Work environment. Statisticians generally work regular hours in an office environment. Sometimes, they may work more hours to meet deadlines.

Some statisticians travel to provide advice on research projects, supervise and set up surveys, or gather statistical data. Although e-mail and teleconferencing make it easier for statisticians to work with clients in different areas, there still are situations that require the statistician to be present, such as during meetings or while gathering data.

Training, Other Qualifications, and Advancement

A master's degree in statistics or mathematics is the minimum educational requirement, but research and academic jobs generally require a Ph.D., while Federal Government jobs require at least a bachelor's degree.

Education and training. A master's degree in statistics or mathematics usually is the minimum educational requirement for most statistician jobs. Research and academic positions usually require a Ph.D. in statistics. Beginning positions in industrial research often require a master's degree combined with several years of experience.

Jobs with the Federal Government require at least a bachelor's degree. The training required for employment as an entry-level statistician in the Federal Government is a bachelor's degree, including at least 15 semester hours of statistics or a combination of 15 hours of mathematics and statistics with at least 6 semester hours in statistics. Qualifying as a mathematical statistician in the Federal Government requires 24 semester hours of mathematics and statistics, with a minimum of 6 semester hours in statistics and 12 semester hours in an area of advanced mathematics, such as calculus, differential equations, or vector analysis.

Many colleges and universities offer degree programs in statistics, biostatistics, or mathematics, while other schools also offer graduate-level courses in applied statistics for students majoring in biology, business, economics, education, engineering, psychology, and other fields. Acceptance into graduate statistics programs does not require an undergraduate degree in statistics, although good training in mathematics is essential. Many schools also offer degrees in fields that include a sufficient number of courses in statistics to qualify graduates for some entry-level positions with the Federal Government. Required subjects for statistics majors include differential and integral calculus, statistical methods, mathematical modeling, and probability theory. Additional recommended courses for undergraduates include linear algebra, design and analysis of experiments, applied multivariate analysis, and mathematical statistics.

Because computers are used extensively for statistical applications, a strong background in computer science is highly recommended. For positions involving quality and improvement in productivity, training in engineering or physical science is useful. A background in biological, chemical, or health science is important for positions involving the preparation and testing of pharmaceutical or agricultural products. Courses in economics and business administration are valuable for many jobs in market research, business analysis, and forecasting.

Advancements in technology have made a great impact on statistics. Statistical modeling continues to become quicker and easier because of increased computational power and new analytical methods or software. Continuing education is important for statisticians, who need to stay abreast of emerging technologies to perform well.

Other qualifications. Good communication skills are important for statisticians who seek a job in private industry, because these statisticians often need to explain technical matters to persons without statistical expertise. An understanding of business and the economy also is valuable for those who plan to work in private industry.

Advancement. Beginning statisticians generally are supervised by an experienced statistician. With experience, they may advance to positions with more technical responsibility and, in some cases, supervisory duties. Opportunities for promotion are greater for people with advanced degrees. Master's and Ph.D. degree holders usually enjoy independence in their work and may engage in research, develop statistical methods, or, after a number of years of experience in a particular area, become statistical consultants.

Employment

Statisticians held about 22,600 jobs in 2008. About 20 percent of these jobs were in the Federal Government, where statisticians were concentrated in the Departments of Commerce, Agriculture, and Health and Human Services. Another 10 percent were found in State and local governments. Most of the remaining jobs were in private industry, especially in scientific research and development services, insurance carriers, and pharmaceutical and medicine manufacturing.

Job Outlook

Average employment growth is projected. Individuals with a degree in statistics should have opportunities in a variety of fields.

Employment change. Employment of statisticians is projected to grow 13 percent from 2008 to 2018, about as fast as the average for all occupations. The demand for individuals with a background is statistics is projected to grow, although some jobs will be in occupations with titles other than statistician.

The use of statistics is widespread and growing. Statistical models aid in decision making in both private industry and government. There will always be a demand for the skills statisticians provide. Technological advances are expected to spur demand for statisticians. Ever-faster computer processing allows statisticians to analyze greater amounts of data much more quickly and to gather and sort through large amounts of data that would not have been analyzed in the past. As data processing continues to become more efficient and less expensive, an increasing number of employers will want to employ statisticians to take advantage of the new information available.

Biostatisticians should experience employment growth, primarily because of the growing pharmaceuticals business. As pharmaceutical companies develop new treatments and medical technologies, biostatisticians will be needed to do research and clinical trials.

Job prospects. Individuals with a degree in statistics have opportunities in a variety of fields. For example, many jobs involve the analysis and interpretation of data from economics, biological science, psychology, computer software engineering, education, and other disciplines. Additional job openings will become available as currently employed statisticians transfer to other occupations, retire, or leave the workforce for other reasons.

Among graduates with a master's degree in statistics, those with a strong background in an allied field, such as finance, biology, engineering, or computer science, should have the best prospects of finding jobs related to their field of study.

Earnings

Median annual wage-and-salary wages of statisticians were $72,610 in May 2008. The middle 50 percent earned between $52,730 and $95,170. The lowest 10 percent earned less than $39,740, while the highest 10 percent earned more than $117,190.

The average annual salary for statisticians in the Federal Government was $92,322 in March 2009, while mathematical statisticians averaged $107,015.

MATH & SCIENCE

—◆—

Biological Scientists

Nature of the Work

Biological scientists study living organisms and their relationship to the environment. They perform research to gain a better understanding of fundamental life processes and apply that understanding to developing new products or processes. Research can be broken down into two categories: basic and applied. Basic research is conducted without any intended aim; the goal is simply to expand on human knowledge. Applied research is directed towards solving a particular problem. Most biological scientists specialize in one area of biology, such as zoology (the study of animals) or microbiology (the study of microscopic organisms).

Basic research in biological sciences advances our knowledge of living organisms so that we can develop solutions to human health problems and improve the natural environment. These biological scientists mostly work in government, university, or private industry laboratories, often exploring new areas of research. Many expand on specialized research they started in graduate school.

Many biological scientists involved in basic research must submit grant proposals to obtain funding for their projects. Colleges and universities, private foundations, and Federal Government agencies, such as the National Institutes of Health and the National Science Foundation, contribute to the support of scientists whose research proposals are determined to be financially feasible and to have the potential to advance new ideas or processes.

Significant Points

❖ Biotechnological research and development should continue to drive much faster than average employment growth.

❖ A Ph.D. is usually required for independent research, but a bachelor's degree is sufficient for some jobs in applied research or product development; temporary postdoctoral research positions are common.

❖ Competition for independent research positions in academia is expected.

Biological scientists who work in applied research or product development apply knowledge gained through basic research to develop new drugs, treatments, and medical diagnostic tests; increase crop yields; and develop new biofuels. They usually have less freedom than basic researchers do to choose the emphasis of their research, and they spend more time working on marketable treatments to meet the business goals of their employers. Biological scientists doing applied research and product development often work in teams, interacting with engineers, scientists of other disciplines, business managers, and technicians. Those working in private industry may be required to describe their research plans or results to nonscientists who are in a position to veto or approve their ideas. These scientists must consider the business effects of their work. Some biological scientists also work with customers or suppliers and manage budgets.

Scientists usually conduct research in laboratories using a wide variety of other equipment. Some conduct experiments involving animals or plants. This is particularly true of botanists, physiologists, and zoologists. Some biological research also takes place outside the laboratory. For example, a botanist might do field research in tropical rain forests to see which plants grow there, or an ecologist might study how a forest area recovers after a fire. Some marine biologists also work outdoors, often on research vessels from which they study fish, plankton, or other marine organisms.

Swift advances in knowledge of genetics and organic molecules spurred growth in the field of biotechnology, transforming the industries in which biological scientists work. Biological scientists can now manipulate the genetic material of animals and plants, attempting to make organisms more productive or resistant to disease. Those working on various genome (chromosomes with their associated genes) projects isolate genes and determine their function. This work continues to lead to the discovery of genes associated with specific diseases and inherited health risks, such as sickle cell anemia. Advances in biotechnology have created research opportunities in almost all areas of biology, with commercial applications in areas such as medicine, agriculture, and environmental remediation.

Most biological scientists specialize in the study of a certain type of organism or in a specific activity, although recent advances have blurred some traditional classifications.

Aquatic biologists study micro-organisms, plants, and animals living in water. *Marine biologists* study salt water organisms, and *limnologists* study fresh water organisms. Much of the work of marine biology centers on molecular biology, the study of the biochemical processes that take place inside living cells. Marine biologists are sometimes called oceanographers, a broader field that also includes the study of the physical characteristics of oceans and the ocean floor.

Biochemists study the chemical composition of living things. They analyze the complex chemical combinations and reactions involved in metabolism, reproduction, and growth.

Biochemists do most of their work in biotechnology, which involves understanding the complex chemistry of life.

Biophysicists study how physics, such as electrical and mechanical energy, relates to living cells and organisms. They perform research in fields such as neuroscience or bioinformatics (the use of computers to process biological information, usually at the molecular level).

Microbiologists investigate the growth and characteristics of microscopic organisms such as bacteria, algae, or fungi. Most microbiologists specialize in environmental, food, agricultural, or industrial microbiology; virology (the study of viruses); immunology (the study of mechanisms that fight infections); or bioinformatics. Many microbiologists use biotechnology to advance knowledge of cell reproduction and human disease.

Physiologists study life functions of plants and animals, both in the whole organism and at the cellular or molecular level, under normal and abnormal conditions. Physiologists often specialize in functions such as growth, reproduction, photosynthesis, respiration, or movement, or in the physiology of a certain area or system of the organism.

Botanists study plants and their environments. Some study all aspects of plant life, including algae, fungi, lichens, mosses, ferns, conifers, and flowering plants; others specialize in areas such as identification and classification of plants, the structure and function of plant parts, the biochemistry of plant processes, the causes and cures of plant diseases, the interaction of plants with other organisms and the environment, and the geological record of plants.

Zoologists and wildlife biologists study animals and wildlife—their origin, behavior, diseases, and life processes. Some experiment with live animals in controlled or natural surroundings, while others dissect dead animals to study their structure. Zoologists and wildlife biologists also may collect and analyze biological data to determine the environmental effects of current and potential uses of land and water areas. Zoologists are usually identified by the animal group they study—ornithologists study birds, for example, mammalogists study mammals, herpetologists study reptiles, and ichthyologists study fish.

Ecologists investigate the relationships among organisms and between organisms and their environments. They examine the effects of population size, pollutants, rainfall, temperature, and altitude. Using knowledge of various scientific disciplines, ecologists may collect, study, and report data on the quality of air, food, soil, and water.

Work environment. Most biologists spend their time in laboratories conducting research and in offices writing up results and keeping up with the latest research discoveries. Some biological scientists, particularly botanists, ecologists, and zoologists, do field studies that involve strenuous physical activity and primitive living conditions for extended periods of time. Biological scientists in the field may work in warm or cold climates, in all kinds of weather. Biological scientists usually are not exposed to unsafe or unhealthy conditions.

Those who work with dangerous organisms or toxic substances in the laboratory must follow strict safety procedures to avoid contamination.

Many biological scientists, particularly those employed in academic settings, depend on grant money to support their research. They may be under pressure to meet deadlines and to conform to rigid grant-writing specifications when preparing proposals to seek new or extended funding.

Biological scientists typically work regular hours. While the 40-hour workweek is common, some biological scientists work longer hours. Some researchers may be required to work odd hours in laboratories or other locations (especially while in the field), depending on the nature of their research.

Training, Other Qualifications, and Advancement

Most biological scientists need a Ph.D. in biology or one of its subfields to work in independent research or development positions. Other positions are available to those with a master's or bachelor's degree in the field.

Education and training. A Ph.D. is usually necessary for independent research, particularly in academia, as well as for advancement to administrative positions. A bachelor's or master's degree is sufficient for some jobs in applied research, product development, management, or inspection; it also may be sufficient to work as a research technician or a teacher. Many with a bachelor's degree in biology enter medical, dental, veterinary, or other health profession schools, or find jobs as high school science teachers.

In addition to required courses in chemistry and biology, undergraduate biological science majors usually study allied disciplines such as mathematics, physics, engineering, and computer science. Computer courses are beneficial for modeling and simulating biological processes, operating some laboratory equipment, and performing research in the emerging field of bioinformatics. Those interested in studying the environment also should take courses in environmental studies and become familiar with applicable legislation and regulations.

Most colleges and universities offer bachelor's degrees in biological science, and many offer advanced degrees. Advanced degree programs often emphasize a subfield, such as microbiology or botany, but not all universities offer curricula in all subfields. Larger universities frequently have separate departments specializing in different areas of biological science. For example, a program in botany might cover agronomy, horticulture, or plant pathology. Advanced degree programs typically include classroom and fieldwork, laboratory research, and a thesis or dissertation. A master's degree generally takes 2 years, and a doctoral degree 5-6 years of full-time study.

Biological scientists with a Ph.D. often take temporary postdoctoral positions that provide specialized research experience. Postdoctoral positions may offer the opportunity to publish research findings. A solid record of published research is essential in obtaining a permanent position performing basic research, especially for those seeking a permanent college or university faculty position.

Other qualifications. Biological scientists should be able to work independently or as part of a team and be able to communicate clearly and concisely, both orally and in writing. Those in private industry, especially those who aspire to management or administrative positions, should possess strong business and communication skills and be familiar with regulatory issues and marketing and management techniques. Those doing field research in remote areas must have physical stamina. Biological scientists also must have patience and self-discipline to conduct long and detailed research projects.

Advancement. As they gain experience, biological scientists typically gain greater control over their research and may advance to become lead researchers directing a team of scientists and technicians. Some work as consultants to businesses or to government agencies. However, those dependent on research grants are still constrained by funding agencies, and may spend much of their time writing grant proposals. Others choose to move into managerial positions and become natural science managers. They may plan and administer programs for testing foods and drugs, for example, or direct activities at zoos or botanical gardens. Those who pursue management careers spend much of their time preparing budgets and schedules. Some leave biology for nontechnical managerial, administrative, or sales jobs.

Employment

Biological scientists held about 91,300 jobs in 2008. In addition, many biological scientists held biology faculty positions in colleges and universities but are not included in these numbers. Those whose primary work involves teaching and research are considered postsecondary teachers.

About 40 percent of all biological scientists were employed by Federal, State, and local governments. Federal biological scientists worked mainly for the U.S. Departments of Agriculture, Interior, and Defense and for the National Institutes of Health. Most of the rest worked in scientific research and testing laboratories, the pharmaceutical and medicine manufacturing industry, or educational institutions.

Job Outlook

Employment of biological scientists is expected to increase much faster than the average for all occupations although there will continue to be competition for some basic research positions.

Employment change. Employment of biological scientists is projected to grow 21 percent over the 2008—18 decade, much faster than the average for all occupations, as biotechnological research and development continues to drive job growth. Biological scientists enjoyed very rapid employment gains over the past few decades—reflecting, in part, the growth of the biotechnology industry. Employment growth will moderate somewhat as the biotechnology industry matures, with fewer new firms being founded and existing firms merging or being absorbed by larger biotechnology or pharmaceutical firms. However, much of the basic biological research done in recent years has resulted in new knowledge, including the isolation and identification of genes. Biological scientists will be needed to take this knowledge to the next stage, understanding how certain genes function within an entire organism, so that medical treatments can be developed to treat various diseases. Even pharmaceutical and other firms not solely engaged in biotechnology use biotechnology techniques extensively, spurring employment for biological scientists. For example, biological scientists are continuing to help farmers increase crop yields by pinpointing genes that can help crops, such as wheat, grow in more extreme climate conditions.

In addition, efforts to discover new and improved ways to clean up and preserve the environment will continue to add to job growth. More biological scientists will be needed to determine the environmental impact of industry and government actions and to prevent or correct environmental problems, such as the negative effects of pesticide use. Some biological scientists will find opportunities in environmental regulatory agencies, while others will use their expertise to advise lawmakers on legislation to save environmentally sensitive areas. New industrial applications of biotechnology, such as new methods for producing biofuels, also will spur demand for biological scientists.

The Federal Government is a major source of funding for basic research and development, including many areas of medical research that relate to biological science. Large budget increases at the National Institutes of Health in the early part of the decade led to increases in Federal basic research and development expenditures, with research grants growing both in number and dollar amount. However, the increase in expenditures slowed substantially in recent years. Going forward, the level of Federal funding will continue to impact competition for winning and renewing research grants.

There will continue to be demand for biological scientists specializing in botany, zoology, and marine biology, but opportunities will be limited because of the small size of these fields. Marine biology, despite its attractiveness as a career, is a very small specialty within biological science.

Job prospects. Doctoral degree holders are expected to face competition for basic research positions in academia. Furthermore, should the number of advanced degrees awarded continue to grow, applicants for research grants are likely to face even more competition. Currently, about 1 in 4 grant proposals are approved for long-term research projects. In general, applied research positions in private industry are somewhat easier to obtain, but may become more competitive if increasing numbers of scientists seek jobs in private industry because of the difficulty finding positions in colleges and universities.

Prospective marine biology students should be aware that those who would like to enter this specialty far outnumber the very few openings that occur each year for the type of glamorous research jobs that many would like to obtain. Almost all marine biologists who do basic research have a Ph.D.

People with bachelor's and master's degrees are expected to have more opportunities in nonscientist jobs related to biology, in fields like sales, marketing, publishing, and research management. Non-Ph.D.s also may fill positions as science or engineering technicians or as medical health technologists and technicians. Some become high school biology teachers.

Biological scientists are less likely to lose their jobs during recessions than those in other occupations, because many are employed on long-term research projects. However, an economic downturn could influence the amount of money allocated to new research and development efforts, particularly in areas of risky or innovative research. An economic downturn also could limit the possibility of extension or renewal of existing projects.

Earnings

Median annual wages of biochemists and biophysicists were $82,840 in May 2008. The middle 50 percent earned between $59,260 and $108,950. The lowest 10 percent earned less than $44,320, and the highest 10 percent earned more than $139,440. Median annual wages of biochemists and biophysicists employed in scientific research and development services were $85,870 in May 2008.

Median annual wages of microbiologists were $64,350 in May 2008. The middle 50 percent earned between $48,330 and $87,040. The lowest 10 percent earned less than $38,240, and the highest 10 percent earned more than $111,300.

Median annual wages of zoologists and wildlife biologists were $55,290 in May 2008. The middle 50 percent earned between $43,060 and $70,500. The lowest 10 percent earned less than $33,550, and the highest 10 percent earned more than $90,850.

According to the National Association of Colleges and Employers, beginning salary offers in July 2009 averaged $33,254 a year for bachelor's degree recipients in biological and life sciences.

In the Federal Government in March 2009, microbiologists earned an average annual salary of $97,264; ecologists, $84,283; physiologists, $109,323; geneticists, $99,752; zoologists, $116,908; and botanists, $72,792.

MATH & SCIENCE

—m—

Geoscientists & Hydrologists

Nature of the Work

Geoscientists and *hydrologists* study the composition, structure, and other physical aspects of the Earth, and the Earth's geologic past and present by using sophisticated instruments to analyze the composition of earth, rock, and water. Many geoscientists and hydrologists help to search for natural resources such as groundwater, minerals, metals, and petroleum. Others work closely with environmental and other scientists to preserve and clean up the environment.

Geoscientists usually study and work in one of several closely related geosciences fields, including geology, geophysics, and hydrology. *Geologists* study the composition, processes, and history of the Earth. They try to find out how rocks were formed and what has happened to them since their formation. They also study the evolution of life by analyzing plant and animal fossils. *Geophysicists* use the principles of physics, mathematics, and chemistry to study not only the Earth's surface, but also its internal composition, ground and surface waters, atmosphere, oceans, and magnetic, electrical, and gravitational forces. Hydrologists study the quantity, distribution, circulation, and physical properties of water and the water cycle.

Within these major geoscience fields, there are numerous subspecialties. For example, *petroleum geologists* map the subsurface of the ocean or land as they explore the terrain for

> ### Significant Points
>
> ❖ Work at remote field sites is common.
>
> ❖ Twenty-three percent of all geoscientists and hydrologists are employed in government.
>
> ❖ Employers prefer applicants with a master's degree for most positions; a Ph.D. degree is required for most research and college teaching positions.
>
> ❖ Excellent job opportunities are expected for geoscientists with a master's degree.

oil and gas deposits. They use sophisticated instrumentation and computers to interpret geological information. *Engineering geologists* apply geologic principles to the fields of civil and environmental engineering, offering advice on major construction projects and assisting in environmental remediation and natural hazard-reduction projects. *Mineralogists* analyze and classify minerals and precious stones according to their composition and structure, and study the environment surrounding rocks in order to find new mineral resources. *Sedimentologists* study the nature, origin, distribution, and alteration of sediments, such as sand, silt, and mud. These sediments may contain oil, gas, coal, and many other mineral deposits. *Paleontologists* study fossils found in geological formations to trace the evolution of plant and animal life and the geologic history of the Earth. *Stratigraphers* examine the formation and layering of rocks to understand the environment which formed them. *Volcanologists* investigate volcanoes and volcanic phenomena to try to predict the potential for future eruptions and hazards to human health and welfare. *Glacial geologists* study the physical properties and movement of glaciers and ice sheets. *Geochemists* study the nature and distribution of chemical elements in groundwater and earth materials.

Geophysicists specialize in areas such as geodesy, seismology, and magnetic geophysics. *Geodesists* study the Earth's size, shape, gravitational field, tides, polar motion, and rotation. *Seismologists* interpret data from seismographs and other geophysical instruments to detect earthquakes and locate earthquake-related faults. *Geomagnetists* measure the Earth's magnetic field and use measurements taken over the past few centuries to devise theoretical models that explain the Earth's origin. *Paleomagnetists* interpret fossil magnetization in rocks and sediments from the continents and oceans to record the spreading of the sea floor, the wandering of the continents, and the many reversals of polarity that the Earth's magnetic field has undergone through time. Other geophysicists study atmospheric sciences and space physics.

Hydrologists often specialize in either underground water or surface water. They examine the form and intensity of precipitation, its rate of infiltration into the soil, its movement through the Earth, and its return to the ocean and atmosphere. Hydrologists use sophisticated techniques and instruments. For example, they may use remote sensing technology, data assimilation, and numerical modeling to monitor the change in regional and global water cycles. Some surface-water hydrologists use sensitive stream-measuring devices to assess flow rates and water quality.

Oceanographers use their knowledge of geosciences, in addition to biology and chemistry, to study the world's oceans and coastal waters. They study the motion and circulation of ocean waters; the physical and chemical properties of the oceans; and how these properties affect coastal areas, climate, and weather. (*Biological oceanographers,* often called marine biologists, study the distribution and migration patterns of the many diverse forms of sea life in the ocean.

Geoscientists in research positions with the Federal Government or in colleges and universities frequently are required to design programs and write grant proposals in order to fund their research. Geoscientists in consulting jobs face similar pressures to market their skills and write proposals so that they will have steady work.

Work environment. Geoscientists and hydrologists can spend a large part of their time in the field, identifying and examining geological formation, studying data collected by remote sensing instruments, conducting geological surveys, constructing field maps, and using instruments to measure the Earth's gravity and magnetic field. They often perform seismic studies, for example, which involve bouncing energy waves off buried layers of rock, to search for oil and gas or to understand the structure of the subsurface layers. Similarly, they use seismic signals generated by an earthquake to determine the earthquake's location and intensity. In laboratories, they examine the chemical and physical properties of specimens. They study fossil remains of animal and plant life or experiment with the flow of water and oil through rocks.

Some geoscientists and hydrologists spend the majority of their time in an office, but many others divide their time between fieldwork and office or laboratory work. Work at remote field sites is common. Some specialists, such as volcanologists, often take field trips that involve significant physical activity and some risk. In the field they work in warm or cold climates and in all kinds of weather. In their research, they may dig or chip with a hammer, scoop with a net, and carry equipment in a backpack. Oceanographers may spend considerable time at sea on academic research ships. Geologists frequently travel to remote field sites by helicopter or 4-wheel-drive vehicles and cover large areas on foot. Many exploration geologists and geophysicists work in foreign countries, sometimes in remote areas and under difficult conditions. Travel often is required to meet with prospective clients or investors. Fieldwork often requires working long and irregular hours.

Training, Other Qualifications, and Advancement

A master's degree is the primary educational requirement for most positions. A Ph.D. is necessary for most research and college teaching positions.

Education and training. A bachelor's degree is adequate for a few entry-level positions, but most geoscientists and hydrologists need a master's degree, which is the preferred educational requirement for most research positions in private industry, Federal agencies, and State geological surveys. A Ph.D. is necessary for most high-level research and college teaching positions, but is generally not required for other jobs.

Many colleges and universities offer bachelor's and graduate degrees in the geosciences. Traditional geoscience courses emphasizing classical geologic methods and topics (such as mineralogy, petrology, paleontology, stratigraphy, and structural geology) are important for all geoscientists. People who study physics, chemistry, biology, mathematics, engineering, or computer science may also qualify for some geoscience positions if their course work includes geology.

Most universities do not offer degrees in hydrology, but instead offer concentrations in hydrology or water studies in their geoscience, environmental science, or engineering departments. Students interested in hydrology should take courses in the physical sciences, geophysics, chemistry, engineering science, soil science, mathematics, aquatic biology, atmospheric science, geology, oceanography, hydrogeology, and the management or conservation of water resources.

Licensure and certification. A number of States require geoscientists and hydrologists who offer their services directly to the public to obtain a license from a State licensing board. Licensing requirements vary by State but typically include education and experience requirements and a passing score on an examination. In States that do not require a license, workers can obtain voluntary certifications. For example, the American Institute of Hydrology offers certification programs in professional hydrology that have similar requirements to State licensure programs.

Other qualifications. Computer skills are essential for prospective geoscientists and hydrologists; students who have experience with computer modeling, data analysis and integration, digital mapping, remote sensing, and Geographic Information Systems (GIS) will be the most prepared entering the job market. Knowledge of the Global Positioning System (GPS)—a locator system that uses satellites—has also become essential. Some employers seek applicants with field experience, so a summer internship is often helpful.

Because geoscientists and hydrologists usually work as part of a team with other geoscientists and with environmental scientists, engineers, and technicians, they must have good interpersonal skills. Strong oral and written communication skills also are important because writing technical reports and research proposals and explaining research results in person are important aspects of the work. Some jobs, particularly for petroleum geologists, require foreign travel, and for these positions knowledge of a second language is beneficial.

These workers must be inquisitive, able to think logically, and capable of complex analytical thinking, including spatial visualization and the ability to infer conclusions from sparse data. Geoscientists and hydrologists involved in fieldwork must have physical stamina.

Advancement. Geoscientists and hydrologists often begin their careers in field exploration or as research assistants or technicians in laboratories or offices. As they gain experience, they take on more complex and difficult assignments. Eventually, some are promoted to project leader, program manager, or to a senior research position. Those who choose to work in management will spend more time scheduling, budgeting, and reporting to top executives or clients.

Employment

Geoscientists held about 33,600 jobs in 2008, while another 8,100 were employed as hydrologists. Many more individuals held geoscience faculty positions in colleges and universities, but they are classified as college and university faculty.

About 23 percent of geoscientists were employed in architectural, engineering, and related services and 19 percent worked for oil and gas extraction companies. State agencies such as State geological surveys and State departments of conservation employed another 9 percent of geoscientists. Eight percent worked for the Federal Government, including geologists, geophysicists, and oceanographers, mostly within the U.S. Department of the Interior for the U.S. Geological Survey (USGS) and within the U.S. Department of Defense.

Among hydrologists, 26 percent were employed in architectural, engineering, and related services, and 19 percent worked for management, scientific, and technical consulting services. The Federal Government employed about 27 percent of hydrologists, mostly within the U.S. Department of the Interior for the U.S. Geological Survey (USGS) and within the U.S. Department of Defense.

Job Outlook

Employment of geoscientists and hydrologists is expected to grow faster than the average for all occupations. Graduates with a master's degree in geoscience can expect excellent job opportunities, but Ph.D.s may face competition for research and college teaching jobs.

Employment change. Employment growth of 18 percent is expected for geoscientists and hydrologists between 2008 and 2018, which is faster than the average for all occupations. The need for energy, environmental protection, and responsible land and water management will spur employment demand. Employment in management, scientific, and technical consulting services should continue to grow as more geoscientists work as consultants. These services have increased their hiring of geoscientists in recent years because of increased government contracting and private corporations' need for technical assistance and environmental management plans. Moreover, many geoscientists and hydrologists monitor the quality of the environment, checking for problems such as deteriorating coastal environments and soil and water contamination—all of which will create employment growth for them. An expected increase in highway building and other infrastructure projects will also be a source of jobs for engineering geologists.

Many geoscientists work in the exploration and production of oil and gas. Historically, employment of petroleum geoscientists has been cyclical and affected considerably by the price of oil and gas. When prices are low, oil and gas producers curtail exploration activities and may lay off geologists. When prices are high, companies have the funds and incentive to renew exploration efforts and to hire geoscientists in larger numbers. In the long term, continued high oil prices are expected to maintain demand for workers who can find new resource deposits. Geoscientists who speak a foreign language and who are willing to work abroad should enjoy the best opportunities, as the need for energy, construction materials, and a broad range of geoscience expertise grows in developing nations.

Demand for hydrologists should also be strong as the population increases and moves to more environmentally sensitive locations. As people increasingly migrate toward coastal regions, for example, hydrologists will be needed to assess building sites for potential geologic hazards and to mitigate the effects of natural hazards such as floods, landslides, and hurricanes. Hydrologists also will be needed to study hazardous-waste sites and determine the effect of pollutants on soil and ground water so that engineers can design remediation systems. Increased government regulations, such as those regarding the management of storm water, and issues related to water conservation, deteriorating coastal environments, and rising sea levels also will stimulate employment growth for these workers.

Job prospects. Graduates with a master's degree in geoscience should have excellent opportunities, especially in consulting firms and in the oil and gas industry. In addition to demand resulting from job growth, replacing those who leave the occupation for retirement, managerial positions, or other careers will generate a number of jobs. A significant number of geoscientists are approaching retirement age, and without increases in the number of students earning master's degrees in the geosciences, job openings may exceed the number of qualified jobseekers over the 2008-18 projection period. However, geoscientists with doctoral degrees, who primarily work as college and university faculty or do research, may face competition. There are few openings for new graduates with only a bachelor's degree in geoscience, but these graduates may have favorable opportunities in related occupations, such as high school science teacher or science technician.

Job prospects for hydrologists should be favorable, particularly for those with field experience. Demand for hydrologists who understand both the scientific and engineering aspects of waste remediation should be strong.

There will be fewer opportunities for geoscientists and hydrologists in Federal and State government, mostly because of budget constraints at key agencies, such as the U.S. Geological Service, and the trend among governments toward contracting out to consulting firms instead of hiring new government employees. However, departures of geoscientists who retire or leave the government for other reasons will result in some job openings over the next decade.

Geoscientists may face layoffs during periods of economic recession, but the prices of commodities are a much more important source of volatility; for those working in the oil and gas or mining industries, the cyclical nature of commodity prices determines demand. When prices are high, jobs are plentiful, but when prices fall, positions become scarce.

Earnings

Median annual wages of geoscientists were $79,160 in May 2008. The middle 50 percent earned between $54,470 and $113,390; the lowest 10 percent earned less than $41,700, and the highest 10 percent more than $155,430.

The petroleum, mineral, and mining industries offer higher salaries, but less job security, than other industries because economic downturns sometimes cause layoffs.

Median annual wages of hydrologists were $71,450 in May 2008. The middle 50 percent earned between $54,910 and $89,200; the lowest 10 percent earned less than $44,410, and the highest 10 percent more than $105,010.

In March 2009, the Federal Government's average salary was $94,085 for geologists, $108,118 for geophysicists, $89,404 for hydrologists, and $105,671 for oceanographers.

MATH & SCIENCE

—ɯ—

Physicists & Astronomers

Nature of the Work

Physicists and astronomers conduct research to understand the nature of the universe and everything in it. These scientists observe, measure, interpret, and develop theories to explain celestial and physical phenomena using mathematics. From the vastness of space to the infinitesimal scale of subatomic particles, they study the fundamental properties of the natural world and apply the knowledge gained to design new technologies.

Physicists explore and identify basic principles and laws governing the motion, energy, structure, and interactions of matter. Some physicists study theoretical areas, such as the nature of time and the origin of the universe; others apply their knowledge of physics to practical areas, such as the development of advanced materials, electronic and optical devices, and medical equipment.

Physicists design and perform experiments with sophisticated equipment such as lasers, particle accelerators, electron microscopes, and mass spectrometers. On the basis of their observations and analysis, they attempt to discover and explain laws

---

Significant Points

❖ Scientific research and development services firms and the Federal Government employ over half of all physicists and astronomers.

❖ Most jobs in basic research usually require a doctoral degree; master's degree holders qualify for some jobs in applied research and development; bachelor's degree holders often qualify as research assistants or for other physics-related occupations, such as technicians.

❖ Applicants may face competition for basic research positions due to limited funding; however, those with a background in physics or astronomy may have good opportunities in related fields, such as engineering and technology.

describing the forces of nature, such as gravity, electromagnetism, and nuclear interactions. Experiments also help physicists find ways to apply physical laws and theories to problems in nuclear energy, electronics, optics, materials, communications, aerospace technology, and medical instrumentation.

Astronomers use the principles of physics and mathematics to learn about the fundamental nature of the universe and its components, including the sun, moon, planets, stars, and galaxies. As such, astronomy is sometimes considered a subfield of physics. They also apply their knowledge to solve problems in navigation, space flight, and satellite communications and to develop the instrumentation and techniques used to observe and collect astronomical data.

Most physicists and astronomers work in research and development. Some conduct basic research with the sole aim of increasing scientific knowledge. Others conduct applied research and development, which builds upon the discoveries made through basic research to develop practical applications of this knowledge, such as new devices, products, and processes. For example, knowledge gained through basic research in solid-state physics led to the development of transistors and, then, integrated circuits used in computers.

Physicists also design research equipment, which often has additional unanticipated uses. For example, lasers are used in surgery, microwave devices function in ovens, and measuring instruments can analyze blood or the chemical content of foods.

A small number of physicists work in inspection, testing, quality control, and other production-related jobs in industry.

Much physics research is done in small or medium-sized laboratories. However, experiments in plasma, nuclear, and high-energy physics, as well as in some other areas of physics, require extremely large and expensive equipment, such as particle accelerators and nuclear reactors. Physicists in these subfields often work in large teams. Although physics research may require extensive experimentation in laboratories, research physicists still spend much time in offices planning, recording, analyzing, and reporting on research.

Physicists generally specialize in one of many subfields, such as elementary particle physics, nuclear physics, atomic and molecular physics, condensed matter physics, optics, acoustics, space physics, or plasma physics. Some specialize in a subdivision of one of these subfields. For example, within condensed-matter physics, specialties include superconductivity, crystallography, and semiconductors. However, all physics involves the same fundamental principles, so specialties may overlap, and physicists may switch from one subfield to another. Also, growing numbers of physicists work in interdisciplinary fields, such as biophysics, chemical physics, and geophysics.

Almost all astronomers do research. Some are theoreticians, working on the laws governing the structure and evolution of astronomical objects. Others analyze large quantities of data gathered by observatories and satellites and write scientific papers or reports on their findings. Some astronomers actually operate large space-based or ground-based telescopes, usually as part of a team. However, astronomers may spend only a few weeks each year making observations with optical telescopes, radio telescopes, and other instruments.

For many years, satellites and other space-based instruments, such as the Hubble space telescope, have provided prodigious amounts of astronomical data. New technology has lead to improvements in analytical techniques and instruments, such as computers and optical telescopes and mounts, and is creating a resurgence in ground-based research.

A small number of astronomers work in museums housing planetariums. These astronomers develop and revise programs presented to the public and may direct planetarium operations.

Work environment. Most physicists and astronomers do not encounter unusual hazards in their work. Some physicists temporarily work away from home at national or international facilities with unique equipment, such as particle accelerators. Astronomers who make observations with ground-based telescopes may spend many hours working in observatories; this work usually involves travel to remote locations and may require working at night. Physicists and astronomers whose work depends on grant money often are under pressure to write grant proposals to keep their work funded.

Physicists often work regular hours in laboratories and offices. At times, however, those who are deeply involved in research may work long or irregular hours. Astronomers may need to work at odd hours to observe celestial phenomena, particularly those working with ground-based telescopes.

Training, Other Qualifications, and Advancement

Because most jobs are in basic research and development, a doctoral degree is the usual educational requirement for physicists and astronomers. Master's degree holders qualify for some jobs in applied research and development, whereas bachelor's degree holders often qualify as research assistants or for jobs in other fields where a physics background is good preparation, such as engineering and technology.

Education and training. A Ph.D. degree in physics or closely related fields is typically required for basic research positions, independent research in industry, faculty positions, and advancement to managerial positions. Graduate study in physics prepares students for a career in research through rigorous training in theory, methodology, and mathematics. Most physicists specialize in a subfield during graduate school and continue working in that area afterwards.

Additional experience and training in a postdoctoral research appointment, although not required, is important for physicists and astronomers aspiring to permanent positions in basic research in universities and government laboratories. Many physics and astronomy Ph.D. holders ultimately teach at the college or university level.

Master's degree holders usually do not qualify for basic research positions, but may qualify for many kinds of jobs requiring a physics background, including positions in manufacturing and applied research and development. Increasingly, many master's degree programs are specifically preparing students for physics-related research and development that does not require a Ph.D. degree. These programs teach students specific research skills that can be used in private-industry jobs. In addition, a master's degree coupled with State certification usually qualifies one for teaching jobs in high schools or at 2-year colleges.

Those with bachelor's degrees in physics are rarely qualified to fill positions in research or in teaching at the college level. They are, however, usually qualified to work as technicians or research assistants in engineering-related areas, in software development and other scientific fields, or in setting up computer networks and sophisticated laboratory equipment. Increasingly, some may qualify for applied research jobs in private industry or take on nontraditional physics roles, often in computer science, such as systems analysts or database administrators. Some become science teachers in secondary schools.

Holders of a bachelor's or master's degree in astronomy often enter an unrelated field where their strong analytical background provides good preparation. However, they are also qualified to work in planetariums running science shows, to assist astronomers doing research, and to operate space-based and ground-based telescopes and other astronomical instrumentation.

Many colleges and universities offer a bachelor's degree in physics. Undergraduate programs provide a broad background in the natural sciences and mathematics. Typical physics courses include electromagnetism, optics, thermodynamics, atomic physics, and quantum mechanics.

Approximately 190 universities offer Ph.D. degrees in physics; more than 60 additional colleges offer a master's as their highest degree in physics. Graduate students usually concentrate in a subfield of physics, such as elementary particles or condensed matter. Many begin studying for their doctorate immediately after receiving their bachelor's degree; a typical Ph.D. program takes about 6 years to complete.

About 75 universities grant degrees in astronomy, either through an astronomy, physics, or combined physics-astronomy department. About half of all astronomy departments are combined with physics departments, while the remainder are administered separately. With about 40 doctoral programs in astronomy, applicants face considerable competition for available slots. Those planning a career in the subject should have a strong physics background. In fact, an undergraduate degree in either physics or astronomy is excellent preparation, followed by a Ph.D. in astronomy.

Many physics and astronomy Ph.D. holders begin their careers in a postdoctoral research position, in which they may work with experienced physicists as they continue to learn about their specialties or develop a broader understanding of related areas of research. Initial work may be under the close supervision of senior scientists. As they gain experience, physicists perform increasingly complex tasks and achieve greater independence in their work. Experience, either in academic laboratories or through internships, fellowships, or work-study programs in industry, also is useful. Some employers of research physicists, particularly in the information technology industry, prefer to hire individuals with several years of postdoctoral experience.

Other qualifications. Mathematical ability, problem-solving and analytical skills, an inquisitive mind, imagination, and initiative are important traits for anyone planning a career in physics or astronomy. Prospective physicists who hope to work in industrial laboratories applying physics knowledge to practical problems should broaden their educational background to include courses outside of physics, such as economics, information technology, and business management. Good oral and written communication skills also are important because many physicists work as part of a team, write research papers or proposals, or have contact with clients or customers who do not have a physics background.

Certain sensitive research positions with the Federal Government and in fields such as nuclear energy may require applicants to be U.S. citizens and to hold a security clearance.

Advancement. Advancement among physicists and astronomers usually takes the form of greater independence in their work, larger budgets, or tenure in university positions. Others choose to move into managerial positions and become natural science managers. Those who pursue management careers spend more time preparing budgets and schedules. Those who develop new products or processes sometimes form their own companies or join new firms to develop these ideas.

Employment

Physicists and astronomers held about 17,100 jobs in 2008. Physicists accounted for about 15,600 of these, while astronomers accounted for only about 1,500 jobs. In addition, there were about 15,500 physicists employed in faculty positions.

About 39 percent of physicists and astronomers worked for the scientific research and development services industry, which includes employees of the 36 Federally Funded Research and Development Centers. These centers, sometimes referred to as national laboratories, perform a significant amount of basic research in the physical sciences. They are funded by government agencies such as the Department of Energy and the Department of Defense, but are administered by universities or private corporations. The Federal Government directly employed another 22 percent, mostly in the U.S. Department of Defense, but also in the National Aeronautics and Space Administration (NASA) and in the U.S. Departments of Commerce, Health and Human Services, and Energy. Other physicists and astronomers worked in nonfaculty research positions at educational institutions and hospitals.

Although physicists and astronomers are employed in all parts of the country, most work in areas in which universities, large research laboratories, or observatories are located.

Job Outlook

Physicists and astronomers should experience faster than average job growth, but may face competition for basic research positions due to limited funding. However, those with a background in physics or astronomy may have good opportunities in related occupations.

Employment change. Employment of physicists and astronomers is expected to grow 16 percent, faster than the average for all occupations during the 2008-18 decade.

Federal research expenditures are the major source of physics-related and astronomy-related research funds, especially for basic research. For most of the past decade there has been limited growth in Federal funding for physics and astronomy research as most of the growth in Federal research funding has been devoted to the life sciences. However, the America COMPETES Act, passed by Congress in 2007, sets a goal to double funding for the physical sciences through the National Science Foundation and the Department of Energy's Office of Science by the year 2016, and recent budgets for these agencies have seen large increases. If these increases continue, it will result in more opportunities in basic research for Ph.D. physicists and astronomers.

Although research and development expenditures in private industry will continue to grow, many research laboratories in private industry are expected to continue to reduce basic research, which includes much physics research, in favor of applied or manufacturing research and product and software development. Nevertheless, people with a physics background continue to be in demand in information technology, semiconductor technology, and other applied sciences. This trend is expected to continue; however, many of the new workers will have job titles such as computer software engineer, computer programmer, or systems analyst or developer, rather than physicist.

Job prospects. In addition to job growth, the need to replace physicists and astronomers who retire or otherwise leave the occupation permanently will account for many job openings. In recent years the number of doctorates granted in physics has been somewhat greater than the number of job openings for traditional physics research positions in colleges and universities and in research centers. Recent increases in undergraduate physics enrollments may also lead to growth in enrollments in graduate physics programs, so that there may be an increase in the number of doctoral degrees granted that could intensify the competition for basic research positions. However, demand has grown in other related occupations for those with advanced training in physics. Prospects should be favorable for physicists in applied research, development, and related technical fields.

Opportunities should also be numerous for those with a master's degree, particularly graduates from programs preparing students for related work in applied research and development, product design, and manufacturing positions in private industry. Many of these positions, however, will have titles other than physicist, such as engineer or computer scientist.

People with only a bachelor's degree in physics or astronomy are usually not qualified for physics or astronomy research jobs, but they may qualify for a wide range of positions related to engineering, mathematics, computer science, environmental science, and some nonscience fields, such as finance. Those who meet State certification requirements can become high school physics teachers, an occupation in strong demand in many school districts. Some States require new teachers to obtain a master's degree in education within a certain time. Despite competition for traditional physics and astronomy research jobs, graduates with a physics or astronomy degree at any level will find their knowledge of science and mathematics useful for entry into many other occupations.

Despite their small numbers, astronomers can expect good job prospects in government and academia over the projection period. Since astronomers are particularly dependent upon government funding, Federal budgetary decisions will have a sizable influence on job prospects for astronomers.

Earnings

Median annual wages of physicists were $102,890 in May 2008. The middle 50 percent earned between $80,040 and $130,980. The lowest 10 percent earned less than $57,160, and the highest 10 percent earned more than 159,400.

Median annual wages of astronomers were $101,300 in May 2008. The middle 50 percent earned between $63,610 and $133,630, the lowest 10 percent less than $45,330, and the highest 10 percent more than $156,720.

The average annual salary for physicists employed by the Federal Government was $118,971 in March 2009; for astronomy and space scientists, it was $130,833.

MATH & SCIENCE

—⚍—

Psychologists

Nature of the Work

Psychologists study mental processes and human behavior by observing, interpreting, and recording how people and other animals relate to one another and the environment. To do this, psychologists often look for patterns that will help them understand and predict behavior using scientific methods, principles, or procedures to test their ideas. Through such research studies, psychologists have learned much that can help increase understanding between individuals, groups, organizations, institutions, nations, and cultures.

Like other social scientists, psychologists formulate theories, or hypotheses, which are possible explanations for what they observe. But unlike other social science disciplines, psychologists often concentrate on individual behavior and, specifically, in the beliefs and feelings that influence a person's actions.

Research methods vary with the topic which they study, but by and large, the chief techniques used are observation, assessment, and experimentation. Psychologists sometimes gather information and evaluate behavior through controlled laboratory experiments, hypnosis, biofeedback, psychoanalysis, or

Significant Points

❖ About 34 percent of psychologists are self-employed, mainly as private practitioners and independent consultants.

❖ Employment growth will vary by specialty; for example, clinical, counseling, and school psychologists will have 11 percent growth; industrial-organizational psychologists, 26 percent growth; and 14 percent growth is expected for all other psychologists.

❖ Acceptance to graduate psychology programs is highly competitive.

❖ Job opportunities should be the best for those with a doctoral degree in a subfield, such as health; those with a master's degree will have good prospects in industrial-organization; bachelor's degree holders will have limited prospects.

psychotherapy, or by administering personality, performance, aptitude, or intelligence tests. Other methods include interviews, questionnaires, clinical studies, surveys, and observation—looking for cause-and-effect relationships between events and for broad patterns of behavior.

Research in psychology seeks to understand and explain thought, emotion, feelings, or behavior. The research findings of psychologists have greatly increased our understanding of why people and animals behave as they do. For example, psychologists have discovered how personality develops and how to promote healthy development. They have gained knowledge of how to diagnose and treat alcoholism and substance abuse, how to help people change bad habits and conduct, and how to help students learn. They understand the conditions that can make workers more productive. Insights provided by psychologists can help people function better as individuals, friends, family members, and workers.

Psychologists may perform a variety of duties in a vast number of industries. For example, those working in health service fields may provide mental healthcare in hospitals, clinics, schools, or private settings. Psychologists employed in applied settings, such as business, industry, government, or nonprofit organizations, may provide training, conduct research, design organizational systems, and act as advocates for psychology.

Psychologists apply their knowledge to a wide range of endeavors, including health and human services, management, education, law, and sports. They usually specialize in one of many different areas.

Clinical psychologists—who constitute the largest specialty—are concerned with the assessment, diagnosis, treatment, and prevention of mental disorders. While some clinical psychologists specialize in treating severe psychological disorders, such as schizophrenia and depression, many others may help people deal with personal issues, such as divorce or the death of a loved one. Often times, clinical psychologists provide an opportunity to talk and think about things that are confusing or worrying, offering different ways of interpreting and understanding problems and situations. They are trained to use a variety of approaches aimed at helping individuals, and the strategies used are generally determined by the specialty they work in.

Clinical psychologists often interview patients and give diagnostic tests in their own private offices. They may provide individual, family, or group psychotherapy and may design and implement behavior modification programs. Some clinical psychologists work in hospitals where they collaborate with physicians and other specialists to develop and implement treatment and intervention programs that patients can understand and comply with. Other clinical psychologists work in universities and medical schools, where they train graduate students in the delivery of mental health and behavioral medicine services. A few work in physical rehabilitation settings, treating patients with spinal cord injuries, chronic pain or illness, stroke, arthritis, or neurological conditions. Others may work in community mental health centers, crisis counseling services, or drug rehabilitation centers, offering evaluation, therapy, remediation, and consultation.

Areas of specialization within clinical psychology include health psychology, neuropsychology, geropsychology, and child psychology. *Health psychologists* study how biological, psychological, and social factors affect health and illness. They promote healthy living and disease prevention through counseling, and they focus on how patients adjust to illnesses and treatments and view their quality of life. *Neuropsychologists* study the relation between the brain and behavior. They often work in stroke and head injury programs. *Geropsychologists* deal with the special problems faced by the elderly. Work may include helping older persons cope with stresses that are common in late life, such as loss of loved ones, relocation, medical conditions, and increased care-giving demands. Clinical psychologists may further specialize in these fields by focusing their work in a number of niche areas including mental health, learning disabilities, emotional disturbances, or substance abuse. The emergence and growth of these, and other, specialties reflects the increasing participation of psychologists in direct services to special patient populations.

Often, clinical psychologists consult with other medical personnel regarding the best treatment for patients, especially treatment that includes medication. Clinical psychologists generally are not permitted to prescribe medication to treat patients; only psychiatrists and other medical doctors may prescribe most medications. However, two States—Louisiana and New Mexico—currently allow appropriately trained clinical psychologists to prescribe medication with some limitations.

Counseling psychologists advise people on how to deal with problems of everyday living, including problems in the home, place of work, or community, to help improve their quality of life. They foster well-being by promoting good mental health and preventing mental, physical, and social disorders. They work in settings such as university or crisis counseling centers, hospitals, rehabilitation centers, and individual or group practices.

School psychologists work with students in early childhood and elementary and secondary schools. They collaborate with teachers, parents, and school personnel to create safe, healthy, and supportive learning environments for all students. School psychologists address students' learning and behavioral problems, suggest improvements to classroom management strategies or parenting techniques, and evaluate students with disabilities and gifted and talented students to help determine the best way to educate them.

They improve teaching, learning, and socialization strategies based on their understanding of the psychology of learning environments. They also may evaluate the effectiveness of academic programs, prevention programs, behavior management procedures, and other services provided in the school setting.

Industrial-organizational psychologists apply psychological principles and research methods to the workplace in the interest of improving the quality of worklife. They also are involved in research on management and marketing problems. They screen, train, and counsel applicants for jobs, as well as perform organizational development and analysis. An industrial psychologist might work with management to reorganize the work setting in order to enhance productivity. Industrial psychologists frequently act as consultants, brought in by management to solve a particular problem.

Developmental psychologists study the physiological, cognitive, and social development that takes place throughout life. Some specialize in behavior during infancy, childhood, and adolescence, or changes that occur during maturity or old age. Developmental psychologists also may study developmental disabilities and their effects. Increasingly, research is developing ways to help elderly people remain independent as long as possible.

Social psychologists examine people's interactions with others and with the social environment. They work in organizational consultation, marketing research, systems design, or other applied psychology fields. Many social psychologists specialize in a niche area, such as group behavior, leadership, attitudes, and perception.

Experimental or *research psychologists* work in university and private research centers and in business, nonprofit, and governmental organizations. They study the behavior of both human beings and animals, such as rats, monkeys, and pigeons. Prominent areas of study in experimental research include motivation, thought, attention, learning and memory, sensory and perceptual processes, effects of substance abuse, and genetic and neurological factors affecting behavior.

Forensic psychologists use psychological principles in the legal and criminal justice system to help judges, attorneys, and other legal professionals understand the psychological findings of a particular case. They are usually designated as an expert witness and typically specialize in one of three areas: family court, civil court, and criminal court. Forensic psychologists who work in family court may offer psychotherapy services, perform child custody evaluations, or investigate reports of child abuse. Those working in civil courts may assess competency, provide second opinions, and provide psychotherapy to crime victims. Criminal court forensic psychologists often conduct evaluations of mental competency, work with child witnesses, and provide assessment of juvenile or adult offenders.

Work environment. Psychologists' work environments vary by subfield and place of employment. For example, clinical, school, and counseling psychologists in private practice frequently have their own offices and set their own hours. However, they usually offer evening and weekend hours to accommodate their clients. Those employed in hospitals, nursing homes, and other healthcare facilities may work shifts that include evenings and weekends, and those who work in schools and clinics generally work regular daytime hours. Most psychologists in government and industry have structured schedules.

Psychologists employed as faculty by colleges and universities divide their time between teaching and research and also may have administrative responsibilities; many have part-time consulting practices.

Increasingly, a good number of psychologists work as part of a team, consulting with other psychologists and medical professionals. Many experience pressures because of deadlines, tight schedules, and overtime.

Training, Other Qualifications, and Advancement

A master's or doctoral degree, and a license, are required for most psychologists.

Education and training. A doctoral degree usually is required for independent practice as a psychologist. Psychologists with a Ph.D. or Doctor of Psychology (Psy.D.) qualify for a wide range of teaching, research, clinical, and counseling positions in universities, healthcare services, elementary and secondary schools, private industry, and government. Psychologists with a doctoral degree often work in clinical positions or in private practices, but they also sometimes teach, conduct research, or carry out administrative responsibilities.

A doctoral degree generally requires about 5 years of full-time graduate study, culminating in a dissertation based on original research. Courses in quantitative experimental methods and research design, which include the use of computer-based analysis, are an integral part of graduate study and are necessary to complete the dissertation. The Psy.D. degree may be based on practical work and examinations rather than a dissertation. In clinical, counseling, and school psychology, the requirements for the doctoral degree usually include an additional year of post-doctoral supervised experience.

A specialist degree or its equivalent is required in most States for an individual to work as a school psychologist, although some States credential school psychologists with master's degrees. A specialist (Ed.S.) degree in school psychology requires a minimum of 2 years of full-time graduate study (at least 60 graduate semester hours) and a 1-year full-time internship during the third year. Because their professional practice addresses educational and mental health components of students' development, school psychologists' training includes coursework in both education and psychology.

People with a master's degree in psychology may work as industrial-organizational psychologists. They also may work as psychological assistants conducting research under the direct supervision of doctoral-level psychologists. A master's degree in psychology requires at least 2 years of full-time graduate study. Requirements usually include practical experience in an applied setting and a master's thesis based on an original research project.

Competition for admission to graduate psychology programs is keen. Some universities require applicants to have an undergraduate major in psychology. Others prefer only coursework in basic psychology with additional courses in the biological, physical, and social sciences, and in statistics and mathematics.

A bachelor's degree in psychology qualifies a person to assist psychologists and other professionals in community mental health centers, vocational rehabilitation offices, and correctional programs. Bachelor's degree holders may also work as administrative assistants for psychologists. Many, however, find employment in other areas, such as sales, service, or business management.

In the Federal Government, candidates must have a bachelor's degree with a minimum of 24 semester hours in psychology, or a combination of education and experience to qualify for entry-level positions. However, competition for these jobs is keen because this is one of the few ways in which one can work as a psychologist without an advanced degree.

The American Psychological Association (APA) presently accredits doctoral training programs in clinical, counseling, and school psychology, as well as institutions that provide internships for doctoral students in school, clinical, and counseling psychology. The National Association of School Psychologists, with the assistance of the National Council for Accreditation of Teacher Education, helps to approve advanced degree programs in school psychology.

Clinical psychologists in Louisiana and New Mexico who prescribe medication are required to complete a post-doctoral master's degree in clinical psychopharmacology and pass a National exam approved by the State Board of Examiners of psychologists.

Licensure. Psychologists in a solo or group practice or those who offer any type of patient care—including clinical, counseling, and school psychologists—must meet certification or licensing requirements in all States and the District of Columbia. Licensing laws vary by State and by type of position and require licensed or certified psychologists to limit their practice to areas in which they have developed professional competence through training and experience. Clinical and counseling psychologists usually need a doctorate in psychology, an approved internship, and 1 to 2 years of professional experience. In addition, all States require that applicants pass an examination. Most State licensing boards administer a standardized test, and many supplement that with additional oral or essay questions. Some States require continuing education for renewal of the license.

The National Association of School Psychologists (NASP) awards the Nationally Certified School Psychologist (NCSP) designation, which recognizes professional competency in school psychology at a national, rather than State, level. Currently, 31 States recognize the NCSP and allow those with the certification to transfer credentials from one State to another without taking a new certification exam. In States that recognize the NCSP, the requirements for certification or licensure and those for the NCSP often are the same or similar. Requirements for the NCSP include the completion of 60 graduate semester hours in school psychology; a 1,200-hour internship, 600 hours of which must be completed in a school setting; and a passing score on the National School Psychology Examination.

Other qualifications. Aspiring psychologists who are interested in direct patient care must be emotionally stable, mature, and able to deal effectively with people. Sensitivity, compassion, good communication skills, and the ability to lead and inspire others are particularly important qualities for people wishing to do clinical work and counseling. Research psychologists should be capable of detailed work both independently and as part of a team. Patience and perseverance are vital qualities, because achieving results in the psychological treatment of patients or in research may take a long time.

Certification and advancement. The American Board of Professional Psychology (ABPP) recognizes professional achievement by awarding specialty certification in 13 different areas, such as psychoanalysis, rehabilitation, forensic, group, school, clinical health, and couple and family. To obtain board certification in a specialty, candidates must meet general criteria which consist of having a doctorate in psychology, as well as State licensure. Each candidate must then meet additional criteria of the specialty field, which is usually a combination of postdoctoral training in their specialty, several years of experience, and professional endorsements, as determined by the ABPP. Applicants are then required to pass the specialty board examination.

Psychologists can improve their advancement opportunities by earning an advanced degree and by participation in continuing education. Many psychologists opt to start their own private practice after gaining experience working in the field.

Employment

Psychologists held about 170,200 jobs in 2008. Educational institutions employed about 29 percent of psychologists in positions other than teaching, such as counseling, testing, research, and administration. About 21 percent were employed in healthcare, primarily in offices of mental health practitioners, hospitals, physicians' offices, and outpatient mental health and substance abuse centers. Government agencies at the State and local levels employed psychologists in correctional facilities, law enforcement, and other settings.

After several years of experience, some psychologists—usually those with doctoral degrees—enter private practice or set up private research or consulting firms. About 34 percent of psychologists were self-employed in 2008—mainly as private practitioners.

In addition to the previously mentioned jobs, many psychologists held faculty positions at colleges and universities and as high school psychology teachers.

Job Outlook

Employment of psychologists is expected to grow as fast as average. Job prospects should be the best for people who have a doctoral degree from a leading university in an applied specialty, such as counseling or health, and those with a specialist or doctoral degree in school psychology. Master's degree holders in fields other than industrial-organizational psychology will face keen competition. Opportunities will be limited for bachelor's degree holders.

Employment change. Employment of psychologists is expected to grow 12 percent from

2008 to 2018, about as fast as the average for all occupations. Employment will grow because of increased demand for psychological services in schools, hospitals, social service agencies, mental health centers, substance abuse treatment clinics, consulting firms, and private companies.

Demand for school psychologists will be driven by a growing awareness of how students' mental health and behavioral problems, such as bullying, affect learning. School psychologists will also be needed for general student counseling on a variety of other issues, including working with students with disabilities or with special needs, tackling drug abuse, and consulting and managing personal crisis.

Spurring demand for clinical psychologists will continue to be the rising healthcare costs associated with unhealthy lifestyles, such as smoking, alcoholism, and obesity, which have made prevention and treatment more critical. An increase in the number of employee assistance programs, which help workers deal with personal problems, also should lead to employment growth for clinical and counseling specialties. More clinical and counseling psychologists will be needed to help people deal with depression and other mental disorders, marriage and family problems, job stress, and addiction. The growing number of elderly will increase the demand for psychologists trained in geropsychology to help people deal with the mental and physical changes that occur as individuals grow older. There also will be increased need for psychologists to work with returning veterans.

Industrial-organizational psychologists also will be in demand to help to boost worker productivity and retention rates in a wide range of businesses. Industrial-organizational psychologists will help companies deal with issues such as workplace diversity and antidiscrimination policies. Companies also will use psychologists' expertise in survey design, analysis, and research to develop tools for marketing evaluation and statistical analysis.

Job prospects. Job prospects should be best for people who have a doctoral degree from a leading university in an applied specialty, such as counseling or health, and those with a specialist or doctoral degree in school psychology. Psychologists with extensive training in quantitative research methods and computer science may have a competitive edge over applicants without such background.

Master's degree holders in fields other than industrial-organizational psychology will face keen competition for jobs because of the limited number of positions that require only a master's degree. Master's degree holders may find jobs as psychological assistants or counselors, providing mental health services under the direct supervision of a licensed psychologist. Still, others may find jobs involving research and data collection and analysis in universities, government, or private companies.

Opportunities directly related to psychology will be limited for bachelor's degree holders. Some may find jobs as assistants in rehabilitation centers or in other jobs involving data collection and analysis. Those who meet State certification requirements may become high school psychology teachers.

Earnings

Median annual wages of wage and salary clinical, counseling, and school psychologists were $64,140 in May 2008. The middle 50 percent earned between $48,700 and $82,800. The lowest 10 percent earned less than $37,900, and the highest 10 percent earned more than $106,840.

Median annual wages of wage and salary industrial-organizational psychologists were $77,010 in May 2008. The middle 50 percent earned between $54,100 and $115,720. The lowest 10 percent earned less than $38,690, and the highest 10 percent earned more than $149,120.

In 2008, about 31 percent of all psychologists were members of a union.

ENGINEERING

—ɯ—

Architects

Nature of the Work

People need places in which to live, work, play, learn, worship, meet, govern, shop, and eat. Architects are responsible for designing these places, whether they are private or public; indoors or out; rooms, buildings, or complexes. Architects are licensed professionals trained in the art and science of building design who develop the concepts for structures and turn those concepts into images and plans.

Architects create the overall look of buildings and other structures, but the design of a building involves far more than its appearance. Buildings also must be functional, safe, and economical and must suit the needs of the people who use them. Architects consider all these factors when they design buildings and other structures.

> ### Significant Points
> ❖ About 21 percent of architects are self-employed—almost 3 times the proportion for all occupations.
>
> ❖ Licensing requirements include a professional degree in architecture, at least 3 years of practical work, training, and passing all divisions of the Architect Registration Examination.
>
> ❖ Architecture graduates may face competition, especially for jobs in the most prestigious firms.

Architects may be involved in all phases of a construction project, from the initial discussion with the client through the final delivery of the completed structure. Their duties require specific skills—designing, engineering, managing, supervising, and communicating with clients and builders. Architects spend a great deal of time explaining their ideas to clients, construction contractors, and others. Successful architects must be able to communicate their unique vision persuasively.

The architect and client discuss the objectives, requirements, and budget of a project. In some cases, architects provide various predesign services: conducting feasibility and environmental impact studies, selecting a site, preparing cost analysis and land-use studies, or specifying the requirements the design must meet. For example, they may determine space requirements by researching the numbers and types of potential users of a building. The architect then prepares drawings and a report presenting ideas for the client to review.

After discussing and agreeing on the initial proposal, architects develop final construction plans that show the building's appearance and details for its construction. Accompanying these plans are drawings of the structural system; air-conditioning, heating, and ventilating systems; electrical systems; communications systems; plumbing; and, possibly, site and landscape plans. The plans also specify the building materials and, in some cases, the interior furnishings. In developing designs, architects follow building codes, zoning laws, fire regulations, and other ordinances, such as those requiring easy access by people who are disabled. Computer-aided design and drafting (CADD) and building information modeling (BIM) technology has replaced traditional paper and pencil as the most common method for creating design and construction drawings. Continual revision of plans on the basis of client needs and budget constraints is often necessary.

Architects may also assist clients in obtaining construction bids, selecting contractors, and negotiating construction contracts. As construction proceeds, they may visit building sites to make sure that contractors follow the design, adhere to the schedule, use the specified materials, and meet work quality standards. The job is not complete until all construction is finished, required tests are conducted, and construction costs are paid. Sometimes, architects also provide post-construction services, such as facilities management. They advise on energy efficiency measures, evaluate how well the building design adapts to the needs of occupants, and make necessary improvements.

Often working with engineers, urban planners, interior designers, landscape architects, and other professionals, architects in fact spend a great deal of their time coordinating information from, and the work of, other professionals engaged in the same project.

They design a wide variety of buildings, such as office and apartment buildings, schools, churches, factories, hospitals, houses, and airport terminals. They also design complexes such as urban centers, college campuses, industrial parks, and entire communities.

Architects sometimes specialize in one phase of work. Some specialize in the design of one type of building—for example, hospitals, schools, or housing. Others focus on planning and predesign services or construction management and do minimal design work.

Work environment. Usually working in a comfortable environment, architects spend most of their time in offices consulting with clients, developing reports and drawings, and working with other architects and engineers. However, they often visit construction sites to review the progress of projects. In 2008, approximately 1 in 5 architects worked more than 50 hours per week, as long hours and work during nights and weekends is often necessary to meet deadlines.

Training, Other Qualifications, and Advancement

There are three main steps in becoming an architect: completing a professional degree in architecture; gaining work experience through an internship; and attaining licensure by passing the Architect Registration Exam.

Education and training. In most States, architects must hold a professional degree in architecture from one of the 117 schools of architecture that have degree programs accredited by the National Architectural Accrediting Board (NAAB). However, State architectural registration boards set their own standards, so graduation from a non-accredited program may meet the educational requirement for licensing in a few States.

Most architects earn their professional degree through a 5-year Bachelor of Architecture degree program, which is intended for students with no previous architectural training. Others earn a master's degree after completing a bachelor's degree in another field or after completing a pre-professional architecture program. A master's degree in architecture can take 1 to 5 years to complete depending on the extent of previous training in architecture.

The choice of degree depends on preference and educational background. Prospective architecture students should consider the options before committing to a program. For example, although the 5-year bachelor of architecture offers the most direct route to the professional degree, courses are specialized, and if the student does not complete the program, transferring to a program in another discipline may be difficult. A typical program includes courses in architectural history and theory, building design with an emphasis on CADD, structures, technology, construction methods, professional practice, math, physical sciences, and liberal arts. Central to most architectural programs is the design studio, where students apply the skills and concepts learned in the classroom and create drawings and three-dimensional models of their designs.

Many schools of architecture also offer post-professional degrees for those who already have a bachelor's or master's degree in architecture or other areas. Although graduate education beyond the professional degree is not required for practicing architects, it may be useful for research, teaching, and certain specialties.

All State architectural registration boards require architecture graduates to complete a training period—usually at least 3 years—before they may sit for the licensing exam. Every State follows the training standards established by the Intern Development Program, a program of the American Institute of Architects and the National Council of Architectural Registration Boards (NCARB). These standards stipulate broad training under the supervision of a licensed architect. Most new graduates complete their training period by working as interns at architectural firms. Some States allow a portion of the training to occur in the offices of related professionals, such as engineers or general contractors. Architecture students who complete internships while still in school can count some of that time toward the 3-year training period.

Interns in architectural firms may assist in the design of one part of a project, help prepare architectural documents or drawings, build models, or prepare construction drawings on CADD. Interns also may research building codes and materials or write specifications for building materials, installation criteria, the quality of finishes, and other related details.

Licensure. All States and the District of Columbia require individuals to be licensed (registered) before they may call themselves architects and contract to provide architectural services. During the time between graduation and becoming licensed, architecture school graduates generally work in the field under the supervision of a licensed architect who takes legal responsibility for all work. Licensing requirements include a professional degree in architecture, a period of practical training or internship, and a passing score on all divisions of the Architect Registration Examination. The examination is broken into nine divisions consisting of either multiple choice or graphical questions. The eligibility period for completion of all divisions of the exam varies by State.

Most States also require some form of continuing education to maintain a license, and many others are expected to adopt mandatory continuing education. Requirements vary by State but usually involve the completion of a certain number of credits annually or biennially through workshops, formal university classes, conferences, self-study courses, or other sources.

Other qualifications. Architects must be able to communicate their ideas visually to their clients. Artistic and drawing ability is helpful, but not essential, to such communication. More important are a visual orientation and the ability to understand spatial relationships. Other important qualities for anyone interested in becoming an architect are creativity and the ability to work independently and as part of a team. Computer skills are also required for writing specifications, for 2-dimensional and 3- dimensional drafting using CADD programs, and for financial management.

Certification and advancement. A growing number of architects voluntarily seek certification by the National Council of Architectural Registration Boards. Certification is awarded after independent verification of the candidate's educational transcripts, employment record, and professional references. Certification can make it easier to become licensed across States. In fact, it is the primary requirement for reciprocity of licensing among State Boards that are NCARB members. In 2009, approximately one-third of all licensed architects had this certification.

After becoming licensed and gaining experience, architects take on increasingly complex assignments, eventually managing entire projects. In large firms, architects may advance to supervisory or managerial positions. Some architects become partners in established firms, while others set up their own practices. Some graduates with degrees in architecture also enter related fields, such as graphic, interior, or industrial design; urban planning; real estate development; civil engineering; and construction management.

Employment

Architects held about 141,200 jobs in 2008. Approximately 68 percent of jobs were in the architectural, engineering, and related services industry. A small number worked for residential and nonresidential building construction firms and for government agencies responsible for housing, community planning, or construction of government buildings, such as the U.S. Departments of Defense and Interior and the General Services Administration. About 21 percent of architects are self-employed.

Job Outlook

Employment is expected to grow faster than the average for all occupations. Competition is expected, especially for positions at the most prestigious firms, and opportunities will be best for those architects who are able to distinguish themselves with their creativity.

Employment change. Employment of architects is expected to increase by 16 percent between 2008 and 2018, which is faster than the average for all occupations. Current demographic trends will lead to an increase in demand for architects. As the population of Sunbelt States continues to grow, the people living there will need new places to live and work. As the population continues to live longer and baby boomers retire, there will be a need for more healthcare facilities, nursing homes, and retirement communities. In education, buildings at all levels are getting older and enrollments continue to increase, which will require many school districts and universities to build new facilities and renovate existing ones.

In recent years, some architecture firms have outsourced the drafting of construction documents and basic design for large-scale commercial and residential projects to architecture firms overseas. This trend is expected to continue and may have a negative impact on employment growth for lower-level architects and interns who would normally gain experience by producing these drawings.

Job prospects. Besides employment growth, additional job openings will arise from the need to replace architects who transfer to other occupations or stop working for other reasons. A growing number of students are graduating with architectural degrees and some competition for entry-level jobs can be anticipated. Competition will be especially keen for jobs at the most prestigious architectural firms as prospective architects try to build their reputation. Prospective architects who have had internships while in school will have an advantage in obtaining positions after graduation. Opportunities will be best for those architects who are able to distinguish themselves from others with their creativity.

There should be demand for architects with knowledge of "green" design. Green design, also known as sustainable design, emphasizes the efficient use of resources such as energy and water, waste and pollution reduction, conservation, and environmentally friendly design, specifications, and materials. Rising energy costs and increased concern about the environment has led to many new buildings being built green.

Employment of architects is strongly tied to the activity of the construction industry and some types of construction are sensitive to cyclical changes in the economy. For example, during recessions nonresidential construction of office and retail space tends to fall as funding for these projects becomes harder to obtain and the demand for these spaces falls. Firms involved in the design of institutional buildings, such as schools, hospitals, nursing homes, and correctional facilities, will be less affected by fluctuations in the economy. Residential construction makes up a small portion of work for architects, so major changes in the housing market would not be as significant as fluctuations in the nonresidential market.

Opportunities are also geographically sensitive, and some parts of the Nation may have fewer new building projects. Also, many firms specialize in specific buildings, such as hospitals or office towers, and demand for these buildings may vary by region. Architects may find it increasingly necessary to gain reciprocity in order to compete for the best jobs and projects in other States.

Earnings

Median annual wages of wage-and-salary architects were $70,320 in May 2008. The middle 50 percent earned between $53,480 and $91,870. The lowest 10 percent earned less than $41,320, and the highest 10 percent earned more than $119,220. Those just starting their internships can expect to earn considerably less.

Earnings of partners in established architectural firms may fluctuate because of changing business conditions. Some architects may have difficulty establishing their own practices and may go through a period when their expenses are greater than their income, requiring substantial financial resources.

Many firms pay tuition and fees toward continuing education requirements for their employees.

ENGINEERING

—ɰ—

Engineers

Nature of the Work

Engineers apply the principles of science and mathematics to develop economical solutions to technical problems. Their work is the link between scientific discoveries and the commercial applications that meet societal and consumer needs.

Many engineers develop new products. During the process, they consider several factors. For example, in developing an industrial robot, engineers specify the functional requirements precisely; design and test the robot's components; integrate the components to produce the final design; and evaluate the design's overall effectiveness, cost, reliability, and safety. This process applies to the development of many different products, such as chemicals, computers, powerplants, helicopters, and toys.

In addition to their involvement in design and development, many engineers work in testing, production, or maintenance. These engineers supervise production in factories, determine the causes of a component's failure, and test manufactured products to maintain quality. They also estimate the time and cost required to complete projects. Supervisory engineers are responsible for major components or entire projects.

Engineers use computers extensively to produce and analyze designs; to simulate and test how a machine, structure, or system operates; to generate specifications for parts; to

Significant Points

❖ Employment is projected to grow about as fast as the average for all occupations, although growth will vary by specialty; overall job opportunities for engineers are expected to be good.

❖ A bachelor's degree in engineering is required for most entry-level jobs, but some research positions may require a graduate degree.

❖ Starting salaries are among the highest of all college graduates.

❖ Continuing education is critical for engineers in order to keep up with improvements in technology.

monitor the quality of products; and to control the efficiency of processes. Nanotechnology, which involves the creation of high-performance materials and components by integrating atoms and molecules, also is introducing entirely new principles to the design process.

Most engineers specialize. Following are details on the 17 engineering specialties covered in the Federal Government's Standard Occupational Classification (SOC) system. Numerous other specialties are recognized by professional societies, and each of the major branches of engineering has numerous subdivisions. Civil engineering, for example, includes structural and transportation engineering, and materials engineering includes ceramic, metallurgical, and polymer engineering. Engineers also may specialize in one industry, such as motor vehicles, or in one type of technology, such as turbines or semiconductor materials.

Aerospace engineers design, test, and supervise the manufacture of aircraft, spacecraft, and missiles. Those who work with aircraft are called *aeronautical engineers,* and those working specifically with spacecraft are *astronautical engineers.* Aerospace engineers develop new technologies for use in aviation, defense systems, and space exploration, often specializing in areas such as structural design, guidance, navigation and control, instrumentation and communication, and production methods. They also may specialize in a particular type of aerospace product, such as commercial aircraft, military fighter jets, helicopters, spacecraft, or missiles and rockets, and may become experts in aerodynamics, thermodynamics, celestial mechanics, propulsion, acoustics, or guidance and control systems.

Agricultural engineers apply their knowledge of engineering technology and science to agriculture and the efficient use of biological resources. Accordingly, they also are referred to as *biological and agricultural engineers.* They design agricultural machinery, equipment, sensors, processes, and structures, such as those used for crop storage. Some engineers specialize in areas such as power systems and machinery design, structural and environmental engineering, and food and bioprocess engineering. They develop ways to conserve soil and water and to improve the processing of agricultural products. Agricultural engineers often work in research and development, production, sales, or management.

Biomedical engineers develop devices and procedures that solve medical and health-related problems by combining their knowledge of biology and medicine with engineering principles and practices. Many do research, along with medical scientists, to develop and evaluate systems and products such as artificial organs, prostheses (artificial devices that replace missing body parts), instrumentation, medical information systems, and health management and care delivery systems. Biomedical engineers also may design devices used in various medical procedures, imaging systems such as magnetic resonance imaging (MRI), and devices for automating insulin injections or controlling body functions. Most engineers in this specialty need a sound background in another engineering specialty, such as mechanical or electronics engineering, in addition to specialized biomedical training. Some specialties within biomedical engineering are biomaterials, biomechanics, medical imaging, rehabilitation engineering, and orthopedic engineering.

Chemical engineers apply the principles of chemistry to solve problems involving the production or use of chemicals and other products. They design equipment and processes for large-scale chemical manufacturing, plan and test methods of manufacturing products and treating byproducts, and supervise production. Chemical engineers also work in a variety of manufacturing industries other than chemical manufacturing, such as those producing energy, electronics, food, clothing, and paper. In addition, they work in healthcare, biotechnology, and business services. Chemical engineers apply principles of physics, mathematics, and mechanical and electrical engineering, as well as chemistry. Some may specialize in a particular chemical process, such as oxidation or polymerization. Others specialize in a particular field, such as nanomaterials, or in the development of specific products. They must be aware of all aspects of chemical manufacturing and how the manufacturing process affects the environment and the safety of workers and consumers.

Civil engineers design and supervise the construction of roads, buildings, airports, tunnels, dams, bridges, and water supply and sewage systems. They must consider many factors in the design process from the construction costs and expected lifetime of a project to government regulations and potential environmental hazards such as earthquakes and hurricanes. Civil engineering, considered one of the oldest engineering disciplines, encompasses many specialties. The major ones are structural, water resources, construction, transportation, and geotechnical engineering. Many civil engineers hold supervisory or administrative positions, from supervisor of a construction site to city engineer. Others may work in design, construction, research, and teaching.

Computer hardware engineers research, design, develop, test, and oversee the manufacture and installation of computer hardware, including computer chips, circuit boards, computer systems, and related equipment such as keyboards, routers, and printers. The work of computer hardware engineers is similar to that of electronics engineers in that they may design and test circuits and other electronic components; however, computer hardware engineers do that work only as it relates to computers and computer-related equipment. The rapid advances in computer technology are largely a result of the research, development, and design efforts of these engineers.

Electrical engineers design, develop, test, and supervise the manufacture of electrical equipment. Some of this equipment includes electric motors; machinery controls, lighting, and wiring in buildings; radar and navigation systems; communications systems; and power generation, control, and transmission devices used by electric utilities. Electrical engineers also design the electrical systems of automobiles and aircraft. Although the terms *electrical* and *electronics engineering* often are used interchangeably in academia and industry, electrical engineers traditionally have focused on the generation and supply of power, whereas electronics engineers have worked on applications of electricity to control systems or signal processing. Electrical engineers specialize in areas such as power systems engineering or electrical equipment manufacturing.

Electronics engineers, except computer, are responsible for a wide range of technologies, from portable music players to global positioning systems (GPS), which can continuously provide the location of, for example, a vehicle. Electronics engineers design, develop, test, and supervise the manufacture of electronic equipment such as broadcast and communications systems. Many electronics engineers also work in areas closely related to computers. However, engineers whose work is related exclusively to computer hardware are considered computer hardware engineers. Electronics engineers specialize in areas such as communications, signal processing, and control systems or have a specialty within one of these areas—control systems or aviation electronics, for example.

Environmental engineers use the principles of biology and chemistry to develop solutions to environmental problems. They are involved in water and air pollution control, recycling, waste disposal, and public health issues. Environmental engineers conduct hazardous-waste management studies in which they evaluate the significance of the hazard, advise on its treatment and containment, and develop regulations to prevent mishaps. They design municipal water supply and industrial wastewater treatment systems, conduct research on the environmental impact of proposed construction projects, analyze scientific data, and perform quality-control checks. Environmental engineers are concerned with local and worldwide environmental issues. Some may study and attempt to minimize the effects of acid rain, global warming, automobile emissions, and ozone depletion. They also may be involved in the protection of wildlife. Many environmental engineers work as consultants, helping their clients to comply with regulations, prevent environmental damage, and clean up hazardous sites.

Health and safety engineers, except mining safety engineers and inspectors, prevent harm to people and property by applying their knowledge of systems engineering and mechanical, chemical, and human performance principles. Using this specialized knowledge, they identify and measure potential hazards, such as the risk of fires or the dangers involved in handling toxic chemicals. They recommend appropriate loss prevention measures according to their probability of harm and potential damage. Health and safety engineers develop procedures and designs to reduce the risk of illness, injury, or damage. Some work in manufacturing industries to ensure that the designs of new products do not create unnecessary hazards. They must be able to anticipate, recognize, and evaluate hazardous conditions, as well as develop hazard control methods.

Industrial engineers determine the most effective ways to use the basic factors of production—people, machines, materials, information, and energy—to make a product or provide a service. They are concerned primarily with increasing productivity through the management of people, methods of business organization, and technology. To maximize efficiency, industrial engineers study product requirements carefully and then design manufacturing and information systems to meet those requirements with the help of mathematical methods and models. They develop management control systems to aid in financial planning and cost analysis, and they design production planning and control systems to coordinate activities and ensure product quality. They also design or improve systems for the physical distribution of goods and services and determine the most efficient plant locations. Industrial engineers develop wage and salary administration systems and job evaluation programs. Many industrial engineers move into management positions because the work is closely related to the work of managers.

Marine engineers and naval architects are involved in the design, construction, and maintenance of ships, boats, and related equipment. They design and supervise the construction of everything from aircraft carriers to submarines and from sailboats to tankers. Naval architects work on the basic design of ships, including the form and stability of hulls. Marine engineers work on the propulsion, steering, and other systems of ships. Marine engineers and naval architects apply knowledge from a range of fields to the entire process by which water vehicles are designed and produced. Other workers who operate or supervise the operation of marine machinery on ships and other vessels sometimes may be called marine engineers or, more frequently, ship engineers, but they do different work.

Materials engineers are involved in the development, processing, and testing of the materials used to create a range of products, from computer chips and aircraft wings to golf clubs and snow skis. They work with metals, ceramics, plastics, semiconductors, and composites to create new materials that meet certain mechanical, electrical, and chemical requirements. They also are involved in selecting materials for new applications. Materials engineers have developed the ability to create and then study materials at an atomic level, using advanced processes to replicate the characteristics of those materials and their components with computers. Most materials engineers specialize in a particular material. For example, metallurgical engineers specialize in metals such as steel, and ceramic engineers develop ceramic materials and the processes for making them into useful products such as glassware or fiber-optic communication lines.

Mechanical engineers research, design, develop, manufacture, and test tools, engines, machines, and other mechanical devices. Mechanical engineering is one of the broadest engineering disciplines. Engineers in this discipline work on power-producing machines such as electric generators, internal combustion engines, and steam and gas turbines. They also work on power-using machines such as refrigeration and air-conditioning equipment, machine tools, material-handling systems, elevators and escalators, industrial production equipment, and robots used in manufacturing. Some mechanical engineers design tools that other engineers need for their work. In addition, mechanical engineers work in manufacturing or agriculture production, maintenance, or technical sales; many become administrators or managers.

Mining and geological engineers, including mining safety engineers, find, extract, and prepare coal, metals, and minerals for use by manufacturing industries and utilities. They design open-pit and underground mines, supervise the construction of mine shafts and tunnels in underground operations, and devise methods for transporting minerals to processing plants. Mining engineers are responsible for the safe, economical, and environmentally sound operation of mines. Some mining engineers work with geologists and metallurgical engineers to locate and appraise new ore deposits. Others develop new mining equipment or direct mineral-processing operations that separate minerals from the dirt, rock, and other materials with which they are mixed. Mining engineers frequently specialize in the mining of one mineral or metal, such as coal or gold. With increased emphasis on protecting the environment, many mining engineers are working to solve problems related to land reclamation and to water and air pollution. Mining safety engineers use their knowledge of mine design and practices to ensure the safety of workers and to comply with State and Federal safety regulations. They inspect the surfaces of walls and roofs, monitor air quality, and examine mining equipment for compliance with safety practices.

Nuclear engineers research and develop the processes, instruments, and systems used to derive benefits from nuclear energy and radiation. They design, develop, monitor, and operate nuclear plants to generate power. They may work on the nuclear fuel cycle—the production, handling, and use of nuclear fuel and the safe disposal of waste produced by the generation of nuclear energy—or on the development of fusion energy. Some specialize in the development of nuclear power sources for naval vessels or spacecraft; others find industrial and medical uses for radioactive materials—for example, in equipment used to diagnose and treat medical problems.

Petroleum engineers design methods for extracting oil and gas from deposits below the earth. Once these resources have been discovered, petroleum engineers work with geologists and other specialists to understand the geologic formation and properties of the rock containing the reservoir, to determine the drilling methods to be used, and to monitor drilling and production operations. They design equipment and processes to achieve the maximum profitable recovery of oil and gas. Because only a small proportion of oil and gas in a reservoir flows out under natural forces, petroleum engineers develop and use various enhanced recovery methods, including injecting water, chemicals, gases, or steam into an oil reservoir to force out more of the oil and doing computer-controlled drilling or fracturing to connect a larger area of a reservoir to a single well. Because even the best techniques in use today recover only a portion of the oil and gas in a reservoir, petroleum engineers research and develop technology and methods for increasing the recovery of these resources and lowering the cost of drilling and production operations.

Work environment. Most engineers work in office buildings, laboratories, or industrial plants. Others may spend time outdoors at construction sites and oil and gas exploration and production sites, where they monitor or direct operations or solve onsite problems. Some engineers travel extensively to plants or worksites here and abroad.

Many engineers work a standard 40-hour week. At times, deadlines or design standards may bring extra pressure to a job, requiring engineers to work longer hours.

Training, Other Qualifications, and Advancement

Engineers typically enter the occupation with a bachelor's degree in an engineering specialty, but some basic research positions may require a graduate degree. Engineers offering their services directly to the public must be licensed. Continuing education to keep current with rapidly changing technology is important for engineers.

Education and training. A bachelor's degree in engineering is required for almost all entry-level engineering jobs. College graduates with a degree in a natural science or mathematics occasionally may qualify for some engineering jobs, especially in specialties that are in high demand. Most engineering degrees are granted in electrical and electronics engineering, mechanical engineering, and civil engineering. However, engineers trained in one branch may work in related branches. For example, many aerospace engineers have training in mechanical engineering. This flexibility allows employers to meet staffing needs in new technologies and specialties in which engineers may be in short supply. It also allows engineers to shift to fields with better employment prospects or to those which more closely match their interests.

Most engineering programs involve a concentration of study in an engineering specialty, along with courses in both mathematics and the physical and life sciences. Many programs also include courses in general engineering. A design course, sometimes accompanied by a computer or laboratory class or both, is part of the curriculum of most programs. Often, general courses not directly related to engineering, such as those in the social sciences or humanities, also are required.

In addition to the standard engineering degree, many colleges offer 2-year or 4-year degree programs in engineering technology. These programs, which usually include various hands-on laboratory classes that focus on current issues in the application of engineering principles, prepare students for practical design and production work, rather than for jobs that require more theoretical and scientific knowledge. Graduates of 4-year technology programs may get jobs similar to those obtained by graduates with a bachelor's degree in engineering. Engineering technology graduates, however, are not qualified to register as professional engineers under the same terms as graduates with degrees in engineering. Some employers regard technology program graduates as having skills between those of a technician and an engineer.

Graduate training is essential for engineering faculty positions and some research and development programs, but is not required for the majority of entry-level engineering jobs. Many experienced engineers obtain graduate degrees in engineering or business administration to learn new technology and broaden their education. Numerous high-level executives in government and industry began their careers as engineers.

The Accreditation Board for Engineering and Technology (ABET) accredits college and university programs in engineering and engineering technology. ABET accreditation is based on a program's faculty, curriculum, and facilities; the achievement of a program's students; program improvements; and institutional commitment to specific principles of quality and ethics. Graduation from an ABET-accredited program may be required for engineers who need to be licensed.

Although most institutions offer programs in the major branches of engineering, only a few offer programs in the smaller specialties. Also, programs with the same title may vary in content. For example, some programs emphasize industrial practices, preparing students for a job in industry, whereas others are more theoretical and are designed to prepare students for graduate work. Therefore, students should investigate curricula and check accreditations carefully before selecting a college.

Admissions requirements for undergraduate engineering schools include a solid background in mathematics (algebra, geometry, trigonometry, and calculus) and science (biology, chemistry, and physics), in addition to courses in English, social studies, and humanities. Bachelor's degree programs in engineering typically are designed to last 4 years, but many students find that it takes between 4 and 5 years to complete their studies. In a typical 4-year college curriculum, the first 2 years are spent studying mathematics, basic sciences, introductory engineering, humanities, and social sciences. In the last 2 years, most courses are in engineering, usually with a concentration in one specialty. Some programs offer a general engineering curriculum; students then specialize on the job or in graduate school.

Some engineering schools have agreements with 2-year colleges whereby the college provides the initial engineering education and the engineering school automatically admits students for their last 2 years. In addition, a few engineering schools have arrangements that allow students who spend 3 years in a liberal arts college studying preengineering subjects and 2 years in an engineering school studying core subjects to receive a bachelor's degree from each school. Some colleges and universities offer 5-year master's degree programs. Some 5-year or even 6-year cooperative plans combine classroom study with practical work, permitting students to gain valuable experience and to finance part of their education.

Licensure. All 50 States and the District of Columbia require licensure for engineers who offer their services directly to the public. Engineers who are licensed are called professional engineers (PEs). This licensure generally requires a degree from an ABET-accredited engineering program, 4 years of relevant work experience, and completion of a State examination. Recent graduates can start the licensing process by taking the examination in two stages. The initial Fundamentals of Engineering (FE) examination can be taken upon graduation. Engineers who pass this examination commonly are called engineers in training (EITs) or engineer interns (EIs). After acquiring suitable work experience, EITs can take the second examination, called the Principles and Practice of Engineering exam. Several States have imposed mandatory continuing education requirements for relicensure. Most States recognize licensure from other States, provided that the manner in which the initial license was obtained meets or exceeds their own licensure requirements. Many civil, mechanical, and chemical engineers are licensed PEs. Independently of licensure, various certification programs are offered by professional organizations to demonstrate competency in specific fields of engineering.

Other qualifications. Engineers should be creative, inquisitive, analytical, and detail oriented. They should be able to work as part of a team and to communicate well, both orally and in writing. Communication abilities are becoming increasingly important as engineers interact more frequently with specialists in a wide range of fields outside engineering.

Engineers who work for the Federal Government usually must be U.S. citizens. Some engineers, particularly nuclear engineers and aerospace and other engineers working for defense contractors, may need to hold a security clearance.

Certification and advancement. Beginning engineering graduates usually work under the supervision of experienced engineers and, in large companies, also may receive formal classroom or seminar-type training. As new engineers gain knowledge and experience, they are assigned more difficult projects with greater independence to develop designs, solve problems, and make decisions. Engineers may advance to become technical specialists or to supervise a staff or team of engineers and technicians. Some eventually may become engineering managers or enter other managerial or sales jobs. In sales, an engineering background enables them to discuss a product's technical aspects and assist in product planning, installation, and use.

Numerous professional certifications for engineers exist and may be beneficial for advancement to senior technical or managerial positions. Many certification programs are offered by the professional societies listed as sources of additional information for engineering specialties at the end of this statement.

About 36 percent of engineering jobs were found in manufacturing industries, and another 30 percent were in the professional, scientific, and technical services industries, primarily in architectural, engineering, and related services. Many engineers also worked in the construction, telecommunications, and wholesale trade industries.

Federal, State, and local governments employed about 12 percent of engineers in 2008. About 6 percent were in the Federal Government, mainly in the U.S. Departments of Defense,

Transportation, Agriculture, Interior, and Energy, and in the National Aeronautics and Space Administration. Many engineers in State and local government agencies worked in highway and public works departments. In 2008, about 3 percent of engineers were self-employed, many as consultants.

Engineers are employed in every State, in small and large cities and in rural areas. Some branches of engineering are concentrated in particular industries and geographic areas; for example, petroleum engineering jobs tend to be located in States with sizable petroleum deposits, such as Texas, Louisiana, Oklahoma, Alaska, and California. Other branches, such as civil engineering, are widely dispersed, and engineers in these fields often move from place to place to work on different projects.

Job Outlook

Employment of engineers is expected to grow about as fast as the average for all occupations over the next decade, but growth will vary by specialty. Biomedical engineers should experience the fastest growth, while civil engineers should see the largest employment increase. Overall job opportunities in engineering are expected to be good.

Overall employment change. Overall engineering employment is expected to grow by 11 percent over the 2008–18 decade, about as fast as the average for all occupations. Engineers traditionally have been concentrated in slower growing or declining manufacturing industries, in which they will continue to be needed to design, build, test, and improve manufactured products. However, increasing employment of engineers in engineering, research and development, and consulting services industries should generate most of the employment growth. The job outlook varies by engineering specialty, as discussed later.

Competitive pressures and advancing technology will force companies to improve and update product designs and to optimize their manufacturing processes. Employers will rely on engineers to increase productivity and expand output of goods and services. New technologies continue to improve the design process, enabling engineers to produce and analyze various product designs much more rapidly than in the past. Unlike the situation in some other occupations, however, technological advances are not expected to substantially limit employment opportunities in engineering, because engineers are needed to provide the ideas that lead to improved products and more productive processes.

The continued globalization of engineering work will likely dampen domestic employment growth to some degree. There are many well-trained, often English-speaking, engineers available around the world who are willing to work at much lower salaries than U.S. engineers. The rise of the Internet has made it relatively easy for part of the engineering work previously done by engineers in this country to be done by engineers in other countries, a factor that will tend to hold down employment growth. Even so, there will always be a need for onsite engineers to interact with other employees and clients.

Overall job prospects. Overall job opportunities in engineering are expected to be good, and, indeed, prospects will be excellent in certain specialties. In addition to openings from job growth, many openings will be created by the need to replace current engineers who retire; transfer to management, sales, or other occupations; or leave engineering for other reasons.

Many engineers work on long-term research and development projects or in other activities that continue even during economic slowdowns. In industries such as electronics and aerospace, however, large cutbacks in defense expenditures and in government funding for research and development have resulted in significant layoffs of engineers in the past. The trend toward contracting for engineering work with engineering services firms, both domestic and foreign, also has made engineers more vulnerable to layoffs during periods of lower demand.

It is important for engineers, as it is for workers in other technical and scientific occupations, to continue their education throughout their careers, because much of their value to their employer depends on their knowledge of the latest technology. Engineers in high-technology areas, such as biotechnology or information technology, may find that their technical knowledge will become outdated rapidly. By keeping current in their field, engineers will be able to deliver the best solutions and greatest value to their employers. Engineers who have not kept current in their field may find themselves at a disadvantage when seeking promotions or during layoffs.

Employment change and job outlook by engineering specialty. Aerospace engineers are expected to have 10 percent growth in employment over the projections decade, about as fast as the average for all occupations. New technologies and new designs for commercial and military aircraft and spacecraft produced during the next decade should spur demand for aerospace engineers. The employment outlook for aerospace engineers appears favorable. Although the number of degrees granted in aerospace engineering has begun to increase after many years of declines, new graduates continue to be needed to replace aerospace engineers who retire or leave the occupation for other reasons.

Agricultural engineers are expected to have employment growth of 12 percent over the projections decade, about as fast as the average for all occupations. Employment growth should result from the need to increase crop yields to feed an expanding population and to produce crops used as renewable energy sources. Moreover, engineers will be needed to develop more efficient agricultural production and to conserve resources. In addition, engineers will be needed to meet the increasing demand for biosensors, used to determine the optimal treatment of crops.

Biomedical engineers are expected to have employment growth of 72 percent over the projections decade, much faster than the average for all occupations. The aging of the population and a growing focus on health issues will drive demand for better medical devices and equipment designed by biomedical engineers. Along with the demand for more sophisticated medical equipment and procedures, an increased concern for cost-effectiveness will boost demand for biomedical engineers, particularly in pharmaceutical manufacturing and related industries. Because of the growing interest in this field, the number of degrees granted in biomedical engineering has increased greatly. Many biomedical engineers, particularly those employed in research laboratories, need a graduate degree.

Chemical engineers are expected to have an employment decline of 2 percent over the projections decade. Overall employment in the chemical manufacturing industry is expected to continue to decline, although chemical companies will continue to employ chemical engineers to research and develop new chemicals and more efficient processes to increase output of existing chemicals. However, there will be employment growth for chemical engineers in service-providing industries, such as professional, scientific, and technical services, particularly for research in energy and the developing fields of biotechnology and nanotechnology.

Civil engineers are expected to have employment growth of 24 percent over the projections decade, much faster than the average for all occupations. Spurred by general population growth and the related need to improve the Nation's infrastructure, more civil engineers will be needed to design and construct or expand transportation, water supply, and pollution control systems, and buildings and building complexes. They also will be needed to repair or replace existing roads, bridges, and other public structures. Because construction industries and architectural, engineering, and related services employ many civil engineers, employment opportunities will vary by geographic area and may decrease during economic slowdowns, when construction is often curtailed.

Computer hardware engineers are expected to have employment growth of 4 percent over the projections decade, slower than the average for all occupations. Although the use of information technology continues to expand rapidly, the manufacture of computer hardware is expected to be adversely affected by intense foreign competition. As computer and semiconductor manufacturers contract out more of their engineering needs to both domestic and foreign design firms, much of the growth in employment of hardware engineers is expected to take place in the computer systems design and related services industry.

Electrical engineers are expected to have employment growth of 2 percent over the projections decade. Although strong demand for electrical devices—including electric power generators, wireless phone transmitters, high-density batteries, and navigation systems—should spur job growth, international competition and the use of engineering services performed in other countries will limit employment growth. Electrical engineers working in firms providing engineering expertise and design services to manufacturers should have better job prospects.

Electronics engineers, except computer, are expected to experience little to no employment change over the projections decade. Although rising demand for electronic goods—including communications equipment, defense-related equipment, medical electronics, and consumer products—should continue to increase demand for electronics engineers, foreign competition in electronic products development and the use of engineering services performed in other countries will limit employment growth. Growth is expected to be fastest in service-providing industries—particularly in firms that provide engineering and design services.

Environmental engineers are expected to have employment growth of 31 percent over the projections decade, much faster than the average for all occupations. More environmental engineers will be needed to help companies comply with environmental regulations and to develop methods of cleaning up environmental hazards. A shift in emphasis toward preventing problems rather than controlling those which already exist, as well as increasing public health concerns resulting from population growth, also are expected to spur demand for environmental engineers. Because of this employment growth, job opportunities should be favorable.

Health and safety engineers, except mining safety engineers and inspectors, are expected to have employment growth of 10 percent over the projections decade, about as fast as the average for all occupations. Because health and safety engineers make production processes and products as safe as possible, their services should be in demand as concern increases for health and safety within work environments. As new technologies for production or processing are developed, health and safety engineers will be needed to ensure that they are safe.

Industrial engineers are expected to have employment growth of 14 percent over the projections decade, faster than the average for all occupations. As firms look for new ways to reduce costs and raise productivity, they increasingly will turn to industrial engineers to develop more efficient processes and reduce costs, delays, and waste. This focus should lead to job growth for these engineers, even in some manufacturing industries with declining employment overall. Because their work is similar to that done in management occupations, many industrial engineers leave the occupation to become managers. Numerous openings will be created by the need to replace industrial engineers who transfer to other occupations or leave the labor force.

Marine engineers and naval architects are expected to have employment growth of 6 percent over the projections decade, slower than the average for all occupations. Continued demand for naval vessels and recreational small craft should more than offset the long-term decline in the domestic design and construction of large oceangoing vessels. Good prospects are expected for marine engineers and naval architects because of growth in employment, the need to replace workers who retire or take other jobs, and the limited number of students pursuing careers in this occupation.

Materials engineers are expected to have employment growth of 9 percent over the projections decade, about as fast as the average for all occupations. Growth should result from increased use of composite and other nontraditional materials developed through biotechnology and nanotechnology research. As manufacturing firms contract for their materials engineering needs, most employment growth is expected in professional, scientific, and technical services industries.

Mechanical engineers are expected to have employment growth of 6 percent over the projections decade, slower than the average for all occupations. Mechanical engineers are involved in the production of a wide range of products, and continued efforts to improve those products will create continued demand for their services. In addition, some new job opportunities will be created through the effects of emerging technologies in biotechnology, materials science, and nanotechnology. Additional opportunities outside of mechanical engineering will exist because the skills acquired through earning a degree in mechanical engineering often can be applied in other engineering specialties.

Mining and geological engineers, including mining safety engineers, are expected to have employment growth of 15 percent over the projections decade, faster than the average for all occupations. Following a lengthy period of decline, strong growth in demand for minerals is expected to create some employment growth over the 2008–18 period. Moreover, many currently employed mining engineers are approaching retirement age, a factor that should create additional job openings. Furthermore, relatively few schools offer mining engineering programs, resulting in good job opportunities for graduates. The best opportunities may require frequent travel or even living overseas for extended periods as mining operations around the world recruit graduates of U.S. mining engineering programs.

Nuclear engineers are expected to have employment growth of 11 percent over the projections decade, about as fast as the average for all occupations. Most job growth will be in research and development and engineering services. Although no commercial nuclear power plants have been built in the United States for many years, increased interest in nuclear power as an energy source will spur demand for nuclear engineers to research and develop new designs for reactors. They also will be needed to work in defense-related areas, to develop nuclear medical technology, and to improve and enforce waste management and safety standards. Nuclear engineers are expected to have good employment opportunities because the small number of nuclear engineering graduates is likely to be in rough balance with the number of job openings.

Petroleum engineers are expected to have employment growth of 18 percent over the projections decade, faster than the average for all occupations. Petroleum engineers increasingly will be needed to develop new resources, as well as new methods of extracting more from existing sources. Excellent opportunities are expected for petroleum engineers because the number of job openings is likely to exceed the relatively small number of graduates. Petroleum engineers work around the world, and in fact, the best employment opportunities may include some work in other countries.

Earnings

Earnings for engineers vary significantly by specialty, industry, and education. Variation in median earnings and in the earnings distributions for engineers in a number of specialties is especially significant.

In the Federal Government, mean annual salaries for engineers ranged from $81,085 in agricultural engineering to $126,788 in ceramic engineering in March 2009.

As a group, engineers earn some of the highest average starting salaries among those holding bachelor's degrees.

ENGINEERING

—m—

Construction and Building Inspectors

Nature of the Work

Construction and building inspectors examine buildings, highways and streets, sewer and water systems, dams, bridges, and other structures. They ensure that their construction, alteration, or repair complies with building codes and ordinances, zoning regulations, and contract specifications. Building codes and standards are the primary means by which building construction is regulated in the United States for the health and safety of the general public. National model building and construction codes are published by the International Code Council (ICC), although many localities have additional ordinances and codes that modify or add to the National model codes. To monitor compliance with regulations, inspectors make an initial inspection during the first phase of construction and follow up with further inspections throughout the construction project. However, no inspection is ever exactly the same. In areas where certain types of severe weather or natural disasters—such as earthquakes or hurricanes—are more common, inspectors monitor compliance with additional safety regulations designed to protect structures and occupants during those events.

There are many types of inspectors. Building inspectors inspect the structural quality

Significant Points

❖ About 44 percent of inspectors worked for local governments, primarily municipal or county building departments.

❖ Many home inspectors are self-employed.

❖ Training requirements vary widely; some States require a license or certificate.

❖ Opportunities should be best for those with construction-related work experience; training in engineering, architecture, construction technology, or related fields; or certification as a construction inspector.

and general safety of buildings. Some specialize in for example, structural steel or reinforced-concrete structures. Before construction begins, plan examiners determine whether the plans for the building or other structure comply with building codes and whether they are suited to the engineering and environmental demands of the building site. To inspect the condition of the soil and the positioning and depth of the footings, inspectors visit the worksite before the foundation is poured. Later, they return to the site to inspect the foundation after it has been completed. The size and type of structure, as well as the rate at which it proceeds toward completion, determine the number of other site visits they must make. Upon completion of the project, they make a final, comprehensive inspection.

In addition to structural characteristics, a primary concern of building inspectors is fire safety. They inspect structures' fire sprinklers, alarms, smoke control systems, and fire exits. Inspectors assess the type of construction, the building's contents, adequacy of fire protection equipment, and any risks posed by adjoining buildings.

Electrical inspectors examine the installation of electrical systems and equipment to ensure that they function properly and comply with electrical codes and standards. They visit worksites to inspect new and existing sound and security systems, wiring, lighting, motors, and generating equipment. They also inspect the installation of the electrical wiring for heating and air-conditioning systems, appliances, and other components.

Elevator inspectors examine lifting and conveying devices such as elevators, escalators, moving sidewalks, lifts and hoists, inclined railways, ski lifts, and amusement rides.

Home inspectors conduct inspections of newly built or previously owned homes, condominiums, town homes, manufactured homes, apartments, and commercial buildings. Home inspection has become a standard practice in the home-purchasing process. Home inspectors are most often hired by prospective home buyers to inspect and report on the condition of a home's systems, components, and structure. Although they look for and report violations of building codes, they do not have the power to enforce compliance with the codes. Typically, they are hired either immediately prior to a purchase offer on a home or as a contingency to a sales contract. In addition to examining structural quality, home inspectors inspect all home systems and features, including roofing as well as the exterior, attached garage or carport, foundation, interior, plumbing, and electrical, heating, and cooling systems. Some home inspections are done for homeowners who want an evaluation of their home's condition, for example, prior to putting the home on the market or as a way to diagnose problems.

Mechanical inspectors examine the installation of heating, ventilation, air conditioning, and refrigeration systems and equipment to insure they are installed and function properly. This may include the inspection of commercial kitchen equipment, gas-fired appliances, and boilers.

Plumbing inspectors examine the installation of piping systems to insure the safety and health of the drinking water system, chemical process piping for industrial uses, and the sanitary disposal of waste. On most construction sites this will involve at least three inspections, including the piping layout, venting, backflow protection, and setting of fixtures.

Public works inspectors ensure that Federal, State, and local government water and sewer system, highway, street, bridge, and dam construction conforms to detailed contract specifications. They inspect excavation and fill operations, the placement of forms for concrete, concrete mixing and pouring, asphalt paving, and grading operations. They record the work and materials used so that contract payments can be calculated. Public works inspectors may specialize in highways, structural steel, reinforced concrete, or ditches. Others specialize in dredging operations required for bridges and dams or for harbors.

The owner of a building or structure under construction employs *specification inspectors* to ensure that work is done according to design specifications. Specification inspectors represent the owner's interests, not those of the general public. Insurance companies and financial institutions also may use their services.

Details concerning construction projects, building and occupancy permits, and other documentation generally are stored on computers so that they can easily be retrieved and updated. For example, inspectors may use laptop computers to record their findings while inspecting a site. Most inspectors use computers to help them monitor the status of construction inspection activities and keep track of permits issued, and some can access all construction and building codes from their computers on the job site, decreasing the need for paper binders. However, many inspectors continue to use a paper checklist to detail their findings.

Although inspections are primarily visual, inspectors may use tape measures, survey instruments, metering devices, and equipment such as concrete strength measurers. They keep a log of their work, take photographs, and file reports. Many inspectors also use laptops or other portable electronic devices onsite to facilitate the accuracy of their written reports, as well as e-mail and fax machines to send out the results. If necessary, they act on their findings. For example, government and construction inspectors notify the construction contractor, superintendent, or supervisor when they discover a violation of a code or ordinance or something that does not comply with the contract specifications or approved plans. If the problem is not corrected within a reasonable or otherwise specified period, government inspectors have authority to issue a "stop-work" order.

Many inspectors also investigate construction or alterations being done without proper permits. Inspectors who are employees of municipalities enforce laws pertaining to the proper design, construction, and use of buildings. They direct violators of permit laws to obtain permits and to submit to inspection.

Work environment. Construction and building inspectors usually work alone. However, several may be assigned to large, complex projects, particularly because inspectors tend to specialize in different areas of construction. Although they spend considerable time inspecting construction worksites, inspectors also spend time in a field office reviewing blueprints, answering letters or telephone calls, writing reports, and scheduling inspections.

Many construction sites are dirty and may be cluttered with tools, materials, or debris. Inspectors may have to climb ladders or many flights of stairs or crawl around in tight spaces. Although their work generally is not considered hazardous, inspectors, like other construction workers, wear hardhats and adhere to other safety requirements while at a construction site.

Inspectors normally work regular hours. However, they may work additional hours during periods when a lot of construction is taking place. Also, if an accident occurs at a construction site, inspectors must respond immediately and may work additional hours to complete their report. Non-government inspectors—especially those who are self-employed—may have a varied work schedule, at times working evenings and weekends.

Training, Other Qualifications, and Advancement

Although requirements vary considerably, construction and building inspectors should have a thorough knowledge of construction materials and practices. In some States, construction and building inspectors are required to obtain a special license or certification, so it is important to check with the appropriate State agency.

Education and training. Most employers require at least a high school diploma or the equivalent, even for workers with considerable experience. More often, employers look for persons who have studied engineering or architecture or who have a degree from a community or junior college with courses in building inspection, home inspection, construction technology, drafting, and mathematics. Many community colleges offer certificate or associate degree programs in building inspection technology. Courses in blueprint reading, algebra, geometry, and English also are useful. A growing number of construction and building inspectors are entering the occupation with a college degree, which often can substitute for previous experience.

The level of training requirements varies by type of inspector and State. In general, construction and building inspectors receive much of their training on the job, although they must learn building codes and standards on their own. Working with an experienced inspector, they learn about inspection techniques; codes, ordinances, and regulations; contract specifications; and recordkeeping and reporting duties. Supervised onsite inspections also may be a part of the training. Other requirements can include various courses and assigned reading. Some courses and instructional material are available online as well as through formal venues.

Licensure and certification. Many States and local jurisdictions require some type of license or certification for employment as a construction and building inspector. Requirements may vary by State or local municipality. Typical requirements for licensure or certification include previous experience, a minimum educational attainment level, such as a high school diploma, and passing a State-approved examination. Some States have individual licensing programs for inspectors, while others may require certification by such associations as the International Code Council, International Association of Plumbing and Mechanical Officials, and National Fire Protection Association.

Similarly, some States require home inspectors to obtain a State-issued license or certification. Currently, 34 States have regulations affecting home inspectors. Requirements for a license or certification vary by State, but may include obtaining a minimum level of education, having a set amount of experience with inspections, purchasing liability insurance of a certain amount, and the passing of an examination. Renewal is usually every few years and annual continuing education is almost always required.

Other qualifications. Because inspectors must possess the right mix of technical knowledge, experience, and education, employers prefer applicants who have both formal training and experience. For example, many inspectors previously worked as carpenters, electricians, or plumbers. Home inspectors combine knowledge of multiple specialties, so many of them come into the occupation having a combination of certifications and previous experience in various construction trades.

Construction and building inspectors must be in good physical condition in order to walk and climb about construction and building sites. They also must have a driver's license so that they can get to scheduled appointments.

Advancement. Being a member of a nationally recognized inspection association enhances employment opportunities and may be required by some employers. Even if it is not required, certification can enhance an inspector's opportunities for employment and advancement to more responsible positions. To become certified, inspectors with substantial experience and education must pass examinations on topics including code requirements, construction techniques and materials, standards of practice, and codes of ethics. The International Code Council offers multiple voluntary certifications, as do many other professional associations. Many categories of certification are awarded for inspectors and plan examiners in a variety of specialties, including the Certified Building Official (CBO) certification, for code compliance, and the Residential Building Inspector (RBI) certification, for home inspectors. In a few cases, there are no education or experience prerequisites, and certification consists of passing an examination in a designated field either at a regional location or online. In addition, Federal, State, and many local governments may require inspectors to pass a civil service exam.

Because they advise builders and the general public on building codes, construction practices, and technical developments, construction and building inspectors must keep abreast of changes in these areas. Continuing education is required by many States and certifying organizations. Numerous employers provide formal training to broaden inspectors' knowledge of construction materials, practices, and techniques. Inspectors who work for agencies or firms that do not conduct their own training programs can expand their knowledge and upgrade their skills by attending State-sponsored training programs, by taking college or correspondence courses, or by attending seminars and conferences sponsored by various related organizations, including professional organizations. An engineering or architectural degree often is required for advancement to supervisory positions.

Employment

Construction and building inspectors held about 106,400 jobs in 2008. Local governments—primarily municipal or county building departments—employed 44 percent. Employment of local government inspectors is concentrated in cities and in suburban areas undergoing rapid growth. Local governments in larger jurisdictions may employ large inspection staffs, including many plan examiners or inspectors who specialize in structural steel, reinforced concrete, and boiler, electrical, and elevator inspection. In smaller jurisdictions, only one or a few inspectors with generalist skills in multiple areas may be on staff.

Another 27 percent of construction and building inspectors worked for architectural and engineering services firms, conducting inspections for a fee or on a contract basis. Many of these were home inspectors working on behalf of potential real estate purchasers. Most of the remaining inspectors were employed in other service-providing industries or by State governments. About 8 percent of construction and building inspectors were self-employed; many of these were home inspectors.

Job Outlook

Inspectors should experience faster than average employment growth. Opportunities should be best for those with construction-related work experience; training in engineering, architecture, construction technology, or related fields; or certification as a construction inspector.

Employment change. Employment of construction and building inspectors is expected to grow 17 percent over the 2008-2018 decade, faster than the average for all occupations. Concern for public safety and a desire for improvement in the quality of construction should continue to stimulate demand for construction and building inspectors in government as well as in firms specializing in architectural, engineering, and related services. As the result of new technology such as building information modeling (BIM), the availability of a richer set of buildings data in a more timely and transparent manner will make it easier to conduct plan reviews. This will lead to more time and resources spent on inspections. In addition, the growing focus on natural and manmade disasters is increasing the level of interest in and need for qualified inspectors. Issues such as green and sustainable design are new areas of focus that will also drive the demand for construction and building inspectors.

The routine practice of obtaining home inspections is a relatively recent development, causing employment of home inspectors to increase rapidly. Although employment of home inspectors is expected to continue to increase, the attention given to this specialty, combined with the desire of some construction workers to move into less strenuous and potentially higher paying work, may result in reduced growth of home inspectors in some areas. In addition, increasing State regulations are starting to limit entry into the specialty only to those who have a given level of previous experience and who are certified.

Job prospects. Those with construction-related work experience; training in engineering, architecture, construction technology, or related fields; or certification as a construction inspector will have the best prospects. Inspectors are involved in all phases of construction, including maintenance and repair work, and are therefore less likely than many construction workers to lose their jobs when new construction slows during recessions. Those who are self-employed, such as home inspectors, are more likely to be affected by economic downturns or fluctuations in the real estate market. However, those with a thorough knowledge of construction practices and skills in areas such as reading and evaluating blueprints and plans will be better off. In addition to openings stemming from the expected employment growth, some job openings will arise from the need to replace inspectors who transfer to other occupations or leave the labor force.

Earnings

Median annual wages of wage and salary construction and building inspectors were $50,180 in May 2008. The middle 50 percent earned between $39,070 and $63,360. The lowest 10 percent earned less than $31,270, and the highest 10 percent earned more than $78,070.

ENGINEERING

—⚏—

Computing Scientists

Nature of the Work

The widespread and increasing use of computers and information technology has generated a need for highly trained, innovative workers with extensive theoretical expertise. These workers, called *computer scientists*, are the designers, creators, and inventors of new technology. By creating new technology, or finding alternative uses for existing resources, they solve complex business, scientific, and general computing problems. Some computer scientists work on multidisciplinary projects, collaborating with electrical engineers, mechanical engineers, and other specialists.

Significant Points

❖ Most computer scientists are required to possess a Ph.D.

❖ Employment is projected to increase much faster than the average for all occupations.

❖ Job prospects are expected to be excellent.

Computer scientists conduct research on a wide array of topics. Examples include computer hardware architecture, virtual reality, and robotics. Scientists who research hardware architecture discover new ways for computers to process and transmit information. They design computer chips and processors, using new materials and techniques to make them work faster and give them more computing power. When working with virtual reality, scientists use technology to create life-like situations. For example, scientists may invent video games that make users feel like they are actually in the game. Computer scientists working with robotics try to create machines that can perform tasks on their own—without people controlling them. Robots perform many tasks, such as sweeping floors in peoples' homes, assembling cars on factory production lines, and "auto-piloting" airplanes.

Computer science researchers employed by academic institutions have job functions that are similar in many ways to those employed by other organizations. In general, researchers in academic settings have more flexibility to focus on pure theory, while those working in business or scientific organizations, covered here, usually focus on projects that have the possibility of producing patents and profits. Some researchers in non-academic settings, however, have considerable latitude in determining the direction of their research.

Work environment. Computer scientists normally work in offices or laboratories in comfortable surroundings. Like other workers who spend long periods in front of a computer terminal typing on a keyboard, computer scientists are susceptible to eyestrain, back discomfort, and hand and wrist problems such as carpal tunnel syndrome.

Training, Other Qualifications, and Advancement

A Ph.D. is required for most jobs, and an aptitude for math is important.

Education and training. Most computer scientists are required to possess a Ph.D. in computer science, computer engineering, or a closely related discipline. For some positions in the Federal Government, a bachelor's degree in a computer-related field may be adequate.

In order to be admitted to a Ph.D. program, applicants generally are required to obtain a bachelor's degree with a strong computer science or computer engineering component. Popular undergraduate majors for Ph.D. program applicants include computer science, computer engineering, software engineering, information systems, and information technology. A bachelor's degree generally takes 4 years to complete. A Ph.D. generally requires at least 5 years of study beyond the bachelor's degree. Ph.D. students usually spend the first two years taking classes on advanced topics, including computer and software systems, artificial intelligence, digital communication, and microprocessors. Students spend the remaining years conducting research on topics in computer science or computer engineering.

Other qualifications. Computer scientists must be able to think logically and creatively. They must possess a strong aptitude for math and other technical topics, as these are critical to the computing field. Because they often deal with a number of tasks simultaneously, the ability to concentrate and pay close attention to detail also is important. Although computer scientists sometimes work independently, they frequently work in teams on large projects. As a result, they must be able to communicate effectively with computer personnel, such as programmers and managers, as well as with users or other staff who may have no technical computer background.

Advancement. After they gain experience with an organization, computer scientists may advance into managerial or project leadership positions. Some choose to leave private industry for academic positions.

Employment

Computer scientists held about 28,900 jobs in 2008. Although they are increasingly employed in every sector of the economy, the greatest concentration of these workers, about

23 percent, was in the computer systems design and related services industry. Many computer scientists were also employed by software publishing firms, scientific research and development organizations, and in education.

Job Outlook

Employment growth is expected to be much faster than the average, and job prospects should be excellent.

Employment change. Employment of computer scientists is expected to grow by 24 percent from 2008 to 2018, which is much faster than the average for all occupations. Employment of these computer specialists is expected to grow as individuals and organizations continue to demand increasingly sophisticated technologies. Job increases will be driven, in part, by very rapid growth in computer systems design and related services industry, as well as the software publishing industry, which are projected to be among the fastest growing industries in the U.S. economy.

Computer scientists develop the theories that allow many new technologies to be developed. The demand for increasing efficiency in areas such as networking technology, computing speeds, software performance, and embedded systems will lead to employment growth. In addition, the growing emphasis on information security will lead to new jobs.

Job prospects. Computer scientists should enjoy excellent job prospects. Graduates from Ph.D. programs in computer science and engineering are in high demand, and many companies report difficulties finding sufficient numbers of these highly skilled workers. In addition to openings resulting from rapid growth in the occupation, some additional job openings will arise from the need to replace workers who move into other occupations or who leave the labor force.

Earnings

Median annual wages of computer and information scientists were $97,970 in May 2008. The middle 50 percent earned between $75,340 and $124,370. The lowest 10 percent earned less than $57,480, and the highest 10 percent earned more than $151,250. Median annual wages of computer and information scientists employed in computer systems design and related services in May 2008 were $99,900.

ENGINEERING

—ɯ—

Computer Software Engineers and Computer Programmers

Nature of the Work

Computer software engineers design and develop software. They apply the theories and principles of computer science and mathematical analysis to create, test, and evaluate the software applications and systems that make computers work. The tasks performed by these workers evolve quickly, reflecting changes in technology and new areas of specialization, as well as the changing practices of employers.

Software engineers design and develop many types of software, including computer games, business applications, operating systems, network control systems, and middleware. They must be experts in the theory of computing systems, the structure of software, and the nature and limitations of hardware to ensure that the underlying systems will work properly.

Computer software engineers begin by analyzing users' needs, and then design, test, and develop software to meet those needs. During this process they create flowcharts, diagrams, and other documentation, and may also create the detailed sets of instructions, called algorithms, that actually tell the computer what to do. They also may be responsible for converting these instructions into a computer language, a process called programming or coding, but this usually is the responsibility of *computer programmers*.

Computer software engineers can generally be divided into two categories: applications engineers and systems engineers. *Computer applications software engineers* analyze end

Significant Points

❖ Computer software engineers are among the occupations projected to grow the fastest and add the most new jobs over the 2008-18 decade, resulting in excellent job prospects.

❖ Employment of computer programmers is expected to decline by 3 percent through 2018.

❖ Job prospects will be best for applicants with a bachelor's or higher degree and relevant experience.

users' needs and design, construct, deploy, and maintain general computer applications software or specialized utility programs. These workers use different programming languages, depending on the purpose of the program and the environment in which the program runs. The programming languages most often used are C, C++, Java, and Python. Some software engineers develop packaged computer applications, but most create or adapt customized applications for business and other organizations. Some of these workers also develop databases.

Computer systems software engineers coordinate the construction, maintenance, and expansion of an organization's computer systems. Working with the organization, they coordinate each department's computer needs—ordering, inventory, billing, and payroll recordkeeping, for example—and make suggestions about its technical direction. They also might set up the organization's intranets—networks that link computers within the organization and ease communication among various departments. Often, they are also responsible for the design and implementation of system security and data assurance.

Systems software engineers also work for companies that configure, implement, and install the computer systems of other organizations. These workers may be members of the marketing or sales staff, serving as the primary technical resource for sales workers, or providing logistical and technical support. Since the selling of complex computer systems often requires substantial customization to meet the needs of the purchaser, software engineers help to identify and explain needed changes. In addition, systems software engineers are responsible for ensuring security across the systems they are configuring.

Computer programmers write programs. After computer software engineers and systems analysts design software programs, the programmer converts that design into a logical series of instructions that the computer can follow. The programmer codes these instructions in any of a number of programming languages, depending on the need. The most common languages are C++ and Python.

Computer programmers also update, repair, modify, and expand existing programs. Some, especially those working on large projects that involve many programmers, use computer-assisted software engineering (CASE) tools to automate much of the coding process. These tools enable a programmer to concentrate on writing the unique parts of a program. Programmers working on smaller projects often use "programmer environments," applications that increase productivity by combining compiling, code walk-through, code generation, test data generation, and debugging functions. Programmers also use libraries of basic code that can be modified or customized for a specific application. This approach yields more reliable and consistent programs and increases programmers' productivity by eliminating some routine steps.

As software design has continued to advance, and some programming functions have become automated, programmers have begun to assume some of the responsibilities that were once performed only by software engineers. As a result, some computer programmers now assist software engineers in identifying user needs and designing certain parts of computer programs, as well as other functions.

Work environment. Computer software engineers and programmers normally work in clean, comfortable offices or in laboratories in which computer equipment is located. Software engineers who work for software vendors and consulting firms frequently travel to meet with customers. Telecommuting is becoming more common as technological advances allow more work to be done from remote locations.

Most software engineers and programmers work 40 hours a week, but about 15 percent of software engineers and 11 percent of programmers worked more than 50 hours a week in 2008. Injuries in these occupations are rare. However, like other workers who spend long periods in front of a computer terminal typing at a keyboard, engineers and programmers are susceptible to eyestrain, back discomfort, and hand and wrist problems such as carpal tunnel syndrome.

Training, Other Qualifications, and Advancement

A bachelor's degree commonly is required for software engineering jobs, although a master's degree is preferred for some positions. A bachelor's degree also is required for many computer programming jobs, although a 2-year degree or certificate may be adequate in some cases. Employers favor applicants who already have relevant skills and experience. Workers who keep up to date with the latest technology usually have good opportunities for advancement.

Education and training. For software engineering positions, most employers prefer applicants who have at least a bachelor's degree and broad knowledge of, and experience with, a variety of computer systems and technologies. The usual college majors for applications software engineers are computer science, software engineering, or mathematics. Systems software engineers often study computer science or computer information systems. Graduate degrees are preferred for some of the more complex jobs.

Many programmers require a bachelor's degree, but a 2-year degree or certificate may be adequate for some positions. Some computer programmers hold a college degree in computer science, mathematics, or information systems, whereas others have taken special courses in computer programming to supplement their degree in a field such as accounting, finance, or another area of business.

Employers who use computers for scientific or engineering applications usually prefer college graduates who have a degree in computer or information science, mathematics, engineering, or the physical sciences. Employers who use computers for business applications prefer to hire people who have had college courses in management information systems and business, and who possess strong programming skills. A graduate degree in a related field is required for some jobs.

In addition to educational attainment, employers highly value relevant programming skills and experience. Students seeking software engineering or programming jobs can enhance their employment opportunities by participating in internships. Some employers, such as large computer and consulting firms, train new employees in intensive, company-based programs.

As technology advances, employers will need workers with the latest skills. To help keep up with changing technology, workers may take continuing education and professional development seminars offered by employers, software vendors, colleges and universities, private training institutions, and professional computing societies. Computer software engineers also need skills related to the industry in which they work. Engineers working for a bank, for example, should have some expertise in finance so that they understand banks' computing needs.

Certification and other qualifications. Certification is a way to demonstrate a level of competence and may provide a jobseeker with a competitive advantage. Certification programs are generally offered by product vendors or software firms, which may require professionals who work with their products to be certified. Voluntary certification also is available through various other organizations, such as professional computing societies.

Computer software engineers and programmers must have strong problem-solving and analytical skills. Ingenuity and creativity are particularly important in order to design new, functional software programs. The ability to work with abstract concepts and to do technical analysis is especially important for systems engineers because they work with the software that controls the computer's operation. Engineers and programmers also must be able to communicate effectively with team members, other staff, and end users. Because they often deal with a number of tasks simultaneously, they must be able to concentrate and pay close attention to detail. Business skills are also important, especially for those wishing to advance to managerial positions.

Advancement. For skilled workers who keep up to date with the latest technology, prospects for advancement are good. Advancement opportunities for computer software engineers increase with experience. Eventually, they may become a project manager, manager of information systems, or chief information officer, especially if they have business skills and training. Some computer software engineers with several years of experience or expertise can find lucrative opportunities working as systems designers or independent consultants, particularly in specialized fields such as business-to-business transactions or security and data assurance.

In large organizations, programmers may be promoted to lead programmer and be given supervisory responsibilities. Some applications programmers may move into systems programming after they gain experience and take courses in systems software. With general business experience, programmers may become programmer-analysts or systems analysts, or may be promoted to managerial positions. Programmers with specialized knowledge and experience with a language or operating system may become computer software engineers. As employers increasingly contract with outside firms to do programming jobs, more opportunities should arise for experienced programmers with expertise in a specific area to work as consultants.

Employment

Computer software engineers and computer programmers held about 1.3 million jobs in 2008. Approximately 514,800 were computer applications software engineers, about 394,800 were computer systems software engineers, and about 426,700 were computer programmers. Although computer software engineers and computer programmers can be found in a wide range of industries about 32 percent were employed in computer systems design and related services. Many also worked for software publishers, manufacturers of computers and related electronic equipment, financial institutions, and insurance providers. About 48,200 computer software engineers and computer programmers were self-employed in 2008.

Job Outlook

Overall, employment of computer software engineers and computer programmers is projected to increase much faster than the average for all occupations. Job prospects should be best for those with a bachelor's degree and relevant experience.

Employment change. Overall, employment of computer software engineers and computer programmers is projected to increase by 21 percent from 2008 to 2018, much faster than the average for all occupations. This will be the result of rapid growth among computer software engineers, as employment of computer programmers is expected to decline.

Employment of computer software engineers is expected to increase by 32 percent from 2008-2018, which is much faster than the average for all occupations. In addition, this occupation will see a large number of new jobs, with more than 295,000 created between 2008 and 2018. Demand for computer software engineers will increase as computer networking continues to grow. For example, expanding Internet technologies have spurred demand for computer software engineers who can develop Internet, intranet, and World Wide Web applications. Likewise, electronic data-processing systems in business, telecommunications, healthcare, government, and other settings continue to become more sophisticated and complex. Implementing, safeguarding, and updating computer systems and resolving problems will fuel the demand for growing numbers of systems software engineers.

New growth areas will also continue to arise from rapidly evolving technologies. The increasing uses of the Internet, the proliferation of Web sites, and mobile technology such as the wireless Internet have created a demand for a wide variety of new products. As more software is offered over the Internet, and as businesses demand customized software to meet their specific needs, applications and systems software engineers will be needed in greater numbers. In addition, the growing use of handheld computers will create demand for new mobile applications and software systems. As these devices become a larger part of the business environment, it will be necessary to integrate current computer systems with this new, more mobile technology.

In addition, information security concerns have given rise to new software needs. Concerns over "cyber security" should result in the continued investment in software that protects computer networks and electronic infrastructure. The expansion of this technology over the next 10 years will lead to an increased need for software engineers to design and develop secure applications and systems, and to integrate them into older systems.

As with other information technology jobs, offshore outsourcing may temper employment growth of computer software engineers. Firms may look to cut costs by shifting operations to foreign countries with lower prevailing wages and highly educated workers. Jobs in software engineering are less prone to being offshored than are jobs in computer programming, however, because software engineering requires innovation and intense research and development.

Employment of computer programmers is expected to decline slowly, decreasing by 3 percent from 2008 to 2018. Advances in programming languages and tools, the growing ability of users to write and implement their own programs, and the offshore outsourcing of programming jobs will contribute to this decline.

Because they can transmit their programs digitally, computer programmers can perform their job function from anywhere in the world, allowing companies to employ workers in countries that have lower prevailing wages. Computer programmers are at a much higher risk of having their jobs offshored than are workers involved in more complex and sophisticated information technology functions, such as software engineering. Much of the work of computer programmers requires little localized or specialized knowledge and can be made routine once knowledge of a particular programming language is mastered.

Nevertheless, employers will continue to need some local programmers, especially those who have strong technical skills and who understand an employer's business and its programming requirements. This means that programmers will have to keep abreast of changing programming languages and techniques. Furthermore, a recent trend of domestic sourcing may help to keep a number of programming jobs onshore. Instead of hiring workers in foreign locations, some organizations have begun to contract with programmers in low-cost areas of the United States. This allows them to reduce payroll expenses, while eliminating some of the logistical issues that arise with offshore outsourcing.

Job prospects. As a result of rapid employment growth over the 2008 to 2018 decade, job prospects for computer software engineers should be excellent. Those with practical experience and at least a bachelor's degree in a computer-related field should have the best opportunities. Employers will continue to seek computer professionals with strong programming, systems analysis, interpersonal, and business skills. In addition to jobs created through employment growth, many job openings will result from the need to replace workers who move into managerial positions, transfer to other occupations, or leave the labor force. Consulting opportunities for computer software engineers also should continue to grow as businesses seek help to manage, upgrade, and customize their increasingly complicated computer systems.

Although employment of computer programmers is projected to decline, numerous job openings will result from the need to replace workers who leave the labor force or transfer to other occupations. Prospects for these openings should be best for applicants with a bachelor's degree and experience with a variety of programming languages and tools. As technology evolves, however, and newer, more sophisticated tools emerge, programmers will need to update their skills in order to remain competitive. Obtaining vendor-specific or language-specific certification also can provide a competitive edge.

In May 2008, median annual wages of wage-and-salary computer applications software engineers were $85,430. The middle 50 percent earned between $67,790 and $104,870. The lowest 10 percent earned less than $53,720, and the highest 10 percent earned more than $128,870. In May 2008, median annual wages of wage-and-salary computer systems software engineers were $92,430. The middle 50 percent earned between $73,200 and $113,960. The lowest 10 percent earned less than $57,810, and the highest 10 percent earned more than $135,780. Median annual wages of wage-and-salary computer programmers were $69,620 in May 2008. The middle 50 percent earned between $52,640 and $89,720 a year. The lowest 10 percent earned less than $40,080, and the highest 10 percent earned more than $111,450. According to the National Association of Colleges and Employers, starting salary offers for graduates with a bachelor's degree in computer science averaged $61,407 in July 2009.

MILITARY

—ɱ—

Armed Forces

Nature of the Work

Maintaining a strong national defense requires workers who can do such diverse tasks as run a hospital, command a tank, program a computer system, operate a nuclear reactor, or repair and maintain a helicopter. The military provides training and work experience in these and many other fields for more than 2.4 million people. More than 1.4 million people serve in the active Army, Navy, Marine Corps, and Air Force, and more than 1.0 million serve in their Reserve components and the Air and Army National Guard. (The Coast Guard, which also is discussed in this statement, is part of the Department of Homeland Security.)

The military distinguishes between enlisted and officer careers. Enlisted personnel, who make up about 82 percent of the Armed Forces, carry out the fundamental operations of the military in combat, administration, construction, engineering, healthcare, human services, and other areas. Officers, who make up the remaining 18 percent of the Armed Forces, are the leaders of the military, supervising and managing activities in every occupational specialty.

The sections that follow discuss the major occupational groups for enlisted personnel

Significant Points

❖ Some training and duty assignments are hazardous, even in peacetime; hours and working conditions can be arduous and vary substantially, and personnel must strictly conform to military rules at all times.

❖ Requirements vary by branch of service, but enlisted personnel need at least a high school diploma or its equivalent while officers need a bachelor's or graduate degree.

❖ Opportunities should be excellent in all branches of the Armed Forces for applicants who meet designated standards.

❖ Military personnel are eligible for retirement after 20 years of service.

and officers.

Enlisted occupational groups. *Administrative careers* include a wide variety of positions. The military must keep accurate information for planning and managing its operations. Both paper and electronic records are kept on personnel and on equipment, funds, supplies, and all other aspects of the military. Administrative personnel record information, prepare reports, maintain files, and review information to assist military officers. Personnel may work in a specialized area, such as finance, accounting, legal affairs, maintenance, supply, or transportation.

Combat specialty occupations include enlisted specialties, such as infantry, artillery, and Special Forces, whose members operate weapons or execute special missions during combat. People in these occupations normally specialize by type of weapon system or combat operation. They maneuver against enemy forces and positions, and fire artillery, guns, mortars, and missiles to destroy enemy positions. They also may operate tanks and amphibious assault vehicles in combat or on scouting missions. When the military has especially difficult or specialized missions to perform, it calls upon Special Forces teams. These elite combat forces maintain a constant state of readiness to strike anywhere in the world on a moment's notice. Team members from the Special Forces conduct offensive raids, demolitions, intelligence, search-and-rescue missions, and other operations from aboard aircraft, helicopters, ships, or submarines.

Construction occupations in the military include personnel who build or repair buildings, airfields, bridges, foundations, dams, bunkers, and the electrical and plumbing components of these structures. Personnel in construction occupations operate bulldozers, cranes, graders, and other heavy equipment. Construction specialists also may work with engineers and other building specialists as part of military construction teams. Some personnel specialize in areas such as plumbing or electrical wiring. Plumbers and pipefitters install and repair the plumbing and pipe systems needed in buildings and on aircraft and ships. Building electricians install and repair electrical-wiring systems in offices, airplane hangars, and other buildings on military bases.

Electronic and electrical equipment repair personnel repair and maintain electronic and electrical equipment used in the military. Repairers normally specialize by type of equipment, such as avionics, computers, optical equipment, communications, or weapons systems. For example, electronic instrument repairers install, test, maintain, and repair a wide variety of electronic systems, including navigational controls and biomedical instruments. Weapons maintenance technicians maintain and repair weapons used by combat forces; most of these weapons have electronic components and systems that assist in locating targets and in aiming and firing the weapon.

Engineering, science, and technical personnel in the military require specific knowledge to operate technical equipment, solve complex problems, or provide and interpret information. Personnel normally specialize in one area, such as space operations, information technology, environmental health and safety, or intelligence. Space operations specialists use and repair ground-control command equipment related to spacecraft, including electronic systems that track the location and operation of a craft. Information technology specialists develop software programs and operate computer systems. Environmental health and safety specialists inspect military facilities and food supplies for the presence of disease, germs, or other conditions hazardous to health and the environment. Intelligence specialists gather and study aerial photographs and use various types of radar and surveillance systems to discover information needed by the military.

Healthcare personnel assist medical professionals in treating and providing services for men and women in the military. They may work as part of a patient-service team in close contact with doctors, dentists, nurses, and physical therapists. Some specialize in providing emergency medical treatment, operating diagnostic tools such as x-ray and ultrasound equipment, laboratory testing of tissue and blood samples, maintaining pharmacy supplies or patients' records, constructing and repairing dental equipment or eyeglasses, or some other healthcare task.

Human resources development specialists recruit qualified personnel, place them in suitable occupations, and provide training programs. Personnel in this career area normally specialize by activity. For example, recruiting specialists provide information about military careers to young people, parents, schools, and local communities, and explain the Armed Service's employment and training opportunities, pay and benefits, and service life. Personnel specialists collect and store information about the people in the military, including information on their previous and current training, job assignments, promotions, and health. Training specialists and instructors teach classes, give demonstrations, and instruct military personnel on how to perform their jobs.

Machine operator and production personnel operate industrial equipment, machinery, and tools to fabricate and repair parts for a variety of items and structures. They may operate engines, turbines, nuclear reactors, and water pumps. Often, they specialize by type of work performed. Welders and metalworkers, for instance, work with various types of metals to repair or form the structural parts of ships, submarines, buildings, or other equipment. Survival equipment specialists inspect, maintain, and repair survival equipment such as parachutes and aircraft life support equipment.

Media and public affairs personnel assist with the public presentation and interpretation of military information and events. They take photographs; film, record, and edit audio and video programs; present news and music programs; and produce artwork, drawings, and other visual displays. Other public affairs specialists act as interpreters and translators to convert written or spoken foreign languages into English or other languages.

Protective service personnel include those who enforce military laws and regulations and provide emergency responses to natural and human-made disasters. For example, military police control traffic, prevent crime, and respond to emergencies. Other law enforcement and security specialists investigate crimes committed on military property and guard inmates in military correctional facilities. Firefighters put out, control, and help prevent fires in buildings, on aircraft, and aboard ships.

Support service personnel provide subsistence services and support the morale and well-being of military personnel and their families. Food service specialists prepare all types of food in dining halls, hospitals, and ships. Counselors help military personnel and their families deal with personal issues. They work as part of a team that may include social workers, psychologists, medical officers, chaplains, personnel specialists, and commanders. Religious program specialists assist chaplains with religious services, religious education programs, and related administrative duties.

Transportation and material-handling specialists ensure the safe transport of people and cargo. Most personnel within this occupational group are classified according to mode of transportation, such as aircraft, motor vehicle, or ship. Aircrew members operate equipment on aircraft. Vehicle drivers operate all types of heavy military vehicles, including fuel or water tank trucks, semitrailers, heavy troop transports, and passenger buses. Quartermasters and boat operators navigate and pilot many types of small watercraft, including tugboats, gunboats, and barges. Cargo specialists load and unload military supplies, using equipment such as forklifts and cranes.

Vehicle and machinery mechanics conduct preventive and corrective maintenance on aircraft, automotive and heavy equipment, heating and cooling systems, marine engines, and powerhouse station equipment. These workers typically specialize by the type of equipment that they maintain. For example, aircraft mechanics inspect, service, and repair helicopters, airplanes, and drones. Automotive and heavy equipment mechanics maintain and repair vehicles, such as humvees, trucks, tanks, self-propelled missile launchers, and other combat vehicles. They also repair bulldozers, power shovels, and other construction equipment. Heating and cooling mechanics install and repair air-conditioning, refrigeration, and heating equipment. Marine engine mechanics repair and maintain gasoline and diesel engines on ships, boats, and other watercraft. They also repair shipboard mechanical and electrical equipment. Powerhouse mechanics install, maintain, and repair electrical and mechanical equipment in power-generating stations.

Officer occupational groups. *Combat specialty officers* plan and direct military operations, oversee combat activities, and serve as combat leaders. This category includes officers in charge of tanks and other armored assault vehicles, artillery systems, Special Forces, and infantry. Combat specialty officers normally specialize by the type of unit they lead. Within the unit, they may further specialize by type of weapon system. Artillery and missile system officers, for example, direct personnel as they target, launch, test, and maintain various types of missiles and artillery. Special operations officers lead their units in offensive raids, demolitions, intelligence gathering, and search-and-rescue missions.

Engineering, science, and technical officers have a wide range of responsibilities based on their area of expertise. They lead or perform activities in areas such as space operations, environmental health and safety, and engineering. These officers may direct the operations of communications centers or the development of complex computer systems. Environmental health and safety officers study the air, ground, and water to identify and analyze sources of pollution and its effects. They also direct programs to control safety and health hazards in the workplace. Other personnel work as aerospace engineers, designing and directing the development of military aircraft, missiles, and spacecraft.

Executive, administrative, and managerial officers oversee and direct military activities in key functional areas, such as finance, accounting, health administration, international relations, and supply. Health services administrators, for instance, are responsible for the overall quality of care provided at the hospitals and clinics they operate. They must ensure that all of the departments work together. As another example, purchasing and contracting managers negotiate and monitor contracts for the purchase of the billions of dollars worth of equipment, supplies, and services that the military buys from private industry each year.

Healthcare officers provide health services at military facilities on the basis of their area of specialization. Officers who examine, diagnose, and treat patients with illness, injury, or disease include physicians, registered nurses, and dentists. Other officers provide therapy, rehabilitative treatment, and additional healthcare services for patients. Physical and occupational therapists plan and administer therapy to help patients adjust to disabilities, regain independence, and return to work. Speech therapists evaluate and treat patients with hearing and speech problems. Dietitians manage food service facilities and plan meals for hospital patients and for outpatients who need special diets. Pharmacists manage the purchase, storage, and dispensing of drugs and medicines. Physicians and surgeons in this occupational group provide the majority of medical services to the military and their families. Dentists treat diseases, disorders, and injuries of the mouth. Optometrists treat vision problems by prescribing eyeglasses or contact lenses. Psychologists provide mental healthcare and also conduct research on behavior and emotions.

Human resource development officers manage recruitment, placement, and training strategies and programs in the military. Recruiting managers direct recruiting efforts and provide information about military careers to young people, parents, schools, and local communities. Personnel managers direct military personnel functions, such as job assignment, staff promotion, and career counseling. Training and education directors identify training needs and develop and manage educational programs designed to keep military personnel current in the skills they need.

Media and public affairs officers oversee the development, production, and presentation of information or events for the public. These officers may produce and direct motion pictures, videos, and television and radio broadcasts that are used for training, news, and entertainment. Some plan, develop, and direct the activities of military bands. Public information officers respond to inquiries about military activities and prepare news releases and reports to keep the public informed.

Protective service officers are responsible for the safety and protection of individuals and property on military bases and vessels. Emergency management officers plan and prepare for all types of natural and human-made disasters by developing warning, control, and evacuation procedures to be used in the event of a disaster. Law enforcement and security officers enforce all applicable laws on military bases and investigate crimes when the law has been broken.

Support services officers manage food service activities and perform services in support of the morale and well-being of military personnel and their families. Food services managers oversee the preparation and delivery of food services within dining facilities located on military installations and vessels. Social workers focus on improving conditions that cause social problems, such as drug and alcohol abuse, racism, and sexism. Chaplains conduct worship services for military personnel and perform other spiritual duties according to the beliefs and practices of various religious faiths.

Transportation officers manage and perform activities related to the safe transport of military personnel and material by air and water. These officers normally specialize by mode of transportation or area of expertise, because, in many cases, they must meet licensing and certification requirements. Pilots in the military fly various types of specialized airplanes and helicopters to execute combat missions and to carry troops and equipment. Navigators use radar, radio, and other navigation equipment to determine their position and plan their route of travel. Officers on ships and submarines work as a team to manage the various departments aboard their vessels. Ships' engineers direct engineering departments aboard ships and submarines, including engine operations, maintenance, repair, heating, and power generation.

Work environment. Specific work environments and conditions depend on the branch of service, the occupational specialty, and other factors. Most military personnel live and work on or near military bases and facilities throughout the United States and the world. These bases and facilities usually offer comfortable housing and amenities, such as stores and recreation centers. Service members move regularly to complete their training or to meet the needs of their branch of service. Some are deployed to defend national interests. Military personnel must be physically fit, mentally stable, and ready to participate in or support combat missions that may be difficult and dangerous and involve time away from family. Some personnel are never deployed near combat areas.

In many circumstances, military personnel work standard hours, but personnel must be prepared to work long hours to fulfill missions, and they must conform to strict military rules at all times. Work hours depend on the occupational specialty and mission.

Training, Other Qualifications, and Advancement

To join the military, applicants must meet age, educational, aptitude, physical, and character requirements. These requirements vary by branch of service and vary between officers, who usually have a college degree, and enlisted personnel, who often do not. People are assigned an occupational specialty based on their aptitude, former training, and the needs of the military. All service members must sign a contract and commit to a minimum term of service. After joining the military, all enlistees receive general and occupation-specific training.

Those considering enlisting in the military should learn as much as they can about military life before making a decision. Doing so is especially important when one is thinking about making the military a career. Speaking to friends and relatives with military experience is a good idea, as is comparing the pros and cons. The next step is talking to a recruiter, who can determine whether the applicant qualifies for enlistment, explain the various enlistment options, and tell which military occupational specialties currently have openings. Applicants must bear in mind that the recruiter's job is to recruit promising applicants into his or her branch of military service, so the information that the recruiter gives is likely to stress the positive aspects of military life in the branch in which he or she serves.

Applicants should ask their recruiter for the branch they have chosen to assess their chances of being accepted for training in the occupation of their choice or, better still, take the aptitude exam to see how well they score. The military uses this exam as a placement exam, and test scores largely determine an individual's chances of being accepted into a particular training program. Selection for a particular type of training depends on the needs of the service and the applicant's general and technical aptitudes and personal preferences. Because all prospective recruits are required to take the exam, those who do so before committing themselves to enlisting have the advantage of knowing in advance whether they stand a good chance of being accepted for training in a particular specialty. The recruiter can schedule applicants to take the Armed Services Vocational Aptitude Battery without any obligation to join. Many high schools offer the exam as an easy way for students to explore the possibility of a military career, and the test also affords an insight into career areas in which the student has demonstrated aptitudes and interests. The exam is not part of the process of joining the military as an officer.

If an applicant decides to join the military, the next step is to pass the physical examination and sign an enlistment contract. Negotiating the contract involves choosing, qualifying for, and agreeing on a number of enlistment options, such as the length of active-duty time, which may vary according to the option. Most active-duty programs have first-term enlistments of 4 years, although there are some 2-year, 3-year, and 6-year programs. The contract also will state the date of enlistment and other options—for example, bonuses and the types of training to be received. If the service is unable to fulfill any of its obligations under the contract, such as providing a certain kind of training, the contract may become null and void.

All branches of the Armed Services offer a delayed entry program (DEP) by which an individual can delay entry into active duty for up to 1 year after enlisting. High school students can enlist during their senior year and enter a service after graduation. Others choose this program because the job training they desire is not currently available, but will be within the coming year, or because they need time to arrange their personal affairs.

The process of joining the military as an officer is different: officers must meet educational, physical, and character requirements, but they do not take an aptitude test. The education and training section that follows includes more information.

Education and training. All branches of the Armed Forces usually require their members to be high school graduates or have equivalent credentials, such as a GED. In 2008, more than 98 percent of recruits were high school graduates. Officers usually need a bachelor's or graduate degree. Training varies for enlisted and officer personnel and varies by occupational specialty. Currently, the U.S. Military is working with several different certifying bodies to ensure that soldiers who separate from the Armed Forces receive formal recognition in the private sector for their military-based technical training.

Enlisted personnel training. Following enlistment, new members of the Armed Forces undergo initial-entry training, better known as "basic training" or "boot camp." Through courses in military skills and protocol, recruit training provides a 6- to 13-week introduction to military life. Days and nights are carefully structured and include rigorous physical exercise designed to improve strength and endurance and build each unit's cohesion.

Following basic training, most recruits take additional training at technical schools that prepare them for a particular military occupational specialty. The formal training period generally lasts from 10 to 20 weeks, although training for certain occupations—nuclear power plant operator, for example—may take as long as a year. Recruits not assigned to classroom instruction receive on-the-job training at their first duty assignment.

Many service people get college credit for the technical training they receive on duty. Combined with off-duty courses, such training can lead to an associate's degree through programs in community colleges such as the Community College of the Air Force. In addition to receiving on-duty training, military personnel may choose from a variety of educational programs. Most military installations have tuition assistance programs for people wishing to take courses during off-duty hours. The courses may be correspondence courses or courses in degree programs offered by local colleges or universities. Tuition assistance pays up to 100 percent of college costs, up to a credit-hour and annual limit. Each branch of the service provides opportunities for full-time study to a limited number of exceptional applicants. Military personnel accepted into these highly competitive programs receive full pay, allowances, tuition, and related fees. In return, they must agree to serve an additional amount of time in the service. Other highly selective programs enable enlisted personnel to qualify as commissioned officers through additional military training.

Warrant officer training. Warrant officers are technical and tactical leaders who specialize in a specific technical area; for example, Army aviators make up one group of warrant officers. The Army Warrant Officer Corps constitutes less than 5 percent of the total Army. Although the Corps is small in size, its level of responsibility is high. Its members receive extended career opportunities, worldwide leadership assignments, and increased pay and retirement benefits. Selection to attend Warrant Officer Candidate School is highly competitive and restricted to those who meet rank and length-of-service requirements. The only exception is for Army aviator warrant officer, which has no requirement of prior military service.

Officer training. Officer training in the Armed Forces is provided through the Federal service academies (Military, Naval, Air Force, and Coast Guard); the Reserve Officers Training Corps (ROTC) program offered at many colleges and universities; Officer Candidate School (OCS) or Officer Training School (OTS); the National Guard (State Officer Candidate School programs); the Uniformed Services University of Health Sciences; and other programs. All are highly selective and are good options for those wishing to make the military a career. Some personnel are directly appointed to attend one of these academies or programs. People interested in obtaining training through the Federal service academies must be unmarried and without dependents in order to enter and graduate, while those seeking training through OCS, OTS, or ROTC need not be single.

Federal service academies provide a 4-year college program leading to a bachelor-of-science (B.S.) degree. Midshipmen or cadets are provided free room and board, tuition, medical and dental care, and a monthly allowance. Graduates receive regular or reserve commissions and have a 5-year active-duty obligation, or more if they are entering flight training.

To become a candidate for appointment as a cadet or midshipman in one of the service academies, applicants are required to obtain a nomination from an authorized source, usually a member of Congress. Candidates do not need to personally know a member of Congress to request a nomination. Nominees must have an academic record of the requisite quality, college aptitude test scores above an established minimum, and recommendations from teachers or school officials; they also must pass a medical examination. Appointments are made from the list of eligible nominees. Appointments to the Coast Guard Academy, however, are based strictly on merit and do not require a nomination.

ROTC programs train students in approximately 270 Army, 130 Navy and Marine Corps, and 140 Air Force units at participating colleges and universities. In addition to taking regular college courses, trainees take 3 to 5 hours of military instruction a week. After graduation, they may serve as officers on active duty for a stipulated period. Some may serve their obligation in the Reserves or National Guard. In the last 2 years of an ROTC program, students typically receive a monthly allowance while attending school, as well as additional pay for summer training. ROTC scholarships for 2, 3, and 4 years are available on a competitive basis. All scholarships pay for tuition and have allowances for textbooks, supplies, and other costs.

College graduates can earn a commission in the Armed Forces through OCS or OTS programs in the Army, Navy, Air Force, Marine Corps, Coast Guard, and National Guard. These programs consist of several weeks of intensive academic, physical, and leadership training. Those who graduate as officers generally must serve their obligation on active duty.

Personnel with training in certain health professions may qualify for direct appointment as officers. In the case of people studying for the health professions, financial assistance and internship opportunities are available from the military in return for specified periods of military service. Prospective medical students can apply to the Uniformed Services University of Health Sciences, which offers a salary and free tuition in a program leading to a doctor-of-medicine (M.D.) degree. In return, graduates must serve for 7 years in either the military or the Public Health Service. Direct appointments also are available for those qualified to serve in other specialty areas, such as the judge advocate general (legal) or chaplain corps. Flight training is available to commissioned officers in each branch of the Armed Forces. In addition, the Army has a direct enlistment option to become a warrant officer aviator.

Other qualifications. In order to join the services, enlisted personnel must sign a legal agreement called an enlistment contract, which usually involves a commitment of up to 8 years of service. Depending on the terms of the contract, 2 to 6 years are spent on active duty and the balance is spent in the National Guard or Reserves. The enlistment contract obligates the service to provide the agreed-upon job, rating, pay, cash bonuses for enlistment in certain occupations, medical and other benefits, occupational training, and continuing education. In return, enlisted personnel must serve satisfactorily for the period specified.

Requirements for each service vary, but certain qualifications for enlistment are common to all branches. In order to enlist, usually one must be at least 17 years old, be a U.S. citizen or an alien holding permanent resident status, not have a felony record, and possess a birth certificate. Applicants who are 17 years old must have the consent of a parent or legal guardian before entering the service. For active service in the Army, the maximum age is 42; for the Navy, 34; for the Air Force and Coast Guard, 27; and for the Marine Corps, 29. All applicants must pass a written examination—the Armed Services Vocational Aptitude Battery—and meet certain minimum physical standards—for example, for height, weight, vision, and overall health. Officers must meet different age and physical standards, depending on their branch of service.

Women are eligible to enter most military specialties; for example, they may become mechanics, missile maintenance technicians, heavy equipment operators, and fighter pilots, or they may enter into medical care, administrative support, and intelligence specialties. Generally, only occupations involving direct exposure to combat are excluded.

Advancement. Each service has different criteria for promoting personnel. Generally, the first few promotions for both enlisted personnel and officers come easily; subsequent promotions are much more competitive. Criteria for promotion may include time in service and in grade, job performance, a fitness report (supervisor's recommendation), and passing scores on written examinations.

People planning to apply the skills they gained through military training to a civilian career should first determine how good the prospects are for civilian employment in jobs related to the military specialty that interests them. Second, they should know the prerequisites for the related civilian job. Because many civilian occupations require a license, certification, or minimum level of education, it is important to determine whether military training is sufficient for a person to enter the civilian equivalent occupation or, if not, what additional training will be required.

Employment

In 2009, more than 2.4 million people served in the Armed Forces. More than 1.4 million were on active duty—about 561,000 in the Army, 327,000 in the Navy, 325,000 in the Air Force, and 202,000 in the Marine Corps. In addition, more than 1.0 million people served in their Reserve components and in the Air and Army National Guard, and 41,000 individuals served in the Coast Guard, which is now part of the Department of Homeland Security.

Military personnel are stationed throughout the United States and in many countries around the world. About half of all military jobs in the U.S. are located in California, Texas, North Carolina, Virginia, Florida, and Georgia. Approximately 265,000 service members were deployed in support of Operations Enduring Freedom and Iraqi Freedom as of June 1, 2009. An additional 378,000 individuals were stationed outside the United States, including 160,000 assigned to ships at sea. About 95,000 were stationed in Europe, mainly in Germany, and another 71,000 were assigned to East Asia and the Pacific area, mostly in Japan and the Republic of Korea.

Job Outlook

Opportunities should be excellent for qualified individuals in all branches of the Armed Forces.

Employment change. The United States spends a significant portion of its overall budget on national defense. The number of active-duty personnel is expected to remain roughly constant through 2018. However, recent conflicts and the resulting strain on the military may lead to an increase in the number of active-duty personnel. The current goal of the

Armed Forces is to maintain a force sufficient to fight and win two major regional conflicts at the same time. Political events, however, could lead to a significant restructuring with or without an increase in size.

Job prospects. Opportunities should be excellent for qualified individuals in all branches of the Armed Forces through 2018. Many military personnel retire with a pension after 20 years of service, while they still are young enough to start a new career. About 184,000 personnel must be recruited each year to replace those who complete their commitment or retire. Since the end of the draft in 1973, the military has met its personnel requirements with volunteers. When the economy is good and civilian employment opportunities generally are more favorable, it is more difficult for all the services to meet their recruitment quotas. When there are economic downturns, recruits may face more competition for various occupational specialties. It is also more difficult to meet these goals during times of war, when recruitment goals typically rise.

Educational requirements will continue to rise as military jobs become more technical and complex. High school graduates and applicants with a college background will be sought to fill the ranks of enlisted personnel, while virtually all officers will need at least a bachelor's degree and, in some cases, a graduate degree as well.

Earnings

The earnings structure for military personnel is shown in table 4. Most enlisted personnel started as recruits at Grade E-1 in 2009; however, those with special skills or above-average education started as high as Grade E-4. Most warrant officers started at Grade W-1 or W-2, depending upon their occupational and academic qualifications and the branch of service of which they were a member, but warrant officer typically is not an entry-level occupation and, consequently, most of these individuals had previous military service. Most commissioned officers started at Grade O-1; some with advanced education started at Grade O-2, and some highly trained officers—for example, physicians and dentists—started as high as Grade O-3. Pay varies by total years of service as well as rank. Because it usually takes many years to reach the higher ranks, most personnel in higher ranks receive the higher pay rates awarded to those with many years of service.

In addition to receiving their basic pay, military personnel are provided with free room and board (or a tax-free housing and subsistence allowance), free medical and dental care, a military clothing allowance, military supermarket and department store shopping privileges, 30 days of paid vacation a year (referred to as leave), and travel opportunities. In many duty stations, military personnel may receive a housing allowance that can be used for off-base housing. This allowance can be substantial, but varies greatly by rank and duty station. For example, in fiscal year 2009, the basic allowance for housing for an E-4 with dependents was $681.90 per month; for a comparable individual without dependents, it was $511.50.

The allowance for an O-4 with dependents was $1,297.80 per month; for a comparable individual without dependents, it was $1,128.60. Other allowances are paid for foreign duty, hazardous duty, submarine and flight duty, and employment as a medical officer. Athletic and other facilities—such as gymnasiums, tennis courts, golf courses, bowling centers, libraries, and movie theaters—are available on many military installations. Military personnel are eligible for retirement benefits after 20 years of service.

The Veterans Administration (VA) provides numerous benefits to those who have served at least 24 months of continuous active duty in the Armed Forces. Veterans are eligible for free care in VA hospitals for all service-related disabilities, regardless of time served; those with other medical problems are eligible for free VA care if they are unable to pay the cost of hospitalization elsewhere. Admission to a VA medical center depends on the availability of beds, however. Veterans also are eligible for certain loans, including loans to purchase a home. Regardless of their health, veterans can convert a military life insurance policy to an individual policy with any participating company upon separation from the military. In addition, job counseling, testing, and placement services are available.

Veterans who participate in the Montgomery GI Bill Program receive education benefits. Under this program, Armed Forces personnel may elect to deduct up to $100 a month from their pay during the first 12 months of active duty, putting the money toward their future education. In fiscal year 2009, veterans who served on active duty for 3 or more years or who spent 2 years in active duty plus 4 years in the Selected Reserve received $1,321 a month in basic benefits for 36 months of full-time institutional training. Those who enlisted and served less than 3 years received $1,073 a month for 36 months of the same. In addition, each service provides its own contributions to the enlistee's future education. The sum of the amounts from all these sources becomes the service member's educational fund. Upon separation from active duty, the fund can be used to finance educational costs at any VA-approved institution. Among those institutions which are approved by the VA are many vocational, correspondence, certification, business, technical, and flight training schools; community and junior colleges; and colleges and universities. The new Post-9/11 GI Bill is an alternative education benefit. There is no deductable for service personnel. The size of the benefit is scaled to the State and to the institution that the veteran is attending. Service personnel must carefully choose which program will be of the most benefit to them in their planned educational future.

APPENDIX 1:

—꘠—

Historic Christian Creeds

THE APOSTLE'S CREED

I believe in God, the Father Almighty,
the Maker of heaven and earth,
and in Jesus Christ, His only Son, our Lord:
Who was conceived by the Holy Ghost,
born of the virgin Mary,
suffered under Pontius Pilate,
was crucified, dead, and buried;
He descended into hell.
The third day He arose again from the dead;
He ascended into heaven,
and sitteth on the right hand of God the
Father Almighty;
from thence he shall come to judge the
quick and the dead.
I believe in the Holy Ghost;
the holy catholic church;
the communion of saints;
the forgiveness of sins;
the resurrection of the body;
and the life everlasting.
Amen.

THE NICENE CREED

I believe in one God, the Father Almighty, Maker of heaven and earth, and of all things visible and invisible.

And in one Lord Jesus Christ, the only-begotten Son of God, begotten of the Father before all worlds; God of God, Light of Light, very God of very God; begotten, not made, being of one substance with the Father, by whom all things were made.

Who, for us men and for our salvation, came down from heaven, and was incarnate by the Holy Spirit of the virgin Mary, and was made man; and was crucified also for us under Pontius Pilate; He suffered and was buried; and the third day He rose again, according to the Scriptures; and ascended into heaven, and sits on the right hand of the Father; and He shall come again, with glory, to judge the quick and the dead; whose kingdom shall have no end.

And I believe in the Holy Ghost, the Lord and Giver of Life; who proceeds from the Father and the Son; who with the Father and the Son together is worshipped and glorified; who spoke by the prophets.

And I believe in one holy catholic and apostolic Church. I acknowledge one baptism for the remission of sins; and I look for the resurrection of the dead, and the life of the world to come. Amen.

THE WESTMINSTER CATECHISM (SHORTER)

Q. 1. *What is the chief end of man?*
Man's chief end is to glorify God, and to enjoy him forever.

Q. 2. *What rule hath God given to direct us how we may glorify and enjoy him?*
The word of God, which is contained in the scriptures of the Old and New Testaments, is the only rule to direct us how we may glorify and enjoy him.

Q. 3. *What do the scriptures principally teach?*
The scriptures principally teach what man is to believe concerning God, and what duty God requires of man.

Q. 4. *What is God?*
God is a spirit, infinite, eternal, and unchangeable, in his being, wisdom, power, holiness, justice, goodness and truth.

Q. 5. *Are there more Gods than one?*
There is but one only, the living and true God.

Q. 6. *How many persons are there in the godhead?*
There are three persons in the Godhead; the Father, the Son, and the Holy Ghost; and these three are one God, the same in substance, equal in power and glory.

Q. 7. *What are the decrees of God?*
The decrees of God are his eternal purpose, according to the counsel of his will, whereby, for his own glory, he hath foreordained whatsoever comes to pass.

Q. 8. *How doth God execute his decrees?*
God executeth his decrees in the works of creation and providence.

Q. 9. *What is the work of creation?*
The work of creation is God's making all things of nothing, by the word of his power, in the space of six days, and all very good.

Q. 10. *How did God create man?*

God created man male and female, after his own image, in knowledge, righteousness and holiness, with dominion over the creatures.

Q. 11. *What are God's works of providence?*

God's works of providence are his most holy, wise and powerful preserving and governing all his creatures, and all their actions.

Q. 12. *What special act of providence did God exercise toward man in the estate wherein he was created?*

When God had created man, he entered into a covenant of life with him, upon condition of perfect obedience; forbidding him to eat of the tree of the knowledge of good and evil, upon the pain of death.

Q. 13. *Did our first parents continue in the estate wherein they were created?*

Our first parents, being left to the freedom of their own will, fell from the estate wherein they were created, by sinning against God.

Q. 14. *What is sin?*

Sin is any want of conformity unto, or transgression of, the law of God.

Q. 15. *What was the sin whereby our first parents fell from the estate wherein they were created?*

The sin whereby our first parents fell from the estate wherein they were created was their eating the forbidden fruit.

Q. 16. *Did all mankind fall in Adam's first transgression?*

The covenant being made with Adam, not only for himself, but for his posterity; all mankind, descending from him by ordinary generation, sinned in him, and fell with him, in his first transgression.

Q. 17. *Into what estate did the fall bring mankind?*

The fall brought mankind into an estate of sin and misery.

Q. 18. *Wherein consists the sinfulness of that estate whereinto man fell?*

The sinfulness of that estate whereinto man fell consists in the guilt of Adam's first sin, the want of original righteousness, and the corruption of his whole nature, which is commonly called original sin; together with all actual transgressions which proceed from it.

Q. 19. *What is the misery of that estate whereinto man fell?*

All mankind by their fall lost communion with God, are under his wrath and curse, and so made liable to all miseries in this life, to death itself, and to the pains of hell forever.

Q. 20. *Did God leave all mankind to perish in the estate of sin and misery?*

God having, out of his mere good pleasure, from all eternity, elected some to everlasting life, did enter into a covenant of grace, to deliver them out of the estate of sin and misery, and to bring them into an estate of salvation by a redeemer.

Q. 21. *Who is the redeemer of God's elect?*

The only redeemer of God's elect is the Lord Jesus Christ, who, being the eternal Son of God, became man, and so was, and continueth to be, God and man in two distinct natures, and one person, forever.

Q. 22. *How did Christ, being the Son of God, become man?*

Christ, the Son of God, became man, by taking to himself a true body and a reasonable soul, being conceived by the power of the Holy Ghost in the womb of the virgin Mary, and born of her, yet without sin.

Q. 23. *What offices doth Christ execute as our redeemer?*

Christ, as our redeemer, executeth the offices of a prophet, of a priest, and of a king, both in his estate of humiliation and exaltation.

Q. 24. *How doth Christ execute the office of a prophet?*

Christ executeth the office of a prophet, in revealing to us, by his word and Spirit, the will of God for our salvation.

Q. 25. *How doth Christ execute the office of a priest?*

Christ executeth the office of a priest, in his once offering up of himself a sacrifice to satisfy divine justice, and reconcile us to God; and in making continual intercession for us.

Q. 26. How doth Christ execute the office of a king?

Christ executeth the office of a king, in subduing us to himself, in ruling and defending us, and in restraining and conquering all his and our enemies.

Q. 27. Wherein did Christ's humiliation consist?

Christ's humiliation consisted in his being born, and that in a low condition, made under the law, undergoing the miseries of this life, the wrath of God, and the cursed death of the cross; in being buried, and continuing under the power of death for a time.

Q. 28. Wherein consisteth Christ's exaltation?

Christ's exaltation consisteth in his rising again from the dead on the third day, in ascending up into heaven, in sitting at the right hand of God the Father, and in coming to judge the world at the last day.

Q. 29. How are we made partakers of the redemption purchased by Christ?

We are made partakers of the redemption purchased by Christ, by the effectual application of it to us by his Holy Spirit.

Q. 30. How doth the Spirit apply to us the redemption purchased by Christ?

The Spirit applieth to us the redemption purchased by Christ, by working faith in us, and thereby uniting us to Christ in our effectual calling.

Q. 31. What is effectual calling?

Effectual calling is the work of God's Spirit, whereby, convincing us of our sin and misery, enlightening our minds in the knowledge of Christ, and renewing our wills, he doth persuade and enable us to embrace Jesus Christ, freely offered to us in the gospel.

Q. 32. What benefits do they that are effectually called partake of in this life?

They that are effectually called do in this life partake of justification, adoption and sanctification, and the several benefits which in this life do either accompany or flow from them.

Q. 33. What is justification?

Justification is an act of God's free grace, wherein he pardoneth all our sins, and accepteth us as righteous in his sight, only for the righteousness of Christ imputed to us, and received by faith alone.

Q. 34. What is adoption?

Adoption is an act of God's free grace, whereby we are received into the number, and have a right to all the privileges of, the sons of God.

Q. 35. What is sanctification?

Sanctification is the work of God's free grace, whereby we are renewed in the whole man after the image of God, and are enabled more and more to die unto sin, and live unto righteousness.

Q. 36. What are the benefits which in this life do accompany or flow from justification, adoption and sanctification?

The benefits which in this life do accompany or flow from justification, adoption and sanctification, are, assurance of God's love, peace of conscience, joy in the Holy Ghost, increase of grace, and perseverance therein to the end.

Q. 37. What benefits do believers receive from Christ at death?

The souls of believers are at their death made perfect in holiness, and do immediately pass into glory; and their bodies, being still united to Christ, do rest in their graves till the resurrection.

Q. 38. What benefits do believers receive from Christ at the resurrection?

At the resurrection, believers being raised up in glory, shall be openly acknowledged and acquitted in the day of judgment, and made perfectly blessed in the full enjoying of God to all eternity.

Q. 39. What is the duty which God requireth of man?

The duty which God requireth of man is obedience to his revealed will.

Q. 40. What did God at first reveal to man for the rule of his obedience?

The rule which God at first revealed to man for his obedience was the moral law.

Q. 41. Where is the moral law summarily comprehended?

The moral law is summarily comprehended in the ten commandments.

Q. 42. What is the sum of the ten commandments?

The sum of the ten commandments is to love the Lord our God with all our heart, with all our soul, with all our strength, and with all our mind; and our neighbor as ourselves.

Q. 43. What is the preface to the ten commandments?

The preface to the ten commandments is in these words, I am the Lord thy God, which have brought thee out of the land of Egypt, out of the house of bondage.

Q. 44. What doth the preface to the ten commandments teach us?

The preface to the ten commandments teacheth us that because God is the Lord, and our God, and redeemer, therefore we are bound to keep all his commandments.

Q. 45. Which is the first commandment?

The first commandment is, Thou shalt have no other gods before me.

Q. 46. What is required in the first commandment?

The first commandment requireth us to know and acknowledge God to be the only true God, and our God; and to worship and glorify him accordingly.

Q. 47. What is forbidden in the first commandment?

The first commandment forbiddeth the denying, or not worshiping and glorifying the true God as God, and our God; and the giving of that worship and glory to any other, which is due to him alone.

Q. 48. What are we specially taught by these words before me in the first commandment?

These words before me in the first commandment teach us that God, who seeth all things, taketh notice of, and is much displeased with, the sin of having any other god.

Q. 49. Which is the second commandment?

The second commandment is, Thou shalt not make unto thee any graven image, or any likeness of anything that is in heaven above, or that is in the earth beneath, or that is in the water under the earth: thou shalt not bow down thyself to them, nor serve them: for I the Lord thy God am a jealous God, visiting the iniquity of the fathers upon the children unto the third and fourth generation of them that hate me; and showing mercy unto thousands of them that love me, and keep my commandments.

Q. 50. What is required in the second commandment?

The second commandment requireth the receiving, observing, and keeping pure and entire, all such religious worship and ordinances as God hath appointed in his word.

Q. 51. What is forbidden in the second commandment?

The second commandment forbiddeth the worshiping of God by images, or any other way not appointed in his word.

Q. 52. What are the reasons annexed to the second commandment?

The reasons annexed to the second commandment are, God's sovereignty over us, his propriety in us, and the zeal he hath to his own worship.

Q. 53. Which is the third commandment?

The third commandment is, Thou shalt not take the name of the Lord thy God in vain: for the Lord will not hold him guiltless that taketh his name in vain.

Q. 54. What is required in the third commandment?

The third commandment requireth the holy and reverent use of God's names, titles, attributes, ordinances, word and works.

Q. 55. What is forbidden in the third commandment?

The third commandment forbiddeth all profaning or abusing of anything whereby God maketh himself known.

Q. 56. What is the reason annexed to the third commandment?

The reason annexed to the third commandment is that however the breakers of this commandment may escape punishment from men, yet the Lord our God will not suffer them to escape his righteous judgment.

Q. 57. Which is the fourth commandment?

The fourth commandment is, Remember the sabbath day, to keep it holy. Six days shalt thou labor, and do all thy work: but the seventh day is the sabbath of the Lord thy God: in it thou shalt not do any work, thou, nor thy son, nor thy daughter, thy manservant, nor thy maidservant, nor thy cattle, nor thy stranger that is within thy gates: for in six days the Lord made heaven and earth, the sea, and all that in them is, and rested the seventh day: wherefore the Lord blessed the sabbath day, and hallowed it.

Q. 58. What is required in the fourth commandment?

The fourth commandment requireth the keeping holy to God such set times as he hath appointed in his word; expressly one whole day in seven, to be a holy sabbath to himself.

Q. 59. Which day of the seven hath God appointed to be the weekly sabbath?

From the beginning of the world to the resurrection of Christ, God appointed the seventh day of the week to be the weekly sabbath; and the first day of the week ever since, to continue to the end of the world, which is the Christian sabbath.

Q. 60. How is the sabbath to be sanctified?

The sabbath is to be sanctified by a holy resting all that day, even from such worldly employments and recreations as are lawful on other days; and spending the whole time in the public and private exercises of God's worship, except so much as is to be taken up in the works of necessity and mercy.

Q. 61. What is forbidden in the fourth commandment?

The fourth commandment forbiddeth the omission or careless performance of the duties required, and the profaning the day by idleness, or doing that which is in itself sinful, or by unnecessary thoughts, words or works, about our worldly employments or recreations.

Q. 62. What are the reasons annexed to the fourth commandment?

The reasons annexed to the fourth commandment are, God's allowing us six days of the week for our own employments, his challenging a special propriety in the seventh, his own example, and his blessing the sabbath day.

Q. 63. Which is the fifth commandment?

The fifth commandment is, Honor thy father and thy mother; that thy days may be long upon the land which the Lord thy God giveth thee.

Q. 64. What is required in the fifth commandment?

The fifth commandment requireth the preserving the honor, and performing the duties, belonging to every one in their several places and relations, as superiors, inferiors or equals.

Q. 65. *What is forbidden in the fifth commandment?*

The fifth commandment forbiddeth the neglecting of, or doing anything against, the honor and duty which belongeth to every one in their several places and relations.

Q. 66. *What is the reason annexed to the fifth commandment?*

The reason annexed to the fifth commandment is a promise of long life and prosperity (as far as it shall serve for God's glory and their own good) to all such as keep this commandment.

Q. 67. *Which is the sixth commandment?*

The sixth commandment is, Thou shalt not kill.

Q. 68. *What is required in the sixth commandment?*

The sixth commandment requireth all lawful endeavors to preserve our own life, and the life of others.

Q. 69. *What is forbidden in the sixth commandment?*

The sixth commandment forbiddeth the taking away of our own life, or the life of our neighbor unjustly, or whatsoever tendeth thereunto.

Q. 70. *Which is the seventh commandment?*

The seventh commandment is, Thou shalt not commit adultery.

Q. 71. *What is required in the seventh commandment?*

The seventh commandment requireth the preservation of our own and our neighbor's chastity, in heart, speech and behavior.

Q. 72. *What is forbidden in the seventh commandment?*

The seventh commandment forbiddeth all unchaste thoughts, words and actions.

Q. 73. *Which is the eighth commandment?*

The eighth commandment is, Thou shalt not steal.

Q. 74. *What is required in the eighth commandment?*

The eighth commandment requireth the lawful procuring and furthering the wealth and outward estate of ourselves and others.

Q. 75. What is forbidden in the eighth commandment?

The eighth commandment forbiddeth whatsoever doth or may unjustly hinder our own or our neighbor's wealth or outward estate.

Q. 76. Which is the ninth commandment?

The ninth commandment is, Thou shalt not bear false witness against thy neighbor.

Q. 77. What is required in the ninth commandment?

The ninth commandment requireth the maintaining and promoting of truth between man and man, and of our own and our neighbor's good name, especially in witness-bearing.

Q. 78. What is forbidden in the ninth commandment?

The ninth commandment forbiddeth whatsoever is prejudicial to truth, or injurious to our own or our neighbor's good name.

Q. 79. Which is the tenth commandment?

The tenth commandment is, Thou shalt not covet thy neighbor's house, thou shalt not covet thy neighbor's wife, nor his manservant, nor his maidservant, nor his ox, nor his ass, nor anything that is thy neighbor's.

Q. 80. What is required in the tenth commandment?

The tenth commandment requireth full contentment with our own condition, with a right and charitable frame of spirit toward our neighbor, and all that is his.

Q. 81. What is forbidden in the tenth commandment?

The tenth commandment forbiddeth all discontentment with our own estate, envying or grieving at the good of our neighbor, and all inordinate motions and affections to anything that is his.

Q. 82. Is any man able perfectly to keep the commandments of God?

No mere man since the fall is able in this life perfectly to keep the commandments of God, but doth daily break them in thought, word and deed.

Q. 83. Are all transgressions of the law equally heinous?

Some sins in themselves, and by reason of several aggravations, are more heinous in the sight of God than others.

Q. 84. What doth every sin deserve?

Every sin deserveth God's wrath and curse, both in this life, and that which is to come.

Q. 85. What doth God require of us that we may escape his wrath and curse due to us for sin?

To escape the wrath and curse of God due to us for sin, God requireth of us faith in Jesus Christ, repentance unto life, with the diligent use of all the outward means whereby Christ communicateth to us the benefits of redemption.

Q. 86. What is faith in Jesus Christ?

Faith in Jesus Christ is a saving grace, whereby we receive and rest upon him alone for salvation, as he is offered to us in the gospel.

Q. 87. What is repentance unto life?

Repentance unto life is a saving grace, whereby a sinner, out of a true sense of his sin, and apprehension of the mercy of God in Christ, doth, with grief and hatred of his sin, turn from it unto God, with full purpose of, and endeavor after, new obedience.

Q. 88. What are the outward and ordinary means whereby Christ communicateth to us the benefits of redemption?

The outward and ordinary means whereby Christ communicateth to us the benefits of redemption, are his ordinances, especially the word, sacraments, and prayer; all which are made effectual to the elect for salvation.

Q. 89. How is the word made effectual to salvation?

The Spirit of God maketh the reading, but especially the preaching, of the word, an effectual means of convincing and converting sinners, and of building them up in holiness and comfort, through faith, unto salvation.

Q. 90. How is the word to be read and heard, that it may become effectual to salvation?

That the word may become effectual to salvation, we must attend thereunto with diligence, preparation and prayer; receive it with faith and love, lay it up in our hearts, and practice it in our lives.

Q. 91. *How do the sacraments become effectual means of salvation?*

The sacraments become effectual means of salvation, not from any virtue in them, or in him that doth administer them; but only by the blessing of Christ, and the working of his Spirit in them that by faith receive them.

Q. 92. *What is a sacrament?*

A sacrament is an holy ordinance instituted by Christ; wherein, by sensible signs, Christ, and the benefits of the new covenant, are represented, sealed, and applied to believers.

Q. 93. *Which are the sacraments of the New Testament?*

The sacraments of the New Testament are baptism and the Lord's supper.

Q. 94. *What is baptism?*

Baptism is a sacrament, wherein the washing with water in the name of the Father, and of the Son, and of the Holy Ghost, doth signify and seal our ingrafting into Christ, and partaking of the benefits of the covenant of grace, and our engagement to be the Lord's.

Q. 95. *To whom is baptism to be administered?*

Baptism is not to be administered to any that are out of the visible church, till they profess their faith in Christ, and obedience to him; but the infants of such as are members of the visible church are to be baptized.

Q. 96. *What is the Lord's supper?*

The Lord's supper is a sacrament, wherein, by giving and receiving bread and wine according to Christ's appointment, his death is showed forth; and the worthy receivers are, not after a corporal and carnal manner, but by faith, made partakers of his body and blood, with all his benefits, to their spiritual nourishment and growth in grace.

Q. 97. *What is required to the worthy receiving of the Lord's supper?*

It is required of them that would worthily partake of the Lord's supper, that they examine themselves of their knowledge to discern the Lord's body, of their faith to feed upon him, of their repentance, love, and new obedience; lest, coming unworthily, they eat and drink judgment to themselves.

Q. 98. *What is prayer?*

Prayer is an offering up of our desires unto God, for things agreeable to his will, in the name of Christ, with confession of our sins, and thankful acknowledgment of his mercies.

Q. 99. *What rule hath God given for our direction in prayer?*

The whole word of God is of use to direct us in prayer; but the special rule of direction is that form of prayer which Christ taught his disciples, commonly called the Lord's prayer.

Q. 100. *What doth the preface of the Lord's prayer teach us?*

The preface of the Lord's prayer, which is, Our Father which art in heaven, teacheth us to draw near to God with all holy reverence and confidence, as children to a father able and ready to help us; and that we should pray with and for others.

Q. 101. *What do we pray for in the first petition?*

In the first petition, which is, Hallowed be thy name, we pray that God would enable us and others to glorify him in all that whereby he maketh himself known; and that he would dispose all things to his own glory.

Q. 102. *What do we pray for in the second petition?*

In the second petition, which is, Thy kingdom come, we pray that Satan's kingdom may be destroyed; and that the kingdom of grace may be advanced, ourselves and others brought into it, and kept in it; and that the kingdom of glory may be hastened.

Q. 103. *What do we pray for in the third petition?*

In the third petition, which is, Thy will be done in earth, as it is in heaven, we pray that God, by his grace, would make us able and willing to know, obey and submit to his will in all things, as the angels do in heaven.

Q. 104. *What do we pray for in the fourth petition?*

In the fourth petition, which is, Give us this day our daily bread, we pray that of God's free gift we may receive a competent portion of the good things of this life, and enjoy his blessing with them.

Q. 105. What do we pray for in the fifth petition?

In the fifth petition, which is, And forgive us our debts, as we forgive our debtors, we pray that God, for Christ's sake, would freely pardon all our sins; which we are the rather encouraged to ask, because by his grace we are enabled from the heart to forgive others.

Q. 106. What do we pray for in the sixth petition?

In the sixth petition, which is, And lead us not into temptation, but deliver us from evil, we pray that God would either keep us from being tempted to sin, or support and deliver us when we are tempted.

Q. 107. What doth the conclusion of the Lord's prayer teach us?

The conclusion of the Lord's prayer, which is, For thine is the kingdom, and the power, and the glory, forever, Amen, teacheth us to take our encouragement in prayer from God only, and in our prayers to praise him, ascribing kingdom, power and glory to him. And in testimony of our desire, and assurance to be heard, we say, Amen.

THE LAUSANNE COVENANT (1974)

INTRODUCTION

We, members of the Church of Jesus Christ, from more than 150 nations, participants in the International Congress on World Evangelization at Lausanne, praise God for his great salvation and rejoice in the fellowship he has given us with himself and with each other. We are deeply stirred by what God is doing in our day, moved to penitence by our failures and challenged by the unfinished task of evangelization. We believe the Gospel is God's good news for the whole world, and we are determined by his grace to obey Christ's commission to proclaim it to all mankind and to make disciples of every nation. We desire, therefore, to affirm our faith and our resolve, and to make public our covenant.

1. THE PURPOSE OF GOD

We affirm our belief in the one-eternal God, Creator and Lord of the world, Father, Son and Holy Spirit, who governs all things according to the purpose of his will. He has been calling out from the world a people for himself, and sending his people back into the world to be his servants and his witnesses, for the extension of his kingdom, the building up of Christ's body, and the glory of his name. We confess with shame that we have often denied our calling and failed in our mission, by becoming conformed to the world or by withdrawing from it. Yet we rejoice that even when borne by earthen vessels the gospel is still a precious treasure. To the task of making that treasure known in the power of the Holy Spirit we desire to dedicate ourselves anew.

(Isa. 40:28; Matt. 28:19; Eph. 1:11; Acts 15:14; John 17:6, 18; Eph 4:12; 1 Cor. 5:10; Rom. 12:2; II Cor. 4:7)

2. THE AUTHORITY AND POWER OF THE BIBLE

We affirm the divine inspiration, truthfulness and authority of both Old and New Testament Scriptures in their entirety as the only written word of God, without error in all that it affirms, and the only infallible rule of faith and practice. We also affirm the power of God's word to accomplish his purpose of salvation. The message of the Bible is addressed to all men and women. For God's revelation in Christ and in Scripture is unchangeable. Through it the Holy Spirit still speaks today. He illumines the minds of God's people in every culture to perceive its truth freshly through their own eyes and thus discloses to the whole Church ever more of the many-colored wisdom of God.

(2 Tim. 3:16; 2 Pet. 1:21; John 10:35; Isa. 55:11; 1 Cor. 1:21; Rom. 1:16, Matt. 5:17, 18; Jude 3; Eph. 1:17,18; 3:10,18)

3. THE UNIQUENESS AND UNIVERSALITY OF CHRIST

We affirm that there is only one Saviour and only one gospel, although there is a wide diversity of evangelistic approaches. We recognise that everyone has some knowledge of God through his general revelation in nature. But we deny that this can save, for people suppress the truth by their unrighteousness. We also reject as derogatory to Christ and the gospel every kind of syncretism and dialogue which implies that Christ speaks equally through all religions and ideologies. Jesus Christ, being himself the only God-man, who gave himself as the only ransom for sinners, is the only mediator between God and people. There is no other name by which we must be saved. All men and women are perishing because of sin, but God loves everyone, not wishing that any should perish but that all should repent. Yet those who reject Christ repudiate the joy of salvation and condemn themselves to eternal separation from God. To proclaim Jesus as "the Saviour of the world" is not to affirm that all people are either automatically or ultimately saved, still less to affirm that all religions offer salvation in Christ. Rather it is to proclaim God's love for a world of sinners and to invite everyone to respond to him as Saviour and Lord in the wholehearted personal commitment of repentance and faith. Jesus Christ has been exalted above every other name; we long for the day when every knee shall bow to him and every tongue shall confess him Lord.

(Gal. 1:6-9; Rom. 1:18-32; 1 Tim. 2:5,6; Acts 4:12; John 3:16-19; 2 Pet. 3:9; 2 Thess. 1:7-9; John 4:42; Matt. 11:28; Eph. 1:20,21; Phil. 2:9-11)

4. THE NATURE OF EVANGELISM

To evangelize is to spread the good news that Jesus Christ died for our sins and was raised from the dead according to the Scriptures, and that as the reigning Lord he now offers the forgiveness of sins and the liberating gifts of the Spirit to all who repent and believe. Our Christian presence in the world is indispensable to evangelism, and so is that kind of dialogue whose purpose is to listen sensitively in order to understand. But evangelism itself is the proclamation of the historical, biblical Christ as Saviour and Lord, with a view to persuading people to come to him personally and so be reconciled to God. In issuing the gospel invitation we have no liberty to conceal the cost of discipleship. Jesus still calls all who would follow him to deny themselves, take up their cross, and identify themselves with his new community. The results of evangelism include obedience to Christ, incorporation into his Church and responsible service in the world.

(1Cor. 15:3,4; Acts 2: 32-39; John 20:21; 1 Cor. 1:23; 2 Cor. 4:5; 5:11,20; Luke 14:25-33; Mark 8:34; Acts 2:40,47; Mark 10:43-45)

5. CHRISTIAN SOCIAL RESPONSIBILITY

We affirm that God is both the Creator and the Judge of all people. We therefore should share his concern for justice and reconciliation throughout human society and for the liberation of men and women from every kind of oppression. Because men and women are made in the image of God, every person, regardless of race, religion, colour, culture, class, sex or age, has an intrinsic dignity because of which he or she should be respected and served, not exploited. Here too we express penitence both for our neglect and for having sometimes regarded evangelism and social concern as mutually exclusive. Although reconciliation with other people is not reconciliation with God, nor is social action evangelism, nor is political liberation salvation, nevertheless we affirm that evangelism and socio-political involvement are both part of our Christian duty. For both are necessary expressions of our doctrines of God and man, our love for our neighbour and our obedience to Jesus Christ. The message of salvation implies also a message of judgment upon every form of alienation, oppression and discrimination, and we should not be afraid to denounce evil and injustice wherever they exist. When people receive Christ they are born again into his kingdom and must seek not only to exhibit but also to spread its righteousness in the midst of an unrighteous world. The salvation we claim should be transforming us in the totality of our personal and social responsibilities. Faith without works is dead.

(Acts 17:26, 31; Gen. 18:25; Isa. 1:17; Psa. 45:7; Gen. 1:26, 27; Jas. 3:9; Lev. 19:18; Luke 6:27, 35; Jas. 2:14-26; John 3:3, 5; Matt. 5:20; 6:33; 2 Cor. 3:18; Jas. 2:20)

6. THE CHURCH AND EVANGELISM

We affirm that Christ sends his redeemed people into the world as the Father sent him, and that this calls for a similar deep and costly penetration of the world. We need to break out of our ecclesiastical ghettos and permeate non-Christian society. In the Church's mission of sacrificial service evangelism is primary. World evangelization requires the whole Church to take the whole gospel to the whole world. The Church is at the very centre of God's cosmic purpose and is his appointed means of spreading the gospel. But a church which preaches the cross must itself be marked by the cross. It becomes a stumbling block to evangelism when it betrays the gospel or lacks a living faith in God, a genuine love for people, or scrupulous honesty in all things including promotion and finance. The church is the community of God's people rather than an institution, and must not be identified with any particular culture, social or political system, or human ideology.

(John 17:18; 20:21; Matt. 28:19,20; Acts 1:8; 20:27; Eph. 1:9,10; 3:9-11; Gal. 6:14,17; 2 Cor. 6:3,4; 2 Tim. 2:19-21; Phil. 1:27)

7. COOPERATION IN EVANGELISM

We affirm that the Church's visible unity in truth is God's purpose. Evangelism also summons us to unity, because our oneness strengthens our witness, just as our disunity undermines our gospel of reconciliation. We recognize, however, that organisational unity may take many forms and does not necessarily forward evangelism. Yet we who share the same biblical faith should be closely united in fellowship, work and witness. We confess that our testimony has sometimes been marred by a sinful individualism and needless duplication. We pledge ourselves to seek a deeper unity in truth, worship, holiness and mission. We urge the development of regional and functional cooperation for the furtherance of the Church's mission, for strategic planning, for mutual encouragement, and for the sharing of resources and experience.

(John 17:21, 23; Eph. 4:3,4; John 13:35; Phil. 1:27; John 17:11-23)

8. CHURCHES IN EVANGELISTIC PARTNERSHIP

We rejoice that a new missionary era has dawned. The dominant role of western missions is fast disappearing. God is raising up from the younger churches a great new resource for world evangelization, and is thus demonstrating that the responsibility to evangelise belongs to the whole body of Christ. All churches should therefore be asking God and themselves what they should be doing both to reach their own area and to send missionaries to other parts of the world. A reevaluation of our missionary responsibility and role should be continuous. Thus a growing partnership of churches will develop and the universal character of Christ's Church will be more clearly exhibited. We also thank God for agencies which labor in Bible translation, theological education, the mass media, Christian literature, evangelism, missions, church renewal and other specialist fields. They too should engage in constant self-examination to evaluate their effectiveness as part of the Church's mission.

(Rom. 1:8; Phil. 1:5; 4:15; Acts 13:1-3, 1 Thess. 1:6-8)

9. THE URGENCY OF THE EVANGELISTIC TASK

More than 2,700 million people, which is more than two-thirds of all humanity, have yet to be evangelised. We are ashamed that so many have been neglected; it is a standing rebuke to us and to the whole Church. There is now, however, in many parts of the world an unprecedented receptivity to the Lord Jesus Christ. We are convinced that this is the time for churches and para-church agencies to pray earnestly for the salvation of the unreached and to launch new efforts to achieve world evangelization. A reduction of foreign missionaries and money in an evangelised country may sometimes be necessary to facilitate the national church's growth in self-reliance and to release resources for unevangelised areas.

Missionaries should flow ever more freely from and to all six continents in a spirit of humble service. The goal should be, by all available means and at the earliest possible time, that every person will have the opportunity to hear, understand, and to receive the good news. We cannot hope to attain this goal without sacrifice. All of us are shocked by the poverty of millions and disturbed by the injustices which cause it. Those of us who live in affluent circumstances accept our duty to develop a simple life-style in order to contribute more generously to both relief and evangelism.

(John 9:4; Matt. 9:35-38; Rom. 9:1-3; 1 Cor. 9:19-23; Mark 16:15; Isa. 58:6, 7; Jas. 1:27; 2:1-9; Matt. 25:31-46; Acts 2:44,45; 4:34,35)

10. EVANGELISM AND CULTURE

The development of strategies for world evangelization calls for imaginative pioneering methods. Under God, the result will be the rise of churches deeply rooted in Christ and closely related to their culture. Culture must always be tested and judged by Scripture. Because men and women are God's creatures, some of their culture is rich in beauty and goodness. Because they are fallen, all of it is tainted with sin and some of it is demonic. The gospel does not presuppose the superiority of any culture to another, but evaluates all cultures according to its own criteria of truth and righteousness, and insists on moral absolutes in every culture. Missions have all too frequently exported with the gospel an alien culture and churches have sometimes been in bondage to culture rather than to Scripture. Christ's evangelists must humbly seek to empty themselves of all but their personal authenticity in order to become the servants of others, and churches must seek to transform and enrich culture, all for the glory of God.

(Mark 7:8, 9, 13; Gen. 4:21,22; 1 Cor. 9:19-23; Phil. 2:5-7; 2 Cor. 4:5)

11. EDUCATION AND LEADERSHIP

We confess that we have sometimes pursued church growth at the expense of church depth, and divorced evangelism from Christian nurture. We also acknowledge that some of our missions have been too slow to equip and encourage national leaders to assume their rightful responsibilities. Yet we are committed to indigenous principles, and long that every church will have national leaders who manifest a Christian style of leadership in terms not of domination but of service. We recognise that there is a great need to improve theological education, especially for church leaders. In every nation and culture there should be an effective training programme for pastors and laity in doctrine, discipleship, evangelism, nurture and service. Such training programmes should not rely on any stereotyped methodology but should be developed by creative local initiatives

according to biblical standards.
(Col. 1:27, 28; Acts 14:23; Tit. 1:5, 9; Mark 10:42-45; Eph. 4:11,12)

12. SPIRITUAL CONFLICT

We believe that we are engaged in constant spiritual warfare with the principalities and powers of evil, who are seeking to overthrow the Church and frustrate its task of world evangelization. We know our need to equip ourselves with God's armour and to fight this battle with the spiritual weapons of truth and prayer. For we detect the activity of our enemy, not only in false ideologies outside the Church, but also inside it in false gospels which twist Scripture and put people in the place of God. We need both watchfulness and discernment to safeguard the biblical gospel. We acknowledge that we ourselves are not immune to worldliness of thoughts and action, that is, to a surrender to secularism. For example, although careful studies of church growth, both numerical and spiritual, are right and valuable, we have sometimes neglected them. At other times, desirous to ensure a response to the gospel, we have compromised our message, manipulated our hearers through pressure techniques, and become unduly preoccupied with statistics or even dishonest in our use of them. All this is worldly. The Church must be in the world; the world must not be in the Church.

(Eph. 6:12; 2 Cor. 4:3, 4; Eph. 6:11, 13-18; 2 Cor. 10:3-5; 1 John 2:18-26; 4:1-3; Gal. 1:6-9; 2 Cor. 2:17; 4:2; John 17:15)

13. FREEDOM AND PERSECUTION

It is the God-appointed duty of every government to secure conditions of peace, justice and liberty in which the Church may obey God, serve the Lord Jesus Christ, and preach the gospel without interference. We therefore pray for the leaders of nations and call upon them to guarantee freedom of thought and conscience, and freedom to practise and propagate religion in accordance with the will of God and as set forth in The Universal Declaration of Human Rights. We also express our deep concern for all who have been unjustly imprisoned, and especially for those who are suffering for their testimony to the Lord Jesus. We promise to pray and work for their freedom. At the same time we refuse to be intimidated by their fate. God helping us, we too will seek to stand against injustice and to remain faithful to the gospel, whatever the cost. We do not forget the warnings of Jesus that persecution is inevitable.

(1 Tim. 1:1-4, Acts 4:19; 5:29; Col. 3:24; Heb. 13:1-3; Luke 4:18; Gal. 5:11; 6:12; Matt. 5:10-12; John 15:18-21)

14. THE POWER OF THE HOLY SPIRIT

We believe in the power of the Holy Spirit. The Father sent his Spirit to bear witness to his Son; without his witness ours is futile. Conviction of sin, faith in Christ, new birth and Christian growth are all his work. Further, the Holy Spirit is a missionary spirit; thus evangelism should arise spontaneously from a Spirit-filled church. A church that is not a missionary church is contradicting itself and quenching the Spirit. Worldwide evangelization will become a realistic possibility only when the Spirit renews the Church in truth and wisdom, faith, holiness, love and power. We therefore call upon all Christians to pray for such a visitation of the sovereign Spirit of God that all his fruit may appear in all his people and that all his gifts may enrich the body of Christ. Only then will the whole church become a fit instrument in his hands, that the whole earth may hear his voice.

(1 Cor. 2:4; John 15:26;27; 16:8-11; 1 Cor. 12:3; John 3:6-8; 2 Cor. 3:18; John 7:37-39; 1 Thess. 5:19; Acts 1:8; Psa. 85:4-7; 67:1-3; Gal. 5:22,23; 1 Cor. 12:4-31; Rom. 12:3-8)

15. THE RETURN OF CHRIST

We believe that Jesus Christ will return personally and visibly, in power and glory, to consummate his salvation and his judgment. This promise of his coming is a further spur to our evangelism, for we remember his words that the gospel must first be preached to all nations. We believe that the interim period between Christ's ascension and return is to be filled with the mission of the people of God, who have no liberty to stop before the end. We also remember his warning that false Christs and false prophets will arise as precursors of the final Antichrist. We therefore reject as a proud, self-confident dream the notion that people can ever build a utopia on earth. Our Christian confidence is that God will perfect his kingdom, and we look forward with eager anticipation to that day, and to the new heaven and earth in which righteousness will dwell and God will reign forever. Meanwhile, we rededicate ourselves to the service of Christ and of people in joyful submission to his authority over the whole of our lives.

(Mark 14:62; Heb. 9:28; Mark 13:10; Acts 1:8-11; Matt. 28:20; Mark 13:21-23; 1 John 2:18; 4:1-3; Luke 12:32; Rev. 21:1-5; 2 Pet. 3:13; Matt. 28:18)

CONCLUSION

Therefore, in the light of this our faith and our resolve, we enter into a solemn covenant with God and with each other, to pray, to plan and to work together for the evangelization of the whole world. We call upon others to join us. May God help us by his grace and for his glory to be faithful to this our covenant! Amen, Alleluia!

APPENDIX 2:

—ɱ—

"God the Communicator"

BY REV. DR. ARNE H. FJELDSTAD

The God of the Bible is the God who communicates with the human being. As Johannes Henrici points out: 'Communication *is deeply rooted in God's nature and it is this nature he imparted to humanity when he created us in his own image* [1].

Communication is a God-given capability given to the created human being and is "the only way to be fully human"[2]. In principle, to be a human is to be a communicator. Communication – the ability to express oneself – remains God's gift to humanity.

This basic understanding of communication as a result of God's creating act in history deepens our understanding of God's own desire for a relationship with His created beings. God wants us to communicate with Him and He with us. Throughout history, as reported in the Bible, we can see how God has communicated through His prophets and then through His Son and how He calls us to respond. Hearing the Good News, living by it and witnessing to it, is the basic calling for all Christians.

The reformer Martin Luther underlines this fundamental link between creation and communication: "he claims that to be created in God's image has to do with relationship and communication …That means I am created for dialogue: God's communication with me takes the form of a conversation. This is the basic theme in all of Scripture: God is continually seeking man (*sic*) out to talk with him, from the story of Eden until the proclamation of the new heavens and the new earth. In the same way the concept of covenant is based on two-way communication" [3].

God moves into the receptor's frame of reference, namely, the culture and the language. "He goes beyond the predictable and the stereotype in his communicative efforts" [4]. He uses the language and thought patterns of those with whom He speaks.

I have been a journalist in mainstream media for more than 30 years. I do think journalists oftentimes in a special way can understand the issue of Gods passion for communication. News reports, articles, presentations or audio/video programs demand a lot of work and oftentimes becomes a "baby" for many journalists. There is an act of "creation" in the very process of communicating a message, directing a program or writing a story.

God has revealed His passionate heart by choosing a significant method of communication, namely incarnation. The almighty, supreme God is really a "God who bends down and, lowering himself, speaks that we might hear and understand This 'bending down' means that all God's communications are incarnational: God reveals Himself in and through the ordinary situations of human life.... And that leads us into history and culture, into created life as well as its vulnerability and brokennes." [5].

God's heartfelt desire to communicate His eternal message of love and redemption has profound consequences for the basic understanding of every Christian's calling to communicate - in any way possible - the good news of salvation. We are called to be "ambassadors of Christ" (2 Corinthians 5:20). Paul's life and work are significantly marked by his skills as a highly effective and successful communicator. Paul's success as a communicator not only in preaching and teaching the gospel, but also in manifesting the truth in daily life brought him into persecution, imprisonment and torture. His methods were dynamic, focused, pastoral and passionate. The apostle related to the needs of people in a particular place and situation. He never lost track of the essential message, the gospel.

All of this comes together in the fact that Paul lived out a holistic theology in his ministry. "Paul showed in many ways and in various situations that he was concerned with people in their total life, and with the effect that the gospel could have on the whole of life. He was, before everything else, the evangelist, calling for the heart and mind to be put right with God. ... practical application of Christian truth was more important to Paul than apprehension of all the content" [6].

Communicating the gospel in today's world also needs to be carried out in a holistic way, with an evangelistic focus, and a pastoral heart authentically caring for people to be reconciled with God. As Christians the Lord Jesus has commissioned us to be his communicators. Our task is to communicate the good news about Jesus Christ in any way possible to every human being (Matthew 28:18-20, John 20:21). This task was given both to the Church as a whole and to every Christian, to the craftsman as well as the journalist.

This understanding of every Christian as a communicator is based upon God as the Creator of the universe. Yet, it is organically woven together with our commission to share the good news of the gospel with other people. Dr. Charles Kraft reminds us "the messenger himself/herself is the major component of the total message. ... We are a major part of the message that we seek to communicate." [7].

Our challenge is to "embody Christ" in our lives, so that not only our words but also our deeds may converge into a holistic testimony of our Lord and Savior Jesus Christ.

In other words, our testimony is our story, our life is our story, and our story must be woven together with God's story. Dr. Leighton Ford has pointed out, the story of God "... goes on forever, weaving its way through countless human lives, countless human stories. We are all part of that great narrative, as we join our stories to His. And we expand that narrative as we call others to join their stories to His" [8].

The heart of all communication is that it takes place in a person-to-person encounter. It is never only a 'transmission' of messages. Communication is to be involved, and must "result in Christ becoming flesh and blood in ever new settings. It is the very nature of the Good News that it will sound differently in Addis Ababa and in London, because it is the Good News about the Word that became a human being. The gospel is the same, but its form will differ according to the situation [9].

This "holistic" and "organic" view of every Christian as a communicator and inevitably a "missionary" is a result of "the two mandates of creation and mission." Dr. Vinay Samuel writes, "As humans made in God's image we are empowered with stewardly responsibility for the earth and for the gospel of the kingdom. It is in the exercise of that stewardship we affirm our identity as God's children and also fulfill our humanity." [10].

Yet, we need to keep in mind that communication is an intrinsic part of the Trinity – Father, Son and Holy Spirit. Some comments have already been made, but let us just note also how God in the Old Testament uses signs to remind His people about the relationship and the covenant: the rainbow for Noah, the blood on the doorframe at Passover, the circumcision to set apart Abraham's descendants.

Jesus Christ is proclaimed as the essence of communication. He is the Word. "In the beginning was the Word, and the Word was with God, and the Word was God. He was with God in the beginning. Through him all things were made; without him nothing was made that has been made. In him was life, and that life was the light of men… The Word became flesh and made his dwelling among us. We have seen his glory, the glory of the One and Only, who came from the Father, full of grace and truth." John 1:1-14

Again, we need to keep in mind a holistic approach: Jesus is not only the spoken Word, but the Word in action. The Kingdom of God is near, He said – and it truly was and is today, through the Holy Spirit. Not only because Jesus Himself was dwelling among us, proclaiming the gospel, but equally so because He acted to heal, feed, comfort and even restore to life.

The Holy Spirit is the Communicator as well. The Bible calls Him "the Counselor" and "the Spirit of truth" who will convince of sin and "guide you into all truth. He will not speak on his own; He will speak only what He hears, and He will tell you what is yet to come. He will bring glory to me by taking from what is mine and making it known to you."

Even more so, to enable us to carry out the task of communicating the Gospel, we have been promised the power of the Holy Spirit. It is this Spirit that can change the Babel of confusion into the Pentecost of genuine understanding. Martin Luther is taking this even further when he explains the 3rd Article of faith in this way: "I believe that I cannot by my own reason or strength believe in Jesus Christ, my Lord, or come to Him; but the Holy Ghost has called me by the Gospel, enlightened me with His gifts, sanctified and kept me in the true faith; even as He calls, gathers, enlightens, and sanctifies the whole Christian Church on earth, and keeps it with Jesus Christ in the one true faith" [11].

Our challenge is to work in the power of the Holy Spirit to reach out to the human heart. We are called to be Spirit-filled communicators linking our personal stories to God's ongoing story in this world. We are called to be humble, honest and transparent communicators always ready to listen, to answer questions and to share the most important story ever told - the real story of our Lord Jesus Christ that can change a life—forever.

END NOTES

[1] Johannes Henrici, "Towards an Anthropological Philosophy of Communication." Communication Resource. March 1983. 1.

[2] Viggo Søgaard, Research In Church and Mission, Pasadena, CA: William Carey Library, 1996, 11.

[3] Knud Jørgensen, "Christian Communication: Remote Control or Incarnation?" World Evangelization. December 1996/January 1997, 5.

[4] Charles Kraft, Communicating the Gospel God's Way, William Carey Library, Pasadena, CA, 1983, 11.

[5] Jørgensen, ibid.

[6] Dean S. Gilliland, Pauline Theology & Mission Practice, Grand Rapids, MI: Baker Book House, 1983, 15.

[7] Kraft, ibid., 31.

[8] Leighton Ford, The Power of Story. Rediscovering the Oldest, Most Natural Way to Reach People for Christ, NavPress: Colorado Springs, CO, 1994, 179.

[9] Jorgensen, ibid., 7.

[10] Vinay Samuel, "Journalism and the Two Mandates: The news profession as vocation. The role of journalism in creation and mission." Available at http://www.gegrapha.org/VinaySamuel.asp

[11] Martin Luther's explanation to the 3rd article of faith. Available at http://cat41.org/WhoWhat/Confessions/SC.htm

Taken from The Oxford Centre for Religion & Public Life. Used by permission.